Risk Management
and Financial Derivatives:

A Guide to the Mathematics

Risk Management and Financial Derivatives

A Guide to the Mathematics

Edited by

SATYAJIT DAS

McGraw-Hill

New York   San Francisco   Washington, D.C.   Auckland   Bogotá
Caracas   Lisbon   London   Madrid   Mexico City   Milan
Montreal   New Delhi   San Juan   Singapore
Sydney   Tokyo   Toronto

First published by The Law Book
Company Limited t/as LBC Information
Services, Sydney, Australia, 1997.

Library of Congress Cataloging-in-Publication Data

Risk management and financial derivatives : a guide to the mathematics
  / edited by Satyajit Das.
    p.   cm.
  Includes index.
  ISBN 0-07-015378-7
    1. Derivative securities—Mathematical models. 2. Risk
management—Mathematical models. 3. Investment analysis—
Mathematical models.   I. Das, Satyajit.
HG6024.A3R577   1998
332.64'5—dc21   97-46822
                                                      CIP

McGraw-Hill

A Division of The McGraw-Hill Companies

    3 4 5 6 7 8 9 DOC/DOC 9 0 2 1 0 9

ISBN 0-07-015378-7

The sponsoring editor for this book was Stephen Isaacs, the editing supervisor was
John M. Morriss, and the production supervisor was Suzanne W. B. Rapcavage.

Printed and bound by R. R. Donnelley & Sons Company.

McGraw-Hill books are available at special quantity discounts to use as premiums
and sales promotions, or for use in corporate training programs. For more
information, please write to the Director of Special Sales, McGraw-Hill, 11 West
19th Street, New York, NY 10011. Or contact your local bookstore.

This book is printed on recycled, acid-free paper containing a
minimum of 50% recycled de-inked fiber.

Preface

1. BACKGROUND AND OBJECTIVES OF THE BOOK

Modern financial management entails an appreciation of a number of key mathematical concepts. This is particularly relevant to risk management and risk management products, such as financial derivatives.

The knowledge of the mathematical concepts and the inherent assumptions underlying these mathematical concepts has tended to be concentrated among a select group of quantitative analysts employed by individual organisations (the so-called *rocket scientists* or *quants*). However, increasingly, the central role played by these products in capital markets is forcing a broader range of personnel to be aware of and utilise these concepts. This may be in a purely supervisory capacity or in using the concepts and products in day-to-day activities. This trend will continue and increase over time.

This increasing emphasis on mathematical finance creates problems for individuals who may not be comfortable with the basic concepts underlying the actual techniques utilised. This is usually caused by either a lack of exposure to the techniques or the absence of use of the concepts since graduation from university or other institutions. Hence, there is a very strong and increasing demand for material which explains the mathematical basis of risk management and financial derivatives in a *non-technical* manner to allow non-specialists to gain an appreciation of the concepts that are utilised.

Risk Management and Financial Derivatives: A Guide To The Mathematics is directed to fill this gap in the literature.

The book consists of a collection of papers from leading market practitioners covering:

(1) the basic mathematics underlying risk management and financial derivatives products; and

(2) application of the basic techniques in a number of common settings to promote understanding of the actual use of the concepts. Applications covered include the most common applications of mathematics to finance, such as:

- yield curve modelling and bond/fixed income pricing;
- pricing derivatives, both forwards and options;
- investment management applications; and
- risk management, in particular, value at risk and portfolio stress simulations based on monte carlo techniques.

The style of the book is as practical as possible. The text avoids mathematical notation to the maximum degree feasible so that an intuitive grasp of the concepts can be gained. The book also includes numerous

v

detailed worked examples, wherever possible, to help the reader understand the concepts and see how the practical calculations are undertaken.

The target audience for this book includes:

- financial institutions, particularly commercial and investment banks, as well as brokers, active in trading activities;
- liability and investment managers who utilise or are looking at utilising trading risk management techniques in the management of trading risk;
- service industries, consultants, IT firms, accountants et cetera, active in advising traders or users of these techniques; and
- regulatory agencies.

The book can also be used as the basis for practical in-house training programs, as well as in post-graduate programs such as MBA or Applied Finance courses in financial markets, either as the primary text or supplementary reading.

2. CONTENT AND STRUCTURE

The book is structured around several themes, which correspond to the parts of the book.

Part 1—Introduction

This consists of a single chapter (Chapter 1) designed to outline the fundamental basis of the application of mathematics to financial markets, in particular the essential risk reward basis of value and the use of risk neutrality and arbitrage as the basis for all valuation or pricing.

Part 2—Interest Rates and Yield Curves

This section and the three which follow it are focused on specific application areas of derivatives in risk management and derivative products. In this part, the focus is on fixed interest markets made: Chapter 2 covers interest rates, the pricing of bonds and measures on interest rate risk, utilising duration and convexity; and Chapter 3 covers yield curve modelling, with coverage of the derivation of zero-coupon rates and the generation of yield curves.

Part 3—Derivative Pricing

Part 3 covers the application of mathematical techniques in the pricing of financial derivatives. Chapter 4 covers the pricing of forward and futures contracts. Chapter 5 examines the pricing of option contracts. Chapters 6 and 7 focus on more advanced issues in option pricing—specifically, the pricing of interest rate options utilising term structure models and the valuation of non-standard or exotic options. Chapter 8 focuses on the estimation of volatility, which is a central issue in the valuation of options. Chapter 9 looks at more complex approaches to estimation of volatility using ARCH/GARCH approaches to modelling volatility changes. Chapters 10 and 11 examine the risk of options: Chapter 10 examines the measurement of option price sensitivity using the Greek alphabet of risk (delta, gamma, theta, vega and rho); and Chapter 11 focuses on the use of option price sensitivities to replicate option profiles (the practice of delta hedging).

Part 4—Investment Management

Part 4 focuses on investment management applications of mathematics. Chapter 12 examines the concept of efficient portfolios and diversification within investment portfolios and the optimisation of portfolio structures. Chapter 13 examines the immunisation of bond portfolio using duration-based hedging techniques. Chapter 14 covers the concept and practice of portfolio insurance, utilising basic option theory to guarantee minimum values of portfolios. Chapter 15 looks at the creation, structuring and management of indexed portfolios.

Part 5—Risk Management

Part 5 covers the mathematics of risk measurement and management. Chapter 16 focuses on the use of value of risk techniques to model trading risk. Chapter 17 examines the use of stress testing, primarily using monte carlo simulation methods to measure risk not captured by traditional models of risk. Chapter 18 extends the framework of risk management to cover credit risk.

Part 6—Mathematical Techniques

Part 6 sets out the mathematical techniques underlying the applications described in previous sections. In Chapter 19 the basic mathematics underlying the financial applications is described, together with material which allows the reader to further her or his knowledge of the techniques and so come to a more complete understanding of the subject matter. The chapter also includes cross-references to built-in mathematical functions found in spreadsheet packages, to allow the reader to program some of these applications.

The book is designed either to be read through from start to finish or as a reference source where individual sections are read as required.

4. ACKNOWLEDGMENTS

I would like to thank all the contributors to the book. They, all busy practitioners, add a practical dimension and real world application focus to the work.

I would like to thank the Publishers—LBC Information Services (Fiona Dixon, Carolyn Uyeda and Julie Burke); Irwin Publishing (Kevin Commins and Stephen Isaacs); and MacMillan Press (Jane Powell and Stephen Rutt). I would also like to thank Kim Paino, who edited the book.

I would like to thank my parents—Sukumar and Aparna Das—for their continued support and encouragement. In particular, I would like to thank my friend Jade Novakovic without whose help, support, patience, tolerance and encouragement this would never have been completed. This book is dedicated to these three people.

SATYAJIT DAS

Sydney
November 1997

Table of Contents

About the Authors

Dr Carol Alexander

After working in the mathematics department of the University of Amsterdam, and later as a bond analyst for Phillips and Drew (UBS), Carol Alexander joined the mathematics faculty at the University of Sussex in 1985. Since 1990 she has developed an international regulation for the time-series analysis of financial markets, specialising in risk measurement and investment analysis. In 1996 she moved to a part-time post at the university, when she became the Academic Director of Algorithmics Inc (www.algorithmics.com) and Editor in Chief of NetExposure, the electronic journal of financial risk (www.netexposure.co.uk).

During the past few years she has been consulting in risk management and time-series analysis for banks, corporates and other financial institutions. As a result, most of her academic research work now concentrates on applied financial econometrics, specialising in volatility and correlation analysis. Carol has developed a large number of general and in-house training courses covering the general areas of risk management and investment analysis for financial institutions.

With Algorithmics Inc, she is developing VAR models for large-scale risk management systems and new methods for historical simulation using pattern recognition. Her pattern recognition algorithm, developed with Dr Ian Giblin (Department of Mathematics, University of Pisa) won the first international non-linear financial forecasting competition in 1996. She also works with Dr Peter Williams (Department of Cognitive Science, University of Sussex) on using neural networks to estimate mixtures of normal distributions to model, "fat-tailed" distributions and term structures of kurtosis. Her research on emerging markets includes the analysis of equity and currency derivatives in the Asia-Pacific region, and the hedging of equities with new cointegration software.

She speaks at many international conferences and on mathematical techniques for risk and investment management and has written numerous articles in both academic and professional journals. Carol's books include the edited *Handbook for Risk Management and Analysis* (1st ed, April 1996; 2nd ed in two volumes, forthcoming February 1998, Wiley). More details of professional and academic publications are given on www.maths.sussex.ac.uk/Staff?COA.html.

Geoffrey Brianton

Geoffrey Brianton has an Honours degree in economics and statistics. He is an independent consultant in the area of investment risk management. For the last ten years he has worked as a Fund Manager in London, Sydney and Melbourne. During that time he has developed and managed a wide variety of quantitative funds, including indexed, capital protected and arbitrage funds. With a background in econometrics and operations research, he has a particular interest in the use of optimisation techniques, both in regard to the problems of portfolio construction and some of the broader problems found in finance such as optional hedging strategies.

Alan Bustany

Alan Bustany is a Principal Consultant in the Financial Services Industry Practice of Price Waterhouse Urwick. He is a Wrangler from Trinity College, Cambridge, and was part of the British team at the 1977 International Mathematical Olympiad in Belgrade. He is an Associate Fellow of the Institute of Mathematics and its Applications, and of the Securities Institute of Australia. Alan has used his mathematical background in a range of technology-related fields, including relational database theory; artificial intelligence; formal methods of software engineering; knowledge-based systems; and financial derivatives.

Mr Bustany has more than 15 years' experience in the computing industry in consulting, commercial, and product development roles. His current focus is strategic consulting in financial markets, risk management, and credit measurement. His clients include Bankers Trust, National Australia Bank, Macquarie Bank and Westpac.

Roger Cohen

Roger Cohen is currently employed at Deutsche Morgan Grenfell, in the Equity Derivatives and Trading Group. His main focus is on the development of structured equity products, pricing and risk management. Roger commenced his career in the financial markets in the Quantitative Applications Division at Macquarie Bank in 1992. Since then he has worked at Natwest Markets in the Global Markets area. He has presented papers at finance conferences in Australia and abroad. Prior to entering the financial markets, Roger was a lecturer in the Faculty of Engineering at the University of Sydney. His main research focus was in the computational modelling of fluid motion.

Frances Cowell

Prior to graduating from university, Frances worked in the biomedical library at the New South Wales Institute of Technology, and then as a Rehabilitation Counsellor for disabled people. After obtaining a Bachelor of Arts degree in psychology and statistics from the University of New South Wales, she worked in the wholesale liquor industry as a Marketing Manager, before completing a Master of Business Administration at the Australian Graduate School of Management.

Frances entered the investment management industry in January 1983 as the Research Analyst for Aetna Life & Casualty, then a major life office. Faced with analysing a portfolio of 300 stocks, she employed a novel approach to stock analysis, using a desktop computer and spreadsheet to simultaneously analyse expected risk-return profiles for a large number of stocks, thereby identifying apparently mispriced issues for closer analysis.

This was combined with industry-wide analyses to estimate industry growth rates and of competitive advantage to identify best performing stocks within industry groups.

In 1984, with the growth of the share price index futures market in Australia, Frances was attracted by the opportunities for SPI arbitrage and joined Australian Bank to exploit these. There she also established and managed an early portfolio protection operation which enabled the bank's borrowers to cap their interest rate risk. This portfolio protection program drew on a variant of Black-Scholes option pricing technology (delta hedging) to hedge the bank's sold option positions.

Later, Frances combined stock index arbitrage principles with delta hedging to exploit underpriced SPI futures contracts with minimal risk. This operation, which was unique at the time, was conducted within a major Australian institutional broking house.

In 1991 Frances began working on indexed portfolios for a major Australian superannuation fund. This work covered domestic and global equities and fixed interest. She managed the derivatives enhanced domestic equities index portfolio, which grew to over A$1 billion. From there she joined County NatWest to take over the management of index portfolios. At County, Frances further developed customising capabilities for indexation clients, with particular focus on adding value by managing after-tax returns to index portfolios.

Satyajit Das

Satyajit Das is an international specialist in the area of financial derivatives, risk management, capital markets, and treasury management.

He presents seminars on financial derivatives/risk management and treasury management/corporate finance in Europe, North America, Asia and Australia. He acts as a consultant to financial institutions and corporations on derivative instruments, risk management, and treasury/financial management issues.

Between 1988 and 1994, Mr Das was the Treasurer of the TNT Group, an Australian-based international transport and logistics company, with responsibility for the Global Treasury function, including liquidity management, corporate finance, capital markets, and financial risk management. He was also involved in the financial restructuring of the TNT Group in the early 1990s. During 1994, Mr Das acted as a consultant to the TNT Group in the areas of financial strategy and policy, capital allocation/management and strategic risk management.

Between 1977 and 1987, he worked in banking with the Commonwealth Bank of Australia, Citicorp Investment Bank and Merrill Lynch Capital Markets, specialising in fundraising for Australian and New Zealand borrowers in domestic and international capital markets and risk management, involving the use of derivative products, including swaps, futures and options.

In 1987, Mr Das was a Visiting Fellow at the Centre for Studies in Money, Banking and Finance, Macquarie University.

Mr Das is the author of *Swap Financing* (IFR Publishing Ltd/The Law Book Company Ltd, 1989); *Swaps and Financial Derivatives: The Global Reference to Products, Pricing, Applications and Markets* (IFR Publishing Ltd/The Law Book Company Ltd/Irwin Professional Publishing, 1994); *Exotic Options* (IFR Publishing Ltd/LBC Information Services, 1996); and *Structured Notes and Derivative Embedded Securities* (Euromoney Publications, 1996). He is also the editor of *The Global Swaps Market* (IFR Publishing Ltd, 1991). He has published on financial derivatives, corporate finance, treasury and risk management issues in professional and applied finance journals.

Mr Das holds Bachelors' degrees in Commerce (accounting, finance and systems) and Law from the University of New South Wales, and a Masters degree in Business Administration from the Australian Graduate School of Management.

Dr Garry de Jager

Garry de Jager holds a PhD in option pricing, a Masters of Business Administration and a Bachelor of Science in mathematics. He is currently the Senior Manager, International Capital Markets Research, for Chase Manhattan Bank, Sydney. His primary interests are modelling derivatives for commodities, foreign exchange and interest rate products. In his role supporting the trading desks, his special emphases are exotic options, hedging strategies, simulation analysis, volatility and correlation analysis, and provision of models for system development. He is a frequent traveller to Chase sites around the world, as well as a regular speaker at seminars on these topics.

Garry has wide commercial experience, having previously been the Director of Research and Development for the specialist financial option company Optech International; Marketing Representative for IBM; and Production Manager in the printing industry. Prior to joining Chase Manhattan he taught finance and Information Systems at the Queensland University of Technology.

Thomas R Gillespie

Thomas Gillespie graduated from the University of Sydney in 1986 with a Bachelor of Science, and in 1988 with a Bachelor of Arts majoring in mathematics and statistics. After graduation, Thomas joined Bankers Trust Australia and specialised in foreign exchange and fixed interest options. In 1989 he moved to James Capel Australia and there specialised in equity derivatives and arbitrage. This led to work with the HSBC group in Sydney, Tokyo and London on a number of projects, including Japanese derivatives arbitrage and automated trading systems. In 1994 Thomas decided to take up part-time studies again, earning a Graduate Diploma in Science in 1994, and is now pursuing a PhD at the University of Sydney. Thomas' current research interests are fitting alternative stochastic processes to financial time series, and the development of new estimation methods. Thomas is currently working with County NatWest Australia, specialising in equity derivatives and structured products.

John Martin

John Martin has worked, taught and published extensively in the areas of treasury, derivatives and financial risk management. He was closely involved in the development of the derivatives industry in both Australia and New Zealand in roles varying from market trader, risk manager, regulator, and educator. John's area of interest is in financial risk management, and he has written numerous articles on this topic, including his recently published book, *Derivatives Maths* (IFR Publishing Ltd, 1996).

Currently, John is a Divisional Director of Australian-based treasury advisory firm Oakvale Capital Ltd. He is responsible for the provision of specialist financial risk management advice to clients across a wide range of industries, including electricity, retailing, agriculture, and financial services.

Prior to joining Oakvale, John was the Risk Manager of the Sydney Futures Exchange from 1991 to 1994, and was then a Director of Financial Risk Management Consulting Pty Ltd. He has also held positions with the Reserve Bank of Australia, and with TNT as Manager, Treasury Planning.

John is regarded throughout the Asia/Pacific region as a leading author and speaker in the areas of treasury and financial risk management, and has lectured extensively to professional groups in the Asia/Pacific region.

John holds a Bachelor's degree in Economics with Honours from the University of Sydney.

Steuart Roe

Steuart Roe is a specialist in equities and finance for County NatWest Securities Australia Ltd, a member of the NatWest Markets Group. He specialises in derivative product development, implementation, and distribution.

Prior to joining County NatWest Securities Australia Ltd, he was an Associate Director, Structured Investments for County NatWest Investment Management Ltd. In this role he was responsible for the design and implementation of tailored investment solutions for individual clients. In particular, he was responsible for the management of in excess of A$2 billion in assets, the bulk of which was in portfolio insurance.

Steuart holds a Bachelor of Science in mathematics and statistics from the University of Melbourne, and a Master of Applied Finance from Macquarie University.

Dr Tim Rowlands

After completing a PhD in theoretical chemistry at Cambridge University in the United Kingdom in 1989, Tim returned to Australia and commenced work for Macquarie Bank in a quantitative analysis role. His work involved supporting the Fixed Interest Division with emphasis on developing and implementing new products, including being part of a team implementing a term structure option pricing model. Tim then moved to the State Bank of New South Wales in 1992, and, from 1993, led the Quantitative Group with work focusing on interest rate options, retail product enhancements (including options incorporating prepayment risk) and risk management methodologies.

In 1995 Tim became Head of Treasury Risk Management, with responsibilities across the full spectrum of market and credit risk, policy and compliance. In mid-1996 Tim moved to Westpac to take responsibility for methodology in the trading risk area. This role has included reviewing and refining the bank's VAR calculations and the implementation of historical simulation capability for risk measurement. In addition, Tim has been involved in research into applying VAR techniques to credit and operational risk to improve capital allocation and risk adjusted performance measurement within the business.

Lance Smith

Lance Smith has a PhD in mathematics from Duke University and was an Assistant Professor of Mathematics at Columbia University prior to joining Salomon Brothers in 1986. At Salomon he worked on the equity proprietary trading desk and was responsible for the development of all the desk's financial pricing and hedging models used for assessing and limiting the risk in a derivatives book. He also developed and implemented several proprietary trading strategies, as well as hedged the more exotic derivative OTC transactions undertaken by the desk. In 1993 he and some of his long-term colleagues founded Imagine Software Inc. Along with developing state of the art risk management technology, he continues to explore new methodologies in pricing derivative securities and quantifying risk in the financial markets.

Selected Bibliography

Chapter 3

Adams, Kenneth J, "Fitting Yield Curves To Market Data" (1994) 1(2) *The Pacific ALM Journal* 27.

Adams, Kenneth J and Van Deventer, Donald R, "Fitting Yield Curves And Forward Rate Curves With Maximum Smoothness" (1994) (June) *The Journal of Fixed Income* 52.

Cox, David, "Yield Curves And How To Build Them" (1995) 4 *Capital Market Strategies* 29.

Flavell, Richard, "Discount Function Construction" *IFR Swaps Weekly*, 27 July 1994, p 4.

—— "Fitting Interest Rate Curves" (1995) *Matlab Financial Computing Brief*.

McEnally, Richard W and Jordan, James V, "The Term Structure of Interest Rates" in Fabozzi, Frank J and Fabozzi, T Dessa (eds), *The Handbook of Fixed Income Securities* (4th ed, Irwin Professional Publishing, Chicago, 1995), pp 779-830.

Smith, David, "By The Bootstraps" (1990) 3(6) *Risk* 40.

—— "Zero Coupon Yields" (1995) 5 *Capital Market Strategies* 51.

Chapter 4

Das, S, *Swaps and Financial Derivatives* (2nd ed, The Law Book Company Ltd, 1994).

Francis, Toy and Whittaker (eds), *The Handbook of Equity Derivatives* (1995).

Hull, J C, *Options, Futures and Other Derivative Securities* (Prentice-Hall, 1993).

Martin, J S, *Derivative Maths* (IFR Publishing Ltd, 1996).

Chapter 5

Black, Fischer, "The Pricing of Commodity Contracts" (1976) 3 (March) *Journal of Financial Economics* 167.

Black, Fischer, "The Holes in Black-Scholes" (1988) 1(3) *Risk* 30.

Black, Fischer, "How We Came Up With the Option Formula" (1989) (Winter) *Journal of Portfolio Management* 4.

Black, Fischer, "How to Use the Holes in Black-Scholes" (1989) 1(4) *Continental Bank Journal of Applied Corporate Finance* 67.

Black, Fischer, "Living Up To The Model" (1990) 3(3) *Risk* 11.

Black, Fischer, Derman, E, and Toy, W, "A One Factor Model of Interest Rates and Its Application to Treasury Bond Options" (1990) (Jan-Feb) *Financial Analysts Journal* 33.

Black, Fischer, and Scholes, Myron, "The Pricing of Options and Corporate Liabilities" (1973) 81 *Journal of Political Economy* 637.

Cookson, Richard, "Moving in The Right Direction" (1993) 6(10) *Risk* 22.

Cox, J and Rubinstein, M, *Options Markets* (Prentice-Hall, Inc, Englewood Cliffs, NJ, 1985).

Derman, Emanuel, "Model Risk" (1996) 9(5) *Risk* 34.

Garman, Mark B and Kohlhagen, Steven W, "Foreign Currency Option Values" (1983) 2 *Journal of International Money and Finance* 231.

Grabbe, J Orlin, "The Pricing of Call and Put Options on Foreign Exchange" (1983) 2 *Journal of International Money and Finance* 239.

Hull, John C, *Options Futures and Other Derivatives Securities* (2nd ed, Prentice-Hall, Inc, Englewood Cliffs, NJ, 1993).

Hull, John C, *Introduction To Futures and Options Markets* (2nd ed, Prentice-Hall, Inc, Englewood Cliffs, NJ, 1995).

Jarrow, Robert A and Rudd, Andrew, *Option Pricing* (Richard D Irwin, Homewood, Illinois, 1983).

Leong, Kenneth, "In the Eye Of The Beholder" (1990) 3(7) *Risk* 38.

Leong, Kenneth, "The Emperor's New Clothes" (1990) 3(8) *Risk* 11.

Leong, Kenneth, "Exorcising The Demon" (1990) 3(9) *Risk* 29.

Leong, Kenneth, "Price Versus Value" (1991) 4(10) *Risk* 22.

Leong, Kenneth, "Model Choice" (1992) 5(11) *Risk* 60.

Mason, R C, "Building On Black Scholes" (1988) 1(11) *Risk* 13.

Meisner, James F and Labuszewski, John W, "Modifying the Black-Scholes Option Pricing Model For Alternative Underlying Instruments" (1984) (Nov-Dec) *Financial Analysts Journal* 23.

Ritchen, Peter, *Options—Theory, Strategy and Applications* (Scott, Foresman and Company, Glenview, Illinois, 1987).

Rowley, Ian, "Pricing Options Using The Black-Scholes Model" (1987) (May) *Euromoney Corporate Finance* 108.

Rowley, Ian, "Option Pricing Models: How Good Is Black-Scholes?" (1987) (June) *Euromoney Corporate Finance* 30.

Smithson, Charles W, "Wonderful Life" (1991) 4(9) *Risk* 37.

Smithson, Charles W with Shang Song, "Extended Family (1) and (2)" (1995) 8(10) *Risk* 19; (1995) 8(11) *Risk* 52.

Swiss Bank Corporation, *Understanding Derivatives* (Prospects Special, Basel, Switzerland, 1994).

Tompkins, Robert, *Options Explained* (MacMillan Press, England, 1994).

Chapter 6

Black, Scholes, (1973) 81 *Journal of Political Economy* 637.

Black, (1976) 3 *Journal of Financial Economics* 167.

Black, Derman, Toy, (1990) *Financial Analysts Journal* 33.

Brace, Gatarek, Musiela, (1995) (Aug) *Risk* 34.

Brennan, Schwartz, (1983) 4 *Finance* 119.

Cox, Ingersoll, Ross, (1985) 53 *Econometrica* 363.

Cox, Ross, Rubinstein, (1979) 7 *Journal of Financial Economics* 229.

Heath, Jarrow, Morton, (1992) 60 *Econometrica* 77.

Ho, Lee, (1986) 41 *Journal of Finance* 1,011.

Ho, (1995) (Summer) *Journal of Derivatives*.

Hull, *Options, Futures and Other Derivatives* (3rd ed, Prentice-Hall, 1997).

Hull, White, (1990) 3 *Review of Financial Studies* 573.

Jamshidian, (1989) 44 *Journal of Finance* 205.

Jarrow, *Modelling Fixed Income Securities and Interest Rate Options* (1996).

Longstaff, Schwartz, (1992) 47 *Journal of Finance* 1,259.

Rebonato, *Interest-Rate Option Models* (Wiley & Sons, 1996).

Rendleman, Bartter, (1979) 34 *Journal of Finance* 1,092.

Smithson, (1995) (Oct-Nov) *Risk*.

Vasicek, (1977) 5 *Journal of Financial Economics* 177.

Chapter 7

Black, F, "The Pricing of Commodity Contracts" (1976) 3(1 and 2) *Journal of Financial Economics* 167.

Black, F, Derman, E and Toy, W, "A One-Factor Model of Interest Rates and Its Application to Treasury Bond Options" (1990) (Jan-Feb) *Financial Analysts Journal* 33.

Black, F and Scholes, M, "The Pricing of Options and Corporate Liabilities" (1973) 81 *Journal of Political Economy* 637.

Conze, A and Viswanathan, "Path Dependent Options: The Case of Lookback Options" (1991) 56(3) *Journal of Finance* 1,893.

Cox, J and Ross, S, "The Valuation of Options for Alternative Stochastic Processes" (1976) (Jan-Mar) *Journal of Financial Economics* 145.

Cox, J C, Ross, S and Rubinstein, M, "Option Pricing: A Simplified Approach" (1979) 7 *Journal of Financial Economics* 229.

Geske, R, "A Note on an Analytical Valuation Formula for Unprotected American Call Options on Stocks with Known Dividends" (1979) 7 *Journal of Financial Economics* 375.

Goldman, M B, Sosin, H B and Gatto, M A, "Path Dependent Options: 'Buy at the Low, Sell at the High' " (1979) 34(5) *Journal of Finance* 1,111.

Grabbe, J O, "The Pricing of Call and Put Options on Foreign Exchange" (1983) 2 *Journal of International Money and Finance* 239.

Heath, D C, Jarrow, R A and Morton, A, "Contingent Claim Valuation with a Random Evolution of Interest Rates" (1990) 9(1) *The Review of Futures Markets* 54.

Hull, J C and White, A, "Efficient Procedures For Valuing European And American Path-dependent Options" (1993) 1(1) *Journal of Derivatives* 21.

Merton, R C, "Option Pricing When Underlying Stock Returns Are Discontinuous" (1976) 3 *Journal of Financial Economics* 125.

Roll, R, "An Analytical Valuation Formula for Unprotected American Call Options on Share with Known Dividends" (1977) 5(2) *Journal of Financial Economics* 251.

Rubinstein, M and Reiner, E, "Barrier Options" in *Exotic Options*, unpublished manuscript by M Rubinstein (1991).

Whaley, R, "On the Valuation of American Call Options on Stocks with Known Dividends" (1981) 9 *Journal of Financial Economics* 207.

Chapter 8

Carrado, Charles and Miller, Thomas, "Volatility Without Tears" (1996) 9(7) *Risk* 49.

Chance, Don, "Leap Into the Unknown" (1993) 6(5) *Risk* 60.

Clarke, Roger C, "Estimating And Using Volatility: Part 1" (1994) (Fall) *Derivatives Quarterly* 40.

Cox, J and Rubinstein, M, *Options Markets* (Prentice-Hall, Inc, Englewood Cliffs, NJ, 1985).

Engle, Robert F, "Statistical Models For Financial Volatility" (1993) (Jan-Feb) *Financial Analysts Journal* 72.

Hargreaves, Guy D, "Volatility in Interest Rate Options", paper presented to a conference, "Options on Interest Rates", IIR Conferences, 9-10 March 1992, Sydney, Australia.

Hull, John C, *Options Futures and Other Derivatives Securities* (2nd ed, Prentice-Hall, Inc, Englewood Cliffs, NJ, 1993).

Hull, John C, *Introduction to Futures and Options Markets* (2nd ed, Prentice-Hall, Inc, Englewood Cliffs, NJ, 1995).

Leong, Kenneth, "Estimates, Guesstimates and Rules Of Thumb" (1991) 4(2) *Risk* 15.

Leong, Kenneth, "Mean Streets" (1991) 4(5) *Risk* 45.

Murphy, Gareth, "When Options Price Theory Meets The Volatility Smile" (1994) (Mar) *Euromoney* 66.

Tompkins, Robert, *Options Explained* (MacMillan Press, England, 1994).

Tompkins, Robert, "Answer in the Cards" (1995) 8(6) *Risk* 55.

Chapter 9

Alexander, C O, "Volatility and correlation forecasting" in C O Alexander (ed), *Handbook of Risk Management and Analysis* (Wiley, 1996).

Alexander, C O, "Evaluating the Use of RiskMetrics™ as a Risk Measurement Tool for Your Operation: What are its Advantages and Limitations" (1996) 2 *Derivatives Use, Trading and Regulation* 277.

Alexander, C O, " 'Splicing' methods for Value-at-Risk" *Derivatives Week*, Learning Curve, June 1997.

Alexander, C O and Leigh, C, "On the Covariance Matrices used in VAR Models" (1997) 4 (Spring) *Journal of Derivatives* 50-62.

Alexander, C O and Chibumba, A M, "Orthogonal factor GARCH", forthcoming, *Journal of Empirical Finance*, 1997.

Alexander, C O and Williams, P M, "Term Structure Forecasts of Foreign Exchange Volatility and Kurtosis: A Comparison of Neural Network and GARCH Methods", forthcoming, *Risk*, 1997.

Becker, S, "A Survey of Risk Measurement, Theory and Practice" in C O Alexander (ed), *Handbook of Risk Management and Analysis* (Wiley, 1996).

Bollerslev, T, "Generalized Autoregressive Conditional Heteroskedasticity" (1986) 31 *Journal of Econometrics* 307.

Broadie, M and Glasserman, P, "Estimating Security Price Derivatives Using Simulation" (1996) 42(2) *Management Science*.

Duan, J, "Cracking the Smile" (1996) 9(12) *Risk* 55-59.

Engle, R F, "Autoregressive Conditional Heteroscedasticity with Estimates of the Variance of United Kingdom Inflation" (1982) 50(4) *Econometrica* 987.

Engle, R F and Mezrich, J, "Grappling with GARCH" (1995) 8(9) *Risk* 112.

Engle, R F and Rosenberg, J, "GARCH Gamma" (1995) 2 *Journal of Derivatives* 47.

Figlewski, S, "Forecasting Volatility Using Historical Data", New York University Salomon Center (Leonard N Stern School of Business), Working Paper, Series No S-94-13, 1994.

Fitzgerald, M D, "Trading volatility" in C O Alexander (ed), *Handbook of Risk Management and Analysis* (Wiley, 1996).

Hull, J C, *Options, Futures, and Other Derivative Securities* (Prentice-Hall, 1993).

Taylor, S J, "Modeling Stochastic Volatility: A Review and Comparative Study" (1994) 4(2) *Mathematical Finance* 183.

Chapter 10

Brown, Stephen J, "Estimating Volatility" in Figlewiski, Stephen, Silber, William L and Subrahmanyam, Marti G, *Financial Options* (Business One Irwin, Homewood, Illinios, 1990), pp 516-537.

Chance, Don M, "Translating The Greek; The Real Meaning Of Call Option Derivatives" (1994) (July-Aug) *Financial Analyst's Journal* 43.

Cox, J and Rubinstein, M, *Options Markets* (Prentice-Hall, Inc, Englewood Cliffs, NJ, 1985).

Hull, John C, *Options Futures and Other Derivatives Securities* (2nd ed, Prentice-Hall, Inc, Englewood Cliffs, NJ, 1993).

Hull, John C, *Introduction To Futures and Options Markets* (2nd ed, Prentice-Hall, Inc, Englewood Cliffs, NJ, 1995).

Tompkins, Robert, *Options Explained* (MacMillan Press, England, 1994).

Chapter 11

Asay, Charles and Edelsburg, Charles, "Can a Dynamic Strategy Replicate the Returns of an Option" (1986) 6(1) *Journal of Futures Markets* 63.

Silber, William L, "Marketmaking In Options: Principles and Implications" in Figlewiski, Stephen, Silber, William L, and Subrahmanyam, Marti G, *Financial Options* (Business One Irwin, Homewood, Illinios, 1990), pp 485-516.

"The Dangers Of Neutrality" (1991) 4(10) *Risk* 48.

Frye, Jon, "Greek Alphabet Soup: A Recipe For Success" (1988) 1(4) *Risk* 26.

Hull, John C, *Options Futures and Other Derivatives Securities* (2nd ed, Prentice-Hall, Inc, Englewood Cliffs, NJ, 1993).

Hull, John C, *Introduction to Futures and Options Markets* (2nd ed, Prentice-Hall, Inc, Englewood Cliffs, NJ, 1995).

Leong, Kenneth, "Solving Mystery" (1990-1991) 4(1) (Dec-Jan) *Risk* 68.

Rubinstein, Mark and Leland, Hayne E, "Replicating Options With Positions In Stock And Cash" (1991) (July-Aug) *Financial Analyst's Journal* 63.

Rutherford, Janette, Sher, Answer, and Fitzgerald, Desmond, "Building Blocks" (1989) 2(7) *Risk* 42.

Smith, A L H, *Trading Financial Options* (Butterworths, London, 1986).

Westminister Equity, "Building Confidence" (1990) 3(4) *Risk* 33.

Chapter 12

Arnott, Robert D and Wagner, Wayne H, "The Measurement and Control of Trading Costs" (1990) (Nov-Dec) *Financial Analysts Journal*.

Black, Fischer, "Universal Hedging: Optimising Currency Risk and Reward In International Equity Portfolios" (1989) (July-Aug) *Financial Analysts Journal*.

Black, Fischer and Litternam, Robert, "Global Portfolio Optimisation" (1992) (Sept-Oct) *Financial Analysts Journal*.

Jeffrey, Robert H and Arnott, Robert D, "Is your Alpha Big Enough to Cover Its Taxes?" (1992) (Sept) *Journal of Portfolio Managament*.

Jobson, D and Korkie, B, "Putting Markowitz Theory to Work" (1981) (Summer) *Journal of Portfolio Management*.

Jobson, J D and Korkie, B, "Improved Estimation for Markowitz Portfolios Using James-Stein Type Estimators", proceedings of the American Statistical Association, Business and Economic Statistic Section, 1979.

Markowitz, Harry, *Mean-Variance Analysis in Portfolio Choice and Capital Markets* (Basil Blackwell Inc, Oxford, 1990).

Markowitz, Harry, "Portfolio Selection: Efficient Diversification of Investments", *Cowles Foundation Monograph No 16* (John Wiley and Sons, New York, 1959).

Perold, A F, "Large Scale Portfolio Optimisation" (1984) 30(10) *Management Science.*

Wolfe, P, "The Simplex Method for Quadratic Programming" (1959) 27(3) *Econometrica.*

Chapter 14

Black, F and Scholes, M, "The pricing of options on corporate liabilities" (1973) 81 (May-June) *Journal of Political Economy* 637.

Hull, J, *Options, Futures, and Other Derivative Securities* (2nd ed, Prentice-Hall International Inc).

Perold, A F and Sharpe, W F, "Dynamic Strategies for Asset Allocation" (1988) (Jan-Feb) *Financial Analyst Journal.*

Chapter 15

Chiang, A C, *Fundamental Methods of Mathematical Economics* (McGraw Hill, New York, 1974).

Kritzman, Mark, *The Portable Financial Analyst* (Probus, Chicago, Ill, 1995).

Lakonishok, Josef, Schleifer, Andre and Vishny, Robert W, *Study of the US Equity Money Manager Performance*, Brookings Institute Study, 1992.

Markowitz, H M, *Portfolio Selection: Efficient Diversification of Investment*, Cowles Foundation Monograph 16 (Yale University Press, New Haven, Ct, 1959).

Rosenberg, B, *Extra Market Components of Covariance in Security Returns* (1974) (Mar) *Journal of Financial and Quantitative Analysis* 263.

Rudd, Andrew, *Optimal Selection of Passive Portfolios* (1980) (Spring) *Financial Management* 57.

Rudd, Andrew and Clasing, Henry K Jr, *Modern Portfolio Theory* (2nd ed, Andrew Rudd, Orinda, CA, 1988).

Sharpe, William F, "Capital Asset Prices: A Theory of Market Equilibrium Under Conditions of Risk" (1970) 19(3) *Journal of Finance* 425.

Sharpe, William F, *Portfolio Theory and Capital Markets* (McGraw Hill, New York, 1970).

Chapter 16

Batlin, Carl, "Regulatory Approaches to Risk Management" (1996) 6 (June) *Financial Derivatives & Risk Management* 69.

Beckstrom, Rod A, Lewis, Don and Roberts, Chris, "VAR: Pushing Risk Management to the Statistical Limit" (1994) 3 *Capital Market Strategies* 9.

Beckstrom, Rod A and Campbell, Alyce R, "Value At Risk: Theoretical Foundations" (1996) 7 *Capital Market Strategies* 44.

Beckstrom, Rod A and Campbell, Alyce R (eds), *An Introduction to Value at Risk* (C.ATS Software Inc, Palo Alto, 1995).

Beder, Tanya Styblo, "VAR: Seductive But Dangerous" (1995) (Sept-Oct) *Financial Analysts Journal* 12.

Bock, Jerome T, "VAR Approaches to Market Risk Management" (1996) 6 (June) *Financial Derivatives & Risk Management* 15.

Cocks, Graham, "Measuring Market Risk Within a Bank" (1996) 1(2) *Journal of Applied Finance and Investment* 63.

Morgan, J P, *RiskMetric™—Technical Document* (3rd ed, J P Morgan, New York, 1995).

Morgan, J P, *RiskMetric™—Technical Document* (4th ed, J P Morgan, New York, 1996).

Lawrence, Dr Colin, Robinson, Gary and Stiles, Matthew, "Incorporating Liquidity Into The Risk Measurement Framework" (1996) 6 (June) *Financial Derivatives & Risk Management* 24.

Lawrence, Dr Colin and Robinson, Gary, "Value at Risk: Addressing Liquidity and Volatility Risks" (1996) 7 *Capital Market Strategies* 24.

Leong, Kenneth, "The Right Approach" (1996) (June) *Risk Value-At-Risk Supplement* 9.

Longerstaey, Jacques, "VAR, RiskMetrics™ And Market Risk Methodology" (1995) 6 *Capital Market Strategies* 9.

Longerstaey, Jacques and Zangari, Peter, "Commoditising the VAR Framework: Incoporating Gamma Risk" (1996) 6 (June) *Financial Derivatives & Risk Management* 49.

Matten, Chris, "The Capital Allocation Challenge for the Banks" (1995) 4-5 *Swiss Bank Corporation Prospects* 2.

Matten, Chris, "Risk Adjusted Performance Measurement" (1996) 6 (June) *Financial Derivatives & Risk Management* 37.

Ramaswami, Murali, "Why Capital at Risk is the Recommended Measure" (1996) 6 (June) *Financial Derivatives & Risk Management* 53.

Salzberg, Mike, "Firmwide Risk Management Systems" (1996) 6 (June) *Financial Derivatives & Risk Management* 62.

Sharma, Jitendra, "Practical Issues of Value-At-Risk" in (1996) *Corporate Finance Risk Management & Derivatives Yearbook* 8.

Shimko, David, "What is VAR?" (1995) 8(12) *Risk* 25.

Shimko, David, "VAR for Corporates" (1996) 9(6) *Risk* 28.

Shimko, David, "Investor's Return On VAR" (1996) 9(7) *Risk* 27.

Smith, Lance C, "Portfolio Simulation: Stress-Testing Techniques" (1996) 6 (June) *Financial Derivatives & Risk Management* 31.

Smithson, Charles and Minton, Lyle, "Value at Risk" (1996) 9(1) *Risk* 25.

Smithson, Charles and Minton, Lyle, "Value at Risk (2)" (1996) 9(2) *Risk* 38.

Spinner, Karen, "Adapting Value at Risk" (1996) (April) *Derivatives Strategy* 14.

Stambaugh, Fred and Cohen, Robert, "Value at Risk: Its Measurement and Uses" (1995) 4 (Dec) *Financial Derivatives & Risk Management* 45.

Taylor, Charles R and MacDonald, William A, "The Future of Market Risk Management" (1996) 6 (June) *Financial Derivatives & Risk Management* 10.

Turner, Chris, "VAR as an Industrial Tool" (1996) 9(3) *Risk* 38.

Wilson, Duncan, "Marriage of Ideals" (1995) 8(7) *Risk* 7.

Wilson, Duncan, "VAR in Operation" (1995) 8(12) *Risk* 24.

Chapter 19

Abramowitz, M and Stegun, I, *Handbook of Mathematical Functions* (9th ed, Dover, 1972).

Bhattacharya, R and Waymire, E, *Stochastic Processes with Applications* (Wiley, 1990).

Black, F and Scholes, M, "The Pricing of Options and Corporate Liabilities" (1973) 81 (May-June) *Journal of Political Economy* 637.

Feller, W, *An Introduction to Probability Theory and Its Applications* (Volume I, 3rd ed, Wiley, 1968).

Feller, W, *An Introduction to Probability Theory and Its Applications* (Volume II, 2nd ed, Wiley, 1971).

Garman, M and Klass, M, "On the Estimation of Security Price Volatilities from Historical Data" (1980) 53 (1) *Journal of Business*.

Hogg, R and Craig, A, *Introduction to Mathematical Statistics* (5th ed, Prentice-Hall, 1995).

Huber, P, *Robust Statistics* (Wiley, 1981).

Hull, J, *Options Futures and Other Derivative Securities* (2nd ed, Prentice-Hall International, 1993).

Hull, J and White, A, "The Pricing of Options on Assets with Stochastic Volatilities" (1987) 42 (June) *Journal of Finance* 281.

Jarrow, R and Rudd, A, *Option Pricing* (Irwin, 1983).

Jarrow, R and Rudd, A, "Approximate Option Valuation for Arbitrary Stochastic Processes" (1982) 10 *Journal of Financial Economics* 347.

Jarrow, R and Rudd, A, "Tests of an Approximate Option Valuation Formula" in Brenner, M (ed), *Option Pricing* (Lexington Mass, DC Heath, 1983, pp 81-100).

Knuth, D, *The Art of Computer Programming: Seminumerical Algorithms* (2nd ed, Vol 2, Addison-Wesley, 1981).

Kreyszig, E, *Advanced Engineering Mathematics* (John Wiley and Sons, 1993).

Launer, R and Wilkinson, G, *Robustness in Statistics* (Academic Press, 1979).

Lawrence, C, Zhou, J and Tits, A, *Users Guide for CFSQP Version 2.4: A C Code for Solving (Large Scale) Constrained Nonlinear (Minimax) Optimisation Problems, Generating Iterates Satisfying All Inequality Constraints* (Electrical Engineering Department and Institute for Systems Research, University of Maryland, College Park, MD 20742 USA, 1996).

Malliaris, A and Brock, W, *Stochastic Methods in Economics and Finance* (North-Holland, 1982).

McKean, H, *Stochastic Integrals* (New York, Academic Press, 1969).

Mendenhall, W, Scheaffer, R and Wackerly, D, *Mathematical Statistics with Applications* (4th ed, Duxbury Press, 1990).

Microsoft Corporation, *Microsoft Excel User's Guide* (1993).

Moro, B, "The Full Monte" (1995) 8(2) *Risk.*

Neter, J and Wasserman, W, *Applied Linear Statistical Models* (Irwin, 1974).

Neter, J, Kutner, M, Nachtsheim, C and Wasserman, W, *Applied Linear Statistical Models* (4th ed, Irwin, 1995).

Papageorgiou, A and Traub, J, "Beating Monte Carlo" (1996) 9(6) *Risk.*

Parkinson, M, "The Extreme Value Method for Estimating the Variance of the Rate of Return" (1980) 53(1) *Journal of Business.*

Press, W, Flannery, B, Teukolsky, S and Vetterling, W, *Numerical Recipes in c* (2nd ed, Cambridge University Press, 1992).

Ross, S, *An Introduction to Probability Models* (4th ed, Academic Press, 1989).

Schuss, Z, *Theory and Application of Stochastic Differential Equations* (Wiley, 1980).

Taha, H, *Operations Research: An Introduction* (5th ed, Macmillan Publishing, 1992).

Tezuka, S, *Uniform Random Numbers: Theory and Practice* (Kluner Academic Publishers, 1995).

Risk Management
and Financial Derivatives:

A Guide to the Mathematics

Part 1

Introduction

Chapter 1

Risk-reward Relationships—Foundations of Derivatives

by Lance Smith

1. INTRODUCTION

Classical portfolio theory examines risk/reward tradeoffs from a "mean-variance' framework. In this model, the "risk" of an individual security is encapsulated by the variance (or, equivalently, *standard deviation*) of its returns. The higher the variance, the more uncertain the return, and therefore the greater the risk. Diversification by assembling a portfolio of securities enables investors to decrease their variance while maintaining their expected profitability target.

The analysis of the risk in derivatives, as well as the pricing methodology, differs from the classical framework in many respects. In fact, in the case of equities, the only point they have in common is the assumption that the risks of an underlying security are characterised by the mean and variance of its returns. At this point, the analysis diverges.

First of all, a derivative security (such as an option) has an asymmetrical return pattern, so that although the risks of the *underlying* security may be summarised by a mean variance model, this description is clearly insufficient to adequately capture the risks in the *option*. We will see that the value of the derivative security is determined chiefly by the price of the underlying and its variance. However, in order to understand this connection, we must first introduce two concepts: *hedging* and *arbitrage*.

2. HEDGING AND ARBITRAGE

The process of reducing or eliminating a particular risk in a portfolio through a trade, or a series of trades, (or contractual agreements) is called *hedging*. The corresponding trades or contractual agreements are referred to as *hedges*. In a typical investment portfolio, there is little or no hedging; rather, the investor simply tries to achieve the greatest upside potential, given an acceptable level of risk. This is the framework of modern portfolio theory.

The pricing of derivatives goes to the other extreme: here, the requirement is to construct a portfolio (the hedging portfolio) that eliminates all of the risks introduced by the derivative security being analysed. In particular, the hedging portfolio is required to replicate a return pattern identical to that of the derivative security, so that, from the point of view of an investor, the two alternatives—replicating portfolio and derivative security—are indistinguishable.

3

This latter point introduces the notion of *arbitrage*. If the replicating portfolio and the derivative security produce the same return pattern, then they should have the same value. If they currently have different values in the marketplace, there is then an opportunity for *arbitrage*, that is, one can sell the higher-valued representation and purchase the lower-valued one, securing a risk free profit.

In the real world, things seldom work out as neatly, and there may be other reasons for an apparent arbitrage opportunity. Most pricing models ignore these secondary issues and focus on the primary risks. It is important, therefore, to understand the underlying assumptions and the implications for the pricing model. In the next section, we will illustrate these points by carefully inspecting two examples.

3. REPLICATING PORTFOLIOS

This section will attempt to provide an intuitive understanding of the "building blocks" of derivatives from a trading and risk management perspective, as opposed to an abstract mathematical one. The basic point of view is that in order to determine the price of a derivative security, one needs to understand how to *hedge* the security, and that the theoretical value is then determined by calculating the cost of the hedge. In this context, *hedging* will refer to a trade, or a series of trades in an appropriate *underlying security* in such a way as to offset the corresponding risk in the derivative security. In practice, there may be alternative choices of hedging security, but these can be compared to this basic case.

By examining the hedging process in some detail, we can arrive at a better appreciation of the risks that are not being adequately hedged; that is, we can better understand "where the model breaks down". The trader's job is then to determine a price for these unhedged risks given the trader's current portfolio. The risk manager's job is to understand and quantify the total unhedged risk in the firm's position and ensure that it is maintained within acceptable limits, given the firm's risk/reward profile.

We will illustrate these points by carefully examining two basic examples.

The first, that of a forward contract on a stock, requires only a *static* hedge. The second, an option on a stock, requires a *dynamic* hedge. In both cases we will see that the price of the security is determined by two considerations:

1. **cost of the hedge (or value of the replicating portfolio); and**

2. **compensation for unhedged risk.**

3.1 **Example 1:** A one year forward contract on a stock

A customer wishes to purchase 100,000 shares of a particular stock from you, one year from today. He wants to determine the price today at which he will purchase the stock in one year.

We will determine the price, the *forward price* of the stock, by examining the cost of the hedge. We seek a trade or series of trades that will exactly offset the risk inherent in the forward contract. We know that in one year we need to have in hand 100,000 shares of stock. One way to achieve this is to purchase the shares of stock today and set them aside for delivery in one year. What will this cost? Let us assume that the current (spot) price of the stock is $100, so that we can purchase the stock at $100 per share today. What must we charge in one year in order to break even? The $100 per share that I have spent on my hedge could have been invested elsewhere, such as in money market securities which earn interest. This is a relatively "risk free" transaction. We wish to place a hedge so that the forward contract is equally risk free. Put another way, as a trader, I will be charged interest on the $100 per share that I have tied up in my hedge. If the rate at which I borrow money for one year is 10% (simple annual), then I will incur $10 per share of interest charges during the life of the forward contract, so I need to receive $110 per share at maturity in order to break even. So, at first pass, the forward price of the stock should be $110.

However, if the stock pays a dividend of, say, $3 over the next year, then I will receive $3 per share in my hedging portfolio. This reduces the cost of my hedge and the customer will expect to be rebated by adjusting the forward price to $107. That is:

$$\text{Total cost of hedge} = \$107 \text{ per share.}$$

At this point we should stop and investigate if there are any risks that we have ignored. One risk is that the $3 of dividends is not guaranteed. We can only *forecast* $3, recognising that the company of the stock could adjust this amount either up or down. For this reason we might modify our price to provide a cushion against this event. An alternative is to simply agree to *pass through* the dividends at the maturity of the contract. In this way neither ourselves nor the customer bear the dividend risk, which is basically unhedgeable. In this case the forward price would remain at $110 per share, and the customer receives any interim dividends.

We have also ignored the effect of changes in interest rates. If we finance our stock hedge overnight, then we are at risk to changes in interest rate levels because our forward price was determined assuming a fixed rate of 10%. This may be overcome by taking term financing for one year at 10%, instead of overnight.

Another risk which has been ignored by our neat analysis is *counterparty* risk; that is, the risk that the counterparty may default on moneys owed to us. Suppose that over the next three months the stock plummets to $25 per share. Let us assume we have a pass-through forward so that the price of the original forward contract has been set at $110. At this point our counterparty will owe us about $85 more per share above the current market price, in nine months (the remaining term of the forward contract). On 100,000 shares this comes out to be $8,500,000. This is essentially the (unrealised) amount of money that we have lost on our hedge, so that if the counterparty defaults we are really out this amount. For this reason there may be collateralisation requirements built in to the contract. We note that futures contracts are exchange-traded forward contracts with a daily collateralisation requirement (that is, variation margin).

Finally, another risk that has been ignored is that of *liquidity*, or the practical limitation of implementing a hedge in the marketplace. In order to hedge our position in this example, we must purchase 100,000 shares of stock. Unless the forward price is calculated off of our average cost of acquiring the stock hedge, we will also be at risk in that the purchase of this much stock may impact on the price.

The main point we are making here is that the theoretical determination of the forward price is as we initially calculated. However, by thinking through what is required to actually hedge the position, we arrive at a better understanding of the risks involved.

Exercise:

Suppose the customer wishes to *sell* a forward contract on the stock. Suppose that in addition the stock can be borrowed or loaned for an annual fee of 2.0%. What should the forward price be?

We next turn to an example of a European style (no early exercise) equity option. Our goal is to understand the hedging process for such a security and its impact upon the theoretical valuation of the option. We will proceed as intuitively as possible.

3.2 Example 2: European style call option on a stock

A customer wishes to purchase a three month call option on 100 shares of stock. The current stock price is $100, as is the exercise (strike) price of the option.

We will begin the analysis with the *expiration diagram* of this security (Exhibit 1.1). That is, a graph of the value of this security at expiration. Clearly, to the extent that the stock price exceeds the exercise price, the excess will be the value of the option, and if the stock price falls below the exercise price, the option will expire worthless. Therefore, the expiration diagram is simply a "hockey stick" as presented below.

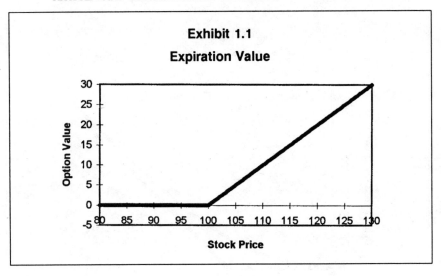

Exhibit 1.1

Expiration Value

We currently have three months to go on this security. What should the graph of the call option value look like when the three months are taken into account? A number of things are easy to see. First of all, for very low stock prices, say around 80, the option has very little value as the possibility of the stock rising 20 points is rather remote (again, we are speaking *intuitively* here). For stock prices around 100, the option has value in that if the stock price drops, there is nothing to lose, but if it rises, there is much to gain, in fact, point for point with the stock price. Finally, for high stock prices, say 120, the option is of course, worth at least 20 points but not a whole lot more because the option has as much to lose as it has to gain depending upon whether the stock falls or rises; put another way, the one-sidedness of the expiration diagram is not as evident with the stock at 120. These intuitive samples indicate that the graph should look something like the following:

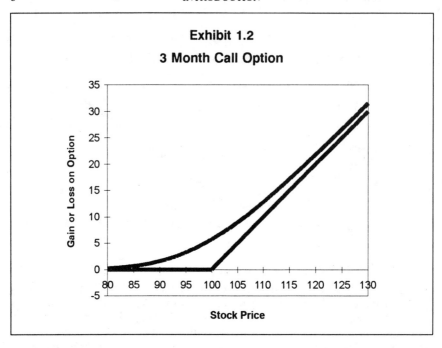

Exhibit 1.2

3 Month Call Option

Note that the graph begins to parallel the hockey stick at both extremes. We see that, on the downside, the graph should approach the expiration diagram. However, on the upside, it will approach a value that is a fixed amount above the expiration diagram. We now will set about to hedge our position. Obviously, as the stock price increases, so does the value of the call option. As we are short the option we will suffer a loss unless we have positioned a hedge that compensates for this loss. One way is to purchase some shares of stock. Then, as the stock price increases, our hedge will make money to offset the losses on the option position. The flip side is of course that if the stock price *drops* our hedge will *lose* money, but our short option position will *gain*. The first question is: How much stock should we purchase? If we make a brief return to first semester calculus we will recall the notion of *tangent line*. The amount of stock we should purchase will correspond to the *slope* of the tangent line. For high stock prices this slope approaches 100%, and for low stock prices it approaches 0%.

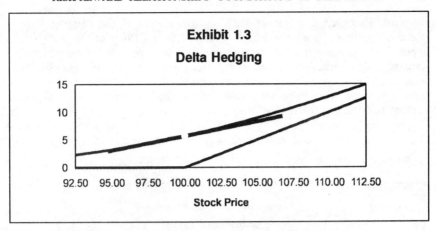

Exhibit 1.3

Delta Hedging

Let us suppose that the current slope, corresponding to the current stock price of 100, is 50%. We should then purchase 50 shares of stock, since the option is actually on 100 shares, not just 1. Suppose next that the stock rallies to 102, where the slope is now 60%. We are underhedged! In order to get hedged again we should purchase another 10 shares, paying 102 per share. Now suppose the stock falls back to 100. Now we are *overhedged* and should sell off 10 shares at 100. Of course we are now back to where we began, except that we have lost 2 points on 10 shares for a $20 loss. If the stock continues to see-saw in this fashion we will continue to "buy high and sell low" in the process of actively hedging our position. This is an odd way to make money, and in fact we appear to be losing. However, the other side of the coin is that, as time passes, the value of the option should "decay". That is, the graph eventually should approach the hockey stick. To the extent that the option decays, we will make back some of the money we are losing by hedging. It is a race between the two effects: trading losses versus time decay. In other words, if the stock is *volatile*, we will be whipsawed more and lose the race, and therefore lose money. If the stock is very quiet, we will win the race and make money. The famous Black-Scholes option pricing formula basically calculates what these hedging costs will be over the life of the option and then asserts that the (present value) of these costs should equal its price. That is, just as in the calculation for the forward contract, *the value should equal the cost of the hedge*. This time it is more complicated, of course, because the hedging process (termed "delta-hedging") is *dynamic*. We summarise this discussion below.

> The theoretical price of an option is equal to the cost of hedging the option.

With this point in mind, we can now examine what *information* is required to price an option. Clearly, the terms of the option (exercise price, expiration date, et cetera) are required. We also need to know various market parameters such as the stock price, dividend information and interest rates, as these are all relevant to calculating the cost of the hedge, just as for the stock forward. However, because of the dynamic nature of the hedging process there is one more parameter which we need: the *volatility* of the stock (or its square, the *variance*). This is a statistical measurement, calculated as an (annualised) standard deviation of the stock price returns that quantifies the extent of the "whipsawing" we can expect when dynamically hedging the option position. The more volatile the stock, the more expensive our hedge, so that the price of the option should increase with the volatility of the stock. Typical values range from 10% to 50%. The lower end corresponds to a stock index, while a blue chip stock is typically in the 20%-35% range.

We summarise the required information in a table:

Inputs for Option Valuation
Contractual Terms
Exercise Price
Expiration Date
Style (American or European)
Market Information
Stock Price
Interest Rates
Dividend Information
Statistical Information
Volatility

At this point it is important to note that all of the inputs are known *except for the volatility* (and to some extent the dividends). That is, the cost of hedging will be influenced by the volatility of the stock *during the life of the option*. This is not really known, but must be predicted. We can certainly measure the past volatility of the stock, but there is no guarantee of the future volatility. This has been compared to "skiing down a slope backwards", watching the trees go by. Because of the inherent intractability of the volatility parameter, there is always a degree of uncertainty in what the hedging costs will be. In short, if we are hedging only by dynamically adjusting our stock hedge, this parameter risk is unhedged. In a typical situation a trader will have a portfolio of options, both long and short of varying maturities, so that the risk of the unknown volatility is netted across the entire portfolio. Then the risk manager needs to be concerned with issues such as three month volatility versus six month volatility; that is, the "term structure" of volatility. We will not explore this aspect here; it is a natural extension of the ideas presented so far.

Exercise:
For very high stock prices, we have stated that the option value approaches a fixed amount above the expiration diagram. Calculate this value by calculating the cost of the hedge (note that the slope is 100%).

4. GLOSSARY OF TERMS

Before we can continue with our discussion, it is important that we define some frequently used technical terms.

A Glossary of Greeks

Delta	Greek symbol δ. This is simply the slope of the tangent line. This risk is *hedgeable* with the underlying stock.
Gamma	Greek symbol γ. This measures how rapidly the slope changes. For a trader, it is used to anticipate how much rehedging will be required for a given move in the stock price. This risk is *unhedgeable*, except with other option-like securities.
Theta	Greek symbol θ. This measures the time decay. In a sense (referring to the "race" mentioned earlier), theta is the flipside of gamma. This risk is also *unhedgeable*, except with other option-like securities.
Sigma	Greek symbol σ. Measures the *volatility* of the stock (expressed as an annualised standard deviation of returns). Also *unhedgeable*, except with other option-like securities.
Kappa	Greek symbol κ (also called "vega"). This measures the sensitivity to the volatility assumption, σ. Again, *unhedgeable* except with other option-like securities.
Rho	Greek symbol ρ (also called "dv01"). Measures the sensitivity to interest rates for (usually) a one "basis point" change (that is, .01%). This is *hedgeable* by trading, for example, an appropriate bond.

5. RISK NEUTRALITY

Up to now, we have examined derivative pricing from the perspective of hedging. As it turns out, there is an alternative method of calculation that is actually a byproduct of the hedging approach, termed the "Risk Neutrality Hypothesis". It states that the price of the derivative security can be calculated by making simplifying assumptions about the underlying process, and then computing its "expected value" under the simplified process, discounting as if it were a known cashflow. We will first illustrate this principle in the case of an ordinary stock option, and then indicate why it is true with a brief foray into the binomial world.

This time we begin again with the hockey stick expiration diagram. We next calculate the "expected value" of this by simply taking each point on the diagram and multiplying by a probability, and then adding them all up. This sounds tedious; fortunately, computers are very good at this. The resulting number is then present valued to today. The probability distribution is obtained by taking the original process for the stock price (that is, *lognormal*—we have carefully avoided actually writing it down) and replacing the *expected return* of the stock—a very subjective number—with the "risk free" rate (actually, our financing rate). We have retained the stock volatility, σ, which is in general a less subjective number than the expected return.

In order to understand why the risk neutral calculation is equivalent to calculating the hedging costs, we will consider a simple one step binomial "tree". That is, suppose that over the next time period the stock, currently at a price of S, can either go up to a price S^+, or go down to a price S^-. We will assume that $S^+ = uS$ and $S^- = dS$ with $0 < d < 1 < u$ (that is, u stands for "up" and d stands for "down"). *We do not assume that we know the probability of either event.* This is tantamount to not knowing the expected return on the stock. Next, we attempt to hedge an option on this stock over the next time period, assuming that at the price S^+ it will equal C^+ and at S^- it will equal C^- (for example, if the option expires in the next time period). We wish to construct a hedge of stock and cash (accruing at a rate of r%) which will "hedge" this option. To that end, we assume that we hold a position of m shares of stock and n units of cash (m will be a fractional share in this calculation). We certainly are not concerned about roundlots right now. Thus, the value of our hedging portfolio is currently

$$mS + nB$$

We will assume that over the next time period that B will grow to FB; F is a "future value" factor; and F—1 is the interest earned per unit of cash during this time period. Our task is to determine m and n so that we are hedged in the two events $S = S^+$ and $S = S^-$. That is, we must determine m and n so that:

$$mS^+ + nFB = C^+$$

and

$$mS^- + nFB = C^-$$

These are two equations in two unknowns which are easily solved. For example, we find that m is just

$$m = (C^+ - C^-)/(S^+ - S^-)$$

which corresponds exactly to the tangent line slope originally discussed. In a similar fashion we can solve for n, and substitute back in to find that, after rearranging terms

$$mS + nB = (pC^+ + qC^-)/F$$

where

$$p = (F - d)/(u — d)$$

and

$$q = (u — F)/(u - d).$$

We note that

$$p + q = 1$$

and

$$0 < p < 1$$
$$0 < q < 1$$

as long as $F < u$. This last assumption simply asserts that the stock must have a chance of outperforming the cash instrument in any time period. (Otherwise, why would anyone ever buy the stock!) These equations imply that p and q can be interpreted as *probabilities* (termed *arbitrage probabilities*) and the value of the hedging portfolio today, which equals the option price today, is simply equal to the expected value of its price over the next time period, using the arbitrage probabilities), discounted by the factor F. This is nothing more than a binomial description of the risk neutrality principle.

The power of the risk neutrality methodology is that once it has been demonstrated that a particular derivative security can be hedged—usually by considering a similar one step binomial tree (or in the case of more complicated multifactor securities, a multinomial tree)—an elaborate mathematical machinery can then be called into play to actually perform the calculation. The main *drawback* of this methodology is that one can be easily seduced into the risk neutral world where none of us actually live, and forget some of the model assumptions that brought us there. This is why, from the point of view of risk management, it is important to understand how the models can break down, and how to best *stress test* them.

6. APPLICATIONS OF THE RISK NEUTRALITY PRINCIPLE

The risk neutrality calculation methodology can be applied to a wide variety of derivative securities. The key point is to verify the hedgeability of the relevant risks; the problem is then reduced to an "expected value" calculation, which is usually quite tractable or at least amenable to a wide variety of mathematical techniques.

6.1 Example: A three month "look back" option

This is a security that will payout in three months the difference between the *maximum* stock price reached over the next three months, S^*, and today's stock price, K. That is, the payment will be:

$$S^* — K.$$

K is currently known, while S^* is not. Is this hedgeable? We resort to binomial logic. With one period to go to expiration, we will know the current maximum S^*, and therefore, the maximum at expiration in either case $S = S^+$

(where the maximum will be the greater of S^+ and S^*), or $S = S^-$ (where the maximum will remain S^*). This means that we can then construct our hedge just as before.

This reasoning can be extended to earlier periods as well, establishing that the security is hedgeable. However, in order to *calculate* the theoretical price, we can now invoke the Risk Neutrality Hypothesis and employ alternative means. Now any mathematician can apply advanced techniques (partial differential equations, Green's functions, stopping times, Monte Carlo as a last resort, et cetera) to solve the problem. Some of these techniques have been around for over 100 years and have become practical with the advent of computer technology. For American style (early exercise) securities, this calculation is performed over a small time interval, after which the security can be tested for early exercise, just as in a binomial option pricing model.

Once the model is in hand, it should be *stress tested* in order to reveal hidden risks that are *unhedgeable* (except with other options or option-like securities).

7. ARBITRAGE—A CLOSER LOOK

As we have noted, the basic premise of all pricing models is that the value of the derivative security should equal that of a replicating portfolio; conversely, if the values differ, than arbitrageurs can play one against the other and obtain a riskless profit. In an efficient market this arbitrage activity should force convergence of market prices to theoretical prices.

All of this is approximately true, and more true for some derivative securities than for others, but there are often legitimate reasons for a "mispricing", usually due to features of the marketplace that have not been adequately incorporated into the pricing model. Obvious features are transaction costs such as brokerage fees and stamp duties. Some others are listed below:

7.1 Counterparty risk (for OTC transactions)

This has been illustrated in the example of the forward contract.

7.2 Cash flow risk

The pricing models usually assume that many can be borrowed whenever it is needed. This may not be really true. If we return to the example of the forward contract, recall the scenario where the stock has fallen to $25 a share. If we have purchased the stock on margin, this would trigger a massive margin call; if we have insufficient funds, our hedge will be liquidated.

7.3 Parameter risk

As discussed in the example of the European style call option, the cost of the hedge will depend largely upon the experienced volatility during the hedging. This parameter can only be estimated.

7.4 Horizon risk

This is a more subtle risk, and has to do with the *rate of convergence* between the market price and the theoretical price; that is, the rate at which the trade increases in profitability. In the case of a three month call option, it will take at most three months. But for, say, a convertible bond, it could take as long as 15 years. This lengthy horizon can easily disincentivize arbritrageurs from stepping in (they tend to have notoriously short time horizons).

8. CONCLUSION

This chapter has discussed the pricing of equity derivatives, but the same techniques apply to other financial derivatives as well. The general procedure is to:

(i) identify the primary risks and a mathematical model for their evolution through time;

(ii) identify underlying "hedging instruments" for the risks;

(iii) verify the hedgeability (this may be done with an appropriate binomial tree, or *multinomial* tree in the case of multiple risks);

(iv) calculate the value by invoking the Risk Neutrality Hypothesis; and

(v) consult a mathematician to actually perform the calculation. Also ask for a list of the model parameters. These will give rise to corresponding sensitivities which should be stress tested in order to develop a better understanding of the unhedged risks.

Part 2

Interest Rates and Yield Curves

Chapter 2

Interest Rates, Bond Pricing, Duration and Convexity

by Roger Cohen

1. WHAT IS AN INTEREST RATE?

The term interest rate is commonly used to describe the growth or earning potential associated with an amount of money. Common occurrences of interest rates include the advertised return on money deposited in a bank account, home loan mortgage rates, financing costs and so forth. The types of rates, and the context in which they are used is often confusing. In this chapter, various representations of interest rates will be introduced and explained. The context in which interest rates are used in the financial markets will be explained.

An interest rate refers to the rate of growth or decay of an asset over time. It is a measure of the value of the asset at the present relative to its value in the future. Although the asset is usually cash, it need not be. Interest rates allow us to quantify questions such as *"is it worth more now or in the future?"* or *"what will this be worth in ten years time?"*. They are a measure of the earning (or expense) associated with deferred consumption. For example, an individual may have a sum of money that is not needed at the present time. Another individual may need money (perhaps to buy food, or to build a house). The two individuals can enter into an agreement where the latter gets the use of the money at the present time. The full amount plus an additional sum will be repaid at a future date. This additional sum is the interest paid by the borrower to the lender. By deferring consumption of the money, the lender is rewarded with extra cash or interest. This is the governing principle of most financial transactions. The financial markets just formalise the mechanics of such transactions. They provide an efficient framework for transferring capital. The underlying principal is that a lender receives interest for the use of capital by a borrower. This applies where the lender is an individual, an organisation or even an entire country. The converse applies to the borrower.

Although varying in complexity, interest rate transactions involve a borrower and a lender. A bank deposit, for example, is effectively a loan by an individual to a bank. The underlying rationale is that the bank is able to use this money to earn income greater than the expense associated with the interest paid to the depositor. An example of this is that home loan mortgage rates (where the bank is the lender and an individual is the borrower) are invariably higher than deposit rates (where the bank is now the borrower). The appropriate rates of interest are dependent on the parties involved in a transaction, the risk of the transaction (that is, whether the borrower will be

19

able to repay the debt), and the amount, structure and timing of the transaction. This will not be discussed further here.

Interest rates are also used to quantify the growth or decay of commodities other than money. This includes gold and other precious metals, and certain financial instruments such as stocks. Interest rates need not be positive. If there are storage costs, or time wastage associated with holding a commodity, then its interest rate may be negative. This means that a lender of such a quantity will pay a fee to the borrower.

1.1 Representations of interest rates

There are many representations of interest rates. Usually (but not always) rates are a positive amount expressed as a percentage. They are measures of the growth or decay of an asset. For example, an advertised rate of 10% paid annually, means that $100 will be worth $110 after one year. Generally a rate is expressed as a percentage, and a basis. The percentage gives the amount of growth that is expected, the basis tells the period over which this growth is compounded. If the 10% of the above example were paid semi-annually (that is, twice a year), then after six months $100 would be worth $105.[1] If the interest is compound, then after a further six months, the $105 is increased by 5% giving $110.25 after one year. From this we can see that 10% semi-annually is then equivalent to 10.25% as an annual rate. Similarly, 10% quarterly would mean a growth of 2.5% is applied each quarter. Simple rates are applied over a period without compounding. An annual simple rate of 10% would increase $100 to $110, $120 and $130 over 1, 2 and 3 years respectively. If the 10% were compounded annually, then $100 would increase to $110, $121 and $133.10 respectively.

1.2 Interest rate arithmetic

There is nothing special about how an interest rate is expressed. Rates can be changed from one basis to any other. The premise for doing this is to realise that, at the end of a period, the final amount must be the same when any rate basis is used. To convert from one basis to another,

$$(1+\frac{r_1}{b_1})^{b1} = (1+\frac{r_2}{b_2})^{b2}$$

where r_1 and r_2 are interest rates with bases b_1 and b_2.

Example:

What is the quarterly equivalent of 7.5% semi-annual?

$$(1+\frac{r}{4})^4 = (1+\frac{0.075}{2})^2$$

This solves to give $r = 0.07431$ or 7.431% as a quarterly rate.

---

1.   By convention, non-annual rates are divided by the number of periods in a year. Thus 10% semi-annually means interest is 5% every half year; 10% quarterly would be 2.5% per quarter and so forth.

An interest rate can be converted from any basis to any other.[2] It is convention to express the periodicity of rates in years. There are various conventions for determining the number of days in a year. These will be discussed below.

Commonly used interest rate bases include

1. *Simple*: This is where the rate is expressed exactly over the period required. For example, 8% over 45 days would mean that $1 grows to $1(1 + 0.08*45/365) = $1.0099 after 45 days.

2. *Daily*: These rates are compounded daily. Cash or overnight rates set by most central banks are daily effective. A daily rate of 10% means that after n days, $100 increases to $100(1+0.1/365)^n$.

3. *Monthly, quarterly and semi-annual*: Rates are compounded 12, four and two times per year.

1.3 Year basis

In financial calculations, the number of days per year used when calculating interest periods is not necessarily the actual number of days in the period. Convention uses either a 365 day or a 360 day year. Months may use the actual number of days or be considered as having a fixed number of days—usually 30. Arithmetic for these conventions can be found in DAS, *Swaps and Financial Derivatives* (2nd ed, 1994), pp 174-178.

1.4 Continuous rates

Another interest rate basis is that of continuous or continuously compounding rates. These never actually appear explicitly in financial instruments or transactions. They are a representation most often used internally in financial calculations. They provide a simple means for performing interest rate arithmetic. Within many financial models, rates are converted to continuous rates. They are converted back to their original basis after manipulation.

In the section above, we showed various compounding periods ranging from one year down to one day. If the compounding period is decreased further, then in the limit (where the period becomes infinitesimal), we have continuously compounding rates. If we had a rate r compounded continuously, then after one year, we would have the following growth:

$$\lim_{n \to \infty}(1+\frac{r}{n})^n = e^r$$

An amount A would grow to Ae^r after one year. For the general case, using rate r for time t (in years), the growth would be e^{rt}. The advantage of continuously compounding rates will become apparent when we introduce

2. It is interesting to note that when rates are advertised, they are commonly expressed in a basis that makes them look attractive to an investor. Deposit rates are often expressed as annual effective even when they are compounded (10.25% annual effective looks more attractive to the uninformed than 10.00% paid semi-annually). For borrowing rates, the converse is often the case. Mortgage rates are often compounded monthly or even daily (a rate of 10% daily is the same as 10.516% annual effective).

forward rates later in this chapter. It is also essential in many models used for option pricing.

Exhibit 2.1

Value of $1 in 1 Year, at 10% Interest Using Various Bases

Basis	Periods Per Year	Rate	Formula	Value
Annual Effective	1	10%	$(1+0.1)$	$1.10000
Semi Annual	2	10%	$(1+0.1/2)^2$	$1.10250
Quarterly	4	10%	$(1+0.1/4)^4$	$1.10381
Monthly	12	10%	$(1+0.1/12)^{12}$	$1.10471
Daily	365	10%	$(1+0.1/365)^{365}$	$1.10516
Daily (360)	360	10%	$(1+0.1/360)^{360}$	$1.10516
Continuous	∞	10%	$e^{0.1}$	$1.10517

10% continuously compounded is the same as 10.517% annual effective.

It is a common perception that continuously compounded rates are complex. This is not true. The reality is that working with continuously compounding rates is simpler than with discrete rates. This is due to the exponential growth and decay used when valuing with continuous rates. The perception of difficulty arises as rates need to be converted to continuous before they can be used, and then often back to simple rates after manipulation. To convert a rate to continuous we use the relationship

$$e^{rt} = (1+R)^T$$

where r is the continuous rate applied over time t years, and R is the periodic rate applied over T periods. The relationship between t and T is $t = T.f$ where f is the number of periods per year over which R is effective.

Example: continuous and discrete rates

What is the continuous and annual equivalent of a semi-annual rate of 7.5%?

When converting a rate from one basis to any other, we will still get the same return. After one year, the semi annual rate R will gross one dollar up to $1(1+R/2)^2$ dollars. A continuously compounded rate r will gross a dollar up to $1.e^r$ dollars. For equivalence, these must be equal. Similarly, the annual rate r' will also gross up to the same dollar value.

$$(1+\frac{R}{2})^2 = e^r = (1+r')$$

Solving when $R = 7.5\%$ gives an annual effective rate of 7.6406% and a continuous rate of 7.3628%.

$$(1+\frac{0.075}{2})^2 = e^{0.073628} = (1+0.076406)$$

The continuously compounded rate can be used in calculations. It is easier to work with exponentials and logarithms rather than the discrete representations.

1.5 Valuing cashflows

From the discussion of interest rates above, we are now in a position to value any cashflow to or from the present day. If we are valuing future cashflows to the present, this is often referred to as *discounting* or obtaining the *net present value* or *NPV*. The reverse—finding the value in the future of an amount of cash at present—is referred to as *grossing up*.

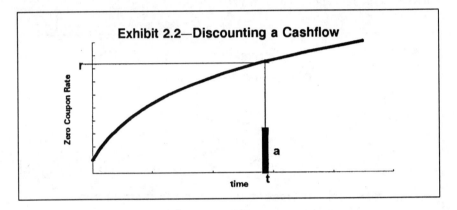

Exhibit 2.2—Discounting a Cashflow

Any cashflow can be valued by discounting at an appropriate rate

$$Val = \frac{a}{(1+r)^t} = e^{-Rt} = a.DF(t)$$

The concepts of discounting and grossing up form the basis of most financial transactions. Investors are trying to maximise their return or the NPV of their assets, while borrowers are seeking the minimum cost for their borrowings. This is all done within a framework where the risks involved and the structure of the transactions are considered.

1.6 Forward rates

As well as being able to express interest rates in many different bases, it is also important to specify the exact period over which the interest rates apply. Rates in the above sections are considered to apply from the present to a date in the future, or vice versa. These are referred to as *spot rates*. The spot date is usually the present date, or the date out of which a transaction begins.

This need not always be the case. Where rates apply over a period that does not involve the present (or spot date), we refer to these rates as *forward rates*. An example—the three month rate in three months time is referred to as the three month forward. There is a deterministic relationship between spot and forward rates. This relationship stems from the principle that a cashflow should have the same NPV no matter how it is discounted. If this does not hold, then there is a basis for increasing the NPV by revaluing the cashflow differently. Such an occurrence is called an *arbitrage* (see the section below). In the financial markets, professional arbitrageurs constantly exploit such occurrences. Because of this, they do not often exist, and if they do then it is only for very short periods.

If it is assumed (usually this is the case) that there is no arbitrage, then over any period, the value of a cashflow will be invariant whether it is discounted by a single rate or a series of forward rates. The general principle

$$\frac{1}{(1+r_{ac})^{t(ac)}} = \frac{1}{(1+r_{ab})^{t(ab)}} \times \frac{1}{(1+r_{bc})^{t(bc)}}$$

where r^{ij} is the rate applicable over period $t(ij)$.

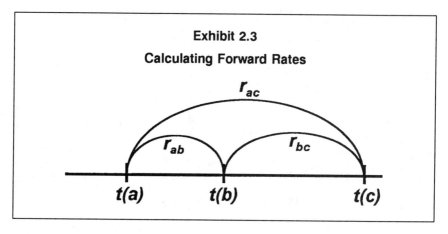

Exhibit 2.3

Calculating Forward Rates

In the market, there may be slight differences in value depending on the path for discounting or grossing up. Usually this will be less than the margin lost if the difference were to be exploited.

Example: forward rates

What is the forward rate from three months to six months given the following spot rates?

	Spot Rate
1 month	7.49
3 Month	7.75
6 Month	7.82

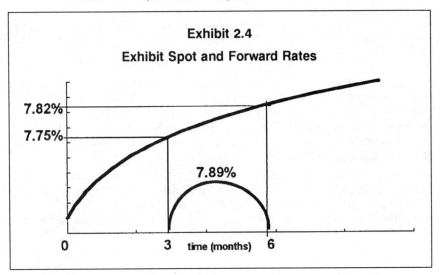

Exhibit 2.4

Exhibit Spot and Forward Rates

To solve for the forward rate from three to six months, we note that under the no arbitrage principal, one dollar in six months must have the same NPV if it is discounted by the six month spot rate, or by the forward rate from three to six months then the three month spot rate. If these are annual effective rates, then

$$\frac{1}{(1+r_{06})^{\frac{6}{12}}} = \frac{1}{(1+r_{03})^{\frac{3}{12}}} \times \frac{1}{(1+r_{36})^{\frac{3}{12}}}$$

The subscripts on the rates above refer to the start and end of the period over which the rates apply. Spot rates all have a subscript starting with zero (the spot date). Solving this gives $r_{36} = 7.8900\%$

Continuously compounded make calculations of forward rates extremely simple. In the example above, we can do the calculation using continuous rates.

	Spot Rate	Continuous
1 month	7.49	7.2228
3 Month	7.75	7.4644
6 Month	7.82	7.5293

The forward rate from three to six months in the continuous representation is given by

$$e^{-r_{06}\frac{6}{12}} = e^{-r_{03}\frac{3}{12}} \times e^{-r_{36}\frac{3}{12}}$$

This simplifies to

$$e^{-r_{36}\frac{3}{12}} = e^{-(r_{06}\frac{6}{12} - r_{03}\frac{3}{12})}$$

or

$$\mathbf{r_{36}} = \frac{12}{3}(r_{06}\frac{6}{12} - r_{03}\frac{3}{12})$$

The forward rate is a simple arithmetic expression, which gives the continuously compounded forward rate from three to six months as 7.5942%. Converted back to an annual effective rate we get 7.8900%, which is exactly the same as when calculated using the annual effective rates directly. Once the conversion to the continuously compounding domain is made, calculations are generally simpler.

Futures contracts are common manifestations of forward rates. In most markets participants have access to a strip of bill futures. These are usually three month instruments which start at various dates in the future. Forward rate agreements or FRAs are instruments which provide a guaranteed forward rate.

Digression: an arbitrage

The calculations from above are based on the principle of *no arbitrage*. To illustrate what happens when there is an arbitrage opportunity, we use the spot rates of the example above, but instead of solving for the forward rate of 7.89%, assume that there exists some instrument which will pay a rate of, say, 8.5% for the forward period from three months to six months.

	Rate
1 month	7.49
3 month	7.75
6 month	7.82
3-6m fwd	8.5

Using these rates, consider the value of a cashflow (say $1,000,000) in six months time. If it were discounted by the six month rate of 7.82%, its NPV would be $963,053. If the NPV were calculated by discounting from six to three months at the forward rate of 8.5%, then from three months to spot at the three month spot rate 7.75%, the NPV is now $961,697 (or $1,356 less than using the six month spot rate). If these rates were all available to a market participant, and the risk associating with borrowing or lending at them were equivalent, then an investor can borrow money for six months—the first three at the three month spot rate, the latter at the forward. This money would be lent at the six month spot rate. At the end of six months the investor would be $1,356 better off, with no net outlay. This represents an arbitrage opportunity. In reality if such an opportunity were to occur, it would quickly be exploited. This would cause the rates to be adjusted until the arbitrage disappears.

Theoretically, there should be no difference to the NPV of a future cashflow, no matter what path the discounting follows. Over one year 365 one day rolls should be the same as one year roll and so forth. This forms the basis of arbitrage free pricing theory. It is a foundation for the pricing of many complex instruments, including options.

1.7 Discount factors

Whenever we use an interest rate, we need to specify the period over which the rate applies, and the basis in which the rate is expressed. This applies to both spot and forward rates. Often this leads to undue complexity. Another way to express rates is as *discount factors*. A discount factor or DF is just the value of one dollar when discounted over the required period. As an example, if the NPV of a dollar at some future date is 94 cents, then the discount factor at this date is 0.94. Discount factors have the advantage that they do not depend on any specific basis. Using discount factors means the complexity of keeping track of whether a rate is annual, semi-annual or continuous is no longer necessary. The only aspect that needs to be tracked is the period over which the discount factor applies. Discount factors can be related to both spot and forward rates.

For compounding rates the discount factor is

$$df = \frac{1}{(1+r)^t}$$

where r is the applicable rate over time t (r must be expressed in the same basis as t—for example, if r is semi annual, then t must be the number of semi annual periods over which r applies). Where the rate r is simple (annual), the discount factor is

$$df = \frac{1}{(1+r\dfrac{d}{365})}$$

where d is the number of days over which discounting takes place. For continuous rates, the discount factor is $df = e^{-rt}$.

A curve can be drawn which gives the discount factor corresponding to any rate. These discount curves show the NPV of $1 at any time when discounted by the applicable rate.

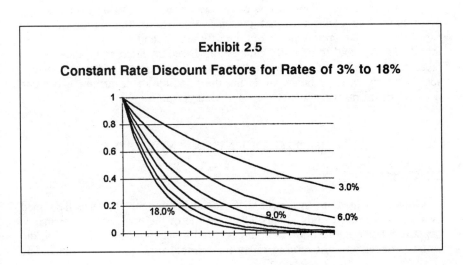

Exhibit 2.5

Constant Rate Discount Factors for Rates of 3% to 18%

Discount factors are also applicable to forward rates. If r_{ab} is a forward rate from time t_a to t_b, then a forward discount factor df_{ab} can be generated. It provides the discounted value at t_a of one dollar at t_b. The relationship between spot and forward discount factors is straightforward.

$$df_{0b} = df_{0a} \times df_{ab}$$

where the subscripts are as described above.

1.8 Putting it all together—the term structure of interest rates

The interest rates used in the above sections are all considered in isolation. In the marketplace, we are constantly bombarded with different rates or types of rates. These are represented in a multitude of different bases. It is only meaningful to compare these rates if they are converted into a uniform basis, and have a consistent underlying type. When this is done, we obtain an *interest rate term structure* or *yield curve*. The interest rate term structure is just a time consistent view of interest rates. Usually it is a curve showing the rates which are effective over different time periods. For example, if we have a set of annual effective rates specified for periods of one, two, three years and so forth, then a curve through these is a representation of an interest rate term structure. Please refer to Chapter 3 for examples.

There is no single universal term structure. Rates differ depending on the currency, types of instrument and the way the rates are represented. Within a single currency, there are different term structures for classes of interest rates. The interest rate term structure may also be derived from market rates rather than using them directly. These aspects will be discussed further in the chapter on the yield curve.

1.9 Summary—interest rates

In this chapter so far we have covered various forms of interest rates. We have shown the different bases that rates can be expressed in, and how to convert from one base to another. The process of discounting and grossing up have been illustrated. These allow cashflows at any time to be valued at any other time. The concept of net present value shows the worth of future cashflows at the spot date. Continuously compounding rates have been introduced as a tool to simplify calculation. Discount factors are also used to represent the value of cashflows at various times. The difference between spot and forward rates is shown. Using the principle of no arbitrage, we can derive forward rates from spot rates and vice versa.

2. BOND PRICING, DURATION AND CONVEXITY

2.1 Bonds

A bond is a medium to long-term financial instrument. It is usually issued by a party in order to raise funds. Over the life of the bond, the issuer makes periodic interest payments. These are referred to as coupons. At maturity, the issuer is under an obligation to repay the original principal of the bond. The life of a bond is usually not less than one year (bills or short-term notes are used for shorter periods). It is not uncommon for bonds to have maturities in excess of 20-30 years. Coupon payments are generally made quarterly, semi-annually or annually.

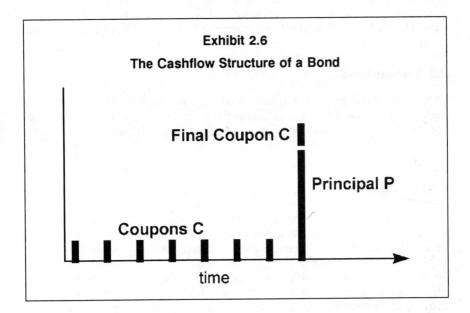

Exhibit 2.6

The Cashflow Structure of a Bond

The value of a bond is determined by the size and timing of the cashflows. It is also highly dependent on the quality of the bond. For example, government or sovereign bonds are usually regarded as high quality instruments. They will be more expensive than lower quality bonds such as those issued by a corporation or an individual.

Some of the factors that affect the value of a bond include:

1. *Coupon size and timing*: the larger and more frequent the coupons, the greater the value of the bond.

2. *Maturity*: this is the period over which coupon payments are made.

3. *Issuer quality*: the risk associated with default is relatively lower if the issuer is of high quality. Such bonds will attract a premium.

4. *Current interest rates and outlook*: these affect the value of the bond on the secondary market.

5. *Liquidity*: there can be a premium for bonds that are easily tradeable.

Bonds are referred to as *fixed interest or fixed income instruments*. This is because, once the bond has been issued, all future payments are known. The only disruption to these will be if there is some sort of crisis event where the issuer cannot make an interest or principal payment, or a payment is delayed. The probability of such a default event is priced into most bonds. As this probability of default changes, the premium or discount associated with it will vary.

Many bonds, once issued, trade in the secondary market. Their market value will depend on prevailing economic conditions as well as the current state of the issuer. To enable bonds to trade, the market has developed conventions for their valuation. These all derive from the principle of discounting cashflows (which is discussed earlier in this chapter). This makes sense, as a bond is just a collection of cashflows. The only additional parameter is the risk to the bond holder associated with actually receiving these cashflows.

2.2 Pricing bonds

In the market place, bonds are usually quoted on the basis of either a yield, or a capital price. Either method can be derived from the other. The choice of method of quotation is just a convention of each particular market.

2.3 Bond yields

The yield of a bond—commonly referred to as its yield to maturity—is basically a measure of the return the bond holder can expect for the outlay involved in purchasing the bond. Yield is quoted as a rate in the same basis as the coupon payments that make up the bond. Most government and investment bonds pay semi-annual coupons—thus the quoted yield is semi-annual. There are a number of representations of the formula for pricing bonds. These generally differ in terminology only. They represent the net present value of the cashflows that make up the bond when they are all discounted by the bond yield.

Bonds are commonly priced as a value per $100 of principal. If the current price is above $100, the bond is said to be valued at a premium. If it is less, then the bond is at a discount. Whether a bond is at a premium or a discount depends on the relativity of the current yield to the coupon size of the bond. Where the yield is greater than the coupon, the bond will be at a discount. Where it is less, the bond is said to trade at a premium.

The price per $100 principal is

$$P = v^{\frac{f}{d}}\left(c(x+a_n)+100v^n\right)$$

where

c = the periodic coupon payment in dollars per $100 principal
$\qquad$ *c = coupon/(coupons per annum)*

n = the number of complete periods from the next coupon to maturity

f = the number of days to the next coupon date

d = the number of days from the last coupon date to the next

v = $1/(1+i)$ where i is the periodic effective interest rate (i = *yield/frequency* ie: $i = yield/2$ for semi annual coupon bonds)

x =　　0 if ex-interest, x = 1 if cum-interest[3]

a_n =　　$(1-v^n)/i$

To value a bond, the above formula is used. Given a yield and the structural details, the value of the bond can be determined.

Example: pricing a bond

What is the price per $100 of a bond with the following characteristics:

Maturity: 15 January, 2001

Settlement: 14 March, 1997

Coupon: 8.5% paid semi-annually

Yield to maturity: 7.14%?

The following quantities can be derived from the above data:

Next Coupon	15/7/97
Previous Coupon	15/1/97
i	3.570%
v	0.965531
n	7
a_n	6.098603
f	123
d	181
c	4.25

Substituting these into the bond formula, and using $x = 1$ (the bond is *cum*-interest), the price of the bond is $105.844 per $100 principal. This means that an investor would pay $105.844 to receive semi annual coupons of $4.25 every six months from 15 July, 1997. A final payment of $104.25 (the $100 principal plus a final coupon) is received by the investor on 15 January, 2001. At this stage, the bond ceases to exist.

The effect on the price of the bond at different yield levels can be seen in the table below.

Yield	Price
7.00%	$106.321
7.14%	**$105.844**
7.50%	$104.628
8.00%	$102.969
8.50%	$101.343
9.00%	$ 99.748
9.50%	$ 98.185

As the yield increases, the cashflows are discounted at a higher rate. This means that the bond will have a lower net present value.

3.　Ex-interest means that the next interest payment is not included in the price of the bond. By convention, there is an ex-interest period before any coupon payment. The duration of this is set by market convention. If the bond trades during this period, the original holder, rather than the purchaser, still gets the coupon.

2.4 Characteristics of bonds

To understand the characteristics of a bond, it is useful to understand how the pricing formula works, and the sensitivity of the bond to various parameters. This allows the risks of the bond to be quantified and managed. It also allows the effect of market conditions to be observed and reacted to.

2.5 Principal and interest

As time progresses, a bond will accrue interest. At coupon dates, this interest is paid out, and the process repeats. The value of a bond can be split into principal and interest components. Interest accrues by the same amount each day. The daily accrual is equal to c/d using the terminology from the example above. Thus, on any day (before the bond goes ex-interest), the accrued interest is:

$$Accrued\ Interest = c[\frac{d-f}{d}]$$

The capital price is just the gross price less the accrued interest

$$Gross\ Price = Capital\ Price + Accrued\ Interest$$

For the bond in the example above, with $f = 123$ and $d = 181$, the accrued interest is $1.362. The capital price is $104.482.

Because of the process of accruing interest over a period, then paying it at coupon dates, the gross price of a bond will sawtooth with time if the yield is constant. The capital price will move much more smoothly.

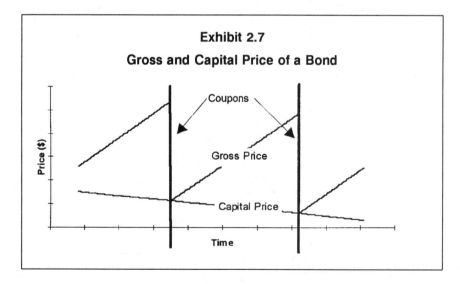

Exhibit 2.7
Gross and Capital Price of a Bond

In many markets, bonds are quoted using capital price rather than yield. From the example above, this bond would be quoted as having a (capital) price of $104.482. The capital price is usually rounded to an even multiple (often eighths, sixteenths or thirty-seconds) of a dollar. The convenience of doing this is that the settlement proceeds can easily and unambiguously be agreed upon, without the use of a pricing formula.[4] In cases where bonds are quoted this way, participants in the market still need to obtain yields. This allows them to compare different bonds, and to gauge their returns. In order to calculate the yield given the price of a bond, the formula for the bond price needs to be solved iteratively. There is no closed form solution for the yield of a bond given its price.

2.6 The bond pricing formula

It is useful to examine the bond pricing formula in more detail. This gives an understanding of the fundamental principle of how bonds are valued. It provides a basis for valuing bond-like instruments, where there may be special conditions on the cashflows (for example, uneven coupon periods or partial principal repayment).

The bond formula discounts all cashflows at the yield to maturity. This is done in two stages. First, cashflows are discounted to the next coupon payment date. These are then discounted from the payment date to the settlement date. The term

$$v^{\frac{f}{d}} = (\frac{1}{1+i})^{\frac{f}{d}}$$

is a discount factor from the next coupon date to the settlement date. The rest of the equation discounts all cashflows to this date.

---

4.   The reason for using capital price to quote bond prices is mostly historical. Before computers or financial calculators were available, market participants rarely agreed on settlement proceeds when only a yield was agreed. To remove this problem, price was quoted directly. Accrued interest is easily and unambiguously determined. It is still the case that for complex instruments such as prepayable securities—where the notion of yield is ambiguous or dependent on other factors or assumptions—that capital price is a more convenient way to quote instruments.

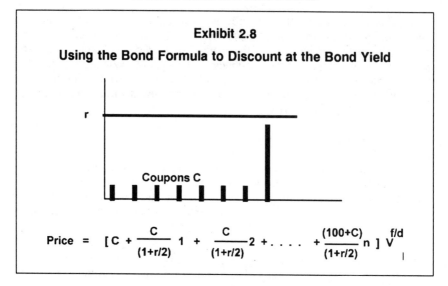

Exhibit 2.8

Using the Bond Formula to Discount at the Bond Yield

$$\text{Price} = [\, C + \frac{C}{(1+r/2)^1} + \frac{C}{(1+r/2)^2} + \ldots + \frac{(100+C)}{(1+r/2)^n} \,] \; V_i^{f/d}$$

Discounting each bond cashflow by the yield to maturity of the bond gives its market value in dollars. It assumes that each cashflow is reinvested at the yield to maturity. In reality, the cashflows will all be reinvested at rates available in the market. If a bond were issued with a ten year maturity, then the first cashflow would be paid nine and a half years to maturity, the second at nine years and so on. The first cashflow could thus be reinvested at a 9.5 year rate, the second at a 9 year rate. The penultimate coupon would be reinvested for just six months. The rates for all these periods are definitely not the same. They may not even equal the bond yield. To reflect a more accurate reinvestment assumption, the zero coupon curve is used. A zero coupon curve constructed out of bonds of similar characteristics would be appropriate for this purpose. The short end of the curve would reflect cash and bill rates, further out, the bonds would be used.

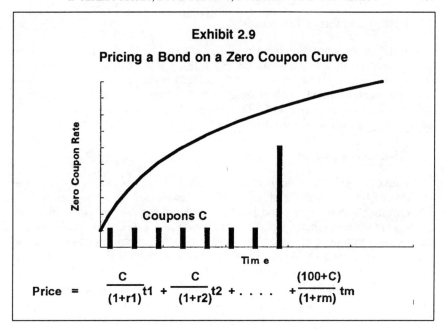

Exhibit 2.9

Pricing a Bond on a Zero Coupon Curve

$$\text{Price} \quad = \quad \frac{C}{(1+r1)}^{t1} + \frac{C}{(1+r2)}^{t2} + \dots + \frac{(100+C)}{(1+rm)}^{tm}$$

If the zero coupon curve is used, then each cashflow is discounted at the appropriate zero coupon rate. If the curve is constructed for bonds of the type being valued, then this price should be exactly the same as the market price of the bond calculated using the yield to maturity and the bond formula. If there is a difference between the price using the formula, and that using the zero coupon curve, it either represents a difference in the type of instrument being valued compared to those on which the curve is based,[5] or a mispricing in the market.[6]

The zero coupon framework for valuing bonds is not used in the marketplace directly by traders. This is because it requires significant information in its derivation. It is well suited to risk management, relative value, arbitrage analysis and other purposes. It is also very useful for the valuation of non-standard bonds. At the expense of losing the convenience of using a single yield to maturity (or capital price), a more realistic reinvestment assumption can be applied. This is much closer to what would be attained in reality if all cashflows were to be reinvested.

When the zero curve is upward sloping, the yield to maturity will be lower than the zero coupon yield at maturity. This is because, when discounting on the zero curve, earlier cashflows are discounted at low yields. The latter ones will require a higher yield if the market price of the bond is to be retrieved. The converse is true for an inverse yield curve.

---

5. For example, a corporate bond valued on a government bond curve will have its price overstated. The government curve does not reflect the higher credit risk—and hence discount—associated with corporate bonds compared to government issues.
6. This may be where a bond is relatively cheap compared to similar bonds. If this occurs, an *arbitrage* opportunity may be exploited.

2.7 Risk parameters for bonds

The holder of a bond or bond portfolio is exposed to changes in the value of the instruments that make up the portfolio. These changes may be due to structural issues such as liquidity or the creditworthiness of the issuer. Other risks are market-related, such as the effect of changing yields, or variations in the interest rate term structure. These risks are quantified and managed by calculating various sensitivity parameters for bonds.

2.8 Risk management

An investor holding a bond or a portfolio of bonds is exposed to changes in value of the components of the portfolio. Unless the investor plans to hold all instruments to maturity, and is not reinvesting the interest cashflows from coupon payments, then exposure to prevailing rates and other market conditions must be considered. There are also structural exposures such as the creditworthiness of the issuer which will not be considered further here. The focus is on interest rate risk-related issues.

The fundamental measures which are used by most portfolio managers to quantify the interest rate risk or exposure in their portfolio is the sensitivity to rate or yield changes, and the timing or length of the cashflows in their portfolio. The former is usually quantified by calculating the sensitivity to a yield shift of one basis point. This is referred to in the market as the PVBP or *present value per basis point*. The PVBP is calculated for bonds by shifting the yield to maturity and measuring the dollar change in the bond price. It is usually quoted as an amount per million dollars face value of the bond.[7] A measure commonly used to express the length of a bond or portfolio is the *modified duration*.

2.9 Duration and modified duration

Measures of duration are useful in that they give a simple means for judging the length of time exposure of a bond or portfolio. These measures aggregate all the bond or portfolio cashflows. Because of this aggregation, they give no information about the structure and timing of cashflows. They are a first order measure, whose use is widespread in the financial industry.

Duration is a concept introduced by Frederick R Macaulay and is one that bears his name.[8] *Macaulay duration* is essentially the time weighted average of the cashflows of a bond. Graphically, it is illustrative to consider the duration as the fulcrum point on a timeline where the cashflows balance. At the duration point, exactly half the dollar value of a bond will have been paid when referenced to the present.

---

7.   In some markets, the PVBP is referred to as the DV01 or *dollar value of one basis point*.
8.   For examples, see Das, *Swaps and Financial Derivatives* (2nd ed, 1994), pp 1055-1060, and references contained therein.

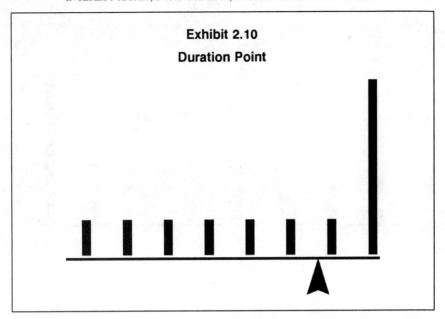

Exhibit 2.10

Duration Point

Duration is useful in that it illustrates where the cashflows occur. A zero coupon bond would have a duration exactly equal to its time to maturity. Using the fulcrum analogy, the pivot point would be where the cashflow occurs. If coupons are included, then, as the coupon size increases, the fulcrum would need to be brought closer to the settlement date. An annuity (a stream or equal cashflows) would have the fulcrum halfway to maturity if the first cashflow were on the settlement date. There is no effect on duration calculations due to the yield to maturity or reinvestment of coupons.

A more useful duration-type measure is the *modified duration*. Extending the balance analogy above, this is the pivot point where the net present value of the cashflows balance. The modified duration is the point where an investor would receive half the present market value of a bond.

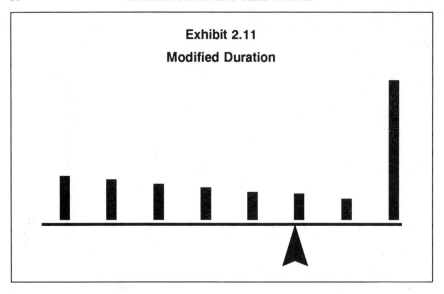

Exhibit 2.11

Modified Duration

Under the discounting process, cashflows at later dates will be worth less proportionally than near flows. This serves to bring the balance point closer to the settlement date. The modified duration is less than the Macaulay duration for any coupon bond (they are equal for a zero coupon bond).

Numerically, both modified and Macaulay duration are simple calculations.

$$DMac = \frac{\sum_i c_i t_i}{\sum_i c_i}$$

where

$DMac$ =   Macaulay duration

c_i =   cashflow that occurs at time t_i.

$$DMod = \frac{\sum_i t_i \dfrac{c_i}{(1+r)^{ti}}}{\sum_i \dfrac{c_i}{(1+r)^{ti}}} = \frac{\sum_i t_i \dfrac{c_i}{(1+r)^{ti}}}{price}$$

$DMod$ is the modified duration. All symbols are as above, and r is an appropriate rate by which the cashflows are discounted. The *price* can be either the capital price or the gross price of the bond. The modified duration will vary depending on which is chosen.[9] If the modified duration is calculated using zero coupon rates then r is replaced by the zero coupon rate

9.   *Capital price modified duration* is often chosen as its behaviour with time is more regular than when gross price is used. This is because of the discontinuity in the gross price of a bond when a coupon is paid. When this occurs, the gross price modified duration will increase discontinuously.

appropriate to each cashflow. Modified duration based on yield to maturity will differ slightly from that based on zero coupon rates.

Example: duration and modified duration

What is the duration and modified duration of the following bond

Maturity: 25 January, 2001

Settlement: 25 June, 1996

Coupon: 8.25% paid annually

Yield to maturity: 7.90%?

Date	Time (y)	Cashflow (c_i)	$c_i t_i$	Discounted Value $(DV_i)_i$	$DV_i t_i$
13/06/96	0	-	-	-	-
25/01/97	0.619	8.250	5.108	7.871	4.873
25/01/98	1.619	8.250	13.358	7.294	11.811
25/01/99	2.619	8.250	21.608	6.760	17.706
25/01/00	3.619	108.250	391.776	82.209	297.528
	Total	133.000	431.851	104.134	331.918

This gives a value for the Macaulay duration of $431.851/133.0 = 3.247$ years, and a modified duration of $331.918/104.134 = 3.187$ years. Note that the bond price from above is $104.134.[10] The maturity of the bond is 3.619 years. As the coupon size decreases, the duration of the bond will approach maturity.

Exhibit 2.12

Effect of Coupon Size on Duration and Modified Duration

Coupon	DMac	Dmod	Maturity
0%	3.619	3.619	3.619
2%	3.508	3.488	3.619
4%	3.412	3.376	3.619
6%	3.329	3.280	3.619
8%	3.256	3.197	3.619
8.25%	3.247	3.187	3.619
10%	3.191	3.124	3.619

---

10. Using the bond formula, the price is $104,147. This difference is exactly one day's worth of accrued interest. This is because of the leap year 1996, which means an extra day's accrual. This is picked up in the formula, but not by direct discounting of cashflows.

2.10 Duration of portfolios

As for a single bond, duration and modified duration can be calculated for portfolios. The method of calculation is exactly as for the single bond case. A portfolio duration is just the weighted average of the component durations.

$$Duration\ (total) = \frac{\sum_n Duration_n\, price_n}{\sum_n price_n}$$

This applies for both Macaulay and modified duration (the two must not be combined).

It is useful to know the (modified) duration for a portfolio, as this gives an approximation for its aggregate life. Duration is important for portfolio managers who are benchmarked against bond indices.

2.11 Interest rate sensitivity—PVBP

When yields (or zero coupon rates) change, bonds change in value. The PVBP quantifies sensitivity to this change. Usually this is done by shifting the yield and valuing the bond. The difference between the shifted and original price suitably normalised gives the PVBP. When hedging bonds with futures or switching from one bond to another, traders often make sure that they stay PVBP matched. This means that their sensitivity to yield changes (assuming that the yields all change by the same amount) is not altered, provided the changes are small.

The theoretical value for PVBP is

$$PVBP = \frac{\partial P}{\partial i}$$

This can be related to the modified duration:

$$DMod = \frac{PVBP}{Capital\ Price} = \frac{1}{Capital\ Price}\frac{\partial P}{\partial i}$$

Modified duration is a useful risk management measure. It gives an aggregate length for a bond or portfolio. The interest rate sensitivity will be similar to that for a zero coupon bond maturing at the modified duration. The sensitivity will not be exactly the same as the cashflow timing can be very different. This is especially prevalent if a portfolio contains bonds across the complete maturity spectrum. The similarity is only first order. Portfolio managers are often set modified duration limits within which their portfolios must be maintained. This sets the basic risk profile of the portfolio, whilst still leaving the manager the flexibility to choose specific instruments or maturity profile.

2.12 PVBP for zero coupon bonds

The value of a zero coupon bond is

$$\frac{\$100}{(1+r)^t}$$

So, per $100:

$$PVBP \approx 100 \left[\frac{1}{(1+r)^t} - \frac{1}{(1+r+\Delta r)^t} \right]$$

where

Δr is a perturbation to the zero coupon rate.

Using a Taylor series expansion of this, it can be shown that $PVBP \propto t$. As the length of the zero coupon bond increases, its PVBP will increase proportionally. This is a useful rule of thumb. Most coupon bonds pay coupons substantially less than the final payment at maturity, so the PVBP for such bonds also increases with time to maturity.

2.13 Convexity

Modified duration and PVBP are useful measures of the sensitivity of bonds to changes in the underlying yield. They are calculated for small yield changes. What happens when the change in yield is large? It is normally the case that most of the time markets only move a few basis points from day to day. Occasionally, there are shocks where the market can move tens or even hundreds of basis points. What happens to the value of bonds under such moves?

The relationship between bond price and yield is not linear. A yield move up will not produce the same magnitude of price change as the same move downwards. The price change for a ten basis point move will not be exactly ten times more than for a one basis point move. The PVBP is not constant over all yields. Convexity is a measure of how the PVBP changes with yield. It is a measure of the non-linearity of the price behaviour of bonds:

$$Convexity = \frac{\partial^2 P}{\partial i^2} = \frac{\partial PVBP}{\partial i}$$

Convexity becomes useful when bonds with similar PVBP are being compared. A larger convexity implies that the PVBP will change more with yield than does a lower convexity. This is a useful property, and can provide benefit to a portfolio manager. This will be illustrated in the section on portfolio management.

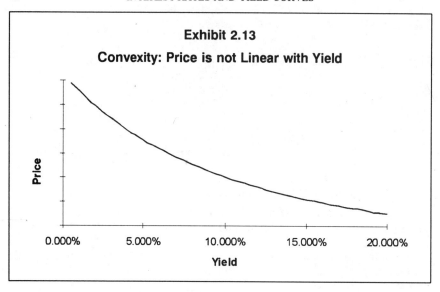

Exhibit 2.13

Convexity: Price is not Linear with Yield

Exhibit 2.14

Convexity for a 20% Coupon Bond

Yield	Yield Change (bp)	Gross Price ($)	Price Change ($)	PVBP per $m
10.00%	—	181.004	—	—
10.01%	1	180.888	0.116108	116.108
10.10%	10	179.848	1.155831	115.583
11.00%	100	169.950	11.053433	110.534

The more convex a bond or portfolio is, the more the PVBP will change as yield changes become large. This has major implications when hedging bond portfolios.

2.14 Evaluating Duration, PVBP and Convexity

Although there exist derivative formulae for modified duration, PVBP and convexity, in practice it is more convenient to evaluate them numerically. This also has the advantage of quantifying them over a yield change that is realistic in the market.[11] The following are suggested for these calculations

$$PVBP = \frac{1}{2\Delta i}[P(i - \Delta i) - P(i + \Delta i)]$$

11. The market is more likely to move, say, 1, 2 or 5 basis points than the infinitesimal move that the differential formulae apply to.

$$Convexity = \frac{1}{\Delta i^2}[P(i - \Delta i) - 2P(i) + P(i + \Delta i)]$$

$$DMod = \frac{PVBP}{Capital\ price}$$

The bond price needs to be calculated at only three yield levels to obtain all these quantities. This is simple to implement, and gives values that are relevant to market moves.

2.15 Time effects

As a bond moves towards maturity, it accrues interest. On coupon payment dates, this interest is shed. The capital price will also change. When the bond matures, its capital price will be exactly $100. If a bond is trading at a premium, its capital price will decrease; while the converse is true for discount bonds. This drift towards a capital price of $100 is called the *pull to par*.

Exhibit 2.15

Pull to Par for Various Coupon Bonds (Yield 8% Semi-Annual)

Maturity (y)	Coupon		
	6%	8%	10%
10	86.410	100.000	113.590
8	88.348	100.000	111.652
6	90.615	100.000	109.385
4	93.267	100.000	106.738
2	96.370	100.000	103.630
0	100.000	100.000	100.000

Over time, components that change the price of a bond are the pull to par, interest accrual and yield changes. It is useful to split any change into these components. Pull to par depends on the difference between the coupon and the yield to maturity. Where this difference is large, the pull will be greater. The pull to par also increases as the bond gets closer to maturity.

2.16 Non-standard bonds

2.16.1 Constant accrual bonds

It is often the case that a bond is not exactly the same as the standard bonds described above. The standard bond pays a fixed coupon every period. Interest accrues each day, and is paid at the coupon date. The coupon size is always the same. If there are differences in the number of days per period (there invariably are as a standard year has an odd number of days), the interest accrued per day will differ slightly.

With constant accrual bonds, the daily accrual is specified. This means that the actual interest payment will differ depending on the number of days in the period.

Example: constant accrual bond

A bond pays a coupon—nominally 10% per annum. The coupon is paid semi-annually, with the same accrual per day.

With this bond, the accrual is based on a standard year of 365 days. The daily accrual (per $100 face value) is $10/365 = $0.027397 per day. If the coupon periods are 182 days and 183 days long in a normal year, then the interest payments are $4.986 and $5.014 respectively. In a leap year, both periods have 183 days. The payments are 5.014% for both periods. In leap years, the bond pays $10.028 in interest.[12]

Pricing of these bonds is commonly done with the bond formula modified slightly for the first coupon.

$$P = v^{\frac{f}{d}}\left((c_n dx + ca_n) + 100v^n\right)$$

Here c_n is the daily interest accrual. The next coupon will be $c_n d$. Pricing assumes that subsequent coupons are all c. Other terms are as per the standard formula. Technically, the value of each coupon should be accrued separately. This is not done, as it will make only a small difference to the bond price, with a large amount of extra complexity.

2.16.2 Bonds with long or short first coupon

The coupon of a standard bond is paid periodically. It is often the case that, when a bond is first issued, the time to the first coupon payment is not an exact period. In this case, the first coupon will accrue interest over either more or less days than if the bond were continuing from a normal payment. In such cases, the initial coupon is usually based on a daily accrual (as described in the section above). The term d (the number of days in the period) is adjusted for the non-standard period. Once this coupon is paid, the bond is priced as a standard bond.

$$P = v^{\frac{f}{d1}}\left((c_n d1.x + ca_n) + 100v^n\right)$$

for the first period of $d1$ days, after which the standard formula is used.

Example: Short first period bond

A bond paying an annual coupon of 8.25% each year on 15 July is initially issued on 1 March. How much will the first coupon payment be?

The standard accrual for this bond is $8.25/365 = $0.022603 per day. The first period is 136 days long, so the first coupon will be $3.074 instead of $8.250. After this is paid, all subsequent coupons will be $8.25.

---

12. For a conventional bond, the interest payment would be $5.00 irrespective of the period length. In 183 day periods, the daily accrual is $5.00/183 = $0.02732, and for 182 day periods it is $0.02747.

2.16.3 Short/long last period

As with a non-standard first period, the last coupon may be delayed or paid early. The final principal repayment may also be shifted. In this case, the formula is adjusted for this. If the last coupon is shifted by l days, and the final payment is shifted by m days, the standard bond formula becomes:

$$P = v^{\frac{f}{d}}\left(c(x + ca_{n-1}) + cv^{(n+l/365)} + 100v^{(n+m/365)}\right)$$

2.16.4 Bonds with amortising principal

The bonds considered so far all pay periodic interest. The principal is paid at maturity. It is often the case that some or all of the principal will be repaid during the life of the bond. If the repayment schedule is known, the bond can be priced as a series of bonds of different periods. This is best illustrated by example.

Example: An amortising bond

Consider a bond with the following characteristics:

Maturity	5 years
Coupon	10%
Frequency	Semi-Annual
Amortisation	20% every year

The cashflows per $100 principal for this bond are

Period	Interest	Principal Paid	Remaining Principal	Total Cashflow
1	$ 5.00		$100.00	$ 5.00
2	$ 5.00	$ 20.00	$100.00	$ 25.00
3	$ 4.00		$80.00	$ 4.00
4	$ 4.00	$ 20.00	$80.00	$ 24.00
5	$ 3.00		$60.00	$ 3.00
6	$ 3.00	$ 20.00	$60.00	$ 23.00
7	$ 2.00		$40.00	$ 2.00
8	$ 2.00	$ 20.00	$40.00	$ 22.00
9	$ 1.00		$20.00	$ 1.00
10	$ 1.00	$ 20.00	$20.00	$ 21.00

To price this bond, we can split it into a series of five bonds each of face value \$20. These bonds mature ar the end of years 1, 2, 3, 4 and 5 respectively. The cashflows for these bonds are as follows:

Period	Bond 1	Bond 2	Bond 3	Bond 4	Bond 5	Total Cashflow
1	\$ 1.00	\$ 1.00	\$ 1.00	\$ 1.00	\$ 1.00	\$ 5.00
2	\$ 21.00	\$ 1.00	\$ 1.00	\$ 1.00	\$ 1.00	\$ 25.00
3		\$ 1.00	\$ 1.00	\$ 1.00	\$ 1.00	\$ 4.00
4		\$ 21.00	\$ 1.00	\$ 1.00	\$ 1.00	\$ 24.00
5			\$ 1.00	\$ 1.00	\$ 1.00	\$ 3.00
6			\$ 21.00	\$ 1.00	\$ 1.00	\$ 23.00
7				\$ 1.00	\$ 1.00	\$ 2.00
8				\$ 21.00	\$ 1.00	\$ 22.00
9					\$ 1.00	\$ 1.00
10					\$ 21.00	\$ 21.00

Each of these is a standard bond of \$20.00 face value. The price of the complete amortising bond is the sum of the prices of each of the component bonds.

Any fixed amortisation of principal can be priced by decomposing the bond into a series of standard bonds of different maturities.

2.16.5 Unknown amortisation of principal

There is a major class of amortising securities where the exact schedule for repayment of the principal is not specified when the bond is issued. There will probably be minimum and maximum boundaries for repayment, but within these, repayment is not known. Such instruments are usually asset-backed securities. These are based on interest payments provided by asset holders. The most common asset-backed securities are mortgage-backed bonds. A mortgage-backed bond is funded by mortgage repayments from property owners. Because a property holder can repay principal at a rate faster than the minimum required under the loan agreement, the holder of a bond backed by these repayments has an uncertain schedule for principal repayment. There are many different structures for mortgage-backed securities. These will not be covered here.

In order to price securities where the principal repayment schedule is unknown, the repayment rate needs to be modelled. This can be a very complex process. In the case of mortgage-backed securities, some models will examine the underlying pool of assets, the demographics of the mortgagees and the prevailing economic environment.

Asset-backed securities that are prepayable contain an additional risk to the investor over the normal risks associated with bonds. This is prepayment risk. This is because the actual repayment rate will differ from that used in the model by which prepayable bonds are priced. If these securities are trading at a premium, then where prepayments are faster than anticipated, the bond holder will be penalised. Where the bond is at a discount, faster repayment will be of benefit to the holder.

Chapter 3

Interest Rate and Yield Curve Modelling

*by Satyajit Das (with a contribution from Roger Cohen)**

1. INTRODUCTION

Interest rates and the process of discounting future cash flows to price and value financial transactions is fundamental to capital markets. Accurate, consistent and reliable interest rates are therefore essential to all financial transactions. This is true irrespective of the type and complexity of the instrument.

In essence, interest rates are the pure price of time designed, through the discounting process, to equate cash flows occurring at different future dates to facilitate valuation and comparison of different transactions. In practice, interest rates are used for the following range of transactions:

1. Pricing and valuation of financial instruments or transactions—entailing the valuation of instruments, such as bonds or derivatives on fixed income instruments, by allowing analysis of the returns from different sets of cash flows through comparison of their discounted present value. In addition, the use of interest rates to value and price derivatives in other asset classes, such as currency, equity, and commodities.

2. Relative value and arbitrage—covering the use of interest rates and discounting to assess the relative value of traded or untraded instruments and to identify arbitrage opportunities.

3. Assessing or forecasting economic expectations—involving the analysis of various types of information available from the yield curve, such as forward rates, to assess market expectations of the path of future interest rates and the term structure of future interest rates which allow the formation and testing of expectations about future economic activity and inflation rates.

However, the process of deriving interest rates or discount factors is far from simple and unambiguous. A whole body of work has developed to assist in the determination of the interest rates to be utilised for the various identified purposes. In this chapter the basic issues relating to the derivation of interest rates and yield curves for use in the pricing and valuation of transactions is examined.

The structure of this chapter is as follows: the interest rates to be utilised are first considered, including identification of the concept of discount factors and the various types of interest rates (par, forward and zero) and their interrelationship, as well as the calculation of forward and zero coupon rates from the available yield curve. The second part of the chapter deals with the

---

*This chapter is written by Satyajit Das. Roger Cohen contributed Exhibits 3.14 and 3.21.

problems of deriving a suitable yield to enable the calculation of the various interest rates, including approaches to interpolation (linear and splines) and the issues in practical curve construction. The chapter concludes with a review of current best practice in interest rate and yield curve modelling.

2. INTEREST RATES

2.1 The concept of interest rates and discount factors

The concept of interest rates and discount factors or present value are interrelated. Central to the concept of interest rates and discount factors is the fact that value in financial transaction is given by cash flow, which is defined in terms of two vectors: amount and the time at which the cash flow occurs.[1]

The concept of discounting these cash flows which may occur at different points of time is designed to enable the value of these individual items to be calculated at a determined point of time (for example, today) to allow comparability. In essence, this requires the cash flow to be moved in time to determine an *equivalent* cash flow as at the relevant date. Using the fundamental homogeneity and uniformity of cash, the current value of cash can be given by its present value, which is intuitively an amount which, if invested at the relevant interest rate, will give a value equivalent to the stated cash flow as at the date on which the cash flow occurs in the futures.

This can be stated more precisely as:

$$C_{t0} = C_{t1} * DF_{t1}$$

Where

C_{t0} = Cash flow at time t0

C_{t1} = Cash flow at time t1

DF_{t1} = Discount factor (or present value) for cash flows as at time t1.

The discount factor (DF) generated or utilised to calculate a discount factor is essentially the present value of $1 at a specific future time. In theoretical terms, this is merely the price of the relevant zero coupon bond, discounted at the zero coupon rate (or, if appropriate, the par or coupon yield to maturity).

Exhibit 3.1 sets out mathematically the relationship of discount factors to the relevant interest rate for each future period. Discount factors, under conditions of positive interest rates, will be less than 1 and greater than 0 and are inversely related to yield with reference to maturity. *Exhibit 3.2* sets out the shape of the interest rate curve and the discount rate curve.

---

1.   To be strictly accurate an additional vector which is required to define value is any contingency or conditionality relating to the cash flow, eg, in the case of an option.

Exhibit 3.1

Discount Factors and Interest Rates

1. Simple Interest

$$DF = 1/(1 + R_{t1} * t/N)$$

Where

DF   =   Discount factor for time t1 at rate R_{t1}

R_{t1} =   Interest rate as at time t1

t   =   Number of days (or t1 − t0)

N   =   Number of days in a year (360 or 365)

2. Compound Interest

$$DF = 1/(1 + R_{t1})^{(t/N)}$$

3. Continuously Compounded Interest

$$DF = e^{-Rt1 * t/N}$$

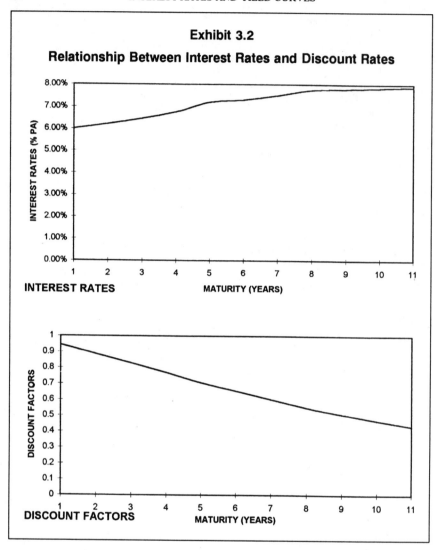

Exhibit 3.2

Relationship Between Interest Rates and Discount Rates

The advantage of discount factors is that each discount factor is unique. It is not affected by market quotation conventions prevalent in relation to interest rates such as the periodicity of compounding (annual, semi-annual, quarterly or continuous) or the day count basis utilised (actual/365, actual/360 or bond basis).

In effect, the problem of yield curves can be expressed as the problem of either deriving term structure of interest rates or discount factors.

2.2 Types of interest rates

2.2.1 Overview

There are in practice three separate types of interest rates:

1. *Par rate*—which is defined as the interest rate on a coupon paying instrument out of today which is the standard interval rate of return formulae which discounts all payments on a coupon bond or instrument at the same interest rates.

2. *Forward rate*—which is defined as the interest rate on a coupon paying instrument out of a nominated date in the future.

3. *Zero rate* (also known as zero coupon rates, spot rates or pure interest rates)—which is defined as the interest rate on an instrument which pays no coupon and entails the exchange of a cash flow today for another (larger) cash flow at a nominated future date.

The par rate is the only observable interest rate in markets. Forward rates and zero rates are more difficult to observe directly. However, in jurisdictions where there are traded markets in interest rate futures and/or zero coupon securities,[2] it may be possible to directly observe certain forward and zero rates.

The three types of rates are clearly and unambiguously interrelated as they are, in effect, different perspectives on the same set of interest rates. In practice, the par interest rates which are observable are utilised to calculate the implied forward and zero rates.

The formal interrelationship between par, forward and zero rates can be stated as follows:

- forward interest rates are the interest rates at which par yields are reinvested;
- zero rates are the par interest rates with the reinvestment risk removed; and
- forward rates as between two points in time are implied by the zero rates at those two points.

Exhibit 3.3 sets out diagrammatically this relationship.

---

2. For example, the US Treasury STRIPS market which allows the unbundling of a bond into individual coupon and principal components and allows separate trading in these components.

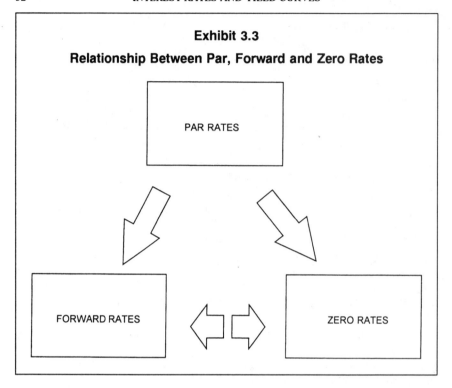

Exhibit 3.3

Relationship Between Par, Forward and Zero Rates

The difference between the rates (in particular, par and zero rates) can be seen from a consideration of their role in valuation. Valuation of all financial transactions assumes the use of identified and specific interest rates or discount/present value factors to discount or present value cash flows identified with individual transactions. The two alternative types of interest rates available are:

1. par rates to maturity; and
2. zero rate to maturity.

As noted above, the par rate to maturity is usually directly observable, being the market quoted rate for the relevant securities of the required maturity. In the case of derivative or swap transactions, the relevant par rate to maturity is, typically, the quoted swap rate for the relevant maturity or, if unavailable, the interpolated yield based on available swap yield curve information. In contrast, the zero rate is not directly observable and is usually estimated from the existing par rate curve for the relevant instrument.

Traditionally, financial instruments have been valued utilising par yield to maturity. However, use of par rates creates a number of problems:

*   coupon effect;
*   assumptions on reinvestment rates; and
*   absence of an unambiguous and unique interest rate for each maturity.

The coupon effect refers to the phenomenon observed in markets that the par interest rates of bonds or other financial instruments with the same maturity but different coupons may vary significantly. These differences may be caused by factors such as the interest rate risk or differential interest rate volatility of the securities, tax or clientele effects.

Utilisation of the par rate implies that the actual realised return only equals the normal redemption par yield to maturity if reinvestment rates on all intermediate cash flows, typically the coupons, are actually equal to the redemption yield. The realised yield, therefore, would only be equal to the par yield where the security is a zero coupon security, that is, a security which has no intermediate cash flows, as there is no potential reinvestment risk in the transaction. In practice, reinvestment rates on coupon cash flows will not equal the redemption yield. Theoretical forward rates are the only true measure of available reinvestment rates, and even then, the forward rates implicit in the yield curves at any point in time do not guarantee that these reinvestment rates are actually achieved.

In addition, the use of coupon of par rates creates an ambiguous relationship between yields and maturities. The use of par rate technology does not facilitate the identification of an *unique* interest rate and, by implication, discount factor for a particular maturity.

For example, assume the following yield curve exists:

Maturity (years)	Par yield % pa
0.25	7.25
0.50	7.55
1.00	7.92
1.50	8.23
2.00	9.05

Under these circumstances, a two year security, which pays intermediate coupons, say, every six months, will be valued by discounting all payments at 9.05% pa. However, for an identical security, with a maturity of 1.5 years, all cash flows, including intermediate coupons, would be discounted at a different rate, namely, 8.23%. Consequently, the rates applicable for years 0.5, 1.00 and 1.5 can be, either, 9.05 or 8.23% pa depending, solely, on the final maturity of the security. Because of these problems, par rate to maturity valuation does not imply an unambiguous relationship between the interest rate and the relevant maturity.

The identified problems of par rate to maturity technology are substantially overcome by utilising zero rates. As noted above, the zero rate can be defined as the interest or discount rate which applies between a cash flow now and a cash flow at a single date in the future, which is equivalent to the yield on a pure discount bond or zero coupon security (hence, the reference to zero rate). Utilising zero rates allows, for example, a two year yield to be directly related to a pure two year security, being a pure zero coupon security with a single cash flow in two years time.

The zero rate eliminates the coupon effect. The use of zero rates to discount or present value cash flows does not involve any assumptions as to the reinvestment rate applicable to any intermediate cash flows. In addition, the zero coupon rate has the advantage that each maturity is identified with a single unambiguous interest rate, being the rate of a pure single payment instrument. These factors allow zero rates to be utilised to value and ultimately manage entire portfolios of financial instruments (bonds and derivatives) as a series of cash flows, each of which is valued at a unique rate.

2.3 Derivation of forward rates

Forward interest rates can be calculated from the current yield curve. If suitably spaced yields and either synthetic or actual securities are available, then forward rates can be estimated.

The forward rates can be calculated based on the theoretical construct that securities of different maturities can be expected to be substitutes for one another. Investors at any time have three choices. They may invest in an obligation having a maturity corresponding exactly to their anticipated holding period. They may invest in short-term securities, reinvesting in further short-term securities at each maturity over the holding period. They may invest in a security having a maturity longer than the anticipated holding period. In the last case, they would sell the security at the end of the given period, realising either a capital gain or a loss.

According to a version of the pure expectations theory of interest rate term structure (see discussion below), investors' expected return for any holding period would be the same, regardless of the alternative or combination of alternatives they chose. This return would be a weighted average of the current short-term interest rate plus future short rates expected to prevail over the holding period; this average is the same for each alternative.

Forward rates may be calculated from the currently prevailing cash market yield curve, as any deviation from the implied forward rates would create arbitrage opportunities which market participants would exploit. This arbitrage is undertaken by buying and selling securities at different maturities to synthetically create the intended forward transaction. By simultaneously borrowing and lending the same amount in the cash market but for different maturities it is possible to lock in an interest rate for a period in the future. If the maturity of the cash lending exceeds the maturity of the cash borrowing the implied rate over the future period, the forward-forward rate, is a bid rate for a forward investment. Similarly, if the maturity of the cash borrowing exceeds the maturity of the cash lending, then the resulting forward-forward rate is an offer rate for a forward borrowing. This process of generating forward rates is set out in *Exhibit 3.4*.

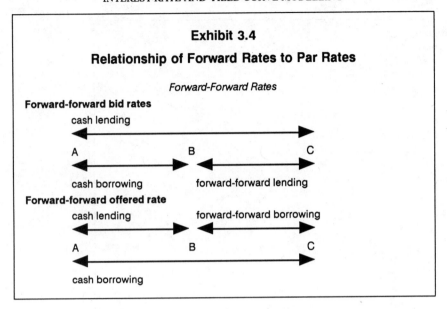

Exhibit 3.4

Relationship of Forward Rates to Par Rates

Forward-Forward Rates

Exhibit 3.5 sets out the mathematical relationship between par interest rates and forward rates. Exhibit 3.6 sets out examples of calculating forward rates.

Exhibit 3.5

Derivation of Forward Rates

$$(1 + R_{t1})^{t1} * (1 + R_{t1 \times 2})^{t2 - t1} = (1 + R_{t2})^{t2}$$

Where

R_{t1} = Par interest rate to time t1

R_{t2} = Par interest rate to time t2

R_{t1x2} = Forward interest rate between time t1 and t2

t1,t2 = Time to maturity in days from the present divided by 365

Rearranging to solve for the forward interest rate:

$$R_{t1 \times 2} = [(1 + R_{t2})^{t2} / (1 + R_{t1})^{t1}]^{1/(t2 - t1)} - 1$$

The above assumes that all rates are expressed in consistent time units, usually annual effective rates.

Exhibit 3.6

Derivation of Forward Rates—An Example

CALCULATION OF FORWARD/FORWARD INTEREST RATES   23-Jul-96

DAYS	(3) RATES (ANNUAL)	(4) $(1+Rt2)^{t2}$	(5) $(1+Rt1)^{t1}$	(6) (4)/(5)	(7) $1/(t2-t1)$	FORWARD RATES FOR PERIOD t1TOt2 $(6)^{(7)}-1$
0						
31	6.2500%					
92	6.5000%	1.01600	1.00516	1.01078	5.98361	6.627%
184	6.8000%	1.03372	1.01600	1.01744	3.96739	7.101%
274	7.1000%	1.05284	1.03372	1.01850	4.05556	7.716%
365	7.4000%	1.07400	1.05284	1.02010	4.01099	8.308%
457	7.5000%	1.09478	1.07400	1.01934	3.96739	7.898%
549	7.5500%	1.11570	1.09478	1.01911	4.05556	7.799%
639	7.6000%	1.13682	1.11570	1.01894	4.05556	7.906%
730	7.9500%	1.16532	1.13682	1.02507	4.01099	10.440%

FORWARD RATE MATRIX

DAYS	RATES (ANNUAL)								
0	6.2500%								
31	6.5000%								
92	6.8000%	6.627%							
184	7.1000%	6.912%	7.101%						
274	7.4000%	7.209%	7.405%	7.716%					
365	7.5000%	7.507%	7.705%	8.013%	8.308%				
457	7.5500%	7.592%	7.754%	7.974%	8.102%	7.898%			
549	7.6000%	7.628%	7.763%	7.930%	8.000%	7.848%	7.799%		
639	7.9500%	7.669%	7.786%	7.925%	7.977%	7.867%	7.852%	7.906%	
730		8.026%	8.161%	8.340%	8.464%	8.503%	8.708%	9.172%	10.440%

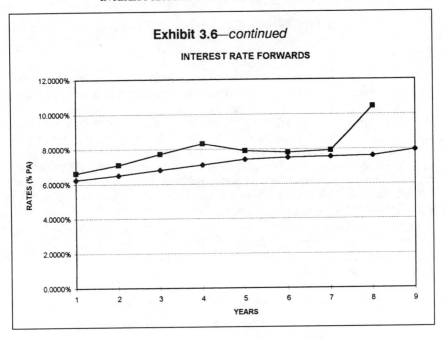

Exhibit 3.6—*continued*

INTEREST RATE FORWARDS

The following characteristics of forward rates should be noted:

1. Forward rates lie above (below) the par rates where the yield curve is positive (negative). This means that the forward rates cross from one side to the other of the par curve where the yield curve changes shape.

2. Forward rates have greater momentum than par rates; that is, the rate of change of the forward rates is more attenuated than that of the par curve.

3. Forward rates can be more volatile than par rates; that is, a small change in par rates can lead to a proportionately larger change in the forward rate.

It is important to note that forward rates, when regarded as forecasts of future short-term interest rates, require a number of theoretical and practical assumptions. From a theoretical perspective, this approach assumes the absence of transaction costs and assumes the validity of the pure expectations theory of the term structure of interest rates. In particular, the forward rate as calculated from the current cash market yield curve contains no compensation for risk and, in particular, includes no liquidity premium. In practice, the last condition is violated as forward rates are generated from the observed interest rate term structure, which, typically, incorporates a liquidity premium.

2.4 Derivation of zero rates

2.4.1 Basic methodology

The actual computation of the zero rate yield curve is complex. In theory, for each future payment of a coupon security, there exists a zero rate that discounts that payment to its present value. These rates constitute the zero rate curve, points along which represent the yield to maturity of a zero coupon bond for the appropriate maturity rate. This zero coupon yield curve is estimated from the existing par or coupon yield curve. This is completed by calculating equilibrium zero coupon rates which value each component of the cash flow of conventional coupon securities in an internally consistent fashion, such that all par bonds would have the same value as the sum of their cash flow components.

The zero coupon rates are calculated using an iterative methodology whereby the zero coupon rate is determined from a known yield curve for the successive points in time (often referred to as bootstrapping). An alternative technique for deriving the zero rates is using the implied forward rates.

2.4.2 Calculating zero coupon rates through bootstrapping

The bootstrapping approach involves a series of distinct steps:

• separate a coupon bond into a series of zero coupon bonds;
• utilise available zero rates to price components; and
• solve for the unknown zero rate within the constraint that the market value of the bond must be equal to the value of the components using zero rates.

Exhibit 3.7 shows the simple calculation of a zero coupon rate. Given that a one year bond has a coupon and yield to maturity of 8.00% pa semi-annual, a total price of $1m is derived. However, if the six month discount security has a yield of 7.00% (not 8.00%) and the first coupon is discounted accordingly at 7.00% (which is a known zero coupon rate), then the 12 month payments must be discounted at a rate higher than the rate (8.02% pa semi-annual in this case) to maintain the equilibrium price of $1m.

In a similar way, break even zero rates for each subsequent maturity can be derived through iteration. Known zero rates are used to derive the succeeding zero using the same logic to generate a complete yield curve of zero rates from the par rate curve.

The zero rate could, in theory, also have been derived from the discount factor. The relevant discount factor for the 1 year rate is in fact the present value of the final cash flow in 1 year divided by the final cash flow which can be used to solve for the zero rate. This is shown in *Exhibit 3.7*.

Exhibit 3.7

Derivation of Zero Rates—Bootstrapping Technique

CALCULATING BREAK-EVEN ZERO RATES—BOOTSTRAPPING

YEARS	PAR RATES (%PA SA)	PAR RATES (%PA A)	CASH FLOWS			ZERO RATE		PRESENT VALUE AT		DIFFERENCE	DISCOUNT FACTORS FROM	
			PRINCIPAL	COUPON @8.000%	TOTAL	(%PA ANNUAL)	(%PA S/A)	ZERO RATE	PAR RATE 0.0816		ZERO RATES	BOOTSTRAPPING
0.00			(1,000,000)		(1,000,000)							
0.50	7.00%	7.12%		40,000	40,000	7.12%	7.00%	38,647	38,462	186	0.966184	
1.00	8.00%	8.16%	1,000,000	40,000	1,040,000	8.18%	8.02%	961,353	961,538	(186)	0.924378	0.924378
								1,000,000	1,000,000			

2.4.3 *Calculating zero coupon rates through implied forward rates*

As an alternative method, it is possible to determine the zero coupon rate curve by using the forward rates implicit in the current yield curve and assuming compounding of intermediate cash flows at the implicit forward rates. The basic concept is to use forward rates to reinvest intermediate cash flows to synthesise a zero coupon bond and derive the zero rate which equates the two cash flows. *Exhibit 3.8* sets out an example using the same data as in *Exhibit 3.7*. In theory, both approaches should yield identical results provided a consistent yield curve is utilised.

The zero rate using the forward rate through the pyramid technique can also be derived using discount factors. This is done by taking the six month discount factor and multiplying it by the discount factor calculated from the forward rate for 6 × 12 forward rate (in the above example). The product is effectively the zero rate discount factor for 1 year. This is shown in *Exhibit 3.8*.

Exhibit 3.8

Derivation of Zero Rates—Implied Forward Technique

CALCULATING BREAK-EVEN ZERO RATES—FORWARD RATES

YEARS	PAR RATES (%PA SA)	PAR RATES (%PAA)	FORWARD RATES (%PAA)	DISCOUNT FACTOR	CASH FLOWS BOND	CASH FLOWS RE-INVEST-MENT	CASH FLOWS FINAL	ZERO RATE (%PA ANNUAL)	ZERO RATE (%PA S/A)	DISCOUNT FACTORS FROM ZERO RATES	DISCOUNT FACTORS FROM FORWARD RATES
0.00					(1,000,000)						
0.50	7.00%	7.12%			40,000		($1,000,000)	7.12%	7.00%	0.966184	
1.00	8.00%	8.16%	9.208%	0.956916	1,040,000	$1,801	$1,081,801	8.18%	8.02%	0.924384	0.924556

2.4.4 Characteristics of zero coupon rates

Exhibit 3.9 sets out examples of zero rates for hypothetical yield curves.

Exhibit 3.9
Zero Rate Curves—Examples

The accompanying graphs set on the derivation of zero coupon rates from a given yield curve utilising the iterative methodology specified. The tables are calculated using the following assumptions:

1. linear interpolation is used to determine the full yield curve; and

2. coupons (payable semi-annually) are assumed to equal the par yield applicable to a specified maturity.

YEAR	DAYS TO PAYMENT	PAR RATE	ZERO RATE
0.50	182	6.0000%	6.0000%
1.00	365	6.1500%	6.1523%
1.50	547	6.2000%	6.2031%
2.00	730	6.2500%	6.2548%
2.50	912	6.3750%	6.3871%
3.00	1095	6.5000%	6.5210%
3.50	1278	6.5750%	6.6011%
4.00	1461	6.6500%	6.6825%
4.50	1643	6.6750%	6.7076%
5.00	1826	6.7000%	6.7336%
5.50	2008	6.7750%	6.8202%
6.00	2191	6.8500%	6.9080%
6.50	2373	6.9250%	6.9972%
7.00	2556	7.0000%	7.0880%
7.50	2739	7.0667%	7.1695%
8.01	2922	7.1333%	7.2525%
8.50	3104	7.2000%	7.3373%
9.01	3287	7.2667%	7.4239%
9.50	3469	7.3333%	7.5124%
10.01	3652	7.4000%	7.6030%

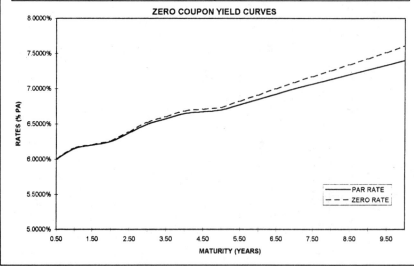

Exhibit 3.9—*continued*

YEAR	DAYS TO PAYMENT	PAR RATE	ZERO RATE
0.50	182	9.0000%	9.0000%
1.00	365	8.7500%	8.7445%
1.50	547	8.6500%	8.6420%
2.00	730	8.5500%	8.5375%
2.50	912	8.4750%	8.4585%
3.00	1095	8.4000%	8.3781%
3.50	1278	8.3250%	8.2964%
4.00	1461	8.2500%	8.2135%
4.50	1643	8.1250%	8.0710%
5.00	1826	8.0000%	7.9275%
5.50	2008	7.9500%	7.8735%
6.00	2191	7.9000%	7.8181%
6.50	2373	7.8500%	7.7616%
7.00	2556	7.8000%	7.7039%
7.50	2739	7.7500%	7.6452%
8.01	2922	7.7000%	7.5856%
8.50	3104	7.6500%	7.5250%
9.01	3287	7.6000%	7.4635%
9.50	3469	7.5500%	7.4012%
10.01	3652	7.5000%	7.3381%

ZERO COUPON YIELD CURVES

The following characteristics of zero coupon rate and the corresponding zero coupon yield curve should be noted:

1. Theoretical zero coupon rates are always above (below) the relevant par or coupon yield curve for a normal or positively (inverse or negatively) sloped yield curve. This reflects the fact that a coupon bond is a collection of zero coupon bonds and the yield to maturity on a coupon bond is simply the average of the zero coupon rates on the constituent zero coupon securities. Consequently, if yield is increasing in a normally sloped yield curve, then each constituent zero element of the coupon bond will have a yield which is less than or equal to that on a zero with a

maturity that is the same as the coupon bond dictating that the yield on the coupon bond must be less than a zero of the maturity. A reverse logic is applicable in the case of negatively sloped or inverse yield curves.

2. The steeper the curve the more steep is the zero coupon rate curve.

3. Zero coupon rates can be more volatile than par rates as each zero rate is dependent on each forward rate leading up to the maturity of the zero coupon rate. A movement in any of the rates results in a movement in the zero coupon rate.

3. YIELD CURVE MODELLING

3.1 Overview

All par rates and zero rates assume and require the existence of a known yield curve. However, much of the problems in derivation of interest rates and discount factors revolves around the issues in generating a complete yield curve of rates for generation of the suitable zero rates used for valuation.

Exhibit 3.10 sets out a typical yield curve which illustrates the difficulties with defining the complete yield curve under most conditions. The curve highlights the following problems:

• data noise—the yield curve may be obscured by the presence of noisy data points whereby there may be a number of yields for similar or identical maturities, which has the effect of increasing the difficulty of determining the *true* interest rate for any maturity; and

• data sparseness—the yield curve may be sparse; that is, it may have significant gaps between observable interest rates. This makes it difficult to specify interest rates for maturities *between* the observed data points.

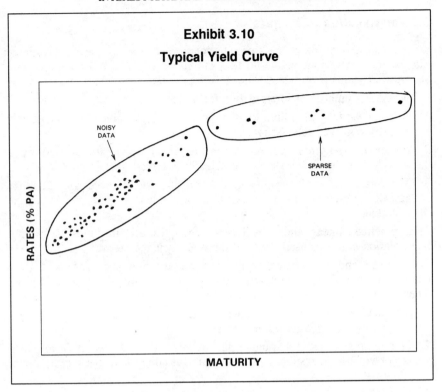

Exhibit 3.10

Typical Yield Curve

The yield curve described is fairly typical with the problem of noise at the shorter maturity and sparseness in longer maturities. The problems described may be caused by a number of factors including the institutional structure of the market, such as the regulatory framework and liquidity factors, as well as tax factors which may affect trading and valuation of financial instruments.

It should be noted that the above assumes homogeneity in terms of default risk or credit quality of the complete set of interest rates; that is, the rates are all risk free rates or of an identical credit quality. In practice, the interest rates may not be homogenous. This problem is considered below in the context of yield curve construction in practice.

The yield curve modelling problem is separable into two separate and distinct problems:

1. interpolation—that is, the generation of a complete yield curve from the data available; and

2. term structure of interest rates—that is, an understanding of the yield curve shapes and interest rate evolution over time.

The second naturally influences the first process.

3.2 Interpolation techniques

As noted above, the process of interpolation requires the use of available interest rates at various points in the yield curve to generate a complete term structure of yields from which the relevant zero rates can be stripped.

There are a number of interpolation techniques:

1. *Stepped model*—all points on the yield curve are given by the nearest actually observed interest rates.

2. *Linear interpolation*—all points on the yield curve are created by a straight line drawn between each actually observed interest rate.

3. *Non-linear interpolation*—all points on the yield curve are fitted to actually observed interest rates using either regression or spline techniques.

In practice, linear and non-linear techniques are the most important interpolation practices used. Each of these is discussed below.

The need and importance of creating an accurate and consistent yield curve using the choice of interpolation techniques available is best achieved when the yield curve generated satisfies the following criteria:

1. · *Fit*—that is, the yield curve generated is consistent with and closely tracks *observed market interest rates*.

2. *Low in noise*—that is, the curve has the appropriate degree of fit in that it is not volatile in response to noisy data (usually where the curve is over fitted).

3. *Consistent*—that is, the par, forward and zero rate derived from the curves are consistent with the observed and theoretical behaviour of these rates. In essence, they are arbitrage free.

4. *Smoothness*—that is, the par, forward and zero rates derived are smooth in that they do not show sudden and unexpected changes and volatility.

In practice, all the criteria identified are unlikely to be satisfied *simultaneously*. In addition, the appropriate trade-off between the criteria is not readily definable. This necessarily introduces a substantial degree of subjectivity in the choice of method and the generation of the yield curve.

3.3 Linear interpolation

Linear interpolation requires the use of straight lines as between any two points of the observed yield curve to estimate the interest rate between these points. *Exhibit 3.11* sets out an example of linear interpolation.

Exhibit 3.11

Linear Interpolation

Given the following seven and ten year interest rates, the benchmark interpolated bond rate for an eight year rate is calculated as follows:

Maturity	Yield
7 Years	7.30% pa
10 Years	7.47% pa

Interpolated yield is calculated as follows:

Interest Rates	Maturity	Days (between)	Blending Factor
7 year rate	15/4/19X4		556/(389 + 556) = 0.588
		389	
8 year rate	9/5/19X5		
		556	
10 year rate	15/11/19X6		389/(389 + 556) = 0.412

Maturity	Interest Rate (%pa)	Blending Factor	Blended Rate (%pa)
7 year rate	7.30	0.588	4.292
10 year rate	7.47	0.412	3.078
		8 year Interpolated Yield	7.37

It is important to note that linear interpolation *on interest rates* is equivalent to *exponential interpolation* on discount factors. Consequently, it is usually done with interest rates rather than discount factors.

The major advantage of linear interpolation is its simplicity and ease of calculation. The disadvantages include:

- the tendency to produce inaccurate rates where the yield curve is changing slope reflecting an inherent tendency for discontinuity (kinks) at each maturity point where the yield curve is not linear in slope;

- the difficulty of generating rates where there is sparse or noisy data; and

- the prospect of generating yield curves which are inconsistent with term structure models of interest rates and also inconsistent with the concept of yield curves which change shape continuously.

3.4 Non-linear interpolation models

3.4.1 Introduction

The concept of non-linear interpolation is predicated on the use of mathematical techniques to generate a fitted yield curve through observed interest rate points. This is undertaken with the objective of fitting a yield curve which reflects the optimality criteria identified and is consistent with the term structure of interest rate assumptions usually made. As noted above, two types of models are generally utilised: regression-based models; and cubic spline-based models.

3.4.2 Regression-based models

A number of models have emerged which seek to use regression techniques, usually non-linear least square regression techniques, to create a fitted yield curve. The models are generally similar in approach, differing in:

- the form of the equation; and
- the number of terms.

Two popular models are the Bradley-Crane model (described in *Exhibit 3.12*) and the Elliot-Echols model (described in *Exhibit 3.13*).

Exhibit 3.12

Regression-based Yield Curve Models—Bradley-Crane Model

The Bradley-Crane model has the following form:

$$\ln(1 + R_M) = a + b_1(M) + b_2\ln(M) + e$$

Where

R_M = Observed interest rate for maturity M

M = Maturity of the interest rate

The model implies that the natural logarithm (ln) of one plus the observed yields for term to maturity of length M are regressed on two variables, the term to maturity and the natural log of the term of maturity. The last term (e) represents the unexplained yield variation. Once the estimated values of a, b_1 and b_2 are obtained, specific maturities of interest can be substituted to obtain estimated yields at these maturity points.

Source: Stephen P Bradley and Dwight B Crane, "Management of Commercial Bank Government Security Portfolios: An Optimisation Approach under Uncertainty" (1973) (Spring) *Journal of Bank Research* 18.

Exhibit 3.13

Regression-based Yield Curve Models—Elliot-Echols Model

The Elliot-Echols model has the following form:

$$\ln (1 + R_i) = a + b_1 (1/M_i) + b_2 (M_i) + b_3 (C_i) + e_i$$

Where

R_i = Yield to maturity

M_i = Term to maturity

C_i = Coupon rate of the ith bond

The model implies that the natural logarithm (ln) of one plus the observed yields are regressed on three variables, the inverse of maturity, the term to maturity and the coupon. The last term (e) represents the unexplained yield variation. Once the estimated values of a, b_1, b_2 and b_3 are obtained, specific maturities and coupons can be substituted to obtain estimated yields at these maturity points.

The Elliot-Echols Model is useful where it is sought to fit yield curves directly to yield data for individual bonds rather than to an homogenised yield series. This might be desirable as a means of avoiding possible distortions created in the process of arriving at the synthetic yield series.

Source: Michael E Echols and Jan Walter Elliot, "A Quantitative Yield Curve Model for Estimating the Term Structure of Interest Rates" (1976) *Journal of Financial and Quantitative Analysis* 87.

An example using a regression-based model is set out in *Exhibit 3.14*.

Exhibit 3.14

Example of Regression-based Model

Regression-based models require the fitting of a functional form to the yield curve. The function is chosen so that it reflects the general shape of the term structure. Parameters that specify the exact form of the function are evaluated to minimise the difference between observed market data and the values given by the function.

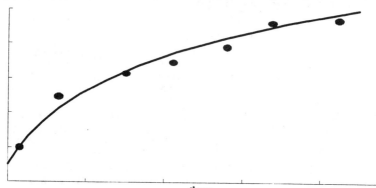

time

Fitting a Curve

The yield curve is specified as a function of rates $r1$, $r2$, $r3$ . . . rn and time t.

$$df(t) = F(t, r1, r2, r3, \ldots, rn)$$

Where $df(t)$ is the discount factor at time t. The form of the function is found by a least squares minimisation of the differences between the observed market rates and the values given by the function. This requires minimisation of:

$$\sum_{i=1}^{n} [F(ti, r1, r2, \ldots, rn) - Market\ Price\ (ti)]^2$$

This now gives a function for which discount factors can be obtained for any term.

Example: An Exponential Curve for Yield

Here we specify the curve of the form:

$$df(t) = a_1 e^{-r1t} + a_2 e^{-r2t} + \ldots + a_n e^{-rnt}$$

To obtain the term structure function, values for the coefficients $a_1, a_2, \ldots a_n$ must be found. This is done using the least squares minimisation shown above. Once these are obtained, we have a function for the yield at any time.

To illustrate this consider a term structure function containing seven terms

$$df(t) = a_1 e^{-r1t} + a_2 e^{-r2t} + \ldots + a_7 e^{-r7t}$$

The values of $r_1, r_2, r_3, r_4, r_5, r_6$ and r_7 are specified. Market rates for 1 through 10 years are used as observations. To define the yield curve, only the coefficients $a_1, a_2, a_3, a_4, a_5, a_6$ and a_7 need to be found. This is done using the minimisation above.

Exhibit 3.14—*continued*

Time (y)	Yield
1	7.52
2	7.57
3	7.7
4	7.8
5	7.88
6	7.95
7	7.995
8	8.03
9	8.05
10	8.06

Market Observed Rates

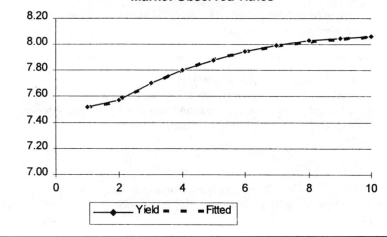

Exhibit 3.14—*continued*

Coefficient (I)	ai	ri
1	5.627834	0.00274
2	4.530894	0.019178
3	−1.28394	0.082192
4	−0.25905	0.246575
5	−0.69042	1
6	2.108328	2
7	4.998892	10

This gives a smooth curve through the known data points. At each known rate, the difference between the market and that given by the curve is small (less than 0.006).

The defined discount function is:

$$df(t) = 5.627834e^{-0.00274t} + 4.530894e^{-0.019178t} - 1.28394e^{-0.082192t} - 0.25905e^{-0.246575t} - 0.69042e^{-t} + 2.108328e^{-2t} + 4.998892e^{-10t}$$

Using this function, discount factors—and hence yields—can be obtained for any time t.

These regression-based models are generally useful in avoiding some of the problems of linear interpolation techniques. In practice, the models represent a compromise between too few terms (which tends to create a smooth curve) and too many terms (which tends to overfit the curve creating a noisy curve).

3.4.3 Cubic splines

A number of models have emerged which use polynomial functions to model and create a fitted yield curve. The basic technique used is that of a cubic spline.

The concept of spline techniques is based on creating a yield curve which does not oscillate to a significant degree (that is, it is not noisy) and is relatively smooth. In practice, this is created using splines which are pieces of elastic material which are constrained so as to pass through a given series of points but are allowed to assume other shapes in between the points specified. In theory, the spline will take the shape that minimises its strain energy which is consistent with the mathematical definition of smoothness specified in determining the fit of the yield curve.

Using splines there are two choices in fitting a yield curve:

1. Use a single high order polynomial—this is generally not favoured because there is an inherent tendency for the curve to take untractable shapes between data points.

2. Use a number of lower order polynomials which are then linked to create a complete yield curve—this is generally the favoured methodology because of its inherent flexibility and its inherent satisfaction of the condition that it go through all observed interest rate data points.

The latter technique is referred to as a piecewise cubic spline technique. Using this technique, the complete yield curve is generated as follows:

1. The observed yield curve in terms of observed data points is divided into a series (n-1 where n is the number of observed data points) of pairs; in effect, a series of paired adjacent yield curve points and rates.

2. The yield curve between any of these observed pairs is then specified as a polynomial which is unique.

3. Each polynomial which specifies the yield curve shape between two unique points is related to the adjacent or neighbour polynomial so that the slope and/or the rate of change of slope is equal at the common data point between the two polynomials. In effect, the first and (optionally) the second derivative of the two polynomials are equated.

Exhibit 3.15 sets out the mechanics of implementing a piecewise cubic spline methodology of interpolation.

Exhibit 3.15

Piecewise Cubic Spline Technique of Interpolation

The piecewise cubic spline is calculated for the following three interest rates (R) as at time t_1, t_2 and t_3. The technique is also applicable to discount factors. The yield curve segment is set out in the following diagram:

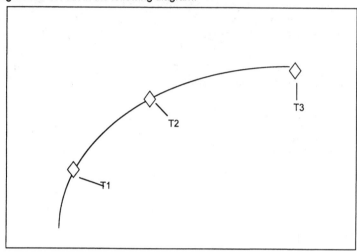

TERM TO MATURITY (YEARS)

The yield curve is divided into two separate pieces, which are described by unique splines.

The section between t_1 and t_2 is described by:

$$R t_1 = a + b t_1 + c t_1{}^2 + d t_1{}^3$$

The section between t_2 and t_3 is described by:

$$R t_3 = m + n t_3 + p t_3{}^2 + q t_3{}^3$$

There are eight constants within the two polynomials which must be calculated. It is now necessary to ensure that the two polynomials go through the common data point and that their slope and the rate of change of slope is equal. This is done as follows:

The section at t_2 is described by both the above polynomials:

$$R t_2 = a + b t_2 + c t_2{}^2 + d t_2{}^3$$
$$R t_2 = m + n t_2 + p t_2{}^2 + q t_2{}^3$$

The first and second derivatives at t_2 must be equal, therefore:

$$b + 2 c t_2 + 3 d t_2{}^2 = n + 2 p t_2 + 3 q t_2{}^2$$
$$2 c + 6 d t_2 = 2 p + 6 q t_2$$

To ensure that the change in slope is equal to zero at the ends, the following equation must also be satisfied:

$$2 c + 6 d t_2 = 2 p + 6 q t_2 = 0$$

There are now six equations that can be solved using multiple regression techniques to generate the optimal piecewise cubic spline.

The above process generates a spline which passes through the data points which by definition is the smoothest interpolated function which fits the observed data.

The major advantages of piecewise cubic splines include:

- the fitted yield curve passes through observed data points and avoids the discontinuity or kinks where the yield curve changes slope;
- the curve is generally smooth; and
- the curve provides a robust estimation technique in a variety of market conditions.

The disadvantages of piecewise cubic splines include:

- the need for sufficient data points to allow a good fitted curve to be generated;
- the computation is somewhat complex; and
- the solution of cubic polynomials with multiple regression techniques exhibit the problems of multi-collinearity (that is, the function introduces uncertainty due to the linkages between each segment of the yield curve) and when solved using multiple regression techniques the definition of accuracy of the result is not unambiguous.

3.4.4 Other forms of yield curve interpolation

Two other forms of interpolation models are sometimes used: basis splines and Laguerre functions.

Basis splines are similar to the piecewise cubic spline technique described. The major benefit in using basis splines is that they avoid some of the problems with piecewise cubic splines described above. This is the result of the fact that basis splines go to zero at defined points reducing the linkage issues identified above. Typically, the third order basis splines are used, as they satisfy the required criteria of smoothness.

Basis splines are generated in a systematic manner with second order splines being generated from first order splines and third order splines being generated from second order splines. *Exhibit 3.16* sets out the mechanics of using basis splines to create a yield curve. The process follows the following logic:

- Each spline function is specified with a defined range. Outside this range it has a zero value. The points at which the spline is zero are referred to as knot points.
- One spline will end where another spline commences across the yield curve.
- Where knot points have been specified, each spline is weighted using multiple regression techniques. This is predicated on the fact that market bond prices can be expressed in terms of the sum of the discounted bond cash flows and the discount factor at each point in the yield curve coinciding with a cash flow is capable of definition in spline functions and weights. This will allow the bond price today to be expressed as a function of unknown function weights and the product of the spline function values and the bond cash flows. This allows the regression to be performed

nominating the bond price as the dependent variable and the function cash
flows products as the independent variable. The regression process is then
used to estimate the function weights.

Exhibit 3.16

Basis Spline Technique of Interpolation

The basis spline is calculated by specifying the following:

First, discount factors are specified as the sum of weighted spline functions:

$$DF(t) = \sum_{l=1}^{e} W_1 S_1(t)$$

Where

DF (t) = Discount factor for time t

W_1 = Function weight

S_1 = Spline function 1

Secondly, the bond price is specified as the sum of the discounted bond cash
flows:

$$P_i = \sum_{j=1}^{1} C_i \sum_{l=1}^{e} W_1 S_1(t)$$

Where

P_i = Price of bond i

C_i = Bond I cash flow at time j

Finally, prices are expressed as the function weights and cashflow function product
which allow determination of the unknown weights:

$$P_i = \sum_{e=1}^{e} W_i \sum_{j=1}^{n} C_i S_1(t)$$

Source: David Cox, "Yield Curves And How To Build Them" (1995) 4 *Capital Market
Strategies* 29-33.

The basis spline, some commentators have argued, has better properties for
fitting yield curves than the simpler piecewise cubic spline techniques.
However, the basis spline techniques have a number of disadvantages:

- they are complex and computationally difficult;

- the shape of the fitted yield curve is sensitive to the location of the knot
  points. It appears necessary to ensure an even number of bonds are
  available between the knot points, which, in practice, is difficult to satisfy;
  and

- basis splines demonstrate instability and volatility and provides inaccurate
  estimates where there are gaps in the yield curve and sparse data.

An alternative interpolation technique is to utilise Laguerre functions.
Exhibit 3.17 sets out a description of interpolation techniques using Laguerre
functions.

Exhibit 3.17

Polynomial-based Yield Curve Models—Laguerre Model

Laguerre functions consist of a polynomial multiplied by a polynomial decay function in the following form:

$$I_t = (a_0 + a_1 * t_1 + a_2 * t_2 + \ldots\ldots + a_n * t_n) * e^{-b * t}$$

Where

I_t = Interest rate for maturity t

t_n = Time to maturity

a_n, b = Constants

Where Laguerre functions are utilised for term structure modelling the decay function eventually dominates the polynomial component. This means that the long term rates stabilises, as predicted by a Laguerre function. This property provides Laguerre models with an advantage over other models where the estimates of long term rates continues to increase or decrease with time.

The advantages of Laguerre functions include:

• they provide a range of flexible shapes which are consistent with observable interest rate data; and

• they are consistent with theoretical work on yield curve shape and there is some evidence for their applicability to interest rate data.

Source: B F Hunt, "Modelling The Term Structure", paper presented at Conference on Options on Interest Rates (organised by IIR Pty Ltd), Sydney, March 1992.

3.4.5 Interest rate models

A newer approach to modelling the yield curve entails the use of term structure models. The key feature of these models is the use of assumed stochastic processes to drive the term structure of interest rates.

These models have the following characteristics:

• the models entail explicit recognition of the uncertain element in interest rate structure; that is, interest rates are probabilistic rather than deterministic;

• the models entail linking the term structure of interest rates to specified stochastic processes and nominated stochastic factors;

• the evolution of these factors over time in accordance with the assumed process determines interest rates; and

• the model generated interest rates satisfy certain no arbitrage conditions.

There are a large number of competing models.[3] *Exhibit 3.18* sets out an example of these types of interest rate models.

---

3. See John Hull, *Futures Options and Other Derivatives* (3rd ed, Prentice Hall, Englewood Cliffs, New Jersey, 1997), Ch 17.

Exhibit 3.18

Interest Rate Models

The Vasichek model specifies the following stochastic model for interest rates:

$$dr = \alpha \, (\gamma - r) \, dt + \sigma \, dz$$

Where

dr = Change in the short-term interest rate

α   = Parameter (greater than 0) which describes the speed at which r revert to a long-run average value

γ   = Long-run value of r

r   = Short-term interest rate

dt = Short-term interval

σ   = Volatility of r

dz = Random variable chosen from a normal distribution with mean 0 and variance dt

The process specified identifies that the change in the short term rate r over the internal dt will have two components:

1. A deterministic component ($\alpha \, (\gamma - r) \, dt$) whereby r will revert to a long run value at a speed parameter (α).

2. A stochastic component ($\sigma \, dz$) which will change randomly.

The structure of the first term implies that if r is close to (away from) its long run value, the deterministic term will be small (large). This term reflects the premise of mean reversion whereby interest rates tend towards some normal rate. The stochastic term will be larger as the time over which change occurs increases. The structure is designed to be consistent with the general pattern of evolution of interest rates in capital markets.

The specified process for interest rate changes allows the derivation of valuation formula for a discount bond, which in turn facilitates the solution for the value of interest rate derivative products.

Source: O A Vasichek, "An Equilibrium Characterisation of the Term Structure" (1977) 5 *Journal of Financial Economics* 177-188.

The model described is a relatively simple single factor model incorporating mean reversion. The major variations include two factor models (such as a short term and a long term interest rate), the inclusion or exclusion of mean reversion, and the imposition of arbitrage free conditions. Models commonly utilised include the Heath-Jarrow-Morton[4] model and the Hull-White model.[5]

The major application of these models is in pricing interest rate derivatives, in particular, options. The research into interest rate models is largely predicated on these demands. They are also related integrally to the non-linear interpolation techniques identified above. This relationship is predicated on the fact that an appropriate curve is fitted to observed market data. The fitted curve then allows the construction of an interest rate yield curve model which obtains estimates which are consistent with the market

4. See D Heath, R Jarrow and A Morton, "Contingent Claim Valuation With A Random Evolution Of Interest Rates" (1991) *Review of Futures Markets* 54-76; "Bond Pricing and the Term Structure of Interest Rates: A New Methodology" (1992) *Econometrica* 60 at 1, 77-105.
5. See Hull, op cit n 3.

data. In this sense, the interest rate models reflect an extension of the interpolation techniques to allow the provision of solutions, both analytical or numerical, for the value of interest rate derivative products.

4. TERM STRUCTURE OF INTEREST RATES

Interest rates deal with the process of valuation of cash flows at different future times. Term structure deals with the pure price of time in the application of different interest rates at different future times. The process of interpolation assumes implicitly or explicitly a term structure model of interest rates. Understanding of the term structure of interest rates is essential in yield curve modelling.

The term structure of interest rates can be defined as the structure of interest rate applicable for cash flows of a homogenous credit quality for different maturities. The types of term structure (or yield curve shapes) observed (see *Exhibit 3.19*) include:[6]

- positive—interest rates increase with maturity;
- negative—interest rates decrease with maturity;
- flat—interest rates are the same across all maturities; and
- humped—interest rates increase with maturity but peak and decrease from their maximum level with further increases in maturities.

6. For a summary of interest rate term structure theories see Richard W McEnally and James V Jordan, "The Term Structure of Interest Rates" in Frank J Fabozzi and T Dessa Fabozzi (eds), *The Handbook of Fixed Income Securities* (4th ed, Irwin Professional Publishing, Chicago, 1995), pp 779-830.

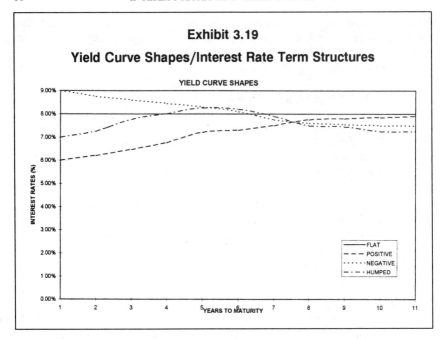

Exhibit 3.19

Yield Curve Shapes/Interest Rate Term Structures

The following theories of the determinants of the term structure of interest rates are usually considered:

1. *Expectations Hypothesis*—in its pure form, the expectations hypothesis states that expected interest return from securities of all maturities are equal. This implies that the return for a particular maturity represents the expected holding period return from investing in shorter term securities which are reinvested at maturity at the implied forward rates. This is based on the implicit assumption that the implied forward rate is the market consensus expected short term interest rate as of the future date. In effect, this theory is consistent with the assumption that longer term interest rates are an average of expected short term interest rates.

2. *Liquidity Preference Hypothesis*—this states that investors prefer shorter maturities in preference to longer maturities and require a premium in the form of a higher interest rate or lower price (the liquidity premium). This is consistent with the assumption of increased price risk with increases in maturity reflecting the potential instability in their capital values upon liquidation prior to maturity if required. The liquidity premium is usually assumed to increase with maturity but at a decreasing rate.

3. *Preferred Habitat/Market Segmentation Hypothesis*—this assumes that the market for shorter dated securities is segmented from that for longer dated securities reflecting the investment preferences of the underlying investors arising from their asset liability matching requirements and risk preferences. This implies that differences in the market structure as embodied in differential demand/supply equilibrium for securities of different maturities dictate the interest rate term structure.

The theories of interest rate term structure are not mutually exclusive. Newer attempts to develop models to encompass the key determinants of term structure usually combine elements of each of the theories. For example, the biased expectations hypothesis states that interest rates reflect the combined impact of future interest rate expectations and also liquidity premia for increased maturities.

The interest rates models described above are not true term structure theories but represent new ways of modelling the yield curve. In reality, the interest rate models are consistent with the key theoretical approaches identified because each represents a special case of stochastic processes used to generate the yield curve.

Exhibit 3.20 sets out a summary of the relationship between the observable interest rate term structures and the theoretical models identified.

Exhibit 3.20
Summary of Interest Rate Term Structure

Type Of Term Structure	Flat	Positive	Negative	Humped
Expectation Theory	Short-term interest rates are expected to remain the same	Short-term interest rates are expected to increase	Short-term interest rates are expected to decrease	Short-term interest rates are expected to increase and then decrease
Liquidity Premium	No liquidity premia	Positive liquidity premia	Negative liquidity premia	Positive liquidity premia followed by negative liquidity premia
Preferred Habitat/Market Segmentation	Equilibrium in demand supply across all maturities	Excess of supply over demand in longer maturities	Excess of supply over demand in shorter maturities	Excess of supply over demand in intermediate maturities
Biased Expectations	Short-term rates are expected to decrease but are offset by increasing liquidity premia	Short-term rates are expected to remain the same or increase moderately and are accentuated by increasing liquidity premia	Short-term rates are expected to decrease but the rate of decrease is offset by an increasing liquidity premia	Short-term rates are expected to stay the same or increase and then decrease (the decrease being sharper than the increase), with the increase being accentuated by and the fall retarded by an increasing liquidity premia

In practice, the yield curve interpolation model utilised must be consistent with the observed interest rate term structure prevalent in the relevant market to avoid inaccuracies and poor predictive performance.

5. YIELD CURVE CONSTRUCTION IN PRACTICE

The process of derivation of appropriate interest rates and discount factors can, as shown above, be reduced into two separate and distinct processes. The first process entails the use of yield curve modelling processes to derive a complete set of interest rates. The second process entails the generation of zero rates from the yield curve which can be utilised for the valuation of financial instruments.

In practice, a number of additional considerations are relevant. A major factor underlying these uncertainties is the incomplete and imperfect nature of financial markets generally and the difficulties in nominating objective criteria to select optimal models for constructing accurate yield curves. These problems include the following:

• The difficulty in identifying yield curves which are homogenous in terms of credit or default risk. In practice, a series of interest rates derived from similar but not perfectly credit homogenous yield curves are combined.

• The problems of defining the characteristics of fit for an estimated yield curve because the criteria of fit, consistency and smoothness can be applied at different levels. For example, there are in reality multiple curves which can be fitted to satisfy the smoothness criteria: the par curve; the forward curve; the zero curve; or the discount factors generated off any of these curves. Linear interpolation often creates irregular forward curves while splines can create regular smooth curve, for one or more of these sets of interest rates or discount factors, *but not for all curves.*

The problems identified are not necessarily capable of perfect solution. In practice, practitioners use compromises reflecting trade-offs between market structure, data integrity, estimation accuracy, computational efficiency and cost effectiveness. A major criteria is the issue of hedge-ability; that is, the capacity to hedge the components of the yield curve and the interest rate risks assumed in the course of pricing, valuing and trading financial instruments off the selected yield curve. In essence, practitioners will favour the construction of a yield curve which not only is nearest the theoretical paradigm but one which also facilitates trading and hedging activities.

Against this set of constraints, most practitioners utilise two separate yield curves for valuation purposes:

1. A risk free curve—usually constructed from the available series of interest rates on government securities of the relevant tenor.

2. A risk adjusted (the swap) curve—usually constructed from a mixture of instruments (including short term inter-bank rates, near term short term interest rate futures contracts or forward rate agreement (FRA) prices/rates, and interest rate swap rates. The swap curve is used to value credit risk affected (that is, non government risk financial instruments) where appropriate, incorporating adjustment spreads where the underlying

instrument is considered to have fundamentally different risk or other characteristics.

The derivation of the risk free curve follows the established procedures identified. Key considerations include, depending on the market, noisy data (reflecting a large number of government securities of identical or similar maturities with different coupons trading at different yields) and data sparseness (whereby there may be significant gaps in the yield curve). In practice, these are overcome by constructing a fitted curve (using one or other of the techniques identified) and generating the required zero rates from that curve.

The generation of the swap curve is more complex. As noted above, this curve is constructed by combining a series of interest rates from different instruments. The following example, which uses the US market, is indicative of both the approach and the key considerations which are relevant. It should be noted that the problem of yield curve construction in other markets is necessarily more complex and less readily soluble than those in the US example, reflecting the relative maturity, liquidity and efficiency of that market.

In practice, the swap curve in US$ is constructed as follows:

- The cash rate (usually based on an interbank rate such as LIBOR) to the first IMM eurodollar delivery date (the near month contract) is taken. Some interpolation is usually required, as the period may not coincide with the traded maturities for cash, which are usually overnight, one week, one, three, six et cetera months.

- The next series of rates taken are the eurodollar futures rates. The number of successive eurodollar futures contracts varies but in practice will be between 12 and 20 quarterly contracts (three to five years).[7] For each contract, the traded futures price is deducted from 100 to determine the forward rate which is then incorporated into the yield curve. This process is repeated for each contract.

- Beyond the futures contracts, available interest rate swap rates are utilised to complete the yield curve.

- Certain dominance rules are specified; for example, the eurodollar rates may or may not be overridden by the relevant swap rates.

The curve once derived is fitted and zero rates generated in the established manner. *Exhibit 3.21* sets out a simple example of the process described.

---

7. It is likely in currencies other than US$ the number of futures contracts used would be lower, say four to eight contracts (one to two years), reflecting the fact that the futures markets in the relevant currency do not allow trading beyond this maturity and/or the liquidity of the market. Technically, in the US$ market, it is theoretically possible to trade eurodollar futures out to 10 years (40 successive quarters), which would mean it would be possible to derive a 10 year yield curve from the futures rates.

Exhibit 3.21

Constructing a Zero Coupon Curve

This is an example of how to construct a zero coupon curve using bills, bill futures and swaps. We use the bootstrap method. Interpolation is based on keeping the forward rates constant. Internal calculations will be in terms of continuously compounding rates and discount factors.

The instruments

For the curve, we use instruments whose prices are available in the marketplace. These are bills, bill futures and swaps. We will assume that the bill futures take precedence where there is any overlap.[i]

To keep the procedure general, all times will be in days or years. This means that dates can be omitted. In a real application, dates would be converted to days. The spot date is assumed to be day zero. All days/years are relative to the spot date unless otherwise specified.

Bills

These are pure discount instruments whose maturity is a fixed number of days out from the spot date.

# Days	Rate
1	6
30	6
60	5.98
150	6

The price of a bill is just its face value discounted over the appropriate number of days. Thus we can directly obtain discount factors for bills. If the bill has d days to maturity then the discount factor is

$$df = \frac{1}{(1 + r\frac{d}{365})}$$

This gives a continuously compounded zero rate of

$$r(zero) = \frac{-365}{d}\ln(df)$$

---

i. This is a realistic assumption as they are the most liquid of the instruments used. Also, short dated swaps are usually hedged using bill futures.

Exhibit 3.21—*continued*

# Days	Rate	df	Cts Zero Rate
1	6	0.999836	5.999507
30	6	0.995093	5.985254
60	5.98	0.990266	5.950799
150	6	0.975936	5.927221

Bill futures

Bill futures are just like bills, except that they start out of a forward date. In this example, we have a strip of bill futures. Where one bill future matures, the next begins. From the table below, the first bill future starts at day 40 and matures on day 132. The next starts on day 132 and expires on day 223 and so forth. The yield of a bill future is just 100 minus its price.

Days to Start	Days to Expiry	Price	Yield
40	132	94.000	6
132	223	93.920	6.08
223	314	93.660	6.34
314	405	93.350	6.65
405	496	93.110	6.89
496	587	92.940	7.06
587	678	92.790	7.21
678	769	92.640	7.36
769	860	92.520	7.48
860	951	92.420	7.58
951	1042	92.330	7.67
1042	1133	92.220	7.78

It is a simple matter to get the forward discount factor and the forward rate continuously compounded for a bill future. These are given by the same formulae as for bills. If the bill future starts at d_s and expires at d_e, then

$$df^e_s = \frac{1}{(1 + r\frac{(d_e - d_s)}{365})}$$

$$r^e_s(zero) = \frac{-365}{(d_e - d_s)}\ln(df^e_s)$$

Exhibit 3.21—*continued*

These are forward discount factors and rates. They need to be linked to spot rates. This will be illustrated below when we combine all the components of the curve.

Days to Start	Days to Expiry	Price	Yield	Cts Zero Rate	df
40	132	94.000	6	5.955082	0.985102
132	223	93.920	6.08	6.034379	0.985068
223	314	93.660	6.34	6.290415	0.984439
314	405	93.350	6.65	6.595475	0.983691
405	496	93.110	6.89	6.831492	0.983112
496	587	92.940	7.06	6.998586	0.982703
587	678	92.790	7.21	7.145964	0.982342
678	769	92.640	7.36	7.293288	0.981981
769	860	92.520	7.48	7.411109	0.981693
860	951	92.420	7.58	7.509266	0.981452
951	1042	92.330	7.67	7.597587	0.981236
1042	1133	92.220	7.78	7.705509	0.980972

Swaps

Swaps are priced as fixed coupon instruments whose coupon is equal to the swap rate. In other words they are par bonds. Conventionally, swaps of three years and less pay quarterly coupons while swaps of longer maturity pay coupons semi annually. It is convention to quote rates for swaps of maturity one to five years, then for seven and ten year swaps. For maturities of six, eight and nine years, we shall interpolate the rates linearly.[ii]

# Years	Rate	Freq
1	6.5	4
2	7	4
3	7.2	4
4	7.25	2
5	7.35	2
6	7.415	2
7	7.48	2
8	7.52	2
9	7.56	2
10	7.6	2

The swaps will be priced when the curve is assembled.

ii.   It may be more appropriate to use higher order interpolation. Alternatively, the curve can be built using only the quoted swap rates. The other rates obtained from the curve.

Exhibit 3.21—*continued*

Putting it together

We have chosen to construct the curve giving precedence to bill futures where there is overlap. Thus the bill of 150 days will be omitted. The 60 day bill will not be used explicitly, but will be used to obtain a bill rate to the beginning of the bill futures strip. Swaps of three years and less are not needed either.

Up to 30 days, the bills provide zero coupon instruments directly. Once a rate at 40 days is known, the bill futures can be used to compute the curve out to 1133 days. The swaps are then required for further dates.

As we know zero rates from the bills to 30 and 60 days, a 40 day bill rate can be implied by interpolation. In this example we assume that forward rates are constant. Using the 30 and 60 day bill rates, the discount factor and forward rate from 30 to 60 days is given by:

$$df_{30}^{60} = \frac{df_0^{60}}{df_0^{30}} = \frac{0.990266}{0.995093} = 0.995149$$

$$r_{30}^{60} = \frac{365}{(60-30)} \ln(df_{30}^{60}) = 5.916344\%$$

This forward rate is used from 30 to 40 days (as the interpolation keeps the forward rates flat). Thus the 40 day discount factor and zero rate can be obtained.

$$df_{30}^{40} = df_0^{30} e^{-0.05916344 \cdot 10/365} = 0.993481$$

The process so far has used bill rates directly to obtain the zero curve to 30 days. The 60 day bill is used to obtain the curve to the beginning of the bill futures strip. The futures can be combined directly to generate the curve out to 1133 days.

	Days (Start)	Days (Expiry)	Zero Rate	Spot DF	Fwd DF	Fwd Rate
Bill	30	60	5.985254	0.995093	0.995149	
Bill	60		5.950799	0.990266		5.916344
Futures Splice	40	60	5.968027	0.993481	0.99838	5.916344
Futures	40	132	5.968027	0.993481	0.985102	5.955082
	132	223	5.959005	0.97868	0.985068	6.034379
	223	314	5.989763	0.964067	0.984439	6.290415
	314	405	6.076895	0.949065	0.983691	6.595475

Exhibit 3.21—*continued*

The forward discount factors for the bill futures have already been obtained above. These can be combined with the discount factor to the beginning of the futures strip to build the curve. For the first future

$$df_0^{132} = df_0^{40} df_{40}^{132} = 0.993481 \times 0.985102 = 0.97868$$

and the continuous zero rate is

$$r_0^{132} = \frac{-365}{132} \ln(0.97868) = 5.959005\%$$

This can be continued for all the bill futures.

# Days	df	Cts Zero Rate
1	0.999836	5.999507
30	0.995093	5.985254
60	0.990266	5.950799
150	0.975936	5.927221
132	0.985102	5.955082
223	0.985068	6.034379
314	0.984439	6.290415
405	0.983691	6.595475
496	0.983112	6.831492
587	0.982703	6.998586
678	0.982342	7.145964
769	0.981981	7.293288
860	0.981693	7.411109
951	0.981452	7.509266
1042	0.981236	7.597587
1133	0.980972	7.705509

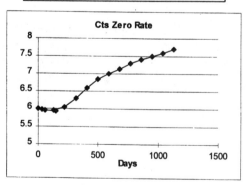

Exhibit 3.21—*continued*

The Zero Curve to the End of the Bill Futures Strip

The swaps are now required. The first swap to be used is the four year swap. The swap rate of 7.25% implies the following cashflows

Years	Cashflow
0	−100.000
0.5	3.625
1	3.625
1.5	3.625
2	3.625
2.5	3.625
3	3.625
3.5	3.625
4	103.625

As the curve has already been generated out to 1133 days (or 3/104 years), this can be used to value the cashflows to three years. The remaining two cashflows are required to generate the curve.

Years	Days	Cashflow	DF	NPV
0	0	−100.000	1	−100
0.5	182	3.625	0.970623	3.51851
1	366	3.625	0.940189	3.408186
1.5	547	3.625	0.908889	3.294723
2	731	3.625	0.876684	3.177981
2.5	912	3.625	0.845036	3.063255
3	1096	3.625	0.81323	2.947957
3.5	1278	3.625		
4	1462	103.625		

The NPV of the swap must equal exactly zero if the cashflow on the spot date is included. Of the cashflows where the curve is available, the NPV is −80.5894. The complete equation is

$$df_{1278} \times 3.625 + df_{1462} \times 103.625 = 80.5894$$

This cannot be solved directly as there are two unknown discount factors. If we use our interpolation rule keeping the forward rate constant, then an iterative solution can be generated.[iii]

This gives a solution for the forward rate of $r^{1462}_{1096} = 8.022778$ and discount factors

$df_{1278} = 0.781339328$ and $df_{1462} = 0.750369643$. This solves the equation for the swap price above. This procedure is then repeated for all the other swaps.

---

iii. Any common numerical method such as Newton-Raphson can be used.

Exhibit 3.21—continued

Instrument	Years[iv]	Discount Factor	Continuous Forward Rate	Continuous Zero Rate
Spot		1		
1 Day Bill	0.003	0.9998	5.9995	5.9995
30 Day Bill	0.082	0.9951	5.9848	5.9853
Futures	0.110	0.9935	5.9163	5.9680
	0.362	0.9787	5.9551	5.9590
	0.611	0.9641	6.0344	5.9898
	0.860	0.9491	6.2904	6.0769
	1.110	0.9336	6.5955	6.1934
	1.359	0.9178	6.8315	6.3105
	1.608	0.9019	6.9986	6.4172
	1.858	0.8860	7.1460	6.5150
	2.107	0.8701	7.2933	6.6071
	2.356	0.8541	7.4111	6.6922
	2.605	0.8383	7.5093	6.7703
	2.855	0.8226	7.5976	6.8426
	3.104	0.8069	7.7055	6.9119
	3.501	0.7813	8.1037	7.0471
4y Swap	4.005	0.7504	8.0228	7.1699
	4.501	0.7223	7.6876	7.2269
5y Swap	5.005	0.6948	7.6876	7.2733
	5.501	0.6689	7.6782	7.3098
6y Swap	6.005	0.6435	7.6782	7.3407
	6.501	0.6190	7.8404	7.3789
7y Swap	7.005	0.5950	7.8404	7.4121
	7.504	0.5725	7.7330	7.4334
8y Swap	8.008	0.5506	7.7330	7.4523
	8.504	0.5295	7.8649	7.4763
9y Swap	9.008	0.5089	7.8649	7.4981
	9.504	0.4892	7.9816	7.5233
10y Swap	10.008	0.4699	7.9816	7.5464

iv. Note that the number of years is not exactly integral for the swaps. This is because when this example was generated, it was assumed that there were 365 days per year. Exact calendar dates were used.

Exhibit 3.21—*continued*

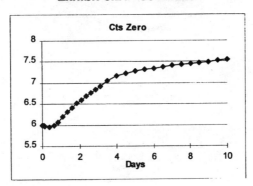

The graph showing the forward rates illustrates the interpolation method. The forward rates are stepped. They change discontinuously. Where there are frequent and liquid instruments (the bills and bill futures), the change is regular. Once the instruments become less liquid, there is some irregularity in these rates. The zero coupon rates are much smoother. It is rare that a long dated forward instrument will require pricing. If it does, the spread will have to be large to account for the irregularity in the forward rates. Alternatively an interpolation method where the forwards are kept smooth will need to be employed.

Obtaining discount factors

Once the curve has been generated, we have discount factors (and rates) at the points where cashflows from the underlying instruments occur. The curve will price these instruments. This in itself is not useful as the prices are already used in the curve construction. Indeed this is a circular situation. The value of the zero curve is in having a model which gives discount factors at any time in the future. To obtain these, we can either graphically retrieve them, or use the interpolation method implicit in the curve.

Exhibit 3.21—*continued*

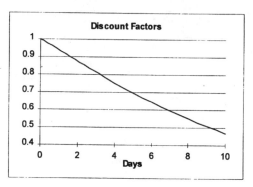

Discount Factors

The Discount Factors

Using the interpolation method to obtain discount factors requires minor calculation. As an example, we will obtain the discount factor at 7.4 years.

Instrument	Years[v]	Discount Factor	Continuous Forward Rate	Continuous Zero Rate
7y Swap	7.005	0.5950	7.8404	7.4121
	7.504	0.5725	7.7330	7.4334
8y Swap	8.008	0.5506	7.330	7.4523

We know the discount factor to 7.005 years. We also know that the forward rate for any period between 7.005 and 8.008 years is 7.7330% (as our interpolation method keeps the forward constant). We can obtain the discount factor from 7.005 to 7.4 years.

$$df_{7.005}^{7.4} = e^{-0.07733t} = 0.969952$$

This then allows the discount factor and zero rate to be calculated.[vi]

Instrument	Years[vii]	Discount Factor	Continuous Forward Rate	Continuous Zero Rate
7y Swap	7.005	0.5950	7.8404	7.4121
7.4y	7.4	**0.577089**	**7.7330**	**7.429182**
	7.504	0.5725	7.7330	7.4334
8y Swap	8.008	0.5506	7.7330	7.4523

Discount factors can be obtained to any dates by this process.

---

v.   Note that the number of years is not exactly integral for the swaps. This is because when this example was generated, it was assumed that there were 365 days per year. Exact calendar dates were used.

vi. In this equation, $t = 0.394520$.

vii. Note that the number of years is not exactly integral for the swaps. This is because when this example was generated, it was assumed that there were 365 days per year. Exact calendar dates were used.

Exhibit 3.21—*continued*

Pricing cashflows

Arbitrary cashflows can now be valued by obtaining the discount factors to the dates where the cashflows occur. To price any instrument, decompose it into cashflows, then use this method. If there are liquidity or other conditions, the zero curve can be modified to account for these. Also the difference between market prices and the price on the curve can be calculated. This is useful to assess the premium or discount the market is building in to non standard instruments. As an example, corporate bonds can be valued on a zero coupon curve built using government bonds. The discount for credit liquidity and other factors can be quantified.

The approach described requires careful consideration of the following factors:

- The nature of the instruments is different, including differences in credit risk and instrument features. For example, the use of futures contracts introduces the following factors: the payment of deposits and margins; the differential credit risk of the clearing house; and, in the case of eurodollar futures, the problems of the fixed tick point value (0.01% is equal to US$25) or the negative convexity.

- The problem of overlapping dates. This can be illustrated by comparing and contrasting the use of FRAs versus futures. The FRAs out of spot will trade at regular runs (3 × 6; 6 × 9 et cetera) which allows the calculation of the relevant forward interest rates and discount factors which are incorporated in the yield curve. In contrast, the eurodollar futures contracts are standardised. They are traded to pre-specified dates and are cash settled against three month LIBOR. As these dates may not be precisely three months apart, the prospect exists for gaps or overlaps between the end of the reference period and the maturity date of the next eurodollar contract. The practical import of this is that the discount factors cannot be multiplied or forward rates compounded as the interest periods are not exactly linked. This requires adjustments to the futures rates.

- The forward rates embodied in eurodollar futures prices reflect some of the inherent biases in futures prices, including the impact of margin payments and the negative convexity. Where interest rates are expected to increase, the holder of a short (long) futures position will receive (be required to pay) margin payments which can be invested (must be funded) at higher interest rates. This uncertainty forces the futures rate to trade above the theoretical arbitrage free forward rate. In practice, the bias in futures prices and the negative convexity necessitate additional adjustments based on the expected volatility of interest rates.

- The selection of the transition point between the futures curves and the swap curve is relatively arbitrary reflecting institutional and market considerations as well the margining and convexity issues identified.

The presence of these factors means that the generation of the relevant yield curve is unlikely to be an objectively verifiable activity.

The major practical problem to arise relates to the fact that more than one equally tractable yield curve can be created from the same set of market data reflecting differences in interest rate selection and mode of adjustment for the problems identified. In reality, the problems are generally likely to be confined to the shorter end, particularly the transition points from one set of interest rates to the next source. A major area is the transition from the futures or FRA rates to the swap rates.

Given that the zero rates are likely to be different, either a selection must be made between the yield curves or adjustment made to the set of rates to be used. One possible basis for selection between the curves is by application. Where an adjustment is to be made it is necessary to either segment the curve to ensure the absence of overlap or create blended curves. There are problems with each approach:

- the use of different curves differentiated by application will create different values and prices for different transactions opening up the possibility of value loss; and
- the adjustments will either create severe discontinuity in the curve and irregularities in the rates or require complex and highly subjective adjustments.

In practice, there is little uniformity in approach to these issues. Each institution generally employs its own set of techniques to deal with the problem, reflecting the nature of the market and the purpose for which the generated zero rates are to be utilised.

5. SUMMARY

The pricing, valuation and trading of financial instruments, irrespective of whether it is a simple fixed income security or a derivative transaction, requires and assumes the availability of interest rate or discount factors extending across the maturity spectrum. In practice, the practitioner is required to choose between different interest rates to value these transactions. The best practice method now applied universally in capital markets is to discount the transaction cash flows using zero rates derived from the relevant yield curve. The zero rate itself requires the construction of the yield curve using sophisticated mathematical techniques within a framework of economic theory which is consistent with observed interest rate behaviour. While the requirement for accurate zero rates is now recognised, deficiencies in market structure and data availability present significant challenges to the derivation of accurate, consistent and computationally efficient yield curves.

Part 3

Derivative Pricing

Chapter 4

Pricing Forwards and Futures Contracts[1]

by John Martin

1. INTRODUCTION

A forward is any contract which obliges you to buy or sell a financial instrument or physical commodity at some date in the future at an agreed price. For our purposes, forwards includes OTC forward contracts and exchange-traded futures contracts, and includes instruments such as:

- foreign exchange forward contracts;
- forward rate agreements;
- forward bonds;
- short-term interest rate futures;
- bond futures;
- stock index futures; and
- commodity futures contracts.

Forward contracts represent an extremely useful starting point for all derivative valuation. As we will see in other parts of this book, more complex derivatives such as swaps and options can be decomposed into portfolios of forward contracts. As a consequence, the valuation of these more complex instruments will be based partly on the forward valuation techniques developed in the following chapters.

While forward contracts are the simplest form of derivative, they represent the largest derivative type by outstanding face value and volume. *Exhibit 4.1* highlights the relative importance of forwards versus swaps and options.

---

1. Parts of this chapter are based on the discussion on forward contracts in J S Martin, *Derivative Maths* (IFR, 1996).

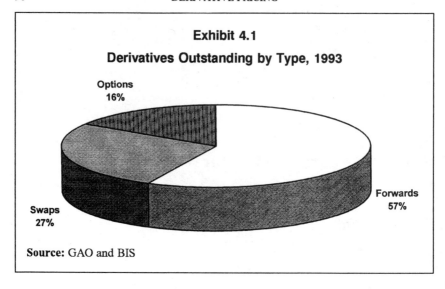

Exhibit 4.1

Derivatives Outstanding by Type, 1993

Options 16%

Forwards 57%

Swaps 27%

Source: GAO and BIS

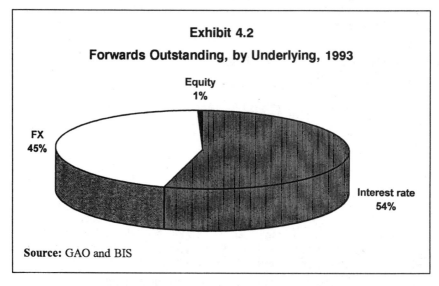

Exhibit 4.2

Forwards Outstanding, by Underlying, 1993

Equity 1%

FX 45%

Interest rate 54%

Source: GAO and BIS

As *Exhibit 4.2* demonstrates, foreign exchange and interest rate products dominate forward transactions. It is interesting to note that most of this volume is comprised of OTC foreign exchange forwards and exchange traded interest rate futures. The volume of equity forwards is relatively low and is mainly stock index futures. Like all derivatives markets, forward markets have seen very rapid growth since the mid 1980s.

2. CHARACTERISTICS OF FORWARDS

2.1 Forwards versus cash transactions

The definition of when a transaction is a cash transaction and when it is a forward is important. We might expect any transaction which settles today to be a cash transaction and a forward is anything settling from tomorrow onward. Unfortunately this is not always the case and, depending on the underlying financial asset, a "cash" transaction can range from today for a money market transaction to several weeks, or longer, in some securities markets. Some examples of cash instrument settlement days are listed below:

Cash Market	Settlement Date
Money market transactions	Today
Euromarkets	Today + 2 business days
Foreign exchange	Today + 2 business days
Stock exchanges	Today + 5 business days
Crude oil	Today + 1 month
Some property markets	Today + 6 weeks

All of these represent "cash" transactions, however, in each market the convention applying to the settlement of these transactions changes according to market convention. The market convention usually reflects the ease with which settlement can be arranged and/or the relative complexity of changing ownership of a financial asset. For example, money market instruments in most currencies are lodged on electronic networks, where both payment and transfer of ownership can occur in a matter of minutes—same day settlement is easily possible. However, where change of ownership involves different time zones and bank accounts such as in foreign exchange, or the shipment of commodities in the oil market, or the completion of legal documentation as in property, the time to settlement becomes longer.

When considering a forward, the market convention on the time to settlement underlying a cash or spot price has to be known. A forward transaction does not commence till the settlement day passes the cash settlement date. So, in the foreign exchange market, a forward is a transaction which settles after two business days.

2.2 Forward price and value

A forward contract gives us the right to buy or sell a financial asset at some date after the normal cash settlement date at an agreed price. The attraction of forward contracts is that they provide a method of obtaining a fixed price on an asset regardless of movements in the cash price between the trade date and the settlement date.

As in the cash market, a forward *price* is agreed between the buyer and seller which reflects the relative cost or benefits to both parties of delaying settlement of that transaction. Once this price is agreed then the market replacement cost, or the *value* of reversing, will also change as market conditions change. An important feature of forwards, and derivative valuation in general, is that there are always two components to valuation:

1. What is the forward price?

2. What is the value of an open transaction based on this price?

The forward price and cash price are usually different. When valuing a forward transaction we first need to determine the prevailing market price for a forward, and then determine the present value based on that forward price. This is simplified in futures markets, as a transparent forward price is the subject of trading and, in liquid markets, is a fair reflection of the price at which open contracts can be reversed.

Determining the forward price is not only a requirement of valuation. It is also an essential tool in comparing different forward instruments such as forwards and futures, whether you are a market maker, arbitrager or hedger. For example, suppose you know that the true "fair" forward price of a security is $100 and the futures market is trading at $99. This suggests that an arbitrage opportunity of $1 exists if you buy the futures contract and enter into another contract to sell it forward. Similarly, if you are a market maker in forward instruments you need to be able to calculate a constantly updated forward price to quote to your clients.

In this chapter we review the following:

- general forward pricing and valuation (Section 3);
- interest rate forwards and futures (Section 4);
- foreign exchange forwards (Section 5); and
- equity forwards (Section 6).

2.3 Terminology

In these chapters on forwards and futures we will use the following standardised terminology:

Term	Description
Valuation Date	The date on which a valuation is being performed (usually today)
Forward Expiry Date	The date on which the forward contract expires and the obligation to buy or sell forward falls due
Forward Settlement Date	The date on which the forward obligations arising from the forward contract must be settled in cash (usually the forward expiry date or soon after)
Forward Period	The number of days between the valuation date and the forward expiry date
Cash or Spot Price	The price paid on the valuation date for a "cash" purchase of the underlying asset
Forward Price	The price agreed to be paid for the underlying asset on the forward expiry date
Asset Income	The income paid to the owner of a financial asset—usually during the forward period. Examples of asset income include coupons and dividends.

3. GENERAL FORWARD PRICING AND VALUATION

3.1 Deriving the forward price

The easiest way to understand forward pricing is to break it down into its underlying components. Like most derivatives, forward transactions can be reproduced by a series of physical positions. This can probably be best explained by some simple examples.

3.1.1 Example: buying a painting

Calculating the forward pricing is the same question as how much should I pay to buy something in the futures. To remove the complications sometimes presented by financial instruments it is often easier to understand derivative pricing using a tangible good such as a piece of artwork. In both of these examples we ignore any compounding effects and assume that there are no other benefits from the asset apart from any described.

Suppose an art dealer offers to sell you a painting today for US$1 million today or US$1.2 million in one year's time. Would you buy it today or in one year? (As a hint the current one year interest rate is 10% pa.)

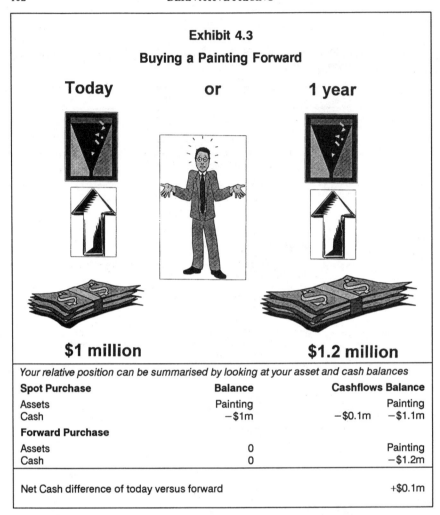

Exhibit 4.3

Buying a Painting Forward

Your relative position can be summarised by looking at your asset and cash balances

Spot Purchase	Balance	Cashflows	Balance
Assets	Painting		Painting
Cash	−$1m	−$0.1m	−$1.1m
Forward Purchase			
Assets	0		Painting
Cash	0		−$1.2m
Net Cash difference of today versus forward			+$0.1m

In *Exhibit 4.3* the problem is represented diagrammatically. The art dealer is offering to buy the painting at a cash price of $1 million or a forward price of $1.2 million. We wish to take the deal which is financially beneficial.

A useful way of looking at the transaction is in terms of the cash and asset balances. If we buy the painting today we give up $1 million. This is either financed by borrowing the funds or reducing our existing cash balances, which at the end of the year incurs an interest cost or reduces interest income by $0.1 million. While the forward purchase avoids spending cash today, it requires paying $1.2 million in one year. At the end of one year both deals give us the same asset, however the cash cost of the forward purchase is $0.1 million higher than the spot purchase—so we would buy the painting today.

While a simple example, it displays an important idea: a forward transaction can be replicated by purchasing the asset today and borrowing the money to finance it. The "fair" forward price is then the cash price plus the interest cost over the life of the forward transaction. In this example, the fair one year forward price is $1.1 million.

This example shows the forward price on an asset that provides no cash return in the form of coupons or dividends. Most financial assets provide an income so we need to incorporate that into our pricing framework. In the following example we use another simple tangible asset.

3.1.2 Example: buying a warehouse

You are given the opportunity to buy a warehouse as an investment for DEM 1 million today or DEM 1.1 million in one year's time. Would you buy it today or in one year? (As a hint, the warehouse is currently earning rental income of 2% pa and you can borrow DEM for 1 year at 14% pa.)

This time we need to take account of the cash income. In this case, if we buy the property today we receive DEM 0.02 million in income, which we do not receive if we purchase the warehouse forward. The rent has the effect of reducing the net cost of "carrying" that property.

Exhibit 4.4

Buying a Warehouse Forward

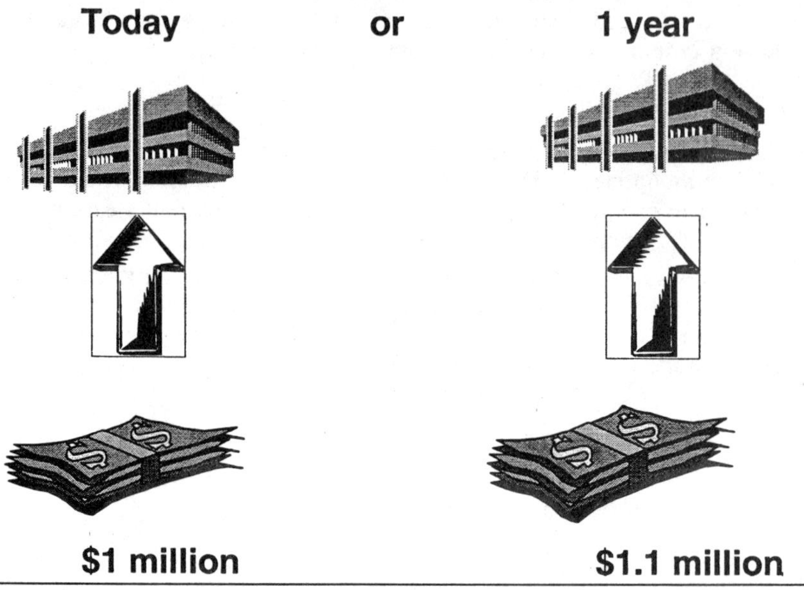

Today	or	1 year

$1 million		**$1.1 million**

Spot Purchase	Balance	Net Cashflows Balance
Assets	Warehouse	Warehouse
Cash	−$1m	−$0.12m −$1.1m
Forward Purchase		
Assets	0	Warehouse
Cash	0	−$1.1m
Net Cash difference of today versus forward		−$0.02m

Using the same cash balance approach as in the above example we can see from *Exhibit 4.4* that, while the rental income reduces the net cost of buying the property the net cash cost, and the "fair" forward price, at the end of the year is DEM 1.12 million. So, in this example we would buy the property forward.

3.2 Some conclusions regarding the forward price

While simple, these two examples display the fundamentals of forward pricing. Essentially the "fair value" forward price makes buyers and sellers indifferent between buying and selling the underlying asset today or in the future based on the current market cash price, cost of financing the asset and the expected return on the asset. In other words the forward price is essentially a summary of the net financial obligations of owning an asset.

The examples also highlight four of the key features of the forward prices:

1. *Replication*: A forward purchase of an asset can be replicated by buying the asset in the cash market, financing the purchase by borrowing the cash required and then receiving any asset income.

2. *Fair price*: The "fair" forward price is given by the cash price plus the net cost of financing the asset over the term of the forward contract.

3. *Interest effect*: The interest cost tends to *increase* the forward price versus the cash price.

4. *"Dividend" or "coupon" effect*: Any cash return on the asset over the term of the forward contract tends to *decrease* the forward price versus the cash price.

These four general rules should apply to all forward prices on financial assets regardless of whether it is an interest rate, foreign exchange or equity product provided they operate in freely operating markets. It is worth noting that these relationships start to break down when you move away from financial assets, particularly to consumable commodities such as agricultural and energy products. This is because the decision to have the physical commodity today or in the future is not just a financial or investment decision, the decision to buy a commodity today or in the future also has to take into consideration when the commodity is required for consumption.

While these examples were from the point of view of a forward purchase, the same logic applies to a forward sale except it works in reverse. Looking at the painting example, if we agree to sell the painting forward we forgo receiving the cash today and any interest earned over the year. Correspondingly, if we sell the painting forward we want to ensure that we will receive a cash amount, which is, at least, equivalent to the cash price plus interest—giving us the same price as suggested by the "buy" example.

The forward price can be "synthetically replicated" using physical transactions. A forward purchase can be replicated by buying today and financing the purchase over the forward term by borrowing. While economically, the price achieved by the replication is equivalent to a forward which usually makes the derivative more attractive. First, the transaction costs of the physical replication are often greater due to the number of extra "legs" and also physical transactions often have higher execution costs than derivatives. Secondly, forward transactions are a future commitment and are "off-balance" sheet. The transactions in the physical replication are included in the balance sheet which has the effect of increasing assets and liabilities and possibly increasing capital costs.

3.3 Cashflow timing and the cost of carry

A cash and forward purchase provide ownership of the asset at different times. However, providing the only benefit offered by these assets is their income stream, and the repayment of principal in debt instruments, then this benefit of ownership now or in the future is only notional.[2] As we have seen the forward price incorporates both the net interest cost of holding the asset

---

2. This is an important condition of forward pricing. If there are other tangible or intangible benefits of owning an asset such as the appreciation of artwork, or the ability to use it for consumption, then, unless these factors can be quantified, the forward price is unknown.

as well as the asset return. As a result the difference between cash and forward transactions is only a difference of cashflow profiles:

1. *Cash purchase cashflow profile*: Requires cash today, however, it will provide income between today and the forward date.

2. *Cash sale cashflow profile*: Receives cash today but will miss out on any income between today and the forward date.

3. *Forward purchase cashflow profile*: Does not require cash till the forward settlement date and as such misses out on any asset income.

4. *Forward sale cashflow profile*: Forgoes receiving cash till the forward settlement date, however it will provide income between today and the forward date.

These cashflow profiles are interesting and explain an important part of the use of forward transactions. Any of the four alternatives represent the exchange of cash and an asset. However, if opposite spot and forward transactions are combined (for example, a spot sale and a forward purchase) then two offsetting cashflows at different points in time are created. In effect, we are creating transactions, using an underlying financial asset, which have the cashflow profile of a borrowing or lending. This is a fundamental driving force in forward markets globally and is a key reason for transactions such as "repos" (see section 4) and FX swaps (see section 5).

Suppose you are a small merchant bank which owns $100 million of liquid government securities. Your organisation has a requirement for $100 million in short-term funding needs over the next three months. The traditional way to finance this would be to borrow in the short-term money market. This creates three problems: your ability to borrow is dependant on your credit standing, as is the cost of borrowing, and the transaction will increase gearing. If, however, you entered into an agreement to sell the securities today and then buy them back in three months, you have created the underlying borrowing required. Further, the ability to raise the funds, and the cost of those funds, is primarily determined by the government securities, not your own credit rating. This type of transaction is often described as "security lending", "sell and buy", "repurchase or reciprocal purchase agreement (repo)", or as a "liquidity swap"—we will refer to it as a "repurchase agreement". Both the money market and "sell and buy" transactions are summarised in *Exhibit 4.5*. The cashflows are identical, however, the balance sheet and gearing consequences are very different—with the money market doubling total assets and liabilities while the other security transaction has no effect on the totals, just the composition.

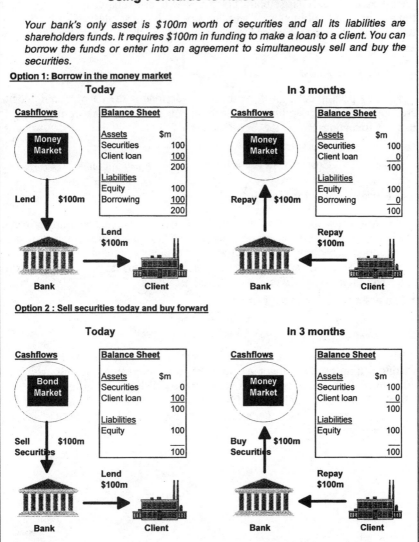

Exhibit 4.5

Using Forwards to Raise Finance

Your bank's only asset is $100m worth of securities and all its liabilities are shareholders funds. It requires $100m in funding to make a loan to a client. You can borrow the funds or enter into an agreement to simultaneously sell and buy the securities.

Whereas the cost of borrowing in the money market is given by its interest rate, in the security transaction it will be given by the difference between the spot and forward price. As we know the forward price of the securities is determined by the current cash price plus the net cost of financing those positions. Given the forward purchase can offer the government securities as collateral the implied interest cost should be lower than the direct money market borrowing.

From the point of view of large holders of financial assets repurchase agreements are a balance sheet efficient and, potentially, low-cost form of financing. For example, an investment bank which is a market maker in securities and holds large bond portfolios will use repurchase agreements to finance its bond holdings in a similar way to the example in *Exhibit 4.5*. We will discuss the intricacies of these agreements in the interest rate and foreign exchange forward chapters.

3.3.1 Cost of carry

The key pricing concept in forward transactions is the net financing cost of creating a synthetic replica using cash instruments. The usual terminology for this net financing cost is the "cost of carry".

$$\text{Forward Price} = \text{Cash Price} + \text{Cost of Carry}$$

$$\text{Cost of Carry} = \text{Interest Cost} - \text{Asset Income}$$

3.4 Forward pricing formulae

We now know the general relationship between cash and forward prices. In this section we will develop three simple formulae for pricing forward transactions depending on the nature of the income stream generated by the underlying financial asset during the period of time to the forward expiry date. The three forms of asset considered are:

- an asset which pays *no* income;
- an asset which pays *constant* income; and
- an asset which pays *"lumpy"* income.

The difference in these three income streams is summarised in *Exhibit 4.6*. Distinguishing by asset income allows us to develop three models which can price most financial assets. As a result, we find that we can apply the same "lumpy" pricing models to bonds and shares—even though, apart from the income streams, the underlying instruments have very different characteristics.

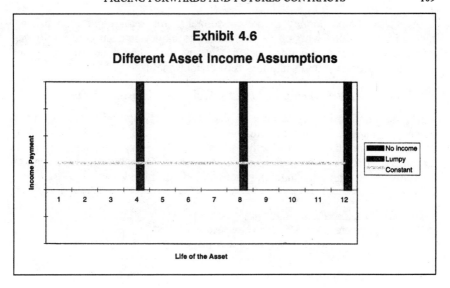

Exhibit 4.6

Different Asset Income Assumptions

3.4.1 Forward pricing on an asset which pays no income

If the asset pays no income between the day we calculate the forward price and the expiry of that forward contract, then the forward price is the cash price adjusted for the interest cost only. Examples of these types of financial assets includes precious metals, some commodities, and artwork.

It is worth noting that this formula also applies to financial assets which pay an uneven or "lumpy" income (see section 3.4.3 below), but will not pay any income between the pricing date and the forward expiry date.

Forward Price: Asset Pays No Income

Using simple interest the calculation is as follows

$$F = S \times (1 + r \times f / D)$$

Where

F   =   Forward price

S   =   Cash or spot price of the underlying instrument

r   =   Interest rate to forward date (preferably zero-coupon rate)

D   =   Day count basis (365 or 360)

f   =   Number of days to the forward expiry date

Examples of underlying assets: precious metals; artwork; and some commodities.

An important assumption in all of the forward formulae is that the interest rate, r, is a simple interest rate over the term to expiry of the forward. Formally this means the interest rate in the model is an effective zero-coupon rate. While zero-coupon rates will be discussed in detail in later chapters the important point about zero-coupon rates is that they pay no interest between today and the maturity date, and there is no risk associated with the re-investment of coupons.

In practice, most money market instruments are zero-coupon. So pricing forward transactions with up to six months to expiry is accurate. For longer terms, pricing using a coupon paying interest rate should be viewed as an estimate—accurate pricing requires zero-coupon yields.

3.4.2 Forward pricing on an asset which pays constant income

The assumption in this formula is that the underlying financial asset pays income at an even, constant rate over the life of the forward contract. In practice that means the asset will pay income for every day that it is held. Examples of this type of instrument include discount money market instruments, foreign exchange and broad-based equity indexes.

Forward Price : Asset Pays Constant Income

Using simple interest, the calculation is as follows

$$F = S \times (1 + (r-q) \times f / D)$$

Where

F = Forward price

S = Cash or spot price of the underlying instrument

r = Interest rate to the forward expiry date

D = Day count basis (365 or 360)

f = Number of days to the forward expiry date

q = Asset income expressed as a % per annum

Examples of underlying assets: money market instruments; foreign exchange; and broad-based equity indexes.

3.4.3 Forward pricing on an asset which pays "lumpy" income

In this formula it is assumed that the underlying financial asset pays income only at certain points over its life. Typically, the asset income is accrued over a period and then paid at the end of the period—this gives a "lumpy" appearance to the income cashflows. From the point of view of forward pricing the important consideration is how many income payments will occur during the life forward term.

Some examples of this type of instrument include bonds and shares.

Forward Price: Asset Pays "Lumpy" Income

Using simple interest and one income payment, the calculation is as follows

$$F = S \times (1 + r_1 \times f_1 / D) - c \times (1 + r_2 \times f_2 / D)$$

Where

F	=	Forward price
S	=	Cash or spot price of the underlying instrument
r_1	=	Interest rate to the forward expiry date
r_2	=	Interest rate between the income payment and forward expiry dates
D	=	Day count basis (365 or 360)
f_1	=	Number of days to the forward expiry date
f_2	=	Number of days between the income payment and forward expiry dates
c	=	Asset income expressed in the same units as the cash price

Examples of underlying assets: bonds and shares.

Sample calculations are provided in *Exhibit 4.7*, where the forward price is calculated on a security under each of the three asset income assumptions.

Exhibit 4.7

Forward Price Example

You intend to buy a security 180 days forward. The current spot price is $90 and the six month interest rate is 6.7% pa (A/360). Calculate the forward price under the following three asset income scenarios:

- *no income;*

- *income paid at rate of 8% pa on a constant basis; and*

- *a lump sum of $4.50 will be paid in 91 days—assume the three month interest rate in three months is also 6.7% pa.*

i) No income

$S = \$90 \qquad r = .067 \qquad f = 180 \qquad D = 360$

$$
\begin{aligned}
F &= S \times (1 + r \times f / D) \\
&= 90 \times (1 + .067 \times 180 / 360) \\
&= 93.015
\end{aligned}
$$

ii) Income = 8% pa constant

$S = \$90 \qquad r = .067 \qquad f = 180 \qquad D = 360 \qquad q = .08$

$$
\begin{aligned}
F &= S \times (1 + (r - q) \times f / D) \\
&= 90 \times (1 + (.067 - .08) \times 180 / 360) \\
&= 89.415
\end{aligned}
$$

iii) Income = lump payment of $4.50

$S = \$90 \qquad r1 = .067 \qquad r2 = .067 \qquad f1 = 180 \qquad f2 = 89 \qquad D = 360 \qquad c = 4.50$

$$
\begin{aligned}
F &= S \times (1 + r1 \times f1 / D) - c \times (1 + r2 \times f2 / D) \\
&= 90 \times (1 + .067 \times 180 / 360) - 4.5 \times (1 + .067 \times 89 / 360) \\
&= 88.44046
\end{aligned}
$$

As the results demonstrate, the nature of the income payment has a considerable impact on the forward price. And as the cost of carry concept tells us, where the asset income exceeds the cost of financing the security (scenarios i and ii) the forward price is lower than the cash price.

3.5 Valuation of forward contracts

In the previous sections we have examined how to determine a forward price based on cash market information. Now that we can generate a forward price we can determine the present value of open forward contracts. We divide this calculation into two steps: determining the value on the forward expiry date; and then determining the present value.

3.5.1 Valuation on the forward expiry date—the forward value

In the financial mathematics of financial assets, value is given by the present value of all future coupon and principal cashflows. As a result, the present value generally represents a premium or discount to the face value of the asset. This is not the case with forward contracts—when a forward contract is initially executed its value is zero, as the forward price this value can change to be positive or negative.

A forward contract represents a commitment to purchase or sell a financial asset, they are not financial assets in their own right. Unlike a financial asset which has value arising from future cashflows, the value of a forward contract only arises from the benefit or loss arising from the obligation to buy or sell the underlying asset.

If we think of the cashflows of a forward contract on an interest bearing security, then as well as the future coupon and principal repayments there is the initial cashflow associated with the purchase or sale of the security on the forward settlement date. So, if a bond is purchased forward, the cashflows consist of a cash payment on the forward settlement date and then cash receipts in the form of coupons and principal repayments over the remaining life of the bond.

At the time a forward contract is executed the forward price and the value of all of the future cashflows created by the bond after the forward expiry date are equal. However, as interest rates change the relative values of the forward price and all of the future cashflows are different. This relationship for a forward purchase of a bond contract can be summarised as follows:

Forward Value = Forward Bond Value − Forward Contract Price

where forward bond value is the value of all of the cashflows created by the bond after the forward expiry date and the forward contract price is the price agreed under the forward contract. As the forward price is fixed, the contract value will change as the forward bond value changes: if the yield to maturity on the bond falls (increasing the forward bond value) then the forward contract value will rise above zero and if bond yields rise the forward contract value will fall below zero.

Over the life of the contract the forward contract price is fixed. The forward bond value is simply calculated by determining the current forward price using the appropriate formula from Section 3.4 above. So, if the forward contract price was $110 and the current forward price is $120, the value of a forward purchase on the forward expiry date would be positive $10.

This relationship holds for all forward contracts. The value as at the forward expiry date is the difference between the forward contract price and the current forward price. This relationship also explains the risk profile, or potential for profit or loss, of forward contract. This relationship is described as the "pay-off" of the forward contract and the graphical representation as a "pay-off diagram". We will utilise this concept regularly in our investigation of derivative value.

Exhibit 4.8 provides an example of a full forward pricing and valuation exercise. It also illustrates the sensitivity of the contract value to changes in the current forward price using a pay-off graph.

3.5.2 *Forward contract valuation today—present value*

A common mistake in using forward contracts is forgetting that the forward valuation occurs on the forward expiry date. As we know from the time value of money, cash today is worth more than in the future. The implication is that, depending on the time period involved, the forward valuation overstates the true present value. We need to be very careful when dealing with forward contracts to ensure we know whether we are calculating forward or present values. This is an important consideration when comparing futures and forwards and is discussed in Section 3.6 below.

Calculating the present value of a forward contract can be performed using one of the present value formulae from Chapter 3. If we can apply a simple interest rate, then the present value of the forward contract value is:

$$\text{Present Value} = \text{Forward value} \, / \, (1 + r \times f \, / \, D)$$

where r is a simple interest zero-coupon rate between today and the forward expiry date. As already noted, if the interest rate that is being used is a money market interest rate it already is zero-coupon interest rate and can be entered directly into this calculation.

The distinction between forward and present values is demonstrated in *Exhibit 4.8*.

Exhibit 4.8

Forward Price and Valuation

You have entered into the forward contract discussed in Exhibit 4.7 where the asset pays no income at a price of $93.015. You decide to calculate the value of this contract after 30 days have passed. In that time interest rates have risen to 8% pa and the cash price of the security has declined to $84.2. Calculate the current forward price, the forward valuation and then the present value of this contract.

Current forward price

S = $84.2   r = .08   f = 150   D = 360

F	=	S × (1 + r × f / D)
	=	84.2 × (1 + .08 × 150 / 360)
	=	<u>87.0067</u>

Value at forward expiry date

Forward value	=	Current forward price − forward contract price
	=	87.0067 − 93.0150
	=	<u>−6.0083</u>

Present value of forward contract

Present value	=	forward value / (1 + r × f / D)
	=	−6.0083 / (1 + .08 × 150 / 360)
	=	<u>−5.81448</u>

Profit and loss risk profile of the forward contract — the pay-off diagram

Forward Purchase - Payoff Diagram

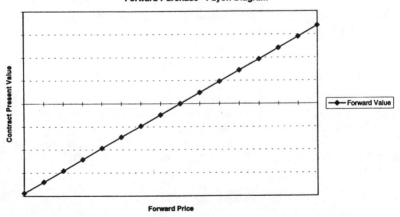

3.6 Valuation differences between forwards and futures

Futures contracts are a standardised form of forward contracts: a futures contract represents a commitment to buy or sell a fixed amount of the underlying financial asset, at a single date in the future. An OTC and futures contract with the same forward expiry date should have the same forward price.

While the pricing and valuation methodologies for the forwards and futures are similar, there are some key differences that need to be considered. In the following two chapters we will deal with specific differences between comparable OTC and exchange traded contracts.

The differences arise from the fact that futures contracts are subject to daily mark-to-markets and upfront initial margins (or performance bonds). These margining requirements have been created to minimise the risk that the clearing house of futures exchanges take to position takers. The effect of these margins, however, is to alter the valuation of futures versus forwards as they cause cashflows prior to the forward expiry date. In terms of the forward valuation/present valuation distinction in Section 3.5, a futures contract generates present values rather than forward values.

3.6.1 The impact of daily mark-to-markets on valuation

While equivalent forward and futures contracts will have the same value at the forward expiry date, it is often not realised that prior to the expiry date they have different present values. It is still common practice in many organisations to directly compare the valuations of forward and futures contracts without recognising that there is a difference in timing.

The valuation effect of daily mark-to-markets is to create a cashflow timing difference: in essence the forward values are being paid early. On any given day, the present value of a futures contract (represented by the mark-to-market gain or loss) is the same as the forward value on an equivalent forward contract.

For example, suppose we buy identical futures and forward contracts for expiry in one year. Today the difference between the current forward price and contract price at which we bought both contracts gives a value equivalent to $100 profit. The present value of these two instruments will reflect the relative timing of the values. If the one year rate is 10%, then the present values are:

$$\text{Futures Profit} \quad = \quad \$100$$
$$\text{Forward Profit} \quad = \quad \$100 \,/\, (1 + 10\%)$$
$$= \quad \$90.91$$

The difference in these values is important, as the futures contract in fact demonstrates greater sensitivity to movements in the forward price. In this example we can say that for every $1 movement in the forward value, the futures contract will generate a present value change of $1, while the present value of the forward contract will only change by 0.9091.

3.6.2 The impact of initial margins on valuation

Initial margins are a security deposit that must be paid by both buyers and sellers of futures contracts to the clearing house. These initial margins are held to cover any losses incurred by a defaulting position holder. In general the initial margins are set to cover the losses generated by a very large movement in the futures price over a 24 hour period. As a result the more volatile the futures price, the higher the level of initial margins.[3]

The impact of initial margins on valuation is not as straightforward to quantify as the daily mark-to-market because it depends on the level of initial margins and the rules of the futures exchange clearing house with respect to the types of collateral (for example, cash, government securities, precious metals, shares) allowed and the interest payment policy. These costs can be divided into two categories: interest cost and capital cost.

3.6.2.1 Interest cost

If the clearing house only accepts cash then the cost of initial margins is equivalent to the interest spread between the cost of funding the initial margin deposits and the interest paid on that deposit by the clearing house:

Interest Cost = Initial Margin × (Funding Cost − Clearing House Rate)

Suppose you enter a futures contract with a face value of $100 million and an initial margin requirement of $3 million. Your company borrows at the overnight money market rate while the clearing house pays the overnight rate minus 0.50% pa on your initial margin deposit. The additional funding cost of these initial margins is equivalent to 0.75% pa or $15,000 annually. In terms of the total contract value this has increased the cost of financing the position by 0.015% pa or 1.5 basis points.

To incorporate the interest cost into the forward pricing formula we need to increase the cost of carry to reflect the additional financing cost of the initial margin. In this example we would add 1.5 basis points to the interest rate, which will have very little effect on the forward price, as is shown in the calculation below where the forward price from *Exhibit 4.8* is recalculated using an interest rate of 8.015% pa:

$$F = S \times (1 + r \times f / D)$$
$$= 84.2 \times (1 + .08015 \times 150 / 360)$$
$$= 87.0119$$

This represents a change in the forward price of 0.0052—a very small impact. Often the interest cost is ignored by market participants because it is viewed as relatively unimportant.

If the clearing house accepts the lodgment of other forms of collateral such as bonds, shares and money market instruments without imposing any charges—a common practice in most large exchanges—then the interest cost will be the difference between the return on the asset and your organisation's cost of funds.

It is quite common for financial institutions to consider that providing securities as initial margin collateral incurs no cost. This is because they

---

3. For more detail on how initial margins are derived, see the Appendix to Chapter 7 in Martin, op cit n 1.

already hold the assets used for collateral for regulatory or investment reasons—they are simply re-using assets already held.

3.6.2.2 Capital cost

Whether initial margin collateral is in the form of cash or some form of security, there is a capital cost. By providing this collateral to the clearing house, the position taker is potentially transferring ownership of the assets and there is the possibility that those assets will not be repaid—initial margins represent a credit risk to the clearing house and some capital has to be set aside for that possibility.

The capital cost will depend on the capital allocation policies of the organisation involved. However, for a bank the Bank for International Settlements (BIS) Capital Adequacy Standards would view the initial margins deposited with the clearing house as a deposit with a corporation—requiring an allocation of capital equivalent to 8% of the deposit. Given the assumed cost of capital of an organisation then we can calculate the capital cost as follows:

$$\text{Capital Cost} = \text{Initial Margin} \times 8\% \times \text{Cost of Capital}$$

So, on the example above, if the cost of capital is assumed to be 20% pa then the annual capital cost is as follows:

$$\begin{aligned} \text{Capital Cost} \;&=\; \$3{,}000{,}000 \times 8\% \times 20\% \\ &=\; \$48{,}000 \text{ pa} \end{aligned}$$

In the same manner as the interest cost, the capital cost is considered an additional cost in financing the futures position and increases the cost of carry. Once again the capital cost is often viewed as too small to worry about and is ignored by some market participants.

4. INTEREST RATE FORWARDS AND FUTURES

4.1 Introduction

As we saw in the previous section, interest rate forwards and futures represent the largest single category of volume in financial derivatives. This is a recognition of the importance of these instruments as a day-to-day hedging and trading tool for all participants of the financial market place. While the volume of OTC forward contracts in some currencies is substantial (for example, US$ Treasury Bonds), *Exhibit 4.9* shows that the global volume of interest rate futures is considerably higher than forwards. This is a reflection of the fact that short-term and long-term interest rate futures are the primary forward interest rate instruments in most currencies, whereas OTC forwards tend to be for more specialised use.

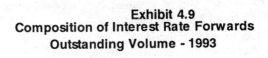

Exhibit 4.9
Composition of Interest Rate Forwards
Outstanding Volume - 1993

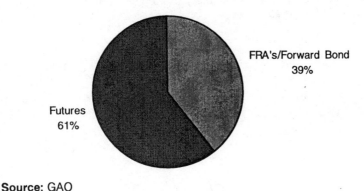

FRA's/Forward Bond
39%

Futures
61%

Source: GAO

In this chapter we will develop pricing and valuation models for forward and futures contracts on interest bearing financial assets.[4] These models will be divided into categories reflecting the different characteristics of forwards on short-term and long-term debt securities. The categories used are as follows:

- forward rate agreements (section 4.2);
- short-term interest rate futures (section 4.3);
- bond forwards (section 4.4); and
- long-term interest rate futures (section 4.5).

For each model our starting point is the generalised model developed in Section 3. These models will then be adapted to the specific cashflow and convention characteristics of each instrument.

4.2 Forward rate agreements

4.2.1 General description

Forward rate agreements (FRAs) are the predominant form of OTC forward on short-term interest rate securities. They represent an agreement between two parties who wish to "fix" the interest rate on an underlying short-term security at a future date. FRAs do not have physical delivery, instead, any profits and losses are realised by way of a cash settlement at the end of the forward period. While the underlying instrument in an FRA is usually a short-term instrument with a term of three or six months, the forward period can range from one month to several years. An FRA is agreed

4.   Another description of the underlying assets is "debt securities".

in terms of a forward interest rate as opposed to a forward price and the pricing formulae need to be adjusted to reflect this.

The liquidity of FRAs in most countries is very high, with most financial institutions providing market making services. Reflecting the level of activity, standard documentation and dealing terms and conditions have been developed in most countries.[5] A summary of the general terms and conditions is provided in *Exhibit 4.10*.

---

5.   Examples of this documentation and terms and conditions can be obtained from most bankers' associations or the local branch of ISDA in the relevant country. Otherwise, see S Das, Swaps and Financial Derivatives (2nd ed, IFR, 1994), pp 89-96.

Exhibit 4.10

General FRA Terms and Conditions

Item	Description
Broken period	A settlement period which differs in length from that used in fixing the interest settlement rate.
Buyer/borrower	The party wishing to protect against a rise in interest rates.
Cash settlement	There is no delivery under an FRA, instead any profits or losses are realised as a cash settlement on the settlement date.
Contract amount	The notional sum on which the FRA is based (that is, the principal).
Contract/trade date	The date the FRA is entered into.
Contract rate	The rate of interest agreed between the parties on the contract date (that is, the forward rate).
Maturity date	The date that the settlement period ends (that is, the maturity date of the security which notionally underlies the FRA).
Run	The period or term of the notional underlying security, usually three or six months.
Seller/lender	The party wishing to protect against a fall in interest rates.
Settlement date	The expiry of the forward period, the start of the notional underlying security and the day the settlement sum is paid.
Settlement period	The term of the notional underlying security represented by the number of days between the settlement date and the maturity date.
Settlement rate	The mean rate quoted by the specified reference banks for the settlement period of the notional underlying security. In US$ based FRAs this is commonly given by the Reuters page "LIBO".
Settlement sum	The amount representing the difference between interest calculated at the contract rate and the settlement rate.

Source: BBA and AFMA

Under an FRA the two parties agree the interest rate (the "forward rate") applying to a notional principal amount of an underlying money market security at a forward settlement date. Depending on how the relevant interest rate moves between the trade date and the forward settlement date, one of the parties will owe the other party a net settlement amount equivalent to the difference between the forward rate and the actual rate for the forward settlement date. The party which benefits from a fall in interest rates is defined as the "lender" or "seller". The other party which benefits from a rise in interest rates is the "borrower" or "buyer".

FRAs are normally quoted in terms of monthly combinations of the time to the forward settlement date and the time to maturity of the notional underlying security. For example, an FRA with one month to forward settlement on a three month security is referred to as a "1 × 4". On quote vendor services such as Reuters, FRA dealers generally provide indications of FRA rates in terms of the standard combinations set out below:

Tenor	Rate	Description of Forward
1 × 4	7.35	A three month security starting in one month
3 × 6	7.25	A three month security starting in three months
6 × 9	7.23	A three month security starting in six months
3 × 9	7.24	A six month security starting in three months
6 × 12	7.20	A six month security starting in six months

An example of an FRA transaction starting in three months on a three month security is summarised in *Exhibit 4.11*.

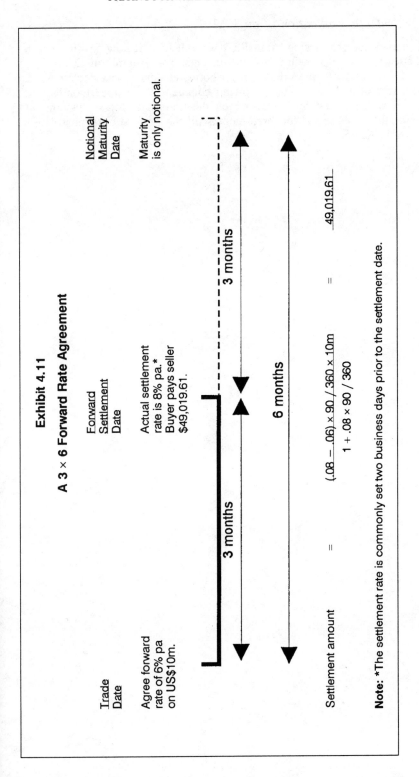

Exhibit 4.11
A 3 × 6 Forward Rate Agreement

4.2.2. Synthetic replication of an FRA

To understand the pricing of an FRA we will look at how an FRA can be synthetically replicated using cash instruments. The example in *Exhibit 4.11* is from the point of view of the buyer/borrower, and it is agreeing on the interest rate of a three month borrowing commencing in three months time. This can be replicated by borrowing on the trade date for six months and investing the funds raised for three months till the forward settlement date as is shown in *Exhibit 4.12*.

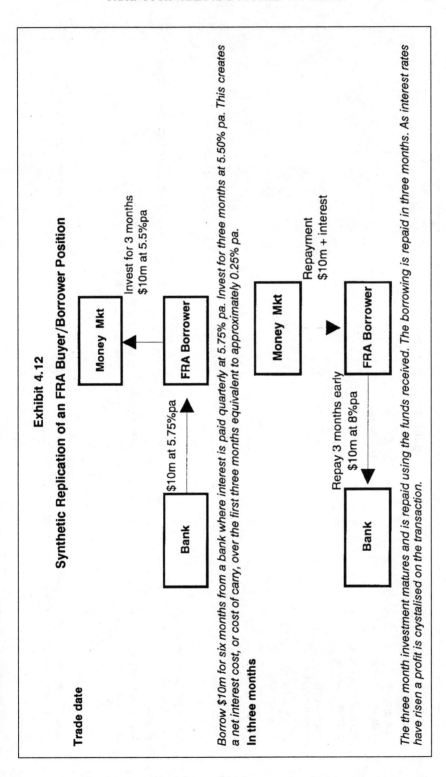

Exhibit 4.12

Synthetic Replication of an FRA Buyer/Borrower Position

Trade date

Invest for 3 months
$10m at 5.5%pa

Money Mkt

FRA Borrower

$10m at 5.75%pa

Bank

Borrow $10m for six months from a bank where interest is paid quarterly at 5.75% pa. Invest for three months at 5.50% pa. This creates a net interest cost, or cost of carry, over the first three months equivalent to approximately 0.25% pa.

In three months

Repayment
$10m + interest

Money Mkt

FRA Borrower

Repay 3 months early
$10m at 8%pa

Bank

The three month investment matures and is repaid using the funds received. The borrowing is repaid in three months. As interest rates have risen a profit is crystalised on the transaction.

Exhibit 4.12—*continued*

Forward rate calculations

Investment
at three months
= 10m × (0.055 × 90 / 360)
= 137,500.00

Borrowing interest
at three months
= (1 + 0.0575 × 90 / 360)
= 143,750.00

Net cost at
three months
= 6,250.00

Principal left at
three months
= 9,993,750.00

Borrowing at
six months
= 10,143,750.00

Forward rate
= (10,143,750 / 9,993,750 − 1) × 360 / 90
= 6.00%

Settlement sum calculation

In the synthetic replication the settlement sum will be equivalent to the net cashflows after the borrowing has been repaid early at three months.

Settlement amount
at three months
= Principal left at three months minus the present value of the remaining interest on the borrowing (at 8% pa)
= 9,993,750 − 10,143,750 / (1 + .08 × 90 / 360)
= 48,897.06 *

Note: * There is a small rounding difference of $122.55 between this calculation and Exhibit 4.11. This arises because the forward interest rate in this example is actually 6.00375% pa.

As with any forward transaction, a cost of carry will be created depending on the difference between the three and six month interest rates. The forward interest rate will be given by the six month interest rate adjusted for the cost of carry. So, if the six month interest rate is 5.75% pa[6] and the three month rate is 5.5% pa then the cost of carry is 0.25% pa. The forward interest rate is consequently 6.00% pa. At the end of three months there has been a net interest cost of $6,250 which effectively means the principal amount of the original borrowing remaining is $9,993,750.

To replicate the cash settlement of the FRA on the forward settlement date, the borrowing is repaid three months early using the principal amount available at three months. The cost of repaying this borrowing is the present value of the principal or interest accrued at the end of the borrowing. The net cashflow arising from repaying the borrowing is $48,897.06, or approximately the same as the same strategy using an FRA in *Exhibit 4.11.*

Using the terminology developed in Sections 2 and 3:

1. The forward rate in this example is the forward price and is derived using the now familiar cost of carry concept.

2. The settlement sum or amount is the same as the forward value.

3. The present value of an FRA is given by taking the present value of the settlement sum.

4.2.3 A model for FRA forward interest rates

FRAs and interest rate futures introduce a number of new characteristics for the general model developed in Section 3:

- an underlying instrument with a limited life, where
- the calculation is expressed in terms of interest rate not price.

In this section we will convert the generalised price formulae from Section 3 into a formula that generates a forward interest rate on a security which accrues interest for a limited period.

An FRA is an instrument in which the underlying asset is cash provides a constant income in the form of interest payments. We know that the underlying asset is a security which pays interest on a principal amount, S, from today until its maturity date. This future value of the cashflows on this security can be expressed as:

$$FV = S \times (1 + q \times d / D)$$

where the asset income, q, is the yield to maturity on the asset expressed as a per cent per annum and d is the number of days from today until maturity of the asset.

Using the forward pricing model with constant income in Section 3.4.2 we know this can be expressed as:

$$F = S \times (1 + (r-q) \times f / D)$$

where r, the financing cost, is the interest rate over the forward period. The cash price, S, is the principal value of the security and the forward price is

---

6.   To avoid compounding differences this rate, while fixed for a term of six months, is
     compounded quarterly.

this amount adjusted for the cost of carry. Our aim is to express this same concept in terms of a forward interest rate calculation. Essentially we need to incorporate the cost of carry over the forward period into the interest calculation from the forward settlement date to the maturity date of the underlying security.

In simplistic terms, the interest on the forward security will be equivalent to the difference between the interest earned between today and the forward settlement date and between today and the maturity date of the underlying security. Given that we know the values of q and r, then the amount of interest earned by the forward security can be expressed as:

$$\text{Forward Interest} = S \times (q \times d / D - r \times f / D)$$

The forward interest rate can then be expressed as:

$$\text{Forward Rate} = \frac{\text{Forward Interest}}{\text{Forward Price}} \times \frac{D}{(d-f)}$$

If we insert the formulae above then we have:

$$\text{Forward Rate} = \frac{S \times (q \times d / D - r \times f / D)}{S \times (1 + (r-q) \times f / D)} \times \frac{D}{(d-f)}$$

which simplifies to:

$$\text{Forward Rate } (r_f) = \frac{(q \times d / D - r \times f / D)}{(1 + (r-q) \times f / D)} \times \frac{D}{(d-f)}$$

This formula approximates the calculation performed in *Exhibit 4.12*. However, it ignores the timing of cashflows and the compounding of interest. In most forward interest rate calculations interest rates r and q have different compounding frequencies, which means they cannot be directly compared.

A common method of avoiding the compounding problems is to convert the interest rates into continuously compound rates. This avoids any compounding differences and simplifies the forward rate calculation. We know that the future value of using a continuous rate is as follows:

$$FV = S \times \exp (q \times d / D)$$

Further, we know that the future value of an amount invested for the full term d and an amount invested for the combined term of f and (d−f) must be the same. Using the future value formula we can express this as follows:

$$S \times \exp (q \times d / D) = S \times \exp (r \times f / D + r_f \times (d-f) / D)$$

If we cancel S and take the natural logarithm of both sides of this equation, this simplifies to:

Forward Interest Rate: Continuous Compounding

$$r_f = \frac{q \times d/D - r \times f/D}{d/D - f/D}$$

Where

r_f	=	Forward interest rate % pa
r	=	Interest rate to the forward settlement date % pa
q	=	Interest rate to the maturity date % pa
D	=	Day count basis (365 or 360)
f	=	Number of days to the forward expiry date
d	=	Number of days to the maturity date of the underlying instrument

Examples of underlying assets: FRAs and short-term interest rate futures

Market interest rates are rarely quoted in continuously compounded form, to use this model we need to convert to and from continuously compounded rates. *Exhibit 4.13* provides an example of a spreadsheet which calculates forward interest rates using the continuous compounding method.

Exhibit 4.13

Forward Rate Agreement Calculator

Spreadsheet example

Field	Cell	Cell: Formula
Inputs		
Trade date	01-Nov-95	$E$8 :
Forward settlement date	30-Jan-96	$E$9 :
Underlying maturity date	29-Apr-96	$E$10 :
Spot rate to forward settlement date %	5.5000	$E$11 :
Frequency (1, 2 or 4)	4	$E$12 :
Interest rate for maturity %	5.8050	$E$13 :
Frequency (1, 2 or 4)	2	$E$14 :
Outputs		
Term to forward settlement in days — f	90	$N$16 : +E9-E8
Term to maturity in days — d	90	$N$17 : +E10-E8
Continuous rate to settlement date % — r	5.4625	$N$18 : =LN(E6/(E7*100)+1)*E7*100
Continuous rate to maturity % — q	5.7224	$N$19 : =LN(E8/(E9*100)+1)*E9*100
Forward rate % —continuous compounding	5.9822	$N$20 : =(E11*(E5-E3)-E10*(E4-E3))/(E5-E4)
—quarterly compounding	6.0271	$N$21 : =4*(EXP(E12/(4*100))-1)*100
—semi-annual compounding	6.0725	$N$22 : =2*(EXP(E12/(2*100))-1)*100
—annual compounding	6.1647	$N$23 : =(EXP(E12/100)-1)*100

The approach in this model is to take the interest rates based on market rates and adjust them to continuous rates to calculate the forward rate. Once the continuously compounded rate has been calculated this can be re-converted to any compounding basis required.

4.2.4 A model for FRA valuation

The value of an FRA on the forward settlement date is the difference between the agreed contract rate in the FRA and the prevailing reference interest rate for the remaining term to maturity of the underlying security (the "settlement rate").

There are two general methods of calculating the forward amount, depending on the conventions in the money market. In most markets where money market securities are traded in terms of face value or discounted using the discount method, such as in the United States and United Kingdom, the settlement formula is as follows:

FRA Settlement Calculation: Full Face Value

If $r_s > r_c$ then the settlement sum is

$$\text{seller pays buyer} = \frac{(r_s - r_c) \times d / D \times S}{1 + r_c \times d / D}$$

If $r_s < r_c$ then the settlement sum is

$$\text{buyer pays seller} = \frac{(r_c - r_s) \times d / D \times S}{1 + r_c \times d / D}$$

Where

r_c = Contract rate % pa

r_s = Settlement rate % pa

d = Settlement period (days till maturity of underlying security)

D = Day count basis (365 or 360)

S = The contract amount

FRA markets commonly using this method: US$ and most European currencies

---

This calculation is derived so that all obligations of the FRA can be terminated on the forward settlement date rather than the maturity date of the notional underlying security. That explains why the difference between the contract and settlement interest amounts is calculated at the maturity of the notional underlying security and then present values this difference to the forward settlement date.

In markets where money market securities are traded at a discount to face value using the yield method, such as in Australia and New Zealand, the forward value is based on a discounted proceeds calculation as follows:

FRA Settlement Calculation: Discounted Face Value

If $r_s > r_c$ then the settlement sum is

$$\text{seller pays buyer} = \frac{S}{1 + r_c \times d / D} - \frac{S}{1 + r_s \times d / D}$$

If $r_s < r_c$ then the settlement sum is

$$\text{buyer pays seller} = \frac{S}{1 + r_c \times d / D} - \frac{S}{1 + r_s \times d / D}$$

Where

r_c	=	Contract rate % pa
r_s	=	Settlement rate % pa
d	=	Settlement period (days till maturity of underlying security)
D	=	Day count basis (365 or 360)
S	=	The contract amount

FRA markets commonly using this method: A$ and NZ$

4.2.4.1 Forward value

Prior to the forward settlement date, the forward value is given by the relevant settlement calculation above. However, instead of the settlement rate, r_s, the prevailing forward rate, r_f, is used. As we noted in Section 3, at initial execution the forward value of an FRA will be zero as the contract rate and the prevailing forward rate are the same. As time passes and the forward rate changes so will the forward value of the FRA. To illustrate this point, *Exhibit 4.14* extends the previous example and examines the change in value of the FRA contract over the forward period using both settlement calculations.

Exhibit 4.14

Forward and Present Value of an FRA

You have entered into the FRA from Exhibit 4.11 as the buyer/borrower. Two months have passed. Calculate the forward rate, the forward value and the present value using the market date provided. Calculate values using both the full face value and discounted face value settlement methods.

Forward Period Remaining

3 months → Enter into 3 × 6 buyer/borrower FRA at 6% pa

1 month	Market data	1 month rate	=	6.00%
		4 month rate	=	6.50%

Forward rate calculation

f = 30

d = 120

r = 5.99% pa (continuous compounded rate)

q = 6.43% pa (continuous compounded rate)

rf = $.0643 \times 120/360 - .0599 \times 30/360$

$120/360 - 30/360$

= 6.58% pa (continuous compounded rate)

Then converted to a quarterly rate

rf = 6.63%

Exhibit 4.14—*continued*

Forward values

rc = 6.00%

dc = 90

Full face value $= \dfrac{(0.0663 - 0.06) \times 90/360 \times 10m}{1 + 0.663 \times 90/360}$

$= 15,493.20$

Discounted face value $= \dfrac{10m}{1 + .06 \times 90/360}$ $\dfrac{10m}{1 + .06 \times 90/360}$

$= 15,264.24$

Present values

Discount the forward values to today using the prevailing one month interest rate

Full face value $= \dfrac{15,493.20}{1 + .06 \times 30/360}$

$= 15,416.12$

Discounted face value $= \dfrac{15,262.24}{1 + .06 \times 30/360}$

$= 15,188.30$

4.2.4.2 Present value

The present value of an FRA is easily calculated once the forward value has been generated using the standard present value formulae. An example of this calculation is provided in *Exhibit 4.14*. The present value should be calculated using a zero-coupon interest rate.

4.2.5 FRA risk characteristics

A forward rate agreement is the right to purchase or sell a short-term money market instrument at some date in the future. Correspondingly, the sensitivity to movements in interest rates of an FRA is very similar to the money market instruments.

In the case of an FRA the duration and convexity is equivalent to the underlying instrument. The point value of a basis point (PVBP), however, is less than that of the underlying instrument. An FRA generates gains and losses on the forward settlement date equivalent to the underlying security, however, these amounts are present valued in the PVBP and so are consequently smaller.

An example of the PVBP is provided later in the chapter in *Exhibit 4.18*, where an FRA PVBP is calculated and compared to short-term interest rate futures contracts.

4.3 Short-term interest rate futures

4.3.1 General description

Short-term interest rate futures represent standardised, exchange traded forward contracts on money market instruments. In general, most major currencies have one futures contract on a tradeable short-term money market instrument such as a bank deposit or bank bill. The pricing and valuation of these instruments is very similar to FRAs and the two markets can often be viewed as direct substitutes. The global volume in these instruments is enormous, representing the largest single category of futures contract. A list of the major short-term interest rate futures contracts are listed in *Exhibit 4.15* along with total volume for 1994.

Exhibit 4.15

List of Short-term Interest Rate Contracts and Volumes

Contract	Currency	Exchange(s)	1994 Futures Volumes	
			No of contracts	Face Value (Bn)
Bank accepted bills*	A$	SFE	9,369,008	6,933
3 month Euro-Swiss franc	CHF	LIFFE	1,698,736	1,493
FIBOR futures	DEM	DTB	428,516	305
3 month Euro-deutschmark	DEM	LIFFE	29,312,222	62,575
3 month ECU interest rate	ECU	LIFFE	622,457	814
PIBOR 3 month	FFR	MATIF	13,176,354	2,717
3 month Sterling interest rate	GBP	LIFFE	16,603,152	25,821
3 month Euro-yen	JPY	TIFFE	37,425,846	367
3 month Euro-yen	JPY	SIMEX	6,820,673	67
3 month Euro-lira	ITL	LIFFE	3,456,437	2
Bank accepted bills	NZ$	NZFOE	608,460	393,963
MIBOR 90	ESP	MEFF	3,730,008	155
3 month Eurodollar	US$	CME	104,823,245	524,116
3 month Eurodollar (fungible with CME)	US$	SIMEX	8,687,969	4,344
3 month Eurodollar	US$	LIFFE	91,738	9,174
1 month Eurodollar	US$	CME	1,911,184	191,118
90 day T-bills	US$	CME	1,020,491	510
		Total	239,786,496	1,224,476

Note: *SFE contract upsized from 500,000 to 1,000,000 in April 1995

The benchmark contract for short-term contracts is the Eurodollar contract traded on the Chicago Mercantile Exchange (CME). As the table in *Exhibit 4.15* shows the Eurodollar contract is the most heavily traded reflecting its status as the primary hedging vehicle for short to medium term exposures. It is also traded on the London International Financial Futures and Options Exchange (LIFFE) and the Singapore International Money Exchange (SIMEX). The SIMEX contract is "fungible" with the CME contract, which means contracts traded on the two exchanges can be offset.

The Eurodollar contract was the first of the short-term futures contracts when it was listed in 1981. Most other short-term interest rate futures contracts have been a copy of the Eurodollar contract with only the currency, settlement interest rate and face value changed. The A$ and NZ$ bank bill contracts traded on the Sydney Futures Exchange (SFE) and the New Zealand Futures and Options Exchange (NZFOE) respectively, are the only contracts which have different valuation formulae.

In order to familiarise ourselves with short-term interest rate contracts we will firstly review the features of the Eurodollar contract and then examine the differences with other contracts.

4.3.1.1 Eurodollars

The Eurodollar is a cash settled contract on a three month Eurodollar time deposit. The name "Eurodollar" derives from the fact that it is a forward contract on a US dollar money market instrument traded in Europe (or London to be more specific). The importance of the contract reflects the importance of the US$ in global financing and the willingness of US-based market participants to use futures.

The CME lists contracts to expire in quarterly rests in March, June, September and December. Currently, there are 40 consecutive quarters listed, that is, expiries out to 10 years. The Eurodollar has obvious appeal to corporations, banks and fund managers with short-term interest rate exposures. However, a substantial driving force behind Eurodollar volumes is from organisations with medium-term exposures such as interest rate swap market makers.

The contract expires on the third Monday of the delivery month and is cash settled against a three-month London Interbank Offered Rate (LIBOR) in a similar fashion to a US$ FRA. If the current month is not a quarterly delivery month then a single "spot" contract is also listed to ensure traders have a very short-term instrument. For example, after the March contract expires an April contract is listed. This "spot" contract concept is currently only offered on the Eurodollar.

The price of a contract is expressed as:

$$\text{Futures Price} = 100 - \text{Interest Rate} \times 100$$

So, if the current interest rate for a Eurodollar deposit starting on the futures expiry date is 5.00% pa, then the futures price is 95.00. The aim of quoting in terms of price rather than yield is primarily to keep interest rate contracts in line with other price-based contracts on bonds, shares and commodities.

A buyer of a Eurodollar contract gains if the futures price rises (interest rate falls) above the price at which they purchase and the seller gains if the price falls (interest rate rises). Be careful when comparing futures to FRAs as the terminology is opposite; a Eurodollar futures buyer is equivalent to an FRA seller/lender as they both benefit from a fall in interest rates.

While the detailed contract specifications of all short-term interest rate futures contracts are provided in the Appendix to this chapter the major features of the Eurodollar contract are summarised below:

Summary of Eurodollar Futures Specifications	
Feature	**Description**
Underlying	90 day Eurodollar time deposit
Face Value	US$1,000,000
Delivery Months	March, June, September, December and spot month
Delivery Method	Cash settled
Settlement Rate	LIBOR rate for three month Eurodollar deposits on the last trading day
Last Trading Day	Third Wednesday of the delivery month
Quotation Method	100 minus the rate of interest
Valuation Formula	Term deposit
Tick Size	The value of each price point is $25
Margining	Initial margin (currently $500/contract) and daily mark-to-market

The details of most of the other short-term interest rate contracts are similar except for differing face values as is summarised below:

Contract	Exchange	Face Value
90 Day T-Bills	CME	1,000,000
Bank Accepted Bills	SFE	1,000,000
3 Month Euro-Swiss Franc	LIFFE	1,000,000
FIBOR Futures	DTB	1,000,000
3 Month Euro-deutschmark	LIFFE	1,000,000
3 Month ECU Interest Rate	LIFFE	1,000,000
MIBOR 90	MEFF	10,000,000
PIBOR 3 Month	MATIF	5,000,000
3 Month Sterling Interest Rate	LIFFE	500,000
3 Month Euro-Yen	TIFFE	100,000,000
Bank Accepted Bills	NZFOE	500,000

For most contracts the underlying instrument is the same as the Eurodollar, that is, a three month deposit on a discount security where interest is calculated using the discount method. However, in the case of the SFE and NZFOE contracts the underlying instrument is a bank bill, which is a discount security valued using the yield formula.[7] This has an impact on valuation, as discussed in section 4.3.3.

4.3.2 A model for futures prices

The price of a futures contract is equal to 100 minus the forward interest rate. So, the futures pricing model will be based on the forward pricing models from section 3 and the FRA model from section 4.2.3.

The method of synthetically replicating a futures contract is exactly the same as an FRA (see section 4.2.2). However, as we have already noted, futures contracts have a different cashflow profile to similar forward contracts because of initial margins and the daily mark-to-market of gains and losses.[8] As a result of initial margins, futures may need to incorporate a small funding cost, while the impact of the mark-to-market is unknown, as it will depend on the level of interest rates over the life of the futures contract.

In summary, the short-term futures contract price is primarily determined by the prevailing forward rate using the formula in section 4.2.3 above. There is, however, an element of the interest rate which will not be known till expiry of the contract due to the unknown funding requirements during the life of the contract. This can be summarised as follows:

Futures Price = 100 − (Forward Rate + Funding Adjustment)

For contracts with a forward period of up to six months the differences between short-term interest rate futures and FRAs are very small, as well as unknown, and can often be ignored.[9] However, for longer term futures consideration should be given to incorporating the possible funding consequences of a futures contract. It has to be remembered that this is just an estimate; it is common for market users to estimate the "worst case" funding cost requirement and incorporate that into their estimate of the effective forward rate given by short-term interest rates.

---

7. A discount formula calculates interest based on the future face value and then deducts this from the face value of instrument. A yield formula is a present value of the future face value of the contract. For more on this distinction see Martin, op cit nl, Ch 3.
8. See section 3.6 for a more detailed discussion on this point.
9. In this case the spreadsheet model provided in Exhibit 4.13 is appropriate.

Exhibit 4.16

Synthetic Replication of a Sold Eurodollar Futures Position

In the following example the forward interest rate provided by a sold Eurodollars position is compared against the forward interest rate provided by a forward rate agreement. The Eurodollar contract expires in 1 year's time for a term of 90 days and it is sold today at a price of 92.74. Over the year interest rates fall and the futures price converges to a three month rate of 5% pa. The table summarises the resulting cashflows by quarter.

To simplify the analysis all interest rates are continuously compounded and converted to a 365 day basis. Also, the futures price is assumed to remain steady until the end of the quarter, at which time it falls to the price shown in the table.

Dates	
Trade date	24-Oct-96
Forward settle	24-Oct-97
Maturity date	22-Jan-98

Market Rates	
Overnight/3 month/1 year =	6.00%
1.25 year rate =	6.25%

Implied FRA Rate Calculations	
f	365
d	455
r	6.00%
q	6.25%

Forward rate =	7.2639%

Exhibit 4.16—continued

		Interest Rates			Synthetic Replication		Futures Replication				
	Qtr	Overnight rate and 3 mth rate	Futures Price	Current fwd rate	Borrow for 1.25 years @ 6.25%	Invest for 1 year	Mark-to-Market	Funding requirement	Interest on initial margins (o/n - 1% pa)	Quarterly interest	Total interest
Today	0	6.00%	92.74	7.26%	1,000,000.00	(1,000,000.00)		(500.00)			
	1	6.75%	92.30	7.70%			1,100.00	600.00	8.51	18.72001	
	2	7.50%	91.86	8.14%			1,100.00	1,718.72	9.46	41.99346	
	3	8.25%	91.42	8.58%			1,100.00	2,860.71	10.42	70.03446	
Forward	4	9.00%	91.00	9.00%		1,061,836.55	1,050.00	3,980.75	11.38	101.9596	
Maturity	5	9.00%			(1,081,026.40)			4,082.71	11.38	104.2797	336.9872

Effective Forward Rate from Futures Contract

Investment return after 1 year =	1,061,836.55
Initial borrowings after 1.25 years =	1,081,026.40
Extra funding cost of futures =	(336.99)
Total borrowings after 1.25 years =	1,080,689.41
Effective interest cost =	7.1374%
Difference between FRA and futures =	−0.1264%

Exhibit 4.16 gives an example of the impact that the funding requirements of a futures contract can have on the effective forward rate. In this case we examine the synthetic replication of a single sold Eurodollar contract. As with the FRA synthetic replication we borrow till the maturity date of the underlying (1.25 years) and invest for the forward period (1 year). The additional complication of the future contract is the upfront initial margin of $500 and the mark-to-markets based on the prevailing forward price. In the example the Eurodollar future is sold at a price of 92.74 with one year till expiry. It is assumed that the forward price rises over the life of the futures contract to settle at 95.00 (a three month interest rate of 5.00% pa). As well as the initial margin this generates substantial funding requirements for a sold position. The interest costs of funding these cashflows is incorporated into the effective futures forward rate calculation. Under this scenario, the effective interest rate by nearly 10 bp over the equivalent FRA forward rate.

The difference between the FRA and the effective forward rate in the futures contract is dependant on the actual path taken by interest rates over the forward period. The effective forward rate on the example above is calculated for a range of outcomes in *Exhibit 4.17*.

Exhibit 4.17

Effective Futures Rate Over a Range of Outcomes

Using the example from Exhibit 4.16, the effective forward rate given by the futures contract is calculated for a range of final three month interest rates.

3 Month Rate After 1 Year	Effective Futures Rate	FRA/Futures Difference
5%	7.3620%	0.0981%
6%	7.3273%	0.0634%
7%	7.2784%	0.0146%
8%	7.2152%	−0.0487%
9%	7.1374%	−0.1264%

It is important to note that these funding issues also face the buyer of a futures contract. However, in the case of the buyer a fall in rates generates positive cashflows and improves the effective forward interest rate.

It is important to realise that these funding problems effect both buyers and sellers of futures contracts. The effective forward rates achieved are the same but they have a different effect. For a seller, if interest rates fall the higher effective forward rate increases its cost of borrowing. However, for a buyer, if interest rates fall, the higher effective forward rate represents an improvement in their investment yield.

This difference in cashflows also gives rise to so-called "convexity adjustments" when hedging OTC products such as FRAs and swaps. This issue will be discussed in the following section on valuation.

4.3.3 Valuation of short-term interest rate futures contracts

As we saw above, the valuation of futures contracts can be a source of considerable confusion. It is important to remember that futures contracts have the peculiar property of constant PVBP—there is no distinction between present and future values. Whereas in cash financial assets and OTC derivatives there is a difference equivalent to the time value of money.

In this section we will consider the formulae for determining the contract value of futures contracts and then examine the impact of constant PVBP when using FRAs.

4.3.3.1 Contract values

All open futures contracts are subject to at least a daily mark-to-market, sometimes more.[10] Whenever a mark-to-market is made the valuation method is unchanged and is based on the same formula used to determine the final settlement value of the futures contract. In the case of a Eurodollars contract, the underlying security is the interest on a 90 day deposit—each point change in the futures price is equivalent to a 0.01% pa change in the interest rate in the underlying security. We can then express the value of this type of contract as:

$$\text{Contract Value}_{ED} = \text{Face Value} \times (100 - \text{Price}) \times d / D / 100$$

where price is the prevailing futures price. So if the futures price is 96.24 then the contract value of a Eurodollar contract is:

$$= \quad 1,000,000 \times (100 - 96.24) \times 90 / 360 / 100$$
$$= \quad 9,400.$$

On any given day the mark-to-market gain or loss will be equivalent to the difference in the contract value at the previous mark-to-market price and today's market price.

Most market participants recognise that the contract value formula always implies a constant PVBP, commonly known as the "tick value" in futures markets, equivalent to $25, regardless of the time to expiry of the futures contract. As we saw in section 3.5.3, this is quite an unusual property, and is commonly referred to as "non-convexity". In fact it represents a form of slightly negative convexity as convexity relates to the percentage change in price and in these contracts the PVBP is declining as a percentage of the present value as interest rates fall. It is more appropriate to describe this property as "non-dollar convexity".

This formula can be applied to all short-term interest rate contracts except the two SFE and NZFOE bank bill contracts. In the case of these contracts the contract value is given by a discount security formula using the yield method:

$$\text{Contract Value}_{BB} = FV / (1 + (100 - \text{Price}) \times d / D / 100)$$

10. Some exchanges such as the CME and CBOT mark-to-market twice a day, once at the close of business and once at the end of morning trading. Further, most exchange clearing houses require "intra-day" margins when market conditions are volatile—effectively marking-to-market during the day.

So in the case of the SFE contract a price of 96.24 is:

$$= \quad 1{,}000{,}000 \ / \ (1 + (100 - 96.24 \ ) \times 90 \ / \ 365 \ / \ 100)$$
$$= \quad 990{,}813.93.$$

In these instruments the PVBP is not constant as it changes slightly according to the level of interest rates. At the price in the example above the tick value is \$24.21, however, at a price of 86.24 the tick value is \$23.06. In practice most market participants assume the tick value is approximately \$24. Because of the underlying yield discount method, bank bill future contracts are displaying a "positive" PVBP relationship as PVBP rises with a fall in yields. It is important to realise that this convexity is arising just from the valuation of the underlying three month bank bill contract—it is not related to the term to forward expiry at all and is just a reflection of the bank bills convexity on the futures expiry date. As such, it shares the same property as the Eurodollar contract: at a given yield the PVBP of the futures contract will be the same regardless of the number of days to the future's expiry date. In the following section we will refer to this property as "constant PVBP".

4.3.3.2 Time value of money, hedge ratios and convexity adjustments

Futures contracts do not appear to obey the rules of the time value of money (TVM). At a given yield the value of a contract is the same today as in the future—there seems to be no compensation for the passing of time. Of course, this is not the case. We need to remember that futures contracts represent a highly structured form of financial derivative. The constant PVBP is a result of the risk management practices of exchange clearing houses; it has not been specifically designed to work this way.

One of the "cornerstones" of valuation is that all derivatives must obey the TVM. As a result, when using futures contracts they must be used to conform with the TVM characteristics for the purpose they are being used. So, when using futures contracts to hedge an instrument such as physical financial assets or OTC derivatives, the number of futures contracts needs to be adjusted in accordance with the TVM characteristics of the instrument being hedged. This is an extremely important rule, and if it is not followed then it will lead to over or under-hedging.

In this section we will consider using short-term interest rate futures to hedge FRAs. For a future and FRA with the same forward settlement date and notional maturity date, the forward interest rate represents is very similar—with differences arising due to the funding consequences of the futures contract. So, as market interest rates change the current forward interest rate used to determine both FRA rates and futures prices can be viewed as identical. Any differences in the two contracts will result from the different treatment of present values.

This is highlighted in *Exhibit 4.18* where the PVBP of an A\$ FRA and equivalent bank bill future are compared. While the future value is the same, the FRA PVBP is lower, reflecting the TVM. If we wish to hedge the FRA with futures contracts the aim is to ensure that any profits and losses today on the FRA are offset by the futures contracts. The appropriate amount of futures to hedge the FRA is that amount which equates the PVBPs of the two instruments—in this case 91 contracts. This equating of PVBPs is often referred to as determining the "hedge ratio". (Note that as time passes the

PVBP of the FRA will rise toward the futures PVBP and the number of futures contracts will need to rise correspondingly.)

Exhibit 4.18

Futures and FRAs: Dealing with Different PVBPs

It is 13 June 1995. Calculate today's PVBP on bank bill futures (BAB) contract and FRA is listed below for face values of A$1 million. Using this information if you had bought $100 million face value of FRAs, how many futures contracts would you sell to hedge the price risk?

Current Market Data

Instrument	Tenor	Underlying Days	Expiry Date	Current Yield	PVBP Yield
1. FRA	15/18	90	13-Sep-96	7.58%	7.59%
2. BAB	Sep-96	90	13-Sep-96	7.58%	7.59%

Note: Zero coupon rate to 13 Sep 96 = 7.90%

Calculations

Instrument	Current Value	PVBP Value	Future Value	Present Value	PVBP
1. FRA	981,652.51	981,628.75	(23.76)	(21.61)	21.61
2. BAB	981,652.51	981,628.75	(23.76)	(23.76)	23.76
	Difference			(2.15)	

Exhibit 4.18—*continued*

Number of futures contract to hedge $100m FRAs.

We assume that the futures price and FRA are very closely correlated. And then apply the hedge ratio formula developed in section 3.5.3.

Hedge Ratio

$$= \text{PVBP(FRA)} / \text{PVBP}$$
$$= 21.61 / 23.76$$
$$= 0.9093$$

So for every $1 face value of FRA we would sell 0.9099 BAB contracts.

Number of contracts

$$= \text{FRA face value} \times \text{Hedge Ratio} / \text{BAB face value}$$
$$= \$100,000,000 \times 0.9093 / \$1,000,000$$
$$= 90.93$$
$$= 91 \text{ contracts (rounded to nearest whole contract)}$$

This analysis suggests that FRAs and futures can be equated by adjusting for the differences in PVBP. This is generally true, however, there is another small effect that FRA and swap market makers call the "convexity adjustment".[11] As the name implies it is an adjustment to take account of the differences in the convexity characteristics of futures contracts and other closely related OTC derivatives. This adjustment starts with the recognition that the interest earned on futures mark-to-markets is negatively correlated with the futures price. That is, as interest rates fall futures prices rise. From the point of view of a short-seller of futures contracts this means if interest rates fall then they will pay mark-to-market losses. However, the interest rate to fund these losses is *lower* than the rate prevailing when they executed the transaction. On the other hand, if interest rates rise, the seller receives mark-to-market profits and earns a *higher* rate of investment interest. This creates a natural bias in futures contracts which favours short-sellers whether interest rates rise or fall. This bias works against a buyer of short-term futures contracts.

As with the funding adjustment, the exact effect of this convexity effect is not known till the expiry of the futures contracts. Estimating the convexity adjustment depends on determining an expected path for interest rates over the life of the futures contract—not a straightforward task. As with the funding adjustment the approach is to make an estimate of the net convexity approach and convert it into a forward interest rate equivalent. The implied futures yield should then be equivalent to the FRA rate plus the convexity adjustment.

A simple example of showing how the convexity adjustment can be calculated is provided in *Exhibit 4.19*. In this case we look at the outcome of the previous hedging example assuming interest rates either increase or decrease by 1% pa. The convexity effect can be seen at work in this example—regardless of whether interest rates rise or fall the futures generate a net benefit of around 1 bp. This is an extremely simple example as it assumes that the zero-coupon and forward rates rise or fall by 1% pa on the first day and stay there. It is a complex estimation problem for a small increase in accuracy and as such is generally of concern only to FRA and swap market makers.

---

11. Convexity is a measure of the sensitivity of duration to a movement in the yield on the underlying instrument. For more details see Martin, op cit n 1, Ch 3.

Exhibit 4.19

Futures and FRAs: Estimating Convexity Adjustments

To see the convexity adjustment at work let us look at the cashflows generated by the transactions in Exhibit 4.18. We will examine the cashflows impact if interest rates rose by 1% pa or fell by 1% pa on the trader date and then stayed there till the forward expiry and examine the relative costs of futures and FRAs.

Original Transactions — 23 June 95

Instrument	Amount		Forward Settlement	Maturity Date	Traded Rate/Price
1. FRA	100,000,000	Seller/investor	13-Sep-96	12-Dec-96	7.58%
2. BAB	91 contracts	Seller	13-Sep-96	12-Dec-96	92.42

Interest Rates

	Original	After 1% rise	After 1% fall
FRA	7.58%	8.58%	6.58%
BAB	7.58%	8.58%	6.58%
1.25 year ra	7.90%	8.90%	6.90%

Calculations for 1% Rise in Rates

Instrument	Traded value Value (1)	Settlement Value	Settlement Amount	Present Value (2)
1. FRA	98,165,251.11	97,928,214.59	(237,036.52)	(215,545.25)
2. BAB	(89,330,378.51)	(89,114,675.28)	215,703.23	215,703.23
		Difference		157.98

Exhibit 4.19 — continued

Calculations for 1% Fall in Rates

Instrument	Traded value Value (1)	Settlement Value	Settlement Amount	Present Value (2)
1. FRA	98,165,251.11	98,403,437.92	238,186.80	215,545.25
2. BAB	(89,330,378.51)	(89,547,128.51)	(216,749.99)	(216,749.99)
		Difference		(158.75)

Notes: (1) A long position is shown as a positive, a short position is negative
(2) The futures present value is the mark-to-market, where a gain is positive and a loss is negative.

Transaction Cashflows and Net Benefit of Futures

Date/Cashflows		Interest Rates Up 1% pa		Interest Rates Down 1% pa	
		Futures	FRA	Futures	FRA
Trade date	13-Jun-95				
Traded Contract value		(89,330,379)		(89,330,379)	
Value after rate change		(89,114,675)		(89,547,129)	
Mark-to-Market		215,704		(216,750)	
Expiry date	13-Sep-96				
Settlement		0	(237,036.52)	0	238,186.80
Interest on mark-to-market		24,258.32		(18,853.23)	
Total Future value		239,962.32	(237,036.52)	(235,603.22)	238,186.80
Futures Benefit – $		2,925.80		2,583.58	
Futures Benefit – % pa		0.0120%		0.0105%	
Futures Benefit – bp		1.20		1.05	

This example displays the futures/FRA convexity effect. Given the simple scenario used, the convexity adjustment suggests that the futures yield should be a little more than 1 bp greater than the FRA rate.

In practice, the amount of the convexity adjustment is ignored for forward period of up to one year. For longer forward terms the adjustment is in the order of 1 or 2 basis points—gradually rising as the forward period increases.

4.3.3.3 A complete futures pricing model

If we incorporate all of the special features of a futures contract relative to a forward contract we can summarise the "complete" short-term interest rate futures pricing model as follows:

Futures Price = 100 − (Forward Rate + Funding Adjustment + Convexity Adjustment)

4.4 Forward bonds

4.4.1 General description

Forward bonds are an OTC forward contract on fixed interest bearing bonds and can be likened to an FRA on a long-term interest rate security. Under a forward bond agreement the two parties agree to deliver a specified bond series at a fixed price at a future date. While FRAs relate to a generic money market interest rate such as LIBOR, forward bond agreements relate to a specific bond issue. So, every forward bond agreement must reflect the characteristics (such as issuer, maturity date, coupon and yield) of the underlying bond. This variety of issues combined with the more complex valuation formula, tend to make forward bonds a more complex and specialised transaction than FRAs.

Typically the forward bond market revolves around government and other high quality bond issues as there is already considerable activity in the underlying securities. As we will see, cash, forward and futures transactions in the bond market are closely related.

4.4.2 Synthetic replication

A forward bond purchase can be synthetically replicated in the same way as an investor FRA by purchasing the security today and financing the bond for the forward period. This is illustrated in *Exhibit 4.20*.

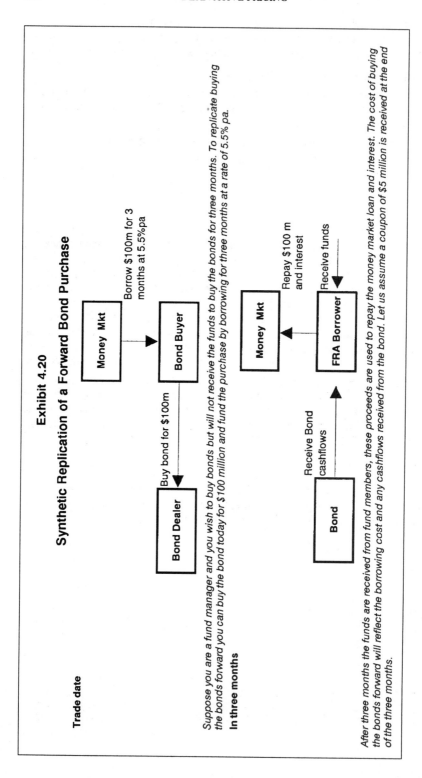

Exhibit 4.20

Synthetic Replication of a Forward Bond Purchase

Trade date

Suppose you are a fund manager and you wish to buy bonds but will not receive the funds to buy the bonds for three months. To replicate buying the bonds forward you can buy the bond today for $100 million and fund the purchase by borrowing for three months at a rate of 5.5% pa.

In three months

After three months the funds are received from fund members, these proceeds are used to repay the money market loan and interest. The cost of buying the bonds forward will reflect the borrowing cost and any cashflows received from the bond. Let us assume a coupon of $5 million is received at the end of the three months.

Exhibit 4.20—*continued*

Forward Rate calculations

Original cash cost	=	100,000,000.00
Bond value at three months	=	95,000,000.00	The bond value is reduced by the coupon payment
Borrowing interest at three months	=	100m × (1 + 0.0575 × 90 / 360)
	=	1,437,500.00
Asset cashflows	=	5,000,000.00
Net Cash value at three months	=	96,437,500.00
Forward Price	=	96.4375

As with all forward transactions the forward price represents the current cash price adjusted for the cost of carry. In this case the cost of carry is the difference between the coupons received on the bond and the cost of financing the bond:

Cost of Carry = Financing Cost − Bond Coupons

A common mistake in forward bond calculations is to use the yield to maturity as the asset return instead of the bond coupon. A forward calculation is concerned with actual cashflows that take place during the forward term—a yield to maturity reflects the asset return over the whole life of the underlying security.

While the example uses a money market interest rate to determine the financing cost this provides only an estimate. If a bond is a government bond then the credit quality of that instrument is likely to be better than most money market instruments. In a synthetic forward purchase the buyer could offer the bond as security and borrow at an interest rate appropriate to the credit quality of the bond. This will be discussed more in the section below on repurchase agreements.

4.4.3 A model for forward bond prices

The synthetic replication indicates that the forward bond price conforms with the "lumpy" income model developed in section 3.6.3, where the lumpy income is the coupon payment on the bond. If the bond does not pay any coupon during the forward period then we use the "no income" model from section 3.6.1.

Forward Bond Price Model—One Coupon Payment

The forward price per $100 can be expressed as:

$$F = S \times (1 + r_1 \times f_1 / D) - c \times (1 + r_2 \times f_2 / D)$$

Where

F = Forward price per $100 face value including accrued interest ("dirty price")

S = Cash bond price including accrued interest

r_1 = Interest rate to the forward expiry date

r_2 = Interest rate between the coupon payment and forward expiry dates

D = Day count basis (365 or 360)

f_1 = Number of days to the forward expiry date

f_2 = Number of days between the coupon payment and forward expiry dates

c = Periodic coupon payment per $100 of face value

It is interesting to note that the forward calculation is based purely on cashflows between today and the forward settlement date. Apart from calculating the initial cash price, S, there is no reference to the bond pricing formula. As with all forward calculations the aim of the model is reflect the cashflow consequence of entraining into a forward transaction.

This formula solves for the forward price. To determine the forward yield, enter the forward price into the bond price calculator and solve for the yield on the forward settlement date. This yield will reflect the cost of carry, however, it is not just a function of the difference between the financing cost and coupon rate, it also reflects the timing and payment of coupons.

This model only allows the incorporation of one coupon payment. Including other coupon payments is simply a matter calculating the future value of each extra coupon using the same methodology as the first coupon. In practice the bulk of forward bond transactions have a forward term of three months or less, so encountering more than one coupon is uncommon.

The best way of building forward bond pricing models is to combine them with a cash bond price calculator. This allows you to automatically generate the current cash price, as well as the next coupon dates and coupon amounts. An example of a forward bond pricing spreadsheet is provided in *Exhibit 4.21*. This spreadsheet assumes that the two short-term interest rates, r_1 and r_2, are the same.

Exhibit 4.21
Forward Bond Price and Yield Calculator

Spreadsheet Example

Field	Cell	Cell Address: Formula (blank for input cells)
Inputs		
Trade date	20-Dec-95	$F$11 :
Forward settlement date	15-Jun-96	$F$12 :
Maturity date	15-Jul-99	$F$13 :
Coupon rate %	8.0000	$F$14 :
Number of periods/year (1, 2 or 4)	2	$F$15 :
Current yield to maturity	6.0000	$F$16 :
Repo rate till forward settlement	4.8500	$F$17 :
Repo rate day count basis (360 or 365)	365	$F$18 :
30/360 days count (y or n)	n	$F$19 :
Underlying Bond Details		
Settlement date	20-Dec-95	$Q$22 : =F11
Forward date	15-Jun-96	$Q$23 : =F12
Maturity date	15-Jul-99	$Q$24 : =F13
Last coupon date	15-Jul-95	$Q$25 : =COUPPCD(F22,F24,F28,F30)
Next coupon date 1	15-Jan-96	$Q$26 : =COUPNCD(F22,F24,F28,F30)
Coupon rate %	8.0000	$Q$27 : =F14
Number of periods/year (1, 2 or 4)	2.0000	$Q$27 : =F15
Current yield to maturity % pa	6.0000	$Q$29 : =F16
MS excel day count method	1	$Q$30 : =IF(F19="n",1,0)
Clean price	106.3361	$Q$31 : =PRICE(F22,F24,F27/100,F29/100,100,F28,F30)
Accrued interest at trade rate	3.4348	$Q$32 : =IF(F22=F25,0,ACCRINT(F25,F26,F22,F27,1,F28,F30))

Exhibit 4.21 — continued

Field	Cell	Cell Address: Formula (blank for input cells)
Financing (or Repo) Details		
Current financing rate	4.85	$Q$35 : =F17
Repo rate day count	365	$Q$36 : =F18
Dirty bond price on trade date	109.7708	$Q$37 : =F32+F31
Number of coupons during repo	1	$Q$38 : =IF(F23>F26,1,0)
Number of repo days in forward period	178	$Q$39 : =F23-F22
Number of days from coupon date to fwd date	152	$Q$40 : =IF(F38=1,F23-F26,0)
Repo finance cost of bond	112.3671	$Q$41 : =F37*(1 + F35/(F36*100))*F39)
Forward Price Calculation		
Cumulative coupon 1 value at forward date	4.0808	$Q$44 : =F27/F28*(1 + F35/(100*F36)*F40)*F38
Dirty forward price	108.2864	$Q$45 : =F41-F44
Last coupon at forward date	15-Jan-96	$Q$46 : =COUPPCD(F23,F24,F28,F30)
Next coupon date at forward date	15-Jul-96	$Q$47 : =COUPNCD(F23,F24,F28,F30)
Accrued interest at forward date	3.3407	$Q$48 : =ACCRINT(F46,F47,F23,F27,1,F28,F30)
Clean forward price	104.9457	$Q$49 : =F45-F48
Forward yield % pa	6.2093	$Q$50 : =YIELD(F12,F13,F14/100,F49,100,F15,F30)*100

To appreciate the impact of a different coupon, *Exhibit 4.22* takes the bond in the previous example and applies different coupon levels. While the yield to maturity and financing rate on each bond is the same, the forward yield at each coupon level is different. In general, as the coupon rate increases the absolute level of the cost of carry increases.

Exhibit 4.22

The Impact of Coupons on Forward Bond Yields

Using the example in Exhibit 4.21, determine the impact on the forward yield of different coupon levels leaving all other inputs unchanged.

Original bond

Trade date	20-Dec-95
Forward settlement date	15-Jun-96
Maturity date	15-Jul-99
Coupon rate %	8
Number of periods/year (1, 2 or 4)	2
Cash yield to maturity % pa	6
Financing/repo rate % pa	4.85
Forward price	104.9457
Forward yield — % pa	6.209315
Yield cost of carry	−0.20931

Impact of Coupons

Coupon % pa	Forward Yield % pa	Cost of Carry % pa
4	6.1973	(0.1973)
8	6.2093	(0.2093)
12	6.2199	(0.2199)
16	6.2292	(0.2292)

4.4.4 A model for forward bond valuation

The forward value of a forward bond is the difference between the contract price in the forward bond agreement and the prevailing forward bond price:

Forward Value = Forward Bond Price − Contract Price

When determining the present value of the forward bond we need to be wary of the discounting interest rate used. While it is common practice to use the prevailing short-term money market rate to the forward term to determine the present value, it is not strictly correct. Determining the present value involves converting a known future cashflow with specific characteristics into a known amount today. A forward bond forward value is obviously characterised by the difference between the current forward price and the contract price. However, these cashflows are also dependent on the characteristics of the underlying bond—most notably the credit quality of the bond. Consequently, the interest rate used to present value these cashflows should be a short-term interest rate on the bond. So, in simplistic terms the interest rate used for government bonds should be equivalent to a treasury bill rate, while the interest rate for bank bonds should be the same as bank-related money market instruments.

In summary, the present value interest rate should be the same as the financing interest rate, r_1, used in the forward bond price formula. So, on a simple interest basis the formula is as follows:

$$\text{Present Value} = \text{Forward Value} / (1 + r_1 \times f / D)$$

In *Exhibit 4.23* an existing forward bond position is marked-to-market by calculating the current forward price and then determining the forward and present value of the forward bond. The forward value can be determined with reference to the "dirty" or "clean" price of the bond. Either method is acceptable as the difference in the two is simply accrued interest. In this example we use the clean price, which gives just the capital gain or loss on the position.

Exhibit 4.23

Forward Bond Valuation

Suppose you have purchased forward $100 m face value of bonds on the following basis:

Original forward purchase

Trade date		17-Jun-96
Forward settlement date		02-Nov-96
Maturity date		15-Dec-05
Coupon rate %		6.5000
Number of periods/year (1, 2 or 4)		2
Current yield to maturity		7.2500
Repo rate till forward settlement		8.0000
Repo rate day count basis (360 or 365)		360
30/360 days count (y or n)	n	
Dirty forward price		97.8629
Clean forward price		95.3765
Forward yield % pa		7.1988

Exhibit 4.23—continued

On 20 September interest rates have risen and you decide to mark the position to market (that is, calculate its present value). The forward price is now as follows:

Forward price on 20 September

Valuation date	20-Sep-96
Forward settlement date	02-Nov-96
Maturity date	15-Dec-05
Coupon rate %	6.5000
Number of periods/year (1, 2 or 4)	2
Current yield to maturity	7.7000
Repo rate till forward settlement	8.4000
Repo rate day count basis (360 or 365)	360
30/360 days count (y or n)	n
Dirty forward price	94.8213
Clean forward price	92.3350
Forward yield % pa	7.6829

In general the forward value is calculated excluding the effects of accrued interest, that is using the "clean" price.

$$
\begin{aligned}
\text{Forward value} &= (\text{forward price} - \text{contract price}) \,/\, 100 \times \text{face value} \\
&= (92.335 - 95.3765)/100 \times 100{,}000{,}000 \\
&= (3{,}041{,}500)
\end{aligned}
$$

$$
\begin{aligned}
\text{Present value} &= \text{forward value} \,/\, 1 + \text{repo rate} \times f \,/\, D) \\
&= -\,3{,}041{,}500 \,/\, (1 + .084 \times 43 \,/\, 360) \\
&= (3{,}011{,}287)
\end{aligned}
$$

4.4.5 Repurchase agreements

In any forward bond market, a large proportion of forward transactions are linked to repurchase (repo) and reverse repurchase (reverse repo) agreements. In some markets it is estimated that the majority of bond dealer transactions is some form of repo or reverse repo. The bulk of bond repos are very short-term—in the order of one day to one week. Even in very liquid markets such as the US treasury bond market, repos for longer than six months are relatively rare.

A repo is the simultaneous execution, with one counterparty, of the sale of a cash bond and a forward bond purchase. That is, it is an agreement to sell a bond today and repurchase it at a date in the future at a fixed price.[12] A reverse repo is the simultaneous purchase of a cash bond and forward bond sale. A repo is arranged so that the sale of the bond today is at the prevailing cash price for the bond and the future repurchase of the bond is based on the forward bond price. Given that we know the cash price of the bond, the forward period and the coupon on the bond the only unknown in a repo is the financing interest rate. This makes the financing interest rate the key variable in any repurchase agreement and explains why this financing interest rate in the forward pricing formula is referred to as the "repo rate".[13]

Exhibit 4.24 diagrammatically illustrates the mechanics of a repo.

12. Other names for repo transactions include buy-backs, reciprocal purchase agreements and bond lending. All have similar economic results, however, the mechanics can be different. For more detail see T Shanahan, "The Repo Market" (1991) (Summer) *Journal of International Securities Markets*.
13. In some markets this is referred to as the "cash" or "term" rate. Both of these terms can be confused with other interest rates, so they will be avoided in the remainder of this book.

Exhibit 4.24

Repurchase and Reverse Repurchase Agreements

A bond dealer decides to execute a Repurchase Agreement on a $100 million bond holding with a bank. The current cash price of the bond is 110 per $100 face value. The first leg of the transaction consists of the bond dealer selling the $100 million face value of bonds and the bank paying $110 million in cash for the bond. At the same time the bond dealer agrees to buy the bonds back from the bank in 1 month's time. Note that the bank is executing a reverse repo.

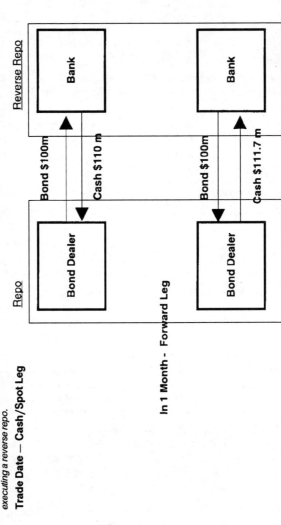

Trade Date — Cash/Spot Leg

Repo   Reverse Repo

Bond Dealer   Bond $100m →   Bank
                   ← Cash $110 m

In 1 Month - Forward Leg

Bond Dealer   Bond $100m →   Bank
                   ← Cash $111.7 m

At the end of 1 month the dealer buys the bond back. The price that they pay will be equivalent to the forward price — in this case a price of 111.7. The effect of this transaction is to allow the bond dealer to borrow money but retain a forward ownership of the bonds. The bank has invested cash with the dealer and holds the bonds as a form of security.

As we discussed in Section 3,[14] the effect of a repo is to shift cashflows from one point of time to another—it does not actually change the participant's exposure to changes in the value of bonds. In *Exhibit 4.24*, the repo has provided a very efficient method of funding its bond positions, as it retains the same long exposure to bond price movements. However, it is able to finance this bond holding at a rate which is usually lower than its normal funding rate. Notice that by continually using repos, that is executing a new repo as soon as each repo matures, the dealer could fund its bond holding over long periods at an attractive rate. This explains why the judicious use of repos is a fundamental aspect of dealing in bonds.

Some of the reasons behind entering into repos and reverse repos are summarised as follows.

4.4.5.1 Repos

1. Obtaining funding at an attractive rate.
2. "Grossing up" investment returns—selling bonds already owned into a repo and then using the cash to invest in more securities.
3. Both repos and reverse repos offer a method of liquidity management to central banks. Repos are widely used to manage the cash position of the banking system. A repo allows the central bank to withdraw cash from the economy today and then re-inject that cash at a date in the future when it will be required.

4.4.5.2 Reverse repos

1. Investors wishing to invest cash and obtaining the underlying bond as security.
2. Often banks are required to hold government bonds for regulatory reasons. Under a reverse repo, the bank could obtain ownership of the bond. However, it is not exposed to the potential price volatility of the underlying bond.
3. An organisation which has created a short position in bonds (for example from the maturity of a forward sale or from an option transaction) could cover this position temporarily through a reverse repo.

A fascinating aspect of repos is that for every term to maturity there are multiple repo rates. Every bond series issued has its own characteristics such as the issuer, the maturity date, the coupon payment dates, and the coupon amounts. As we saw in *Exhibit 4.22*, just by varying the size of the coupon changes the forward yield to maturity on otherwise identical bonds. Given these different characteristics, the market can have greater or less interest in owning bonds. If a particular bond series is in demand, then the cost of financing it will be lower than less in demand bonds. This is because reverse repo counterparties will be willing to invest cash at a lower rate to obtain temporary ownership of highly favoured bonds.

The US treasury bond market is the most liquid cash and forward bond market in the world. While the issuer is constant and the terms similar the repo rate on different bond issues can vary substantially depending on the level of demand for specific issues. As an example, in late October 1995

---

14. See section 3.3.

while the overnight US$ interest rate was 5.75% pa, the repo rate for treasury bonds varies from 5.50% pa down to 1.75% pa for the series, which are in heavy demand. Reasons for these very low repo rates reflects the existence of large short positions in these securities relative to their supply. These short positions are covered with reverse repos, and as the availability of bonds declines the short-position holders are willing to accept a lower return on the cash invested in a reverse repo.

We can solve for the repo rate implied in a forward bond transaction by re-arranging the formula from section 4.4.3 as follows (if we assume r_1 and r_2 are the same):

Calculating the Implied Repo Rate

The repo rate in the forward leg of a repo can be solved as follows:

$$r_1 = \frac{F - S + c}{S \times f_1 / D - c \times f_2 / D}$$

Where

F = Forward price per $100 face value including accrued interest at futures date (dirty price)

S = Cash bond price including accrued interest

r_1 = Repo rate to the forward expiry date

D = Day count basis (365 or 360)

f_1 = Number of days to the forward expiry date

f_2 = Number of days between the coupon payment and forward expiry dates

c = Periodic coupon payment per $100 of face value

Exhibit 4.25 calculates the implied repo rate on a forward bond transaction using this formula.

Exhibit 4.25

Repo Rate Calculation

Calculate the implied repurchase rate in the following forward bond transaction.

Cash Bond Details

Trade date	20-Dec-95
Forward settlement date	15-Jun-96
Maturity date	15-Jul-99
Coupon rate %	8.0000
Number of periods/year　(1, 2 or 4)	2
Current yield to maturity	6.0000
Dirty cash price	109.7708
Day count basis	Act/Act

Forward Details

Dirty forward price	108.2864
Repo rate day count basis (360 or 365)	365
Number of days in forward period	178
Coupon payment on 15-Jan-95	4.0000
Number of days from coupon date to fwd date	152

Repo calculation

Inputs:

$S =$	109.7708	$f_1 =$	178
$F =$	108.2864	$f_2 =$	152
$c =$	4.0000	$D =$	365

Formula:

$$r = \frac{F - S + c}{(S \times f_1 / D - c \times f_2 / D)}$$

$$= 4.8500\%$$

4.5 Bond futures

4.5.1 General description

Bond futures represent a standardised, exchange-traded forward bond contract. Like short-term interest rate futures contracts they have become an integral part of most financial markets, and typically represent a benchmark for long-term interest rate transactions.

The pricing and valuation of these instruments is derived from the forward bond calculations in section 4.4 above. As with all futures contracts, adjustments may need to be made for margin funding costs. The users of both bond futures and forward bonds are usually very similar and the reasons these products are used are closely related. In those countries where the underlying cash market is liquid, the volume in bond futures is substantial.

A list of the major bond futures contracts are listed in *Exhibit 4.26* along with the total volume for 1994.

Exhibit 4.26
List of Bond Futures Contracts and Volumes

Contract	Currency	Quote Method	Delivery Method	Exchange(s)	No of contracts	Face Value (Bn)
A$ 3 year bond	A$	Yield	Cash settled	SFE	9,709,791	719
A$ 10 year bond	A$	Yield	Cash settled	SFE	800,263	59
Medium term notional bond (BOBL)	DEM	PPH	Physical delivery	DTB	5,647,859	402
German government bond (Bund)	DEM	PPH	Physical delivery	LIFFE	37,335,437	6,642
German government bond (Bund)	DEM	PPH	Physical delivery	DTB	14,160,460	2,519
Spanish government bond	ESP	PPH	Physical delivery	MEFF	13,191,835	548
10 year government French bond	FFR	PPH	Physical delivery	MATIF	50,153,150	5,171
Long gilt future	GBP	PPH	Physical delivery	LIFFE	19,048,097	1,481
Italian government bond (BTP)	ITL	PPH	Physical delivery	LIFFE	11,823,741	1,492
Japanese government bond (JGB)	JPY	PPH	Cash settled	LIFFE	610,925	599
10 year Japanese government bond (JGB)	JPY	PPH	Cash settled	TSE	12,999,698	12,754
10 year Japanese government bond (JGB)	JPY	PPH	Cash settled	SIMEX	443,564	218
NZ$ 3 year bond	NZ$	Yield	Cash settled	NZFOE	101,229	7
NZ$ 10 year bond	NZ$	Yield	Cash settled	NZFOE	42,541	3
Swiss government bond	SFR	PPH	Physical delivery	SOFFEX	949,657	14
2 Year treasury notes	US$	PPH	Physical delivery	CBOT	939,043	188
5 Year treasury notes	US$	PPH	Physical delivery	CBOT	12,462,838	1,246
10 Year treasury notes	US$	PPH	Physical delivery	CBOT	24,077,828	2,408
US treasury bonds (T-bonds)	US$	PPH	Physical delivery	CBOT	99,959,881	9,996
US treasury bonds	US$	PPH	Physical delivery	MIDAM	1,385,904	69
					315,843,741	46,535

Notes:

1. "PPH" means the bond futures contracts are quoted in price terms as price per hundred units of face value.

2. "Yield" quotes mean the futures are quoted in terms of yield to maturity where the futures price is equivalent to 100 minus the yield.

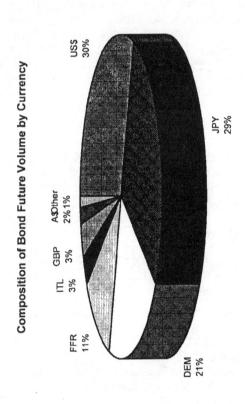

Exhibit 4.26—continued

Composition of Bond Future Volume by Currency

US$ 30%

JPY 29%

A$ 2% Other 1%

GBP 3%

ITL 3%

FFR 11%

DEM 21%

Two important differences between these futures contracts is highlighted in the table in *Exhibit 4.26*:

1. *Quote method*: The price of most bond futures contracts is quoted as the current price per 100 units of face value (shown in the table as "PPH"). For these contracts, the futures price is essentially the same as the forward price previously calculated in section 4.4.3. The other alternative is the "yield" method. Futures prices are quoted as 100 minus the yield to maturity of the underlying forward bond. The futures quotation method is usually a reflection of the local bond market convention for quoting cash bond prices.

2. *Delivery method*: There are two alternative methods with which bond contracts are terminated: physical delivery and cash settlement. As its name implies, physical delivery requires that all open contracts at expiry must deliver (the futures contract seller), or take delivery of (the buyer), a defined amount and type of bonds. In the case of cash settlement, at expiry, all open contracts are reversed at the final settlement price of the contract (usually on the last day of trading). That is, all obligations under the futures contract are cancelled upon payment or receipt of the cash difference between the original traded price and the final settlement price of the futures contract.

In the case of some contracts, notably the A$ and NZ$ bond futures, they are quoted using the yield method and are cash settled against a basket of underlying bonds. This creates some additional pricing complexities for the forward bond formula, which are highlighted below.

4.5.2 Pricing and valuing bond futures

Conceptually, the pricing and valuation tools developed in section 4.4 can be applied directly to bond futures with the same sort of adjustments as were applied to short-term interest rate futures:

Futures Price = Forward Price + Funding Adjustment +

Convexity Adjustment

As with all futures, there is no distinction between forward and present values and this should be incorporated into any hedging transaction using the PVBP in the same manner as the short-term futures contract.[15]

While the funding and convexity adjustments discussed in relation to short-term futures should strictly be applied, they are often ignored by market participants. The reason for this is twofold:

1. *Short forward period*: Most of the traded volume in bond futures across all contracts have a relatively short forward period (up to six months). As we have seen in earlier sections the funding and convexity adjustment calculations are usually extremely small for forward periods of under one year.

---

15. See section 4.3.3 for an example of dealing with the constant PVBP characteristics of futures contracts.

2. *Long-term instrument*: If the funding or convexity adjustment is calculated and spread over the fairly long life of the underlying bond, the impact of the adjustment tends to be fairly small.

Unfortunately, while it describes the conceptual relationship, deriving the final quoted futures price is not quite as simple as the formula above implies. In all bond futures additional adjustments are required depending on the nature of the delivery process. We can divide the futures price calculations into two general groups:[16]

1. *Delivery and conversion factors*—At the expiry of most bond futures contracts (for example, CBOT treasury notes and bonds) a physical delivery of bonds takes place. There is a specified list of approved bonds which can satisfy delivery and a "conversion factor" which is indented to convert each bond to the equivalent of the notional bond underlying the contract. This conversion process is not perfect and usually one of the approved bonds becomes the "cheapest" to deliver. Effectively, the price of the futures contract is based off the forward price per hundred (multiplied by the conversion factor) of the cheapest to deliver bond.

2. *Yield quotes and basket bonds*—These bonds are cash settled against the average yield on a basket of bonds on the last day of trading of the futures contract. The futures price is given by 100 minus the forward yield of the basket of bonds underlying the futures contract. Because each futures price point is one basis point in yield, and given bonds exhibit convexity, as the futures price changes so does the dollar, or "tick" value of each futures price point—the higher the futures price the higher the tick value. Both the SFE and NZFOE's bond contracts trade on this basis.

5. FOREIGN EXCHANGE FORWARDS

5.1 Introduction

The interesting feature about foreign exchange transactions is that they are purely about cashflows. In interest rate markets there is typically an underlying security which has specific interest paying and maturity characteristics and it may be in limited supply. With a foreign exchange transaction there is no specific underlying instrument; any organisation can create its own tailor-made foreign exchange transaction.

Additionally, foreign exchange transactions are a homogenous product and completely fungible.[17] That is, if a company enters into a foreign exchange transaction with a bank which settles in two days time, this can be offset by entering into an opposite transaction with another bank—the only difference will be the profit or loss due to differences in the exchange rate on the original and offsetting deals.

---

16. For more on this see Martin, op cit n 1, Ch 5.
17. If two financial instruments are fungible then they are perfect substitutes and can be used to replace one another.

Combining the underlying demand to execute foreign exchange deals for trade and capital transactions with this flexibility to create and manage foreign exchange positions, the enormous size and success of the OTC foreign exchange market can be understood. While currency futures exist, their volume is small relative to the OTC market.

The global foreign exchange market is the epitome of the "global financial village"—it is a huge marketplace spread across numerous financial centres and time zones. No matter what the time of day, it is possible to execute foreign exchange transactions involving major currencies. The BIS conducts a survey of global turnover every three years and the results from April 1995 are set out in *Exhibit 4.27*.

Exhibit 4.27
Global Foreign Exchange Turnover

Daily averages in billions of US Dollars (1)

Transaction	Apr-89 % share		Apr-92 % share		% change 1989-92	Apr-95 % share		% change 1992-95
Spot	350	56%	400	45%	14%	535	41%	34%
Forward (2)	240	39%	420	48%	75%	695	53%	65%
OTC Sub-Total	590		820		39%	1230		50%
Futures (3)	30	5%	60	7%	100%	72	6%	20%
Total	620		880		42%	1,302		48%

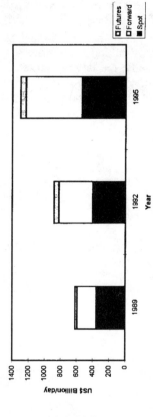

Foreign Exchange Volume

Notes:
(1) Figures have been adjusted for double counting.
(2) Includes outright forwards and forwards which are one leg of an FX swap.
(3) The Apr 95 volume was not provided with the BIS survey. Growth has been estimated from futures turnover growth of 20% from 1992 to 1995 (**Source:** FIA).

Source: BIS

In 1995 total daily volume for spot and forward FX instruments was US$1.3 trillion. This represents an increase in volume of 48% from 1992, an increase on the 1989-1992 change of 42%. The proportion of transactions executed as forwards has steadily increased since the survey was commenced. In 1989 forwards and futures represented 44% of total volume, but by 1995 this has risen to 59%.

An important feature of the market is that the bulk of volume is made up of FX swap transactions—a simultaneous execution of spot and forward or forward and forward transactions. The BIS do not include hard data in the survey but they do note that only 14% of forwards are outright, the remaining 86% are part of an FX swap transaction. This implies FX swap volume of US$ 598 billion per day in April 1995.

Reflecting the global nature of the FX market the survey also points to expanding turnover in most countries, as can be seen from *Exhibit 4.28*. Though, interestingly, the largest market, London, has grown at a more rapid rate since the survey started than its nearest rivals, the United States and Japan. In terms of geographical regions, the importance of Europe has grown in each survey, and it now represents more than half the total global volume.

Exhibit 4.28

Geographic Composition of Global FX Volume

Total OTC turnover by country

Transaction	Apr-89 % share		Apr-92 % share		% change 1989-92	Apr-95 % share		% change 1992-95
1 United Kingdom	184	26%	290.5	27%	58%	464.5	30%	60%
2 United States	115.2	16%	166.9	16%	45%	244.4	16%	46%
3 Japan	110.8	15%	120.2	11%	8%	161.3	10%	34%
4 Singapore	55	8%	73.6	7%	34%	105.4	7%	43%
5 Hong Kong	48.8	7%	60.3	6%	24%	90.2	6%	50%
6 Switzerland	56	8%	65.5	6%	17%	86.5	6%	32%
7 Germany		0%	55	5%	—	76.2	5%	39%
8 France	23.2	3%	33.3	3%	44%	58	4%	74%
9 Australia	28.9	4%	29	3%	0%	39.5	3%	36%
10 Denmark	12.8	2%	26.6	2%	108%	30.5	2%	15%
11 Canada	15	2%	21.9	2%	46%	29.8	2%	36%
12 Belgium	10.4	1%	15.7	1%	51%	28.1	2%	79%
13 Netherlands	12.9	2%	19.6	2%	52%	25.5	2%	30%
14 Italy	10.3	1%	15.5	1%	50%	23.2	1%	50%
15 Sweden	13	2%	21.3	2%	64%	19.9	1%	-7%
Other	21.6	3%	61.3	6%	184%	89.2	6%	46%
Total (1)	717.9		1076.2		50%	1572.2		46%

Note: (1) The total in this table is higher than the actual turnover in Exhibit 4.27 because this table has cross-border double counting. For example, a transaction executed by a bank in the UK and a bank in the USA would be recorded in both countries.

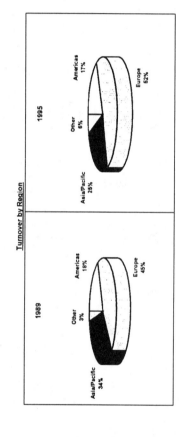

Exhibit 4.28—*continued*

Turnover by Region

1989

Asia/Pacific
34%

Other
3%

Americas
18%

Europe
45%

1995

Asia/Pacific
25%

Other
6%

Americas
17%

Europe
52%

Exhibit 4.29 demonstrates the declining importance of the US$. In 1989 the US$ was one of the legs in 90% of FX transactions but by 1995 this had fallen to 83%. Most of the US$ share has been lost to non-DEM European Economic Union currencies.

Exhibit 4.29
Currency Composition of Global OTC FX Volume

Total OTC turnover by currency as a percentage

Currency	Apr-89 % share		Apr-92 % share		% change 1989-92	Apr-95 % share		% change 1992-95
1 US Dollar	531	90%	672.4	82%	27%	1020.9	83%	52%
2 Deutschemark	159.3	27%	328	40%	106%	455.1	37%	39%
3 Japanese Yen	159.3	27%	188.6	23%	18%	295.2	24%	57%
4 Pound Sterling	88.5	15%	114.8	14%	30%	123	10%	7%
5 French Franc	11.8	2%	32.8	4%	178%	98.4	8%	200%
6 Swiss Franc	59	10%	73.8	9%	25%	86.1	7%	17%
7 Canadian Dollar	5.9	1%	24.6	3%	—	36.9	3%	50%
8 ECU	5.9	1%	24.6	3%	317%	24.6	2%	0%
9 Australian Dollar	11.8	2%	16.4	2%	39%	36.9	3%	125%
10 Other EMS currencies	17.7	3%	73.8	9%	317%	159.9	13%	117%
11 Other	129.8	22%	90.2	11%	-31%	123	10%	36%
Total (2)	590	200%	820	200%		1230	200%	

Note: (1) The % share is expressed as a proportion of the global volume.
        (2) As each FX deal involves two currencies the sum of the total volume in each currency is double the estimated global turnover.

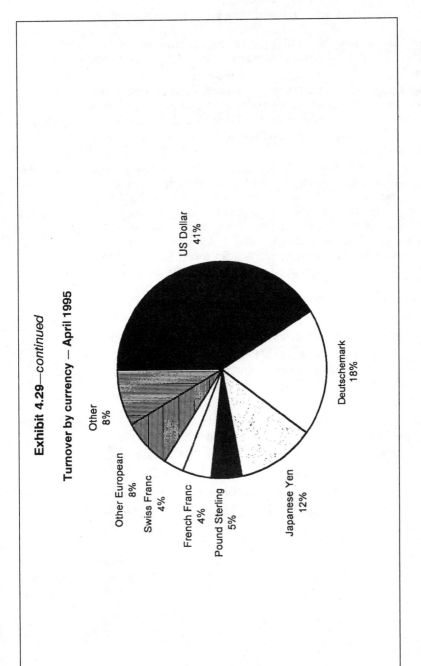

Exhibit 4.29—*continued*

Turnover by currency — April 1995

US Dollar
41%

Deutschemark
18%

Japanese Yen
12%

Pound Sterling
5%

French Franc
4%

Swiss Franc
4%

Other European
8%

Other
8%

5.2 A model for the forward foreign exchange price

In this section we will convert the generalised price formulae from Section 3 into a formula that generates a forward foreign exchange rate.

A forward FX transaction is an instrument in which a cash in one currency is exchanged for cash in another currency. Either currency can be thought of as the underlying asset. These assets provide constant and known incomes in the form of interest payments. We know that these assets can be exchanged on a spot basis at a rate of 1 unit of the base currency for S units of the terms currency.

The spot exchange rate is the current rate of exchange of two currencies. The synthetic replication above indicates that the forward exchange rate of two currencies is dependant on their respective interest rates. The forward FX pricing formula has a lot in common with the general forward models developed in Section 3, however, the formula needs to be adjusted for the fact that the interest amounts, r and q, are calculated on different currency amounts—1 unit of the base currency for every S units of the terms currency. We also need to incorporate the possibility that the calculation basis underlying each interest rate may differ. Generally for short-term forwards the main differences between money market interest rates are:

- the assumed number of days per annum (either 360 or 365); and
- whether the rate is based on a discount or yield calculation.[18]

The simplest approach is to look at the forward value of cash in each currency. As we have already discussed, cash by itself earns no income so we can apply the general "no-income" pricing model:

$$F = S \times (1 + r) \times f / D$$

This can be rewritten as follows for the forward cash value for the base (F_B) and the terms currency (F_T) as follows:

$$\text{Base Currency: } F_B = 1 \times (1 + r_B) \times f / D_B$$

$$\text{Terms Currency: } F_T = S \times (1 + r_T) \times f / D_T$$

where S is the exchange rate. The forward rate of exchange between these two currencies will be given by the ratio of these two forward amounts. This is summarised below:

---

18. See Martin, op cit n 1, Ch 3.

Short-term Forward Foreign Exchange Price

Using simple interest, the calculation is as follows:

$$F = \frac{S \times (1 + r_T) \times f / D_T}{(1 + r_B) \times f / D_B}$$

Where

F	=	Forward exchange rate
S	=	Spot exchange rate
r_T	=	Terms currency interest rate to forward date
r_B	=	Base currency interest rate to forward date
D_T	=	Terms currency day count basis (365 or 360)
D_B	=	Base currency day count basis (365 or 360)
f	=	Number of days to the forward expiry date from the spot settlement date.

An example of this calculation is set out in *Exhibit 4.30.*

Exhibit 4.30

Forward Pricing Example

The current spot rate for US$/CAD is 1.3513. Calculate the rate of a forward FX deal settling in 30 days from the spot date. The 1 month US$ interest rate is 6.25% pa and the CAD rate is 8.2% pa. Calculate the implied forward FX rate.

S = 1.3513   f = 30

rT = 8.20%   DT = 365

rB = 6.25%   DB = 360

$$F = \frac{S \times (1 + rT) \times f / DT}{(1 + rB) \times f / DB}$$

$$= \frac{1.3513 \times (1 + .082) \times 30 / 365}{(1 + .0625) \times 30 / 360}$$

$$= \mathbf{1.3534}$$

Forward Points   =   0.0021 premium

There are a number of assumptions underlying this calculation, which, if they do not hold, may require an adjustment to the formula:

1. *Simple interest*: There is assumed to be no compounding in the interest calculation. This can be adjusted for by applying the compound interest calculation.

2. *Zero-coupon*: The interest rates are assumed to be zero-coupon rates. This is generally a satisfactory assumption for forward FX deals of up to six

months, most interest rates longer than that contain re-investment risk. This assumption is relaxed in the section on long-term foreign exchange below.

3. *Interest rates are yields*: The formula assumes that interest rates are yields; that is, the interest amount is given by multiplying the principal value today. If an interest rate is from a discount security which calculates interest on a discount basis, then this will need to be converted to a yield basis.[19]

4. *Calculations from spot date*: The forward period is from the spot settlement date to the forward settlement date. Strictly speaking, the interest rates that should be used are the two day forward interest rates, however, this is usually ignored as the impact is minimal.

Bids and Offers

A forward FX rate is derived from three market rates: the spot FX rate and the interest rate in both currencies. In each case the appropriate bid and offer rate has to be identified. In FX markets the "bid" is the rate at which a dealer is willing to buy the base currency; and the "offer" is where the dealer will sell the base currency—the bid rate is lower than the offer rate. As its counterparty we do the opposite of the dealer so we will sell the base currency at the bid and buy it at the offer. As we noted earlier, from an end-user's point of view a rule of thumb is that we will always lose money from the bid-offer spread, that is you "buy high and sell low".

Unfortunately, in money markets bids and offers can have two meanings, depending on the underlying money market instrument. If the underlying instrument is a direct term deposit with a bank, then the bid will be where you can invest funds with the bank, and the offer is where you can borrow from the bank—the bid interest rate is lower than the offer interest rate. However, if the instrument is a tradeable security, such as a bank bill, where the underlying security is bought and sold according to its present value, the bids and offers are expressed in terms of interest rates. As a lower price implies a higher yield, the "bid" interest rate is higher that the "offer" interest rate. One way of avoiding confusion with these conventions is to apply the rule of thumb to interest rates: an end-user will invest at the lower interest rate and borrow at the higher interest rate.

Assuming that we are end-users rather than FX dealers, the simplest method of identifying the appropriate rates is to make use of the synthetic replication concept to identify whether to use the bid or offer. If we wish to buy the base currency forward in three months, the synthetic replication is to buy the base currency in the spot FX market, borrow in the terms currency and invest in the base currency. Using this, then, we use the appropriate rates as follows for a forward purchase or sale:

19. Ibid.

Calculating Forward Rates (End-User Perspective): Bids and Offers

Leg	Buy Base Currency Forward	Sell Base Currency Forward
Spot Foreign Exchange	offer	bid
Base Money Market[1]	bid (low rate)	offer
Terms Money Market[1]	offer (high rate)	bid

Note: The quote convention in this table assumes underlying instruments are bank deposits

An example of using the correct bids and offers is set out in the first part of *Exhibit 4.31*.

5.3 A model for forward FX valuation

The forward value of a forward FX transaction is the difference between the original contract price and the prevailing market forward price. A forward FX transaction is usually expressed in terms of a constant amount of the base currency, while the terms currency is left to vary and all gains and losses are generated in the commodity currency. The forward value in the terms currency of a forward FX where the base currency is purchased/terms currency sold, the deal can be expressed as follows:[20]

$$\text{Forward Value}_{TERMS} = \text{Base Amount} \times F_M - \text{Base Amount} \times F_C$$

where F_M is the prevailing forward market rate and F_C is the contract rate.

If, instead, the terms currency is held constant then the situation is inversed as follows for a bought base currency position:

$$\text{Forward Value}_{BASE} = \text{Terms Amount} / F_C - \text{Terms Amount} / F_M$$

The mark-to-market on a forward FX position will be given by present valuing these forward value calculations. It is essential that we correctly identify the currency in which the forward value is generated. As it is usually the case that the interest rate differs between the two currencies, the present value of a forward cashflow in either currency will be different. So, if the forward value is calculated in the terms currency it should be present valued using the terms currency interest rate:

$$\text{Present Value}_{TERMS} = \text{Forward Value}_{TERMS} / (1 + r_T \times f / D)$$

otherwise if the forward value is in the base currency:

$$\text{Present Value}_{BASE} = \text{Forward Value}_{BASE} / (1 + r_B \times f / D)$$

Exhibit 4.31 provides a complete worked example for determining the current mark-to-market revaluation of a forward FX position.

20. A sold base currency/purchased terms currency has the same formula with the forward rates F_M and F_C reversed.

Exhibit 4.31

Forward FX Transaction

You currently hold a forward FX position where you buy GBP/sell USD 10 million at 1.5340. This contract will settle in 92 days time. Given the market rates below calculate the current revaluation of this position.

Market rates		
Spot GBP/USD:	bid	offer
	1.5629	1.5634

Three Month Money Market rates (Deposit rates)

	Bid	Offer
GBP	6.55	6.65
USD	5.53	5.75

1. Calculate current forward FX price

We wish to revalue a bought GBP forward FX position. The current market value will be given by the forward FX price at which an offsetting position can be put in place. Consequently we need to generate a three month forward price to sell GBP/buy USD. The inputs to the forward price model will be the FX spot rate bid, the GBP money market offer and the USD money market bid.

S	=	1.5629	f	=	90
rT	=	5.53%	DT	=	360
rB	=	6.65%	DB	=	365

$$F = \frac{S \times (1 + rT) \times f / DT}{(1 + rB) \times f / DB}$$

$$= \frac{1.5629 \times (1 + .0553) \times 90 / 360}{(1 + .0665) \times 90 / 365}$$

$$= \mathbf{1.5589}$$

---

2. Calculate the forward and present values

The principal value of the transaction is expressed in the terms currency, that is, USD 10 million so we use the formula:

Forward Value = Terms Amount / Fc − Terms Amount / Fm

Where

Terms Amount	=	10,000,000 USD
Fc	=	1.5340
Fm	=	1.5589

Forward Value	=	10,000,000 / 1.5340 − 10,000,000 / 1.5589
	=	104,125 USD
	=	66,794 GBP
Present Value	=	Forward Value / (1 + rT × f / DT)
	=	102,705 USD
	=	65,715 GBP

The mark-to-market revaluation on this position is a profit of USD 102,705.

5.4 Foreign exchange swaps

The BIS survey in section 5.1 identified that a very large percentage of global foreign exchange volume is in the form of FX swaps—the simultaneous execution of offsetting spot and forward foreign exchange transactions.[21] These transactions need to be distinguished from cross-currency interest rate swaps ("currency swaps"). FX swaps are generally short-term in nature and consist of just a spot and forward leg. Currency swaps are longer-term instruments, typically in the range of 1 to 10 years, and involve a series of periodic interest exchanges. While they are different instruments, the overall economics of the two transactions have the same effect of switching one currency exposure to another for the life of the instrument.

The popularity of FX swaps is a reflection of the important tasks for which it can be used:

- the temporary conversion of one currency to another without creating an exposure to foreign exchange movements;
- extending existing forward FX positions;
- a vehicle for trading the pure interest differential of two currencies without an exposure to exchange rates; and
- arbitrage related activities such as covered interest arbitrage.

Like a bond repurchase agreement, an FX swap allows the two counterparties to temporarily exchange one asset for another—in this case one currency for another. By itself, the transaction does not create an outright

---

21. An FX swap can also be the simultaneous execution of offsetting forward transactions with different terms.

foreign exchange exposure, as any gains or losses on the initial spot currency exchange are offset by gains and losses on the final forward exchange.

A useful example of the impact of an FX swap is the extension of an existing forward position which expires on the current spot settlement date. The mechanics of an extension or rollover of an existing FX position consist of two legs:

1. *The spot leg*: a spot FX deal is executed which offsets the cashflows from the original forward deal. This will typically crystallise a gain or loss equivalent to the difference between the original forward rate and the current spot rate.[22]

2. *The forward leg*: a forward FX deal is executed at the prevailing forward rate. The net cost of this transaction will be the spot and forward spreads and the forward points.

If these two legs are executed separately then there is a risk that the spot foreign exchange rate moves between executing the spot and forward legs. An FX swap reduces a rollover to one deal and removes the foreign exchange risk by simultaneously executing both legs. In an FX swap the transaction becomes insensitive to the spot exchange rate used, and the important variable in the transaction is the forward points—it is for this reason that forward points are also referred to as swap points or the swap rate.

Exhibit 4.32 demonstrates how a forward FX position expiring in two days can be extended for another three months with one FX swap transaction.

22. Some countries still allow "historic rate rollovers". In these transactions the gain or loss is not crystallised on the rollover date and is carried till the forward transaction finally matures. This introduces another component to calculating the forward FX price—an interest adjustment for any gains or losses funded by the FX dealer. In many countries these transactions have been banned due to the possibility of concealing trading losses for long periods of time.

Exhibit 4.32

Extending a Forward FX Deal With an FX Swap

A company has a sold GBP 20 million/bought USD transaction expiring in two business days time. It wishes to extend this position for three months and decides to use an FX swap to do so where it buys GBP spot and sells GBP forward. The effect of the FX swap is to fund the settlement of the original transaction in two days time and create a new sold GBP/buy USD forward FX transaction in three months time. The net cost of this transaction is the forward or swap points over the next three months. Note that to simplify cashflows the original sold GBP position and the current spot FX rate are assumed to be same—this happy state of affairs rarely occurs in reality.

Current market rates:	Spot GBP/USD:	1.5629
	3 month Forward GBP/USD:	1.5589
	Forward or Swap Points:	(40)

Diagramatic representation of FX swap

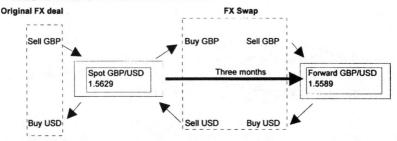

Cashflows of original deal and FX swap

Cashflows		GBP	USD
Day 0	Execute FX Swap		
Day 2	Settle Original FX deal	(20,000,000)	(31,258,000)
	Spot Leg of FX swap	20,000,000	31,258,000
	Net cashflows	—	—
Day 92	Forward leg of FX swap	(20,000,000)	31,178,000

Net Cost of FX swap =	(80,000)

5.5 Long-term forward foreign exchange transactions

5.5.1 General description

As the name implies long-term forward foreign exchange (LTFX) transactions are a longer-term version of the forward FX transaction. It is an agreement between two parties who wish to agree on an exchange of currency cashflows at some date, possibly years in the future. For our purposes, we will consider an LTFX as any forward contract longer than six months.

LTFX contracts are relatively small proportion of total FX market volume. The BIS foreign exchange turnover statistics indicate that only 1% of FX volume is for longer than one year. While most FX dealers will quote LTFX transactions out for five years, given the lower liquidity of these instruments the bid-offer spread is wider than short-term forwards and reversing the position will not be as straightforward.

Typically, LTFX contracts are associated with hedging the FX exposures created by long-term borrowings or income streams created by assets in foreign currencies. Often LTFX transactions and currency swaps can be used interchangeably, the advantage of LTFX is that they can be more easily tailored to meet uneven future cashflows.

5.5.2 Pricing and valuing LTFX transactions

The synthetic replication of an LTFX is the same as a forward FX transaction—the borrowing and lending legs are just for a longer term. Similarly, the valuation procedure is identical. However, the valuation of LTFX is complicated by the following two effects:

1. *Zero-coupon yield*: The forward pricing and valuation models assume that there are not interest cashflows during the forward period—that is, the interest rates are zero coupon rates. This is a reasonable assumption when using money market interest rates, however, the quoted yields in most currencies which have a term to maturity of more than one year, usually are coupon-paying interest rates. The difficulty with coupon-paying yields is that there is a re-investment risk associated with each coupon payment. To price LTFX this risk has to be removed by deriving zero-coupon interest rates.

2. *Compounding*: Longer-term interest rates typically are expressed as compound interest rates—accordingly, compounding also needs to be incorporated into the model.

If we ignore either effect the LTFX price will be wrong, particularly if the yield curves in each currency have opposite shapes as this will exacerbate the difference between the zero-coupon and coupon interest differentials. *Exhibit 4.33* highlights the difference in forward price of a one year A$/US$ LTFX example when correctly calculated and when the short-term model is used.

Exhibit 4.33

LTFX Pricing: Using Zero Coupon Yields

To demonstrate the impact of using zero-coupon versus coupon yield curves, calculate the LTFX using the two sets of interest rates provided below.

Current Market Rates

FX Rate	0.7202
1 year, US$ coupon (sa)	5.50%
1 year, US$ zero coupon (sa)	5.56%
1 year, A$ coupon (ann)	7.60%
1 year, US$ zero coupon (ann)	7.79%

Correct Forward Price

Using zero-coupon rate & compounding sa rate	**0.7063**	
Incorrect Forward Prices (Short-term model)		Difference
Using coupon rate ignoring compounding	0.7067	−0.0003
Using coupon rate & compounding sa rate	0.7072	−0.0008

The three components of a short-term forward FX model are a spot exchange rate and two money market instruments; whereas the LTFX model is comprised of a spot FX deal and two zero-coupon bond transactions. That is, a LTFX purchase of the base currency can be synthetically replicated by buying the base currency in the spot market, funding the spot settlement of the terms currency by borrowing using a zero-coupon bond and investing the base currency proceeds in a zero-coupon bond which expires on the forward settlement date.

To incorporate this into our forward pricing model, the interest rate legs will calculate the forward value of a single amount (compounded using zero coupon rates).[23] If we incorporate these concepts into the forward pricing model we can express the LTFX model as follows:

---

23. Zero coupon rates are often not observable as a market quote, so the rates will need to be generated from coupon paying, or par, yields such as prevailing swap rates. See Martin, op cit n l, Ch 8 for more detail on calculating zero coupon interest rates from par rates.

Long-term Forward Foreign Exchange (LTFX) Price

Using simple interest, the calculation is as follows:

$$F = \frac{S \times (1 + r_T / m_T)^{n_T}}{(1 + r_B) / m_B)^{n_B}}$$

Where

F = Forward exchange rate

S = Spot exchange rate

r_T = Terms currency zero coupon interest rate to forward date

r_B = Base currency zero coupon interest rate to forward date

m_T = Terms currency payment frequency (that is, 1, 2, 4, 12)

m_B = Base currency payment frequency

n_T = Terms currency # of payment periods to the forward date

n_B = Base currency # of payment periods to the forward date

An important characteristic of LTFX contracts is the impact of the interest differential on the forward price. Compared to a short-term forward FX contract, the interest rate legs of LTFX have considerably more impact on the forward price.

Exhibit 4.34

LTFX Pricing and Sensitivities

The graph below shows the sensitivity of a 5 year JPY/USD LTFX deal to changes in both the interest differential and the spot exchange rate. A feature of LTFX transactions is the increasing importance of the interest differential the longer the term to expiry. In this 5 year deal the impact of a move in the exchange rate of 1% is approximately equal to a change in the interest differential of 0.20% pa

Market Data	
Spot FX rate	101.00
USD 5 Year rate % pa (sa)	6.20
JPY 5 Year rate % pa (sa)	2.50
Interest Differential % pa	3.70

$$\text{LTFX Price} = \frac{S \times (1 + rT / mT)^{nT}}{(1 + rB / mB)^{nB}}$$

$$= \frac{101 \times (1 + 0.025/2)^{10}}{(1 + 0.062/2)^{10}}$$

$$= \mathbf{84.27}$$

The sensitivities of this position in foreign exchange points are as follows

PVBP   = -0.0368

That is, a 1 bp rise in the interest differential will decrease the present value of the position by 0.0368 fx points.

PVFP   =   0.0074

That is, a 0.01 change in the spot FX rate will alter the present value by 0.0074

PVD   =   0.0075

Each day that passes increases the present value by 0.0075 fx points.

LTFX Price Sensitivity

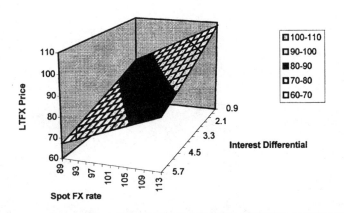

Exhibit 4.34 calculates the LTFX price of a five year JPY/US$ transaction and then graphs the sensitivity of the forward price to movements in the interest differential and the spot price. In this example a movement of 1% in the exchange rate has the same impact as a 0.20% pa change in the interest differential.

The forward value of a LTFX contract is the same as for a short-term forward FX contract: the difference between the contract value and the current market value. However, when calculating the present value we need to take account of the same yield considerations as the LTFX price. As a result we calculate the present value of the LTFX contract by using a zero coupon yield and applying the following compound interest, present value formula:[24]

$$\text{Present Value}_{BASE} = \text{Forward Value}_{BASE} / (1 + r_B / m_B)^n{}_B$$

5.6 Par forwards

5.6.1 Instrument description

Another form of LTFX is the par forward. It is a series of LTFX contracts with regularly spaced settlement dates (for example, monthly or quarterly) at a constant exchange rate. *Exhibit 4.35* compares the exchange rate of a five year CHF/US$ par forward transaction with a series of LTFX contracts which would achieve the same effect. The benefit from the point of view of an end user is that it allows the benefit or cost of a forward discount or premium to be spread out over the life of the transaction. In the example provided, from the point of view of a buyer of US$, in the first two years of the transaction you buy US$ at a substantially lower exchange rate than that implied by traditional forward instruments. The downside of course is that after two years the exchange rate is higher.

---

24. This is the base currency present value, to generate the terms currency PV just substitute terms currency variables for the base currency variables used.

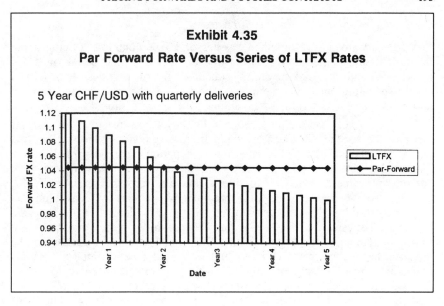

Exhibit 4.35

Par Forward Rate Versus Series of LTFX Rates

5 Year CHF/USD with quarterly deliveries

In terms of the present value of these transactions the economics of a par forward and a series of LTFX are the same (as we will see below the pricing of par forwards ensures that this is the case). While in terms of the FX transaction alone there seems to be little added value in a par forward, the attraction of these instruments is that they can be very useful for cashflow management and also tax planning.

For example, suppose a Swiss-based distribution company is about to commence importing equipment from the United States. It has signed a five year contract which will require you to buy US$10 million of equipment every quarter. The initial set-up costs associated with selling this equipment will be substantial and at current exchange rates you are likely to have negative CHF cashflows for the first two years, after which time cashflows will turn positive. You talk to your banker and he or she is concerned about financing the new project given its long lead time and currency exposures and suggests that you consider covering the exposures using the forward FX rates outlined in *Exhibit 4.35*. From the Swiss manufacturer's point of view a par forward would be more attractive than a series of LTFX contracts. Par forwards provide and immediately lower CHF cost for the equipment imports and possibly create a positive cashflow in the first two years. The downside is that the CHF cost of the equipment is relatively higher than a series of LTFX contracts. The par forward has allowed the Swiss company to obtain forward FX cover and also smooth out its cashflows.

A par forward is also interesting as it also shares some similarities with fixed-to-fixed cross currency interest rate swaps as it involves a constant exchange of currency cashflows as opposed to the variable cashflows of LTFX contracts. We will see that in our discussion of currency swaps that par forwards can be a useful tool in managing swap exposures.

5.6.2 Pricing and valuing par forwards

A par forward is a "smoothed" series of LTFX contracts. Pricing a par forward involves determining the cashflows from a similar series of LTFX transactions and then making an adjustment for the funding cost or benefit of evenly spreading out the currency cashflows. As is the case for any forward transaction the present value of executing a par forward should be zero.

The spreadsheet set out in *Exhibit 4.36* shows how to solve for the par forward rate for the CHF/US$ example from the previous section. The first step is to calculate the LTFX rates for each periodic par forward date. We then need to determine what constant CHF delivery amount has an equivalent net present value to the CHF delivery amounts from the series of LTFX amounts. As can be seen the CHF par forward amounts will save the end user substantial CHF amounts—in effect the FX dealer is lending the difference between the LTFX rate and the par forward rate and having it repaid in the later delivery amounts. The dealer deserves a return on the money it has loaned to the end-user and so the par forward rate will include a funding cost. The solution of the par forward rate is to solve for a par forward rate which ensures that the total net present value of all of the funding differences is equal to zero. It is at this point that we know the money lent in the early par forward deliveries is re-couped, with interest, in the later deliveries.[25]

---

25. In practice FX dealers will want to ensure that the interest rates used reflect market bids and offers and that they earn a positive funding NPV on the transaction. This can be achieved in this model by setting the target NPV at a rate which provides the dealers required return. For example, in Exhibit 4.36 if the required NPV was CHF100,000 then the par forward rate would be 1.0476.

Exhibit 4.36

Pricing a Par Forward Transaction

Transaction Details

Spot FX Rate	1.13
Term (Yrs)	5
Delivery Frequency	Quarterly
Quarterly Amount	10,000,000

Solution

Unrounded Par Forward	1.04701178	Change

	B	C	D	E	F		G	H	I
	Market Parameters				LTFX Cashflows		Par Forward	Net CHF	Net CHF
	Zero USD Rate	Zero CHF Rate	Forward FX rate		USD Amount	CHF Amount	CHF Amount	Funding Difference	Funding NPV
1	5.7500	2.0000	1.1196		10,000,000	11,195,564	10,470,118	−725,446	(721,837)
2	5.7500	2.0000	1.1092		10,000,000	11,092,093	10,470,118	−621,975	(615,802)
3	5.7817	2.0628	1.0992		10,000,000	10,992,155	10,470,118	−522,037	(515,043)
4	5.8134	2.1257	1.0895		10,000,000	10,894,820	10,470,118	−424,702	(415,793)
5	5.8358	2.2508	1.0810		10,000,000	10,809,644	10,470,118	−339,526	(330,133)
6	5.8582	2.3759	1.0731		10,000,000	10,730,621	10,470,118	−260,504	(251,409)
7	6.6166	2.8575	1.0589		10,000,000	10,588,703	10,470,118	−118,585	(112,821)
8	7.3751	3.3391	1.0435		10,000,000	10,434,820	10,470,118	35,297	33,026
9	7.2463	3.4347	1.0383		10,000,000	10,383,014	10,470,118	87,104	80,653
10	7.1175	3.5304	1.0343		10,000,000	10,342,908	10,470,118	127,210	116,508
11	7.0405	3.6254	1.0300		10,000,000	10,299,796	10,470,118	170,322	154,230
12	6.9634	3.7205	1.0266		10,000,000	10,265,579	10,470,118	204,539	183,032
13	6.9159	3.8062	1.0227		10,000,000	10,227,428	10,470,118	242,690	214,577
14	6.8685	3.8920	1.0196		10,000,000	10,196,121	10,470,118	273,997	239,261

Exhibit 4.36—continued

| | Market Parameters | | | LTFX Cashflows | | Par Forward | Net CHF | Net CHF |
	Zero USD Rate	Zero CHF Rate	Forward FX rate	USD Amount	CHF Amount	CHF Amount	Funding Difference	Funding NPV
15	6.8380	3.9668	1.0161	10,000,000	10,161,093	10,470,118	309,025	266,506
16	6.8076	4.0416	1.0131	10,000,000	10,131,450	10,470,118	338,668	288,347
17	6.7881	4.1057	1.0098	10,000,000	10,097,918	10,470,118	372,200	312,883
18	6.7686	4.1697	1.0069	10,000,000	10,068,646	10,470,118	401,472	333,110
19	6.7534	4.2142	1.0032	10,000,000	10,032,394	10,470,118	437,724	358,691
20	6.7382	4.2587	0.9999	10,000,000	9,999,221	10,470,118	470,897	381,012

Net CHF NPV (Target) 0

Summary of Results

Average LTFX rate =	1.0477
Funding Cost =	0.0023
Par Forward rate =	1.0470

How this Spreadsheet works

1. Generate the Zero Coupon interest rates (on a quarterly basis for columns B and C).
2. Calculate the LTFX rates in Column C.
3. Calculate the USD and CHF cashflows for each quarterly roll for column E and F.
4. Enter a "guess" of the Par Forward Rate and enter into the cell labelled "Unrounded Par Forward".
5. Calculate the Par Forward CHF amount in column H by multiplying the USD amount by the Unrounded Par Forward Amount.
6. The Net CHF amount is simply the difference between columns F and G.
7. Calculate the NPV in column I by taking the present value of column H using the CHF zero interest rates and the compound interest present value formula.
8. From the Tools menu invoke the "Solver" function.
9. Make the Net NPV cell (column I) the target by changing the cell with the Unrounded Par Forward rate so that the target becomes Zero and then press solve, this will iteratively solve for the Unrounded Par Forward Rate which makes the NPV zero.

Once a par forward price can be generated then the valuation procedures are identical to an LTFX contract. However, while a series of LTFX positions can be valued individually, all of the par forward legs should be valued together, because of the interdependence between the series of deliveries.

6. EQUITY FORWARDS

6.1 Introduction

In their relatively short lifetime equity forwards have gained a reputation as a highly risky instrument. The October 1987 stock market crash, and 1989 "mini-crash", prompted considerable conjecture that stock index futures exacerbated the market fall and, given the losses sustained by long position holders, were too risky an instrument to be used by the general public.[26] Then, in 1995, the collapse of British merchant bank Baring Brothers primarily due to unauthorised trading in share price index futures on the Japanese Nikkei index, prompted more regulatory "navel gazing" with respect to these instruments.

Despite the bad press, share price index futures have been an outstanding success if measured by volume growth since they were introduced in the United States in 1982. Stock index futures are a classic example of a derivative which "adds-value" to organisations and individuals with an exposure to share markets, as they provide a method of gaining an exposure to share market or hedging an existing exposure at considerably lower cost than transacting in the physical market. However, like their underlying market, the price volatility in share index futures is generally higher than most interest rate and currency markets—and as a result are a risky instrument in the hands of a novice user or uncontrolled trader.

An interesting feature of derivatives on equity index futures is the relatively high usage of options relative to both cash market volume and forward volume. Whereas in developed interest rate markets, option volume might be 10% of forward volume, in equity index markets the option percentage might be 20% or higher. This is partly explained by the high level of volatility, which encourages market participants to take insurance in the form of options.

Exhibit 4.37 summarises global exchange traded volume in equity forwards. Share price index futures dominate turnover, with very small volume in individual share futures. In the United States this is partly the result of regulatory restrictions, however, even where contracts have been listed on individual shares volume has been low.[27] The bulk of the volume is in US$ denominated indexes, followed by Japan and then Germany.

---

26. Possibly the most spectacular case of the damage done by stock index futures to over-leveraged users was the Hang Seng Stock Index Futures contract traded on the Hong Kong Futures Exchange. The majority of long position holders at the time of the crash were individual speculators. After the crash, most of these "longs" defaulted on payment of their losses and the market was effectively closed.

27. Apart from Sweden, individual share futures contracts are relatively new, and this may also contribute to the low volume.

Exhibit 4.37

List of Share Index and Individual Share Futures Contracts

Contract	Currency	Contract Type	Delivery Method	Exchange	1994 Futures Volumes (1)(2)	
					No of contracts	Face Value (US$ Bn)
Austrian Traded Index (ATX)	ATS	SFI	Cash settled	OTOB	348,291	3.455
All Ordinaries Index	AUD	SFI	Cash settled	SFE	2,552,546	102.708
Share Futures	AUD	ISF	Cash settled	SFE	32,441	0.002
Bel-20	BEF	SFI	Cash settled	BELFOX	154,574	0.795
San Paulo Stock Exchange Index (Ibovespa)	BRL	SFI	Cash settled	BM&F	10,583,594	92.218
Toronto 35 Index	CAD	SFI	Cash settled	TFE	104,209	9.543
Swiss Market Index (SMI)	CHF	SFI	Cash settled	SOFFEX	1,694,260	239.743
DAX Stock Index Future	DEM	SFI	Cash settled	DTB	5,140,803	804.121
Danish KFX Stock Index Future	DKK	SFI	Cash settled	CSE	429,466	8.162
IBEX 35	ESP	SFI	Cash settled	MEFF RV	27,020,886	39.362
CAC 40 Stock Index	FFR	SFI	Cash settled	MATIF	7,464,449	582.178
FTSE 100 Stock Index	GBP	SFI	Cash settled	LIFFE	4,227,490	595.662
Hang Seng Index	HKD	SFI	Cash settled	HKFE	4,192,574	257.324
Nikkei 225	JPY	SFI	Cash settled	OSE	6,208,821	1,109.523
Nikkei 300	JPY	SFI	Cash settled	OSE	4,684,480	124.362
Nikkei Index	JPY	SFI	Cash settled	SIMEX	5,801,098	518.331
Tokyo Stock Price Index (TOPIX)	JPY	SFI	Cash settled	TSE	2,623,067	371.105
Forty Index (3)	NZD	SFI	Cash settled	NZFOE	7,397	0.206
Swedish OMX Index	SEK	SFI	Cash settled	OM	1,706,984	44.518
Stock Futures	SEK	ISF	Physical Delivery	OM	234,250	0.002

Exhibit 4.37—*continued*

Contract	Currency	Contract Type	Delivery Method	Exchange	1994 Futures Volumes (1)(2)	
					No of contracts	Face Value (US$ Bn)
Standard & Poors 400	USD	SFI	Cash settled	CME	285,962	79.640
Standard & Poors 500	USD	SFI	Cash settled	CME	18,708,599	5,612.299
Nikkei 225 (Settled in USD)	USD	SFI	Cash settled	CME	548,233	49.930
Russell 2000	USD	SFI	Cash settled	CME	36,239	–
Eurotop Index (Settled in USD)	USD	SFI	Cash settled	COMEX	62,231	–
Value Line Stock Index	USD	SFI	Cash settled	KCBT	50,259	14.123
Mini Value Line Stock Index	USD	SFI	Cash settled	KCBT	51,901	2.917
NYSE Composite	USD	SFI	Cash settled	NYFE	729,231	116.823
South African All Share Index	ZAR	SFI	Cash settled	SAFEX	2,185,672	–
Totals					107,870,007	10,779

Notes: 1. The Face Value has been estimated by multiplying the tick size by the/an estimated average value of the index and as such should be treated as a rough approximation only.

2. If the Face Value is a dash then there was insufficient information to make the estimate.

3. The NZFOE replaced the Forty Index with the NZSE-10 Contract in late 1995.

4. While the LEPO products traded on the ASX and SOFFEX are direct competitors of share futures they are strictly an option and have been included with equity options. This has little impact on any totals as LEPO volume is also very small.

Source: FIA

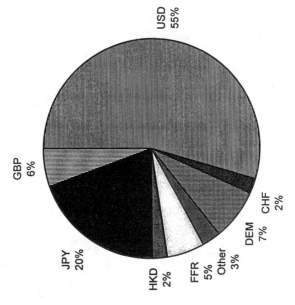

Exhibit 4.37–*continued*
Composition of Equity Futures by Currency

USD 55%

GBP 6%

JPY 20%

HKD 2%

FFR 5%

Other 3%

DEM 7%

CHF 2%

Most statistics on derivatives show that equity derivative turnover is considerably smaller than for interest rate and currency derivatives. While this is in line with lower cash market volume in shares when compared with interest rate and foreign exchange markets, many market commentators suggest that the development of equity derivatives has lagged behind. As a result, it is widely perceived that equity derivatives will be the high growth derivatives areas in the remainder of the 1990s.[28]

In the following sections we will review the pricing and valuation of:

* share price index futures (Section 6.2); and

* individual share futures (Section 6.3).

6.2 Share index futures

6.2.1 General description

A share price index (SPI) future is an exchange-traded contract based on a broad-based share price index. A buyer of an SPI future contract benefits from a rise in the value of the underlying index and loses from a fall in the index; the opposite applies for the seller. SPI futures are not deliverable; at expiry they are cash settled against the underlying index. Over the life of a contract the buyer should receive or pay the difference between the original purchase price and the final settlement price depending on whether the price has moved higher or lower.

For example, if a Standard and Poors (S&P) 500 futures contract is bought at a price of 600 and the price rises to 625, then the buyer will receive the gain equivalent to 25 index points. In this case each index point is worth US$ 500, so the total gain is US$ 2,500 per contract. The seller of this position is in the opposite situation, that is, it is facing a loss of US$ 2,500.

An SPI futures contract is a more esoteric product than other forward contracts we have examined, in that the underlying is not a tradeable security and is not deliverable.[29] Many market observers often describe these products as purely a bet on whether the value of the underlying index will be higher or lower than the traded price on the expiry date, with a payoff linked to how right or wrong you are. In fact, when the S&P 500 contract was launched in 1982 it was widely perceived as a gimmick with little chance of success—by the end of the 1980s its notional daily volume exceeded all of the stocks traded on the New York Stock Exchange (NYSE). Despite its more esoteric nature the SPI future is a pure form of forward contract and its price is determined by the same cost of carry factors as any forward instrument. Further, the description of the SPI as a form of bet is just another way of defining a forward contract and can equally be applied to interest rate and equity futures.

---

28. See Francis, Toy and Whittaker (eds), *The Handbook of Equity Derivatives* (1995).
29. While the profit and loss behaviour of the SPI can be replicated by a portfolio of shares, this portfolio will not have exactly the same characteristics as the SPI future. For example, the SPI future price is based on an index whose value is related to its original base and how long it has been in existence.

As there is no underlying security, it is up to the futures contract specification to convert the "bet on a stock index" into a form which can easily be employed by equity market participants. The basic specification developed in the original US SPI futures contracts has been applied all over the world. The value of each contract is determined by multiplying the traded futures price by a fixed multiple. For example, the multiple in the FTSE 10 is GBP25, so if the futures price is 3,600 then the total contract value will be GBP90,000, and for every 1 index point change in price the value of this contract will change by GBP25. The Appendix to this chapter provides a summary of the contract specifications for listed SPI futures contracts.

6.2.2 Synthetic replication of share price index futures

As with any forward contract, an SPI future can be replicated by using cash instruments. In this case the underlying asset is a portfolio of shares with the same weightings as the underlying index.

Suppose you are a fund manager operating in a share market without an SPI futures contract.[30] You intend to buy shares in three months time but wish to buy at prices prevailing today. The synthetic replication of an SPI futures contract would be to borrow funds to buy the portfolio of shares today and then repay the borrowing in three months time with the funds you intended to buy the shares with. The price of this forward purchase will be given by the current spot price minus the net financing cost of the portfolio. In this case the cost of carry is given by the borrowing cost minus dividends received on the portfolio.

---

30. This is a problem faced in a number of countries—while they may have active share markets, an SPI future does not exist and the only method of obtaining forward exposure to these markets is with a synthetic position.

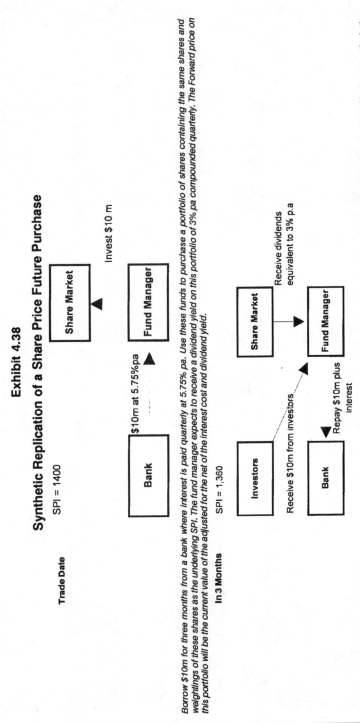

Exhibit 4.38

Synthetic Replication of a Share Price Future Purchase

Borrow $10m for three months from a bank where interest is paid quarterly at 5.75% pa. Use these funds to purchase a portfolio of shares containing the same shares and weightings of these shares as the underlying SPI. The fund manager expects to receive a dividend yield on this portfolio of 3% pa compounded quarterly. The Forward price on this portfolio will be the current value of the adjusted for the net of the interest cost and dividend yield.

After three months the fund manager receives funds from its investors and repays the borrowing. The effective price at which the portfolio was purchased in three months is the original value plus the cost of carry. From the buyers point of view the dividends received effectively reduce the forward purchase price while the interest cost increases the forward cost.

Exhibit 4.38—continued

Forward rate calculations—portfolio

Original cash cost	=	10,000,000
Borrowing interest at three months	=	10m × (1 + 0.0575 × 90 / 360)
		143,750
Dividends received at three months	=	10m × (1 + 0.003 × 90 / 365)
		73,973
Net Cost of carry	=	69,777
Forward Price	=	10,069,777
Forward Premium	=	0.6978%

Forward rate calculations—index

Suppose we wish to express the forward price in terms of the SPI index. Essentially the index is another way of expressing the current value of a portfolio — in this case the value is 1,400 rather than $10 million. The forward price calculation is then exactly the same as for the portfolio and is given by the net cost of carry. Using the premium as a summary of the net cost of carry then the three month forward SPI price will be:

Forward SPI	=	Cash SPI × cost of carry
	=	(1 + 0.006978)
		1,409.77
Cost of carry	=	9.77

Gain or loss on forward purchase

The actual value of the index in three months time is 1,360—the value of the original portfolio has declined by 2.85%. The loss on your forward position is even greater because the cost of carry has increased your effective purchase price.

Loss	=	Index value − Forward purchase value
	=	1360 − 1409.77
	=	49.77 index points or −3.53%

Exhibit 4.38 provides an example of a synthetic purchase of SPI futures. As this example demonstrates, the index can be considered the current value of a portfolio of shares and the forward price of that index is given by the interest cost of financing that portfolio minus the expected dividends to be received on that portfolio.

6.2.2.1 Imperfections: slippage, transaction costs and short selling

Most SPI futures have "broad-based" underlying indices—that is, the index is made up of a large number of stocks, which are intended to replicate the performance of the whole stock market or the stock market leaders.[31] Even in the case of the "leader" type indices the number of shares involved can create logistical execution problems for synthetic replication. For example, executing an order for 20 shares simultaneously, even on an electronic trading network, may be difficult. It is likely that the portfolio will suffer from "slippage" as you wait for the underlying shares to be purchased—so the index value you achieve may differ from the index value at the time you commenced the strategy.

As synthetic replication is the cornerstone of arbitrage activities, this requirement to buy or sell a large number of stocks can lead to arbitrage problems. This is one of the reasons why SPI futures can trade away from "fair market value", or the forward price implied by synthetic replication. If an arbitrage exists it has to be of significant magnitude to overcome the risks of slippage and any other imperfections.

This deviation from fair market value is a characteristic that is most pronounced in less liquid futures markets or underlying share markets which have not developed methods of effectively purchasing portfolios. A common complaint by fund managers in all markets is that unless they hold futures contracts till expiry (and the futures price converges to the cash price), then the hedge provided by the futures contract can over- or under-perform the underlying index due to this mis-pricing.[32] *Exhibit 4.39* shows the deviation from fair value of the world's largest SPI futures contract, the S&P 500, from its inception to 1994. Not surprisingly the mis-pricing was greatest in the contract's early days and during the stock market crash. Since 1992 the discrepancy has fallen significantly, as mechanisms for executing the cash market leg of an arbitrage improved and the market became less one-sided.

---

31. For example, the all ordinaries and all share indexes basically includes all shares with their market weightings while the BEL-20 and Toronto 35 Index are based on the top 20 and 35 shares respectively. The S&P 500, Nikkei 225 and FTSE 100 are somewhere in between.
32. In fact, a motivating factor behind the development of equity swaps was fund managers wishing to obtain a tailor made method of linking their performance to the underlying index without the mis-pricing risk with futures.

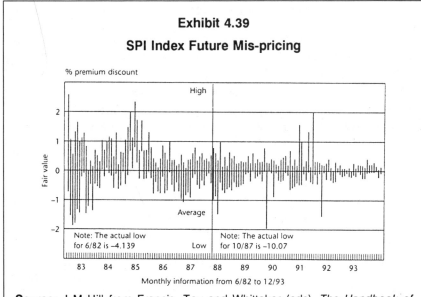

Exhibit 4.39

SPI Index Future Mis-pricing

Note: The actual low for 6/82 is –4.139

Note: The actual low for 10/87 is –10.07

Monthly information from 6/82 to 12/93

Source: J M Hill from Francis, Toy and Whittaker (eds), *The Handbook of Equity Derivatives* (1995).

There are various methods that have been developed for decreasing the risk of slippage including:

1. *Imperfect portfolios*: This involves creating a portfolio with fewer stocks than the index but with a close correlation to the index. The obvious risk in this strategy is that any differences in price movements between the portfolio and the index undermine the arbitrage gains.

2. *Index portfolios*: In some share markets index portfolios are a traded instrument. Typically these are arranged by market makers and transaction costs are higher than for shares.

3. *Portfolio trades in electronic trading networks*: The development of electronic trading networks at futures and stock exchanges has improved the possibility of executing multiple stock buy and sell orders simultaneously—providing there is reasonable liquidity in each market. Many of the activities of so-called ''program'' traders involves a computer program monitoring share price levels, and then if an arbitrage appears automatically generating buy or sell orders for an electronic trading network. The crucial element in this type of operation is liquidity; even if a buy order can be executed instantaneously, unless there is a corresponding sell order at the same price the transaction will not be executed.

Another imperfection in synthetic replication is the transaction cost. As already noted, the transaction costs in stock markets tend to be higher than equity derivatives markets. While this tends to encourage the use of futures and options it also creates an additional cost in synthetic replication and hence arbitrage opportunities. In fact, even in well-developed markets which have introduced the measures above to reduce slippage, some mis-pricing still occurs because of transaction costs. For example, if the share brokerage is 1%, then the futures price must move by more than 1% from fair value to make an arbitrage worthwhile.[33]

Exhibit 4.40 compares the mis-pricing of the Australian all ordinaries index against the transaction costs of executing an arbitrage. As the graph demonstrates, the mis-pricing generally stays with the transaction cost hurdle.

---

33. It is important to note that the mis-pricing tends to be less than the arbitrage gap, because the major arbitrage players are often associated with share market-makers and their cost of execution is usually lower than customer executions.

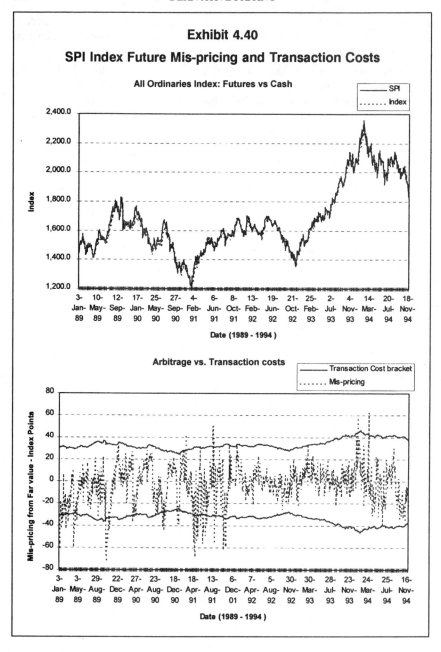

Exhibit 4.40

SPI Index Future Mis-pricing and Transaction Costs

Another important regulatory constraint on the synthetic replication of a sold forward position is any limitation on short selling and stock lending. A synthetic sold position requires the ability to sell a portfolio of stock without owning them and then funding the settlement of this transaction by borrowing the underlying shares till the forward expiry date. Short-selling is viewed suspiciously in many share markets and is occasionally sighted as a factor which leads to share price volatility and manipulation. Accordingly, there can be considerable regulation around short-selling and share lending. In some markets, including Asian "tiger" countries such as Thailand, short-selling is not permitted in any form—meaning that a forward sale cannot be replicated. In these markets the fact that one side of the market is "missing" will undermine the development of an equity derivatives market.

From the point of view of synthetic replication and forward pricing, the greater the restrictions on short-selling and stock lending the more likely is mis-pricing of forward contracts. A market maker which buys a futures contract cannot hedge itself using a synthetic forward purchase and must sell another futures contract. If this tends to force down the price relative to fair value then this mis-pricing is likely to persist, as arbitragers will not be able to take advantage of the discrepancy.

In most markets the restrictions that apply to short-selling are considerably less onerous and consist of the following types of requirements:

1. *Eligible security*: Typically, stock exchanges only wish to allow short-selling in stock where manipulation is difficult and there is considerable liquidity. As a result, for a share to be eligible for short-selling it needs to meet minimum market capitalisation and turnover requirements.[34]

2. *Limit on short-sales*: To avoid manipulation, the cumulative short sales of a particular stock by a group of related companies is limited to some percentage of the outstanding shares on issue (for example, 10% is used by a number of exchanges).

3. *Uptick and downtick rules*: In a number of exchanges a short sale must be identified and it cannot be made at a price lower than the last sale price. This can be referred to as both the uptick and downtick rule. Its effect is to constrain short-selling in a falling market.

These types of restrictions allow short-selling to occur with a minimum of constraints, and they will generally not be a cause of a divergence between futures prices and the fair forward price.[35] If the restrictions are more onerous for the index you wish to price, attempt to quantify the cost to the short-seller and incorporate this in another form of transaction cost.

6.2.3 A model for the share price index futures price

As the synthetic replication discussion in the section above indicates the forward price of an SPI future is based on the generalised price formulae from section 3. In this case the asset is the share and the asset return is the dividend. The funding cost will typically reflect the prevailing wholesale interest rate at which market makers and arbitragers can borrow for the forward term—typically a bank credit money market interest rate.

---

34. For example, in Australia the shares must have a market capitalisation in excess of A$100 million, 50 million shares on issue and a ratio of share turnover to shares on issue in excess of 7 to 8%.

35. The downtick rule may cause some discrepancies where the price is free-falling (such as in a market crash), as the short-sellers will not be permitted to execute transactions. Though, in these conditions, forward mis-pricing is generally the least of anyone's worries!! This can be seen in Exhibit 4.39 by the 10% discount in the futures price to fair value in October 1987.

Our generalised models can specify dividends as a constant percentage per annum or else as a lump sum. While dividends are generally paid at a fixed amount per share regardless of the price of that share, calculating this could become extremely complicated in an SPI future as there are potentially hundreds of dividends paid on different dates. However, the fact that there can be hundreds of stocks means that dividend payments throughout the year and in fact this stream of dividends is more like a continuous yield than a series of lumpy payments. For this reason, broad-based index models typically express dividends in terms rather than cents or pfennig per share.

Fortunately, this task is made somewhat easier by the fact that actual historical dividend yields are provided for most share indexes, and these yields tend to be fairly stable. For SPI futures pricing purposes we need to be able to estimate the expected dividends over the forward period and express it as a yield on the prevailing index price. Many market practitioners simplify this by taking the historical dividend yield and using this in the forward pricing model.

If we incorporate dividends as a per annum yield, the SPI futures pricing model is an extension of the constant income model as follows:

Share Price Index Futures Price (for Broad-Based Index)

Using simple interest, the calculation is as follows

$$F = S \times (1 + (r - q) \times f / D)$$

Where

F	=	Forward SPI price
S	=	Cash or spot price of the share price index
r	=	Interest rate to the forward expiry date
D	=	Day count basis (365 or 360)
f	=	Number of days to the forward expiry date
q	=	Dividend yield expressed as a % per annum on the same day count basis as the interest rate

This same model could be applied to an OTC share price index forward contract.

Exhibit 4.41 provides a spreadsheet model for calculating short-term SPI futures prices as well as any implied arbitrage opportunities. The example shown is for the FTSE-100, while a mis-pricing of 1.81 index points is calculated this represents a tiny proportion of the index (0.04%) and cannot be considered an arbitrage opportunity. In fact, in this example we have set the "arbitrage gate", or minimum mis-pricing requirement at 10 index points—reflecting our anticipated transaction costs.

Exhibit 4.41

Share Price Index Futures Price Calculator

Spreadsheet example—broad-based index only

Field	Cell	Cell: Formula
Inputs		
Underlying SPI index	FTSE-100	
Current Cash Index Price	3680.4000	$E$9 :
Today's Date	01-Dec-95	$E$10 :
Forward Delivery Date	15-Mar-96	$E$11 :
Current Interest Rate (% pa)	6.4000	$E$12 :
Annual Dividend yield (% pa)	4.0000	$E$13 :
Current Futures Price	3704.0000	$E$14 :
Arbitrage "gate" (fut price equiv)	10.0000	$E$15 :
Contract "Tick size"	25.0000	$E$16 :
Outputs		
Implied Futures Price	3705.81	$K$18: =E9* (1 + (E12-E13)*(E11-E10)/36500)
Contract Value	92,600	$K$19: =E16*E14
Cost of Carry (index points)	25.41	$K$20: =E18-E9
Implied Arbitrage Opportunity (Indication only)	25.41	$K$21: =ABS(E18-E14)
Potential Arbitrage	NO ARBITRAGE	$K$22: =IF(E21>E15,IF(E18>E14, "BUY FUTURES, SELL PHYSICAL", "SELL FUTURES, BUY PHYSICAL"), "NO ARBITRAGE")

Exhibit 4.41—*continued*

Pricing sensitivity graphs

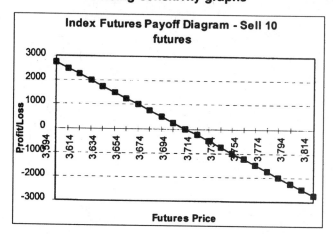

Index Futures Payoff Diagram - Sell 10 futures

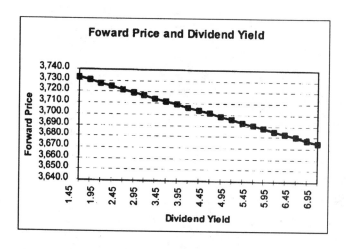

Foward Price and Dividend Yield

While this model provides a simple and generally accurate model there are some features of the model that need explanation:

- funding of margins;
- continuous dividends;
- forward price contango and dividend yield;
- dividend seasonality; and
- leader indexes.

These are discussed in the remainder of this section.

As with all futures contracts there will be a funding impact arising from the initial margins and daily mark-to-market gains and losses. Given most SPI futures' volume is concentrated in the first delivery month, these funding issues can generally be ignored. If, however, you do wish to include the funding effects, then follow the same interest adjustment steps as outlined in Section 4.9.

It is important to realise that this is a simple interest model, so the interest rate has no compounding and is a zero coupon interest rate. As we have noted elsewhere, this means most money market interest rates can be directly entered into the model. However, a feature of most calculated dividend yields is that they are equivalent to a continuous yield. While the difference on the forward price is usually insignificant, it is sometimes necessary to convert the dividend yield from a continuous rate to a simple interest rate appropriate for the period.

The implication of this model is that as long as dividend yields are lower than prevailing interest rates, which is the "usual" situation, then the futures prices will be higher than the cash index price—referred to as futures price "contango". As we noted in the synthetic replication discussion the futures price can mis-price relative to the "fair value" of the forward index and, as the cash value of the index is known as well as the interest rate, then this mis-pricing is often expressed as the expected dividend yield. It is a useful exercise to use this model to solve for the implied dividend yield in futures prices and look for any pricing discrepancies. *Exhibit 4.42* shows the SPI futures price curve for the S&P 500 in December 1995 and calculates the implied dividend yield.[36] The implied dividend yield can be solved by rearranging the SPI future price formula as follows:

$$q = \frac{(1 + r \times f/D - F/S)}{f/D}$$

---

36. This futures model and the implied "dividend yields" exercise can also be applied directly to commodity futures where the shape of the forward price can often be highly volatile. Obviously commodities do not pay dividends, so in the case of a commodity the asset return is relabelled the "convenience yield", which reflects the convenience of owning the asset today as opposed to some date in the future.

Exhibit 4.42

SPI Futures and Implied Dividend Yields

CME S&P 500

Futures Month	Days to Expiry	Futures Price	Interest Rate A/365	Implied Dividend Yield % pa
Cash Index		613.70		
Dec-95	11	614.80	5.893	−0.05%
Mar-96	102	620.40	5.727	1.82%
Jun-96	194	625.45	5.640	2.04%
Sep-96	291	630.20	5.636	2.26%

382
Historical 1 year dividend yield   2%

S&P Futures Curve and Dividend Yield

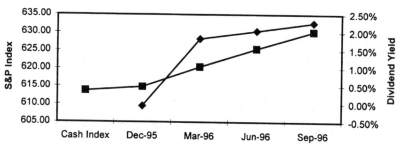

Note: 1.   LIBOR rates used and multiplied by 365/360 to make them comparable to the dividend yield result.

We have assumed that the dividend yield is a constant rate throughout the year. While a convenient assumption, there is often a ''seasonality'' in the payment of dividends. So, while the dividend yield for a whole year may be 4% pa, this may be made up of an effective yield of 4.5% pa in the first half of the year and 3.5% pa in the second half of the year. Depending on where the forward period occurs in these dividend seasons, the dividend yield should be altered. More sophisticated users will actually make forecasts of the dividend yield and take account of this seasonality. The dividend yield calculated in *Exhibit 4.42* tends to show very rough seasonality.

The first contract month has a dividend yield of effectively zero[37]—the market expects no dividend effect on the index in the 11 days remaining to expiry. However, the remaining three delivery months have a dividend yield of approximately 2%, which closely resembles the dividend yield over the

---

37. The exhibit actually calculated in Exhibit 4.42 is −0.05%. The prospect of a negative dividend is highly unlikely—it is purely rounding error if the futures price is reduced by the minimum tradeable unit of 0.05 then the dividend yield is 0.22%, which is the closest the market can get to a zero dividend yield.

past year calculated as a percentage of the prevailing index price. This suggests that there is little seasonality in the S&P 500 dividend yield and/or the market as a whole ignores it.

The assumption of the dividend as yield is reasonable for broad-based indexes, however, for leader style indexes with a small number of shares (for example, 20 or less) this assumption may lead to errors as the dividend stream will start to take on a "lumpy" appearance. In fact, it is possible that for short-term SPI futures on a narrow-based index, there may be no dividend payments at all during the forward period. This model can be used as an estimate, however, the more appropriate solution is to use the individual share price model in section 6.3 to calculate the futures price of each share and then weight these prices using the underlying index weightings.

6.2.4 Valuation of share price index futures

The forward valuation of an SPI future is straightforward, reflecting the difference between the original contract futures price and the prevailing futures price. As with all futures contracts, all profits and losses are paid as they occur—accordingly, there is no difference between present and future values.[38] As a result the present value sensitivities of an SPI future are greater than an equivalent OTC forward by the size of the present value discount over future values.

Determining the risk characteristics of an SPI future follows the same PVBP concepts used previously: calculate the present value impact of a 1 point change in each of the pricing variables—cash SPI, interest rates and dividend yields—as well as the impact of 1 day passing.

6.3 Individual share futures

6.3.1 General description

While *Exhibit 4.37* shows that the volume in individual share futures (ISF) contracts is very small, there has been considerable interest by market participants and exchanges globally in this product over recent years. It is also a product which is worth understanding, as it represents the basic building block for pricing equity options and for narrowly-based index options.

An ISF is an agreement to buy or sell the underlying shares at an agreed date in the future. The buyer of a share future is not entitled to any dividends (that is, the ISF trades "ex-dividend") over the forward period however the share futures will take part in any corporate events such as bonuses, stock splits and rights issues.[39]

At present, ISFs are listed on the Swedish Exchange OM and the Sydney Futures Exchange. The OM contracts have physical delivery while the SFE contracts are currently cash settled. ISFs are directly comparable to the low exercise price option (LEPO) contracts listed on the Australian Stock

---

38. To review the valuation of a futures contract and differences with forwards see the discussion on short-term interest rate futures in section 4.
39. See the chapter on equity options in Martin, op cit n 1, to see the effect of these adjustments.

Exchange Derivatives and SOFFEX markets. LEPOs are call options on a stock with an exercise price close to zero. While LEPOs are strictly an option, the low exercise price makes it very likely that the option will be exercised and the LEPO behaves like a futures contract.

As with SPI futures the advantage of an ISF over cash market transactions is that it provides an exposure to share price movements at a lower transaction cost. *Exhibit 4.43* provides an example comparing the cost of trading shares versus ISFs.

Exhibit 4.43

Comparing ISF and Cash Market Transaction Costs

How could you have used share futures in the March quarter

Undertake a spread trade to capitalise on Newscorp's outperformance

One of the most outstanding events that has occurred in the sharemarket in the first three months of this year has been the outperformance of News Corporation shares against the sharemarket (as illustrated in the chart below).

To benefit from this, a trader could have undertaken a spread trade between NCP Share Futures and SPI futures contracts.

Scenario:

In January, a share trader believed that News Corporation shares would perform the sharemarket during the March quarter. To benefit from this expected scenario, the trader undertakes a spread transaction, by buying News Corporation (NCP) Share Futures contracts and simultaneously selling Share Price Index (SPI) futures and later closing not the futures position by undertaking a reserve spread transaction.

Spread implementation:

On 3 January, NCP Share Futures were trading at $5.12 and the SPI was trading at 1927.

As illustrated in the table, this produces a contract value of $7,270 ($5.12 × 1,420*) for one SPI contract. This means that 6.6 NCP Share Futures contracts will be required for every one SPI contract sold (ie $48,175/$7,270).

The trader must however, allow for the volatility of NCP shares versus the overall market ie, the beta of NCP. At the time of implementing the spread transaction, NCP had a beta of 1.02. Therefore the number of Share Futures contracts required would be less and is calculated as 6.5 (6.6/1.02 − 6.5). The trader therefore buys 6 NCP Share Futures contracts at $5.12 with a value of $43,622 ($5.12 × 1,420 × 6) and simultaneously sells 1 SPI contract at 1927 with a value of $48,175.

Closing the spread:

On 21 March, the trader's expectation comes to fruition, with NCP Share Futures rising $1.49 to $6.61 (an increase of 0.3%). The share trader closes out the futures position by undertaking a reserve spread by selling 6 NCP Shares contracts and buying 1 SPI contract.

Exhibit 4.43—*continued*

News corporation outperforms the market in March quarter

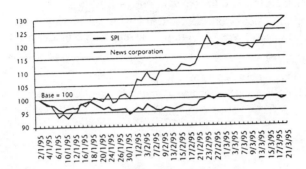

Calculations required		NCP share futures	SPI
Actual prices	3/1/95	$5.12	1927
	21/3/95	$6.61	1932
	% change	+29.1%	+0.3%
Contract value:	@ 3/1/95	$7,270 ($5.12 × 1,420)	$48,175 (1927 × $25)
No of contracts required		6.6 ($48,175/$7,270)	
Adjusted for NCP beta @ 1.02		6.5 (6.2/1.02)	
Nearest whole contracts required		6	

Result of the spread

The trader realises a profit of 149 cents on each NCP Share Futures contract and given that each 1 cent movement = $14.20, this represents a profit of $12,695 (ie 149 cents × $14.20 × 6 contracts). This more than offsets the 5 point loss incurred on the SPI contract, which given each 1 point movement = $25, translates into a loss of $125 (ie 5 points × $25 × 1 contract).

Overall the trader realised a net profit on this spread transaction of $12,570, (before transaction costs). The trader has thus benefited from trading relative performance which has less risk than trading absolute performance.

Source: J S Martin, *Derivative Maths* (IFR, 1996).

6.3.2 A pricing model for individual share futures

The synthetic replication of an ISF is the same as for an SPI future, however, instead of the underlying being a portfolio of shares it is a single stock. The major impact from a pricing point of view is that the dividend payment is "lumpy". Depending on the dividend payment policy of the underlying company, the owner of shares will receive a dividend amount on a quarterly, semi-annual or annual basis. As a result the ISF model requires the magnitude and payment date of any dividends in the forward period.

While companies generally attempt to maintain a fairly stable dividend payment policy, it is dependant on the profitability of the company and its own internal cashflow requirements. In very general terms the dividend payment of an individual company is not as stable as for a broad-based stock index. As a result, more effort is required in estimating the expected dividend on the underlying share in the forward period—a potentially difficult task if the ISF has an expiry date longer than one year.

The ISF pricing behaviour has something in common with a forward bond contract and the same type of "lumpy" asset income model can be applied:

Individual Share Future Pricing Model

Using simple interest and one income payment, the calculation is as follows

$$F = S \times (1 + r_1 \times f_1 / D) - c - (1 + r_2 \times f_2 / D)$$

Where

F	=	Forward price
S	=	Cash share price
r_1	=	Interest rate to the forward expiry date
r_2	=	Interest rate between the dividend "ex" and forward expiry dates
D	=	Day count basis (365 or 360)
f_1	=	Number of days to the forward expiry date
f_2	=	Number of days between the dividend "ex" and forward expiry dates
c	=	Dividend expressed in the same units as the cash price

Note: This model is also applicable to OTC share forwards.

In this model the dividend adjustment takes place on the date the underlying share is deemed "ex-dividend", and shares purchased on that date are no longer entitled to that dividend. The dividend received then earns interest between the "ex" date and the futures expiry date.

As with SPI futures, longer term ISFs should take account of potential funding costs associated with holding the futures position.

Another interesting feature of ISFs is that they have to reflect the pricing behaviour of the underlying share in the case of a dividend payment. A feature of the Australian share market is that for a company which pays the full company tax rate a tax credit, known as a "franking credit", is attached to the dividend payment.

Effectively, the company has pre-paid some tax owing on the share for the share holder. An example provided by the SFE on calculating the effective cost of physically hedging an ISF, incorporating the "franking" credit, is shown in *Exhibit 4.44*.

Exhibit 4.44

Cost of Hedging an SFE ISF

How to calculate the hedge price of SFEs share futures

On 1 May, 1995 assume a futures broker, who is also a market maker received a call from a client interested in buying June BHP Share Futures (going long). As a market maker (which means they also take principal positions), the broker will take the other side of the deal and thus will sell (go short) BHP Share Futures. To protect his/her futures position, the market maker will simultaneously go long on physical BHP shares.

To quote the BHP Share Futures price, the market maker needs to calculate the fair price of the BHP Share Futures contract. There are two pricing formulas used to calculate the fair price of Share Futures, which are based on two standard arbitrage positions that a market maker can establish:

(1) long the underlying shares and short the Share Futures

(2) short the underlying shares and or long the Share Futures

In this particular example, the market maker has established position (1) and therefore will calculate the effective hedge price on the basis of being long shares and short Share Futures using the following formula.

Share futures effective price = (SP + (SP*CC*Days/365)) − DIV + Stamp duty Y. F.C. + T

Whereby

SP	=	PURCHASE PRICE OF THE UNDERLYING SHARES
	=	ON 1 MAY BHP SHARES WERE TRADING AT $18.18
CC	=	THE COST TO CARRY THE POSITION FOR THE DURATION OF THE TRANSACTION EXPRESSED AS AN ANNUAL PERCENTAGE RATE (SIMPLISTICALLY THIS IS THE RISK FREE RATE OF RETURN AVAILABLE IN THE MONEY MARKET FOR AN INVESTMENT WITH A SIMILAR DURATION)
	=	60%
DAYS	=	THE NUMBER OF DAYS THE CAPITAL IS INVESTED
	=	59 DAYS [1 MAY TO 29 JUNE (DAY OF EXPIRY OF JUNE BHP SHARE FUTURES CONTRACT)]
DIV	=	THE AMOUNT OF CASH DIVIDEND WAS PAID ON THE LAST DAY OF THE CONTRACT
STAMP DUTY	=	THIS IS THE 0.3% STATE GOVERNMENT LEVY ON THE PRINCIPAL SHARE VALUE
	=	$18.18 * 0/003 * 2 (ROUND TURN)
	=	$0.11 PER SHARE
F.C.	=	THE AMOUNT OF FRANKING CREDITS ATTACHED TO THE CASH DIVIDEND
	=	GIVEN THE 26 CENT DIVIDEND IS FULLY FRANKED AND THE TAX RATE IS 33%, THE AMOUNT OF FRANKING CREDIT IS:
	=	$0.26 * 0.33/(1 − 0.33) * 100%
	=	$0.1281 PER SHARE
T	=	TOTAL TRANSACTION COST PER SHARE
	=	ARE APPROXIMATELY $0.023 ROUND TURN

Based on the above factors, the "all-up" price for a hedge for the June 1995 BHP Share Futures contract as at 1 May 1995 would thus be:

$18.18 * 6% * 59/365 − 0.26 + 0.11 − 0.1281 + 0.023 − $18.10

As expected the fair value of the June 1995 BHP Share Futures is priced at a discount to the physical shares due to the fact that the cash settlement process means Share Futures do not attract dividends and thus are quoted on an ex-dividend basis.

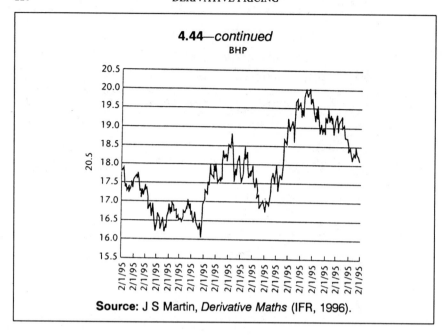

Source: J S Martin, *Derivative Maths* (IFR, 1996).

The valuation requirements of ISFs are the same as for SPI futures.

Chapter 5

Pricing Options

by Satyajit Das

1. OVERVIEW

Option contracts provide the purchaser with the right to either buy from (a call option) or sell to (a put option) the writer of the option at an agreed price (the strike price) a fixed amount of an underlying asset on (European style exercise) or any time before (American style exercise) a pre-nominated date (the expiry date). The purchaser pays the writer a fee (the premium) in return for effectively guaranteeing a maximum purchase price (call option) or minimum sales price (put option). Option valuation is concerned with the determination of the fair value of the premium.

The distinguishing feature of option valuation is the asymmetric nature of the payoff of the instrument. *Exhibit 5.1* sets out the pay-offs of option and forward contracts, highlighting this feature of option contracts.

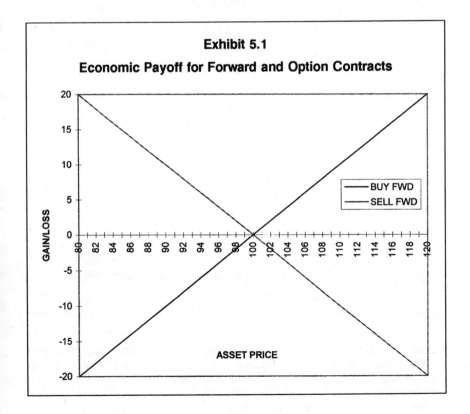

Exhibit 5.1

Economic Payoff for Forward and Option Contracts

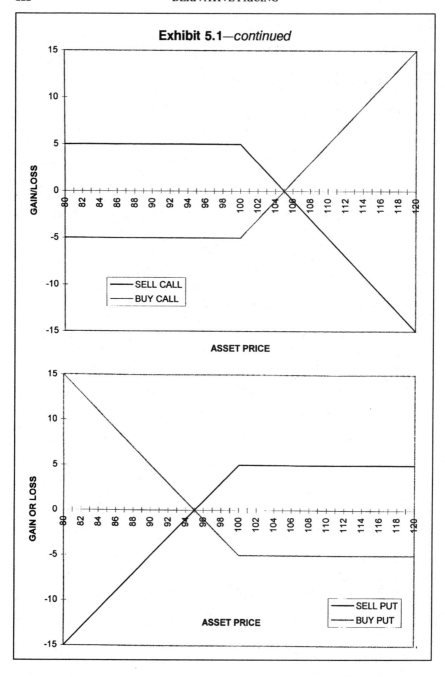

Exhibit 5.1—*continued*

The structure of the payoff dictates that the purchaser has unlimited potential profit with the loss limited to the premium paid. The writer in contrast has a limited gain (the premium received) but an unlimited loss. The structure of the payoffs means the actual value of the option is contingent on the future asset price either at maturity (for a European option) or the *path* or sequence of asset prices between the entry into the option and the option expiry (for an American option because of the risk of early exercise).

This position complicates the process of risk neutral valuation for option instruments. In the case of a forward, the forward instrument payoffs can be replicated by a spot position in the asset, which is then financed or invested. For example, a forward purchase is hedged by a spot purchase of the asset which is the financed through till the forward maturity. This replication is allowed by the *symmetric* nature of the payoffs to the parties entering into the forward. In the case of an option, the asymmetric nature of the payoff dictates both a more complex method of replication of the option position and the determination of the fair value of the instrument.

In this chapter, the process of option valuation is examined. The process of option replication through trading in the spot asset is considered in Chapter 11. Two other aspects of option valuation, the sensitivities of the value of the option to each of the parameters used to value the option and the estimation of volatility, are considered in Chapters 10 and 8 respectively.

The structure of this chapter is as follows:

- the basic concepts of option valuation, including the key determinants of option value, are considered first;
- the concept of risk neutral option value is developed, using a simple probability based framework;
- the approach of risk neutral mathematical option valuation is introduced;
- two approaches to option valuation—the Black-Scholes model and the binomial model—are examined;
- the assumptions underlying the model and their violation in financial markets are then analysed; and
- the adaptations of the basic model for different problems of valuation—early exercise, dividend paying stock as well as the different asset classes—are then detailed.

2. OPTION VALUATION CONCEPTS

2.1 Option pricing nomenclature

The value of an option is known as at maturity because one of the key determinants of option value, namely, the asset price at maturity, is known. As at maturity, the price of an option is usually given as:

Call option

$$P_C = \text{Maximum } [0; S_m - K]$$

Put option

$$P_P = \text{Maximum } [0; K - S_m]$$

Where

P_C = Premium/value of call option

P_P = Premium/value of put option

S_m = Spot price of asset at maturity

K = Strike price of option

The maximum function is necessitated by the choice of option exercise, which rests with the purchaser who will not exercise the option unless it is economically advantageous to do so.

In determining the value of an option, it is usual to distinguish between:

- the *intrinsic value*; and
- the *time value* of an option.

An option's intrinsic value is based on the difference between its exercise price and the current price of the underlying debt instrument. If the option is currently profitable to exercise, it is said to have intrinsic value, that is, a call (put) option has intrinsic value if the current price of the instrument is above (below) the option's exercise price. The intrinsic value is given by:

For a call option

$$S_t - K$$

For a put option

$$K - S_t$$

Where

S_t = Spot price at time t

The concept of intrinsic value requires additional clarification in the context of the applicable exercise rules. In the case of a European option, as exercise is only permitted as at maturity, intrinsic value prior to that date requires the strike price to be discounted to the relevant date. This is usually given as $Ke^{-rf.t}$ (that is, the strike price discounted back to the date of valuation at the continuously compounded risk free rate). The discounted strike price is then compared to the spot price of the asset. To a degree the concept of an intrinsic value of a European option prior to maturity is redundant as the option is incapable of being exercised prior to maturity. The computation of the *theoretical* intrinsic value of the European option prior to maturity is only relevant as a means for identifying the *sources* of value for the option.

In the case of an American option where the possibility of early exercise is present and permissible, the exercise price does not need to be discounted as it will be paid in full at the date of exercise.

Whether or not the option has intrinsic value, it may have time value. Time value is defined as:

Option Premium = Intrinsic Value + Time Value

Therefore

Time Value = Option Premium − Intrinsic Value

The time value of the option reflects the amount buyers are willing to pay for the possibility that, at some time prior to expiration, the option may become profitable to exercise.

The values identified are subject to a number of value constraints:

Option Premium ≥ 0

Intrinsic Value ≥ 0

Time Value ≥ 0

Three other option valuation terms merit comment:

- in-the-money;
- at-the-money; and
- out-of-the-money.

It is customary for market participants to refer to particular options as belonging to one of the three groups. An option with an exercise price at or close to the current market price of the underlying security is said to be at-the-money. An option with intrinsic value is referred to as being in-the-money, while an out-of-the-money option is one with no intrinsic value, but presumably with some time value.

2.2 Factors affecting option values

The fundamental direct determinants of option value include:

1. the current price of the underlying asset (S);
2. the exercise price of the option (K);
3. interest rates (Rf);
4. the time to expiry (T); and
5. the volatility of prices on the underlying asset (σ).

Other factors affecting option valuation include the type of option (that is, whether the option is American or European) as well as payouts from holding the underlying instrument.

The general effect of each of the five major relevant variables on the value of an option (where all other variables are held constant) is summarised in *Exhibit 5.2*.

Exhibit 5.2

Factors Affecting Option Valuation

Factor	Effect of increase in factor on value of	
	Call	Put
Strike price	Decrease	Increase
Spot price	Increase	Decrease
Interest rate	Increase	Decrease
Time to expiry	Increase	Increase
Volatility	Increase	Increase

The effect of changes in the spot price of the instrument, option strike prices, and time to expiry on the pricing of options are relatively easily understood.

In the case of a call option, the higher the price of the underlying instrument, the higher the intrinsic value of the option if it is in-the-money and hence the higher the premium. If the call is out-of-the-money, then the higher the underlying instrument's price the greater the probability that it will be possible to exercise the call at a profit and hence the higher the time value, or premium, of the option. In the case of put options, the reverse will apply.

The impact of changes in exercise price is somewhat similar. For an in-the-money call option the lower the exercise price, the higher the intrinsic value, while for an out-of-the-money call the lower the exercise price the greater the probability of profitable exercise and hence the higher the time value. A similar but opposite logic applies in the case of put options.

The impact of time to expiration and option valuation is predicated on the fact that the longer an option has to run, the greater the probability that it will be possible to exercise the option profitably, hence the greater the time value of the option.

The impact of volatility derives from the fact that the greater the expected movement in the price of the underlying instrument, the greater the probability that the option can be exercised at a profit and hence the more valuable the option or its time value. In essence, the higher the volatility, the greater the likelihood that the asset will either do very well or very poorly, which is reflected in the price of the option.

The impact of interest rates is less clear intuitively. The role of interest rates in the determination of option premiums is complex and varies from one type of option to another. In general, however, the higher the interest rate, the lower the *present value* of the exercise price the call buyer has contracted to pay in the event of exercise. In essence, a call option can be thought of as the right to buy the underlying asset at the discounted value of the exercise price. Consequently, the greater the degree of discount the more valuable is the right, hence, as interest rates increase and the degree of discount increases commensurately, the corresponding option value increases. In fact, a higher interest rate has a similar influence to that of a lower exercise price. A similar but opposite logic applies in the case of a put option. The higher interest rate decreases the value of the put option as it reduces the current (present valued or discounted) value of the exercise price that the buyer has contracted to receive.

An alternative way of looking at the impact of changes in interest rates is to view the option as a means for replicating the exposure to the asset. For example, a call option provides exposure to the asset in a manner analogous to a purchase of the asset. If interest rates increase, than the call option increases in attractiveness as a means of replicating the asset exposure. This is because the lower cash outlay entailed by the premium means that the cost (in forgone interest) is lower if the option is utilised. This means that the price of the call option is bid up. In the case of a put option, such a transaction can be viewed as an alternative to selling the asset. In this case an increase in interest rates reduces the premium of a put option as the proceeds of the sale are not received until the option is exercised and entails higher opportunity costs where interest rates increase. Decreases in interest rates have a similar impact but in reverse.

3. RISK NEUTRAL OPTION VALUATION

The development of a formal model for the valuation of options requires an understanding of the concept of risk neutral valuation techniques. The application of risk neutral valuation arguments is identical to that used in the context of the valuation of forward contracts.

The risk neutral approach is predicated on two central premises:

1. The value of any option must be equal to the expected payoffs under the instrument.

2. The value of the option can be determined by replicating the payoff or economic profile of an option using a position in the underlying asset and cash. This means that a short (long) position in the option can be hedged by the offsetting position in the asset and cash to create a riskless portfolio which should return the risk-free rate of interest.

The risk neutral valuation approach allows determination of the value of an option by arbitrage arguments which, very importantly, implies that the value of the option can be determined independent of risk preferences of the parties to the transaction as well as any expectations about the *direction* of underlying asset prices.

As in the case of pricing of forward contracts, the creation of this risk neutral portfolio to replicate the payoff profile of the derivative allows the value of the derivative instrument to be determined, because both the asset and the derivative contract have the same value driver—the changes in the price of the underlying asset.

The use of risk neutrality is central to both the valuation and trading or synthetic creation of options. In this chapter, the concept of risk neutrality is used to derive the value of the option contract. The process of using the concept of risk neutrality to synthesise option instruments is discussed in Chapter 11.

4. A BASIC OPTION PRICING MODEL

Within the framework of risk neutrality outlined, a very simple intuitive option pricing model can be derived. This model, in fact, exhibits all the characteristics and dimensions of option valuation generally.

The central unknown in valuing an option is the *forward* asset price as of the expiry date (this assumes a European style exercise). As with any other unknown variable in financial valuation, determination of value of the underlying contract is feasible by estimating the range of possible values and the probabilities attaching to individual possible outcomes.

Exhibit 5.3 sets out a basic option pricing model utilising this fundamental approach.

Exhibit 5.3

Simple Option Pricing Model

Assume the following scenario:

Current Spot Price of Asset (S) = 100

1 year Risk Free Interest Rate (Rf) = 10.00% pa

This implies an arbitrage free forward of 110 assuming that the asset does not pay any income. The *actual* spot price of the asset in one year's time is not known but is expected to be in the range set out below and the probability of the asset price being at any particular level is also specified:

Expected Asset Price In 1 Year	Probability (%)
90	10
100	20
110	40
120	20
130	10

The above table assigns a designated probability to all possible forward asset price states (effectively, the assumed distribution of forward asset prices).

This data can now be utilised to price the following call option:

K = 110

T = 1 year

Rf = 10.00% pa

The fair value of the option today should consistent with the risk neutral argument be the expected payoff of the option contract which is as follows:

Expected Asset Price In 1 Year	Probability (%)	Value of Call Option	Probability Adjusted Expected Value of Call Option
90	10	0	0
100	20	0	0
110	40	0	0
120	20	10	2
130	10	20	2
		Total	4

The expected value of the call option in this case is 4 at maturity of the option which must be discounted back at 10.00% pa for 1 year to provide the present value of the option. The current value of the option is 3.64.

The basic model requires, consistent with all option valuation models, the following input parameters:

1. the possible values or prices that can be assumed by the underlying asset as at option expiry;

2. the probabilities attaching to the possible values that can be assumed by the asset as at option expiry; and

3. the risk free interest rate to allow discounting of the expected values of the option.

In the basic option pricing model described, the asset price as at the forward date is restricted to five possible values. In reality, for a real world transaction, the range of possible values is large and theoretically infinite, although in reality many of the value states are unlikely or have very low probabilities. However, the requirement dictated by this model for both identification of each of the possible asset price states and the probability attaching to each possible asset price state is tedious.

In practice, the process of generating the possible forward asset prices and their probabilities is simplified by the introduction of an assumed asset price distribution.

5. ASSET PRICE DISTRIBUTIONS

The concept of a distribution of forward prices is central to option pricing theory. The seminal work of Black and Scholes in their path-breaking option pricing model is as much about their seminal work in simplifying the generation of the forward asset price as it is about the valuation of options.

Black and Scholes introduces a breathtakingly simple but robust assumption in generating the forward asset price distribution. In effect, they assumed that if the spot price of the asset and the *distribution of asset price changes (the asset returns)* are known, then it would be possible to determine the complete distribution of forward asset prices. To generate the distribution of asset price changes Black and Scholes assumed that the stock prices follow a process which is termed a continuous *random walk*. The introduction of this assumption means that the changes in the price of or continuously compounded returns on the underlying asset are normally distributed and that the forward asset price is lognormally distributed.

The introduction of these assumptions has a number of very significant implications. The forward asset prices and the probabilities of a particular asset price can now be calculated utilising the characteristics of a normal distribution. The major features of a normal distribution is that the *complete* distribution of asset prices and probabilities can be expressed in terms of two variables:

- the mean expected return (μ); and

- the standard deviation of the expected return (σ).

In the Black-Scholes approach, the mean expected return is taken to be the risk free rate of interest. In effect, the price of the underlying asset is expected to drift towards the forward price. The standard deviation of the expected return which equates to the volatility of asset prices (identified above as a key determinant of option values) is defined to be the standard deviation of the logarithmic returns on the underlying asset to the maturity of the option. The estimation of volatility is a particularly vexed issue and is dealt with in detail separately in Chapter 8. In the remainder of this chapter, volatility is assumed to be a known term.

The advantage of utilising a normal distribution is evident in that the two variables identified can also be used to infer the probability of the asset price taking on particular values. For example, once the mean and standard deviation are known, the following probabilities are also known:

- 67% probability that the forward asset price will be between the mean (the forward price) ± 1 s;

- 95% probability that the forward asset price will be between the mean (the forward price) ± 2 s; and

- 99% probability that the forward asset price will be between the mean (the forward price) ± 3 s.

The introduction of the concept of log normality should also be explained. *Exhibit 5.4* sets out the comparative shape of a normal as against lognormal distribution.

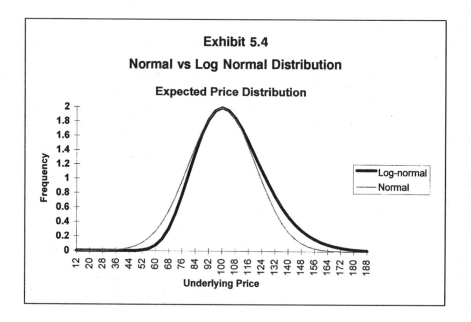

The lognormal distribution differs from the symmetrical normal distribution in that it exhibits a skew with its mean, median and mode all differing from that in a normal distribution. The major advantage of using a lognormal distribution is that a lognormally distributed variable can only take positive values (between zero and infinity) in contrast to a normal distribution which allows variables to take on both positive and negative values.

The introduction of the assumptions allows the generation of a *complete distribution* of forward asset prices and their probabilities. This in turn allows *all* possible positive intrinsic values of option as at maturity to be generated. The intrinsic values are then weighted by their respective probabilities to determine the expected value of the option, which is then discounted to the present to calculate the option's fair value.

The introduction of the concept of the distribution of forward asset prices transforms the problem of option valuation in several respects:

- it makes the valuation of the option independent of the *direction* of asset price movements; and

- it converts the problem of option valuation into a problem of estimation of the *volatility* of the returns on the asset (more particularly, the annualised standard deviation of the log of the price changes).

The introduction of the asset price distribution assumption allows the development of mathematical option pricing models.

6. OPTION PRICING THEORY

6.1 Approaches to mathematical option pricing

Mathematical option pricing models seek to calculate the price of particular options, utilising the identified fundamental determinants of option value and incorporating these within a defined formalised mathematical framework. The technological approach of formal valuation is the same regardless of the type of option being evaluated, whether it be an option on commodities, equity stock or market index currencies, or a debt instrument as well as futures contracts on each of these assets. The fundamental approach also extends to non-standard or exotic options. The approach to valuation of these types of instruments is discussed in Chapter 7.

The development of mathematical option pricing models requires the following distinct steps:

1. specific assumptions as to market structure and behaviour of the underlying instrument;

2. definition of certain arbitrage boundaries on the potential value of the option; and

3. derivation of a pricing solution.

6.2 Market assumptions

Mathematical option pricing models can be developed to synthesise the many factors which affect the option premium within identified arbitrage boundaries. In order to develop such mathematical option pricing models, it is necessary to make a number of restrictive assumptions, including:

- asset trading is continuous, with all asset prices following continuous and stationary stochastic processes;

- asset has no intermediate cash flows (for example, dividends, interest et cetera);

- the asset price moves around in a continuously random manner;

- the distribution of the asset's return is log normal;

- the variance of the return distribution is constant over the asset's life;

- the risk free rate of interest is constant over the option's life;

- the option is European;

- no restrictions or costs of short selling; and

- no taxes or transaction costs.

Most of these assumptions are self-explanatory and are consistent with efficient capital market theory. Stochastic process refers to the evolution of asset prices through time modelled as random, characterised by continuous series of price changes governed by the laws of probability as prescribed. By continuous processes, it is usually implied that the price of the underlying asset can vary over time but does not have discontinuities or jumps, that is, the price movement over time of the asset could be graphed without lifting the pen from the paper.

The stochastic process, as assumed, is one that is determined the same way for all time periods of equal length. Specifically, the traditional approach to option valuation assumes that the price of the underlying asset has a particular type of probability distribution, assumed to be a log normal distribution. It is also assumed that the standard deviation of this distribution is constant over time.

6.3 Boundary conditions

Mathematical option pricing requires identification of certain boundaries that can be placed on the values of options based on arbitrage considerations. The concept of arbitrage in this context relies upon dominance whereby a portfolio of assets is said to dominate another portfolio if, for the same cost, it offers a return that will, at least, be the same. The underlying assumption, in this context, is that if these boundary conditions are breached, arbitrage activity would force the prices of the underlying assets and options within the arbitrage boundaries as arbitragers would enter into transactions designed to take advantage of riskless profit opportunities.

Exhibit 5.5 sets out the major boundary conditions on the price of an option. In the interest of clarity, in this section, the boundary conditions to option value are stated with reference to generalised assets. There are nine major arbitrage boundaries discussed in *Exhibit 5.5*. Put-call parity for options is a special arbitrage condition, which is discussed below.

Exhibit 5.5

Boundary Restrictions on the Value of an Option*

Notation

The following notation is used in outlining the boundary conditions:

S = asset price

Sm = asset price at maturity

K = strike price

T = time to maturity

Rf = risk free interest rate

σ = volatility of returns from asset

P_{ca} = price of American call

P_{ce} = price of European call

P_{pa} = price of American put

P_{pe} = price of European put

$PV(K)$ = present value of amount K (that is, $Ke^{-Rf.T}$)

C = Intermediate cash flow on asset

Arbitrage Boundaries

$$P_{ce} \text{ or } P_{ca} \geq 0$$
$$P_{pe} \text{ or } P_{pa} \geq 0$$

This states that the value of an option is greater than or equal to 0. Option exercise is voluntary, consequently, purchasers will never exercise an option if the value of the option entails a loss and therefore option prices cannot take on negative values.

At maturity of the option:

$$P_{ce} \text{ or } P_{ca} = 0 \text{ or S-K}$$
$$P_{pe} \text{ or } P_{pa} = 0 \text{ or K-S}$$

The value of a call or put option will be either 0 or its intrinsic value at maturity. If this conditions is not satisfied, arbitrage opportunities exist. For example, if a call at maturity sells for less than S-K, arbitragers could lock in a profit by borrowing enough to purchase the call and exercising it immediately making a riskless profit after paying back the loan.

Prior to maturity of the option:

$$P_{ca} \geq 0 \text{ or S-K}$$
$$P_{pa} \geq 0 \text{ or K-S}$$

If at any time prior to maturity, an American option contract sells for less than its intrinsic value, an arbitrage opportunity exists to purchase the option and exercise immediately while buying or selling the physical asset to lock in a riskless profit.

Exhibit 5.5—continued

$$P_{ca} \geq P_{ce}$$
$$P_{pa} \geq P_{pe}$$

An American option cannot sell for a premium value less than an identical European option. The American style of option confers all the benefits of the European contract plus the capacity of early exercise.

For an asset which has no intermediate cash flow, it can be economically demonstrated that it is superior to sell the option prior to maturity rather than being exercised early.

The validity for this arbitrage condition can be established by constructing the following two portfolios:

1. Buy a European call for P_{ce} and invest PV of strike price PV(K).
2. Buy S.

The payoff from these two portfolios as at maturity of the options is:

Portfolio Value	Out-of-the-money (Sm < K)	In-the-money (Sm ≥ K)
P_{ce} + PV(K)	0 + K	(Sm − K) + K
S	Sm	Sm

At maturity, the portfolio consisting of the European call and the present value of the strike price is never worth less than the asset, so the current cost of the first portfolio can never be less than that of the second. This implies that an American call option will usually never be exercised prior to maturity as the investor would only receive the intrinsic value of the option (S-K), which is less than S-Ke$^{-Rf.T}$ for any positive interest rate. Consequently, a rational investor will always sell a call option to somebody else rather than exercise the option.

For an asset which has intermediate cash flows, it can be economically demonstrated that early exercise is possible.

The proof of this strategy can be established by constructing portfolios which are similar to above. The two portfolios are as follows:

1. Buy a European call for P_{ce} and invest PV of strike price PV(K +C) where C is the intermediate cash flow from holding the asset.
2. Buy S.

The payoff from these two portfolios is set out below as at maturity of the options is:

Portfolio Value	Out-of-the-money (Sm < K)	In-the-money (Sm ≥ K)
P_{ce} + PV(K + C)	0 + K + C	(Sm − K) + K + C
S	Sm + C	Sm + C

The payout table indicates that at maturity the portfolio of the call and cash never pays less than the second portfolio consisting of the stock. The first portfolio gives a higher return when the option expires out-of-the-money. Consequently, the first portfolio cannot sell for less than the second portfolio. This means that whenever a European call is in-the-money prior to maturity the lowest value it can trade for will be equal to the stock price minus the investment required to receive an amount equal to the strike price plus any intermediate cash flow at maturity; that is, S − PV (K + C). The lower limit on the value of the European call must be the lower limit on an American option's value.

This implies an optimal exercise policy for an American option on the asset with intermediate cash flows. If the lower limit on the call's value [S − PV (K + C)] is greater than the amount received by exercising (S − K), then it is better to sell than exercise. However, if [S − PV (K + C)] is less than (S − K), then the American call should be exercised rather than sold prior to maturity.

Exhibit 5.5—continued

An American call should therefore only be exercised early where the discounted value of the strike price and intermediate cash flows are greater than the strike price. In essence, it is PV(C) that determines whether the option is sold or exercised. This implies that an American option where the underlying asset has high intermediate cash flows is more likely to be exercised early.

$$P_{ce} \text{ or } P_{ca} \leq S$$
$$P_{pe} \text{ or } P_{pa} \leq S$$

This can be illustrated with an example. A call option cannot be worth more than the underlying asset because if the option were worth more than the asset, then a riskless arbitrage profit could be made by writing a call and using the proceeds to buy the asset. If the call is exercised, the asset can be delivered and the strike price received in return, while if the call is unexercised at maturity the asset which has a positive value will be held, thereby allowing the arbitrager to make a positive profit without incurring any risk.

P_{ce} or P_{ca} must be worth less than an identical option with a lower exercise price; and P_{pe} or P_{pa} must be worth less than an identical option with a higher exercise price.

In this case, the call with the low exercise price offers a greater chance of being in-the-money; consequently, it cannot sell for a price which is lower than an option which has less chance of being in-the-money. The reverse is true for put options.

P_{ce} or P_{ca} or P_{pe} or P_{pa} cannot be worth less than an identical option with a shorter time to maturity.

Intuitively, the longer the maturity on the option, the greater the opportunity for there to be a sufficiently large change in the asset price to push the option into the money. Consequently, an option with a longer maturity cannot sell for less than an equivalent option with a shorter maturity. If this condition is violated, an arbitrage can be set up whereby the arbitrager writes the shorter-dated option while purchasing the option with the longer maturity to lock in a riskless arbitrage profit.

* The description of option boundary conditions draws on Ian Rowley, "Pricing Options Using the Black-Scholes Model" (1987) (May) *Euromoney Corporate Finance* 108.

6.4 Put-call parity

Put-call parity which defines the relationship between the price of a European call option and a European put option with the same exercise price and time to expiration is an additional arbitrage boundary on option values. Utilising the same notation as that used previously, put-call parity can be stated as follows:

$$P_{ce} + PV(K) = P_{pe} + S$$

This implies that buying a call and investing PV of K is identical to buying a put and buying the asset.

The proof of this relationship can be established by setting up two portfolios:

1. buy a European call for premium P_{ce} and invest PV(K); and
2. buy a European put for premium P_{pe} and buy the asset for S.

The payoffs on the two portfolios at maturity are as follows:

Portfolio value	Out-of-the-money (Sm < K)	In-the-money (Sm > K)
P_{ce} + PV(K) P_{pe} + S	0 + K (K − Sm) + Sm	(Sm − K) + K 0 + Sm

At maturity, the two portfolios are equal irrespective of whether the option expires in or out-of-the-money.

The put-call parity condition can be restated as follows:

Synthetic call (reversal)

$$P_{ce} = P_{pe} + S - PV(K)$$

Synthetic put (conversion)

$$P_{pe} = P_{ce} - S + PV(K)$$

Long asset/forward

$$S = P_{ce} - P_{pe} + PV(K)$$

Short asset/forward

$$-S = P_{pe} - P_{ce} - PV(K)$$

For European options, arbitrage possibilities will exist if the put-call parity conditions are not fulfilled. An example of put-call parity arbitrage is set out in *Exhibit 5.6*.

Exhibit 5.6

Put-Call Parity Arbitrage

Assume that the a forward on an asset is trading for 1 month forward at 86.14/86.15. Call options on the contract with strike price 86.00 on the contract are trading at 0.28/0.33. Put options with an identical strike price are trading at 0.02/0.07. Both options are on the forward contract. In these circumstances, it is possible to create a synthetic 86.00 call at less than 0.28 as follows:

- buy 86.00 put at 0.07;
- buy forward at 86.15; and
- sell 86.00 call at 0.28.

This transaction effectively creates a call at less than the 0.28 received. This can be proved as follows: the sold call and the bought put are equivalent to a synthetic short forward position at a price of 86.00. The position creates a net cash flow to the grantor of 0.21. Of the 0.21, 0.15 is lost through the bought forward position at 86.15 which is above the synthetic short price of 86.000. However, the forward loss of 0.15 is more than offset by the 0.21 gain on the option.

Where the underlying asset pays out a cash flow of C, put-call parity can be restated as:

$$P_{ce} + PV(K + C) = P_{pe} + S$$

It is important to note that the put-call parity theorem is only valid for European options. Synthetic positions for American options are not always pure. For example, if S decreases and an American put is exercised, then you would lose the difference between K and S immediately, not at the forward date.

This means that put-call parity for American options can be stated as follows:[1]

$$P_{ca} - S + PV(K) < P_{pa} < P_{ca} - S + K$$

6.5 The concept of a riskless hedge

The derivation of the mathematical option pricing model also requires understanding of the concept of a riskless hedge. A riskless portfolio by definition consists of an asset and a corresponding option held in proportion to the prescribed hedge ratio, continuously adjusted, whereby the portfolio is perfectly hedged against movements in asset prices as changes in the call price and the asset price are mutually offsetting.

Certain riskless portfolio positions are set out below:

Position	Hedge
long position in calls	short Δ assets for each call held
short position in calls	long Δ assets for each call sold
long position in puts	long Δ assets for each put held
short position in puts	short Δ assets for each put sold

Delta $(\Delta)^2$ refers to the sensitivity of the option premium to changes in the asset price.

Utilising the constructs of portfolio theory or the capital asset pricing model, it can be predicted that a riskless portfolio should earn no more than a risk free rate of return. It is important to note that outside the context of this riskless hedge construct, the values derived by mathematical option pricing models are not meaningful.

Mathematical option pricing models, such as Black-Scholes, utilise the concept of the riskless hedge to set up portfolios of the asset and cash which are managed dynamically over time to replicate the payoff of an option. It is then possible to utilise the techniques of stochastic calculus to derive a mathematical solution to the valuation problem.

7. THE BLACK-SCHOLES OPTION PRICING MODEL

Black and Scholes[3] were the first to provide a close form solution for the valuation of European call options. The mathematical derivation of the Black-Scholes Option Pricing Model is beyond the mathematical capabilities assumed for this Chapter. A detailed derivation of Black-Scholes is set out in Chapter 19.

1. For a mathematical proof see John C Hull, *Introduction to Futures and Options Markets* (Second edition, Prentice Hall, Englewood Cliffs, NJ, 1995), pp 210-218.
2. See detailed discussion in Chapter 10.
3. Fischer Black and Myron Scholes, "The Pricing of Options and Corporate Liabilities" (1973) 81 *Journal of Political Economy* 637.

Black-Scholes option pricing model is usually specified as follows:

$$P_{ce} = S. N(d1) - K e^{-Rf.T} . N(d2)$$

Where

$d1 = [\ln (S/ K) + (Rf + \sigma^2/ 2) T] / \sigma \sqrt{T}$

$d2 = [\ln (S/ K) + (Rf - \sigma^2/ 2) T] / \sigma \sqrt{T}$

$\quad = d1 - \sigma \sqrt{T}$

A number of aspects of the formula require explanation:

- N (d1) and N (d2) are cumulative normal distribution functions for d1 and d2. *Exhibit 5.7* sets out the concept of the cumulative normal distribution function diagrammatically. In the diagram, the area given is the probability that a variable with a normal distribution will be less than d1;

- ln is the logarithm of the relevant number; and

- $Ke^{-Rf.T}$ is the amount of cash needed to be invested over period or time T at a continuously compounded interest rate of Rf in order to receive K at maturity.

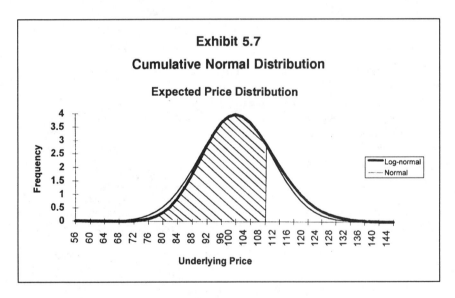

The price of a European put option can be derived by utilising put-call parity:

$$P_{pe} = K e^{-Rf.T} . N(- d2) - S. N(- d1)$$

Two aspects of the Black-Scholes' Option Pricing Model require comment:

1. The calculation of the cumulative normal distribution function [N(d)] is undertaken either utilising a N(d) table or directly utilising numerical procedures. *Appendix A* to this chapter sets out the methodology for calculating cumulative normal distribution function.

2. The model requires specification of the volatility of prices on the underlying instrument (parameter σ in the above equation). Techniques

for the estimation of volatility, including discussion of the various issues thereto, is detailed in Chapters 8 and 9.

Exhibit 5.8 sets out an example of utilising the Black and Scholes Option Pricing Model to calculate the price of an option.

Exhibit 5.8

Using Black-Scholes Option Pricing Model

Calculate the price for a call and put option on an asset based on the following information:

$S = 105.00$

$K = 100.00$

$T =$ six months (0.5 yrs)

$RF = 10\%$ pa (0.10)

$\sigma = 20\%$ (0.20)

Using the above inputs, we can compute the call option price as follows:

$$d1 = [\ln (105/100) + (0.1 + 0.20^2/2) \, 0.5]$$

$$= 0.769$$

$$d2 = 0.769\text{-}0.141 = 0.628$$

Using the normal cumulative distribution table:

$$N(0.769) = 0.7791$$

$$N(0.628) = 0.7349$$

Therefore, the call option value is:

$$P_{ce} = 105 \times 0.7791 - 100 \times e^{-0.10 \times 0.50} \times 0.7349$$

$$= 11.900$$

The value of the call option is $11.90 or 11.33% of Asset Price.

The value of the call can be dissected as follows:

$$\text{Intrinsic value} = 105 - 100 \times e^{-0.10 \times 0.50} = 9.877$$

$$\text{Time value} = 11.90\text{-}9.877 = 2.023$$

The corresponding put option value is:

$$N(-0.769) = 0.2209$$

$$N(-0.628) = 0.2651$$

$$P_{pe} = 100 \times e^{-0.10 \times 0.50} \times 0.2651 - 105 \times 0.2209$$

$$= 2.023$$

The value of the put option is $2.023 or 1.9261% of asset price. The put value is all time value as the option is out-of-the money.

The actual components of the formula show how the value of the option is determined by the combination of asset and borrowing that replicates the payoff profile of an option.

The formula actually represents the replication of the call option through investment in the asset and borrowing to finance the position with the position being adjusted over time in line with asset price movements.

- The term S. N (d1) represents the amount of asset which must be held and financed. The term N (d1) is effectively the delta of the option.

- The term $Ke^{-Rf.T}$ represents the amount that must be borrowed to finance the holding of the asset.
- The actual premium represents the difference between the terms which ensures cash neutrality of the portfolio.

Intuitively, assuming physical settlement of the option, if the option is exercised, then the seller will have to transfer to the buyer assets valued at Sm. In effect, the strike price K will need to be satisfied through delivery of assets valued at Sm. This means that the S.N (d1) is, intuitively, the present value of receiving the asset in the event of exercise. The second term—$Ke^{-Rf.T}$ would under this approach represent the present value cost of the strike price in the event of exercise. In a risk neutral world, if the option is likely to be exercised, then the difference between the two terms would represent the expected payout of the option which in turn would equate to the premium to render the transaction a zero return transaction.

This is evidenced by the fact that if the option is deep in-the-money then both N(d1) and N(d2) approach 1. This means that the call value approaches $S - Ke^{-Rf.T}$. Similarly, as the option approaches expiry, that is, T approaches 0, both N(d1) and N(d2) approach 1 and $e^{-Rf.T}$ also approaches 1. This means that the call value approaches $S - K$.

8. BINOMIAL OPTION PRICING MODEL

8.1 Concept

The binomial option pricing model utilises an identical logical approach to Black-Scholes. However, in contrast to Black-Scholes, the binomial approach assumes that the security price obeys a binomial generating process. The binomial approach also assumes that the option cannot or will not be exercised prior to expiration (that is, the option is European).

The valuation process begins by considering the possibility that the price can move up or down over a given period by a given amount. This enables calculation of the value of the call option at expiration of the relevant period (which is always the greater of zero or the price of the instrument minus the exercise price). The riskless hedge technique starts at expiration and works backwards in time to the current period for a portfolio consisting of the physical security sold short or one sold futures contract on the relevant asset and one bought call option on the relevant asset.

Since the portfolio is riskless, it, consistent with Black-Scholes, must return the risk free rate of return over the relevant period. The derivation of the value of the call option using this approach is predicated on the fact that the call option must be priced so that the risk free hedge earns exactly the risk free rate of return.

Exhibit 5.9 sets out a simple example of a 1 step binomial model.

Exhibit 5.9

One Step Binomial Option Pricing Model

In order to illustrate the logic of a binomial option pricing model, consider the following example:

$$S = 100$$

The asset price is expected to increase or decrease by 10% to 110 or 90 respectively over the next year. Assume a call option utilising the following parameters:

$$S = 105$$
$$T = 1 \text{ year}$$
$$Rf = 10\% \text{ pa}$$

The value of the call option can be ascertained based on the expected increase or decrease in the asset price as follows:

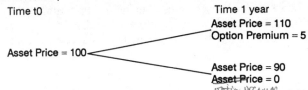

Time t0

Time 1 year

Asset Price = 110
Option Premium = 5

Asset Price = 100

Asset Price = 90
Asset Price = 0

To determine the fair value of the option it is necessary to create a riskless hedge, entailing investment in the asset to offset the position in the call, such that the portfolio value is known with certainty *irrespective of whether the aset price increases or decreases*.

The construction of the riskless portfolio requires the following steps:

1. Assume the position consists of 1 sold call which is offset by holding Δ units of the asset.

2. The value of Δ is determined on the basis that it will be equate to a value which makes the portfolio riskless. This entails that the value of portfolio will be the same for both an increase and a decrease in the asset price. Therefore:

$$110 \Delta - 5 = 90 \Delta$$
$$\Delta = 0.25$$

This means that to hedge or replicate 1 sold call it would be necessary to hold .25 units of the asset. Irrespective of whether the asset price moves up or down, the portfolio has a value of 22.5 as at the expiry of the option.

Based on the intuition that a riskless portfolio should earn the risk free rate of interest, it is now possible to derive the fair value of the option based on the following steps:

3. The value of the riskless portfolio constructed must in present value terms be:

$$e^{-Rf.T} 22.5 = e^{-.10.1} 22.5 = 20.36$$

4. The fair value of the option can now be calculated using the known value of the portfolio of assets at commencement of the transaction (.25 × 100 = 25) as follows:

Value of Asset Portfolio − Option premium = Value of Riskless Portfolio

$$25 - \text{Option Premium} = 20.36$$
$$\text{Option premium} = 4.64$$

Exhibit 5.9—*continued*

The fair value of the call option is 4.64. If the option was trading at a value higher (lower) that the fair value, then the riskless portfolio would cost less (more) than the option premium to create allow the creation of a portfolio which yield more than the risk free rate of return (a mechanism for borrowing at less than the risk free rate). In either case, the value difference would attract arbitrage to realign the value of the option to eliminate the possibilities for arbitrage.

8.2 Generalised binomial option

In the binomial model, the time period to option expiry is divided into a series of discrete intervals. This contrasts with the continuous time model of Black-Scholes. However, as the number of intervals to maturity increases, the resulting increase in final stock prices begins to approximate the continuous log normal distribution. This allows a more generalised version of the model to be created. *Exhibit 5.10* sets out the generalised version of the binomial model.

Exhibit 5.10

Generalised Binomial Option Pricing Model

In order to generalise the Binomial Option Pricing Model it is necessary to define: the factor amount the asset price can go up or down as at each step of the binomial tree and the probability of an up or a down move.

It can be shown that:*

u	$= e^{\sigma \sqrt{t}/n}$	
d	$= e^{-\sigma \sqrt{t}/n}$	
	$= 1/u$	
p	$= (e^{rf.t/n} - d)/(u-d)$	

$$pu + (1-p)d = e^{\frac{rf \cdot t}{n}}$$

risk-free

Where:

u	=	the factor amount the stock price can go up
d	=	the factor amount the stock price can go down
e	=	the exponential term
σ	=	the volatility of logs of the returns of the asset price
t	=	time to expiry of the option
n	=	number of steps
p	=	the probability of an upward move in the asset price
rf	=	the risk free rate of interest

The value of an option in a 1 step tree can therefore be stated as:

$$P = e^{-rf.t/n} [p. P_u + (1 - p) P_d]$$

Where:

P_u	=	the option value on an increase in the asset price
P_d	=	the option vlaue on an decrease in the asset price

The model can be extended using a similar logic for multiple steps.

* See Hull, op cit n1, Chs 10 and 15 for a full proof and derivation of these relationships.

Exhibit 5.11 sets out a multi-step binomial option model using the generalised model created. *Exhibit 5.12* sets out a multi-step binomial model for a put option.

Exhibit 5.11

Multi-Step Binomial Model For European Call Option

Assume the following parameters for a European call option:

S = 100

K = 100

T = 1 year

Rf = 10% pa

σ = 20% pa

Assume also the number of steps (n) to be used is 2.

Exhibit 5.11—*continued*

In order to use the binomial model, it is necessary to calculate u, d, and p.

$$u = e^{.20 \sqrt{1/2}} = 1.151910$$

$$d = 1/u = 0.868123$$

$$p = (e^{.10. \, 1/2} - 0.868123)/ \, (1.151910 - 0.868123) = .645371$$

This allows the construction of the binomial tree as follows:

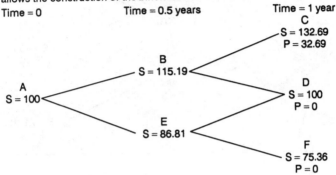

In order to now derive the value of the option, it is necessary to work back through the tree solving for the price of the option as at each node of the tree. In the above case the major node which is relevant is node B where the value of the option can be given as:

$$P = e^{-.10. \, 1/2} \, [.645371(32.69) + (1 - .645371) \, 0 \,]$$

$$= 20.07$$

This allows restatement of the tree as follows:

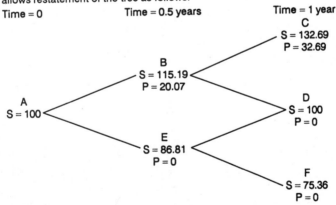

The value of the option at commencement (node A) can now be calculated as follows:

$$P = e^{-.10. \, 1/2} \, [.645371(20.07) + (1 - .645371) \, 0 \,] = 12.32$$

Exhibit 5.11—*continued*

The complete tree therefore is as follows:

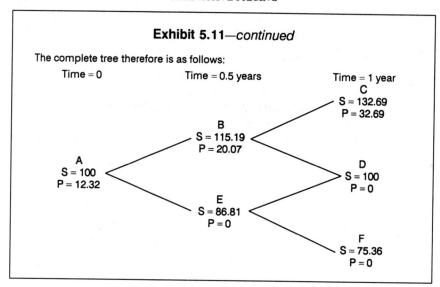

Exhibit 5.12

Multi-Step Binomial Model For European Put Option

The binomial model can be used to value a European put option in an entirely similar way. Assume the same parameters as for the example in *Exhibit 5.12* with the exception that the option is a European put option.

The inputs u, d, and p are as before:

$$u = e^{.20 \sqrt{1/2}} = 1.151910$$

$$d = 1/u = 0.868123$$

$$p = (e^{.10. 1/2} - 0.868123)/ (1.151910 - 0.868123) = .645371$$

This allows the construction of the binomial tree as follows:

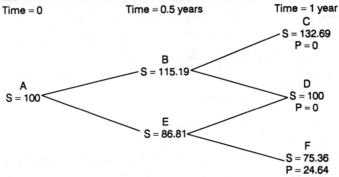

Time = 0   Time = 0.5 years   Time = 1 year

C
S = 132.69
P = 0

B
S = 115.19

A
S = 100

D
S = 100
P = 0

E
S = 86.81

F
S = 75.36
P = 24.64

In order to now derive the value of the option, it is necessary to work back through the tree solving for the price of the option as at each node of the tree. In the above case the major node which is relevant is node E where the value of the option can be given as:

$$P = e^{-.10. 1/2} [.645371(0) + (1 - .645371) 24.64]$$
$$= 8.31$$

This in turn allows calculation of the value of the put at commencement (node A) as:

$$P = e^{-.10. 1/2} [.645371(0) + (1 - .645371) 8.31]$$
$$= 2.80$$

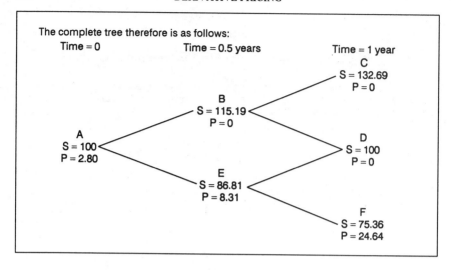

The complete tree therefore is as follows:

8.3 Numerical solution issues

The simple binomial models with small numbers of steps are relatively easy to solve. However, it is necessary to increase the number of steps significantly to increase the accuracy of the estimate of the value of the option.

In general, the minimum number of steps utilised in valuing options is around 50 to 100. This means that there are:

- $n + 1$ terminal stock prices (n = the number of steps) or 51 (50 + 1) terminal stock prices; and
- 2^n possible paths or 2^{50} possible price paths.

The large number of paths places substantial demands on numerical techniques to solve through the tree to estimate the price of the option.

8.4 Features of binomial models

The binomial option pricing model contains the Black-Scholes formula as a limiting case. If, for the binomial option pricing model, the number of sub-periods are allowed to tend to infinity, the binomial option pricing model tends to the option pricing formula derived by Black and Scholes.

The major advantage of the binomial model is that as the time to maturity is segmented into a series of discrete variables the model can take into account specific option values prior to maturity. This allows the binomial approach to be used to provide a solution not only for the closed form European option pricing problem but also for the more difficult American option pricing problems when numerical simulation approaches must be employed (see more detailed discussion below). In essence, the binomial pricing approach is useful as it can accommodate more complex option pricing problems, such as non-constant interest rates and volatility, debt options and exotic options such as path dependent structures.

9. OPTION PRICING MODELS—ISSUES IN APPLICATION

The major attraction of option pricing models, such as Black-Scholes and its binomial variations include:

- the fact that all input variables, other than volatility, are directly observable; and
- the models do not make any reference to the investor's attitudes to risk.

While the model plays a central role in option valuation trading, the underlying assumptions do not necessarily hold true in practice. In particular, violations of the model's assumptions exist in the following areas:

- asset price behaviour;
- constant and measurable volatility;
- constancy of interest rates;
- no intermediate cash flows; and
- the issue of early exercise.

Some of these violations are significant (like assumptions about asset price behaviour), while others are relatively minor (constancy of interest rate except for debt options, intermediate cash flows and early exercise) in terms of their impact on the validity of these models.

The key assumption, that price changes are continuous through time (that is, the assumption that there are no jumps or discontinuities between successive asset prices), independent and log normally distributed over time with constant variance, may be violated in practice. The assumption of independence of asset price changes, as required by efficient market theory, is not wholly convincing. The empirical evidence and support for the log normal distribution of asset prices and its constancy over time is also not completely convincing.[4] It is clear that option prices are sensitive to the stochastic processes assumed and changes in the assumptions produce significant, large percentage changes in option prices.

Empirical research highlights that *true* distributions differ from theoretical normal distribution in two respects:

1. The distributions of actual asset price changes are characterised by *fat tails*, that is these distributions display larger extreme price changes (both positive and negative) than implied by a theoretical normal distribution. This means that the theoretical models would *underprice* out-of-the-money and in-the-money option. This reflects the fact that the theoretical distribution allocates a lower probability to very high intrinsic values than is the case in reality.

2. Asset price behaviour appears to be characterised by discontinuities in the asset price changes or jumps. This contributes to the fat tails of the distribution.

The violation of the asset price behaviour assumptions underlying Black and Scholes has prompted the development of variations on the basic model

---

4. For a discussion of the log normality of asset price changes see Chapter 16 where the evidence is considered in the context of value at risk calculations which also rely on the assumption of log normality.

which make use of alternative stochastic processes, including absolute diffusion, displaced diffusion, jump processes and diffusion-jump processes. Empirical tests have tended to show that these alternative models are not able to provide better predictions of actual prices than the Black-Scholes type of model on a consistent basis. The price differences resulting from differing assumptions as to the underlying asset price movements in fact are *no* greater than the price differences that result from different assumptions of volatility.

The asset price volatility factor required as an input to option pricing models must be forward looking, that is, a forecast of the probable size (although not necessarily the direction) of asset price changes between the present and the maturity of the option. The problem in volatility estimation (the determination of the true constant volatility of the asset price) is, in practice, sought to be overcome by utilising two types of volatility: historical and implied.

Historical volatility is based on past prices of the underlying asset computed as the standard deviation of log relatives of daily price returns (usually annualised) over a period of time. Utilising historical volatility requires the selection of the period over which price data is to be sampled. It is possible to utilise price information over long periods (up to five years or longer) to derive the volatility estimate. This assumes that volatility is constant over long periods. It is also possible to use a much shorter period (less than 30 days) to get a good estimate of the current level of volatility. It is necessary to adjust the volatility input into the option pricing formula on a regular basis where short-term volatility is used on the basis that the volatility actually varies significantly.

Implied volatility is determined by solving an option pricing model (such as Black-Scholes) in reverse, that is, calculating the volatility which would be needed in the formula to make the market price equal to fair value as calculated by the model. Where this method is used, the implied volatility equates the model premium to the actual premium observed in the option market. An interesting problem with implied volatility measures is that options with different strike prices but with the same maturity often have different implied volatility. This is the phenomenon of the volatility smile, which is dealt with in Chapter 10. In addition, volatility appears to illustrate a term structure.

Historical volatility is a measure of past, already experienced, price behaviour. To the extent the option pricing model is validated, implied volatility reflects market expectations of future price behaviour during the life of the option. Both measures are important, and comparing the two can reveal interesting insights into the market in the underlying asset. However, no normative rule for derivation of the volatility estimate is available. This means that in reviewing option premiums, particularly where the value of the option in question is sensitive to the volatility estimate utilised, any option price suggested by an option model must be regarded with caution.

In addition, the models usually assume constant volatility. This assumption is clearly breached in practice, as volatility changes over time often very significantly.

Some attempted solutions to the volatility measurement model have sought to explicitly take into account the stochastic nature of volatility itself by using multi-factor numerical techniques which utilise two stochastic variables, namely, the asset and the volatility. A detailed discussion of issues pertaining to estimation of volatility is set out in Chapters 8 and 9.

The assumption that interest rates are constant is particularly problematic in the case of options on some debt instruments. This is because interest rate changes drive asset price changes where the asset itself is an interest bearing security. In addition, the volatility of asset prices in the case of debt instruments is a function of remaining maturity and, in turn, interest rates, which reflect the shape of the yield curve. As maturity diminishes, the volatility of the asset also diminishes and constant variance cannot be assumed.

The impact of intermediate cash flows depends on the pattern of payments and the certainty with which the cash flows can be predicted. The Black-Scholes model does not appear to be very sensitive to assumptions about intermediate payouts, which are certain. Where the intermediate cash flows are uncertain, however, the closed form Black-Scholes approach appears to break down and it is particularly difficult to compute American call prices.

The Black-Scholes model sets a lower limit for the price of the American call, but the model does not encompass the additional problem of determining the optimal time to exercise the option where the possibility of early exercise is not excluded. However, the model provides a reasonable approximation for the prices of American options.

The problems of both intermediate cash flows and early exercise can be solved with some adjustments to the standard models. These adjustments are examined below in detail.

Empirical tests of the Black-Scholes model indicate that the model is remarkably robust and provides accurate pricing for at-the-money options with medium to long maturity. The model appears to systematically misprice out-of-the-money and in-the-money options and also options where volatility increases or time to maturity is very short. In general, however, the model appears to successfully capture the essential determinants of option prices and United States studies show that traders cannot make consistent above normal returns on an after tax, post commission basis by setting up hedged portfolios.

Different models, which seek to overcome some deficiencies of Black-Scholes, essentially introduce new assumptions and do not necessarily produce improvements in pricing predictions.

The increased effort in improving and developing variations on available theoretical option pricing models creates the added problem of model selection. Clearly, there is no simple basis for selecting between the various techniques as the actual benefit from a particular model will depend on the user's objective. The selection of any model practically depends on the user's assumptions concerning the underlying asset price process. As there is no universal or true underlying process of asset prices, there can be no universal option pricing model and therefore no definitive fair value price for options.

In practice, models (such as Black-Scholes and the binomial price approaches) have remained successful because of their logical simplicity, computational efficiency and their robustness. Market participants have sought to deal with the failure of model assumptions in real markets by a series of adjustments to the models, in practice, including:

- adjusting the volatility utilised for options with different maturities or different strikes to adjust for the undervaluation of in or out-of-the-money options; and

- increasing volatilities for shorter dates options to adjust for the potential impact of large jumps and consequent changes in the price of the underlying asset.

The strength of the option pricing models identified may ultimately lie in their capacity to compress the four observable variables into one other variable, implied volatility, which can then be interpreted. However, the problem of model pricing performance has led to option traders utilising a range of pricing techniques and risk management techniques to manage the risk of writing options.

10. OPTIONS PRICING MODELS—EXTENSIONS TO THE STANDARD MODELS

10.1 Overview

In this section, the amended versions of the basic option pricing model are considered. The basic models are designed to deal with European options on non-income-producing assets. The extensions described extend the basic model in a number of specific areas:

- adjustment for intermediate cash flows;
- the possibility of early exercise;
- a change in the underlying asset to *a forward or futures contract* on the asset; and
- coverage of specific asset classes, such as equity, currency, debt or commodities.

Exhibit 5.13 sets out the hierarchy of option pricing models.

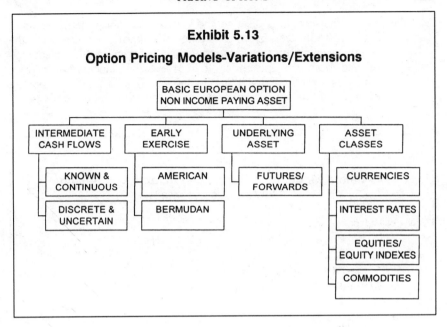

Exhibit 5.13

Option Pricing Models-Variations/Extensions

10.2 Intermediate cash flows

In practice, most assets pay out intermediate cash flows. These take the form of:

Asset Class	Income/Intermediate Cash Flow
Equities/equity market indexes	Dividends
Debt/interest rates	Coupons
Currencies	Interest rate on the foreign currency
Commodities/commodity Price Indexes	Asset lease rates or convenience yields

In practice, there are a number of mechanisms for incorporating the impact of these intermediate cash flows into the option pricing models:

• adjust the holding cost by the yield on the asset, that is, reducing the risk free rate (Rf) by the yield (Y), thereby using the holding cost of Rf − Y in the model.

• adjusting the spot price of the asset by the income expected on the asset. This is done in one of two ways:

(a) Where the income is assumed to be continuous, by adjusting the asset by replacing S by the term $S\ e^{-Y.T}$ where Y = the continuously compounded expected rate of return on the asset. *Exhibit 5.14* sets out a valuation model adapting the standard Black-Scholes model for an asset which pays continuous income. An example of applying this type of model is set out below using a currency option where the risk free interest rate in the foreign currency (Rf_f) is used instead of Y in the formula in *Exhibits 5.19* and *5.20*.

(b) Where the income is discrete and known, the spot price of the asset may be adjusted by discounting the known income to the commencement of the transaction and subtracting the discounted income from the spot price to derive an ex-income asset price which is then used as S in the model. *Exhibit 5.18* sets out an example of this type of adjustment with regard to an equity option.

Exhibit 5.14

Valuation Model for a European Option Asset Paying Continuous Income

For a call option:

$$P_{ce} = S\,e^{-Y.T}.\,N\,(d1) - K\,e^{-Rf.T}.\,N(d2)$$

Where

$d1 = [\ln (S/K) + (Rf - Y + \sigma^2/2)\,T] / \sigma \sqrt{T}$

$d2 = [\ln (S/K) + (Rf - Y - \sigma^2/2)\,T] / \sigma \sqrt{T}$

$= d1 - \sigma \sqrt{T}$

Where all terms are as defined previously and Y = the continuously compounded expected rate of return on the asset.

For a put option:

$$P_{pe} = K\,e^{-Rf.T}.\,N(-d2) - S\,e^{-Y.T}.\,N(-d1)$$

Where a binomial option pricing model is utilised to value the option, the value of the asset must be adjusted at the node at which the income is paid (or, in practice, the date at which the entitlement to the income is lost, such as an ex-dividend or ex-coupon date). The value of the asset is reduced by the amount of the income flow.

This creates a number of problems. The tree of asset prices becomes non-recombining, that is, an up move followed by a down move is no longer the same as a down move followed by an up move in the asset price. The tree also becomes larger as a result of the non-recombining nature of the tree. This is exacerbated where there are several cash flows. A common approach to improve the numerical efficiency of the solution of the binomial tree under these circumstances is to treat the asset as the asset price (ex-dividend), which is modelled through the tree and the present value of the future dividends which is added to the modelled asset price at each node.[5]

10.3 Early exercise/American options

The market for options trades both European and American options. As noted above, an American option will generally not be exercised early as the economic rationale favours the sale of the option. However, as noted above under certain circumstances, early exercise is possible.

---

5. See Hull, op cit n1, pp 365-368.

In practice, the risk of early exercise is particularly evident in the following cases:

- For in-the-money call options where the asset pays a high yield or income payment. This is because the benefit of receiving the high yield or the capture of the cash flow of the income payment on the asset may yield a superior return to the uncertain value of the asset and call at maturity. This is particularly relevant for equity options with a large dividend payable prior to option expiry where payment of the dividend would substantially reduce the value of the asset reducing the value of the call option. A similar logic applies to currency call options on a currency which has high interest rates whereby the option is likely to be exercised early.

- In the case of put options, a deep in-the-money put can economically be exercised early with the proceeds received invested at the risk free rate to yield a superior return to the uncertain intrinsic value of the put at maturity.

The valuation of American options is usually undertaken in two ways:

1. using a modified version of Black-Scholes option pricing model; and

2. using the binomial approach to option pricing.

The Modified Black-Scholes European Option Pricing Formula relies on the intuition that the standard Black-Scholes model provided a lower estimate of the value of the American option. It is identical to Black Scholes except that the formula checks to see if the value it is returning is below the intrinsic value of the option. Where the Black-Scholes European Option value is below the intrinsic price of the option then the Modified Black-Scholes American Formula returns the intrinsic value of the option. That is:

Black-Scholes American Option Value = Maximum (Black-Scholes European Value; Intrinsic Value)

The binomial option pricing model is well suited to estimating the fair value of an American exercise option. This reflects the fact that this approach incorporates all possible paths taken by the asset price as well as the distribution of asset prices as at the expiry of the option. This allows American options to be priced through a process whereby it is possible to calculate option values at each node of the tree and to test for the feasibility of early exercise. If the option at any node has a higher intrinsic value (that is, the value on early exercise) than the theoretical value of the option, the higher intrinsic value is used in the solution back through the tree, effectively incorporating the risk of early exercise.

Exhibit 5.15 sets out an example of using a binomial option pricing model to value an American put option.

Exhibit 5.15

Multi-Step Binomial Model for an American Put Option

The use of a multi-step binomial option pricing model for an American put option can be illustrated with the example given in *Exhibit 5.12*. Assume all the factors stated in that example with the exception that the option is now an American put.

The binomial tree in that case was as follows:

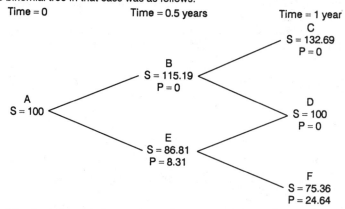

Time = 0	Time = 0.5 years	Time = 1 year

C
S = 132.69
P = 0

B
S = 115.19
P = 0

A
S = 100

D
S = 100
P = 0

E
S = 86.81
P = 8.31

F
S = 75.36
P = 24.64

In solving back through the tree it is feasible to compare the value of a European put option with *the intrinsic value of the option* if the option is exercised at that node.

In this example, as at node E, the value of the European option is 8.31. However, if the option is exercised, it will have an intrinsic value of 13.19 (100 − 86.81). This means that the holder of the option would at this point rationally exercise the put option early.

In order to value the American put, the intrinsic value of the option at node E is substituted for the theoretical European value. This in turn allows calculation of the value of the put at commencement (node A) as:

$$P = e^{-.10 \cdot 1/2} [.645371(0) + (1 - .645371) \, 13.19]$$
$$= 4.45$$

The complete tree therefore is as follows:

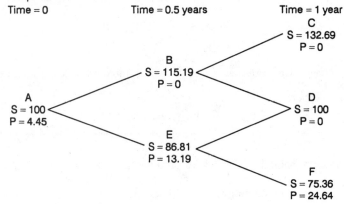

Time = 0   Time = 0.5 years   Time = 1 year

C
S = 132.69
P = 0

B
S = 115.19
P = 0

A
S = 100
P = 4.45

D
S = 100
P = 0

E
S = 86.81
P = 13.19

F
S = 75.36
P = 24.64

The difference between the value of the American put (4.45) and the value of the European put (2.80) of 1.65 can be attributed to the value of the right of early exercise.

An alternative approach is to use quadratic approximation methods to value American options. Under this approach, it is assumed that an American option is equal to a European option plus a separate early exercise option. The quadratic approximation method determines the early exercise option value and then adds it to the value calculated by the Modified Black-Scholes European Formula. The early exercise option value is determined by an iterative process. An example of this approach is that utilised by Barone-Adesi and Whalley.[6]

A variation on the American option is the Bermudan option, which is only capable of exercise on a nominated number of discrete dates prior to expiry. In effect, it is some way between an American and a European option. These types of options are priced using a binomial option pricing model which tests for the risk of early exercise at the relevant nodes of the tree.

10.4 Options on forward/futures contracts

Where the option is on a forward or futures contract, the basic Black-Scholes model can be altered to adjust for the changed nature of the underlying asset. *Exhibit 5.16* sets out Black's version of the original basic Black-Scholes model for a premium paid European option on a futures contract.

6. See G Barone-Adesi and R E Whalley, "Efficient Analytic Approximation Of American Option Values" (1987) 42 (June) *Journal of Finance* 301.

Exhibit 5.16

Black Option Pricing Model for Forward/Futures Contracts

For a call option:

$$P_{ce} = e^{-Rf.T} [F. N(d1) - K . N(d2)]$$

Where

$$d1 = [\ln (F/ K) + (\sigma^2/ 2) T] / \sigma \sqrt{T}$$
$$d2 = [\ln (F/ K) - (\sigma^2/ 2) T] / \sigma \sqrt{T}$$
$$= d1 - \sigma \sqrt{T}$$

Where all terms are as defined previously and F = forward or future prices of the underlying asset.

For a put option:

$$P_{pe} = e^{-Rf.T} [K. N(- d2) - S N(-d1)]$$

The intuition behind the Black reformulation of the Black-Scholes option pricing model in the context of futures is that the investment in a futures contract requires no commitment of funds (deposits, margins et cetera are ignored), whereas investment in the physical asset (for example, a share in the case of an equity option) imposes a cost. Consequently, nothing is paid or received (up-front) in setting up the hedge which entails buying or selling the futures contract.

The value of a call option on a futures contract should be lower than the value of a call option on the physical asset, as the futures price should already impound the carrying costs associated with the physical commodity. That is, the futures price is in essence the forward price, which will naturally reflect any carry costs over the relevant period. The usual qualifications concerning early exercise of American options will, of course, apply.

In general, the mean reverting property of interest rates causes these implied volatilities to decrease with option maturity. Relationships between volatility and maturity of caps, floors and collars et cetera are difficult to observe since most of these over-the-counter instruments have maturities beyond the longest maturity of traded Eurodollar futures. However, in practice, this relationship can be extrapolated.

Exhibit 5.17 sets out an example of utilising the Black option pricing model to derive the price of an option on a forward contract.

Exhibit 5.17

Example of Using the Black Option Pricing Model for Forward/Futures Contracts

Assume the following information:

$$\text{Forward Price} = F = 100$$
$$\text{Strike Price} = K = 100$$
$$\text{Time to Maturity} = T = 12 \text{ months (1.00 yrs)}$$
$$\text{Risk Free Rate} = Rf = 10\% \text{ pa (0.10)}$$
$$\text{Volatility} = \sigma = 20\% \text{ pa (0.20)}$$

Using the above inputs, we can compute the call option price as follows:

$$d1 = 0.10$$
$$d2 = -0.10$$

Using the N(x) table:

$$N(d1) = N(0.10) = 0.5398$$
$$N(d2) = N(-0.10) = 0.4602$$
$$N(-d1) = N(-0.10) = 0.4602$$
$$N(-d2) = N(0.10) = 0.5398$$

Therefore, the call and put prices are as follows:

$$P_{ce} = e^{-0.10 \times 1.00} [100 \times 0.5398 - 100 \times 0.4602]$$
$$= 7.20 \text{ or } 7.20\% \text{ of Future Asset Value}$$
$$P_{pe} = e^{-0.10 \times 1.00} [100 \times 0.5398 - 100 \times 0.4602]$$
$$= 7.20 \text{ or } 7.20\% \text{ of Future Asset Value}$$

The computational method where the Black model is used to price options *on futures contracts* for the price of the relevant options will differ depending on the type of margining system applicable. When the margining system dictates that proceeds are not paid up-front to option writers prices have to be higher to compensate the seller for the fact that the premium is not received at the beginning and consequently it is not available for investment. If it is assumed initially that the premium is paid over to the seller of the option only at maturity, the premium would have to be increased by the additional interest that could have been earned over the life of the option if the premium was available for investment. Consequently, the value of the call option will become:

$$P_{ce} = F.N\ (d1) - K.N\ (d2)$$

In addition, the put-call parity relationship, where proceeds are not paid up-front for open futures contracts, is different:

$$P_{pe} = P_{ce} - F + K$$

In practice, the adjustment process is not simple, because if nothing changes, part of the premium will be paid over to the writer of the option as the time value decays to zero over the life of the option.

11. OPTIONS ON DIFFERENT ASSET CLASSES

11.1 Overview

To date, the focus on option valuation has been general, rather than focused on specific types of assets. In this section, adjustments to the option pricing model dictated by the *type* of underlying asset are examined. The amendments are specifically designed to encompass the particular characteristics of each asset class. The adjustments required for the possibility of early exercise, discussed above, apply uniformly to these cases where the option is American style, allowing the possibility of exercise prior to maturity. Similarly, the use of an amended model where the underlying asset is a futures contract on the asset, as described above, is also applicable to each of the asset classes described.

11.2 Options on equity/equity market index

Options where the underlying asset is an individual equity stock or equity market index require the model to be adjusted for the dividends paid on the underlying asset. The major issue with the income stream attaching to the asset is the uncertainty relating to future dividends both in terms of amounts and their exact timing.

In order to incorporate the potential impact of the income stream the two approaches described above are utilised:

1. Where the dividend income is assumed to be continuous, by adjusting the asset by replacing S by the term $S\ e^{-Y.T}$ where Y = the continuously compounded expected dividend rate on the asset. *Exhibit 5.14* sets out a valuation model adapting the standard Black-Scholes model for an asset which pays continuous income.

2. Where the dividend income is discrete and known, the spot price of the asset may be adjusted by discounting the known dividend to the commencement of the transaction and subtracting the discounted income from the spot price to derive an ex-income asset price which is then used as S in the model. *Exhibit 5.18* sets out an example of this type of adjustment with regard to an equity option.

Exhibit 5.18

Valuation of Equity Option

Assume a $4.00 call option on ABC Ltd (ABC) with an expiry in four months' time is required to be priced. The underlying share price of is $5.00. The risk free return to option expiry is 13.10%. The volatility of the underlying shares' rate of return is 40%. The last dividend paid by ABC Bank Ltd was $0.30 per share. Assume that ABC is expected to pay a dividend of $0.30 per share just prior to option maturity.

In order to value the option, it is necessary to adjust the spot price of the asset for the expected dividend. The present value of this dividend discounted at the risk-free rate of return is $0.287. Therefore, the ex-dividend share price on $4.713 (calculated $5.00 − $0.287).

The inputs into the option pricing model are:

$S = 4.713$

$K = 4.00$

$\sigma = 0.40$

$Rf = .1310$

$T = 0.33$

Using the standard Black-Scholes formula:

$$d1 = 1.017$$
$$d2 = 0.787$$

Therefore:

$$N(1.0177) = 0.846$$
$$N(.787) = 0.785$$

The call option value is determined as follows:

$$P_{ce} = 4.713\,(0.846) - (0.9577)\,(4.00)\,(0.785)$$
$$= \$0.98$$

The Black-Scholes option-pricing model values the ABC option at 98 cents.

In practice, the first approach is used with longer dated equity options while the second approach is used with shorter dated equity options.

A second consideration in relation to equity options is the potential dilutionary impact of conversion. This exists as a problem in the case of equity options or warrants issued by the company. It is not a problem in exchange traded or over-the-counter options *on existing equity securities*. This is because it is only in the first case that the exercise of the option results in the issue of *additional equity*.

As the standard option pricing model assumes that the exercise of the option does not impact the value of the underlying asset, it is necessary to adjust the model for the following effects:

- the exercise of these options increases the number of shares which are on issue; and

- the payment of the exercise price of the option creates an additional cash inflow into the issuer of the options.

The standard model must usually be adjusted in two ways to reflect this impact:

1. The spot price of the asset must be adjusted for dilution as follows:[7]

$$Sd = (S. \; Qs + W. \; Qw)/ \; Qs$$

Where

Sd = the dilution adjusted spot price of the equity

S = the spot price of the equity

W = Market value of warrants

Qs = Number of shares currently on issue

Qw = Number of warrants on issue

2. The value of the theoretical call is adjusted to incorporate the dilution value as follows:

$$Pce \; (adj) = Pce. \; [Qs/ \; (Qs + Qw) \;]$$

Where

Pce (adj) = Dilution adjusted value of the call

Pce = Call option premium

In practice, the expected dilutionary effect of exercise will make the premium on the warrants (call options) lower than for a standard call option.

11.3 Options on currency/foreign exchange

In theory, the Black model for pricing options on forward contracts is capable of being utilised to value currency options. However, in practice, the way several interest rates are involved in ways differing from the assumption of the Black-Scholes model dictate the use of different models.

Garman and Kohlhagen[8] argue that it is the interest rate *differential between domestic and foreign risk free rates* that reflects the expected price drift of the underlying asset rather than a single interest rate that is appropriate in a single asset option.[9] The Garman-Kohlhagen model is set out in *Exhibit 5.19. Exhibit 5.20* sets out an example of pricing a currency option using the model.

7. See Aswanth Damodaran, *Damodaran on Valuation* (John Wiley, New York, 1995), pp 336-339.
8. Mark B Garman and Steven W Kohlhagen, "Foreign Currency Option Values" (1983) 2 *Journal of International Money and Finance* 231.
9. The Black-Scholes model employs interest rates in two different contexts: first, to discount future values; and, secondly, as an arbitrage-based surrogate for the drift of the deliverable instrument. The first use takes place outside the N (.) while the second takes place inside, reflecting the distribution of maturation values. Garman and Kohlhagen (ibid) show that it is only the interest rate differential that controls the distribution features while the interest rates control the discounting of future values.

Exhibit 5.19

Garman-Kohlhagen Model for Valuation of Currency Option

For a call option:

$$P_{ce} = S\, e^{-Rf_f \cdot T} \cdot N(d1) - K\, e^{-Rf_d \cdot T} \cdot N(d2)$$

Where

$d1 = [\ln (S/K) + (Rf_d - Rf_f + \sigma^2/2)\, T] / \sigma \sqrt{T}$

$d2 = d1 - \sigma \sqrt{T}$

Where all terms are as defined previously and

Rf_d = the risk free interest rate in the domestic currency

Rf_f = the risk free interest rate in the foreign currency

   For a put option:

$$P_{pe} = K\, e^{Rf_d \cdot T} \cdot N(-d2) - S\, e^{Rf_f \cdot T} \cdot N(-d1)$$

Exhibit 5.20

Valuation of a Currency Option

Assume the following facts relating to US$/Yen:

$S = 115.00$

$K = 110.00$

$T = 6$ months (0.5 years)

$Rf_f = 3\%$ pa (0.03) (the yen interest rate)

$Rf_{fd} = 6\%$ pa (0.06) (the US$ interest rate)

$\sigma = 12.00\%$ pa (0.12)

The calculations are as follows:

$$d1 = 0.743$$
$$d2 = 0.658$$

Therefore:

$N(0.743) = 0.771$

$N(0.658) = 0.745$

$N(-0.743) = 0.229$

$N(-0.658) = 0.255$

The value of the call option is:

$$P_{ce} = S\,e^{-Rf_f \cdot T} \cdot N(d1) - K\,e^{-Rf_d \cdot T} \cdot N(d2)$$
$$= 115.\,e^{-0.03 \times 0.5} \times 0.771 - 110.\,e^{-0.06 \times 0.5} \times 0.745$$
$$= 7.92$$

The fair value of the call in Yen is 7.92.

The value of the put option is:

$$P_{ce} = K\,e^{-Rf_d \cdot T} \cdot N(-d2) - S\,e^{-Rf_f \cdot T} \cdot N(-d1)$$
$$= 110.\,e^{-0.06 \times 0.5} \times 0.255 - 115.\,e^{-0.03 \times 0.5} \times 0.229$$
$$= 1.28$$

The fair value of the put in Yen is 1.28.

The difference between the Black model and the Garman-Kohlhagen model[10] gains importance where the difference between the two rates is very small or when one or other rate is large. The latter is particularly relevant in the case of American options because the high interest rate may influence the early exercise of the option.

---

10. Garman and Kohlhagen (ibid) also show that by substituting the forward currency price as at the option expiry (relying on the interest parity condition that the fully arbitraged forward rate should equal to the spot rate adjusted by the interest differential between the currencies) into the model it is possible to derive the Black option pricing model on forward/ futures contracts, thereby showing that currency options can be treated on the same basis as options on forwards generally.

11.4 Options on commodities

Options on commodities create issues in pricing primarily through difficulties in the estimation of the convenience yield/asset payout rate. This reflects the substantial difficulties in the estimation of this parameter. In practice, options on commodities may be priced in one of the following ways:

- Options on physical commodities using the continuous income version of the Black-Scholes model (see *Exhibit 5.14*) with the asset convenience yield being used as the income term Y.

- Options on forward commodities using the Black model for options on forward contracts (see *Exhibit 5.16*).

The latter approach has the advantage of already impounding the convenience yield or asset payout rate in the forward commodity price used in the model.

11.5 Options on debt instruments

11.5.1 Distinctive features of debt options

The pricing of options on interest rates and debt instruments are particularly complex and several distinctive features of debt instruments must be incorporated into the pricing of debt options.

The key features which require incorporation in the pricing mechanism include:

- Debt instruments, typically, have a defined maturity and their limited and declining life represents special problems in option pricing.

- The underlying security in the case of debt instruments usually involves payouts in the form of interest during the life of the option.

- The rate of interest cannot be assumed to be constant as, first, interest rate changes drive price changes in the underlying asset, and, secondly, most interest rate security values do not depend on a single random variable but on a number of random interest rates.

- Volatility of the underlying debt instrument cannot be assumed to be constant.

Most debt securities have a defined maturity. This is in contrast to other assets, such as equities, currencies and commodities, which do not have fixed lives.

It is important to distinguish between two classes of options on debt instruments: options on the cash market debt instrument (that is, the actual physical debt security); and futures on the relevant debt instrument. In practice, both types of options coexist and are available. This is despite the fact that in any market, a cash market, a futures market and one options market (either on the cash market instrument or the futures contract) would usually be sufficient to fulfil all risk transfer possibilities since the option on the cash market and the option on the futures market will, generally, serve similar functions.

In practice, options on cash market or physical debt instruments takes one of two forms: *fixed deliverable*, whereby a debt instrument *with specified characteristics* is required to be delivered; or *variable deliverable*, whereby a *specified existing debt issue* is required to be delivered. For example, a six month call option on a 90 day Eurodollar deposit (90 days commencing from the expiry date of the option) is a fixed deliverable option. In contrast, a three month put option on the 8.5% August 2002 US treasury bond, which requires delivery on that specific security—irrespective of remaining term to maturity—is an example of a variable deliverable option.

Variable deliverable options create complex pricing issues. This reflects the fact that unlike other cash market assets which have infinite lives or futures contracts which are not based on a particular, wasting debt security (futures contracts have particular characteristics which are specified and constant), actual physical debt securities are affected by the passage of time in two respects:

1. The underlying debt instrument itself has a shorter tenor or period to maturity as the option itself approaches expiration.

2. At maturity, the value of the interest rate security converges to a known constant value (usually, par or face value) and the volatility of the security approaches zero.

The impact of intermediate cash flows on the underlying debt instrument will depend on whether the underlying asset for the debt option is a cash market debt security or a futures contract on the relevant instrument. Where the option is on a futures contract of the relevant debt instrument, the fact that there are no coupon interest payments and that the maturity of the particular debt securities is fixed, means that the general pricing technology applicable to options on forward/futures contracts (see discussion above) can be utilised. However, where the option is on the physical debt security, the presence of intermediate cash flows can be problematic.

The assumption made by models such as Black and Scholes that there are no intermediate cash payouts can be relaxed using a modification of the formula which allows for payments that are proportional to the price of the underlying security. However, the normal type of adjustment utilised may not be appropriate in the case of debt options. Where the option is on an underlying security which bears a coupon, the accrued interest is continuously added to the full price of the bond representing a continuous payout to the holder of the debt security. As the coupons are fixed in dollar amount not proportional to the price of the underlying debt security, this type of modification proposed would be inappropriate.

As noted above, basic option pricing models assume that only one interest rate, the risk-free rate, is relevant. However, at any given point in time, a variety of risk-free interest rates for different maturities are observable. Each of these interest rates and, consequently, the shape of the yield curve as a whole is subject to change over time.

A major difficulty in relation to the pricing of debt options relates to the fact that the price of the underlying asset (the debt security) itself is a function of interest rates. Moreover, it is unlikely depending on the type of option, that it is a function of the risk-free interest rate utilised to present value the exercise price of the option. An additional complication arises from the fact that where the option is a variable deliverable option (as defined above), the exact interest rate required to value the underlying debt instrument itself is subject to change with the passage of time.

These difficulties mean that the value of options on debt instruments or interest rates do not depend on a single random interest rate variable but may depend on a *number* of different random interest rates (in effect, the complete term structure of interest rates).

The effect of changes in interest rates and the time to expiration are particularly complex. For options on assets, such as shares, as the risk-free rate increases, the value of the call option increases as the present value of the exercise price in the event of exercise declines; that is, if the call option and the security itself are regarded as different ways for an investor to capture any gain on the security price, as rates rise the increased cost of carry on the underlying security will make the call more attractive, leading to an increase in its value.

However, in the case of debt options, it is unreasonable to assume (as is usually done in the case of equity options) that the price of the underlying debt security is independent of the level of interest rates. Significant movements in the prices of the asset will occur as a result of changes in interest rates and, in general, any cost of carry consideration would be minor relative to the change in the value of the underlying security. For example, it would be reasonable to assume that rate increases will usually have a negative impact on the price of call options on debt instruments, as a rise in interest rates will most likely cause a fall in the price of the underlying instrument or futures contract.

The constancy of the variance of volatility of the underlying debt instrument also cannot be assumed. This results from two factors:

- The stochastic process followed by interest rates appears to have a mean reversion quality—that is, there is an inbuilt drift that pulls them back to some long run average level (see *Exhibit 5.21*).

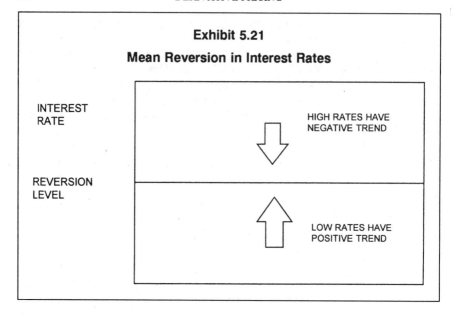

- Volatility of debt securities (in the case of a variable delivery option) is likely to tend to zero, reflecting the fact that at maturity, the value of debt instrument itself must converge to a known value (usually, the par value of the security). An additional factor in this regard is that the price volatility of a security is itself a complicated function of the actual volatility of interest rates of varying maturity and the time to maturity at the security itself (see *Exhibit 5.22*).

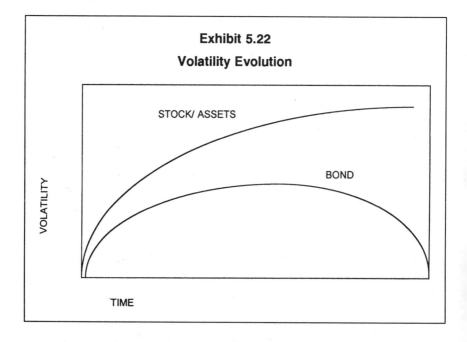

Consequently, the volatility of debt instruments will generally be a function of the assumed stochastic process of interest rate movement, assumptions about the shape and future movement of interest rate across the whole yield curve, and the remaining life of the security at a given point in time. These complexities dictate that constant variance cannot be assumed and it is probable that the volatility, itself, may also be stochastic variable.

The complexity of these interactions can be illustrated with reference to the effect of changes in time to expiration on such options. For options on assets with unlimited lives, an option with a longer time expiration will, generally, be worth more than a comparable option with a short term to expiry on the basis that it has all the attributes of the shorter dated option plus more benefits for the holder, that is, there is greater probability that the option can be profitably exercised. This property need not necessarily hold for debt options, particularly variable deliverable options, as depending on the relative magnitude of the time value and the intrinsic value, it is conceivable that under certain circumstances, an option with a longer time to expiration may be worth less than one with a shorter term. This would reflect the fact that securities usually begin to trade closer to par as the instrument approaches maturity. The greater price stability may affect the value of the option.

11.5.2 Approaches to pricing debt and interest rate options

In practice, the pricing of debt and interest rate options fall into two categories:

1. Options on futures/forwards where the underlying asset is a standardised debt instrument—these types of options are valued in a manner consistent with the types of theoretical option pricing models outlined, in particular, the Black option pricing model, as some of the problems identified can be minimised.

2. Options on physical debt instruments (particularly, on physical bonds)—are more problematic and usually entail the use of various numerical, usually binomial or lattice, option pricing model.

The first type of approach is the one commonly used with pricing caps, floors and collars as well as options on swaps/swaptions (although Bermudan style swaptions or those where the final maturity of the underlying swap is fixed at the time of entry may be more akin to the problems of pricing options on physical debt instruments).

For example, pricing caps, floors and collars utilising the first approach (using the Black model for options on forward/futures rates) entails the following steps:

• The cap, floor or collar agreement is analytically separated into a series of option contracts. For example, an interest rate cap agreement may be split up into a series of put option contracts on the prices of short term debt securities pricing off the relevant interest rate index.

• Each separate option is then valued utilising the identified model. In determining the price of each option, it is important to note that the input for the current spot price of the index is not the physical market price at the time the agreement is entered but the then current futures or forward price on the relevant index.

- The option premium for each contract is calculated and then summed to give the actual price for the overall contract.

Exhibit 5.23 sets out an example of using this approach to price a single period cap.

Exhibit 5.23

Example of Calculating Cap/Floor Prices Using Black's Option Pricing Model

Yield approach

Calculate the premium for a $1m 15% cap on three months LIBOR for one period of three months commencing in three months' time where the forward rate for three month LIBOR in three months' time is 15.016% pa and the three month risk free rate is 15.00% pa. This information can be reformulated for input into the model as follows:

$F = 0.15016$

$K = 0.1500$

$T = 0.25$

$Rf = 0.15$

$\sigma = 0.17$

The price of the cap (call option on yield) can be calculated as follows:

$d1 = 0.055$

$d2 = -0.030$

Therefore:

$N(0.055) = 0.5219$

$N(-0.03) = 0.4880$

The price of the call is calculated as follows:

$$P_{ce} = e^{-0.15 \times .25} [0.15016 \times 0.5219 - .15 \times 0.4880]$$
$$= 0.004978$$

As the asset and strike price were specified in yield terms, it is necessary to restate the option premium as follows:

$$P_{ce} = [t.Fv/ (1 + F.t)] \times P_{ce}$$

Where

t = the interest rate period (.25 years)

FV = face value of the option (1,000,000)

Therefore, the value of the cap is as follows:

$$P_{ce} = [.25 \times 1,000,000/ (1 + .15016 \times .25)] \times .004978$$
$$= \$1,199.54 \text{ or } 0.1199\% \text{ of face value}$$

The price of the equivalent floor (put on interest rates) is as follows:

$N(-0.055) = 0.4781$

$N(-0.03) = 0.5120$

$$P_{pe} = 240,954.57 \times e^{-0.15 \times 0.25} [0.15 \times 0.5120 - 0.15016 \times 0.4781]$$
$$= \$1,162.40 \text{ or } 0.1162\% \text{ of FV}$$

Exhibit 5.23—*continued*

Price approach

Calculate the premium for an 8% cap on three month LIBOR for one year period of three months in one years' time where the forward rate for three month LIBOR in one year is 7% pa. This information can be reformulated for input into the model as follows:

$F = 982,800.98$ (the value of US$1,000,000 face value 3 month security discounted at 7.00% pa)

$K = 980,392.16$ (the value of US$1,000,000 face value 3 month security discounted at 8.00% pa)

$T = $ one year (1.0)

$RF = 6.5\%$ (0.065)

$\sigma = 0.00344$

The price of the cap is calculated as follows:

$d1 = 0.715$

$d2 = 0.712$

Therefore:

$N(0.715) = 0.7627$

$N(0.712) = 0.7616$

$N(-0.715) = 0.2373$

$N(-0.712) = 0.2384$

Therefore, the cap premium (put option on price) is:

$$P_{pe} = e^{-0.065 \times 1} [980,392.16 (0.2384) - 982,800.98 (0.2373)]$$
$$= \$474.92 \text{ or } 0.0475\% \text{ of FV}$$

The Black option pricing model involves the assumption that σ—the volatility of the forward/futures contract—is constant. As noted above, this assumption is unlikely to hold in practice because of the mean reverting process. This dictates that when the period to option expiration is large, the price of the forward or futures contract is not greatly sensitive to current interest rates, but as the time to option expiry decreases, the current level of interest rates becomes progressively more important in determining the forward or futures price with the result that the volatility of the forward or futures price may increase with the effluxion of time.

In practice, the Black option pricing model can be applied if some adjustments designed to minimise impact of this phenomenon are adopted.

Utilising this approach, applied volatility for forward interest rates are calculated usually from traded futures options or from traded caps, floors, et cetera. The debt option being valued is then priced utilising the implied volatilities generated. This multiple use of the Black model, first, to calculate implied volatility and, secondly, to price the option, allows errors that may be caused by the use of the inexact model to be reduced. More importantly, they ensure that the calculated option prices are reasonably consistent with traded option prices.

In general, the mean reverting property of interest rates causes these implied volatilities to decrease with option maturity. Relationship between volatility and maturity of caps, floors and collars, et cetera, are difficult to observe since most of these over-the-counter instruments have maturities beyond the longest maturity of traded Eurodollar futures. However, in practice, this relationship can be extrapolated.

The major identified problems with pricing options on interest rates or debt instruments are most evident in pricing options on physical debt instruments, particularly medium to long-term bonds. A variety of approaches have emerged towards pricing these types of options usually incorporating an interest rate term structure model. Chapter 6 examines interest rate option pricing using these types of approaches.

12. SUMMARY

Option contracts, because of their asymmetric payoff profiles, present a particular challenge in pricing. However, using the standard assumption of risk neutral valuation, it is possible to estimate the fair value of the option contract by determining the expected value of a portfolio consisting of the underlying asset and cash which is adjusted dynamically through time to replicate the payoff of the option. The basic model thus derived can than be adjusted in a number of ways to estimate the fair value of different types of options as well as options on different asset classes.

Appendix A

Cumulative Normal Distribution Function[11]

Tables for the cumulative normal distribution function (N) are attached.
Alternatively, a polynomial approximation can be used:
Where $x \geq 0$

$$N(x) = 1 - N'(x) (a_1 k^1 + a_2 k^2 + a_3 k^3)$$

Where $x < 0$

$$N(-x) = 1 - N(x)$$

Where
$k = 1/ (1 + \alpha x)$
$\alpha = 0.33267$
$a_1 = 0.4361836$
$a_2 = -0.1201676$
$a_3 = 0.9372980$
and
$N^1(x) = (1/ \sqrt{2\Pi}) . e^{-x2/2}$
This provides values for $N(x)$ that are usually accurate to about four decimal
places and are always accurate to within 0.0002.

---

11. See M Abramowitz and I Stegun, *Handbook of Mathematical Functions* (9th ed, Dover Publications, New York, 1972).

Table for N(x)

This table shows values of N(x) for $x \geq 0$. When $x < 0$, the relationship $N(-x) = 1-N(x)$ can be used. For example, $N(-0.12) = 1-0.5478 = 0.4522$.

The table should be used with interpolation. For example:

$$N(0.6278) = N(0.62) + 0.78 [N(0.63) - N(0.62)]$$
$$= 0.7324 + 0.78 \times 0.0033$$
$$= 0.7350$$

x	.00	.01	.02	.03	.04	.05	.06	.07	.08	.09
0.0	0.5000	0.5040	0.5080	0.5120	0.5160	0.5199	0.5239	0.5279	0.5319	0.5359
0.1	0.5398	0.5438	0.5478	0.5517	0.5557	0.5596	0.5636	0.5675	0.5714	0.5753
0.2	0.5793	0.5832	0.5871	0.5910	0.5948	0.5987	0.6026	0.6064	0.6103	0.6141
0.3	0.6179	0.6217	0.6255	0.6293	0.6331	0.6368	0.6406	0.6443	0.6480	0.6517
0.4	0.6554	0.6591	0.6628	0.6664	0.6700	0.6736	0.6772	0.6808	0.6844	0.6879
0.5	0.6915	0.6950	0.6985	0.7019	0.7054	0.7088	0.7123	0.7157	0.7190	0.7224
0.6	0.7257	0.7291	0.7324	0.7357	0.7389	0.7422	0.7454	0.7486	0.7517	0.7549
0.7	0.7580	0.7611	0.7642	0.7673	0.7704	0.7734	0.7764	0.7794	0.7823	0.7852
0.8	0.7881	0.7910	0.7939	0.7967	0.7995	0.8023	0.8051	0.8078	0.8106	0.8133
0.9	0.8159	0.8186	0.8212	0.8238	0.8264	0.8289	0.8315	0.8340	0.8365	0.8389
1.0	0.8413	0.8438	0.8461	0.8485	0.8508	0.8531	0.8554	0.8577	0.8599	0.8621
1.1	0.8643	0.8665	0.8686	0.8708	0.8729	0.8749	0.8770	0.8790	0.8810	0.8830
1.2	0.8849	0.8869	0.8888	0.8907	0.8925	0.8944	0.8962	0.8980	0.8997	0.9015
1.3	0.9032	0.9049	0.9066	0.9082	0.9099	0.9115	0.9131	0.9147	0.9162	0.9177
1.4	0.9192	0.9207	0.9222	0.9236	0.9251	0.9265	0.9279	0.9292	0.9306	0.9319
1.5	0.9332	0.9345	0.9357	0.9370	0.9382	0.9394	0.9406	0.9418	0.9429	0.9441
1.6	0.9452	0.9463	0.9474	0.9484	0.9495	0.9505	0.9515	0.9525	0.9535	0.9545
1.7	0.9554	0.9564	0.9573	0.9582	0.9591	0.9599	0.9608	0.9616	0.9625	0.9633
1.8	0.9641	0.9649	0.9656	0.9664	0.9671	0.9678	0.9686	0.9793	0.9699	0.9706
1.9	0.9713	0.9719	0.9726	0.9732	0.9738	0.9744	0.9750	0.9756	0.9761	0.9767
2.0	0.9772	0.9778	0.9783	0.9788	0.9793	0.9798	0.9803	0.9808	0.9812	0.9817
2.1	0.9821	0.9826	0.9830	0.9834	0.9838	0.9842	0.9846	0.9850	0.9854	0.9857
2.2	0.9861	0.9864	0.9868	0.9871	0.9875	0.9878	0.9881	0.9884	0.9887	0.9890
2.3	0.9893	0.9896	0.9898	0.9901	0.9904	0.9906	0.9909	0.9911	0.9913	0.9916
2.4	0.9918	0.9920	0.9922	0.9925	0.9927	0.9929	0.9931	0.9932	0.9934	0.9936
2.5	0.9938	0.9940	0.9941	0.9943	0.9945	0.9946	0.9948	0.9949	0.9951	0.9952
2.6	0.9953	0.9955	0.9956	0.9957	0.9959	0.9960	0.9961	0.9962	0.9963	0.9964
2.7	0.9965	0.9966	0.9967	0.9968	0.9969	0.9970	0.9971	0.9972	0.9973	0.9974
2.8	0.9974	0.9975	0.9976	0.9977	0.9977	0.9978	0.9979	0.9979	0.9980	0.9981
2.9	0.9981	0.9982	0.9982	0.9983	0.9984	0.9984	0.9985	0.9985	0.9986	0.9986
3.0	0.9986	0.9987	0.9987	0.9988	0.9988	0.9989	0.9989	0.9989	0.9990	0.9990
3.1	0.9990	0.9991	0.9991	0.9991	0.9992	0.9992	0.9992	0.9992	0.9993	0.9993
3.2	0.9993	0.9993	0.9994	0.9994	0.9994	0.9994	0.9994	0.9995	0.9995	0.9995
3.3	0.9995	0.9995	0.9995	0.9996	0.9996	0.9996	0.9996	0.9996	0.9996	0.9997
3.4	0.9997	0.9997	0.9997	0.9997	0.9997	0.9997	0.9997	0.9997	0.9997	0.9998
3.5	0.9998	0.9998	0.9998	0.9998	0.9998	0.9998	0.9998	0.9998	0.9998	0.9998
3.6	0.9998	0.9998	0.9999	0.9999	0.9999	0.9999	0.9999	0.9999	0.9999	0.9999
3.7	0.9999	0.9999	0.9999	0.9999	0.9999	0.9999	0.9999	0.9999	0.9999	0.9999
3.8	0.9999	0.9999	0.9999	0.9999	0.9999	0.9999	0.9999	0.9999	0.9999	0.9999
3.9	1.0000	1.0000	1.0000	1.0000	1.0000	1.0000	1.0000	1.0000	1.0000	1.0000
4.0	1.0000	1.0000	1.0000	1.0000	1.0000	1.0000	1.0000	1.0000	1.0000	1.0000

Chapter 6

Interest Rate Option Pricing Models

by Tim Rowlands

1. INTRODUCTION

With the publication of their benchmark paper, Black and Scholes (BS) provided a means for valuing options on a wide range of financial instruments. Their work gave us an analytic framework that has since been put to many and varied uses. Many extensions and enhancements of their original model have been made, but the basic approach has remained intact. However, when the underlying instrument on which the option is granted or purchased is an interest rate or interest rate product, there is considerable strain put on some of the key BS assumptions.

First, there is the assumption that the rate used to discount the forward option price back to today is constant whilst the interest rates, upon which the underlying depends for its value, are evolving randomly. This represents an inconsistency which is magnified when the life of the option is a significant proportion of the length of maturity of the underlying instrument, for example a three year option on a one year swap. In effect, using this example, this assumption is saying that the forward rate from three to four years is a stochastic (random) quantity yet the spot three year rate is fixed. In other words the four year rate is stochastic while the three year rate isn't. Clearly as the option life grows as a proportion of the overall combined option plus underlying maturity this becomes less palatable. It is possible to imagine circumstances where a three month rate remained relatively constant whilst a ten year rate evolved randomly (as in a three month option on a ten year bond) but a little harder to imagine a three year rate remaining constant whilst a four year rate is expressed as random with its full normal volatility. Stochastic interest rate enhancements to the basic BS model have been used to overcome this in the case of stock options but they become much more difficult for interest rate options.

Secondly, there is the assumption that the annualised volatility of the underlying interest rate is constant for the life of the option. This is a difficult assumption to work with, even in simple options, but in the case of interest rate options there is a well-defined volatility term structure observed in the markets that clearly contravenes this constant volatility assumption. Stochastic volatility models and models involving deterministic, but not constant, volatility have been developed in an attempt to overcome this deficiency.

Thirdly, there is the assumption of an interest rate or bond price process that behaves in a Brownian motion fashion with the consequent growth of the total standard deviation of the underlying rate to be related to the square root of time. This implies that the distribution of rates or prices will spread to infinity as time goes to infinity, thus if you wait long enough an interest rate of any size (for example, 100%, 1000%, even 1000000%) is possible. This is contrary to experience, as there are political and economic forces at work to keep interest rates at "reasonable" levels. This is referred to as "mean reversion"—the process whereby there is a tendency for rates and prices to return to their long-term average levels or average rates of growth that is stronger the further from this long-term average they have strayed. This is a particularly complicated addition to the interest rate modelling process since it links the change of the interest rate over a period of time explicitly with its level, and this is determined by the dynamics of the recent past. In other words, we have to keep track of the path of interest rates because we need to know where it is to determine where it is going. This causes problems in that it makes analytic option pricing solutions tough and numerical solutions typically become much more calculationally intensive (for example, "bushy" trees and lattices instead of clean connected ones). This dependence of movements in future rates or prices on the past is described as the process being non-Markovian. When the rates or prices are independent of the past (we don't need to know where we are to predict how we will move in the future), this is described as Markovian.

Numerous attempts to overcome some or all of these problems have been made, and are continuing to be made, so that the modelling of interest rate processes and interest rate option pricing remains a rich and interesting field of study. In the sections below, we will quickly review the types of models in use, we will look at interest rate processes at a conceptual level and then use these as a starting block to unravel the various different modelling approaches used for interest rate options. Using a binomial lattice for illustration, we will explore what is required to implement an interest rate option pricing model.

2. FAMILIES OF INTEREST RATE MODELS

Although there are many different interest rate models, they can be grouped into various families of models that allow easy comparison at a macro level. The main split in the early chronology of models was into equilibrium models and arbitrage free models. This broad classification is still relevant, but there has been a shift towards arbitrage free models in recent years so that most models these days fit into this category. The fundamental difference between the two categories is that equilibrium models begin with a model for the economy as a whole and derive a suitable process for the time value of money based on estimated economic utility functions for the participants in the economy. From this, interest rates can be modelled and the value of future fixed, floating and contingent cashflows can be determined. The best known of these models is the Cox, Ingersoll, Ross model.

Arbitrage free models begin with the choice of an interest rate process and then development of a description of rates into the future, based on the need to conform with a no arbitrage condition, that is, there should be no self-financing strategy which generates a risk-free profit. This arbitrage-free state is the equivalent of the risk-neutral valuation of the traditional BS model. Consequently, the probability distribution for rates associated with these models is artificially chosen to fit the arbitrage-free condition and current interest rates and is thus not related to that which would be forecast by the market and is generally known as the risk-neutral probability distribution.

The next major division in the family of arbitrage free models is into models which are and are not preference free. Construction of an arbitrage free model (beginning with a simple expression of the interest rate process in a manner similar to the equilibrium models) enables the building of a term structure of interest rates but this will be unlikely to be consistent with the observed market-term structure. This is because some sort of trend will be assumed for the short-term rate and this will prove to be too simplistic to describe the subtleties seen across the whole term structure. In addition, the market observed short rate will not match the "risk-free" rate of the kind used in the BS stock option since this is a value representing the return on a money-market account rather than a bond return. In order to establish consistency with the observed term structure, an estimate must be made for the market price of risk. This represents the premium over the "risk-free" rate that must be returned to match the observed term structure. Unfortunately, this is not a market observable depending basically on the preferences or risk appetite of investors in the economy. In the BS model, this is removed by building a replicating portfolio of a combination of the money market account (growing at the risk-free rate) and the underlying stock. This can't be done for interest rates because the risk-free rate is a tradeable part of the term structure of interest rates. To avoid the problems associated with trying to estimate the market price of risk, there have been developed models which specifically fit the observed term structure of interest rates in an arbitrage-free manner. These models are described as "preference free" since they don't require an estimate of the market price of risk. Unfortunately, this fitting process is done numerically and so there is a loss of analytic tractability. This has led to the preponderance of numerical models such as lattices to accomplish this.

There are also divisions between the models on the basis of the nature of the underlying random process. Some models use a lognormally distributed random process for the interest rates whereas others use a normally distributed random process. A few models use other processes such as a square root process or Bessel process but these are usually for specific analytic solutions in cases where a normal or lognormal distribution doesn't yield an analytic result. Other models have been based on a random description of the bond prices rather than the underlying rates, but these have to be radically adjusted in cases where the maturity of the bond is approached since at this time the price of the bond homes in on the face value and thus does not follow a square-root-of-time volatility process.

Other divisions within the family of interest rate models are based on the number of factors used in the construction of the term structure of interest rates. Many models have been developed which use a single factor, others are multi-factor. Single factor models are based on a single random variable in the interest rate process. This usually corresponds to a short-term interest rate. From this single source of uncertainty the whole term structure is derived, and the manner in which it evolves determined. This means that all other elements depend in some way on this single factor. An analogy can be borrowed from hedging or risk management. Typically in the past, interest rate positions, particularly bond portfolios, had their risk assessed in terms of their "duration". This was a single number that represented the average maturity of the portfolio and, using a basis point sensitivity, gave an indicator of the riskiness of the portfolio. This was based on a parallel shift of the yield curve and its impact on the portfolio. However, it has become clear that although this approach is a reasonable estimate, it is incomplete, because it takes no account of the different behaviour of different parts of the yield curve. This is because there isn't perfect correlation in the movements of interest rates at different maturities on the yield curve—sometimes rates move in opposite directions. Thus, a parallel shift model for a yield curve gives an incomplete picture of the risk of a bond portfolio with bonds of different maturities. In the same way, single factor interest rate models relate all of the interest rates to a single short rate. Though different models build the term structure in different ways, the net result is that the rates are all perfectly correlated across maturities. To move beyond this, additional factors are required and these are based on additional random variables. For example, a two factor model may incorporate random variables (with some, but not perfect, correlation) to represent a short rate and a long-term interest rate (for example, Brennan and Schwarz).

The final family of models is the relatively new generation of yield curve models in which the whole term structure of interest rates is taken as the random variable, for example, Heath, Jarrow and Morton. In the single factor case, rather than a single interest rate varying, a vector of rates (the yield curve across the maturities) is varying, but based on a single random variable. Since the underlying "variable" is the whole yield curve, interest rate instruments can be valued directly at a future time by discounting back the cashflows down the forward curve. In order to preserve an arbitrage-free state in these cases there is generally a loss of the Markovian property. Alternatively, there can be a return to the Markovian nature of the process if specific assumptions are made about the form of the volatility. Generally, this reduces the model to one of the simpler cases, anyway.[1]

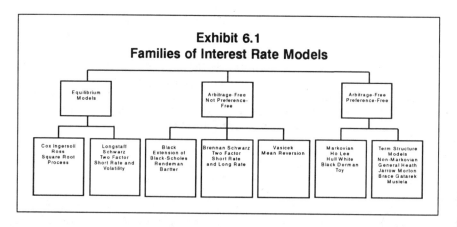

Exhibit 6.1
Families of Interest Rate Models

1. For a more detailed family tree of option pricing models see Smithson (two articles in *Risk* magazine).

3. THE INTEREST RATE PROCESS

The fundamental level of differentiation of interest rate models is the underlying interest rate process. A Brownian motion or Wiener process or random walk all refer to a process by which a quantity such as an interest rate evolves through time in a manner which results in a normal distribution. There will be some drift or trend which is proportional to the length of time that passes and there will be a gradual spreading of the distribution in such a way that the standard deviation of the distribution is proportional to the square root of the length of time that passes. In simplest terms, all of this is represented in the following equation

$$dr = \mu dt + \sigma dz$$

where dr is the change in rates over a short time period dt. The drift coefficient is μ and the spread coefficient is σ, and dz represents a small change in a normal random variable with mean zero and standard deviation equal to the square root of dt.

One of the key elements to understanding different models is being able to interpret this type of stochastic (because it includes a random variable) differential (because it is expressed in terms of small changes or differences) equation (SDE). Since dz is normally distributed and dr is proportional to it, then we know that dr is also normally distributed. The spread of the probability distribution is determined by the constant σ which is usually referred to as the volatility of the rate. This value can be estimated from historic data as the standard deviation of the *absolute changes in rates* over a period containing a number of observations, for example, three months of daily rate movement data. As dz has a mean of zero, the average value for dr over a large number of observations is determined only by the μdt term. If μ is a constant, as in this simple case, then there is a steady linear trend in the average or expected rate changes. This is common for assets that return a steady long-term growth rate (for example, house prices, shares, et cetera) but it is not so appropriate for interest rates, as it means that the rates would continue along the linear upward or downward trend forever, thus reaching very large positive or negative values, given sufficient time. So, in short, the interpretation of a SDE as written above with constant drift and volatility coefficients would be that rates evolve following a normal distribution around a linear trend.

In the above example, if μ was negative then eventually rates would become negative and continue becoming more and more negative as time went on. Alternatively, a large value of σ would allow the random term to overwhelm the drift and again allow (with small but nevertheless finite probability) negative interest rates. Notwithstanding a couple of historic examples of their occurrence, it is generally accepted that negative rates are not a desirable feature in an interest rate process. The use of a lognormal distribution for the changes in rates puts a lower bound of zero on the interest rates. In processes of this type it is the logarithm of the rate that is normally distributed. In this case the SDE could be written as:

$$d \ln(r) = \mu dt + \sigma dz$$

where $\ln(r)$ is the natural (base e) logarithm. An alternative representation of this is to write:

$$dr = \mu rdt + \sigma rdz$$

This is equivalent after a slight change in the drift term (see below). Note that the volatility term contains the rate to the power one. In simple terms, when the volatility term doesn't contain r, the distribution is Normal and if it contains r to the power one it is Lognormal. The Cox, Ingersoll, Ross model has r to the power of a half, hence its description as a square root process. Strictly, the $d\ln(r)$ form of the dr expression above is:

$$d\ln(r) = (\mu - \frac{1}{2}\sigma^2)dt + \sigma dz$$

This can be shown using Ito's Lemma which is an important result in financial modelling. (A simpler, though not rigorous, derivation can be obtained by taking a Taylor's series expansion of the derivative of $\ln(r)$ and noting that dz^2 is equivalent to dt.)

Once again the spread of the distribution is determined by the value of σ, but in this case it can be estimated from historic data by taking the standard deviation of the logarithm of the ratio of rates from one observation to the next. This is true since the equivalent absolute change in the logarithm of the rate from one day to the next is the logarithm of one rate minus the logarithm of the previous rate, and the difference of two logarithms is equal to the logarithm of the ratio of the rates. This is the origin of the seemingly strange definition of historic volatility as the standard deviation of the log-ratio of rates.

If $\ln(r)$ trends down to be a negative number (that is, μ is negative), then this means the rate will still be positive as the exponential of a negative number is positive and lies between zero and one. It is still unbounded on the positive side so that very large rates of interest can be obtained. The BS model uses a lognormal distribution for stock prices since these can grow to large values with time and are always positive. Once again, this is less appropriate for interest rates, as unbridled growth upwards in rates is not likely, due to political and economic factors coming to bear so that they remain at "reasonable" levels.

This effect of rates returning to some long-term average value rather than growing to higher and higher levels is referred to as "mean reversion". This can be built into a SDE as follows:

$$dr = k(\theta - r)dt + \sigma dz$$

where θ is the long-term average value of r and k is a measure of how strong the mean reversion "force" is. As can be seen, if the level of r is above the long-term average, θ, then the drift term will be negative and the rate will trend down. If the level of r is below the long-term average then the drift term will be positive and the rate will trend up. The further the rate is from the long-term average the stronger this drift will be. This can also be applied to a lognormal process leading to a SDE of:

$$d\ln(r) = k[\theta - \ln(r)]dt + \sigma dz$$

The difficulty with the last two SDEs is that the inclusion of the rate or its logarithm in the drift term means that the change in rate is dependent on where the rate is currently, and thus there is a loss of the Markovian property (that is, the size of the next jump is dependent on where we are, rather than being independent, which is the Markovian case). This leads to bushy lattices and difficult analytical solutions to the SDEs.

Thus far we have assumed that the coefficients in the SDEs have been constants but they can be chosen to be time dependent or, just as in the case of mean reversion, rate dependent. We have also only considered r to be a single short-term rate. If we wish to proceed to a multi-factor model so as to explain a greater range of possible term structures and term structure movements there are several different ways we can do so.

One alternative is to use a pair of rates—a short-term and a long-term rate. These can be represented by a pair of related SDEs as follows:

$$dr = k(l - r)dt + \sigma_1 r dw$$
$$dl = \sigma_2 l dz$$

and where

$$dw dz = \rho dt$$

In this case (the model of Brennan and Schwartz), the short rate is a mean reverting lognormally distributed rate that has as long-term average a long-term rate that is also lognormally distributed. The two rates are correlated with correlation coefficient ρ.

There are many examples of models in which the coefficients are time dependent and this allows values to be selected to ensure that the evolving rates fit the market observed term structure of interest rates. What this means is that the average or expected value of the rates at forward dates are consistent with the forward rates observed today. Jamshidian, Hull and White and others have produced models of this type. The SDE in these cases is typically of the form:

$$dr = (\theta(t) - ar)dt + \sigma dz$$

The fitting of the rate process to the current term structure of interest rates and volatilities is a process known as calibration. This will be discussed in more detail in the next section.

The final type of interest process is that used in the yield curve models where the rate itself is a function of maturity rather than a single rate for a single maturity. Heath, Jarrow, Morton and Brace, Musiela, Gatarek are examples of this type of model. The forward rates are modelled in an arbitrage-free manner and calibrated to fit the existing term structures of interest rates and volatilities. The SDE looks like this:

$$df(t,T) = \alpha(t,T)dt + \sigma_f(t,T)dW(t)$$

where the volatility function, σ_f, is the forward volatility function. Models of this type are quite computationally intensive in their purest form as they are non-Markovian leading to bushy lattices. It is possible to make simplifying assumptions about the volatilities which reduce the model to simpler forms. In this way, many of the older and simpler models are special cases of the HJM approach. These are the state-of-the-art models and are likely to be the way of the future for pricing and risk management of interest rate derivative products.

How do we choose an appropriate interest rate process? This is very much a case of personal preference combined with an assessment of the complexity of the uses for which it is to be implemented. The running of a complex book of derivative products by an investment bank is very different to a small corporate treasury that might purchase the occasional cap or floor. Clearly the former will need a high quality implementation of a yield curve model, whereas the latter can get by with one of the simpler BS style pricing models, provided a conceptual understanding of the risks inherent in option products is well understood.

What do we do with it? Once an interest process has been selected we can simulate the evolution of the rate going forward. This can be done in a variety of ways, including binomial or higher order lattices, Monte Carlo simulation or, in some cases, analytically, because the SDE is soluble algebraically as in the BS model.

To conclude the discussion of interest rate processes it is necessary to summarise what we have seen. An interest rate process is a description of the way in which rates evolve into the future. These processes can be described by a Stochastic Differential Equation (SDE). By examining the SDE of a model, or designing one of our own, we can determine the features we want to build into a model. These features include the type of probability distribution, whether or not we will try to fit the current market observables exactly, whether we will include mean reversion and so on. All of this is fundamental to the building of any model and in some senses from then on the rest is just algebra and, often, some numerical mathematics!

4. A BINOMIAL LATTICE ILLUSTRATION OF AN INTEREST RATE MODEL

Binomial (and higher order) lattices provide a means of modelling stochastic processes in a controlled manner and were first applied to option pricing by Cox, Ross and Rubinstein. An alternative approach, Monte Carlo simulation requires large numbers of trials to ensure that there has been a representative coverage of possible outcomes in a random process, whereas the lattice approach has a wide and representative coverage at each stage, and extending the number of steps in the lattice simply increases the resolution of the random process. It also allows for the pricing of American options since it provides a means of stepping back through time from expiry to determine whether it is better to exercise or to hold onto the option.

Let us work through an example, using a lattice model to price a caplet. Extension onto a cap is straightforward as it is merely the sum of a series of caplets. The caplet has an expiry two years hence and is based on a three month interest rate. For simplicity we will use just eight steps in the lattice, each representing one three month period. The interest rate process will be a simple lognormal one with the drift term being time-dependent to allow for the fitting of the current term structure in an arbitrage-free manner and with the volatility term being constant.

$$dr = \mu(t)rdt + \sigma rdz$$

As we stated, above, this is equivalent to:

$$d\ln(r) = (\mu(t) - \tfrac{1}{2}\sigma^2)dt + \sigma dz$$

Integrating both sides (ignoring for the moment the time-dependence of μ) gives:

$$\ln(r_T) - \ln(r_0) = (\mu(T) - \tfrac{1}{2}\sigma^2)T + \sigma\sqrt{T}U(0,1)$$

Or,

$$r_T = r_0 e^{(\mu(T)-\frac{1}{2}\sigma^2)T} e^{\sigma\sqrt{T}U(0,1)}.$$

where $U(0,1)$ is a Standard Normal variable (that is, has mean zero and standard deviation 1).

This expression has three components, the initial interest rate, r_0, the drift term (the first exponential) and the volatility term (the second exponential). We wish to adjust the drift term so that our rate lattice matches our current term structure so we will rewrite the equation above to be:

$$r_T = r_0 a_T e^{\sigma\sqrt{T}U(0,1)}$$

where we will determine the a_T terms to fit the term structure. This fitting process is the reason for not being rigorous with the integration of the time dependent μ term. We will replace the Standard Normal variable $U(0,1)$, with a Binomial variable "$B(0,1)$", as is the usual practice in building a binomial lattice.

A binomial variable, b_{ni}, is represented on a lattice at node i at time step n. It has value:

$$b_{ni} = \frac{(2i - n)}{\sqrt{n}}$$

and probability,

$$P_{ni} = {}^nC_i 2^{-n}$$

where the binomial co-efficient is

$${}^nC_i = \frac{n!}{i!(n-i)!}$$

and assuming a probability of one half for up and down movements. Consequently, this variable has mean zero and standard deviation one. (A further comment on our choice of probabilities is made below.) If we split our time to maturity T into n steps, then each step has length

$$\Delta t = \frac{T}{n}$$

Substituting into our expression for r_T,

$$r_T(n,i) = r_0 a_T e^{\sigma\sqrt{n\Delta t}\frac{(2i-n)}{\sqrt{n}}}$$

Simplifying,

$$r_T(n,i) = r_0 a_T e^{\sigma\sqrt{\Delta t}(2i-n)}$$

So let us now move into the numerical part of the example. We will start with a continuously compounding zero coupon curve with rates for each quarter as below,

Exhibit 6.2

Years	0	0.25	0.5	0.75	1	1.25	1.5	1.75	2	2.25
Zero Rate	6.00%	6.15%	6.28%	6.40%	6.50%	6.58%	6.64%	6.69%	6.72%	6.75%

From this, we can generate a set of rates for each node using the formula above. A volatility of 12% per annum has been assumed.

quarterly $\sigma = 0.06$ $\Delta t = \frac{T}{n} = 1$

Exhibit 6.3

Time Steps (quarters)

Node	0	1	2	3	4	5	6	7	8
0	6.1500%	6.7941%	7.4597%	8.0902%	8.6896%	9.2487%	9.8558%	10.3355%	11.0276%
1		6.0259%	6.6162%	7.1753%	7.7070%	8.2029%	8.7413%	9.1668%	9.7806%
2			5.8680%	6.3639%	6.8355%	7.2753%	7.7529%	8.1302%	8.6746%
3				5.6443%	6.0625%	6.4526%	6.8762%	7.2108%	7.6937%
4					5.3770%	5.7229%	6.0986%	6.3954%	6.8237%
5						5.0758%	5.4090%	5.6723%	6.0521%
6							4.7973%	5.0308%	5.3677%
7								4.4620%	4.7607%
8									4.2224%
a_T	1	1.040403	1.075797	1.098776	1.111456	1.114082	1.118078	1.104214	1.109543

This table represents a set of interest rates of period equal to a quarter of a year. The current spot rate, 6.15%, appears in the first cell corresponding to $r_0(0,0)$ and this is seen to progress either up to 6.7941% or down to 6.0259%. The probability of up or down movements is taken to be 0.5 and this reveals the reason for using a_T. We could use the formula value (from the integration above, done rigorously) for this and adjust the probability of up or down movements to fit the term structure. Alternatively, as has been done here, the probabilities can be chosen beforehand and the rates for the nodes adjusted to fit the term structure. The latter approach means that the formula for the probability at a node is the simple one shown above, rather than depending on a combination of the adjusted probabilities that would arise otherwise. Using probabilities of 0.5 makes a spreadsheet implementation much simpler.

How did we arrive at the values for a_T listed in the table? This is done iteratively. To illustrate using the first step we have rates $r_1(1,0)$ and $r_1(1,1)$ each occurring with probability 0.5. What is the expected two-quarter zero rate, R_2, using these rates?

$$e^{R_2 2\Delta t} = 0.5 * e^{r_0(0,0)\Delta t} * e^{r_1(1,0)\Delta t} + 0.5 * e^{r_0(0,0)\Delta t} * e^{r_1(1,1)\Delta t}$$

But we know that R_2 should equal our two quarter spot rate from our current zero coupon curve (6.28% in this example) so we can adjust the a_1 factor which determines the r_1 rates until the above condition is met. This is easy on a spreadsheet using a solve function (for example "Goal Seek" in Microsoft Excel) or can be done using any well-known numerical zero finding algorithm in a coded version. The two individual terms in the expression correspond to the node specific discount rates. These rates can be used to discount cashflows occurring on the nodes back to zero. This technique for building a lattice follows an approach which is known as forward induction. In this example the discount rate lattice has the following values:

$$\frac{r_0+r_1}{2}, \quad \frac{r_0+r_1+r_2}{3}, \quad \frac{r_0+r_1+r_2+r_3}{4} \quad \cdots$$

Exhibit 6.4

Discount Rates	0	1	2	3	4	5	6	7	8
0	6.1500%	6.4721%	6.8013%	7.1235%	7.4367%	7.7387%	8.0412%	8.3279%	8.6279%
1		6.0879%	6.3921%	6.7413%	7.0873%	7.4188%	7.7448%	8.0522%	8.3668%
2			6.0146%	6.2435%	6.5610%	6.8994%	7.2439%	7.5739%	7.9088%
3				5.9220%	6.0787%	6.3420%	6.6572%	6.9831%	7.3246%
4					5.8130%	5.9087%	6.1215%	6.3901%	6.7018%
5						5.6902%	5.7437%	5.9001%	6.1347%
6							5.5626%	5.5753%	5.6966%
7								5.4250%	5.4180%
8									5.2914%
Expected Value	6.15%	6.28%	6.40%	6.50%	6.58%	6.64%	6.69%	6.72%	6.75%

From the first lattice of rates we can look at the value of our caplet and then using the second "discount" lattice we can get the net present value. If we take as our strike rate, 7.00%, then we need to compare each of our final node rates with this and construct the payoff. We then weight each payoff by the probability of occurrence and then discount back to today. The sum of these contributions is the caplet price.

Exhibit 6.5

Node	Rate	max (r − K,0)	Value per $1m	Discount Rate	Probability	Contrib-ution ($)
0	11.0276%	4.0276%	10,068.96	8.6279%	0.00391	33.10
1	9.7806%	2.7806%	6,951.48	8.3668%	0.03125	183.76
2	8.6746%	1.6746%	4,186.51	7.9088%	0.10938	390.91
3	7.6973%	0.6937%	1,734.21	7.3246%	0.21875	327.66
4	6.8237%	0.0000%	—	6.7018%	0.27344	—
5	6.0521%	0.0000%	—	6.1347%	0.21875	—
6	5.3677%	0.0000%	—	5.6966%	0.10938	—
7	4.7607%	0.0000%	—	5.4180%	0.03125	—
8	4.2224%	0.0000%	—	5.2914%	0.00391	—
				Price ($)		935.43

The value per million is calculated as the percentage payoff applied to one million dollars for one quarter. The discounting raises an interesting point. Here we have discounted each caplet contribution by the discount factor that applies to its node—in effect assuming stochastic discount rates. You may recall that under BS assumptions there is a single constant discount factor for the period, that is discount factors are not stochastic. If we apply the two year spot rate (6.72%) as the discount rate for each contribution to the caplet we end up with a price of $955.69 per $m face value. The difference between $955.69 and $935.43 shows the relative size of the error made under a BS assumption of constant discount rates. A single constant volatility was used for the caplet valuation. Use of different volatilities and thus different lattices for the different caplets in a cap would allow the calibration of the cap price to the volatility term structure as well as the interest rate term structure.

We can make some concluding comments about this example. A simple interest rate process was assumed and from this a binomial process in which we made the assumption of 0.5 as our up and down probabilities. We built the lattice including a variable drift component which we then solved for iteratively to fit the current term structure of interest rates (in zero coupon curve form). Part of this iterative fitting yielded a discount lattice which is useful for discounting individual cashflows back to today from specific nodes. From the quarterly rate lattice we determined the payoff in percentage terms then converted this to a dollar amount. This was discounted back to today to provide us with a caplet price. We observed the different effect of discounting with the stochastic rates as opposed to using a single discount rate.

This approach can easily be extended to a full cap (or floor) and can also be easily implemented on a spreadsheet. Note that to increase the number of steps beyond one per quarter would require the final payoff rate of period one quarter being determined as an expected value from the rates beyond the expiry node.

5. CONCLUSION

In concluding this chapter I hope that I have provided the reader with an overview of the breadth of interest rate option pricing models and the various reasons for this diversity. The underpinning of all of these models is an assumption about the underlying interest rate process and interpreting the SDE allows us to identify what distribution of rates is being assumed, what factors are time-dependent and may thus be used to fit exact term structures, and whether such features as mean reversion have been included.

Through an example we looked at the choices required for building a lattice model and the way in which factors can be adjusted to calibrate the model to existing term structure information. Obviously in such a short chapter there are many things which have been simplified but I hope that the flavour of the topic has been made accessible.

There are a number of books which cover the field of interest rate option pricing but those of Hull and Jarrow are readily accessible to the non-mathematician and the review article by Ho and the chapters in the book by Rebonato provide discussion of individual models.

Chapter 7

Pricing Models for Complex/Exotic Options

by Dr Garry de Jager

1. INTRODUCTION

Until fairly recently, if reference was made to financial options, it almost certainly referred to either a simple call or put, or, in the field of interest rates, a simple cap or floor. Since that time, more complicated options and other derivative instruments have also become popular, notwithstanding the fact that the "vanilla" options and derivatives still constitute the bulk of the trades.

We can think about exotic derivatives, and exotic options in particular, as coming in two "waves". The first wave consisted of products such as average rate options, barrier options and digital options, and these are often now not considered substantially different from the "vanilla" products. The second wave might be considered to be products such as knockout options with limited barrier periods, power options, cross product options, range binaries and spread options. In general we might say that the more difficult it is to understand the details of an option, the more difficult it is to assess a fair price and the more sources of uncertainty or risk, the more likely it is that the option will be considered "exotic".

2. EMERGENCE OF EXOTIC OPTIONS

Exotic options tended to emerge in the face of three influences: customer needs, progress in pricing theory (often led by academics), and improved trader ability to manage risk.

2.1 Client needs

Standard European options have:

(a) a payoff at one point in time, that is, the maturity of the option;

(b) this "payoff" is a standard linear function of the price of the underlying asset; and

(c) this "price" is the underlying's value at maturity.

However, not all clients want to be rewarded only at maturity, nor might they necessarily want to be rewarded according to the level of the price of the underlying asset, and if they do, then it might not necessarily be a linear function. We can readily find examples for each of these three cases.

First, a client may wish to be rewarded when a particular event occurs, for example, at the exact moment when the price of the underlying moves through a particular price level. A knock-in barrier option and knock-out barrier with rebate are examples of such a derivative. Secondly, a client may wish to be rewarded with a specific pre-determined cash sum if the underlying is above (or below) a certain price level at maturity. A digital option is an example of such a derivative. Thirdly, a client may prefer a payoff function that is different from the standard linear function of price at maturity. For instance, he/she may prefer a more generous payoff than the classical $MAX(0,spot-strike)$ for a standard call. Two such payoffs would be:

(a) $MAX(0,spot*spot-strike)$; and

(b) $MAX(0, spot-MIN(spot))$.

In the first case the payoff is usually much greater if the option is in the money at maturity, particularly when the asset price is unexpectedly high. A power option is an example of such an option. In the second case we are dealing with a lookback option, that is, at maturity we "lookback" over the past history of prices and pick the lowest one, and this replaces the standard strike in an ordinary call.

2.2 Progress in pricing theory

Following the publication of the seminal Black-Scholes[1] pricing formula for equity options, there rapidly followed a series of publications, primarily produced by academics, pricing options in other domains, for example, the Black[2] model for pricing options on commodities and futures, the Grabbe[3] model for options on foreign exchange, the Roll/Geske/Whaley[4] model for options on equities with dividends. There also followed a plethora of models to price more complicated styles of options, regardless of what the underlying might be—the Cox, Ross and Rubinstein[5] binomial American option model; the Goldman et al[6] lookback option model, which was further developed by Conze and Viswanathan;[7] the arithmetic average rate and average strike option models; the Rubinstein and Reiner[8] barrier option models; digital options; the de Jager/Winsen[9] generalized power option models, and many more.

As option trading desks began hiring mathematical finance researchers (often referred to as "rocket scientists"), virtually any style of payoff

1. F Black and M Scholes, "The Pricing of Options and Corporate Liabilities" (1973) 81 *Journal of Political Economy* 637.
2. F Black, "The Pricing of Commodity Contracts" (1976) 3(1 & 2) *Journal of Financial Economics* 167.
3. J O Grabbe, "The Pricing of Call and Put Options on Foreign Exchange" (1983) 2 *Journal of International Money and Finance* 239.
4. R Roll, R Geske and R Whaley, "On the Valuation of American Call Options on Stocks with Known Dividends" (1981) 9 *Journal of Financial Economics* 207.
5. J C Cox, S Ross and M Rubinstein, "Option Pricing: A Simplified Approach" (1979) 7 *Journal of Financial Economics* 229.
6. M B Goldman, H B Sosin and M A Gatto, "Path Dependent Options: 'Buy at the Low, Sell at the High' " (1979) 34(5) *Journal of Finance* 1111.
7. Conze and Viswanathan, "Path Dependent Options: The Case of Lookback Options" (1991) 46(5) *Journal of Finance* 1893.
8. M Rubinstein and E Reiner, "Barrier Options" (1991) *Exotic Options* (unpublished manuscript by M Rubinstein).
9. G de Jager and J Winsen (1992), "Power over Gamma: Curved Option Payoffs".

became possible. Further, options depending on the paths followed by more than one asset, also became possible. "Rocket scientists", using various techniques usually derived from the original Black-Scholes PDE ("partial differential equation"), together with established statistical techniques involving the volatilities of, and the correlations between, two, three or even more assets, have been able to provide traders with quite robust pricing models for these "hybrid" style options.

Finally, in the interest rate domain, there has been a flurry of activity to improve on the standard market model which is a simple application of the Black[10] model. These new improved models are usually referred to as "term structure" models, because they create a "tree" structure of possible future interest rates, and the option prices at each of the nodes are discounted depending on the interest rate at that node. These trees theoretically price exotic interest rate options more accurately than do standard formulae.

2.3 Traders and the management of risk

Unless traders feel confident in managing the not inconsiderable risks associated with exotic options, the financial community would be faced with the prospect of having a plethora of theoretical exotic option pricing formulae, but also having traders offering quotations with very wide bid/ask spreads, making it impracticable for clients to transact deals. Fortunately, both the power of computing hardware, and the availability of large-scale computing software systems, have enhanced the ability of traders to risk manage their portfolios more effectively. This increase in computer efficiency coincided with the entrance of exotics into the marketplace. Traders over the years have been able to develop sophisticated techniques to manage their books including vega and gamma immunization, and risks allocated to various "time buckets". The refinement of these techniques, prior to the arrival of exotics, resulted in the management of the latter being more smooth than might otherwise have been the case.

3. WHY EXOTICS ARE DIFFERENT

In the previous section, the implications were that exotics were different from the standard call and put options, and not only different, but far more complex to price and possibly to manage. Exotics are similar to the standard option in that they generally retain the concept of the "right, but not the obligation, to buy or sell a quantity of the underlying for what may prove to be a favourable price". The differences generally revolve around two issues (a) the activation of the option, and (b) the payout function of the option.

---

10. Black, op cit n 2.

3.1 Pricing

When pricing a standard European call or put option, it transpires that, in the words of Robert Merton (one of the doyens of option theory), "there is a trick" thanks to the technique of dynamic hedging:

(a) we can actually assume that all investors are risk neutral—therefore they require only the risk-free rate on any investment—no matter how risky;

(b) therefore in this (unreal) world all underlying assets will be priced on the basis that they will return, on average, no more (or less!) than the risk-free rate;

(c) therefore we need only calculate the probabilities of the underlying's prices at maturity (based on asset growth at the risk-free rate); and

(d) hence in turn calculate the "expected" value of an option at maturity; and

(e) finally, and most importantly, discount this expected value at the risk-free rate, back to today.

A problem with many exotics is that the technique above is not sufficient. We have seen, for instance, that some exotic options do not depend only on the price of the option at maturity. Thus the simple discounting from maturity may not apply—if we have a payoff that may occur at any time, then anticipating the discount factor will not be a trivial matter. Further, with the entire family of "term structure" models, even if we know the time of the payoff (maturity or some other time), we still don't know the appropriate discounting factor since it depends on the path that interest rates have taken to that point. For these and other reasons, more complicated pricing techniques are required. We can see that these changes are basically examples of different "activation" and different "payoff functions".

3.2 Managing risk

If pricing is not a simple matter of a fairly standard closed form mathematical expression, then the risk management is also often more difficult. We have to consider that the most elementary form of hedging is the basic "delta hedge" where a position in the underlying is used to counter the effects on option values of a move in the price of the underlying. "Smooth" option value functions usually lead to smooth hedging functions, that is, relatively small movements in the price of the underlying require relatively small trading strategies. However, with an exotic, the value function may not be "smooth", and relatively small movements in the price of the underlying may lead to substantial changes in option revaluation—and hence to a very substantial trading strategy. These uncertainties make the risks associated with the option potentially more difficult to manage.

4. GOING ABOUT GETTING A FAIR PRICE

The pricing of exotic options needs to incorporate the path dependencies that may activate a payoff or the option itself, as well as the potentially difficult payoff functions. Faced with a difficult option valuation, a number of techniques may be employed by our "rocket scientist". Seven techniques in his/her armory are:

(a) integration of integrals using advanced mathematics;

(b) solving single integrals, or multi-dimensional integrals using numerical techniques;

(c) employing complex binomial or multinomial lattices (or trees);

(d) employing finite difference techniques;

(e) using monte carlo simulations;

(f) creation of term structure trees; and

(g) use of approximating techniques.

4.1 Integration/advanced mathematics

An example of complex integration is the limited period barrier option where the knockout period begins some time after option initiation, and ends some time prior to option maturity. To price such an option a triple integral is required and tedious integration is required to provide a solution. Complex probability distributions, affected by path dependencies, often contribute to the complexity.

4.2 Integrals/numerical techniques

Where integrals are difficult, or impossible, to solve, standard numeric integration techniques may be employed. This is often the case with complex options whose payoffs depend on more than one underlying asset. In the case of multiple integrals, it is often possible to reduce the problem to a single integral which requires a solution using a variant of a standard technique often employed in high school mathematics—calculating an area under a curve. In the high school approach, students plot the curve on graph paper, and physically count the area under the curve. Using computers, the "rocket scientist" will employ standard mathematical techniques such as *Simpson's Rule* or *Romberg Integration* to calculate the area under the curve so as to calculate an option's value.

4.3 Binomial/multinomial lattices

An appealing method for less technical people to cope with is the notion of a complicated *decision tree* with probabilities connecting each of the nodes on the tree. In the case of option pricing these are usually simplified into what we call *recombining trees* rather than *exploding trees*, that is, at each time step nodes are connected to multiple nodes on the next time step. As with decision trees, the calculations begin with option values at the maturity of the option, and we work backwards using the probabilities, until we reach the node at the inception of the option. American options of all types are usually priced in this manner. Activation of options or determination of intermediate payoffs can be calculated more easily in this discrete time environment.

4.4 Finite difference schemes

A similar scheme to the above is the finite difference lattice. Although this system uses *coefficients* rather than *probabilities*, the effect is similar. This particular technique creates a lattice much like a chess board—in this case, rectangular with an identical number of nodes at each time step. The technique is widely used in mathematics, and option pricing fits neatly into a subset of the applications referred to as the *heat equation*. However, in the world of option pricing there is a case for maintaining that almost anything that can be achieved with a finite difference scheme, can be achieved more simply and more accurately with a multinomial tree.[11] The scheme is also used to value American options, and also options which exhibit a *volatility smile*.

4.5 Monte Carlo simulations

There has been an increasing interest in using a fairly "blunt instrument" known as *Monte Carlo* simulation. This method generates a path of prices for the underlying asset, and the option is priced at maturity. The method is repeated, with a second option price determined. Many thousands of trials follow, and the average of all the trials is deemed to be the option price. The field of monte carlo simulations is a science in itself, and many sophisticated techniques can be employed to speed the process or make it more accurate. In recent times the *pseudo random number* approach has been added to the *antithetic technique* to provide fast and relatively accurate option valuation. Typical options that are valued in this fashion include complicated discrete averaging payoffs where perhaps there are criteria for the number of business days that are required to be above or below a certain target price. This method generally avoids the complex mathematics associated with path dependencies.

4.6 Term structure trees

Standard binomial or multinomial trees where the underlying is an interest rate level suffer from a number of disadvantages:

(a) Since interest rates themselves are not traded—products such as bonds and swaps which are dependent on the levels of interest rates are traded—the expected price of a bond some time in the future will be equal to the forward bond price, but the expected interest rate for a forward contract will generally not be equal to the forward interest rate. This gives rise to the well-known *convexity adjustment* between the

---

11. G. de Jager, "Option Pricing With Implicit Finite Difference Methods and Large-Scale Bounded Multinationals" (1994) Proceedings of Asia Pacific Finance Association Conference 1994.

forward yield and the expected yield, which complicates the construction of a tree of interest rates.

(b) If future payoffs on such trees are to be discounted, the discount factors are not at all clear, and, theoretically should reflect the path of interest rates taken to the node in question, that is, path dependency is far more difficult than for other options.

The three most popular term structure methodologies have been the Heath, Jarrow and Morton method,[12] the Hull and White method,[13] and the Black, Derman and Toy[14] (or Black and Karasinski) model.[15] The trees are *calibrated* against cap prices from the market model, and then used to price exotic options of almost every shade.

4.7 Approximating techniques

There will be cases where the problem is difficult to formulate, but there is an obvious connection with a similar problem that has a known answer. Examples include the desired arithmetic average versus the known geometric average; knockouts measured at discrete intervals, versus known probability distributions for continuous knockouts; control variate techniques in monte carlo simulations. The discrete time barrier is an interesting example. Broadie[16] et al showed that a good approximation can be made by using the continuous barrier formula, but altering the barrier input into this formula by a specific multiple. Simulations indicate this approximating technique is effective.

5. BEHAVIOUR OF PRICES AND RISK MEASURES

The behaviour of option prices, deltas, gammas and vegas often distinguishes the exotic from the traditional European call and put and is therefore of particular interest. We illustrate this by graphing option prices and risk measures for three exotics—average rate option, down and out European barrier call, and binary range floater. The delta in the following figures is the traditional fraction of one unit of the underlying stock to buy/sell to hedge the option, but the vegas and gamma risk measures are *real* values rather than *theoretical* values and are calculated as follows:

(a) *Dollar Gamma*: The price moves up 1%, the option delta changes—we sell more of the stock for a call—and then the price moves back to original level resulting in our buying back the extra hedge at a lower price. The gain made is called the *dollar gamma*.

12. D C Heath, R A Jarrow and A Morton, "Contingent Claim Valuation with a Random Evolution of Interest Rates" (1990) 9(1) *The Review of Futures Markets* 54.
13. J C Hull and A White, "Efficient Procedures for Valuing European and American Path-dependent Options" (1993) 1(1) *Journal of Derivatives* 21.
14. F Black, E Derman and W Toy, "A One-Factor Model of Interest Rates and its Application to Treasury Bond Options" (1990) (Jan-Feb) *Financial Analysts Journal* 33.
15. F Black and P Karasinski, "Bond and Option Pricing When Short Rates are Lognormal (1991) Jul/Aug) *Financial Analysts Journal* 52.
16. Broadie, Glasserman and Kov, "A Continuity Correction For Barrier Options" (1995) Proc of European Risk Conference Paris 1996.

(b) *Dollar Vega*: The volatility moves up 1% and we note the change in the option price. The difference in price is termed the *dollar vega*.

5.1 Average rate call

The formula for a call on the geometric average stock price over the period to option maturity (rather than on the stock price at maturity), and without any past history of prices, is:

$$e^{-rT}\left[Se^{mean+0.5\,var}\,N(d1) - KN(d2)\right]$$

Where:

T	=	time to maturity
r	=	risk-free rate to maturity
S	=	current spot price
K	=	strike price
mean =		$0.5*(r-d-0.5*vol*vol)*T$
vol	=	expected volatility to maturity
d	=	dividend yield/foreign exchange rate
var	=	vol*vol/3
d2	=	[log(S/K)+mean]/sqrt(var)
d1	=	d2+sqrt(var)

In practice we usually have to make two adjustments:

(a) first, the traditional average option is calculated using arithmetic, rather than geometric averages, and

(b) secondly, the averages are usually calculated using a discrete, say daily, set of future prices, rather than the "continuous" over time average implicit in the above formula.

We now price an average rate arithmetic call option which has a remaining 42 business days within 60 calendar days to run to maturity and the average is constructed using a 10 am fixing on each business day. Initially there were 142 business days to incorporate into the average, so there have been 100 previous business days, and the average spot on these was $39.85. The option strike is $40, market volatility is now 18.5%, and the risk-free rate to option maturity is 8% (expressed as an annually compounded in arrears rate). *Exhibits 7.1, 7.2, 7.3* and *7.4* plot the option price, delta, gamma and vega respectively, against those of a regular European call. The plottings vary the spot price of the underlying stock with values from $32 to $56 being employed.

It is interesting to see that the price of the average rate call is much more stable than that of its regular European call counterpart, and this is confirmed by the lower delta values in *Exhibit 7.2*. This is clearly intuitive, since the bulk of the averaging has already occurred, and thus changes in current price (which is the major predictor of the remaining 42 prices to be averaged) are somewhat overwhelmed by the history of past prices. This is not the case with the standard European call where the major pricing factor is the spot price of the underlying stock. We note that the standard European call has deltas approaching 1 when the option is deep in the money, whereas for the same stock values, the average rate call deltas level off at just below 30%. The explanation for this is that for every dollar increase in the price of the stock, the average rate call does not increase by a dollar—since only 42 of a total of 142 prices are affected—and hence around a 30% hedge adequately covers changes in the option value.

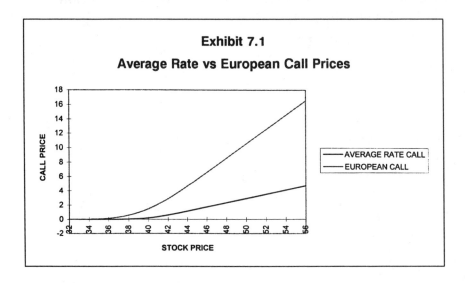

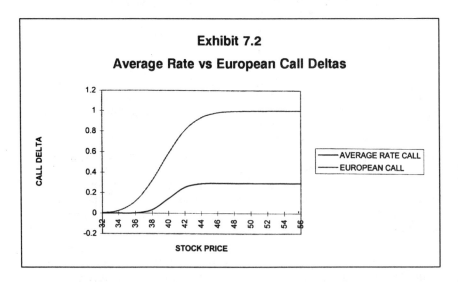

Because the prices of the average rate call option are not as sensitive to price changes in the underlying stock as are standard calls, we would expect the gamma of the option to be less as well, and this proves to be the case in *Exhibit 7.3*. Finally, we would expect that changes in the volatility over the remaining life of the option will also have less effect than normal, since they potentially only affect future prices of the underlying and cannot affect the 100 prices that have already occurred. This is confirmed in *Exhibit 7.4*.

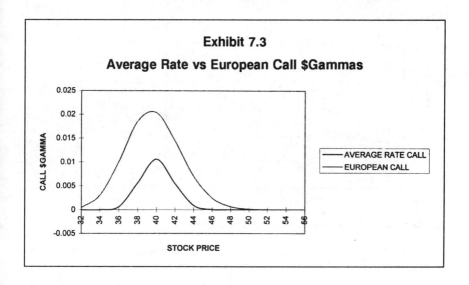

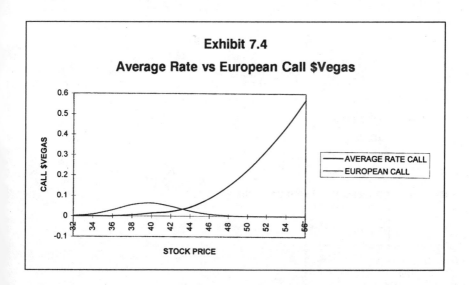

We note that what we might term the "stabilising effects" outlined above are not so dramatic if the ratio of past prices to future prices in the average rate call option is reduced. *Exhibit 7.5* demonstrates that the prices and deltas are much closer when we consider a similar option to the above, but this time with 510 business days across 730 calendar days still to run to maturity, as against 100 past prices to be incorporated into the average.

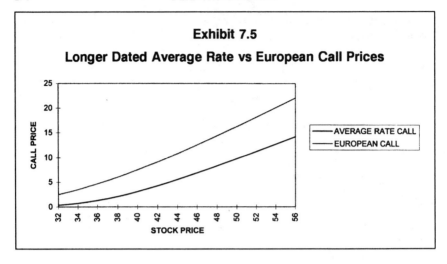

Exhibit 7.5

Longer Dated Average Rate vs European Call Prices

5.2 Down and out European barrier call

The formula for a down and out call on stock varies depending on whether the barrier is above or below the strike. Where the barrier is below the strike, we have:

$$CALL \;-\; e^{-rT}\left[e^{(r-d)T}S\left(\frac{H}{S}\right)^{2\mu/(\sigma^*\sigma)+2}N(d1) \;-\; -K\left(\frac{H}{S}\right)^{2\mu/(\sigma^*\sigma)}N(d2)\right]$$

Where:

T	=	time to maturity
r	=	risk free rate to maturity
S	=	current spot price
K	=	strike price
H	=	barrier price
σ	=	expected volatility to maturity
μ	=	r-d-0.5*σ*σ
d	=	dividend yield/foreign exchange rate

$$d2 \;=\; \left[\frac{\ln\left(\dfrac{H^2}{SK}\right)+\mu T}{\sigma\sqrt{T}}\right]$$

$$d1 \;=\; d2+\sigma\sqrt{T}$$

In practice we usually have to make a price adjustment to this formula, since the barrier is often based on discrete time periods, say daily 10 am fixings, rather than the "continuous" barrier implicit in the above formula.

We now consider a down and out call option on a stock where there are 365 calendar days to maturity, with strike at $40, market volatility at 18.5%, risk-free rate to option maturity at 8%, and a barrier of $36. *Exhibits 7.6, 7.7, 7.8* and *7.9* plot the option price, delta, gamma and vega respectively, against those of a corresponding regular European call. The plottings vary the spot price of the underlying stock from $32 to $44.

The first point of interest to note in *Exhibit 7.6* is that the barrier call price is zero if the spot is below the barrier, that is, the option has already been knocked out. At just above the barrier stock price of $36, the barrier call has a very low value, as would be expected—there is a very good chance the option will be knocked out because the stock price is so close to the barrier. At higher stock prices, the barrier call is worth nearly the same as a standard call since, according to the statistical probabilities of a bell-shaped lognormal curve of future stock prices, there is minuscule probability that the stock price will drop back down to the barrier in the remaining year to option maturity.

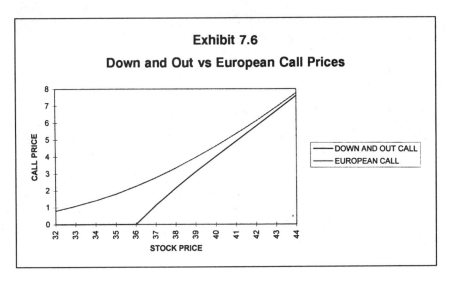

Exhibit 7.6

Down and Out vs European Call Prices

The delta of the barrier option, however, exhibits what at first might seem "bizarre" behaviour. There are two determinants here. First, at high stock prices, the delta should be close to the same as that for a standard option, since there is a low probability of any knockout occurring. Secondly, at a low price, the delta will be either (a) zero for stock prices below the barrier, or (b) rising as the stock price moves away from the barrier. Just how rapidly the delta rises is the interesting thing in *Exhibit 7.7*. We note that it climbs to almost 1.2. This is explained as follows: At $38, the stock price is still only $2 above the barrier and the option is still in substantial danger of being quickly knocked out. To guard against this complete loss in value of the barrier call, the trader would sell 1.2 shares in the underlying stock—a type of "leveraged hedge"—so he/she is compensated for a falling stock price which knocks out, or threatens to knock out, the barrier call.

This rapid rise, and subsequent fall, in the delta as stock prices rise, means we have a large gamma which is initially negative, and then positive, and this is illustrated in *Exhibit 7.8*. (We should also note that there is a discontinuity at the barrier price of $36.) The negative gamma above a stock price of $36 is obvious from *Exhibit 7.7*, which indicates that as stock prices rise, the knock out call delta reduces. Now we can see a clear contrast here as compared to a standard call. If a trader is long the standard call, then typically he will hold a negative position in the stock as a hedge. If the price of the stock rises, the delta rises, and the trader sells more of the stock. However, with a down and out call, although the trader, at stock prices just above $36, will have sold more than one unit of the stock for every option held, if the stock price rises, the trader will actually buy back some of his/her hedge, rather than sell more of the stock. It is well known, that in these circumstances—that is, being negative gamma—a move up and then back in the price of the stock results in a "dollar gamma loss" for the portfolio of the long option and the short hedge.

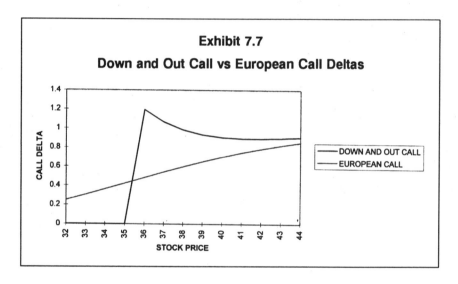

Exhibit 7.7

Down and Out Call vs European Call Deltas

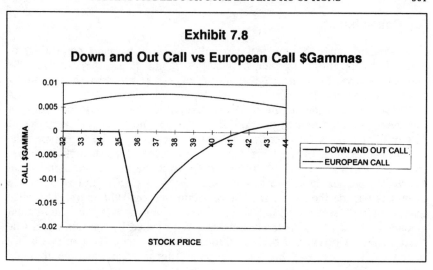

Exhibit 7.8

Down and Out Call vs European Call $Gammas

Finally, we look at the dollar vega of the down and out call. The two determining factors which give rise to the patterns in *Exhibit 7.9* are (a) that the vegas of the European and down and out calls will converge as the stock price increases, and (b) the shape of the vega curve for the down and out call, whilst similar to that for the European call, is of course zero below the barrier, and the vega is always much smaller than that for the regular call, since the price of the option is always smaller.

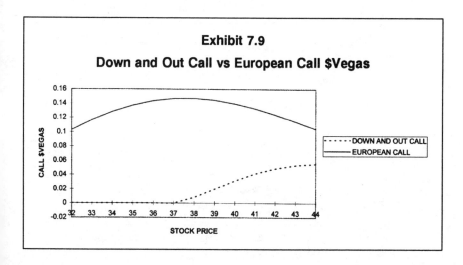

Exhibit 7.9

Down and Out Call vs European Call $Vegas

5.3 Range binary

A standard range binary deal generally involves a client depositing, or notionally depositing, a principal with the trading house, but forgoing the interest thereon. In return, the client receives a payout that is potentially better than the standard libor interest rate, should three months libor remain within a defined band for most of the period. For instance, in one form of this deal, as represented in *Exhibit 7.10*, the client has a principal of $10 million dollars on deposit with the trader, and the client forgoes the current market libor interest rate of 5.5% for the next three months. In return, the client will receive 6.15% for every day over the next three months that the daily libor fixing is within the band 5.15% to 6.15%, and zero for the days it is outside the range. If libor is within this band the entire time, then the client will receive $152,500 in "interest" as opposed to the regular amount of $138,700. This latter amount is represented by the horizontal line "fixed side". However, if halfway through the three months there is a half a per cent fall in rates and this situation persists for the remaining month and a half, then the client would only receive $76,250 in "interest".

The *Exhibit 7.10* plots the expected payout to the client for a given range of volatility expectations. We note that the higher the expected volatility, the lower the expected payout to the client. On reflection, this should be obvious since (a) libor is currently within the range, and (b) a very low actual volatility would almost certainly ensure it stays within the range, and therefore (c) a high actual volatility will dramatically increase the chances of libor moving out of the range for at least part of the next three months.

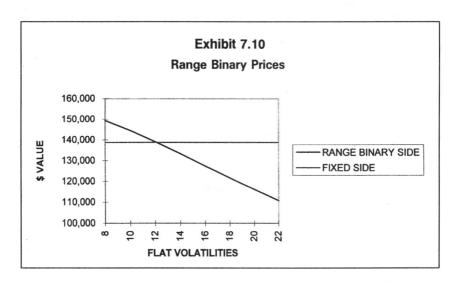

6. CONCLUSION

The essential ingredients of exotic options seem to be path dependency and/or complex payoff functions. They are usually more difficult to price and more difficult to manage in a portfolio. There are many similarities between exotics and standard options, and in one sense we can say that we have merely been stretching the current concepts of optionality a little further. In the future, we might have newer concepts of optionality.

Much of the probability distribution work in option pricing is still based on the original Black-Scholes[17] framework of log-normal brownian motion with constant volatility. As new stochastic processes are developed, we might logically see the emergence of newer exotic style options. Jump processes might logically be involved in such developments.

17. Black and Scholes, op cit n 1.

Appendix

A Glossary of Some Popular Exotic Options

Average Rate

The call or put payoff now depends on the average of the underlying between two specified dates, rather than on the underlying's price at maturity. The two selected dates are usually the option start and expiry. (Also called an Asian option).

Average Strike

The call or put strike is not set at option initiation, but is deferred till option expiry, whence the average of the underlying between two specified dates takes the place of the regular strike.

Barrier Option—In (Single)

An agreement whereby the purchaser obtains a vanilla European option under certain conditions, the central condition being that a particular price level of the underlying is breached. If the timing of the breaching of the barrier is restricted to option maturity, then sometimes it is called a "European barrier". Generally the barrier period is from option inception to option maturity. Some barrier options operate on a discrete basis (for example, the price level of the underlying is observed only once a day, whereas others operate on a continuous time basis). (Also known as "knock-in" options.)

Barrier Option—Out (Single)

The purchaser of the options stands to lose all the claims associated with the option should the price of the underlying breach a predetermined level; that is, the "barrier" level. (Also known as "knock-out" options.)

Barrier Options—Limited Period (Single)

These are similar to the above knock-in and knock-out options, except that the time period over which the barrier may be breached to effect a knock-in or knock-out is limited. If the time period is at the beginning, it is often referred to as a "front-end barrier", whereas if the time period is restricted to a period ending at option maturity, it is often referred to as a "back-end barrier". A more general form allows the barrier period to commence after option inception and end prior to option maturity.

Barrier Option (Double)

Similar to any of the above barrier options except that now we have two barriers—an upper and a lower barrier. For a "double knock-in" option the price of the underlying needs to breach either of the two barriers during the specified time period, whereas for a "double knock-out" option, the underlying needs to avoid breaching either of the two barriers else the option immediately lapses.

Barrier Option (Parisian Style)

This option can take the form of any of the above types of barriers, but now there is an additional requirement, namely that for the barrier to be considered "breached", the underlying must be beyond the barrier for a given number of days.

Ratchet Options

These options have their strikes reset (usually on a favourable basis) during the life of the option, or in the case of a cap, successive caplets may have their strikes reset favourably. Similar concepts underlie the *cliquet* or *resettable* options. The resetting will usually be the result of some level of the underlying being reached, and the possible reset times may be restricted to particular occasions (for example, the end of the previous caplet).

Bermuda Options

Options that may be considered half-way between European and American; that is, Bermudan (also known as mid-Atlantic options). The idea here is that on a number of particular intermediate dates, the option may be exercised.

Digital Options (European Style)

Basically any of the options in this section can also have a digital payoff. Unlike the standard call and put options, digital options have a set dollar payout at maturity if the underlying price is above the strike—for a digital call, or below the strike—for a digital put. Digital versions of barriers and double barriers are also possible.

Digital Options (American Style)

This form of the digital pays out the moment the strike is first reached during the life of the option. This option can be incorporated into the standard knockout option where a "rebate" is paid should the barrier be breached.

Optimal Rate LookBack Option

The call or put payoff depends on the most favourable price the underlying experienced between two specified dates (highest price for a call, lowest price for a put).

Optimal Strike LookBack Option

The setting of the call or put strike is deferred to option maturity whence the most favourable price the underlying experienced between two specified dates (lowest price for a call, highest price for a put) takes the place of the regular strike.

Power Options

A power call will payoff $Max(S^N - K, 0)$ instead of the usual payoff. If the spot is above 1, which it usually will be for these types of options, the payoff can be very high very quickly, especially if N is greater or equal to 2.

Quanto Options

An option where the underlying asset and the payoff calculation are in different currencies (for example, a cap on deutschmark interest rates where the notional principal payoff is in US dollars, and the "option compensation" is US dollars).

Shout Option

This option has some of the aspects of the *optimal rate lookback option* in that a favourable level achieved during the life of the option may be used to replace the underlying's price at option maturity. However, in this instance, the holder is not guaranteed the *most* favourable price of the underlying for the payoff settlement, but gets a single opportunity to nominate this price. Thus, if at any time during the life of the option the holder feels the *top of*

the market has been reached, he or she may nominate that price as a
"fallback" level. Then at maturity, if this fallback level is more favourable
to the outcome than the underlying's price at maturity, it will be used
instead.

Spread Options

These payoff on the difference between the level of two underlying assets. A
wide variety of spreads are possible (for example, the difference between two
interest rates of different tenors, the difference between two metal prices, the
difference between two futures prices on the same commodity).

Chapter 8

Estimating Volatility

by Satyajit Das

1. OVERVIEW

The concept of volatility of asset prices and returns is central to financial markets. Volatility provides essential data about the probability of achieving certain outcomes in terms of price levels which is intrinsic to key decisions in financial markets, such as asset allocation and construction of efficient asset or liability portfolios (in the context of a risk-return trade-off). In the context of option pricing, an estimate of volatility is essential to the valuation of the instrument. This chapter focuses on the problem of volatility estimation in the context of option pricing.

The structure of this chapter is as follows: a framework for volatility, covering causes of volatility in asset markets and the relationship between volatility and option pricing, is first examined. Approaches to volatility estimation are then considered, including historical volatility, implied volatility, as well as alternative approaches to volatility modelling. The behaviour of volatility, particularly the concept of the volatility smile and the term structure of volatility, are analysed. The Chapter concludes with an analysis of volatility estimation in practice.

2. VOLATILITY ESTIMATION—FRAMEWORK

2.1 Introduction

Volatility estimation, in the context of option pricing, must be considered in the broader context of asset price and return volatility generally. The framework for volatility estimation, in reality, must recognise the causes of volatility in asset prices and the inter-relationship between volatility and option pricing models.

2.2 Causes of volatility in asset prices

Price volatility in asset markets is caused by a variety of factors, the most important of which is information release. A second cause of volatility is the process of trading and market-making in financial instruments.

Information release generally fall into two categories: anticipated and unanticipated information. Anticipated information includes economic statistics as well as political or social information. This type of information release is anticipated. Market participants develop expectations regarding the content of the informational release. The impact of the information is, often, driven by whether or not it corresponds to market expectations, reflecting the fact that asset prices will generally incorporate the content of expected information releases. The impact of information releases can be analysed, particularly with reference to past releases. It may be possible to develop probabilistic expectations of anticipated asset price volatility from the historical reaction of the market to prior actual data releases in combination with probabilities in relation to a variety of range outcomes for the relevant information release.

Unanticipated information releases typically relate to international events (wars, natural disasters, et cetera) and other unanticipated or unanticipatable events. This type of information can have substantial and unpredictable impact on asset price volatility. The difficulty in predicting this type of informational release (by definition) makes it extremely complex to incorporate these types of factors in forecasting future asset price volatility.[1]

A newer area of financial economics research (the study of market micro-structure) seeks to isolate the impact of trading on volatility.[2] This research identifies the informational content of trading and its interaction with the institutional structure of markets as a possible source of volatility in asset markets.[3]

In seeking to isolate factors generating asset price volatility, the linkages between volatility in various market segments or across markets should be noted. Analysis indicates that there may be implied and historical volatility relationships between different markets. For example, bond market volatility across various currencies show significant correlation. Similarly, in certain currencies, volatilities in the foreign exchange market are, often, useful indicators of volatility in interest rate markets in the relevant currencies.

2.3 Relationship between asset volatility and option pricing

Mathematical option pricing models, such as the Black Scholes model, require estimation of the future volatility of the underlying asset price, as this item is a parameter which must be input into the model. Binomial models require similar inputs.

The volatility estimate used in option valuation is the annualised standard deviation of the logs of the asset returns (or the continuously compounded

1. For a recent analysis of the impact of release of information of volatility, see Louis Ederington and Ja Hae Lee, "The Impact Of Macroeconomic News On Financial Markets" (1996) 9 (Spring) *Journal of Applied Corporate Finance* 41.
2. For example, a number of studies have found that volatility as between close of trading on Friday and opening of trading the next Monday morning (when there is an interval of around three non-trading days) is only around 20% higher than that as between close of trading on a one day and open of trading the next day (when there are no intervening non-trading days) rather than the predicted three times higher, suggesting that volatility is higher when trading on exchanges is open than when it is closed: see E E Fama, "The Behaviour Of Stock Market Prices" (1965) 38 (Jan) *Journal of Business* 34; K R French, "Stock Returns And The Weekend Effect" (1979) *Journal of Financial Economics* 55.
3. See Kalman J, Cohen, Steven F Maier, Robert A Schwartz and David K Whitcomb (1986) *The Microstructure of Securities Markets* (Prentice-Hall Englewoods Cliffs, New Jersey, 1986); Robert A Schwartz, *Equity Markets* (Harper & Row, New York, 1988).

asset returns). The volatility estimate is a measure of the uncertainty about the returns on the asset. It is used to generate the distribution of asset prices as at the option expiry to calculate the fair value of the option.

There are several aspects of the volatility estimate which should be noted:

1. The volatility parameter required to derive option values is forward looking; that is, the relevant volatility is the asset return volatility in the period to option expiry.

2. Volatility is assumed to be constant as between the pricing date and option expiry.

3. Volatility is assumed to be time homogenous; that is, it is the same over the life of the option.

4. Uncertainty about the asset price at option maturity is assumed to be directly proportional to the asset price at commencement.

The estimation of the volatility of the underlying asset price is particularly problematic because it is the only parameter of most mathematical pricing models which is not observable directly. The sensitivity of the option value to this parameter places additional demands on the estimation of volatility.

3. VOLATILITY ESTIMATION

3.1 Approaches

Estimation of the *true* volatility of the underlying asset price is extremely difficult. In practice, a number of alternative approaches are utilised. The major approaches include:

- historical/empirical approach; or
- implied volatility approach.

In recent times, a number of other approaches to option volatilities have emerged. These include ARCH type volatility models.

3.2 Historical/empirical volatility

3.2.1 Calculation of historical volatility

Under the historical or empirical approach, volatility estimates are calculated as the standard deviation of logs of the price changes of a sample time series of historical data for the asset price.

This calculation procedure entails the following steps:

1. The time series of historical data is specified. This will usually be the series of daily, weekly or monthly price observations for the relevant asset. As discussed in more detail below, for debt securities either price or yield can be utilised.

2. The price changes are calculated to measure the periodic (daily, et cetera) return on the asset. In practice, the price relatives are utilised; that is, one plus the return or the observation at time t1 divided by the observation at the previous point in the time series t0. While the

standard deviation can be calculated for either the returns or the price relatives the first leads to inaccuracies reflecting the nature of the log normal distribution based on the effect of compounding. This means that the calculation using the price relatives is preferred. The difference is not significant for calculations involving relatively short data series but becomes increasingly significant as the data series increases in size.

3.   The standard deviation of the price relatives is then calculated.

The interpretation of the standard deviation is as follows:

- The standard deviation computed equates to the volatility over the relevant time interval (daily, et cetera).

- The periodic observation is then scaled to give the annualised volatility of the asset price returns. This is done using the following relationship:

$$\sigma_{annual} = \sigma_{daily} \times \sqrt{\text{number of days}}$$

where the number of days would be set at either 250 or 260 days.

Exhibit 8.1 shows a possible sequence of asset prices over a 20 day period. The data gives an estimate for the daily volatility of 0.00889 or 0.889%. Assuming that time is measured in trading days and that there are 250 trading days per year, the estimated annual volatility is 0.14051 or 14.051% pa.

Note that the daily volatility is scaled using the square root of the time interval. This reflects the fact that the assumed uncertainty about the asset price does not increase linearly.

Exhibit 8.1

Volatility Estimation—Historical/Empirical Approach

CALCULATING VOLATILITY

Period	Asset Price	Price Relative (St/(St-1))	Daily Return Ui = ln (St/(St − 1))
0	8.2500		
1	8.1800	0.99152	(0.00852)
2	8.2000	1.00244	0.00244
3	8.2000	1.00000	0.00000
4	8.2100	1.00122	0.00122
5	8.1200	0.98904	(0.01102)
6	8.1500	1.00369	0.00369
7	8.0700	0.99018	(0.00986)
8	8.1300	1.00743	0.00741
9	8.1700	1.00492	0.00491
10	8.2000	1.00367	0.00367
11	8.1600	0.99512	(0.00489)
12	8.1900	1.00368	0.00367
13	8.1200	0.99145	(0.00858)
14	8.0400	0.99015	(0.00990)
15	8.1900	1.01866	0.01848
16	8.0900	0.98779	(0.01229)
17	8.1200	1.00371	0.00370
18	8.1800	1.00739	0.00736
19	8.2700	1.01100	0.01094
20	8.1500	0.98549	(0.01462)

STANDARD DEVIATION (PER PERIOD)   0.889%

ANNUALISED VOLATILITY (DAYS)   250   14.051%

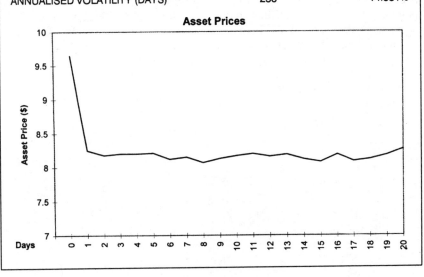

Asset Prices

3.2.2 Calculating historical volatility—adjustments

In calculating the historical volatility of certain assets the asset price sequence must be adjusted to reflect the non-homogenous nature of the data series. A major cause of this non-homogeneity is the entitlement to income on the underlying assets; for example, coupons in the case of debt instruments, and dividends in the case of equity stocks.

The presence of these income flows has the impact of reducing the comparability of succeeding price observations because the transition from cum-interest to ex-interest or cum-dividend to ex-dividend will affect the price of the asset. In theory, the asset price should fall by the amount of the income entitlement (coupon or dividend). This necessitates intervention to adjust the price sequence when an asset goes ex entitlement as follows:

The price relative is restated as $\ln (S_t + D) / S_{t-1}$.

Some practitioners eliminate data around the ex entitlement data, particularly for equities, from the data series reflecting the impact of a variety of factors, such as tax, on asset prices during these transitions and the resultant potential distortion in the volatility estimate.

3.2.3 Calculating historical volatility—asset class extensions

The above analysis focuses on the volatility of asset prices in general. This would encompass equity stocks, equity market indexes, commodity prices, commodity price indexes and currency values. In the case of debt instruments, it is feasible to calculate the volatility of both asset prices (being volatility of the price of the underlying debt security) and yield volatility (being the volatility of the interest rate index itself).

Exhibit 8.2 sets out calculation of both the price and yield volatility for a debt instrument (in this case a three month or 90 day discount instrument). In practice, the two are related with the interest rate changes driving the changes in the price of the debt instrument. Exhibit 8.3 sets out the normal method for converting yield volatility to price volatility. Both yield based and price based measures of volatility are utilised for debt instruments. As described above, in theoretical terms, price volatility is proportional to absolute yield volatility and modified duration.

Exhibit 8.2

Volatility Estimation—Historical/Empirical Approach for Debt Instruments

CALCULATING VOLATILITY—DEBT INSTRUMENTS

$$\frac{P_{t+1}}{P_t} = e^{r_t}$$

EXHIBIT 8.2 VOLATILITY ESTIMATION—HISTORICAL/EMPIRICAL APPROACH FOR DEBT INSTRUMENTS

PERIOD	INTEREST RATE	ASSET PRICE	PRICE VOLATILITY CALCULATIONS		YIELD VOLATILITY CALCULATIONS	
			PRICE RELATIVE (St/(St − 1))	DAILY RETURN u = ln(St/(St − 1))	PRICE RELATIVE (St/(St − 1))	DAILY RETURN ln(St/(St − 1))
0	6.000%	98.5421				
1	6.125%	98.5122	0.99970	(0.00030)	1.02083	0.02062
2	6.350%	98.4584	0.99945	(0.00055)	1.03673	0.03608
3	6.200%	98.4943	1.00036	0.00036	0.97638	(0.02391)
4	6.250%	98.4823	0.99988	(0.00012)	1.00806	0.00803
5	6.400%	98.4464	0.99964	(0.00036)	1.02400	0.02372
6	6.500%	98.4225	0.99976	(0.00024)	1.01563	0.01550
7	6.650%	98.3867	0.99964	(0.00036)	1.02400	0.02372
8	6.750%	98.3629	0.99976	(0.00024)	1.01563	0.01550
9	6.650%	98.3867	1.00024	0.00024	0.98519	(0.01493)
10	6.580%	98.4034	1.00017	0.00017	0.98947	(0.01058)
11	6.600%	98.3987	0.99995	(0.00005)	1.00304	0.00303
12	6.710%	98.3724	0.99973	(0.00027)	1.01667	0.01653
13	6.650%	98.3867	1.00015	0.00015	0.99106	(0.00898)
14	6.700%	98.3748	0.99988	(0.00012)	1.00752	0.00749
15	6.720%	98.3700	0.99995	(0.00005)	1.00299	0.00298
16	6.740%	98.3653	0.99995	(0.00005)	1.00298	0.00297
17	6.780%	98.3557	0.99990	(0.00010)	1.00593	0.00592
18	6.740%	98.3653	1.00010	0.00010	0.99410	(0.00592)
19	6.670%	98.3820	1.00017	0.00017	0.98961	(0.01044)
20	6.700%	98.3748	0.99993	(0.00007)	1.00450	0.00449
STANDARD DEVIATION (PER PERIOD)				0.023%		1.499%
ANNUALISED VOLATILITY (DAYS)		250.0000		0.000%		0.000%

Exhibit 8.3

Relationship Between Price and Yield Volatility

The following formula can be used to convert yield volatility into its price volatility equivalent:

Price Volatility = (Δ Price/ Δ Yield) × Yield × Yield Volatility

For example, the formula can be used as follows to convert yield volatility of 20% for 91 day securities to its equivalent price volatility as follows:

(Δ Price/ Δ Yield) = 24.08 for 0.0001% pa or 1 bps change in yield (per $1,000,000 face value of the security at a yield of 7.00% pa)

Therefore:

Price Volatility = 24.08 × 7.00% × 20.00% = 0.337% pa

An observable feature of the relationship between yield and price volatility is that yield volatility increases in a market with decreasing yields whereas price volatility decreases (for similar movements in outright yield).

In practice, both types of yields are utilised with the preferred volatility estimate parameter being driven, largely, by market convention. In utilising yield volatility estimates, the following points should be noted:

- Yield volatility is usually assumed to be constant for fixed interest instruments of the same yield implying a flat yield curve which does not change shape and trades at constant yield volatility across all maturities.

- The use of yield volatility has the potential to create confusion where the yield curve shape is, itself, volatile.

- Yield volatility is not affected by the changing duration associated with fixed coupon bonds.

Utilising price volatility estimates for debt instruments, the following points should be noted:

- The price volatility constantly changes with changing duration of the underlying fixed interest instrument.

- It is necessary to clarify where the price volatility being calculated are the basis of a "clean" (ex interest) or "dirty"' (cum accrued interest) price.

In practice, price volatility is utilised in markets where the underlying security is traded in price (for example, the US treasury bond market). In addition, yield volatility is utilised in preference to price volatility in a variety of markets for options on short term interest rates because price volatility of these instruments is very low.

3.2.4 Considerations in using historical/empirical volatility

The historical/empirical techniques for volatility estimation seeks to quantify past market volatility and utilise this as a basis for forecasting *future* market volatility for asset prices.

The major difficulties with this approach include:

- assumed stationarity of volatility parameters;

- specifying the number of observations utilised;
- the availability of a variety of price observations;
- specifying the number of days utilised; and
- allocating relative importance to different components of the time series.

A major difficulty relates to the assumption implied by this technique that past volatility is a useful mechanism for deriving future asset price volatility. The assumed stationarity of the volatility estimate is neither logical nor supported by empirical evidence. Volatilities for a variety of assets demonstrate significant changes over time.

The period over which data is utilised to generate historical volatility is constantly debated. Proponents of utilising data over a very long period (say, five years) implicitly assume that volatility is constant over long periods of time or, alternatively, tends towards a quantifiable average level of volatility. This is consistent with a hypothesis regarding the mean reverting nature of volatility.

Proponents of utilising data over a shorter period (between one and three months) base their position on the implied view that volatility itself is not constant but varies significantly and prefer to use a shorter period to obtain a good estimate of the current level of volatility. Adherents to this theory would, as a consequence, adjust the volatility parameter input into option pricing formulas regularly.

It is clear that the larger number of observations utilised to estimate volatility, the higher the probability that changes in, for example, general economic conditions or other exogenous factors, will impact upon the calculated volatility causing a violation of the assumption that the standard deviation of the asset's return is constant over the life of the option. The trade-off between increasing the period over which data is utilised in order to achieve more efficient estimates and the probability that the volatility has altered is essentially not resolvable within the context of the mathematical option pricing models discussed.

A further complication arises from the fact that the price data utilised can take a variety of forms, including:

- close-to-close prices;
- open-to-close prices;
- close-to-open prices; and
- high or low prices.

The use of close-to-close prices is the most common measure utilised. This measure allows the full daily movement of the asset price to be captured and the impact of all information released over the relevant 24 hour period to be captured. The impact of non-trading days (such as holidays and weekends) tends to distort the data series as information may be released and impact upon prices but is not captured until a later date. The process of annualisation utilised (see above) does not adjust for this phenomenon.

Open-to-close prices provide a measure of intra-day volatility, which shows reaction to all information released during the trading day. Use of open-to-close prices creates problems of annualisation as it is necessary, to be accurate, to adjust for the concentration of information released within an average 24 hour period.

Use of close-to-open prices allows a measure of overnight volatility. It shows reaction to information release outside trading hours and, in certain cases, measures the interrelationship between the domestic market and international market in other time zones. The close-to-open price series suffers from the same difficulties as the open-to-close price series because of difficulties of annualisation.

High to low prices again facilitate capturing of the range of a full day's price movements in the volatility estimate. It is typically useful to traders who have intra-day positions or are hedging positions intra-day.

The major value of the variety of price series and the different estimates of volatility that can be derived lies in the capacity to compare the relative price volatility of the various series.

As noted above, the daily volatility is scaled by the square root of the time to maturity to derive the annualised volatility. One commentator.[4] argues that there are at least three relevant choices as to the maturity estimate:

1. *Calendar days*—the number of actual calendar days between the time of valuation and option maturity.

2. *Trading days*—the number of days over the option life on which trading in the relevant asset is open.

3. *Economic days*—the number of days over the option life on which information *likely to impact the asset price* is released.

The last concept requires the information release to be *anticipated*. As noted previously, the asset price seems to react to both anticipated and unanticipated information. In addition, the use of economic days would necessarily require an understanding of and specific identification of information *likely* to affect asset prices.[5]

The distinction between calendar and trading days is more interesting. The volatility estimate utilised for short dated options is particularly problematic. For example, in the case of an option with a time to expiry of, say, seven days where there are intervening non-trading days (a weekend and perhaps a holiday), the proportion of non-trading days as a proportion of the life of the option is significant. Similarly, for a short dated option, there may be *no non-trading days*. In these cases, the use of the same volatility scaled over the *calendar time to maturity* appears inappropriate. In practice, some practitioners adjust the volatility of these option to reflect this factor. A common technique is to adjust the volatility used (see *Exhibit 8.4*).

4.   See Kenneth Leong, "Exorcising the Demon" (1990) 3 (9) (Oct) *Risk* 29.
5.   For discussion of research on economic days, see Galen Burghardt and Gerald A Hanweck Jr, "Calendar-Adjusted Volatilities" (1993) (Winter) *The Journal of Derivatives* 23.

Exhibit 8.4

Adjusting Volatility

Assume an option with seven days to expiry. Of these seven days, four are non-trading days. The market volatility on an annualised basis is 15.00% pa. The volatility of this option is rebased as based as follows to adjust for the short maturity:

1. Rebase the annual volatility to a daily basis:

$$.15/ \sqrt{250} = 0.009487$$

2. Re-annualise the daily volatility to an annualised basis adjusted for the lower number of trading days (three out of seven or 42.86%). The adjustment is based on the fact that normally the annualisation uses 250 days in a year (or 68.49% of the calendar year). Therefore, the daily volatility is scaled by 156.43 days (42.86% of 365 days).

$$.009487 \sqrt{156.43} = .118655$$

The adjusted volatility used would be 11.8655% pa.

If the option had five days to expiry, all of which were trading days, then the adjustment would be to rebase it using 365 days (100% trading days) as follows:

$$.009487 \sqrt{365} = .1812 \text{ or } 18.12\% \text{ pa}$$

An additional problem relates to the impact of high value price changes in the calculation of historical volatility estimates. This problem may also be stated as the problem of allocating relative importance to the sequence of data.

Consider an unweighted set of data which contains a single large price change. If that data point is removed, for example where a trailing average for a fixed number of days of price observations is utilised to calculate the volatility estimate, then the removal of the particular data point will have the impact of substantially altering the volatility either up or down. *Exhibit 8.5* sets out an example of this phenomenon.

Exhibit 8.5

Impact of Changes in Data Series on Volatility Estimate

CALCULATING VOLATILITY

Period	Asset Price	Price Relative (St/(St-1))	Daily Return Ui = ln (St/(St − 1))
0	9.6500		
1	8.2500	0.85492	(0.15674)
2	8.1800	0.99152	(0.00852)
3	8.2000	1.00244	0.00244
4	8.2000	1.00000	0.00000
5	8.2100	1.00122	0.00122
6	8.1200	0.98904	(0.01102)
7	8.1500	1.00369	0.00369
8	8.0700	0.99018	(0.00986)
9	8.1300	1.00743	0.00741
10	8.1700	1.00492	0.00491
11	8.2000	1.00367	0.00367
12	8.1600	0.99512	(0.00489)
13	8.1900	1.00368	0.00367
14	8.1200	0.99145	(0.00858)
15	8.0800	0.99507	(0.00494)
16	8.1900	1.01361	0.01352
17	8.0900	0.98779	(0.01229)
18	8.1200	1.00371	0.00370
19	8.1800	1.00739	0.00736
20	8.2700	1.01100	0.01094

STANDARD DEVIATION (PER PERIOD)   3.587%

ANNUALISED VOLATILITY (DAYS)   250   56.708%

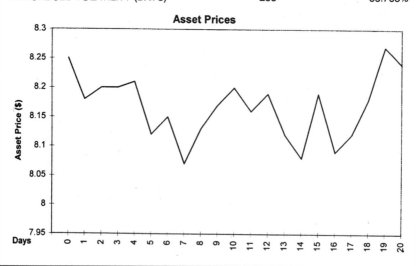

Exhibit 8.5—*continued*

CALCULATING VOLATILITY

Period	Asset Price	Price Relative (St/(St − 1))	Daily Return Ui = ln (St/(St − 1))
0	8.2500		
1	8.1800	0.99152	(0.00852)
2	8.2000	1.00244	0.00244
3	8.2000	1.00000	0.00000
4	8.2100	1.00122	0.00122
5	8.1200	0.98904	(0.01102)
6	8.1500	1.00369	0.00369
7	8.0700	0.99018	(0.00986)
8	8.1300	1.00743	0.00741
9	8.1700	1.00492	0.00491
10	8.2000	1.00367	0.00367
11	8.1600	0.99512	(0.00489)
12	8.1900	1.00368	0.00367
13	8.1200	0.99145	(0.00858)
14	8.0800	0.99507	(0.00494)
15	8.1900	1.01361	0.01352
16	8.0900	0.98779	(0.01229)
17	8.1200	1.00371	0.00370
18	8.1800	1.00739	0.00736
19	8.2700	1.01100	0.01094
20	8.2400	0.99637	(0.00363)

STANDARD DEVIATION (PER PERIOD)   0.752%
ANNUALISED VOLATILITY (DAYS)   250   11.892%

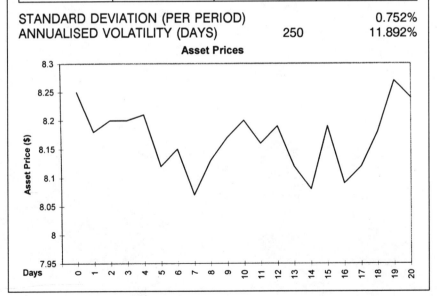

Asset Prices

This problem, together with the desire to give greater weight to more recent data, has lead to a number of weighting schemes being proposed. One example of this is the exponential weighting scheme proposed by J P Morgan in its RiskMetrics™ models. This approach uses a decay factor λ (equal to 0.94) to give greater weight to more recent data. Under this approach, the forecast from the exponential estimator for the variance of returns over the next days for a given set of T returns is given as:

$$\sigma^2 = (1\lambda)\sum_{t=1}^{T} \lambda^{t-1}(R_t - \bar{R})^2$$

Where R_E is the daily return at time t

The decay factor is chosen to minimise the error between actual observed volatility and its forecast over the sample period utilised.[6]

3.3 Implied volatility

3.3.1 Calculation of implied volatility

The implied volatility approach calculates volatility implied by the current market value of options. This is undertaken by specifying the option price and calculating the volatility which would be needed in a mathematical option pricing formula, such as Black-Scholes to derive the specified market price as a fair value of the option. *Exhibit 8.6* sets out an example of the calculation of implied volatility.

---

6.   For a detailed discussion of the exponential scheme, see J P Morgan Reuters, (1995) *RiskMetricTM—Technical Document* (4th ed, J P Morgan Reuters Ltd, New York, 1996) at Chapter 5.

Exhibit 8.6

Volatility Estimation—Implied Volatility

MODEL OUTPUTS	CALL	PUT
OPTION PREMIUM	3.73	8.38
OPTION PREMIUM (% OF ASSET PRICE)	3.73%	8.38%

PRICING INPUTS		
UNDERLYING ASSET PRICE	100.00	
STRIKE PRICE	110.00	
TRADE DATE	1-Jan-X6	
EXPIRY DATE	1-Jul-X6	
RISK FREE RATE	10.00%	
CALL(0)/PUT (1)	0	1
	Call	Put
OPTION PREMIUM	4.50	9.00
OPTION PREMIUM (% OF ASSET PRICE)	4.50%	9.00%

IMPLIED OPTION VOLATILITY (% PA)	22.80%	22.26%

The calculation of implied volatility is usually done using an iterative procedure. *Exhibit 8.7* sets out two examples of iterative procedures commonly utilised.

Exhibit 8.7

Iterative Procedures for Calculation of Implied Volatility

The following are two common methods used to calculate implied volatility:

Bisection method

The process utilised is as follows:

1.   A low estimate for volatility is used to determine an option value.
2.   A high estimate for volatility is used to calculate a second option value.
3.   The next estimate is determined by an interpolation procedure:

$$\sigma_{low} + (P - P_{low}) \times [\,(\sigma_{high} - \sigma_{low})\,/\,(P_{high} - P_{low})\,]$$

Where

σ_{high}; σ_{low} is equal to the high or low volatility estimate

P ; P_{high}; P_{low} is equal to the actual observed option premium, option premium for the high and low volatility estimate

4.   If the interpolated option value is below (above) the actual option premium, then the procedure is repeated with the low (high) volatility estimate with the interpolated estimate.
5.   The procedure entailing the above steps is repeated until the volatility estimate corresponds to the actual price of the option.

Newton Raphson method

This procedure is as follows:

1.   A reasonable estimate for the implied volatility is used to calculate the option premium.
2.   If the option premium does not correspond to the actual observed option price, then the first estimate is adjusted as follows:

$$(P - P_{\text{first estimate}})\,/\,(\delta C / \delta \sigma)$$

Where

$P - P_{\text{first estimate}}$ is the actual observed premium and the premium calculated using the first volatility estimate

$\delta C / \delta \sigma$ is the derivative of the option formula with respect to volatility evaluated at the first estimate of volatility:

$$S \times \sqrt{T}\,(1/\sqrt{2\pi}\,)\,e^{-d12/2}$$

Where

C = Price of a call option

S = Asset Price

D = d_1 in Black-Scholes Option Pricing Formula (refer Chapter 5)

3.   The volatility estimate generated is then used to recalculate the option premium.
4.   The process is repeated until the implied volatility corresponding to the observed market premium is derived.

Source: Mark Kritzman, *The Portable Financial Analyst* (Probus Publishing, Chicago, Illinois, 1995), pp 113-122.

3.3.2 Considerations in using implied volatility

The use of implied volatility is generally deficient in that it intrinsically sanctions a circular process. The volatility implied in options currently trading, which measures the volatility level required to clear the market at a given point in time, is treated as being the true constant asset price volatility parameter.

There are additional technical difficulties:

- A major difficulty with implied volatilities is that options with different strikes with the same maturity often demonstrate different implied volatilities (the so-called "smile" effect which is discussed below).
- Where options of the relevant type or maturity are not traded, this technique is unavailable.

The major value of implied volatility techniques as a method of volatility estimation is that it provides an observable measure of the relevant option market expectations as to volatility.

3.4 Volatility modelling

Historical and implied volatility assume that volatility is stable in that changes in volatility are unpredictable in that volatility *changes* are uncorrelated with previous changes in volatility.

This condition would be satisfied if a regression of the squared value of the differences of the asset price changes or returns and the mean of the time series (the error squared) as at time t(n) and the error squared as at time t(n-1) (the previous observation) showed no significant relationship. This lack of relationship would be evident in:

1. the β or slope of the regression line should not be significantly different from 0;
2. the intercept of the regression line should approximate the average value of the errors squared; and
3. the residuals around the fitted values equal the differences between the actual values for the errors squared and the predicted values from the regression are randomly distributed around a zero expected value.

If these conditions were satisfied the residuals would be described as homoscedastic (that is, they were serially independent).

In practice, the residuals do not, in fact, satisfy the above conditions; that is, they are heteroscedastic. This is evident in the following:

1. the regression coefficients may or may not be significant; but
2. the errors squared are related to prior values (for example, there are clusters of positive as well as negative residuals (where the regression underestimates (overestimates) the actual errors squared));
3. the errors squared are related in usually a non-linear relationship.

The underlying logic of this approach is that of *volatility clustering* (the high value of the errors squared occur in clusters). Volatility clustering which is observable in financial markets suggests that volatility follows a predictable pattern. Large asset price changes seem to be succeeded by a sequence of *further large changes*. This pattern causes volatility to be high after large asset price movements. Increasingly, a variety of statistical/econometric techniques are being applied to volatility estimation. One such technique is known as ARCH (an acronym for Auto Regressive Conditional Heteroskedasticity). A number of variations on ARCH techniques, representing extensions of the basic model, are also increasingly being utilised. A detailed analysis of estimating volatility with these types of models is set out in Chapter 9. In this Chapter a brief overview only is presented.

The basic insight underlying ARCH models is the concept that volatility follows clear patterns. Central to this approach is that the volatility of an asset today depends on the volatility of the asset yesterday and the ''shock'' in the price of the asset yesterday. A central tenet in this approach is that the intertemporal link in volatility changes over time is relatively constant or stationary. This implies that volatility changes are predictable on the basis of historical volatility. This approach is usually allied to an assumption that volatility regresses towards long-term long run means (that is, it shows a basic mean reversion tendency). ARCH models imply that the best estimate of volatility is not the volatility of the asset *today*. These models show how a change in volatility persists and decays gradually. For example, an increase in asset price leads to an underlying increase in asset volatility with a gradual decrease towards a mean level.

The ARCH models are predicated on correcting for the detected non-linearity through regressing the residuals at time t(n) on the errors squared as at time t2. The coefficients of this second regression are then used to adjust (by adding) to the coefficients of the original regression. This assumes that the variance (the average value of errors squared) is *conditional on the heteroskedasticity*. *Exhibit 8.8* sets out the basic procedure for deriving ARCH estimates.

Exhibit 8.8

Arch Procedures

The ARCH methodology requires the following procedure:

1. The observed means are subtracted from their mean.
2. The difference calculated in the previous step (step 1) is squared to calculate the errors squared.
3. Th errors squared as at time t(n) are regressed against the errors squared as at time t(n-1) (regression 1).
4. The fitted errors squared as at time t(n) are subtracted from the observed errors squared as at time t(n-1).
5. The residuals in the previous step as at time t(n) are regressed on the errors squared as at time t(n-1) (regression 2). Under the generalised least square approach, both sides of the regression equation should be divided by the fitted values from regression 1.
6. The regression coefficients (intercept (α) and slope (β)) from the regression 2 are added to the coefficients from regression 1 (regression 3).

The adjusted regression equation (regression 3) provides a more efficient predictor of variance than the original regression equation. The increased efficiency is only to the degree that the residuals from the original model are heteroskedastic.

Source: Mark Kritzman, *The Portable Financial Analyst* (Probus Publishing, Chicago, Illinois, 1995), pp 123-129.

An important element of the ARCH model is that it more readily explains "fat tailed" and leptokurtic distributions of asset price changes. The major applications of ARCH models, have, to date, been modelling correlations between assets and forecasting volatility.

3.5 Risk reversal volatility

Classical volatility estimates are to a degree non-directional. However, there is increasing interest in using observed market volatilities as a mechanism for inferring information about the future direction of volatility and also of the spot asset price. One such technique is that of risk reversal volatilities, which are used for these purposes.

Risk reversal volatilities use implied volatilities as a mechanism for deriving the market's view of the future path and volatility of asset prices. In itself, it is not a mechanism for deriving volatility estimates but is used in parallel with other techniques to provide additional information to calibrate volatility estimates. In particular, it provides valuable information regarding the pattern of volatility, in particular, the volatility smile (which is discussed below).

Risk reversals may be defined as the following transactions:

1. the purchase of an out-of-the-money call with the simultaneous sale of an out-of-the-money put; or
2. the purchase of an out-of-the-money put with the simultaneous sale of an out-of-the-money call.

Typically, both transactions are done, with the two options both usually having the same expiration date and being of equal size.

Transaction 1 above yields a view of the market which biased to increases in the asset price, while transaction 2 evidences a view of the market which is biased to decreases in the asset price. This reflects the economic biases evident in the transactions. *Exhibit 8.9* sets out a diagrammatic view of the transaction using the payoff profiles. *Exhibit 8.10* sets out an example of risk reversal volatilities.

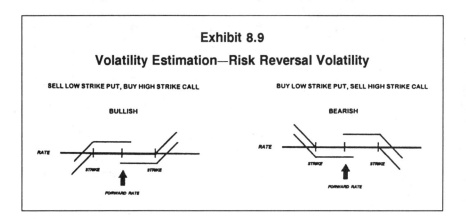

Exhibit 8.9

Volatility Estimation—Risk Reversal Volatility

Exhibit 8.10

Volatility Estimation—Risk Reversal Volatility Example

Assume the market is trading 3 month US$/JPY risk reversals as follows:
- three month US$/JPY volatilities are quoted as 8.50/8.80%; and
- three month US$/JPY 25 delta risk reversals (premium for JPY calls/US$ puts) are quoted as 0.00/0.20%.

These quotes can be interpreted as follows:
- the sale of a low strike US$ put (implied volatility of 8.80%) combined with a purchase of a US$ call (implied volatility of 8.80%) means a net risk reversal volatility of 0.00%; and
- the purchase of a low strike US$ put (implied volatility of 8.70%) combined with the sale of a high strike US$ call (implied volatility of 8.50%) means the client pays a net risk reversal volatility of 0.20%.

The demand and supply of risk reversals supplies valuable information on the following:
- the *expected* movement in implied volatility; and
- the *expected* movement in the spot.

The interpretation of the risk reversal volatilities is usually done within the following format which specifies the preferred trades for particular views of asset price and asset volatility:

Expectation As To Asset Volatility	Decrease	Static	Increase
Expectation As To Asset Price			
Decrease	Sell calls	Sell asset	Buy puts
Static	Sell calls & puts	Sell calls & puts	Buy calls & puts
Increase	Sell puts	Buy asset	Buy calls

3.6 Alternative approaches

One researcher has suggested an alternative approach to the estimation of volatility based on the concept of conservation of volatility.[7]

The basic premise of the theory is that actual observation reveals that there are days with high volatility and there are days with low volatility. Any estimate or forecast of volatility is essentially an average of these two elements based on historical data. Utilising this approach, volatility is defined as follows:

$$\sigma = w_1 \sigma_n + w_2 \sigma_h$$

Where

σ = volatility overall

w_1 = fraction of days of normal volatility

σ_n = normal volatility

w_2 = fraction of days of high volatility

σ_h = high volatility

This concept is similar to the concept of economic days identified above. This is relevant insofar as it would be expected that days when economic information is released would generally be volatile days.

This approach is used to estimate volatility as follows:

1. Existing historical price changes are segmented into two groups—high and normal volatility. This is done using a filter such as changes above a certain threshold level.

2. The volatility for each series is calculated normally.

3. The estimate for volatility is calculated using the traders estimate of the number of days of normal versus high volatility in the period to the expiry of the option. The weights are calculated using this scheme and applied to the historical volatility estimates derived for the respective series.

---

7.   See Robert Tompkins, *Options Explained* (MacMillan Press, England, 1994), Ch 5.

4. BEHAVIOUR OF VOLATILITY

4.1 Key issues

Two aspects of the behaviour of volatility estimates require comment:

- the volatility smile—that is, the behaviour of volatility relative to the strike price or yield of the option; and
- the term structure of volatility—that is, the behaviour of volatility relative to time to expiry.

4.2 The volatility smile

In practice, at-the-money options, generally, are observed to trade with lower implied volatilities relative to out-of-the-money options and to a lesser extent in-the-money options. This phenomenon is described as the volatility smile. *Exhibit 8.11* sets out an example of a typical volatility which highlights both the higher volatilities for in and out-of the-money options and the skew in the smile (usually, in favour of out-of-the money options).

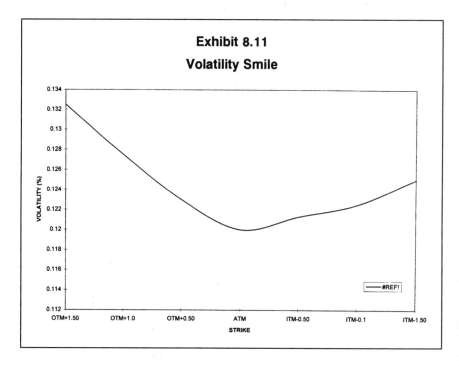

The volatility smile reflects a variety of factors, including:

- adjustments for the distributional assumptions underlying standard option pricing models;
- directional assumptions regarding the movement in the underlying asset prices which are incorporated into the option volatility and price;

- clientele effects and the demand for out-of-the-money options;
- the management of option hedging risks by traders; and
- liquidity effects.

The volatility smile is capable of explanation in terms of the deviation of observed asset price movements from the assumed log normal distribution. In practice, asset price movements seem to be characterised by the following:

- The market distribution of asset prices changes appears to demonstrate fat tails (statistically described as the kurtosis of the distribution). This type of distribution is characterised by more larger value price changes than is consistent with a normal distribution.

- The fat tails are consistent with the presence of "jump" risk, that is, non-stochastic (or discontinuous) changes or movements in the price of the asset which cause deviation from the assumption of a normal distribution.

The *actual* observed pattern of price changes because of the above characteristics would systematically underestimate the value of deep in and out-of-the-money options. This reflects the fact that the log normal distribution *systematically* underestimates the expected values that the option may take at maturity in either tail of the distribution. The volatility smile is consistent with trader behaviour which seeks to adjust the option premium for these deficiencies in an option pricing model such as Black-Scholes.[8] This adjustment is effected through an increase in the volatility for both deep in and out-of-the-money options to equate the premium received to the *expected* payouts under the option incorporating the *true* asset price change distribution.

The volatility smile, particularly the skew in the structure of the smile, may reflect expectations regarding the expected direction of price movements which are incorporated in the option price and by implication the implied volatility. For example, if the US$/JPY is expected to decline from its current level of 110, then US$ puts/JPY calls may be more valuable and US$ calls/ JPY puts with a strike price at or above the spot rate may be correspondingly less valuable. This directional view may be reflected in option price which will be higher than in the absence of this expectation and reflected in the implied volatilities.

The higher price and implied volatilities can be considered to be the higher expected economic cost of hedging or dynamically replicating the option. The smile and the skew are also consistent with the inherent nature of log normal distributions which have a natural skew to the right hand tail, implying a higher probability of a rise than a fall in the asset price. Implied volatilities, if it is sought to adjust for the skew, should be higher for options with strike prices below the implied forward rate (assumed to be the mean of the distribution) than for options with strike prices above the implied forward prices to correct for the natural bias in prices.

The market for options with different strike prices appears to exhibit significant biases in demand and supply (a clientele effect). Out-of-the-money

---

8. This approach is suggested by Fischer Black in "How to Use the Holes in Black-Scholes" (1989) 1 (4) *Continental Bank Journal of Applied Corporate Finance* 59.

options are attractive vehicles for speculative investment demand, reflecting the following factors:

- the gearing or leverage of the out-of-the-money options (expressed as the asset price divided by the option premium) is higher; and
- the low absolute cash investment entailed in the purchase of the option.

The presence of these factors dictates significant demand for these options. The supply for these types of options is constrained by the fact that option traders are reluctant to sell/write these out-of-the-money options because of the difficulty of hedging or replicating these options in the event of a jump in the asset price (high gamma risk).

In contrast, the position for in-the-money options is influenced by different factors. The dominating characteristic of these types of options is that they have a high delta and move closely with movements with the underlying asset prices. This allows in-the-money options to be used as a direct substitute for the asset itself. The primary demand for these options is from participants such as traders who, in replicating options through the process of delta hedging, need to trade in the underlying asset. The high delta of these options may enable these to be substituted for the asset in the replication process. This has the effect of lowering the financing costs in replicating the option synthetically. Similarly, other traders or participants seeking to synthesise positions in the asset at lower cost may find these in-the-money options attractive.

The supply of these options is limited. This reflects the reluctance to write a deep in-the-money option because in the absence of a large or extreme price movement the option will be exercised, requiring the seller to buy or sell the asset at a price which is disadvantageous to them. In addition, such options do not have significant time or volatility value, further reducing their attractiveness to the seller.

The interaction of supply and demand for these deep in-the-money options results in the option price and implied volatilities being bid up above comparable volatilities for at-the-money options of the same maturity.

The volatility smile also appears to incorporate the impact of traders seeking to manage the risk of option transactions. Traders seek to replicate options through a process of trading in the underlying asset. This approach to option portfolio management is consistent with standard option pricing models, such as Black-Scholes, which derive the fair value of the option as the cost of dynamically hedging a short position in the option through a position in the asset which continuously adjusted including the funding cost of the position. This process referred to as delta hedging or dynamic option replication is discussed in detail in Chapter 11.

The process of option replication, in the manner described, is, in practice, not free from risk. The primary risks are the possibility of a sudden gap or jump in asset prices (a large value price change) which requires a substantial adjustment to the position in the asset to be effected. This reflects the fact that the option delta has changed significantly. The option writer is also exposed to changes in volatility which will cause changes in both the value of the options and its delta requiring rehedging through trading in the asset. These risks usually referred to the gamma and vega risk cannot be hedged through trading in the asset. This is because the asset itself has low or no gamma (that is, the convexity of the asset price is significantly lower than the convexity of the option) and no vega risk. Gamma and vega risk can only be offset by trading in an option on the underlying asset.

In practice, the problems in hedging require traders to trade in options to manage the risks in their option portfolios. Traders typically trade in short-dated at-the-money options to manage their gamma and to a lesser extent vega risks. This reflects the fact that gamma and vega are at their highest level for short-dated at-the-money options. This creates a significant demand for these options as traders rebalance their hedges frequently in response to market movements in the asset price and volatility. The supply for these options is also strong reflecting the high volatility or time value of these at-the-money options, which makes them attractive for sellers.

The combination of the above factors results in differential liquidity of options with different strike prices for a given maturity. The volatility of at-the-money options is lower reflecting the higher liquidity of these options from the greater balance between supply and demand for these options. In and out-of-the-money are less frequently traded and the imbalance of demand relative to supply is reflected in the higher implied volatility relative to the at-the-money options. The resultant volatility smile is, as noted above, often skewed with out-of-the-money options demonstrating higher volatilities than both at and in-the-money option. The volatility smile also appears to diminish with maturity reflecting the reduced impact of the factors identified.

4.3 Term structure of volatility

The term structure of volatility encompasses two separate issues:

1. the relationship between volatility and the time to expiry of the option; and

2. the pattern of forward volatilities.

In general terms, volatility for shorter time to expiry option is higher than the volatility for options with longer times to expiry. This usual term structure of volatility is set out in *Exhibit 8.12*.

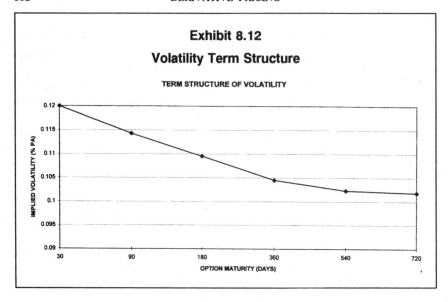

Exhibit 8.12

Volatility Term Structure

TERM STRUCTURE OF VOLATILITY

This pattern of decreasing volatility relative to option maturity essentially reflects:

- the expectations of larger price movements in the very near future which drive the implied volatility levels to higher levels for short-dated options;

- the proportionately larger impact on option values of large asset prices changes in the asset price on short-dated options and the relatively higher risk to the seller of these options, which must be compensated for through higher premiums and higher implied volatilities; and

- the mean reversion nature of volatility which seems to fall (rise) from high (low) absolute level towards a long run mean level.

There are two additional aspects of the term structure of volatilities: the volatility cone and the concept of forward volatilities.

The concept of the volatility cone is based on the fact that in projecting volatility over the life of the option the trader may seek to project, based on history, the highest and lowest volatility that are likely to occur to ensure that the estimated volatility is unlikely to be exceeded (assuming the option is sold). This entails the projection of maximum, minimum, average and (optional) historical implied volatilities for at-the-money options for different maturities. A sample volatility cone is set out in *Exhibit 8.13*. The trader would seek to use a volatility estimate that is favourable within the boundaries indicated by the cone.

Exhibit 8.13

Volatility Cone Structure

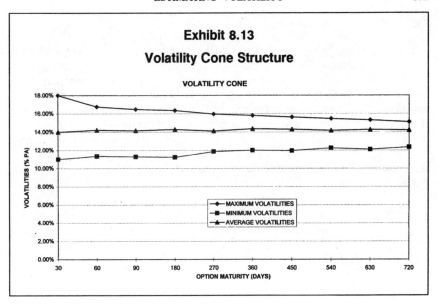

The concept of forward volatilities is analogous to the concept of forward asset prices such as forward interest rates. It focuses on the implied forward volatility calculated as the forward variance. *Exhibit 8.14* sets out an example of the calculation of forward volatilities.

Exhibit 8.14

Forward Volatilities

Assume volatilities are trading as follows:

        0.5 year (184 days):   16.40% pa (.1640)

        1 year (365 days):   15.25% pa (.1525)

The forward volatility is given by the following relationship[9]

$$\sigma_{forward} = \sqrt{[t_m \cdot \sigma_{t\,m}^2 - (t_m - t_n)\sigma_{t\,n}^2]/(t_m - t_n)}$$

Where

$\sigma_{forward}$ = forward volatility

$\sigma_{t\,m}, \sigma_{t\,n}$ = volatility for maturity n or m

t_n = shorter maturity n

t_m = longer maturity m

  Applying the formula to the assumptions case:

      Forward volatility (181 day forward in 184 days time) =

  $\sqrt{[365 \cdot 0.1525^2 - 184 \cdot 0.1640^2]/(365 - 184)} = 0.1398$ or 13.98% pa

---

9.   See Tompkins, op cit n 7, p 191.

4.6 Volatility surfaces

It is increasingly common to combine the patterns of volatility—the smile and term structure—into a volatility surface. *Exhibit 8.15* sets out an example of a volatility surface. The surface is typically generated for the purpose of valuation of portfolios of options which may contain a range of options with substantially different strike prices and maturities. The surface is derived from observed implied volatilities or specified volatilities obtained from other sources with interpolation procedures used to complete points on the surface which are either unavailable or not traded. The volatility estimates generated from the surface are then utilised to determine the value of the options in the portfolio.

Exhibit 8.15
Volatility Surface

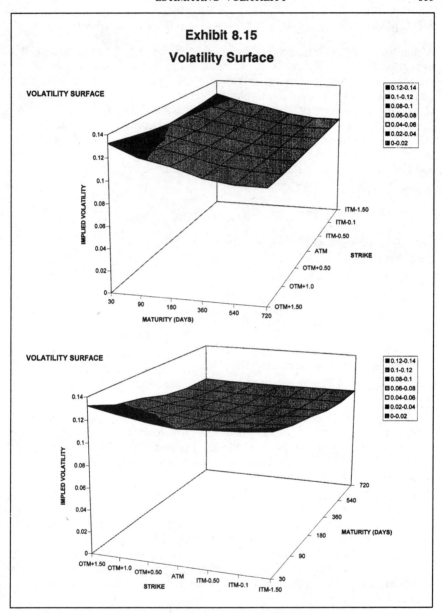

4.7 Option pricing models incorporating stochastic volatility

A number of option pricing models have been developed to incorporate the impact of the volatility smile and term structure.[10] These models effectively introduce a stochastic volatility term into the option pricing process. This replaces the traditional constant volatility term. The stochastic volatility term is usually a function of the strike price and the term of the option. The volatility function is derived from available market prices for options, and is calculated by calculating the implied option volatility using an option pricing model. This allows the construction of an option pricing model which uses and is consistent with historical volatilities structures.

5. VOLATILITY ESTIMATION IN PRACTICE

Volatility estimation in practice is a complex activity; it requires an understanding of the following:

• the various volatility estimates available and their significance; and

• behaviour of volatility parameters.

In practice, market participants take into consideration the following types of volatility:

• implied versus historical volatility;

• implied versus predicted volatility; and

• implied or historical volatility versus actual volatility.

The difference between implied and historical volatility is useful in predicting potential changes in volatility, while differences between implied versus predicted volatility determine a variety of trading strategies utilised by market participants. The relationship of the implied historical volatility versus actual realised volatility provides the basis for adjusting expectations of future asset price volatility.

In practice, the attitude to volatility estimation and the relative importance assigned to each of these methodologies will depend, to some extent, on the activities of the market participant and the risks sought to be managed. For example, an intra-day hedger or trader will take a different view to a participant seeking to hedge longer-term positions. Similarly, volatility estimation for hedging short versus long-dated option may as will generation of volatilities for the purposes of risk management as distinct from option valuation.

The volatility estimates available are, in practice, influenced by the underlying liquidity in assets. The lack of liquidity, signified by wider bid-offer spreads for particular securities, will generally be reflected in the pricing of options (that is, the implied volatility).

---

10. See Bruno Dupire, "Pricing with a Smile" (1994) 7 (1) *Risk* 18; Emanuel Derman and Iraj Kani, "Riding on a Smile" (1994) 7 (2) *Risk* 32.

Chapter 9

Estimating and Forecasting Volatility and Correlation Using ARCH and GARCH Models

by Carol Alexander

1. INTRODUCTION

Estimates and forecasts of volatility and correlation are one of the cornerstones of quantitative financial analysis. They are needed for risk management, investment analysis, capital allocation, trading, pricing and hedging—sometimes in the guise of covariance matrices.[1] In many cases these forecasts will be the only stochastic parameters in the model (as, for example, in certain Value-at-risk models) so their accuracy is crucial to the success of the analysis.

Two methods for generating volatility and correlation estimates and forecasts for financial returns are in common use: moving average methods and GARCH. There are also some more sophisticated mathematical techniques which can be applied (for example, neural networks) but these are beyond the scope of this chapter.[2] Moving average methods are standard statistical estimation techniques, and the estimates generated are taken as forecasts in financial applications. On the other hand GARCH models provide current estimates of volatility and correlation, that are then used to generate distinct forecasts of the whole term structure.

In this chapter the mathematical methods used to generate moving average and GARCH volatility and correlation are described, and the advantages and limitations of each method are explained. This is followed by a short survey of some of the most common applications of volatility and correlation to financial markets.

---

1. The covariance matrix is a square array of numbers with variances along the diagonal and covariances on the off diagonal. Volatility and correlation are just standardised forms of variance and covariance: In particular, if V is the variance of h-day returns, then h-day volatility is $100\sqrt{250V/h}\%$, where we have assumed there are 250 trading days per year. If V_1 and V_2 are the variances of two h-day returns and COV is their covariance, then their correlation is $COV/\sqrt{V_1 V_2}$. Although covariance measures the same thing as correlation—degree of co-movement between two (jointly stationary) returns series—it depends on the units of measurement. Correlation is just a standardised form of covariance, so that it always lies between -1 and $+1$ and so that a correlation near zero is indeed insignificant.

2. C O Alexander and P M Williams, "Term Structure Forecasts of Foreign Exchange Volatility and Kurtosis: A Comparison of Neural Network and GARCH Methods" (1997).

2. MOVING AVERAGE METHODS

A moving average is an average taken over a rolling window of a fixed number of data points. Thus the average is first calculated on data points x_1, x_2, ... x_n, then on data points x_2, x_3, ... x_{n+1} and so on. Each time the window is rolled, one point is knocked off behind and another is added at the end, so that the sample size remains fixed. Recording the average in this way creates a new time series which begins at time period n of the original time series.

To generate variance estimates using moving averages, it is usual to apply the average to squared returns r_t^2 (t = 1,2,3,....) or squared mean deviations of returns $(r_t - \bar{r})^2$ where $\bar{r}$ is the average return over the data window. Although standard statistical estimates of variance are based on mean deviations,[3] empirical research on the accuracy of variance forecasts in financial markets has shown that it is often better not to use mean deviations of returns, but to base variances on squared returns and covariances on cross products of returns.[4]

2.1 "Historic" volatility and correlation

The n-period "historic" estimate of variance at time T is based on an equally weighted moving average of the n past one-period returns squared:

$$\hat{\sigma}_T^2 = \sum_{t=T-n}^{t=T-1} r_t^2 \, / \, n$$

The square root of this (that is, the standard deviation) is then converted into an annualised percentage in the usual way, to obtain the historic volatility.[5] Traditionally, an n-day historic volatility estimate has been used as a volatility forecast over the next n days—for example, to price an option which matures in n days time. The rationale for this is that financial volatility tends to come in "clusters", where tranquil periods of small returns are interspersed with volatile periods of large returns.[6] Long-term volatility predictions should be unaffected by this "clustering" behaviour, and so we need to take an average squared return over a long historic period. But short-term volatility predictions should reflect current market conditions, whether volatile or tranquil, that means that only the immediate past returns should be used.

---

3.   The standard unbiased estimate of sample variance is $\sum(x_i - \bar{x})^2/(n-1)$ where n is the number of observations in the sample. Note that the use of $n-1$ rather than n in the denominator is a bias correction which is not necessary when actual returns rather than mean deviations are used.
4.   S Figlewski, "Forecasting Volatility Using Historical Data", Working Paper, Series No S94-13, Leonard N Stern School of Business, Salomon Center, New York University, 1994; C O Alexander and C Leigh, "On the Covariance Matrices Used in VAR Models" (1997) 4 (Spring) *Journal of Derivatives.*
5.   See above n 1.
6.   As long ago as 1963 Benoit Mandlebrot (of the "Fractal" fame) observed that financial returns time series exhibit periods of volatility interspersed with tranquillity, where "Large returns follow large returns, of either sign. . . ."

Although there is a rationale for using the current n-day volatility estimates as forecasts of average volatility over the next n-days, the equally weighted averaging induces some very misleading properties in historic volatility time series. *Exhibit 9.1* shows two such "historic" volatility series for the FTSE with n=30 and n=60 respectively (and both are calculated using daily returns). The figure illustrates a basic problem with the use of equally weighted averages that has motivated a general shift in methodology towards exponentially weighted moving averages for financial market analysis. First, when there is a jump in market price, an equally weighted average of squared returns will jump up the very next day. This is as an accurate reflection of the "clustering" behaviour of volatility in financial markets. But that one, large, squared return will continue to keep volatility estimates high for exactly 30 days in the 30-day moving average, and exactly 60 days in the 60-day moving average, whereas the underlying volatility will have long ago returned to normal levels. Secondly, exactly 30 days (or 60 days) after a major market event the equally weighted volatility estimate will jump down again as abruptly as it jumped up. What has been seen from the event until that day is just a ghost of what happened 30 days ago. But there was nothing special about that day—it was just the day on which a (long overdue) correction in the estimate occurred. Because the average is taken over fewer observations, this correction will be bigger in short-term volatility estimates. For example, the 30-day FTSE volatility jumped up to 68% for the 30 days after Black Monday before it jumped back to its normal levels around 13%. But the 60-day volatility only jumped up to around 50%—although it took twice as long to correct.

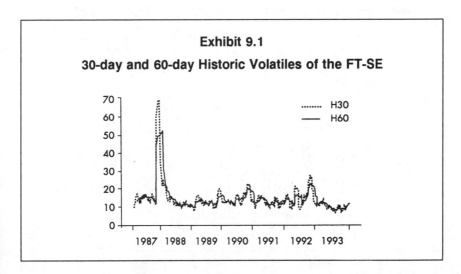

Exhibit 9.1

30-day and 60-day Historic Volatiles of the FT-SE

These "ghost features" are always going to be a problem when equally weighted averages are applied to financial market data.[7] Not only do they keep volatility estimates artificially high for an arbitrary length of time, but they can induce an artificial sense of stability into covariance (and

7. Such as in the current practice of producing market betas or statistical hedge ratios (see section on Applications below).

correlation) estimates. An n-period "historic" covariance estimate between
two one-period returns series $r_{1,t}$ and $r_{2,t}$ is given by

$$\hat{\sigma}_{12,T} = \sum_{t=T-n}^{t=T-1} r_{1,t} r_{2,t} / n$$

and this may be converted to n-period correlation by dividing by the product
of the two n-period standard deviations. Again, it is common practice to use
the current n-day correlation estimate as a forecast of correlation over the
next n days.

Now, unlike volatility, stable correlations do not always exist.[8] If a time
series of instantaneous correlation estimates—such as GARCH
estimates—were generated using a pair of returns series that are not "jointly
stationary", these correlations would be very unstable. However, if an
equally weighted n-period moving average is used instead of GARCH, an
artificial stability is induced in these correlation estimates by the "ghost
features". This feature is evident in *Exhibit 9.2*, which shows 30-day and
60-day historic correlations between MSCI indices for the UK and the US.

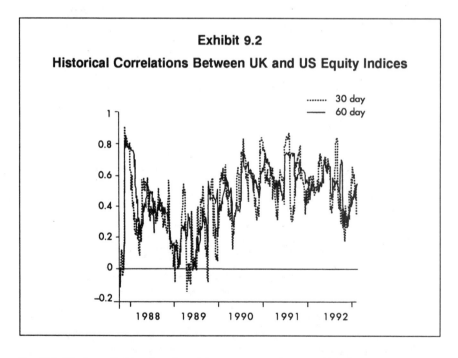

Exhibit 9.2

Historical Correlations Between UK and US Equity Indices

8.   Volatility is applicable when financial returns are stationary—which they usually are—but
     correlations are applicable only when the two returns series are *jointly* stationary. Although
     joint stationarity can often be assumed, for example between two domestic bond returns, it is
     commonly found that two arbitrarily chosen returns are not jointly stationary. For example,
     returns to some South American Brady bonds are unlikely to be jointly stationary with an
     Indian equity—and in this case "correlation" estimates will be very unstable.

2.2 Exponentially weighted moving averages

The "ghost features" produced in equally weighted averages of financial market returns are clearly a problem, which is caused by the fact that all past returns that come into the average are equally important, however long ago. Exponentially weighted moving averages (EWMA) of squared returns do not exhibit these "ghost features" because past returns become less significant as time goes on. An EWMA variance estimate at time T, based on a time series of squared returns is

$$\hat{\sigma}_T^2 = (1-\lambda) \sum_{i=1}^{\infty} \lambda^{i-1} r_{T-i}^2$$

In an EWMA past observations are now weighted by the "smoothing constant" λ, which is between 0 and 1, so an observation n days ago is multiplied by λ^n, which is very small for large n. Thus extreme events have less of an impact on variances and covariances as they move further into the past. Since shocks are smoothed out by the exponential weighting, this technique is sometimes called "exponential smoothing"—the bigger the smoothing constant λ, the more weight is given to past observations and the smoother the resulting time series.

EWMA is a standard statistical estimation technique, but for volatility and correlation forecasting in financial markets it has some limitations. First, it is only really useful as a one-step-ahead forecast. That is, if daily squared returns are smoothed using EWMA, this provides a useful series of one-day variance forecasts (which are in fact similar to GARCH one-day forecasts).[9] However there is only one way in which we can extend the forecast horizon and use EWMA methods for n-day forecasts, and that is to smooth n-day squared returns. Alternative methods—such as using the "square root of time" rule,[10] or applying exponential smoothing to an equally weighted

9. C O Alexander, "Volatility and Correlation Forecasting" in C O Alexander (ed), *Handbook of Risk Management and Analysis* (Wiley, 1996).
10. The "square root of time" rule simply calculates h-day standard deviations as $\sqrt{h}$ times the daily standard deviation. It is based on the assumption that daily log returns are normally, independently and identically distributed, so the variance of h-day returns is just h times the variance of daily returns. But since volatility is just an annualised form of the standard deviation, and since the annualising factor is—assuming 250 days per year—$\sqrt{250}$ for daily returns but $\sqrt{250/h}$ for h-day returns, this simply amounts to the Black-Scholes constant volatility assumption, i.e. that current levels of volatility remain the same.

variance series—are doomed to failure.[11] Another limitation of this technique is that—unlike GARCH—it gives no optimal method of estimating the parameter. Finally, there can be two problems when these methods are applied to generate large covariance matrices:

1. The same value of the smoothing constant needs to be applied to all series, otherwise the matrix will not be "positive semi-definite", that means that it would give negative risk on certain portfolios;

2. EWMA covariance matrices effectively use only the last m data points, where m is such that $\lambda^{m-1} \approx 0$.[12]

Hence covariance matrices with k factors will have many zero eigenvalues when k >> m, and special algorithms to cope with these nearly singular matrices are needed, otherwise many of these zero eigenvalues will be estimated a being negative and the "indefinite" matrices which result will give negative risk measures for certain portfolios anyway.[13]

3. GARCH METHODS

GARCH stands for Generalized Autoregressive Conditional Heteroscedasticity: "Generalized" because it is a general class of ARCH model, "Autoregressive" because the variances generated by ARCH models involve regression on their own past, and "Conditionally Heteroscedastic" literally means changing variance, or "volatility clustering" as it has become known. The first ARCH model was introduced by Rob Engle (1982). Tim Bollerslev (1986) developed the GARCH formulation of the model, which is more commonly used in financial markets.[14]

To understand GARCH we first need to recall the ideas of standard linear regression. Linear regression models are commonplace in financial market analysis; they are used to calculate market betas, statistical hedge ratios, and sensitivities in more general factor models (see the section below on "Applications"); they can be used for prediction, and for confidence limits and other types of statistical inference on model parameters. The innovation in GARCH is to augment the standard linear regression model with another

---

11. C O Alexander, "Evaluating the Use of RiskMetrics™ as a Risk Measurement Tool for your Operation: What are its Advantages and Limitations" (1996) 4 *Derivatives Use, Trading and Regulation.*

12. Let the original data be $X = \begin{bmatrix} Y \\ Z \end{bmatrix}$, $A = \mathrm{diag}(1, \lambda, \lambda^2, ..., \lambda^{t-1})$ $\tilde{X} = AX$

where X is txk, Y is mxk where m is the rank of A'A and Z is (t−m)xk.

Let $\Lambda = diag(1, \lambda, \lambda^2, ..., \lambda^{m-1})$ so that A'A can be partitioned $\begin{bmatrix} \Lambda'\Lambda & 0 \\ 0 & 0 \end{bmatrix}$

Then we can write $\tilde{X}'\tilde{X} = X' A' AX = (Y' Z') A' A \begin{bmatrix} Y \\ Z \end{bmatrix} = Y' \Lambda' \Lambda Y$

This proves that only the first m rows of the original data X are used in the calculation of the EWMA covariance matrix.

13. It also means that the Cholesky decomposition does not exist. The Cholesky decomposition of the covariance matrix is needed for evaluating Value-at-risk of options portfolios.

14. A survey of these models is given in Alexander, op cit n 9.

equation, the "conditional variance" equation—the equation in the original model now being termed the "conditional mean" equation. The parameters in both equations are estimated simultaneously, using maximum likelihood estimation, and the outputs of the GARCH model include two time series: the estimated conditional mean series (the "fitted" series in standard regression) and the estimated conditional variance series (the GARCH variance estimate). The standard input for a GARCH model for financial market volatility is a series of daily returns, r_t.[15] This input is called the dependent variable, and its level is modelled by the conditional mean equation. The conditional mean equation can be anything reasonable,[16] such as

$$r_t = \varphi_0 + \varphi_1 r_{t-1} + \varepsilon_t$$

If we assume that $V(\varepsilon_t) = \sigma^2$ the error process ε_t is called "homoscedastic" (that is, it has constant variance) and then this would just be an ordinary regression model. But in GARCH we allow the residual to have time-varying variance, in particular we have the conditionally heteroscedastic assumption that $V_t(\varepsilon_t) = \sigma_t^2$ and we model this time-varying variance with another equation—the conditional variance equation. The GARCH(1,1) model has the conditional variance equation

$$\sigma_t^2 = \omega + \alpha \varepsilon_{t-1}^2 + \beta\sigma_{t-1}^2$$

where the restrictions $\omega>0$ α, $\beta \geq 0$ are placed on the parameters to ensure that variance is positive. Also $\alpha+\beta<1$ ensures that GARCH volatility forecasts "mean-revert", so that forecasts will get closer to the long-term average volatility as the maturity of the forecast increases.

An important difference between GARCH and the moving average methods described above is that the GARCH volatility estimates are different from the forecasts. GARCH forecasts of volatility of any maturity can be computed in a simple iterative manner: Put

$$\sigma_{t+1}^2 = \omega + \alpha \varepsilon_t^2 + \beta\sigma_t^2$$

and for s>1

$$\sigma_{t+s}^2 = \omega + (\alpha + \beta) \sigma_{t+s-1}^2$$

Then, assuming returns have no autocorrelation the GARCH forecast of variance of h-day returns is

$$\sigma_{t,h}^2 = \sum_{i=1}^{h}\sigma_{t+i}^2$$

and the GARCH h-day volatility forecast is $100\sigma_{t,h}\sqrt{250}$%, assuming 250 trading days per year. GARCH term structures behave in the intuitive "mean-reverting" fashion illustrated in *Exhibit 9.3*. In fact their behaviour can be very similar to implied volatility term structures.[17]

15. The length of historic data needed for GARCH needs to be long enough that the maximum likelihood estimation converges, but not so long that extreme market events that occurred a long time ago have an effect on current long-term GARCH forecasts.
16. However, the more parameters in the model the more flat the likelihood function and so the more difficult it becomes to get the estimation procedure to converge. Often a very parsimonious parameterization is used in the conditional mean equation, such as the AR(1) model in this example.
17. R F Engle and J Mezrich, "Grappling with GARCH" (1995) 8(9) *RISK*.

Exhibit 9.3

GARCH Volatility Term Structures of US$ Rates (28 November 1994)

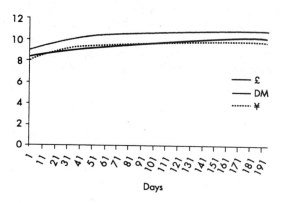

GARCH Volatility Term Structures of US$ Foreign-exchange Rates (2 March 1995)

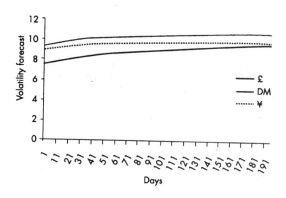

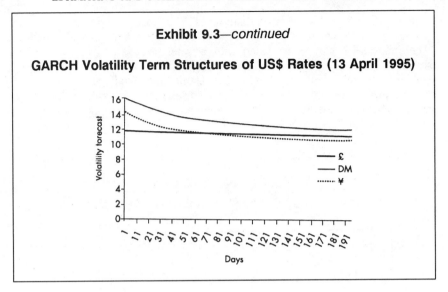

Exhibit 9.3—*continued*

GARCH Volatility Term Structures of US$ Rates (13 April 1995)

Moving average methods, on the other hand, assume constant volatility term structures.[18] Thus current levels of volatility are supposed to persist forever, which is clearly a very unrealistic assumption. There is no doubt of the success of GARCH in volatility forecasting, but when we try to extend the univariate model so that GARCH covariances (and correlations) are obtained, we run into programming problems. The multivariate GARCH model takes as inputs a vector time series of returns r_t, for example the returns to all risk factors in a portfolio. The variance of a vector time series is a matrix time series H_t: the covariance matrix. Since multivariate GARCH models need to output not a single scalar variance but a whole matrix at every point in time, there are a very large number of parameters in a multivariate GARCH model and this makes direct computation of GARCH covariance matrices very difficult. There is a multivariate GARCH method called "orthogonal GARCH" that gets around these programming difficulties by using a combination of principal components analysis and univariate GARCH.[19] This orthogonal GARCH method has additional merits: the lack of dimensional restrictions, and the fact that these matrices are positive definite. Also, by adding or subtracting principal components, the model can be tailored to cut down the "noise" in the data if so desired, and this process makes correlation forecasts more stable. An example explaining the method for just two categories can easily be extrapolated to any number of risk factor categories: Suppose $P = (P_1, \ldots P_n)$ are the principal components of the first system (n risk factors) and let $Q = (Q_1, \ldots Q_m)$ be the principal components of the second system (m risk factors). Denote by A (nxn) and B (mxm) the factor weights matrices of the first and second systems. Within factor covariances are given by $AV(P)A'$ and $BV(Q)B'$ respectively and cross-factor covariances are ACB' where $V(P)$ and $V(Q)$ denote the diagonal matrices of GARCH variances of the principal components and C denotes the

18. See above n 10.
19. C O Alexander and A M Chibumba, "Orthogonal Factor GARCH" (1997).

mxn matrix of GARCH covariances of principal components. As an illustration of the method I have applied it to a system of equity indices (where the S&P has to be taken into a category of its own) and USD exchange rates. The system is small enough to compare the "splicing" method with full multivariate GARCH estimation (just!) and *Exhibit 9.4* shows just one of the resulting correlations obtained by each method—between the GBP/USD exchange rate and the Nikkei during the period 1 Jan 1993 to 17 Dec 1996.

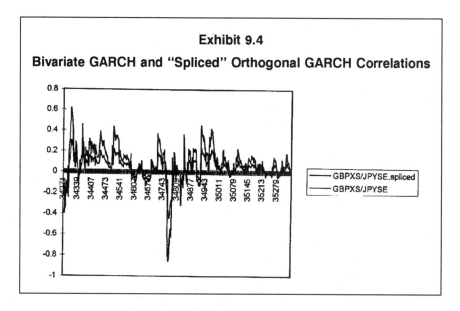

Exhibit 9.4

Bivariate GARCH and "Spliced" Orthogonal GARCH Correlations

However, the model can break down in stress scenarios, so although the stable variances and covariances it provides are perfect for measuring everyday risks they should be used with caution for volatility and correlation forecasting during extreme market conditions.

Although GARCH models are a little more complex than the moving average methods of volatility and correlation estimation, their sound mathematical structure makes them easy to adapt to different environments. For example, correlation estimates and forecasts will be upset if data are asynchronous, which they often are. Rather than invest huge amounts of time in the collection of synchronous data sets, a simple modification of the conditional mean equations in a multivariate GARCH model generates forecasts which are be based on *two* period correlations which allow for feedback between markets which close at different times. This is the "asynchronous" GARCH model being developed by Rob Engle and Joe Mezrich at Saloman Bros, NY.

A final point which distinguishes GARCH from the moving average methods outlined above is that the estimated GARCH model, that is commonly used to generate well-behaved variance and covariance forecasts of any maturity, also provides a stochastic volatility/correlation model that is very effective for pricing and hedging options. The estimated parameters are used in the conditional variance equations, and then Monte Carlo simulations are applied to a two factor model as outlined below (see "Option Pricing and Hedging").

4. SOME APPLICATIONS OF VOLATILITY AND CORRELATION TO MARKET RISK

4.1 Measuring market betas in factor models

Simple factor models describe returns to an asset or portfolio in terms of returns to risk factors and idiosyncratic return. For example, in the simple Capital Asset Pricing Model (CAPM) the return to a portfolio, denoted r_t, is approximated by the linear regression model

$$r_t = \alpha + \beta R_t + \varepsilon_t$$

where R_t is the return to the risk factor, the error process ε_t denotes the idiosyncratic return and β denotes the sensitivity (or "beta") of the portfolio to the risk factor. This beta is estimated by the ratio of the covariance (between the portfolio and the risk factor) to the variance of the risk factor.[20]

More generally, in multivariate factor models, portfolio returns are attributed to several risk factors: the portfolio return is given by

$$\alpha + \beta_1 R_1 + \beta_2 R_2 + \ldots + \beta_3 R_3 + \varepsilon$$

where $R_1, \ldots R_n$ are the returns to different risk factors, $\beta_1, \ldots \beta_n$ are the net portfolio sensitivities (that is, the weighted sum of the individual asset sensitivities) and is the idiosyncratic return of the portfolio (that is, that part of the return not attributed to the different risk factors). The net betas with respect to each risk factor can be calculated from the covariances (between risk factors and between the portfolio and risk factors) and the variances of the risk factors. EWMA or GARCH estimates of these quantities then give time-varying market betas which are a great improvement on the constant betas one usually obtains from standard data suppliers.

4.2 Measuring portfolio risk

It is standard procedure to measure risk in a linear portfolio in terms of variance and covariances.[21] In simple portfolios which can be described by a weighted sum of the constituent assets, all we need to find is the covariance matrix of these asset returns. The return to the portfolio is $\mathbf{w'r}$ where $\mathbf{w}$ is the vector of portfolio weights and $\mathbf{r}$ is the vector of asset returns so the portfolio variance is $\mathbf{w'Vw}$—that is, the variance of the return—where $\mathbf{V}$ is the covariance matrix of $\mathbf{r}$. Provided $\mathbf{V}$ is a positive definite matrix, the portfolio risk will always be positive, whatever the weights in the portfolio.[22]

---

20. So the beta is the correlation times the relative volatility.
21. Variance is not the only measure of portfolio risk—"Value-at-risk", "regret" or "downside risk" are also used (see Beckers, 1996).
22. One of the problems with the RiskMetrics™ data is that they are not positive definite, they are "indefinite", so certain portfolios will have negative VAR (see Alexander, 1996b).

In larger linear portfolios, that are best described not at the asset level but by the factor models described above, the portfolio variance is measured using the covariance matrix of risk factor returns and the vector of sensitivities to different risk factors. If we ignore the idiosyncratic risk, the portfolio variance from the factor model is simply $\beta'V\beta$ where β is the vector of (net) portfolio sensitivities and V is the covariance matrix of risk factor returns. Both V and β are obtained from variances and covariances, so the same remarks apply: it is better to use time-varying estimates such as those obtained from EWMA or GARCH models than the "constant" variances and covariances that one can get from ordinary least squares regression or equally weighted moving averages.

4.3 Constructing hedged portfolios to minimise portfolio risk

When hedging a portfolio with forwards or futures we regard their deltas as weights in the total portfolio. The problem is of choosing a vector of weights ω in a portfolio to minimise its variance. In mathematical notation:

$$\text{Min}_\omega \ \omega' \ V\omega \text{ such that } \Sigma\omega_i = 1$$

where V is the covariance matrix of asset returns. Assuming that weights can be negative or zero this is a straightforward linear programming problem, having the solution

$$\omega_i{}^* = \psi_i \ / \ \Sigma\psi_i \text{ where } \psi_i = \Sigma\text{ith column of } V^{-1}.$$

Suppose we take V to be a time-varying covariance matrix such as the GARCH matrix. This will give time-varying weights $\omega_{i,t}{}^*$ that can be used to re-balance the portfolio as volatilities and correlations between the assets change.

4.4 Option pricing and hedging

There are two types of application of volatility and correlation to pricing and hedging options. Either the relevant forecast of average volatility and/or correlation over the life of the option is "plugged" into the closed form solution (for example, into the Black-Scholes formula for vanilla options), or a two factor model with price diffusion and stochastic volatility model is used to simulate terminal price distributions from which the option price is calculated as the discounted expected option pay-off assuming risk-neutral evaluation.[23] Hedge ratios are also calculated using finite difference approximations on these simulations.[24]

To fix ideas, first recall how simulation can be used to price and hedge a call option on an underlying price S(t) which follows the Geometric Brownian Motion diffusion

$$dS(t)/S(t) = \mu dt + \sigma dZ$$

where Z is a Wiener process. Since volatility σ is constant this is a one factor model, and it is only necessary to use Monte Carlo on the independent increments dZ of the Wiener process to generate price paths $S(t)$ over the life

23. J C Hull, *Options, Futures and Other Derivative Securities* (Prentice Hall, 1993).
24. M Broadie and P Glasserman, "Estimating Security Price Derivatives Using Simulation" (1996) 2 *Management Science* 42.

of the option. This is done on the discrete form of Geometric Brownian Motion, namely

$$S_t = S_{t-1} \exp (\mu - 0.5\sigma^2 + \sigma z_t)$$

where $z_t \sim NID(0,1)$.[25] So, starting from the current price S_0, Monte Carlo simulation of an independent series on z_t for t=1,2,....T will generate a terminal price S_T. Thousands of these terminal prices should be generated starting from the one current price S_0, and the discounted expectation of the option pay-off function gives the price of the call. For example for a plain vanilla option

$$C(S_0) = \exp(-rT) \; E(\max\{S-K,0\})$$

where r is the risk-free rate, T the option maturity and K is the strike. So from the simulated distribution $S_{T,i}(i = 1,...N)$ of terminal prices we get the estimated call price

$$\hat{C}(S_0) = \exp(-rT) \; (\Sigma_i \max\{S_{T,i}-K,0\} \, / \, N)$$

Simulation deltas and gammas are calculated using finite difference approximations, such as the central differences

$$\delta = [C(S_0 + \eta) - C(S_0 - \eta)]/2\eta$$

$$\gamma = [C(S_0+\eta) - 2C(S_0) + C(S_0-\eta)]/\eta^2$$

In this example, with constant volatility GBM for the simulations, the delta and gamma should be the same as those obtained using the Black-Scholes "plug-in" formulae. But in practice, simulation errors can be very large unless the time is taken to run large numbers of simulations for each option price.[26]

Now consider how to extend the standard GBM model to a two factor model, where the second factor is GARCH(1,1) stochastic volatility. The two diffusion processes are

$$S_t = S_{t-1} \exp (\mu - 0.5\sigma_t^2 + \varepsilon_t)$$

$$\sigma_t^2 = \omega + \alpha \, \varepsilon_{t-1}^2 + \beta\sigma_{t-1}^2$$

where $\varepsilon_t = \sigma_t z_t$. Starting with current price S_0 and unconditional standard deviation σ_0, an independent set of Monte Carlo simulations on $z_t(t = 0,1, ... T)$ will now generate σ_t at the same time as S_t for t = 1 ,..., T. Note that the simulated price paths are already based on expected volatility levels, so the GARCH delta and gamma hedge ratios do not require additional vega hedging.[27]

GARCH is not the only way of putting stochastic volatility into option prices and hedge ratios: there are alternatives such as the "autoregressive in variance" model.[28] However, moving average methods do not yield stochastic volatility models and so these methods can only be used to "plug" into closed form solutions; they cannot be used to generate option prices and

25. To derive this from the continuous form use Ito's lemma on logS and then make time discrete.
26. Simulation errors are reduced by using correlated random numbers—the variance of delta estimates is reduced when $C(S_0+\eta)$ and $C(S_0-\eta)$ are positively correlated.
27. R F Engle and J Rosenberg, "GARCH Gamma" (1995) Journal of Derivatives.
28. S J Taylor, "Modelling Stochastic Volatility: A Review and Comparative Study" (1994) 4(2) *Mathematical Finance* 183.

hedge ratios which already account for stochastic volatility, so moving average deltas and gammas do need additional vega hedges.

4.5 Fitting the smile with GARCH

GARCH models can be estimated using cross-section data on the market implied smile surface, and then the dynamics of the GARCH model can be used to predict the smile. Initial values for the GARCH model parameters are fixed, and then GARCH option prices obtained, as explained above, for options of different strikes and maturity. These prices are then put into the Black-Scholes formula, and the GARCH ''implied'' volatility is backed out of the formula (just as one would do with ordinary market implied volatilities, only this time the GARCH price is used instead of the price observed in the market). Comparison of the GARCH smile surface with the observed market smile surface leads to a refinement of the GARCH model parameters (that is, iteration on the root mean square error between the two smiles) and so the GARCH smile is fitted. It turns out that the GARCH parameters estimated this way are very similar to those obtained from time series data, so using the GARCH smile to predict future smiles leads to sensible results.[29]

4.6 Volatility and correlation trading

We have just seen that options prices are based on assumptions about volatility and correlation during the lifetime of the option. Options sellers will account for volatility and correlation in their prices, and each market price of an option has forecasts of volatility and/or correlation implicit in its price. This ''implied'' volatility and correlation needs to be distinguished from the statistical volatility and correlation forecasts which are calculated using moving averages or GARCH. In fact, implied and statistical methods use different data and different models[30] to forecast the same thing: the volatility of the underlying assets over the life of the option.

Implied volatility is like an option price—it contains all the forward expectations of investors about the likely evolution of the underlying. In fact implied volatility is an inverse option price: if we know the market price of the option and all the other parameters in a particular pricing functional used for the option, we can invert this price functional to solve for volatility: this is the implied volatility. If the price functional were an accurate representation of reality, and if the statistical forecasts were known to be accurate, then any observed differences between implied and statistical volatility would reflect inappropriate expectations from investors. So volatility traders use the relationship between statistical and implied measures to form expectations of implied volatility and so also the likely movements in options prices.

---

29. J Duan, ''Cracking the Smile'' (1996) *RISK*.
30. Implied methods use current data on market prices of options—statistical methods use historic data on the underlying asset price. Implied methods use an assumed diffusion process for the underlying asset price—statistical methods assume only (conditional) normality of underlying asset returns.

For example, 95% confidence limits of GARCH n-period volatility forecasts can be generated using the covariance matrix of estimated coefficients in the GARCH model. These are then tracked over a period of time and implied volatility is examined in relation to these limits. A volatility purchase (such as buying an at-the-money straddle) would be appropriate when implied volatility falls below the lower 95% limit. On the other hand, when implied volatility seems too high, above the 95% GARCH upper limit, the volatility trader should rather sell volatility.

The P&L of certain volatility trades may be reduced by trading pairs of options on assets which have been highly correlated historically. For example, a trade on the relative volatility V_1/V_2 of two highly correlated equities may consist of two straddles where one is bought and one is sold in vega neutral proportions.[31] Tracking relative implied volatilities and their statistical historical levels provides a means of determining whether current relative volatility is out of line: If their relative volatility is thought to be too high, the straddle on asset 1 is sold and the straddle on asset 2 is bought, with the opposite trade being relevant for traders who believe relative volatility is undervalued.

4.7 Value-at-risk modelling

Value at risk (VAR) has become central to financial decision making, not just for risk managers and regulators, but for anyone concerned with the actual numbers produced: traders, fund managers, corporate treasuries, accountants etc. Not only is capital set aside for regulatory compliance on the basis of these measures—such things as trading limits or capital allocation decisions may be set. Providing accurate VAR measures therefore becomes a concern for many.

A VAR measure depends on two parameters, the holding period h and the significance level, α. A good VAR model should provide a convergent and consistent sequence of VAR measures for every holding period from one day (or even less than a day) to several years.[32] However the significance level is just a matter of personal choice: Do you want normal circumstances VAR measures to reflect potential losses one day in twenty ($\alpha=0.05$) or one day in a hundred ($\alpha=0.01$)?

The generally accepted methods for linear portfolios ("Covariance" methods) and options portfolios ("Structured Monte Carlo") both require an accurate, positive definite covariance matrix. In the "covariance" method, denote by ΔP_t the forecast P&L over the next h days, and by μ_t and $\sigma^2{}_t$ its mean and variance. Then assuming P&Ls are conditionally normally distributed we have[33]

$$VAR = Z_\alpha \sigma_t - \mu_t$$

31. M D Fitzgerald, "Trading Volatility" in C O Alexander (ed), *Handbook of Risk Management and Analysis* (Wiley, 1996).
32. Currently only GARCH models can really do this effectively—moving average methods have problems because they are too simple, and other more advanced models such as neural networks still have some way to go.
33. Apply the standard normal transformation to ΔP_t.

where Z_α denotes the critical value from the standard normal distribution corresponding to your choice of significance level. It is often assumed that μ_t is zero, and Z_α is just looked up in tables, so the sole focus of this method is on σ_t, the standard deviation of forecast P&L over the holding period. But

$$\sigma^2{}_t = \mathbf{P'VP}$$

where $\mathbf{V}$ is the covariance matrix of asset returns (or risk factor returns) over the holding period and $\mathbf{P}$ is a vector of the current mark-to-market values of the assets (or of the current sensitivities times the current mark-to-market values of the risk factors). Since $\mathbf{V}$ is the only stochastic part of the model it is crucial to obtain good estimates of the parameters in $\mathbf{V}$, that is, the variance and covariance forecasts of asset (or factor) returns over the holding period. For example, the model may give zero or negative VAR measures if $\mathbf{V}$ is not positive definite.

VAR measures for options portfolios are often calculated using Monte Carlo methods to simulate a distribution of P&Ls over the forthcoming holding period. To calculate this distribution, correlated vectors of underlying returns are simulated over the holding period. These are generated using the Cholesky decomposition of the covariance matrix of returns to the underlyings[34] and it is (again) important to obtain positive definite covariance matrices, because otherwise the Cholesky decomposition does not exist.[35] Each set of correlated simulations gives one value of the portfolio at the end of the holding period. Lots of such values are simulated and used to calculate a simulated P&L distribution from which the VAR measure can be read off directly as $\text{Prob}(\Delta P_t < -\text{VAR}) = \alpha$ (see *Exhibit 9.5*).

34. If $\mathbf{r}$ is a vector of standard independent returns, and $\mathbf{C'C} = \mathbf{V}$ where $\mathbf{C}$ is the (triangular) Cholesky matrix, then $\mathbf{C'r}$ is a vector of returns with variance covariance matrix $\mathbf{V}$.
35. So what can be done with the non-positive semi-definite matrices, produced by RiskMetrics™? Ad hoc methods—such as shooting the negative or zero eigenvalues to something small and positive—must be resorted to. Unfortunately this changes the original covariance matrix in an arbitrary way, without control over which volatilities and correlations are being effected.

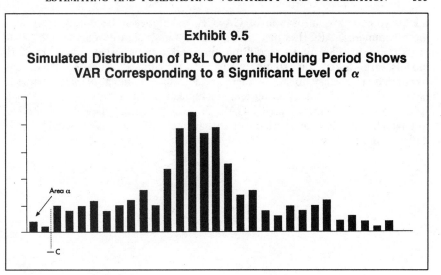

Exhibit 9.5

Simulated Distribution of P&L Over the Holding Period Shows VAR Corresponding to a Significant Level of α

The current emphasis on integrated risk systems, to measure VAR across all the risk positions of a large bank, requires very large covariance matrices indeed. Regulators require the use of at least one year of historic data, so exponentially weighted moving average methods are ruled out. Currently there are only two realistic alternatives: equally weighted moving averages or GARCH. Equally weighted moving average covariance matrices are easy to construct, and should be positive definite (assuming no linear interpolation of data along a yield curve, et cetera) but will be contaminated by any stress events which may have occurred during the last year. These should be filtered out of the data before the moving average is applied, and saved for later use when investigating the effect of real stress scenarios on portfolio P&Ls. Multivariate GARCH models of enterprise-wide dimensions would be computationally impossible. The only way that one can construct large dimension covariance matrices using GARCH is to employ the orthogonal GARCH model and "splice" together the full covariance matrix.[36]

5. SUMMARY

This chapter has described current state-of-the-art techniques for estimating and forecasting covariance matrices, and surveyed some of their applications to financial markets analysis. In the earlier part of the chapter it was shown that one has to be very careful about using moving average techniques, however simple they may appear. Their drawbacks include: "indefiniteness" of covariance matrices estimates, so that certain portfolios will have negative risk measures; "ghost features" in equally weighted average methods; the absence of any model for stochastic volatility; and problems with extending estimates to forecasts—in fact only their one-step ahead forecasts are meaningful. Thus moving average techniques have very limited applicability. On the other hand, although the computational side of GARCH models is

36. C O Alexander, " 'Splicing' Methods for Value-at-Risk" (1997) *Derivatives Week.*

relatively complex, utilisation of GARCH techniques is becoming more and more common. GARCH is just another name for "volatility clustering", so it is particularly relevant to modelling financial returns. Also, since GARCH models are based on sound statistical techniques such as maximum likelihood, it is easy to apply these models in a number of ways without having to resort to bits of string and elastoplast. In the survey of applications it has been shown how elegantly GARCH models can be adapted and applied to enhance a number of areas in the management of risk, investment, pricing, hedging and trading.

Chapter 10

Measuring Option Price Sensitivity—The "Greek Alphabet" of Risk

by Satyajit Das

1. INTRODUCTION

The fair value of an option is a function of five parameters: the price of the asset (S); the option strike price (K); the time to option expiry (T); the risk free rate (Rf); and the volatility of the asset returns (σ). Changes in each of these variables directly impact upon the price of the relevant option (see discussion in Chapter 5). In practice, precise and quantitative estimates can be obtained of the *directional* as well as *quantum* effect of changes in the option pricing input parameters. These sensitivities of the option premium are represented by a number of Greek letters (following the notation conventions of mathematics), which are used to quantify and estimate the risk of options.

In this chapter, the techniques of quantifying the sensitivity of option prices using the Greek alphabet of risk is examined. An overview of option price sensitivities and risk, including potential uses, is first considered. Each of the individual risk elements—delta (Δ), gamma (γ), vega (κ),[1] theta (τ) and rho (ρ)—are separately considered, including their function and significance as well as their behaviour. Other risk factors—such as lambda (λ), charm, speed, colour and fugit—are also identified as well as a generalisation of the concepts to cover option risks where the underlying option involves different assets. The chapter also examines the use of extending the overall conceptual framework to cover risk generally (as distinct from risk in relation to option transactions).

2. OPTION PRICE SENSITIVITIES AND RISKS—AN OVERVIEW

As noted above, the sensitivities and risks of option transactions with references to changes in option pricing parameters are obtained through the mathematical option pricing models which not only provide a closed form means of valuing option contracts, but, in addition, provide a wealth of additional data with respect to the various formula variables. For example, the delta, that is, the derivative of the option premium with respect to asset price, provides investors, portfolio managers or market makers with the exact

---

1. Vega is not a Greek letter and, in practice, the Greek letter kappa (κ) is used to denote the sensitivity of the option premium to changes in volatility. However, the term vega is used in the text to denote this sensitivity. Other Greek letters used to denote this sensitivity include epsilon (ε) and lambda (λ).

hedge ratio required to hedge their portfolio position in options or in the underlying assets.

These derivatives allow market participants to identify the short-term sensitivity of option premiums to changes in the underlying security price, volatility, time to expiration, et cetera. In mathematical terms, these sensitivities are partial derivatives of the premium with respect to these parameters. *Exhibit 10.1* summarises the key partial derivatives in relation to a European option on a non income paying asset. *Exhibit 10.2* sets out the actual mathematical partial derivatives for a European option on a non-income paying asset.

Exhibit 10.1

Option Risk Measures—The Greek Alphabet

Option Derivative	Concept
Delta (Δ)	Delta is the derivative of the option pricing formula with reference to the asset price (S). It measures the estimated change in the option premium for a change in S.
Gamma (γ)	Gamma is the second derivative of the option pricing formula with reference to the asset price (S). It measures the estimated change in the delta of the option for a change in S.
Vega (κ)	Vega is the derivative of the option pricing formula with reference to the volatility of the asset returns (σ). It measures the estimated change in the option premium for a change in σ.
Theta (τ)	Theta is the derivative of the option pricing formula with reference to the time to option expiry (T). It measures the estimated change in the option premium for a change in T.
Rho (ρ)	Rho is the derivative of the option pricing formula with reference to the risk free rate (Rf). It measures the estimated change in the option premium for a change in Rf.

Exhibit 10.2

Option Derivatives—European Options on a Non-income-producing Asset

Option Derivative	Partial Derivative
Delta—Call	$\Delta = N\,(d1)$
Delta—Put	$\Delta = N\,(-d1)$
Gamma—Call & Put	$\gamma = N\,(d1)/S.\,\sigma.\,\sqrt{T}$
Vega—Call & Put	$\kappa = S.\,\sqrt{T}.\,N\,(d1)$
Theta—Call	$\tau = (S.\,\sigma.\,N\,(d1)/2\,\sqrt{T})-Rf.\,K.e^{-Rf.T}\,N(d2)$
Theta—Put	$\tau = (S.\,\sigma.\,N\,(d1)/2\,\sqrt{T})-Rf.\,K.e^{-Rf.T}\,N(-d2)$
Rho—Call	$\rho = K.T.\,e^{-Rf.T}\,N(d2)$
Rho—Put	$\rho = K.T.\,e^{-Rf.T}\,N(-d2)$

The major applications of these measures of risk include:

1. The measurement of the risk of options in terms of its behaviour in response to changes in an individual market parameter, such as the asset price.
2. Facilitating the replication of asset by synthetically creating the option's economic payoffs by trading in the underlying asset.
3. Using the sensitivity and behaviour of the option as a means for precisely defining the hedging or other objectives of the option trader and enabling the creation of more efficient strategies.

In analysing the risk measures, individual components are illustrated using a series of examples based on a consistent set of inputs. The example utilised is set out in *Exhibit 10.3*. The example used is that of a European option on a non-income-paying asset.

Exhibit 10.3
Option Risk Measures—Example

OPTION PRICING MODEL—BLACK SCHOLES

INPUTS/OPTION PRICING/SENSITIVITIES

PRICING INPUTS

UNDERLYING ASSET PRICE	100.00
STRIKE PRICE	100.00
TRADE DATE	1-Jan-95
EXPIRY DATE	1-Jul-95
VOLATILITY	20.00%
RISK FREE RATE	10.00%
INCOME ON ASSET	0%

MODEL OUTPUTS

	CALL	PUT
OPTION PREMIUM	8.23	3.39
OPTION PREMIUM (% OF ASSET PRICE)	8.23%	3.39%

PREMIUM SENSITIVITIES/"GREEKS"	CALL	Description of outputs	
DELTA	0.6637	0.6637	A 1.00 increase in S will change premium by =
GAMMA	0.0259	0.0259	A 1.00 increase in S will change delta by =
VEGA	0.26	0.2569	A 1% increase in vol will change the premium by
THETA (pa)	10.99	10.9950	Divide by 365 to get daily time decay
THETA (per day)	0.03012		
RHO	0.2883	0.2883	A 1% incr. in int rate will change by premium by

PREMIUM SENSITIVITIES/"GREEKS"	PUT	Description of outputs	
DELTA	−0.3363	−0.3363	A 1.00 increase in S will change premium by =
GAMMA	0.0259	0.0259	A 1.00 increase in S will change delta by =
VEGA	0.26	0.2569	A 1% increase in vol will change the premium by
THETA (pa)	1.48	1.4787	Divide by 365 to get daily time decay
THETA (per day)	0.00405		
RHO	−0.1836	−0.1836	A 1% incr. in int rate will change by premium by

3. DELTA

3.1 Concept

Delta is the first derivative of the option pricing formula with respect to the asset price. The delta measures the expected change in the value of the option for a given change in the asset price.

The expected price change is given by:

Change in the asset price times Delta = Expected Change in Option premium

In *Exhibit 10.3* (above) the deltas are as follows:

Call option—0.6637
Put option—(0.3363)

This implies that for a small change of say .10 in the asset price the option value will change by:

Call option—0.6637 times .10 = 0.07
Put option—(0.3363) times .10 = 0.03

Exhibit 10.4 shows the result of the change in terms of its impact on the premium, which is consistent with the predicted changes.

Exhibit 10.4
Option Delta

OPTION PRICING MODEL—BLACK SCHOLES
INPUTS/OPTION PRICING/SENSITIVITIES

PRICING INPUTS	
UNDERLYING ASSET PRICE	100.10
STRIKE PRICE	100.00
TRADE DATE	1-Jan-95
EXPIRY DATE	1-Jul-95
VOLATILITY	20.00%
RISK FREE RATE	10.00%
INCOME ON ASSET	0%

MODEL OUTPUTS	CALL	PUT
OPTION PREMIUM	8.30	3.36
OPTION PREMIUM (% OF ASSET PRICE)	8.29%	3.36%

PREMIUM SENSITIVITIES/"GREEKS"	CALL
DELTA	0.6663
GAMMA	0.0258
VEGA	0.26
THETA (pa)	11.01
THETA (per day)	0.03017
RHO	0.2896

Description of outputs	
A 1.00 increase in S will change premium by =	0.6663
A 1.00 increase in S will change delta by =	0.0258
A 1% increase in vol will change the premium by	0.2564
Divide by 365 to get daily time decay	11.0103
A 1% incr. in int rate will change by premium by	0.2896

PREMIUM SENSITIVITIES/"GREEKS"	PUT
DELTA	-0.3337
GAMMA	0.0258
VEGA	0.26
THETA (pa)	1.49
THETA (per day)	0.00409
RHO	-0.1823

Description of outputs	
A 1.00 increase in S will change premium by =	-0.3337
A 1.00 increase in S will change delta by =	0.0258
A 1% increase in vol will change the premium by	0.2564
Divide by 365 to get daily time decay	1.4941
A 1% incr. in int rate will change by premium by	-0.1823

3.2 Behaviour

The delta of an option is characterised by the following pattern of behaviour:

1. The delta of a call (put) option is positive (negative), reflecting the direction of change of the option value for a given increase in the asset price.

2. The option delta is between 0 and 1 for a call option and 0 and −1 for a put option. The delta of the asset is always 1; a long position has a delta of +1 while a short position has a delta of −1.

3. Deep out-of-the-money options have deltas close to zero because they are not very responsive to changes in the underlying asset price. Deep in-the-money options have deltas close to +1 or −1 because they move in step with the underlying price. At-the-money options tend to have deltas close to 0.5.

4. The higher the delta the closer the option price changes are to the changes in the asset price and consequently are to the gains and losses that would derive from a position in the underlying asset.

Exhibit 10.5 sets out a delta surface which illustrates the behaviour of the delta for the option depicted in *Exhibit 10.3*.

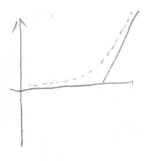

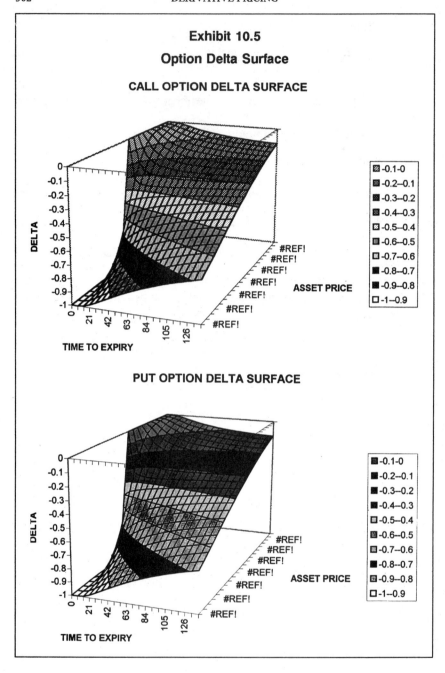

Exhibit 10.5

Option Delta Surface

CALL OPTION DELTA SURFACE

PUT OPTION DELTA SURFACE

In utilising delta, it is important to recognise that it holds for only small movements in the asset price. This can be illustrated by comparing the expected change in the option premium and the *actual change* in the option premium. This comparison is set out in *Exhibit 10.6*.

Exhibit 10.6

Delta Performance

Change in Asset Price	Estimated Change in Call Option Premium Using Commencing Delta	Actual Change in Call Option Premium	Difference
+20	+13.27	+16.92	3.65
+10	+6.64	+7.74	1.10
+5	+3.32	+3.62	0.30
+1	+0.66	+0.68	0.02
+0.10	+0.07	+0.07	0
−0.10	−0.07	−0.06	0.01
−1	−0.66	−0.65	0.01
−5	−3.32	−2.97	0.35
−10	−6.64	−5.21	1.43
−20	−13.27	−7.59	5.68

Change in Asset Price	Estimated Change in Put Option Premium Using Commencing Delta	Actual Change in Put Option Premium	Difference
+20	−6.73	−3.08	3.65
+10	−3.36	−2.26	1.10
+5	−1.68	−1.38	0.30
+1	−0.34	−0.32	0.02
+0.10	−0.03	−0.03	0
−0.10	+0.03	+0.03	0.01
−1	+0.34	+0.35	0.01
−5	+1.68	+2.03	0.35
−10	+3.36	+4.79	1.43
−20	+6.73	+12.42	5.69

Notes:
The calculations are based on the data in *Exhibit 10.3*.

As is evident, for other than relatively small changes in the asset price, the delta predicted changes in option premium over or under estimate the actual change in the option premium.

This reflects the fact that the option delta is, in effect, the slope of the curve which plots the change in the option premium for given changes in asset price. *Exhibit 10.7* shows the curve relating changes in option premium to changes in asset price. The graph illustrates the curvilinear relationship. The slope of the curve changes with respect to the underlying asset price. As the asset price moves by large increments and larger portions of the curve are covered by the jump, the delta estimate becomes increasingly inaccurate as a predictor of option price movements. This is effectively because delta itself changes (see *Exhibit 10.4*). This change is measured by gamma, which is described below.

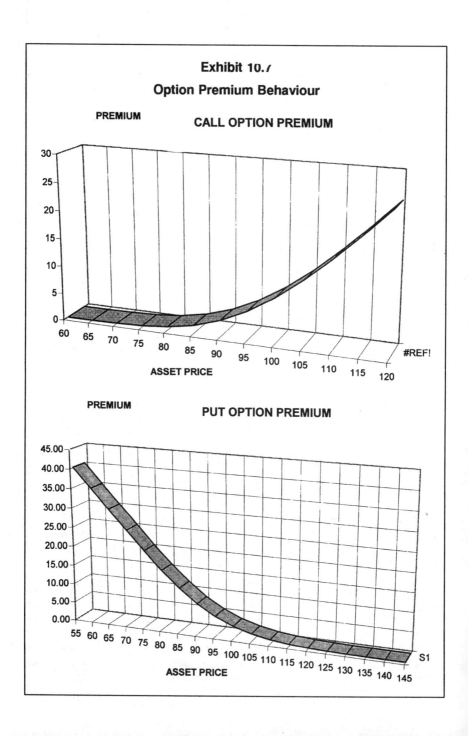

A feature of option deltas is the fact that they are additive; that is, the delta of a portfolio of options is the sum of the face value weighted deltas of the options contained within the portfolio. This relationship can be stated as:

$$\Delta_p = \sum_{n=1}^{n} w_n \cdot \Delta_n$$

Where

Δ_p = the portfolio delta

Δ_n = the delta of the nth option in the portfolio

w_n = the weight for the n the option calculated as the face value of the option divided by the total face value of options in the portfolio

The additive nature of delta greatly facilitates the management of a portfolio of options.

3.3 Application

Delta is the most important measure of option price sensitivity. It conveys a wide range of information, including:

- the asset content of the option; and
- the probability of the option being exercised.

The delta of an option is often referred to as its *equivalent asset position*. This reflects the fact that a holding of delta amount of the asset (say, a long (short) position of .6637 (-0.3363) in the asset) will provide an economic result in terms of gains or losses for small movements in the asset price which are identical to purchases of the option itself.

The delta of an option also gives the probability of the option being exercised. For example, in the example above, the deltas indicate that the call (put) has an approximately 66.37% (33.63%) probability of exercise. The delta in effect gives the probability that the asset price will be above or below the strike price of the option at maturity. This provides important information in terms of enabling the risk of the option to be assessed.

These two properties of the option delta are intrinsic to the application and pricing and trading of options. The asset content implicit in delta allow the assessment and comparison of option strategies. An important aspect of this process is the ability to use the delta equivalence to compare positions as between the *asset* and the *option*.

This equivalence has an important implication for replication of options, which is central to the trading of options. The fact that delta provides the asset content as well as the probability of the option being exercised allows the option to be replicated by maintaining and dynamically adjusting a portfolio consisting of the asset and cash. This asset portfolio will, under certain conditions, give the same economic payoffs as the option being replicated. This relationship is central to the derivation of the option value.[2] This process, which is referred to as delta hedging and forms the basis of all trading and risk management of options, is discussed in detail in Chapter 11.

4. GAMMA

4.1 Concept

Gamma is the second derivative of the option premium (delta is the first derivative) with respect to the underlying security price. It indicates how quickly delta will change as the underlying price changes, that is, the change in the price delta given the unit change in the underlying price.

The expected price change is given by:

Change in the asset price times Gamma = Expected Change in Option Delta

In *Exhibit 10.3* (above) the gammas are as follows:

Call option—0.0259
Put option—0.0259

This implies that for a small change of say 1.00 in the asset price the option value will change by:

Call option—0.0259 times 1.00 = 0.0259
Put option—0.0259 times 1.00 = 0.0259

Exhibit 10.8 shows the result of the change in terms of its impact on the premium, which is consistent with the predicted changes. The slight mis-estimation reflects the curvature of the option premium with respect to asset price, which gives gamma a certain curvature.

---

2. Black-Scholes and other option pricing approaches, such as the binomial models, are predicated on the concept of this replicating portfolio which is free of risk, which allows derivation of the option price as the combined portfolios should only yield the risk free rate of interest.

Exhibit 10.8

Option Gamma

OPTION PRICING MODEL—BLACK SCHOLES
INPUTS/OPTION PRICING/SENSITIVITIES

PRICING INPUTS	
UNDERLYING ASSET PRICE	101.00
STRIKE PRICE	100.00
TRADE DATE	1-Jan-95
EXPIRY DATE	1-Jul-95
VOLATILITY	20.00%
RISK FREE RATE	10.00%
CALL (0)/PUT (1)	0
EUROPEAN (0)/AMERICAN (1) EXERCISE	0
INCOME ON ASSET	0%

MODEL OUTPUTS	CALL	PUT
OPTION PREMIUM	8.91	3.07
OPTION PREMIUM (% OF ASSET PRICE)	8.82%	3.04%

PREMIUM SENSITIVITIES/"GREEKS"	CALL
DELTA	0.6891
GAMMA	0.0248
VEGA	0.25
THETA (pa)	11.14
THETA (per day)	0.03051
RHO	0.3009

Description of outputs	
A 1.00 increase in S will change premium by =	0.6891
A 1.00 increase in S will change delta by =	0.0248
A 1% increase in vol will change the premium by	0.2513
Divide by 365 to get daily time decay	11.1352
A 1% incr. in int rate will change by premium by	0.3009

Exhibit 10.8—*continued*

PREMIUM SENSITIVITIES/"GREEKS"	PUT
DELTA	−0.3109
GAMMA	0.0248
VEGA	0.25
THETA (pa)	1.62
THETA (per day)	0.00444
RHO	−0.1710

Description of outputs	
A 1.00 increase in S will change premium by =	−0.3109
A 1.00 increase in S will change delta by =	0.0248
A 1% increase in vol will change the premium by	0.2513
Divide by 365 to get daily time decay	1.6190
A 1% incr. in int rate will change by premium by	−0.1710

4.2 Behaviour

The gamma of an option is characterised by the following pattern of behaviour:

1. Deep out-of-the-money or in-the-money options have gammas close to zero because they are not very responsive to changes in the underlying asset price.

2. At-the-money options particularly where the time to maturity is relatively short have the highest gammas reflecting the fact the option is likely to be exercised or expire unexercised and the resulting option delta will go to either 1 (in the case of exercise) or 0 (in the case of non-exercise).

3. A low gamma indicates that the option delta changes slowly for a given change in the underlying asset price. A high gamma indicates that the option delta is very sensitive to changes in the price of the underlying asset.

4. Assets have minimal gamma. For most assets, the gamma is zero. The only exception to this is fixed interest securities which have some gamma because of the convex nature of price changes for given changes in interest rates.

Exhibit 10.9 sets out a gamma surface which illustrates the behaviour of the gamma for the option depicted in *Exhibit 10.3*.

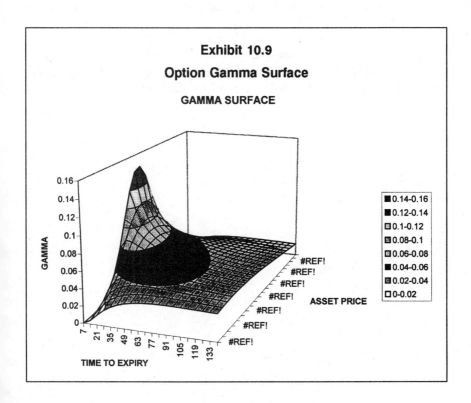

Exhibit 10.9

Option Gamma Surface

GAMMA SURFACE

4.3 Application

Gamma can be best regarded as a measure of the convexity of the option and the resultant hedging risk of replicating the option with a position in the asset through delta hedging.

In this regard it is a measure of hedging risk. It provides information about the sensitivity of the asset equivalent position of the option for given changes in asset prices. Similarly, it provides a measure of the convexity of the option position.

5. VEGA

5.1 Concept

Vega is the first derivative of the option premium with respect to the volatility. The vega measures the expected change in the value of the option for a given change in the volatility parameter.

The expected price change is given by:

Change in the volatility times Vega = Expected Change in Option premium

In *Exhibit 10.3* (above) the vegas are as follows:

Call option—0.26
Put option—0.26

This implies that for a small change of say 1.00% in the volatility the option value will change by:

Call option—0.26 times 1.00 = 0.26
Put option—0.26 times .10 = 0.26

Exhibit 10.10 shows the result of the change in terms of its impact on the premium, which is consistent with the predicted changes.

Exhibit 10.10

Option Vega

OPTION PRICING MODEL—BLACK SCHOLES

INPUTS/OPTION PRICING/SENSITIVITIES

PRICING INPUTS	
UNDERLYING ASSET PRICE	100.00
STRIKE PRICE	100.00
TRADE DATE	1-Jan-95
EXPIRY DATE	1-Jul-95
VOLATILITY	20.00%
RISK FREE RATE	10.00%
CALL (0)/PUT (1)	0
EUROPEAN (0)/AMERICAN (1) EXERCISE	0
INCOME ON ASSET	0%

MODEL OUTPUTS	CALL	PUT
OPTION PREMIUM	8.49	3.65
OPTION PREMIUM (% OF ASSET PRICE)	8.49%	3.65%

PREMIUM SENSITIVITIES/"GREEKS"	CALL
DELTA	0.6588
GAMMA	0.0248
VEGA	0.26
THETA (pa)	11.21
THETA (per day)	0.03071
RHO	0.2846

Description of outputs	
A 1.00 increase in S will change premium by =	0.6588
A 1.00 increase in S will change delta by =	0.0248
A 1% increase in vol will change the premium by	0.2584
Divide by 365 to get daily time decay	11.2098
A 1% incr. in int rate will change by premium by	0.2846

Exhibit 10.10—continued

PREMIUM SENSITIVITIES/"GREEKS"	PUT	Description of outputs	
DELTA	−0.3412	A 1.00 increase in S will change premium by =	−0.3412
GAMMA	0.0248	A 1.00 increase in S will change delta by =	0.0248
VEGA	0.26	A 1% increase in vol will change the premium by	0.2584
THETA (pa)	1.69	Divide by 365 to get daily time decay	1.6936
THETA (per day)	0.00464		
RHO	−0.1873	A 1% incr. in int rate will change by premium by	−0.1873

5.2 Behaviour

The vega of an option is characterised by the following pattern of behaviour:

1. Deep out-of-the-money or in-the-money options have lower vegas because they are not very responsive to changes in volatility, reflecting the fact that these options either have values dominated by the intrinsic value of the option or have low values.

2. At-the-money options, particularly where the time to maturity is long, have the highest vega.

3. A low vega indicates that the option delta changes slowly for a given change in the volatility. A high vega indicates that the option delta is very sensitive to changes in the price of the volatility.

4. Assets have zero vega. This reflects the fact that volatility is not a parameter relevant to pricing of *assets*.

Exhibit 10.11 sets out a vega surface which illustrates the behaviour of the vega for the option depicted in *Exhibit 10.3*.

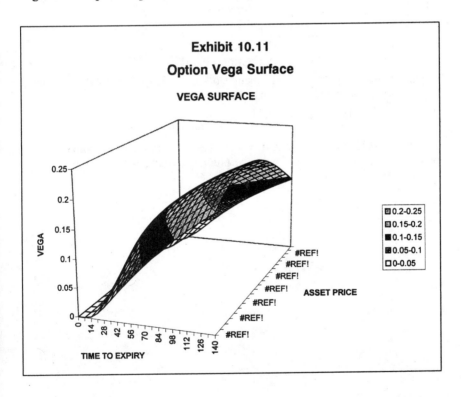

5.3 Application

Vega measures the sensitivity to changes in volatility of a single option or a portfolio. In this regard it measures the exposure or risk to volatility changes present in the position under consideration.

6. THETA

6.1 Concept

Theta is the first derivative of the option premium with respect to the time to expiry. The theta measures the expected change in the value of the option for a given change in the option's time to expiry. The option theta is an annualised estimate and is usually divided by 365 days to get the daily theta estimate.

The expected price change is given by:

Change in the time to expiry times Theta = Expected Change in Option premium

In *Exhibit 10.3* (above) the vegas are as follows:

Call option—0.03
Put option—0.004

This implies that for a small change of say 1 day (7 days) in the time to expiry the option value will change by:

Call option—0.03 times 1.00 = 0.03 (0.21)
Put option—0.004 times 1.00 = 0.004 (0.03)

Exhibit 10.12 shows the result of the change in terms of its impact on the premium, which is consistent with the predicted changes.

Exhibit 10.12

Option Theta

OPTION PRICING MODEL—BLACK SCHOLES

INPUTS/OPTION PRICING/SENSITIVITIES

PRICING INPUTS	
UNDERLYING ASSET PRICE	100.00
STRIKE PRICE	100.00
TRADE DATE	2-Jan-95
EXPIRY DATE	1-Jul-95
VOLATILITY	20.00%
RISK FREE RATE	10.00%
CALL (0)/PUT (1)	0
EUROPEAN (0)/AMERICAN (1) EXERCISE	0
INCOME ON ASSET	0%

MODEL OUTPUTS	CALL	PUT
OPTION PREMIUM	8.20	3.39
OPTION PREMIUM (% OF ASSET PRICE)	8.20%	3.39%

PREMIUM SENSITIVITIES/"GREEKS"	CALL
DELTA	0.6632
GAMMA	0.0260
VEGA	0.26
THETA (pa)	11.01
THETA (per day)	0.03017
RHO	0.2866

Description of outputs	
A 1.00 increase in S will change premium by =	0.6632
A 1.00 increase in S will change delta by =	0.0260
A 1% increase in vol will change the premium by	0.2564
Divide by 365 to get daily time decay	11.0106
A 1% incr. in int rate will change by premium by	0.2866

Exhibit 10.12—*continued*

PREMIUM SENSITIVITIES/"GREEKS"	PUT	Description of outputs
DELTA	−0.3368	A 1.00 increase in S will change premium by = −0.3368
GAMMA	0.0260	A 1.00 increase in S will change delta by = 0.0260
VEGA	0.26	A 1% increase in vol will change the premium by 0.2564
THETA (pa)	1.49	Divide by 365 to get daily time decay 1.4918
THETA (per day)	0.00409	
RHO	−0.1828	A 1% incr. in int rate will change by premium by −0.1828

Exhibit 10.12—continued

OPTION PRICING MODEL—BLACK SCHOLES
INPUTS/OPTION PRICING/SENSITIVITIES

PRICING INPUTS

UNDERLYING ASSET PRICE	100.00
STRIKE PRICE	100.00
TRADE DATE	8-Jan-95
EXPIRY DATE	1-Jul-95
VOLATILITY	20.00%
RISK FREE RATE	10.00%
CALL (0)/PUT (1)	0
EUROPEAN (0)/AMERICAN (1) EXERCISE	0
INCOME ON ASSET	0%

(CALL (0)/PUT (1) row also shows: 1)

MODEL OUTPUTS

	CALL	PUT
OPTION PREMIUM	8.02	3.37
OPTION PREMIUM (% OF ASSET PRICE)	8.02%	3.37%

PREMIUM SENSITIVITIES/"GREEKS"

	CALL
DELTA	0.6607
GAMMA	0.0265
VEGA	0.25
THETA (pa)	11.11
THETA (per day)	0.03043
RHO	0.2767

Description of outputs

A 1.00 increase in S will change premium by =	0.6607
A 1.00 increase in S will change delta by =	0.0265
A 1% increase in vol will change the premium by	0.2528
Divide by 365 to get daily time decay	11.1075
A 1% incr. in int rate will change by premium by	0.2767

Exhibit 10.12—*continued*

PREMIUM SENSITIVITIES/"GREEKS"	PUT	Description of outputs	
DELTA	-0.3393	A 1.00 increase in S will change premium by =	-0.3393
GAMMA	0.0265	A 1.00 increase in S will change delta by =	0.0265
VEGA	0.25	A 1% increase in vol will change the premium by	0.2528
THETA (pa)	1.57	Divide by 365 to get daily time decay	1.5730
THETA (per day)	0.00431		
RHO	-0.1778	A 1% incr. in int rate will change by premium by	-0.1778

6.2 Behaviour

The theta of an option is characterised by the following pattern of behaviour:

1. The theta is negative reflecting the loss of value as the time to expiry diminishes. This fall in value accrues to the seller as a gain which is offset by the loss suffered by the purchaser.

2. The theta of an option typically for a deep in or out-of-the-money option is lower than for a corresponding at-the-money option.

3. The highest theta is for an at-the-money option with a short time to expiry.

Assets, interestingly, will generally have thetas. The source of theta will vary. For example, options on debt instruments will exhibit a theta consistent with the accrual of interest income or expense on the instrument. Similarly, the impact of dividends or commodity interest rates will be reflected in the asset thetas for equities/equity indexes or commodities/commodity indexes. The changes in futures price reflecting changes in the carry cost as a result of changes in the time to delivery/settlement will provide futures/forward contracts with their theta.

Exhibit 10.13 sets out a theta surface which illustrates the behaviour of the theta for the option depicted in *Exhibit 10.3*.

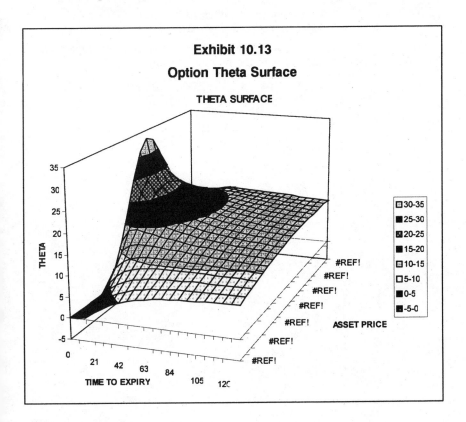

6.3 Application

Theta measures the sensitivity to changes in the time to expiry of a single option or a portfolio. In this regard it measures the exposure or risk to the passage of time present in the position under consideration.

7. RHO

6.1 Concept

Rho is the first derivative of the option premium with respect to the risk free interest rate. The rho measures the expected change in the value of the option for a given change in the risk free interest rate.

The expected price change is given by:

Change in the risk free rate times Rho = Expected Change in Option premium

In *Exhibit 10.3* (above) the vegas are as follows:

Call option 0.29
Put option −0.18

This implies that for a small change of say 1% pa in the risk free rate the option value will change by:

Call option 0.29 times 1.00 = 0.29
Put option −0.18 times 1.00 = 0.18

Exhibit 10.14 shows the result of the change in terms of its impact on the premium, which is consistent with the predicted changes.

Exhibit 10.14

Option Rho

OPTION PRICING MODEL—BLACK SCHOLES
INPUTS/OPTION PRICING/SENSITIVITIES

PRICING INPUTS	
UNDERLYING ASSET PRICE	100.00
STRIKE PRICE	100.00
TRADE DATE	1-Jan-95
EXPIRY DATE	1-Jul-95
VOLATILITY	20.00%
RISK FREE RATE	11.00%
CALL (0)/PUT (1)	0
EUROPEAN (0)/AMERICAN (1) EXERCISE	0
INCOME ON ASSET	0%

MODEL OUTPUTS	CALL	PUT
OPTION PREMIUM	8.52	3.21
OPTION PREMIUM (% OF ASSET PRICE)	8.52%	3.21%

PREMIUM SENSITIVITIES/"GREEKS"	CALL
DELTA	0.6764
GAMMA	0.0255
VEGA	0.25
THETA (pa)	11.60
THETA (per day)	0.03179
RHO	0.2932

Description of outputs	
A 1.00 increase in S will change premium by =	0.6764
A 1.00 increase in S will change delta by =	0.0255
A 1% increase in vol will change the premium by	0.2530
Divide by 365 to get daily time decay	11.6049
A 1% incr. in int rate will change by premium by	0.2932

Exhibit 10.14—*continued*

PREMIUM SENSITIVITIES/"GREEKS"	PUT	Description of outputs	
DELTA	−0.3236	A 1.00 increase in S will change premium by =	−0.3236
GAMMA	0.0255	A 1.00 increase in S will change delta by =	0.0255
VEGA	0.25	A 1% increase in vol will change the premium by	0.2530
THETA (pa)	1.19	Divide by 365 to get daily time decay	1.1888
THETA (per day)	0.00326		
RHO	−0.1764	A 1% incr. in int rate will change by premium by	−0.1764

6.2 Behaviour

The rho of an option is characterised by the following pattern of behaviour:

1. The rho for a call (put) is positive (negative) reflecting the directional impact of an increase in interest rates on the value of the option.
2. The rho decreases with time to maturity, reflecting the diminished impact of the discounting of the exercise price.

Exhibit 10.15 sets out a rho surface which illustrates the behaviour of the rho for the option depicted in *Exhibit 10.3*.

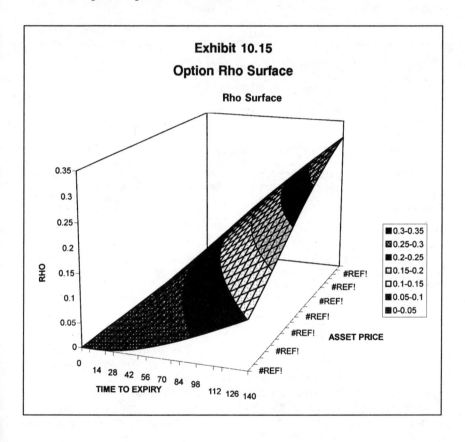

Exhibit 10.15

Option Rho Surface

6.3 Application

Rho measures the sensitivity to changes in the risk free interest rate of a single option or a portfolio. In this regard it measures the exposure or risk to changes in the discount rate present in the position under consideration.

8. INTERACTION OF RISK MEASURES

Exhibit 10.16 summarises the option sensitivities for underlying asset and option positions.

Exhibit 10.16 Option Sensitivities—Summary				
Asset or Option Position	**Delta**	**Gamma**	**Theta**	**Vega**
Purchased Asset	Positive	Not applicable	Not applicable	Not applicable
Sold Asset	Negative	Not applicable	Not applicable	Not applicable
Purchased Call	Positive	Positive	Negative	Positive
Sold Call	Negative	Negative	Positive	Negative
Purchased Put	Negative	Positive	Negative	Positive
Sold Put	Positive	Negative	Positive	Negative

The analysis of the individual risk measures, to date, has been undertaken on a separate basis. In practice, there is substantial interaction between the risk measures. The most significant interactions are between delta, gamma, vega and theta.

Delta and gamma are both affected by changes in volatility. The pattern of interaction is as follows:

• Increases in volatility result in higher deltas for out and at-the-money options. Increases in volatility reduce the delta for in-the-money options. This pattern reflects the fact that delta is, in one sense, a measure of the probability of exercise of the option. The increase in volatility increases or decreases the probability of exercise for out and at-the-money options and in-the-money options respectively.

• Gamma generally decreases with an increase in volatility and vice versa. The change in gamma for a change in volatility is greatest for an at-the-money option, while the change in gamma is much lower for changes in volatility for in and out-of-the-money options.

The relationship between delta and volatility is set out in the delta-volatility surface set out in *Exhibit 10.17*. The relationship between gamma and volatility is set out in the gamma-volatility surface set out in *Exhibit 10.18*. In both cases, an option with a term to expiry of 30 days is utilised.

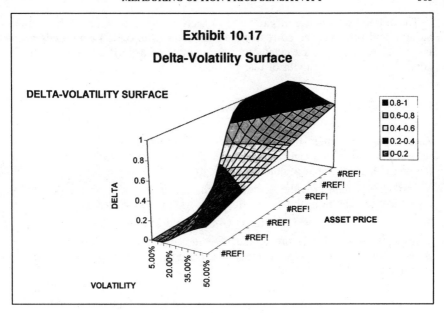

Exhibit 10.17

Delta-Volatility Surface

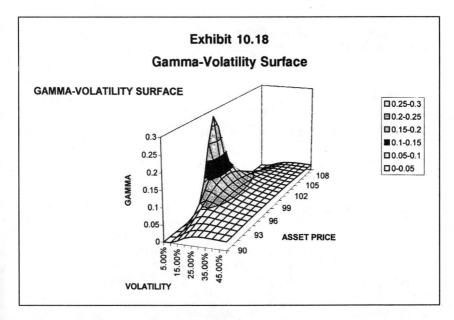

Exhibit 10.18

Gamma-Volatility Surface

The implication of this relationship is that where the delta of an option or portfolio is utilised to hedge or replicate the underlying option, changes in volatility can significantly erode the efficiency of the hedge.

The relationship between gamma and theta is more complex. Where theta is large and positive, the corresponding gamma of the option also tends to be large and negative.[3] This means that the gamma of a portfolio, under certain conditions, offsets the theta of that portfolio.

9. OTHER RISK PARAMETERS

A number of other risk parameters are utilised to obtain additional information about the sensitivity or risk profile of an option. These include: lambda (λ); speed; charm; colour; and fugit.

Lambda (λ) measures the percentage change in the value of the option for a percentage change in the asset price. It is usually calculated as:

Lambda = Delta times (Asset Price/Option Value)

It is effectively a measure of the leverage inherent in the option position. A large lambda indicates a greater sensitivity *in proportional terms* to movements in the asset price.

Speed, charm and colour were all derivatives suggested by Mark Garman.[4] Each of these terms measures additional risk aspects of option transactions:

- *speed* is a measure of the change in gamma for a given change in the asset price;
- *charm* is a measure of the change in delta for a given change in time to expiry; and
- *colour* is a measure of the change in gamma for a given change in time to expiry.

Each of these measures, in particular, charm and colour, have significance for traders seeking to manage a portfolio of options.

Fugit was also suggested by Mark Garman.[5] It is the expected value of the time to exercise of an American option. It is usually calculated using an iterative procedure within a binomial option pricing framework.

10. EXTENSIONS FOR OPTIONS ON DIFFERENT ASSETS

In the above analyses, the focus has been on a European option with non-income-paying asset. The same approach can be extended to cover options on different underlying assets. *Exhibit 10.19* sets out the partial derivatives for these types of options.

---

3. For a formal mathematical proof of this see John C Hull, Options Futures and Other Derivatives (3rd ed, Prentice Hall, Englewood Cliffs, NJ, 1996), pp 327-328.
4. See Mark Garman, "Charm School" (1992) 5(7) *Risk* 53.
5. See Mark Garman, "Semper Tempus Fugit" (1989) 2(5) *Risk* 34; "Semper Tempus Fugit" in "From Black Scholes To Black Holes" (1992) *Risk* 89.

Exhibit 10.19
Option Derivatives—Extensions

Option Derivative	European Option on a Non-asset Paying Asset (Black-Scholes)	European Option on Asset Paying Continuous Income (Y) (Amended Black-Scholes)	European Option on Forward/Futures Contract (Black)	European Option on Currency (Garman-Kohlhagen)
Delta—Call	$\Delta = N(d1)$	$\Delta = e^{-Y.T} N(d1)$	$\Delta = e^{-Y.T} N(d1)$	$\Delta = e^{-Rff.T} N(d1)$
Delta—Put	$\Delta = N(-d1)$	$\Delta = e^{-Y.T} N(-d1)$	$\Delta = e^{-Y.T} N(-d1)$	$\Delta = e^{-Rff.T} N(-d1)$
Gamma—Call & Put	$\gamma = N(d1)/S.\sigma.\sqrt{T}$	$\gamma = N(d1). e^{-Y.T}/S.\sigma.\sqrt{T}$	$\gamma = N(d1). e^{-R.T}/F.\sigma.\sqrt{T}$	$\gamma = N(d1). e^{-Rff.T}/S.\sigma.\sqrt{T}$
Vega—Call & Put	$\kappa = S.\sqrt{T}.N(d1)$	$\kappa = e^{-Y.T} S.\sqrt{T}.N(d1)$	$\kappa = e^{-Rf.T} F.\sqrt{T}.N(d1)$	$\kappa = e^{-Rff.T} S.\sqrt{T}.N(d1)$
Theta—Call	$\tau = (S.\sigma.N(d1)/2\sqrt{T}) - Rf. K.e^{-Rf.T} N(d2)$	$\tau = (S.\sigma.N(d1). e^{-Y.T}/2\sqrt{T}) - Y.S.e^{-Y.T} N(d1) - Rf. K.e^{-Rf.T} N(d2)$	$\tau = (F.\sigma.N(d1). e^{-R.T}/2\sqrt{T}) - Rf. F.e^{-Rf.T} N(d1) - Rf. K.e^{-Rf.T} N(d2)$	$\tau = (S.\sigma.N(d1). e^{-Rff.T}/2\sqrt{T}) - Rff. S.e^{-Rff.T} N(d1) - Rfd. K.e^{-Rfd.T} N(d2)$
Theta—Put	$\tau = (S.\sigma.N(d1)/2\sqrt{T}) - Rf. K.e^{-Rf.T} N(-d2)$	$\tau = (S.\sigma.N(d1). e^{-Y.T}/2\sqrt{T}) - Y.S.e^{-Y.T} N(-d1) - Rf. K.e^{-Rf.T} N(-d2)$	$\tau = (F.\sigma.N(d1). e^{-Rf.T}/2\sqrt{T}) - Rf. F.e^{-Rf.T} N(-d1) - Rf. K.e^{-Rf.T} N(-d2)$	$\tau = (S.\sigma.N(d1). e^{-Rff.T}/2\sqrt{T}) - Rff. S.e^{-Rff.T} N(-d1) - Rfd. K.e^{-Rfd.T} N(-d2)$
Rho—Call	$\rho = K.T. e^{-Rf.T} N(d2)$	$\rho = K.T. e^{-Rf.T} N(d2)$		$\rho = K.T. e^{-Rfd.T} N(d2)$
Rho—Put	$\rho = K.T. e^{-Rf.T} N(-d2)$	$\rho = K.T. e^{-Rf.T} N(-d2)$		$\rho = K.T. e^{-Rfd.T} N(-d2)$
Rho—Call (Foreign Interest Rate)				$\rho = K.T. e^{-Rff.T} N(d2)$
Rho—Put (Foreign Interest Rate)				$\rho = K.T. e^{-Rff.T} N(-d2)$

The options covered include:

1. European option where the underlying asset pays continuous income;
2. European option on a forward or futures contract; and
3. European option on a currency.

The risk measures for a European option on a commodity or equity would be identical to that for either an option where the underlying asset pays continuous income or an option on a currency with the commodity payout or convenience yield or equity dividend yield substituted for either the income of foreign interest rate.

11. SUMMARY

The derivatives of the valuation formula for options provide a quantifiable measure of the sensitivity and risk of the option to changes in one or more of the underlying factors which determine the price of the option. These risk measures are central to the management of the risk of options, hedging options, and using options to manage risk in asset portfolios.

In recent times, the derivative measures of risk have been used more generically to capture and present the risk of *all instruments*. This encompasses *assets* and *forwards,* as well as options. This reflects the fact that the risk or value sensitivities of all instruments are capable of being measured, expressed, and communicated easily using this general vocabulary of risk. *Exhibit 10.20* sets out this generalised language of risk which is increasingly utilised.

Exhibit 10.20

Generalised Risk Measures

Risk Measure	Concept for Options	Concept for General Risk
Delta (Δ)	Delta is the derivative of the option pricing formula with reference to the asset price (S). It measures the estimated change in the option premium for a change in S.	Measures exposure to price change of underlying asset; equivalent to Present Value of Basis Point (PVBP) or Dollar Value of 1 Basis Pointi (DVO1).
Gamma (γ)	Gamma is the second derivative of the option pricing formula with reference to the asset price (S). It measures the estimated change in the delta of the option for a change in S.	Measures exposure to change in delta; equivalent to measure of convexity.
Vega (κ)	Vega is the derivative of the option pricing formula with reference to the volatility of the asset returns (σ). It measures the estimated change in the option premium for a change in σ.	Measures exposure to changes in volatility (only applicable to options).
Theta (τ)	Theta is the derivative of the option pricing formula with reference to the time to option expiry (T). It measures the estimated change in the option premium for a change in T.	Measures exposure to or change in value arising from the effluxion of time; analogous to carry income or expense.
Rho (ρ)	Rho is the derivative of the option pricing formula with reference to the risk free rate (Rf). It measures the estimated change in the option premium for a change in Rf.	Measures exposure to changes in the discount rate(s) applicable.

Chapter 11

Option Replication Utilising Delta Hedging

by Satyajit Das

1. INTRODUCTION

It is feasible to replicate or synthesise the economic return profile of an option transaction by a process of trading in the underlying asset. The capacity to replicate the option using the underlying asset is implicit in the inherent nature of delta which, amongst other information, provides a guide as to the asset content of the option. This concept which is referred to variously as delta hedging, option replication, synthetic options, or dynamic hedging as well as a number of proprietary terms, is central to both the pricing and trading/hedging of options.

The requirement to synthetically replicate the economic profile of an option rather than trading in the underlying option may arise for a number of reasons. These include:

- Financial institutions active in trading may enter into transactions with clients where they either sell or buy options which they must offset the market risk. The dealer can offset the client position with an offsetting option transaction (either on an exchange or over-the-counter). However, where it is not possible to offset the exposure in this way, it may be necessary for the dealer to hold and hedge the position either till maturity or, more often, until an offsetting transaction can be entered into. In the period between the initial transaction and the offsetting transaction, the option dealer would delta hedge its exposure to reduce any exposure to movements in the price of the underlying asset.

- Participants may need to synthesise options where, first, such options are not readily available or traded, or, secondly, it is more cost effective to create such options rather than purchasing the options.

- The creation of structured investment products such as capital protected funds or portfolio insurance products which require either the creation or purchase of options. In these situations, the fund may prefer to synthesise the option for cost or other reasons, such as customisation et cetera. The use of synthetic option technology in portfolio insurance applications is discussed in Chapter 14.

In this chapter, the process of option replication is examined. The process of delta hedging is first explained with a series of examples of increasing complexity. This analysis focuses on the cost of hedging and the risks inherent in synthetically creating the option. The risk and risk management of this methodology for trading and hedging options is then considered.

2. DELTA HEDGING[1]

2.1 Concept

The concept of utilising a position in the underlying asset to replicate the economic profile of an option is central to both the *pricing or valuation* of an option and the trading and hedging of these instruments.

As noted previously, delta, that is, the partial derivative of the option valuation formula with respect to asset price, provides a measure of the change in the option premium for a small change in the asset price. This allows a portfolio, consisting of the asset and the option, to be constructed which is immune in relation to value to small changes in the asset price.

For example, a short call position may be hedged with a long position in the asset. The amount of asset held would be equivalent to delta times the face value of the option.[2] For small changes in the asset price, the change in the value of the asset portfolio would offset equal and opposite changes in the value of the option portfolio. This portfolio would economically be a riskless portfolio which to avoid arbitrage would only earn the risk free rate of interest on the investment in the portfolio. This basic insight is utilised in all option pricing models, such as Black-Scholes and the binomial pricing approaches, to derive the fair value of the option. *Exhibit 11.1* sets out the riskless fully-hedged portfolio positions possible.

Exhibit 11.1

Riskless Hedge Positions

Position	Hedge
long position in calls	short Δ assets for each call held
short position in calls	long Δ assets for each call sold
long position in puts	short Δ assets for each put held
short position in puts	long Δ assets for each put sold

Delta $(\Delta)^3$ refers to the sensitivity of the option premium to changes in the asset price.

Implicit in this approach is the capacity for the final payoff from the option to be replicated by trading in the asset underlying the option to create an instantaneous hedge against small movements in asset price. This approach can then be extended by dynamically adjusting the hedge by altering the holding of the asset and the amount of the borrowing and lending to replicate the option until maturity. This approach, which has been

---

1. For an excellent analysis of delta hedging see Nassim Taleb, *Dynamic Hedging: Managing Vanilla and Exotic Options* (John Wiley & Sons, New York, 1997).
2. Alternatively, the position could be constructed as for each unit of asset held, it would be necessary to sell 1/delta of the call option on the asset.
3. See detailed discussion in Chapter 10.

recognised by a number of writers, allows the synthetic creation of an option by holding delta weight of the asset underlying the option and adjusting the holding of the asset in accordance with changes in the delta of the option.[4] The synthetic option can therefore be created from a portfolio of existing traded instruments, which, with proper management over time, can replicate the return characteristics of an option. This is what is referred to delta hedging.

2.2 Example of delta hedging

Delta hedging entails the creation of a synthetic option by using a portfolio consisting of two instruments:

1. the asset into which the option can be exercised, whether it be a cash market instrument or futures and forwards on the underlying asset; and

2. a risk-free asset, usually cash or high quality securities.

The key to creating a synthetic option is to determine the proportion of cash and asset to maintain in the portfolio. This proportion is adjusted through time in a very specific way to replicate the price behaviour of a call option. In practice, such a portfolio can be created and properly managed to give approximately the same premium and outcome as a traded call option on the underlying asset.

The intuition for synthetic options derives from the fact that, for example, the price behaviour of a call option is similar to that of a portfolio with combined positions involving the underlying asset and cash. Although the price of a call option and the price of the underlying asset change in the same direction, the effect on the price of the call option of a given change in the asset price depends on the current price level of the asset. This is because the number of units of the asset held in the replicating portfolio must be sufficient to equate to the slope of the call option price curve at that particular price level or the particular option's delta.

Exhibit 11.2 sets out a simple example of a delta hedge to replicate a call option.

---

4.   See, for example, Mark Rubinstein and Hayne E Leland (July-August 1991).

Exhibit 11.2

Delta Hedge—Example 1

Assume a call option on a non-income-producing asset where the asset is trading at 100. The call option is on the following terms:

Strike prices = 100

Time to expiry = 0.50

Risk free rate = 10% pa

Volatility = 20% pa

The call option premium (using Black Scholes) is 8.26. The option delta is .6641.

Using this information two portfolios can be constructed:

1. a short position in the options, say 100 options (each on 1 unit of the asset); and
2. a long position in 66.41 units of the asset (calculated as delta times the face value of the options).

The changes in value of the two portfolios for small changes in the asset price are set out below

Increase In Asset Price (from 100 to 100.10)

	Initial Portfolio			Final Portfolio		

Portfolio 1 = Option

	Asset Price = 100			Asset Price = 100.10		
Amount	Value (per Option)	Portfolio Value	Amount	Value (per Option)	Portfolio Value	Change in Portfolio Value
100	8.26	826	100	8.33	833	−7

Portfolio 2 = Assets

	Asset Price = 100			Asset Price = 100.10		
Amount	Value (per Option)	Portfolio Value	Amount	Value (per Option)	Portfolio Value	Change in Portfolio Value
66.41	100	6641	66.41	100.10	6648	7

Change In Overall Portfolio Value   0

Decrease In Asset Price (from 100 to 99.90)

	Initial Portfolio			Final Portfolio		

Portfolio 1 = Option

	Asset Price = 100			Asset Price = 99.90		
Amount	Value (per Option)	Portfolio Value	Amount	Value (per Option)	Portfolio Value	Change in Portfolio Value
100	8.26	826	100	8.20	820	6

Portfolio 2 = Assets

	Asset Price = 100			Asset Price = 100.10		
Amount	Value (per Option)	Portfolio Value	Amount	Value (per Option)	Portfolio Value	Change in Portfolio Value
66.41	100	6641	66.41	99.90	6635	−6

Change in Overall Portfolio Value   0

As is evident, the portfolio of the short call options and the offsetting portfolio of the delta amount of the asset is insulated from small changes in asset price. The change in the value of the options for a given movement in the asset price is offset by an equal but opposite change in the value of the asset. While the example focuses on short call position, an identical logic can be utilised in relation to all option positions. For example, the technique for replicating put options is similar. It entails maintaining a portfolio consisting of cash and a short position in the underlying asset, which is adjusted as the price of the asset changes.

The replicating portfolio must be adjusted as the asset price changes. This will usually entail, in the case of a call option, selling assets as the asset price falls and buying assets as the asset price rises. If the asset price declines, then the holding of the assets is sold, with the proceeds being used to partially repay the borrowings used to finance the position. If the asset price at maturity is below the strike price, then the replication portfolio should end up with no holding of the asset at maturity and no corresponding borrowing. This portfolio would have a value of zero. This corresponds to the value of the option. If the asset price increases, then the holding of the assets is increased, with borrowings being undertaken (for the value of the asset less the premium received) to finance the position. If the asset price at maturity is above the strike price, then the option will be exercised. The replication portfolio should equal the units of asset underlying the option financed by borrowings, which is equal to the strike price. The difference corresponds to the intrinsic value of the option.

The portfolio is never fully invested when the asset price increases, nor fully disinvested when the asset price falls. The process of portfolio adjustment will reduce the initial investment. Theoretically, by the expiration of the call option, the cumulative depreciation should approximately equal the initial theoretical value of the call option.

From a theoretical standpoint, the process of delta hedging entails the final option payoff being replicated by the position in the stock financed by borrowings and the option premium received. This can be seen by examining a model such as Black-Scholes, which can be reduced as follows:

Option Premium = Delta times Asset − Amount of Borrowing

This more formally can be given as:

$$P_{ce} = S. \, N(d1) - K \, e^{-Rf.T} . \, N(d2)$$

The asset holding is dictated by the delta or sensitivity to asset price changes of the option. The amount of borrowings is equivalent to the present value of the exercise price of the option adjusted for the probability that the call option expires at maturity in-the-money. The rationale, in a risk-neutral and arbitrage-free world, being that the expected amount due for repayment to the lender is equivalent to this amount.

Two aspects of the replication process should be noted:

1. the replication portfolio is inherently self financing; and

2. the replication portfolio must be dynamically managed reflecting changes in the factors affecting the option price leading to changes in the relative holding of the asset and the amount of borrowings.

The concept of creating synthetic options permits option granters to replicate not only call options, but many other option positions. Using replicating portfolios the granter of options can, where it has created a risk position by writing options, cover these open positions, creating synthetic options which hedge the existing exposure.

2.2 Costs of replication

The process of replication is not costless. The major costs include:

- financing of the asset position or investment of the proceeds of a short sale;
- trading costs; and
- loss of hedge efficiencies.

The financing cost element is self-explanatory. The holding of assets required to hedge a short call option or a long put option will require financing, with the resulting interest expense being incurred. In contrast, a long call or short put option will require short selling the asset, releasing cash which can be invested and earn interest.

Trading costs cover a variety of items:

- The transaction costs of trading—the bid-offer spread—in actual markets means that each transaction results in a cost to the trader seeking to replicate the option.
- The gains or losses on trading—the process of replication requires the trader to, for a call option, buy high, sell low in the process of dynamic hedge management whereby the holding of assets must be increased as the price goes up and decreased as the price of the asset falls. For a put option, a similar process is applicable, with the short position in the asset having to be increased as the price decreases and decreased as the price increases, resulting in the same pattern of selling low and buying high. This pattern of trading inherently creates losses which will represent the cost of replicating the option.

Loss of hedge efficiency covers a variety of items:

- Delta slippage—as discussed in greater detail below in the context of risk management, it may not be possible to maintain a delta neutral position under all circumstances. This may be the result of either the use of *periodic rebalancing* rather than *continuous rebalancing*, reflecting the incorporation of transaction and trading costs as well as price movements which are discontinuous and introduce lags in adjustment of the delta hedge. The failure to maintain perfect delta neutrality creates exposures to the movement in the *price of the underlying asset* with resulting gains and losses.
- Rebalancing costs—these reflect the impact of the decision to periodically rebalance the portfolio, which creates the delta slippage noted above and the resultant gains and losses from exposure to asset price movements. In this regard, all delta hedging is a compromise between increased frequency of rebalancing the hedge (which incurs additional trading costs) and less frequent rebalancing (which reduces efficiency of the hedge and exposes the portfolio to gains and losses from changes in the asset price).

In perfect, frictionless capital markets, the costs of the delta hedge should exactly equal the theoretical premium of the option. In practice, the factors identified make this unlikely.

2.3 Issues in delta hedging

As illustrated above, in most situations, the value of an option behaves in a manner which is similar to a portfolio consisting of short or long positions in the asset and cash borrowings or investments. This allows the process of replication described.

However, when put to practice, the theory of delta hedging suffers from a number of difficulties:

1. market structure issues, such as the capacity to borrow and finance or lend the asset;
2. the impact of transaction costs;
3. the pattern of changes in the asset price, such as the absence of large jumps or non-continuous price changes;
4. the constancy of volatility and interest rates over the life of the option; and
5. issues arising from the use of forwards or futures contracts on the asset to replicate the option.

The process of option replication inherently assumes that, where the delta hedge requires holding a position in the asset, it is possible to finance. Similarly, where the delta hedge requires a short sale of the asset, it is assumed that, first, it is feasible to effect the short sale, and, secondly, it is possible to borrow the asset to implement the short sale. These conditions may not be able to be met in every market structure.

As noted above, the requirement to trade in the underlying asset results in the trader incurring trading costs. The trading costs are related to the frequency of re-balancing of the hedge. The more frequent the re-balancing the more accurately the replicating portfolio tracks the underlying option being hedged. However, the frequency of trading obviously affects the cost of replication by way of increased transaction costs. A related problem is the inability to accurately predict the *level* of transaction costs. The position in the asset must be adjusted periodically as the option's delta changes. As the delta changes are unknown (being a function of the path of asset prices), the exact number or quantum of hedge adjustments is not known in advance. This means that the transaction costs are not known in advance.

The ability to replicate the value changes in the option through trading in the asset will only be applicable for small changes in the asset price and where the asset price changes are continuous. A large discrete change in the asset price—in effect, a discontinuous movement or gap—will significantly impair the effectiveness of the hedge. This reflects the fact that in the event of a discontinuity or gap the change in the asset position cannot be undertaken sufficiently quickly. The price of the option will adjust immediately but the hedge cost will lag behind the change in the asset price, creating hedging errors and a divergence in the value of the hedge relative to the option.

The theoretical model of delta hedging assumes that both the volatility of asset price changes is negligible and the risk-free interest rate is constant over the life of the option. In reality, both of these variables are uncertain. Changes in each of these terms will, in fact, impact on the efficiency of the hedge. For example, a change in volatility levels may not be accompanied by a change in the price of the asset. In these circumstances, the value of the option will change but will not be accompanied by a corresponding change in the value of the asset position. Changes in volatility will also alter the option delta, resulting in changes in the required hedge which will have an impact on the cost of replicating the option.

Changes in interest rates will affect the process of delta hedging in a number of ways. Changes in interest rates will alter the forward price of the asset and hence the value of the option. In addition, it will affect the cost of the hedge, as it will increase the cost of holding the asset and reduce the cost of shorting.

The final issue relates to the use of forwards or futures on assets to replicate the option. The major rationale for this is the off-balance sheet nature of these instruments and the accompanying efficiencies in the use of capital. However, the use of forwards or futures introduces additional risk factors into the hedging process. The use of forward/futures contracts assumes the fair value pricing of these contracts; that is, their prices are free of arbitrage. In reality, the forward contract may be priced away from fair value, thereby introducing additional errors in the hedging process. The changes in the cash-futures basis (effectively, the cost of carry) may result in higher hedging costs.

Similarly, where the forward or futures contract used is of a different maturity to that of the option, the maturity mismatch introduced creates an exposure to changes in the shape of the yield curve. This reflects the fact that changes in shorter term rates will affect the forward/futures contract value differently from the impact of longer-term rates on the value of the underlying option.

2.4 More complex examples of delta hedging

The concept of utilising option replication techniques is further illustrated in *Exhibit 11.3* with a series of more complex examples. These examples are designed to highlight some of the risks and difficulties in seeking to replicate options through trading in the underlying assets.

Exhibit 11.3
Delta Hedge—Example 2

14-Aug-96

DELTA HEDGING

CALL OPTION EXAMPLE (OPTION EXPIRES IN-THE-MONEY)

INPUTS	
ASSET PRICE	$100.00
STRIKE PRICE	$100.00
TRADE DATE	01-Jan-96
EXPIRY DATE	29-Jan-96
TIME TO EXPIRY (DAYS)	28.00
VOLATILITY (INITIAL)	20.00%
INTEREST RATE	10.00%
HOLDING COST	0.00%

HEDGE PROFIT AND LOSS	
PREMIUM RECEIPT	$21,928
INTEREST ON PREMIUM	$168
HEDGE COSTS	($19,554)
NET	$2,541

NO OF ASSETS:	10,000	10,000	10,000	10,000	10,000
DATE	01-Jan-96	08-Jan-96	15-Jan-96	22-Jan-96	29-Jan-96
TIME TO EXPIRY (DAYS)	28.00	21.00	14.00	7.00	0.00
ASSET PRICE	$100.00	$101.50	$99.00	$100.50	$102.50
VOLATILITY (CURRENT)	20.00%	20.00%	20.00%	20.00%	20.00%
INTEREST RATE (CURRENT)	10.00%	10.00%	10.00%	10.00%	10.00%

OPTION PREMIUM	$2.1928	$2.7542	$1.1014	$1.3729	$2.5000
DELTA	0.5071	0.6273	0.4048	0.5758	1.0000
GAMMA	0.0714	0.0770	0.0996	0.1404	0.0000
THETA (per day)	0.0385	0.0427	0.0532	0.0773	0.0000
VEGA	0.1096	0.0913	0.0749	0.0544	0.0000
RHO	-0.0017	-0.0016	-0.0004	-0.0003	0.0000

Exhibit 11.3—continued

DELTA HEDGE	AMOUNT	PRICE					
HEDGE REQUIREMENT			5,071	6,273	4,048	5,758	10,000
HEDGE TRANSACTIONS							
PURCHASE ASSETS	5,071	$100.00	$507,143	$507,143	$405,935	$405,935	$405,935
PURCHASE ASSETS	1,202	$101.50		$121,980			
PURCHASE ASSETS	(2,225)	$99.00					
PURCHASE ASSETS	1,710	$100.50				$171,860	$171,860
PURCHASE ASSETS	4,242	$102.50					$434,829
VALUE OF HEDGE PORTFOLIO							
NO OF ASSETS			5,071	6,273	4,048	5,758	10,000
AVERAGE VALUE OF ASSETS			$100.00	$100.29	$100.29	$100.35	$101.26
TOTAL			$507,143	$629,123	$405,935	$577,795	$1,012,624
GAIN ON HEDGE ADJUSTMENT					($2,864.99)		($12,624)
INTEREST COST				($972.60)	($1,206.54)	($778.51)	($1,108.10)
CUMULATIVE COST				($972.60)	($5,044.13)	($5,822.63)	($19,554.48)

Exhibit 11.3—continued

DELTA HEDGING

14-Aug-96

CALL OPTION EXAMPLE (OPTION EXPIRES OUT-OF-THE-MONEY)

INPUTS	
ASSET PRICE	$100.00
STRIKE PRICE	$100.00
TRADE DATE	01-Jan-96
EXPIRY DATE	29-Jan-96
TIME TO EXPIRY (DAYS)	28.00
VOLATILITY (INITIAL)	20.00%
INTEREST RATE	10.00%
HOLDING COST	0.00%

HEDGE PROFIT AND LOSS	
PREMIUM RECEIPT	$21,928
INTEREST ON PREMIUM	$168
HEDGE COSTS	($16,121)
NET	$5,975

NO OF ASSETS:	10,000	10,000	10,000	10,000	10,000
DATE	01-Jan-96	08-Jan-96	15-Jan-96	22-Jan-96	29-Jan-96
TIME TO EXPIRY (DAYS)	28.00	21.00	14.00	7.00	0.00
ASSET PRICE	$100.00	$101.00	$99.00	$100.50	$98.50
VOLATILITY (CURRENT)	20.00%	20.00%	20.00%	20.00%	20.00%
INTEREST RATE (CURRENT)	10.00%	10.00%	10.00%	10.00%	10.00%
OPTION PREMIUM	$2.1928	$2.4503	$1.1014	$1.3729	$0.0000
DELTA	0.5071	0.5881	0.4048	0.5758	0.0000
GAMMA	0.0714	0.0797	0.0996	0.1404	0.0000
THETA (per day)	0.0385	0.0439	0.0532	0.0773	0.0000
VEGA	0.1096	0.0936	0.0749	0.0544	0.0000
RHO	-0.0017	-0.0014	-0.0004	-0.0003	0.0000

Exhibit 11.3—continued

	AMOUNT	PRICE					
DELTA HEDGE							
HEDGE REQUIREMENT			5,071	5,881	4,048	5,758	0
HEDGE TRANSACTIONS	**AMOUNT**	**PRICE**					
PURCHASE ASSETS	5,071	$100.00	$507,143	$507,143			
PURCHASE ASSETS	810	$101.00		$81,773			
PURCHASE ASSETS	(1,833)	$99.00			$405,330	$405,330	
PURCHASE ASSETS	1,710	$100.50				$171,860	
PURCHASE ASSETS	(5,758)	$98.50					
VALUE OF HEDGE PORTFOLIO							
NO OF ASSETS			5,071	5,881	4,048	5,758	0
AVERAGE VALUE OF ASSETS			$100.00	$100.14	$100.14	$100.25	
TOTAL			$507,143	$588,916	$405,330	$577,189	$0
GAIN ON HEDGE ADJUSTMENT					($2,085.73)		($10,048.92)
INTEREST COST				($972.60)	($1,129.43)	($777.34)	($1,106.94)
CUMULATIVE COST				($972.60)	($4,187.76)	($4,965.10)	($16,120.96)

Exhibit 11.3—continued

DELTA HEDGING   14-Aug-96

PUT OPTION EXAMPLE (OPTION EXPIRES IN-THE-MONEY)

INPUTS

ASSET PRICE	$100.00
STRIKE PRICE	$100.00
TRADE DATE	01-Jan-96
EXPIRY DATE	29-Jan-96
TIME TO EXPIRY (DAYS)	28.00
VOLATILITY (INITIAL)	20.00%
INTEREST RATE	10.00%
HOLDING COST	0.00%

HEDGE PROFIT AND LOSS

PREMIUM RECEIPT	$21,928
INTEREST ON PREMIUM	$168
HEDGE COSTS	($21,614)
NET	$482

NO OF ASSETS:	10,000	10,000	10,000	10,000	10,000
DATE	01-Jan-96	08-Jan-96	15-Jan-96	22-Jan-96	29-Jan-96
TIME TO EXPIRY (DAYS)	28.00	21.00	14.00	7.00	0.00
ASSET PRICE	$100.00	$98.00	$97.00	$100.50	$97.00
VOLATILITY (CURRENT)	20.00%	20.00%	20.00%	20.00%	20.00%
INTEREST RATE (CURRENT)	10.00%	10.00%	10.00%	10.00%	10.00%
OPTION PREMIUM	$2.1928	$3.0425	$3.4689	$0.8739	$3.0000
DELTA	-0.4852	-0.6506	-0.7728	-0.4223	-1.0000
GAMMA	0.0714	0.0780	0.0785	0.1404	0.0000
THETA (per day)	0.0385	0.0402	0.0395	0.0775	0.0000
VEGA	0.1096	0.0862	0.0566	0.0544	0.0000
RHO	-0.0017	-0.0018	-0.0013	-0.0002	0.0000

Exhibit 11.3—continued

	AMOUNT	PRICE					
DELTA HEDGE							
HEDGE REQUIREMENT			(4,852)	(6,506)	(7,728)	(4,223)	(10,000)
HEDGE TRANSACTIONS							
PURCHASE ASSETS	(4,852)	$100.00	($485,215)	($485,215)	($418,496)	($418,496)	
PURCHASE ASSETS	(1,654)	$98.00		($162,092)	($162,092)		
PURCHASE ASSETS	(1,222)	$97.00			($118,536)		
PURCHASE ASSETS	3,505	$100.50					
PURCHASE ASSETS	(5,777)	$97.00					($560,362)
VALUE OF HEDGE PORTFOLIO							
NO OF ASSETS			(4,852)	(6,506)	(7,728)	(4,223)	(10,000)
AVERAGE VALUE OF ASSETS			$100.00	$99.49	$99.10	$99.10	$97.89
TOTAL			($485,215)	($647,307)	($765,843)	($418,496)	($978,858)
GAIN ON HEDGE ADJUSTMENT				$930.55	$1,241.41	($4,915.63)	($21,141.77)
INTEREST COST						$1,468.74	$802.60
CUMULATIVE COST				$930.55	$2,171.96	($1,274.92)	($21,614.10)

Exhibit 11.3—continued

DELTA HEDGING   14-Aug-96

PUT OPTION EXAMPLE (OPTION EXPIRES OUT-OF-THE-MONEY)

INPUTS

ASSET PRICE	$100.00
STRIKE PRICE	$100.00
TRADE DATE	01-Jan-96
EXPIRY DATE	29-Jan-96
TIME TO EXPIRY (DAYS)	28.00
VOLATILITY (INITIAL)	20.00%
INTEREST RATE	10.00%
HOLDING COST	0.00%

HEDGE PROFIT AND LOSS

PREMIUM RECEIPT	$21,928
INTEREST ON PREMIUM	$168
HEDGE COSTS	($12,729)
NET	$9,366

NO OF ASSETS:	10,000	10,000	10,000	10,000	10,000
DATE	01-Jan-96	08-Jan-96	15-Jan-96	22-Jan-96	29-Jan-96
TIME TO EXPIRY (DAYS)	28.00	21.00	14.00	7.00	0.00
ASSET PRICE	$100.00	$98.00	$97.00	$100.50	$102.00
VOLATILITY (CURRENT)	20.00%	20.00%	20.00%	20.00%	20.00%
INTEREST RATE (CURRENT)	10.00%	10.00%	10.00%	10.00%	10.00%
OPTION PREMIUM	$2.1928	$3.0425	$3.4689	$0.8739	$0.0000
DELTA	-0.4852	-0.6506	-0.7728	-0.4223	0.0000
GAMMA	0.0714	0.0780	0.0785	0.1404	0.0000
THETA (per day)	0.0385	0.0402	0.0395	0.0775	0.0000
VEGA	0.1096	0.0862	0.0566	0.0544	0.0000
RHO	-0.0017	-0.0018	-0.0013	-0.0002	0.0000

Exhibit 11.3—*continued*

	AMOUNT	PRICE					
DELTA HEDGE							
HEDGE REQUIREMENT			(4,852)	(6,506)	(7,728)	(4,223)	0
HEDGE TRANSACTIONS	**AMOUNT**	**PRICE**					
PURCHASE ASSETS	(4,852)	$100.00	($485,215)	($485,215)	($485,215)	($418,496)	
PURCHASE ASSETS	(1,654)	$98.00		($162,092)	($162,092)		
PURCHASE ASSETS	(1,222)	$97.00			($118,536)		
PURCHASE ASSETS	3,505	$100.50					
PURCHASE ASSETS	4,223	$102.00					
VALUE OF HEDGE PORTFOLIO							
NO OF ASSETS			(4,852)	(6,506)	(7,728)	(4,223)	0
AVERAGE VALUE OF ASSETS			$100.00	$99.49	$99.10	$99.10	
TOTAL			($485,215)	($647,307)	($765,843)	($418,496)	$0
GAIN ON HEDGE ADJUSTMENT						($4,915.63)	($12,257.12)
INTEREST COST				$930.55	$1,241.41	$1,468.74	$802.60
CUMULATIVE COST				$930.55	$2,171.96	($1,274.92)	($12,729.45)

Four examples are included: replication of a call option which expires in-the-money; replication of a call option which expires out-of-the-money; replication of a put option which expires in-the-money; and replication of a put option which expires out-of-the-money. The examples entail the assumption that the hedges are rebalanced at the end of every seven days (an arbitrary choice). In the following discussion, the focus is on the replication of the call option which expires in-the-money. However, the issues in respect of the other cases are similar.

As is evident, the hedge profit and loss on this option show a net gain of $2,541. The gain is calculated as the premium receipt, including interest on premium, adjusted for the hedging costs, which incorporates trading gains and losses and the cost of financing the asset positions.

If the option replication position had been consistent with the theory, then the net hedge profit and loss should have been zero; that is, the cost of synthesising the option should have been exactly equal to the option premium. In reality, this will rarely be the case. The difference reflects the following factors:

- actual experienced volatility of asset price changes relative to the volatility implicit in the option premium; and
- inefficiencies in the hedge portfolio and the hedge process.

In this case, the actual experienced volatility of asset price changes was approximately 18.02% pa. This compares to the volatility used to price the option of 20.00% pa. *Exhibit 11.4* sets out the performance of the hedge portfolio where the actual experienced volatility is used to price the option. As would be expected, the net hedge profit and loss is zero. Note also the differences in the hedge requirements, reflecting the changes in the option delta arising from the lower volatility (see more detailed discussion below).

The second factor which may affect the hedge profit and loss is the inefficiencies in the hedge portfolio and the hedging process. This is caused by a number of factors, including the frequency of rebalancing and the presence of discontinuities or gaps in the asset price path, or non-constancy of volatility and/or interest rates.

As noted, the frequency of rebalancing will influence the efficiency of the hedge. As the objective of the hedge is to maintain delta neutrality, each time the asset price changes, the delta of the option will also change, requiring rebalancing of the hedge. However, the presence of transaction costs dictates that the hedge only be readjusted *periodically*. This is designed to minimise the transaction costs while maintaining delta matching to a sufficient degree. This process of periodic rather than continuous rebalancing necessarily means that the trader will have small exposures to the *asset price changes* creating gains and losses which vary from the theoretical option premium.

A further source of hedge costs results from the changes in delta itself. As notes, changes in delta require adjustments in the hedge. However, if the change in the asset price is large, in particular, a discontinuity or sharp jump, the lag in adjusting the hedge will necessarily mean a divergence between the replication costs and the theoretical value of the option. In effect, the delta hedge, as discussed in detail below, does not cover the gamma risk of the strategy.

The theoretical assumptions that both volatility and interest rates remain constant are unlikely to be realised in practice. The non-constancy of these parameters will also affect the performance of the hedge.

Changes in volatility will affect the hedging process in two separate ways:

1. The first impact will be that the movement in volatility will impact upon the value of the option but not the value of the asset position.

2. The second impact will be that the change in volatility will alter the option delta and will thereby affect the costs of the hedge.

The impact of volatility changes is illustrated by the examples in *Exhibit 11.5*. In this example, the hedge performance of the call option is considered where the volatility increases from the original level (20%) to 25% or decreases to 15%. In each case the change occurs after one week and the volatility remains at the higher or lower level for the remainder of the life of the option.

Exhibit 11.4
Delta Hedge— Based on Actual Volatility

26-Aug-96

DELTA HEDGING

CALL OPTION EXAMPLE (OPTION EXPIRES IN-THE-MONEY)

INPUTS	
ASSET PRICE	$100.00
STRIKE PRICE	$100.00
TRADE DATE	01-Jan-96
EXPIRY DATE	29-Jan-96
TIME TO EXPIRY (DAYS)	28.00
VOLATILITY (INITIAL)	18.02%
INTEREST RATE	10.00%
HOLDING COST	0.00%

HEDGE PROFIT AND LOSS	
PREMIUM RECEIPT	$19,758
INTEREST ON PREMIUM	$152
HEDGE COSTS	($19,910)
NET	$0

NO OF ASSETS:					
	10,000	10,000	10,000	10,000	10,000
DATE	01-Jan-96	08-Jan-96	15-Jan-96	22-Jan-96	29-Jan-96
TIME TO EXPIRY (DAYS)	28.00	21.00	14.00	7.00	0.00
ASSET PRICE	$100.00	$101.50	$99.00	$100.50	$102.50
VOLATILITY (CURRENT)	18.02%	18.02%	18.02%	18.02%	18.02%
INTEREST RATE (CURRENT)	10.00%	10.00%	10.00%	10.00%	10.00%
OPTION PREMIUM	$1.9758	$2.5744	$0.9536	$1.2655	$2.5000
DELTA	0.5061	0.6392	0.3932	0.5830	1.0000
GAMMA	0.0793	0.0845	0.1098	0.1552	0.0000
THETA (per day)	0.0347	0.0380	0.0476	0.0694	0.0000
VEGA	0.1096	0.0903	0.0744	0.0542	0.0000
RHO	-0.0015	-0.0015	-0.0004	-0.0002	0.0000

Exhibit 11.4—*continued*

	AMOUNT	PRICE					
DELTA HEDGE							
HEDGE REQUIREMENT			5,061	6,392	3,932	5,830	10,000
HEDGE TRANSACTIONS							
PURCHASE ASSETS	5,061	$100.00	$506,058	$506,058	$394,405	$394,405	$394,405
PURCHASE ASSETS	1,331	$101.50		$135,089			
PURCHASE ASSETS	(2,460)	$99.00					
PURCHASE ASSETS	1,898	$100.50				$190,728	$190,728
PURCHASE ASSETS	4,170	$102.50					$427,469
VALUE OF HEDGE PORTFOLIO							
NO OF ASSETS			5,061	6,392	3,932	5,830	10,000
AVERAGE VALUE OF ASSETS			$100.00	$100.31	$100.31	$100.37	$101.26
TOTAL			$506,058	$641,147	$394,405	$585,134	$1,012,603
GAIN ON HEDGE ADJUSTMENT				($970.52)	($3,228.03)		($12,603)
INTEREST COST					($1,229.60)	($756.39)	($1,122.17)
CUMULATIVE COST				($970.52)	($5,428.15)	($6,184.54)	($19,909.78)

As is evident, the value of the option changes as a result of the changes in volatility levels. The impacts of these changes are only unrealised gains or losses where the option is marked-to-market. There is no realised or cash impact of the change in volatility *unless the option is sold or repurchased.* Where the option position is hedged with a dynamically managed position in the asset, changes in volatility have no direct *cash* impact on the cost of replicating the option other than through the impact on the option deltas.

The change in volatility impacts on the option deltas. An increase (decrease) in volatility decreases (increases) the option delta. This is apparent in *Exhibit 11.5.* The altered position in the asset affects the hedging costs.

Exhibit 11.5

Delta Hedge—Performance Where Volatility is not Constant

26-Aug-96

CALL OPTION EXAMPLE (OPTION EXPIRES IN-THE-MONEY)

INPUTS	
ASSET PRICE	$100.00
STRIKE PRICE	$100.00
TRADE DATE	01-Jan-96
EXPIRY DATE	29-Jan-96
TIME TO EXPIRY (DAYS)	28.00
VOLATILITY (INITIAL)	20.00%
INTEREST RATE	10.00%
HOLDING COST	0.00%

DELTA HEDGING

HEDGE PROFIT AND LOSS	
PREMIUM RECEIPT	$21,928
INTEREST ON PREMIUM	$168
HEDGE COSTS	($18,927)
NET	$3,169

NO OF ASSETS:	10,000	10,000	10,000	10,000	10,000
DATE	01-Jan-96	08-Jan-96	15-Jan-96	22-Jan-96	29-Jan-96
TIME TO EXPIRY (DAYS)	28.00	21.00	14.00	7.00	0.00
ASSET PRICE	$100.00	$101.50	$99.00	$100.50	$102.50
VOLATILITY (CURRENT)	20.00%	25.00%	25.00%	25.00%	25.00%
INTEREST RATE (CURRENT)	10.00%	10.00%	10.00%	10.00%	10.00%
OPTION PREMIUM	$2.1928	$3.2152	$1.4784	$1.6457	$2.5000
DELTA	0.5071	0.6061	0.4266	0.5630	1.0000
GAMMA	0.0714	0.0627	0.0807	0.1130	0.0000
THETA (per day)	0.0385	0.0544	0.0673	0.0972	0.0000
VEGA	0.1096	0.0929	0.0758	0.0547	0.0000
RHO	−0.0017	−0.0018	−0.0006	−0.0003	0.0000

Exhibit 11.5—continued

DELTA HEDGE	AMOUNT	PRICE					
HEDGE REQUIREMENT			5,071	6,061	4,266	5,630	10,000
HEDGE TRANSACTIONS							
PURCHASE ASSETS	5,071	$100.00	$507,143	$507,143	$427,672	$427,672	$427,672
PURCHASE ASSETS	990	$101.50		$100,441			
PURCHASE ASSETS	(1,795)	$99.00					
PURCHASE ASSETS	1,364	$100.50				$137,073	$137,073
PURCHASE ASSETS	4,370	$102.50					$447,906
VALUE OF HEDGE PORTFOLIO							
NO OF ASSETS			5,071	6,061	4,266	5,630	10,000
AVERAGE VALUE OF ASSETS			$100.00	$100.24	$100.24	$100.31	$101.27
TOTAL			$507,143	$607,584	$427,672	$564,745	$1,012,651
GAIN ON HEDGE ADJUSTMENT					($2,234.25)		($12,651)
INTEREST COST				($972.60)	($1,165.23)	($820.19)	($1,083.07)
CUMULATIVE COST				($972.60)	($4,372.09)	($5,192.28)	($18,926.66)

Exhibit 11.5—continued

DELTA HEDGING   26-Aug-96

CALL OPTION EXAMPLE (OPTION EXPIRES IN-THE-MONEY)

INPUTS

ASSET PRICE	$100.00
STRIKE PRICE	$100.00
TRADE DATE	01-Jan-96
EXPIRY DATE	29-Jan-96
TIME TO EXPIRY (DAYS)	28.00
VOLATILITY (INITIAL)	20.00%
INTEREST RATE	10.00%
HOLDING COST	0.00%

HEDGE PROFIT AND LOSS

PREMIUM RECEIPT	$21,928
INTEREST ON PREMIUM	$168
HEDGE COSTS	($20,578)
NET	$1,518

NO OF ASSETS:	10,000	10,000	10,000	10,000	10,000
DATE	01-Jan-96	08-Jan-96	15-Jan-96	22-Jan-96	29-Jan-96
TIME TO EXPIRY (DAYS)	28.00	21.00	14.00	7.00	0.00
ASSET PRICE	$100.00	$101.50	$99.00	$100.50	$102.50
VOLATILITY (CURRENT)	20.00%	15.00%	15.00%	15.00%	15.00%
INTEREST RATE (CURRENT)	10.00%	10.00%	10.00%	10.00%	10.00%
OPTION PREMIUM	$2.1928	$2.3048	$0.7308	$1.1025	$2.5000
DELTA	0.5071	0.6632	0.3702	0.5977	1.0000
GAMMA	0.0714	0.0989	0.1295	0.1848	0.0000
THETA (per day)	0.0385	0.0308	0.0389	0.0572	0.0000
VEGA	0.1096	0.0880	0.0730	0.0537	0.0000
RHO	-0.0017	-0.0013	-0.0003	-0.0002	0.0000

Exhibit 11.5—continued

	AMOUNT	PRICE	5,071	6,632	3,702	5,977	10,000
DELTA HEDGE							
HEDGE REQUIREMENT			5,071	6,632	3,702	5,977	10,000
HEDGE TRANSACTIONS							
PURCHASE ASSETS	5,071	$100.00	$507,143	$507,143	$371,557	$371,557	$371,557
PURCHASE ASSETS	1,561	$101.50		$158,428			
PURCHASE ASSETS	(2,930)	$99.00					
PURCHASE ASSETS	2,275	$100.50				$228,635	$228,635
PURCHASE ASSETS	4,023	$102.50					$412,309
VALUE OF HEDGE PORTFOLIO							
NO OF ASSETS			5,071	6,632	3,702	5,977	10,000
AVERAGE VALUE OF ASSETS			$100.00	$100.35	$100.35	$100.41	$101.25
TOTAL			$507,143	$665,571	$371,557	$600,192	$1,012,501
GAIN ON HEDGE ADJUSTMENT					($3,964.05)		($12,501)
INTEREST COST				($972.60)	($1,276.44)	($712.57)	($1,151.05)
CUMULATIVE COST				($972.60)	($6,213.09)	($6,925.67)	($20,577.57)

The change in interest rates impacts on the cost of replication in two ways:

1. The first is its impact on the option delta, although this is relatively insignificant.

2. The second and more significant impact is by way of higher funding costs in financing the asset holding, or higher investment returns on the proceeds of the short sale.

Exhibit 11.6 sets out an example of the impact of interest rate changes on the process of replication for both increases or decreases.

Exhibit 11.6

Delta Hedge—Performance Where Interest Rates are not Constant

26-Aug-96

CALL OPTION EXAMPLE (OPTION EXPIRES IN-THE-MONEY)

INPUTS	
ASSET PRICE	$100.00
STRIKE PRICE	$100.00
TRADE DATE	01-Jan-96
EXPIRY DATE	29-Jan-96
TIME TO EXPIRY (DAYS)	28.00
VOLATILITY (INITIAL)	20.00%
INTEREST RATE	10.00%
HOLDING COST	0.00%

DELTA HEDGING

HEDGE PROFIT AND LOSS	
PREMIUM RECEIPT	$21,928
INTEREST ON PREMIUM	$168
HEDGE COSTS	($20,356)
NET	$1,740

NO OF ASSETS:	10,000	10,000	10,000	10,000	10,000
DATE	01-Jan-96	08-Jan-96	15-Jan-96	22-Jan-96	29-Jan-96
TIME TO EXPIRY (DAYS)	28.00	21.00	14.00	7.00	0.00
ASSET PRICE	$100.00	$101.50	$99.00	$100.50	$102.50
VOLATILITY (CURRENT)	20.00%	20.00%	20.00%	20.00%	20.00%
INTEREST RATE (CURRENT)	10.00%	12.00%	12.00%	12.00%	12.00%
OPTION PREMIUM	$2.1928	$2.7510	$1.1005	$1.3724	$2.5000
DELTA	0.5071	0.6266	0.4045	0.5756	1.0000
GAMMA	0.0714	0.0769	0.0996	0.1403	0.0000
THETA (per day)	0.0385	0.0425	0.0531	0.0772	0.0000
VEGA	0.1096	0.0912	0.0749	0.0544	0.0000
RHO	−0.0017	−0.0016	−0.0004	−0.0003	0.0000

Exhibit 11.6—continued

	AMOUNT	PRICE					
DELTA HEDGE							
HEDGE REQUIREMENT			5,071	6,266	4,045	5,756	10,000
HEDGE TRANSACTIONS	**AMOUNT**	**PRICE**					
PURCHASE ASSETS	5,071	$100.00	$507,143	$507,143	$405,619	$405,619	$405,619
PURCHASE ASSETS	1,195	$101.50		$121,247			
PURCHASE ASSETS	(2,221)	$99.00					
PURCHASE ASSETS	1,711	$100.50				$171,950	$171,950
PURCHASE ASSETS	4,244	$102.50					$435,055
VALUE OF HEDGE PORTFOLIO							
NO OF ASSETS			5,071	6,266	4,045	5,756	10,000
AVERAGE VALUE OF ASSETS			$100.00	$100.29	$100.29	$100.35	$101.26
TOTAL			$507,143	$628,390	$405,619	$577,568	$1,012,623
GAIN ON HEDGE ADJUSTMENT					($2,856.59)		($12,623)
INTEREST COST				($1,167.12)	($1,466.16)	($933.48)	($1,329.20)
CUMULATIVE COST				($1,167.12)	($5,469.88)	($6,403.35)	($20,355.73)

Exhibit 11.6—continued

DELTA HEDGING

26-Aug-96

CALL OPTION EXAMPLE (OPTION EXPIRES IN-THE-MONEY)

INPUTS	
ASSET PRICE	$100.00
STRIKE PRICE	$100.00
TRADE DATE	01-Jan-96
EXPIRY DATE	29-Jan-96
TIME TO EXPIRY (DAYS)	28.00
VOLATILITY (INITIAL)	20.00%
INTEREST RATE	10.00%
HOLDING COST	0.00%

HEDGE PROFIT AND LOSS	
PREMIUM RECEIPT	$21,928
INTEREST ON PREMIUM	$168
HEDGE COSTS	($18,752)
NET	$3,344

NO OF ASSETS:	10,000	10,000	10,000	10,000	10,000
DATE	01-Jan-96	08-Jan-96	15-Jan-96	22-Jan-96	29-Jan-96
TIME TO EXPIRY (DAYS)	28.00	21.00	14.00	7.00	0.00
ASSET PRICE	$100.00	$101.50	$99.00	$100.50	$102.50
VOLATILITY (CURRENT)	20.00%	20.00%	20.00%	20.00%	20.00%
INTEREST RATE (CURRENT)	10.00%	8.00%	8.00%	8.00%	8.00%
OPTION PREMIUM	$2.1928	$2.7574	$1.1022	$1.3735	$2.5000
DELTA	0.5071	0.6280	0.4051	0.5760	1.0000
GAMMA	0.0714	0.0771	0.0997	0.1404	0.0000
THETA (per day)	0.0385	0.0429	0.0533	0.0774	0.0000
VEGA	0.1096	0.0914	0.0750	0.0544	0.0000
RHO	-0.0017	-0.0016	-0.0004	-0.0003	0.0000

Exhibit 11.6—continued

DELTA HEDGE

	AMOUNT	PRICE					
HEDGE REQUIREMENT			5,071	6,280	4,051	5,760	10,000
HEDGE TRANSACTIONS							
PURCHASE ASSETS	5,071	$100.00	$507,143	$507,143	$406,253	$406,253	$406,253
PURCHASE ASSETS	1,209	$101.50		$122,713			
PURCHASE ASSETS	(2,230)	$99.00					
PURCHASE ASSETS	1,709	$100.50				$171,770	$171,770
PURCHASE ASSETS	4,240	$102.50					$434,602
VALUE OF HEDGE PORTFOLIO							
NO OF ASSETS			5,071	6,280	4,051	5,760	10,000
AVERAGE VALUE OF ASSETS			$100.00	$100.29	$100.29	$100.35	$101.26
TOTAL			$507,143	$629,856	$406,253	$578,022	$1,012,624
GAIN ON HEDGE ADJUSTMENT					($2,873.39)		($12,624)
INTEREST COST				($778.08)	($966.35)	($623.29)	($886.83)
CUMULATIVE COST				($778.08)	($4,617.83)	($5,241.12)	($18,752.27)

3. OPTION REPLICATION—RISK MANAGEMENT

3.1 Risk dimensions

The use of option replication techniques entails significant risks which require management. In practice, these risk are expressed, measured and managed using the sensitivities of options as depicted by the "Greeks" (see Chapter 10). The major risk dimensions include:

- delta/gamma, or exposure to asset price or changes in delta;
- vega/kappa, or volatility risk;
- theta, or time decay risk; and
- rho, or interest rate risk.

These Greek letters provide a measure of the behaviour of option value as market conditions change, and allow evaluation and management of the risk for an individual option or, more realistically, within an option portfolio.

In this section, the risk management process of option replication is considered through consideration of the management of each of the identified risk dimensions.

3.2 Delta-gamma risk

As previously outlined, the delta for derivative securities can be defined as the change of its price with respect to the price of the underlying asset. Delta, as a construct, emerges quite clearly from the Black-Scholes option pricing approach, which implies the possibility of establishing an instantaneous riskless portfolio consisting of a position in the derivative security and a position in the underlying asset.

The option's delta, as is evident from the discussion above, is essential to managing its risk within a hedge portfolio, in which the option is hedged by purchasing or selling delta units of the underlying asset. The risk management function (at least, as noted below, for small price changes) is determined by delta neutrality, whereby the overall portfolio of options and hedges has a delta of zero, thereby immunising the portfolio for changes in value from both price increases and decreases.

The concept of delta also enables one option to be hedged *with another option* on the same underlying asset by creating delta neutral positions. As both options are affected by movements in the price of the underlying asset, to ensure this is necessary to hold the options in the right proportions, in the resulting changes in value to offset.

The delta of the underlying asset is, by definition, 1.0. In practice, delta hedging utilises a futures or forward contract on the underlying asset rather than the asset itself. The principles of delta hedging are equally applicable where a futures or forward position in the underlying asset is utilised. The futures or forward contract utilised as the hedge does not, necessarily, have to have the same maturity as the derivative security. However, the use of futures or forward contracts introduces the fair pricing issues identified above.

Deltas have the property of additivity. The delta of a portfolio of options and other derivative securities on an asset is the sum of the deltas of the individual options and other assets in the portfolio. This facilitates the use of delta to summarise the price sensitivity of even a very complex portfolio of assets and derivative products.

However, delta only holds for very small changes in the asset price. Therefore, any movement in the asset price outside a small range leads to diminished hedge efficiency. This change in the asset price exposes the portfolio to what is commonly referred to as gap/jump risk or gamma risk.

Gamma is the change in delta as the underlying asset price changes. As changes in delta produce exposure in a portfolio, the level of gamma can be utilised to quantify the risk of an option portfolio. The gamma of an option is not stationary, but changes as the asset price changes. Gamma is highest when the option is at-the-money with a short time to expiry.

The basic problem of delta hedging, therefore, is that while the delta of an option varies substantially through its life, the delta of the underlying asset is always fixed. Consequently, in theory, continual rehedging is required to keep the portfolio perfectly delta neutral. This problem is sometimes sought to be averted by a technique known as gamma hedging, whereby the intermediary seeks to match the rate at which the deltas themselves vary with changes in asset prices.

The concept of gamma neutral hedging recognises that adjusting the portfolio to delta neutrality after each asset price change does not give adequate protection to a portfolio. A gamma hedge is a hedge strategy that attempts to reduce the exposure of the portfolio by reducing total portfolio gamma.

A portfolio which is fully hedged will have both a zero delta and a zero gamma. The only means of creating a zero gamma position is to match each option with the offsetting position in that option series. Consequently, gamma is sought to be minimised by changing the composition of the option component of the portfolio. Changing the underlying asset side of the portfolio has no impact on gamma. For example, the gamma impact of selling at-the-money puts can be minimised by buying out-of-the-money puts.

Against this background, the notion of delta and gamma neutrality can be stated more precisely. A delta neutral option or book of options hedged with offsetting positions in the underlying asset is one whose value is unaffected by (small) changes in the price of that underlying asset. A gamma neutral option portfolio is one that remains delta neutral as the price of the underlying asset changes.

In practice, gamma indicates the extent of portfolio rebalancing that will be needed in a delta neutral position. A large gamma position indicates that a portfolio will require substantial rehedging when the asset price alters. In essence, gamma is a measure of the risk exposure of a hedge position that will emerge when the price of the underlying asset changes, particularly where it changes rapidly or in a discontinuous manner or is not or is unable to be adjusted instantaneously. This is particularly the case where the price movement in the underlying asset is non-stochastic, commonly referred to as a price jump. The use of gamma to measure and manage the hedge risk is designed to, in fact, adjust the hedging process for the fact that the position in the underlying asset cannot be adjusted continuously as required by theoretical delta hedging.

As noted above, the gamma risk of a portfolio can only be reduced by purchasing options. An alternative measure of managing the gamma exposure on a portfolio is to restructure the portfolio configuration of options to replicate synthetic positions in the underlying asset itself. That is, create purchased/sold positions in the relevant series of call and put options to create purchased or sold position equivalents in the underlying asset, which by definition have limited gamma exposure.

3.3 Volatility risk

As previously noted, option values are particularly sensitive to changes in the volatility of the underlying asset. This is referred to as vega or volatility risk.

Volatility risk is a particularly important factor in option portfolio management. This reflects the fact that portfolio management, is, in part, an exercise in management of volatility positions. Portfolio managers converse in terms of being short or long volatility. The underlying premise is that the portfolio manager's task is to attempt to position the portfolio volatility exposure to seek to profit from changes in volatility level within pre-specified limits.

An important aspect of managing volatility risk is that it can only be neutralised by taking positions in the same or a different series of options. Volatility is not a determinant of value of the underlying asset and consequently cannot be neutralised through positions in the asset market itself.

3.4 Theta risk

The option theta measures the rate of change in the value of the portfolio with respect to time, where all other value parameters are held constant. In effect, theta measures the rate of time decay for the options or the degree to which it loses its inherent value as a "wasting asset". Theta measures the cost of holding an option and, conversely, the reward of selling an option.

As discussed below, management of theta is particularly important and its interaction with gamma and vega risks constitute a major component of option portfolio management.

3.5 Interest rate risk

Rho measures option portfolio risk with respect to changes in the riskfree interest rate. As previously outlined, the time value for a call option comes partly from the interest that can be earned investing the strike price from the present until the expiration date. Conversely, the purchaser of put loses interest while waiting until option maturity to receive the strike price. Consequently, changes in interest rates will have an impact on the value of the option.

In practice, the rho or riskless interest rate risk of the portfolio can be managed by assuming positions in the underlying interest rate market by traditional interest rate risk management measures.

3.6 Risk interactions

As might be expected, individual risk dimensions identified are substantively interrelated. This necessitates a constant process of trade-offs between the various risk dimensions and the management of an option portfolio. In this section, some key aspects of the trade-offs entailed in option portfolio management are examined.

For the trader, offsetting the price risk of the portfolio of options by delta-based purchases and sales of the underlying asset reduces the risk of the delta-neutral portfolio, whereby the value of the portfolio is insulated from the effects of small price changes in the underlying assets.

However, such a position still exposes the portfolio manager to significant risks. Delta-neutral positions entailing a net purchase of options will have a negative theta; that is, the option position will decline in value over time reflecting the nature of the option as a wasting asset. The value of the option evolves towards its intrinsic value as expiration approaches. In contrast, a delta-neutral position which entails sold options will gain in value as expiration approaches.

Interaction of delta and theta, in this context, dictates that market makers prefer delta-neutral positions that are net sold options so as to enable them earn the erosion in the value of the option; that is, benefit from the option portfolio theta. Structuring a portfolio to benefit from theta entails the portfolio manager assuming gamma and vega risk.

A portfolio which is delta-neutral and short options will require the portfolio manager to rebalance the hedge, in the case of a call by buying when the price of the underlying asset increases and selling the underlying asset where the price falls. Similarly, the portfolio is exposed to increases in value from falls in volatility, but loses value from increases in volatility.

To an extent, some of these risks are offsetting. For example, theta and gamma tend, at least to some degree, to offset the other. A net purchased option portfolio which is delta-neutral simultaneously loses value because of time decay or theta with the passage of time, but improves in value as a result of the movement in price because of the position's gamma risk. Conversely, a delta-neutral position entailing a net sold position in options increases in value because of theta each day, but, generally speaking, decreases in value when the market moves up and down because of the portfolio's gamma risk.

However, the risks are not necessarily entirely offsetting. Theta erosion in option values occurs relatively smoothly over the period to expiration. In contrast, the gains and losses from gamma rebalancing can be large and discontinuous, reflecting the fact that larger gains and losses from gamma occur when there is a sharp change in the price of the underlying asset which prevents the portfolio manager from adjusting or rebalancing the delta hedge appropriately.

The interaction of these risks typically forces portfolio managers to seek to generate earnings/value from an options portfolio by one or other of the following strategies:

1. Maintain delta neutral/net short options portfolio positions where it is anticipated that the underlying price movements will not be discontinuous (that is, the portfolio has low gamma risk) and volatility of the underlying assets are not expected to change substantially (that is, low vega/kappa risk).

2. Operate the portfolio on the basis that portfolio value/earnings derived from the bid-offer spread on purchasing and selling options. By implication, the portfolio manager would, under this strategy, seek to balance the portfolio by purchasing some options and selling others, in contrast to being a net purchaser or seller of options.

3. Managing the option portfolio as a volatility risk management function where portfolio managers seek to benefit from changes in volatility levels in the underlying asset.

The first strategy is fairly self-explanatory, and is consistent with the factors described above.

The second approach is also relatively straightforward and is predicated on the notion that portfolio managers view delta hedging in the underlying asset or option replication techniques as a *temporary* substitute for an offsetting option transaction. In effect, the portfolio manager plans to earn the bid-offer spread without seeking to worry about the erosion in value of the option portfolio or the management of the complex gamma and vega risks entailed.

The last approach, essentially taking views on volatility, seeks to generate profits according to the portfolio manager's capacity to anticipate price volatility changes for the underlying asset market, without taking a large market risk. The major problem for any option portfolio manager is that the volatility of the underlying asset, at least as it is utilised to calculate option values, has a significant level of uncertainty associated with its estimation. Consequently, the expected or true volatility of the asset can change over the life of the option, resulting in changes in portfolio valuation.

In practice, this dictates that portfolio managers may seek to balance the portfolio to earn the bid-offer spread, in volatility terms, whilst managing their portfolio to be delta, gamma, theta and kappa neutral. This is particularly the case where volatility levels in the underlying asset are subject to uncertainty or are experiencing rapid and sudden shifts. In contrast, in a market where volatility is "trending" in one or other direction or the asset price is relatively stable, the portfolio manager may choose to take portfolio positions designed to facilitate increases in portfolio value in the event of the anticipated change in portfolio volatility occurring or from the benefit of accruing time value from selling options. Such positions regarding changes in volatility can be both for outright movements in volatility for a particular class of assets or positions for changes in the implied pattern of volatilities or its term structure.

3.7 Delta hedging in practice

The risk of using delta hedging techniques to replicate options can be assessed from the practice of portfolio insurance. This is a practice whereby asset managers create capital guaranteed (at a pre-agreed level) investments. This is done in two ways:

1. holding the asset and dynamically creating a put option on the asset to establish a minimum investment value; and

2. investing in cash and trading in asset to synthesise a call option on the asset to create exposure to increases in the asset price. The minimum portfolio value is represented by the total portfolio value adjusted for the cost of replicating the portfolio (effectively, the option premium).

This practice, which is quite widespread, performed poorly in the equity market crash in 1987.[5]

Similarly, option hedges, in currency, interest rate and commodity markets, performed below expectation in the ERM crises in 1992, the bond market collapse in 1994 and the Gulf War and the sharp fall in copper prices in 1996 following the disclosure of the Sumitomo copper trading losses.[6]

In each case, the failure of the dynamic hedge to efficiently replicate the option position sought to be hedged can be attributed to a combination of the following factors:

• the sharp, discontinuous jump in asset prices which made it difficult to maintain delta neutrality, creating exposure to the *asset price movements*;

• the sharp and unanticipated changes in volatility which also affected hedge performance; and

• the change in liquidity conditions in the underlying asset markets and the increase in transaction costs, which led to rises in the cost of the hedge over that which had been anticipated.

The use of futures contracts to replicate the option due to significant savings in transaction costs may have exacerbated the problems, as in these stressful conditions the pricing of the futures contracts may have deviated from fair value, creating further hedge slippage.

4. OPTION REPLICATION—DEVELOPMENTS

The risks of replicating options dynamically have led researchers to experiment with different strategies to improve the efficiency of the hedge. Three areas of development merit particular comment:

1. the hedging of short versus long dated options;

2. transaction cost incorporated strategies; and

5. See Jon Taylor and Matthew Smith, "Option Replication" (1987) (Dec) *Intermarket* 16-55; Desmond Fitzgerald and Janette Rutherford, "Variations On A Theme" (1988) 1(7) *Risk* 30-31.

6. For a perspective on practical issues in option hedging see Krystna Kryzak, "Gamma Raison" (1990) 3(5) *Risk* 21-27; Richard Cookson, "Models Of Imperfection" (1992) 5(9) *Risk* 55-61; Richard Cookson and Lilian Chew, "Things Fall Apart" (1992) (Oct) *Risk* 44-53.

3. static option replication techniques.

The distinction between hedging short versus long dated options is driven by the different risk characteristics. For short dated options, the typical option sensitivities (delta, gamma, vega, theta, and rho) may not provide accurate risk measures. This reflects the more significant impact of sharp movements in asset price and volatility in theses options.

This has led to the development of approaches to option portfolio management which segment the portfolio by remaining time to maturity. A typical segmentation would be short (under 30 days), medium (up to 6-12 months) and long (beyond 12 months).

Within this segmented framework, the principal, albeit not the sole, focus is as follows:

• for short options, gamma risk management is important;

• for medium to longer dated options, vega risk management is important.

This segmentation also has implications for the process of replication and the underlying instrument used. The risk of volatility changes for longer dated options favours the use of *options*, rather than the asset, to replicate these positions. This is discussed below in the context of static option replication.

As noted above, the presence of transaction costs impacts on the cost of the hedge, leading to a tradeoff between frequency of rehedging and the transaction costs incurred. The impact of transaction costs is that the trader must, of necessity, select a hedging strategy incorporating a discrete hedging algorithm. This has, as a by-product, implications for the valuation of the option.

A number of models have emerged which provide hedging strategies for the replication of options incorporating transaction costs. These models are based on placing boundaries on the risk of replication measured by the variance of the hedge portfolio. Alternative approaches use utility functions which relate both to the risk and return.[7]

Static portfolio replication entails the use of *options* rather than trading in the underlying asset to replicate the option. The major rationale for this type of replication is that it avoids the risk of underperformance of the hedge where the asset price moves are discontinuous and large or where there are shifts in volatility levels. The major application of static portfolio replication is in relation to longer or more complex options (including exotic options).

The basic approach is to model the option payoff (using an option pricing model) at maturity, using different asset prices and volatilities. The model payoff is then sought to be replicated by a portfolio of options (with different expires and strike prices). The technique usually involves the use of some

---

7. For discussion on different strategies for optimising the cost of hedging options see Elizabeth Whalley and Paul Wilmott, "Counting The Cost" (1993) 6(10) *Risk* 59-66; Elizabeth Whalley and Paul Wilmott, "Hedge With An Edge" (1994) 7(10) *Risk* 82-85.

form of optimisation technique, such as multiple regression, to generate the portfolio of options which best replicates the option sought to be synthesised.[8]

5. SUMMARY

The potential to replicate options through trading in the underlying asset is inherent in the approach to valuation of options. By trading in the asset and either financing the investment or investing the proceeds of a short sale and adjusting the asset position as asset prices, volatilities, interest rates and time to maturity change, it is theoretically possible to replicate the economic profile of an option.

However, this process of delta hedging is only accurate for small movements in asset. In particular, sharp and discontinuous changes in asset prices, changes in volatility or changes in interest rates may expose the trader to the risk of the asset portfolio underperforming the option sought to be replicated. This dictates the use of sophisticated risk control mechanisms to monitor and manage the risk of the replicating portfolio to maintain the accuracy of the hedge and to match its performance to that of the option.

8.   See Jon Frye, "Static Portfolio Replication" (1988) 1(11) *Risk* 22-23; Kenneth S Choie and Frederick Novomestky, "Replication Of Long Term With Short Term Options" (1989) (Winter) *Journal of Portfolio Management* 17-19; Emanuel Derman, Deniz Ergener and Iraj Kani, "Forever Hedged" (1994) 7(9) *Risk* 139-145.

Part 4

Investment   Management

Chapter 12

Portfolio Optimisation

by Geoffrey Brianton

1. INTRODUCTION

This chapter will investigate portfolio optimisation. That is, the construction of portfolios that for some specific criteria are better than all other portfolios. The main area of study will be the model at the heart of Modern Portfolio Theory—the "mean-variance" model.

This model was first proposed in the 1950s by Harry Markowitz. Although his landmark paper is one of the most widely cited in finance, the mean-variance optimisation approach is not as widely used in practice as this would suggest. This chapter will focus on the reasons for this, and investigate some of the practical steps that can be taken to tame the model. It is written from the point of view of a fund manager.

The starting point will be a review of utility theory and risk aversion, as this is the basis for the "mean-variance" model.

2. UTILITY, RISK AVERSION AND PROBABILITY DISTRIBUTIONS

Imagine you are walking down the street and, to your delight, find a dollar on the pavement. Now, if instead of a single dollar you find two dollars, you would be even more delighted. If you found three dollars it would be an even better event. However, as the amount found increases, the additional joy of finding a larger amount of money becomes smaller. The satisfaction in finding $10,000 would be almost indistinguishable from that of finding $10,001. This is known as diminishing marginal utility. That is, at the margin, the utility (benefit) gained reduces with each additional dollar found.

One of the consequences of diminishing marginal utility is that investors are reticent to put at risk existing wealth in order to gain new wealth. This is because the last dollar is more valuable than the next one. Consider an investor who is faced with two options. One is a certain gain of $10, the other is a 50% chance of a $5 return and a 50% chance of gaining $15. Both options will return on average $10, so what would be the choice of an investor with diminishing margin utility? *Exhibit 12.1* shows the amount utility of a return of five, ten and fifteen dollars expressed in term of ticks.

Exhibit 12.1

Utility for Various Returns

Return amount	Utility
$5	✓
$10	✓✓✓
$15	✓✓✓✓

Under the first option ($10 with certainty) the investor has a gain of three ticks worth of utility. With the second option (50% change of $15 and 50% change of $5) the investor will receive either one or four ticks with an equal probability, an expected outcome of two and a half ticks. The investor would always choose the first option due to the extra half a tick of utility. The investor characteristics of choosing a certain return over an uncertain return when, on average, both will produce the same expected return is known as risk aversion. Risk aversion is a direct result of the next one being good, but not quite as good as the last one.

2.1 Utility functions

In solving the problem of portfolio construction, a more complete definition of an investor's utility than the number of ticks for three different returns is required. An investor's utility function defines the relationship between return and the level of utility received. *Exhibit 12.2* shows a typical utility function.

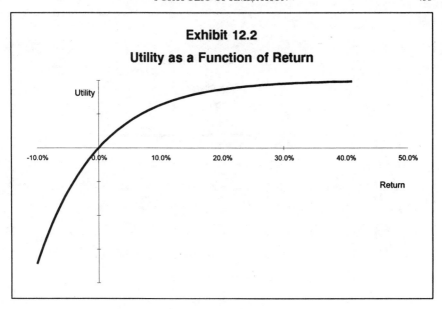

Exhibit 12.2

Utility as a Function of Return

On the horizontal axis is the return (in percentage terms), while the vertical axis indicates the investor's utility for that return. This utility function has three key characteristics that are common to all utility functions:

- it is always positive (known as non-satiation)
- it is upwardly sloping (more is better); and
- the slope decreases as the return increases (diminishing marginal utility).

In mathematical terms, the utility function has a positive first derivative and a negative second derivative. There are a wide variety of utility functions that fit the above criteria. The function used most frequently in portfolio choice problems is known as the exponential utility function. It has the form

$$U(r) = 1 - e^{-\lambda r}$$

Where

λ is a risk aversion parameter (pronounced lambda);

U is the level of utility for a given level of return; and

r is the return.

It has the advantages of having the appropriate properties of a utility function and, by varying the risk aversion parameter, it can model a full range of investor preferences from very risk averse to risk neutral.[1]

---

1. Ultimately there is no clear defining reason why the exponential utility function should be used in preference to other utility functions. As the exponential function is flexible and mathematically simple to manipulate, it is widely used but this does not mean that other functions are inappropriate.

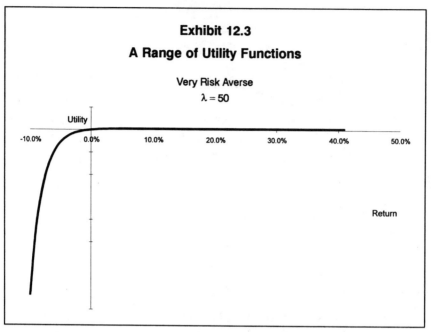

Exhibit 12.3
A Range of Utility Functions

Very Risk Averse
$\lambda = 50$

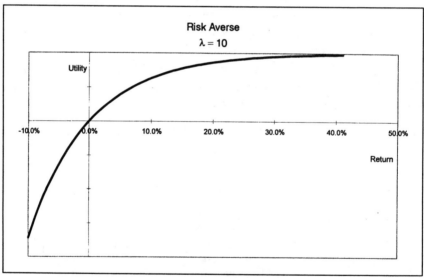

Risk Averse
$\lambda = 10$

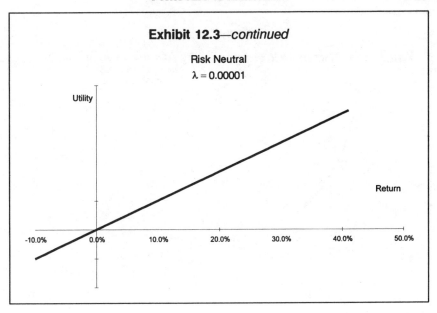

Exhibit 12.3—*continued*

Risk Neutral

$\lambda = 0.00001$

The risk neutral investor treats each additional return as being equally desirable. As a result, this investor's choice is always the asset with highest expected return regardless of the potential losses. The "very risk averse" investor places a very low additional utility from higher returns and would strongly tend toward assets with stable returns and low probabilities of losses. The "risk averse" investor lies between these two.

2.2 What is your λ?—a two asset example

The appropriate risk aversion (λ) for a given investor is not an easy question. It is generally not possible to simply ask most investors "So what is your λ?" Typically an investor's risk aversion needs to be determined indirectly by examining their behaviour and choices. Consider the following example: each year an investor has the choice of two assets. Investment A has a certain return of 3%. Investment B will return either 40%, 10% or −20% with a probability of $\frac{1}{4}$, $\frac{1}{2}$ and $\frac{1}{4}$ respectively. On average, investment B will return 10%, significantly higher than A, but there is a one in four chance of a substantial negative return.

The amount an investor is prepared to put into the risky asset (B) indicates how venturesome is their investment approach. *Exhibit 12.4* shows the relationship between the weight in investment B and the λ that would make that choice optimal (if we assume the investor has an exponential utility function).[2] The larger the investment in the risky asset the less risk averse the investor. (The reader is encouraged to do this exercise from their own point of view.)

---

2.   Appendix II gives the mathematical derivation of this relationship.

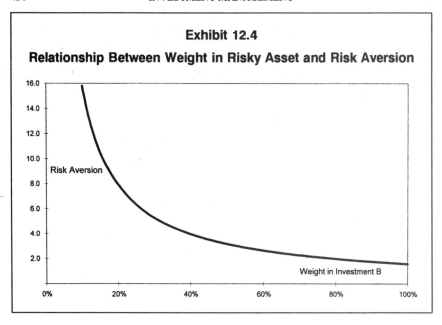

Exhibit 12.4

Relationship Between Weight in Risky Asset and Risk Aversion

For example, consider an investor saving for her retirement. She is in her early fifties and plans to work for another five years or so. She has a moderate level of wealth which (not surprisingly) she would like to grow. She is cautious about putting at risk the retirement lifestyle she has already secured. Assume that she has decided to put 30% of her portfolio in the risky assets. This would equate to a λ of about 5.

The task of modeling an investor's level of risk aversion is complex. However, for the purposes of this chapter we will continue assuming this simple two asset question and the example investor's response and see how far the problem of portfolio optimisation can be progressed.

2.3 Probability distributions

At this stage, half of the problem has been solved, that being a robust model of the investor's utility. A model for behaviour of the assets is also needed.

In the previous two-asset example, the return of asset B in the next period was not known but the likelihood of various returns was known. In statistical terms this is called the *probability distribution* of the returns from B. The most common approach used for asset returns is to model the log of the returns. Log returns $R = \ln(1 + r)$ (where r is the return and ln is the natural logarithm function) are modelled because they are mathematically simpler to deal with than the returns themselves.

Log returns (R) have been shown to approximate a normal distribution. In these cases, the returns (r) have what is known as a *log-normal* distribution. The log-normal distributions can be defined by three sets of parameters:

- the expected (log) return of each asset;
- the *standard deviation* of the (log) return of each asset; and

• the *correlations* between the (log) return of each pair of assets.

For the remainder of this chapter the reader should assume that when returns are being discussed it refers to log-returns.

In the example investor's case she is saving for her retirement; she is interested in maximising the purchasing power of her investment. Hence long-term, real after-tax returns are probably the relevant measure. As an example, (and without loss of generality) this chapter will assume that there are seven assets in which she may invest her wealth. The seven assets and their expected returns are shown in *Exhibit 12.5*. In this case they are forecast returns,[3] but they could be estimated from historical data.

Exhibit 12.5
Expected Asset Returns

Asset	Expected annual, real after tax returns
Equities (EQ)	5.00%
International Equities (IE)	4.00%
Listed Property (PR)	2.75%
Index Bonds (XB)	2.00%
Nominal Bonds (NB)	2.00%
International Bonds—hedged (IB)	1.50%
Cash (CH)	0.50%

The standard-deviation of an asset indicates how widely spread are the returns.

Exhibit 12.6 compares the distribution for nominal bonds and equities. The horizontal axis shows above/below average returns. Equities, being the more volatile asset class, have a much wider distribution of outcomes. Often the term "variance" is used in place of standard-deviation. Variance is simply the square of the standard-deviation.

3. This chapter was written from an Australian tax perspective. The effect of local tax laws such as tax credit received with income earned on domestic equity has been taken into account. The same assumptions would result in a different set of expected returns for non-Australian investors.

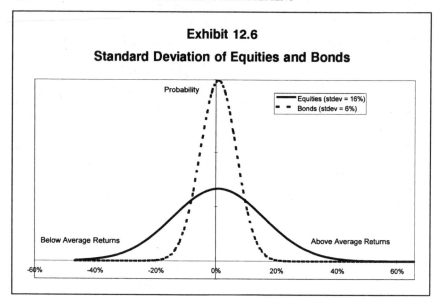

Exhibit 12.6

Standard Deviation of Equities and Bonds

Exhibit 12.7 shows the annualised standard deviations for each asset class. These have been estimated from monthly total real returns over the period 1988 to 1995.

Exhibit 12.7

Standard Deviations of Assets

Asset	Annualised Standard Deviation
Equities (EQ)	15%
International Equities (IE)	16%
Property (PR)	9%
Index Bonds (XB)	6%
Nominal Bonds (NB)	5%
International Bonds—hedged (IB)	4%
Cash (CH)	1%

Correlations between two assets range between minus one and plus one. A negative/positive correlation indicates that when one asset has an above/below average return the other will tend to produce a below/above average return respectively.

Exhibit 12.8 gives a graphical representation of correlations. The dots show the actual monthly joint return for Australian equities and property over the period 1988 to 1995. The correlation calculated over this period is 0.55, a strong positive correlation. The ellipses show how the joint returns should be distributed assuming a log-normal distribution. For example, 10% of all observations should fall in the smallest ellipse. The effect of the high correlation between equities and property is to elongate the ellipses such that when equity returns are above/below average, property returns are more likely to be above/below average as well.

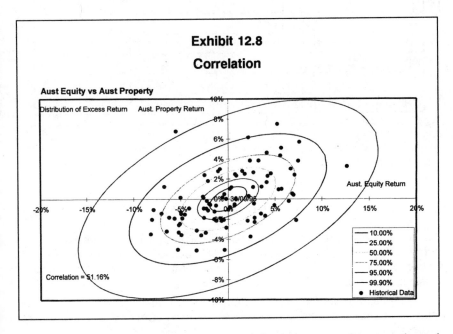

Exhibit 12.8

Correlation

Exhibit 12.9 shows the correlation between the seven asset classes, estimated over the same period as the standard-deviations. Only half the matrix needs to be shown since the correlation of, for instance CH with IE, is the same as that of IE with CH (−2%).

Exhibit 12.9

Asset Correlations

	EQ	IE	PR	XB	NB	IB	CH
EQ	1.00						
IE	0.29	1.00					
PR	0.51	0.28	1.00				
XB	0.18	0.13	0.28	1.00			
NB	0.37	0.20	0.41	0.40	1.00		
IB	0.19	0.48	0.26	0.31	0.55	1.00	
CH	−0.01	−0.02	0.00	−0.14	0.19	−0.21	1.00

In statistics jargon the combination of the variances and correlations is called the co-variance matrix.

3. MEAN-VARIANCE OPTIMISATION

Armed with both a tractable model of investor preferences (the exponential utility function), and the probability distribution of returns (the log-normal distribution), the problem of selecting an optimal portfolio (one which is better than all other portfolios) can be solved.

The problem of portfolio optimisation is to maximise the expected value of utility given the expected distribution of returns. Mathematically this can be expressed as:

$$E[U(r)] = \int (1 - e^{-\lambda r})(2\pi\sigma)e^{\left(-\frac{1}{\sigma^2}\right)(r-\mu)(r-\mu)} dr$$

Surprisingly, this rather fearsome piece of mathematics can be simplified down to:[4]

$$\text{Maximise } \mu_p - \left(\frac{\lambda}{2}\right)\sigma_p^2$$

Where

μ_p is the expected return (mean) of the portfolio; and

σ^2_p is the expected variance of the portfolio.

This equation is known as the mean-variance criteria for an optimal portfolio. The criteria lends itself to a relatively simple interpretation. The optimal portfolio is the one that maximises the expected return of the portfolio, subject to a penalty for any increase in the expected variance. The higher the investor's risk aversion (λ) the greater the penalty for any variance in the portfolio return. Essentially, the variance of the portfolio becomes the

---

4.   Refer to Appendix I for more details.

proxy for risk. For this reason, the co-variance matrix is often referred to as the risk matrix. For the remainder of this chapter the word "risk" will be used as a short-hand way of saying the standard-deviation of returns.

One of the major criticisms of the mean-variance model is that variance may not be a complete measure of risk. To an extent, this criticism is misguided as the use of variance as a measure of risk has been derived *indirectly* by assuming that returns have a log-normal distribution. Hence, the questioning of variance as a valid risk measure is really asking a deeper question of whether the log-normal distribution is a robust model of portfolio returns.

3.1 Indifference curves

The mean-variance criteria ($\mu_p - \lambda/2\sigma^2_p$) provides a way of comparing two portfolios. Suppose a portfolio is picked at random and its expected return and variance is calculated. Assume we have another portfolio with a higher return (say 1% higher) but with a higher variance (say $\lambda/2\%$ higher). The investor would be indifferent between the two portfolios. This is because the increase in utility due to the increase in the expected return is exactly offset by the decrease in utility due to the higher portfolio variance. If all portfolios with the same level of utility are joined, they form what is known as an indifference curve (IC). All portfolios on the IC are equally attractive to the investor. *Exhibit 12.10* shows a single IC. Most importantly, all portfolios that lie above/below the indifference curve are unambiguously better/worse than those on the IC.

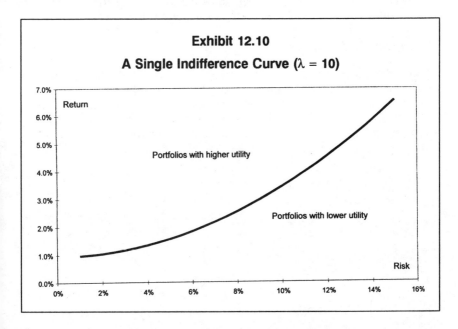

For each level of utility there will be an IC containing all portfolios that have that level of utility. *Exhibit 12.11* shows a range of utility curves.

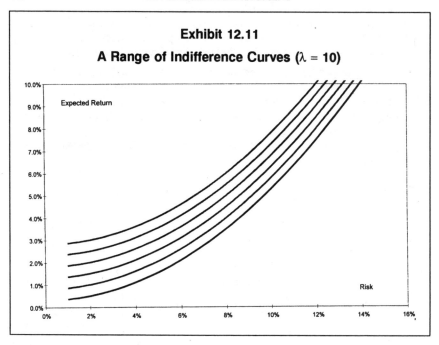

Exhibit 12.11

A Range of Indifference Curves ($\lambda = 10$)

The investor's goal would to be on the highest possible IC. However, not all combinations of returns and variances are possible. For example, a portfolio with a very high return and no risk is highly desirable but, unfortunately, impossible to achieve. In order to determine the optimal portfolio we need to combine the IC with the range of portfolios that are feasible.

3.2 The efficient frontier

Using the values for the assets' expected returns, standard-deviation and correlations, the expected return and risk of any portfolio can be calculated. For example, *Exhibit 12.12* shows the expected return and risk of a hypothetical starting portfolio. Assume that this is the portfolio the investor is starting with before she has considered the problem of whether it is optimal.

Exhibit 12.12

Expected Risk and Return of the Starting Portfolio

Asset	Weight in Starting Portfolio
Equities	2.7%
International Equities	54.3%
Property	2.5%
Index Bonds	3.7%
Nominal Bonds	33.5%
International Bonds—hedged	3.3%
Cash	0.0%
Total	100.0%
Expected return	3.2%
Risk	9.5%

The risk and return can be plotted on the same axes on which the indifference curves were plotted.

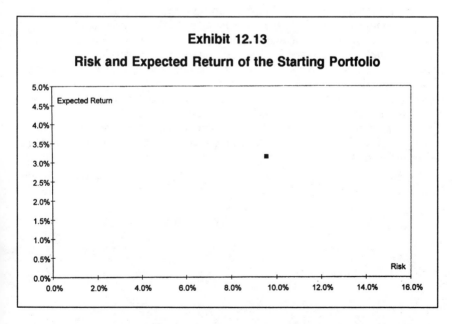

Exhibit 12.13

Risk and Expected Return of the Starting Portfolio

Being able to plot the risk and return characteristics of the starting portfolio is not very illuminating as it does not give an indication as to whether this portfolio is better or worse than other portfolios picked at random. A broader comparison is required. *Exhibit 12.14* shows the risk and return characteristics of 1000 portfolios selected at random along with the initial random portfolio.

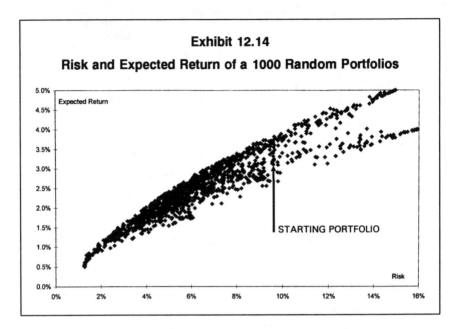

Exhibit 12.14

Risk and Expected Return of a 1000 Random Portfolios

It is clear from this figure that the starting portfolio is not a candidate for being an optimal portfolio as there are many portfolios that have the same (or lower) levels of risk but a higher return. The starting portfolio is therefore said to be "sub-optimal" because there are portfolios which are unambiguously better. Note that the starting portfolio can be ruled out even before the risk aversion of the investor is considered. Once all the sub-optimal portfolios have been removed, the remaining portfolios each have the characteristic of the highest possible return for their level of risk. This set of portfolios is known by the slightly heroic name of "the efficient frontier". The "optimal" portfolio, for a given investor, will be somewhere along the efficient frontier.

Exhibit 12.15 shows the risk and return characteristics of the efficient frontier.

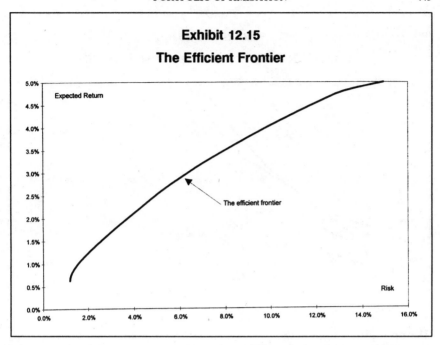

Exhibit 12.15

The Efficient Frontier

Fortunately, it is not necessary to create 1000 random portfolios to find the efficient frontier. A mathematical algorithm using *quadratic programming* can calculate the frontier. Further reading on the mechanics of calculating the efficient frontier can be found in the bibliography.

3.3 The optimal portfolio

The final question to answer is, given an investor's level of risk aversion, which portfolio on the efficient frontier is optimal? This can be answered by combining the efficient frontier with the investor's indifference curve. Recall that the investor's aim would be to have a portfolio that lies on the highest possible IC. *Exhibit 12.16* shows the efficient frontier along with the utility curves for an investor with $\lambda = 10$.

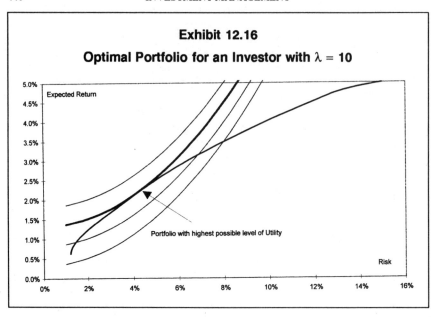

The optimal portfolio is the point on the efficient frontier where the IC just touches. Higher IC are impossible to achieve and lower IC have a lower level of utility. The example investor has a λ of 5, with the optimal portfolio on the efficient frontier shown in *Exhibit 12.17*.

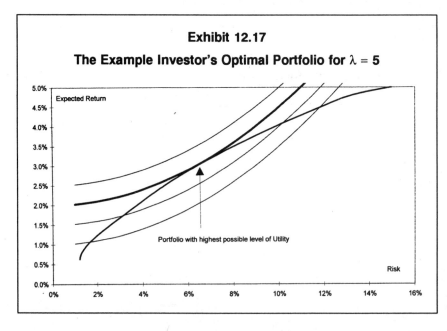

Note the different shape of the IC due to the lower level of risk aversion. As the risk aversion decreases, portfolios with progressively higher returns (and risk) are selected. The weights of the portfolio are shown in *Exhibit 12.18* and the test portfolio is shown for comparison purposes.

Exhibit 12.18

Expected Risk and Return of the Optimal Portfolio $\lambda = 5$

Asset	Weight in Optimal Portfolio	Weight in Starting Portfolio
Equities	25.7%	2.7%
International Equities	13.5%	54.3%
Property	3.7%	2.5%
Index Bonds	33.4%	3.7%
Nominal Bonds	23.7%	33.5%
International Bonds—hedged	0.0%	3.3%
Cash	0.0%	0.0%
Total	100.0%	100.0%
Expected return	3.1%	3.2%
Risk (standard deviation of return)	6.6%	9.5%

Compared to the test portfolio the optimal portfolio has a significantly lower risk with only a slight fall in the expected return.

3.4 How reliable is the optimal portfolio?

If you saw a dice for the very first time and you knew nothing about the underlying probabilities of various numbers occurring on each roll, how could you determine the likelihood of each number occurring? One way would be to roll the dice 100 times and see how frequently each number comes up. The results of such an experiment are shown in *Exhibit 12.19*.

Exhibit 12.19

Frequency of Numbers in 100 Dice Rolls

Number	Frequency	Estimated Probability
1	17	0.17
2	9	0.09
3	22	0.22
4	13	0.13
5	18	0.18
6	21	0.21

The true probability of any number occurring is 0.1667 (1 in 6) but the estimated probabilities are significantly different from this. In the above experiment the estimated chances of a two are less than 1 in 10 and the estimated chances of a six are better than 1 in 5. This type of inaccuracy is called *estimation error*. If you were to base the strategy for playing a dice-based game on these probabilities your approach would not be optimal.

The optimal portfolio for the example investor seems to be quite reasonable. It has a good spread of assets and, *based on the estimates for return and risk*, it is has a higher utility than any other portfolio. Unfortunately, the estimates of risk and return are just that—estimates. As with the dice, actual underlying risks and returns are still unknowns. They can only be estimated either by some forecasting method and/or observation of historical behaviour. An important question to explore is how much does estimation error affect the optimal portfolio?

The simple answer is that it affects the portfolio quite substantially. For example, consider the following experiment. Here the optimal portfolio has been calculated 100 times—each time with a slightly different co-variance matrix, in order to simulate the effects of sampling error.[5] *Exhibit 12.20* shows the range of outcome for each asset class. *Exhibit 12.21* shows the actual weights for the 100 simulated portfolios.

---

5.   The additional co-variance matrices were calculated using a bootstrap method. Random samples of the multi-variate normal distribution were created based on the original co-variance matrix. From these samples the new co-variance matrix was estimated.

Exhibit 12.20

Range of Optimal Asset Weights in Sampling Error Experiment

Asset	Minimum Weight	Maximum Weight	Average Weight
Equities	20.5%	37.2%	26.6%
International Equities	8.0%	19.1%	13.3%
Property	0.0%	15.7%	3.7%
Index Bonds	22.5%	49.4%	33.3%
Nominal Bonds	3.4%	39.0%	21.5%
International Bonds—hedged	0.0%	14.4%	1.6%
Cash	0.0%	0.0%	0.0%

Exhibit 12.21

Range of Optimal Asset Weights in Sampling Error Experiment

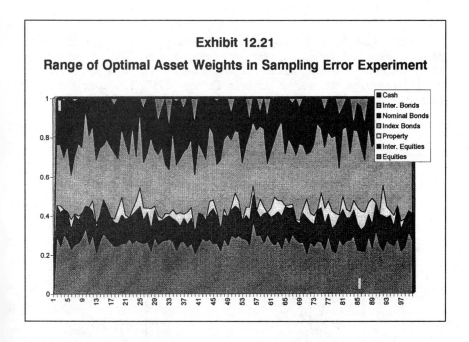

The average weights are close to the original optimal portfolio but the range that the optimal weights can take is quite startling. Take, for example, the optimal weight for Australian equities which varies between 20.5% and 37.2%. Also, the optimiser has not taken into account such features as transaction costs and the lack of liquidity in some asset classes. Note that none of the underlying assumptions of the model (such as returns having a log-normal distribution) has been questioned in this experiment.

The sensitivity and lack of reality of the mean-variance optimised portfolios are well known to practitioners and are the primary reasons why, despite the appealing theory, the mean-variance optimisers are not widely used in portfolio construction. In a chapter entitled portfolio optimisation this is a rather disappointing observation. The next section investigates methods by which the mean-variance model can be tamed.

4. PRACTICAL PORTFOLIO OPTIMISATION

When the mean-variance model is given a set of expected returns and a co-variance matrix *and nothing* else it is not surprising that the output is sensitive to these inputs and lacking in realism to such issues as liquidity and transaction costs. It was not told anything about them. Broadly, the mean-variance model can be improved in two ways. First, by stabilising the variability in the inputs and, secondly, by expanding the model to include other information.

4.1 Robust risk estimation

Exhibit 12.22 shows the rolling correlation between Australian equity and property measured, using five years of monthly returns. There are a number of instances of the correlation jumping substantially in a single month, notably just after the market crash in October 1987. The correlation also changes significantly in October 1992 when the 1987 crash drops out of the sample period.

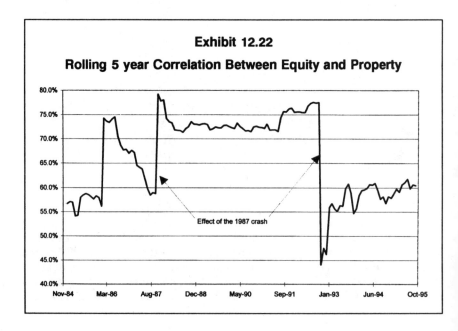

Exhibit 12.22

Rolling 5 year Correlation Between Equity and Property

It could be argued (tenuously) that the rise in correlation in October 1987 was real, but it is very difficult to support the idea that the correlation between equity and property fell by 50% in October 1992 just because it was 5 years and 1 month after the crash. In the previous section it was noted that the output from a mean-variance model can vary significantly with change in the risk measures. It can be rather disturbing to an analyst to find the optimiser suggesting a substantially different portfolio when there have been no significant changes to the forecast returns.

In choosing the methods to calculate the co-variance matrix, there should be two goals:

- ensure that the risk measure does not change dramatically from one period to another when there has been no significant change in the market; and

- ensure that the co-variance matrix is free from extreme values that unduly affect the optimisation process.

This is known as robust estimation. A detailed description of the methods for robustly estimating a co-variance matrix are beyond the scope of this book. To illustrate the idea, a simple approach, that can dramatically improve the stability of the risk measures, is to exclude extreme market moves (such as October 1987). *Exhibit 12.23* shows the correlation between equity and property over the same period after the two most extreme months have been removed.

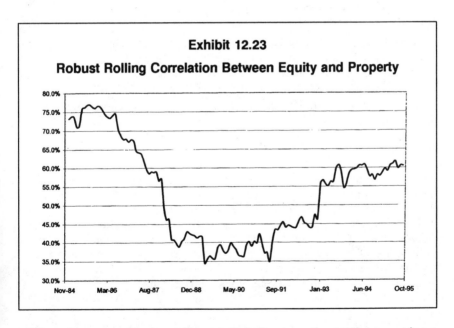

Exhibit 12.23

Robust Rolling Correlation Between Equity and Property

The advantage of using robust techniques to estimate the co-variance matrix is that it will allow the mean-variance model to produce consistent results over time, and limit the extent to which output will be greeted with the response "why is it doing that?" The co-variance matrix will still be subject to estimation error but, because it is more stable over time, analysts can learn to work with the model.

4.2 Optimisation to a benchmark and asset/liability modelling

The two-asset problem, introduced earlier, is good for illustrating the idea of risk aversion but in practice a more detailed analysis of the investor's requirements is needed to determine their level of risk aversion.

For example, consider a young man with at least thirty years before retirement. For such a person the "safe" investment A could well represent an extremely risky prospect. Assume that the basket of goods the young man is aiming to consume[6] was increasing in cost at a rate of 4% per annum over the next 30 years. In this case investment A would result in a slow but steady erosion of the future purchasing power of his nest egg. The young man would be certain of the amount of money he would have, but uncertain if he could afford anything. His best course of action would be to invest substantially in the "risky" investment B.

This type of analysis is known as asset/liability modelling. In this case the liability is the basket of goods to be consumed in retirement in 30 years time. The aim of asset/liability modelling is to create a long-term portfolio which, as closely as possible, matches the liability profile of the investor.

Such a portfolio can be used as the starting point for a mean-variance model. When used in this way the long-term portfolio is called a benchmark, strategic or a normal portfolio (is this chapter it will be referred to as a benchmark). The benchmark embodies the long-term assumptions about the behaviour of the investor's liabilities and the assets in which he or she can invest.

Asset/liability modelling is not the only source of benchmarks. Frequently, fund managers are given an implicit benchmark of the average allocation of their peers. Specialist managers (those managing one asset class) typically are given the broad market index as their benchmark.

The use of a long-term benchmark transforms the mean-variance problem in a number of ways. First, risk is defined in terms of variance in returns relative to the benchmark return. This variance is often called *tracking error*. Secondly, the expected returns may need to be expressed in terms of deviations from the long-term returns. For example, if the forecast for Australian equities for the next year was 4% this is 1% below the long-term expected return (assuming the benchmark has been constructed using returns from *Exhibit 12.5*). Hence, the relevant expected return for the optimiser is −1%. The reason for this is that the long-term expectation of Australian equities earning an after-tax return of 5% is already embodied in the benchmark. If the long-term return was included in the optimisation relative to the benchmark it would be double counted. *Exhibit 12.24* shows an example long-term benchmark and forecast asset returns.

---

6. The basket may consist of such goods as a house by the beach, health care, luxury motor cars and overseas trips. The CPI may be a poor indicator of rate of change in the price of this basket.

Exhibit 12.24

Benchmark and Forecast Expected Returns

Asset	Forecast Expected Returns (relative to long-term returns)	Benchmark Weight (%)
Equities	−2%	40.0
International Equities	−5%	25.0
Property	−3%	10.0
Index Bonds	2.5%	5.0
Nominal Bonds	1.5%	15.0
International Bonds—hedged	1%	0.0
Cash	0%	5.0
Expected return		−2.0%

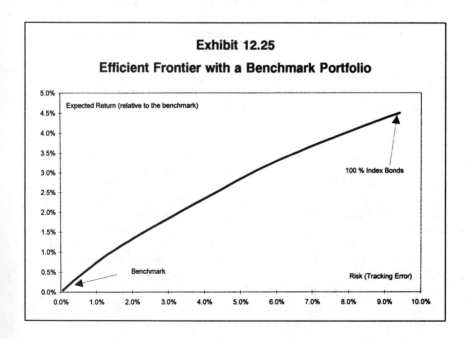

Exhibit 12.25

Efficient Frontier with a Benchmark Portfolio

Optimising to a benchmark produces significantly more stable results than optimising the absolute portfolio weights. The starting point for the efficient frontier will *always* be the benchmark, regardless of the forecast returns and estimated co-variance matrix.

Exhibit 12.26
Selected Portfolios on the Efficient Frontier

Asset	Lowest Risk (Benchmark) (%)	Medium Risk (%)	Highest Risk (%)
Equities	40.0	36.4	
International Equities	25.0	13.5	
Property	10.0	0.0	
Index Bonds	5.0	25.3	100.0
Nominal Bonds	15.0	24.8	
International Bonds—hedged	0.0	0.0	
Cash	5.0	0.0	
Risk (tracking error)	0.0	2.5	9.4
Expected return	−2.0	0.4	2.5

Note that returns in this table returns are relative to the benchmark.

4.3 Transaction costs, turnover constraints and asset bounds

In *Exhibit 12.26* the portfolios on the efficient frontier contained significant amounts of index bonds. This is understandable as index bonds have the highest expected return. However, index bonds are not very liquid and consequently the costs of investing (and divesting at a later date) are high. This has not been taken into account in the optimiser.

The mean-variance model can easily be extended to include the cost of transactions. This is achieved by effectively reducing the expected return of a portfolio by the costs involved in trading from the existing portfolio to the new one. A further refinement is to place differential transaction costs depending on whether the portfolio weight is being moved towards or away from the benchmark. The costs of moving away from the benchmark are double the actual cost, whereas the costs of moving towards the benchmark are zero. The logic of this is that the portfolio will only move away from the benchmark if the expected return can cover the round trip costs of investment.

The optimal portfolio can be further constrained by limiting overall turnover of the portfolio. For example, it could be decided that the total turnover should be no more than some pre-set limit, for instance 20%.

The bluntest technique for controlling portfolio turnover is to apply bounds to the asset classes. For example, it could be decided independently of the optimisation process that the maximum weight in which the portfolio could realistically be invested in index bonds is 10%. Ideally, if the expected returns, transactions costs and overall risk aversion have being properly specified then explicit bounds on assets should not be required. Overuse of asset bounds can lead to the optimal portfolio being primarily defined by the bounds rather than by the optimisation process.

On the other hand, fund managers are often given explicit guidelines in terms of how much they can invest in a particular asset. Bounds play a very useful role when they represent such pre-defined (and often legally binding) restrictions on a fund.

4.4 Bayesian Inference—allowing for imperfect forecasts

So far, very little has been said about the estimated expected returns. They are the most important input of the model. A model with a poorly constructed or unstable co-variance matrix could still produce a portfolio that will add value to the benchmark—*if the expected returns are accurate*. If the expected returns are poor, the resultant portfolio will almost certainly under-perform its benchmark.

One of the most persistent criticisms of the mean-variance model from an investment analyst's point is that there is no allowance for some forecasts to be better than others. For example, an analyst asked to forecast equities and property might say:

> "Well, I'm fairly confident the equities will kick on and return 10%. On property—I guess it might ease a bit—but in this market it's difficult to call."

The exasperated person in charge of running the optimiser will press the analyst to give an unambiguous, single forecast for each asset. Assume, in this case, the forecasts end up being equities up 10% and property down 2%. Is this the best interpretation of the analyst's views? There are two elements missing from this final forecast. First, the analyst is clearly uncertain of the property forecast. The mean-variance model would treat these two forecasts as being equally valid. Secondly, there is a known strong positive correlation between equity and property which is not necessarily being taken into account.

The problem of combining imperfect knowledge with sample information is an area of statistics known as Bayesian Inference. An approach suggested by Black and Litterman is particularly novel and innovative. It notes that there are two competing sources of returns, the underlying long-run returns and the analyst's view. Both sources of information are imperfect and best expressed in probabilistic terms. Also, the co-variance matrix gives information about the pattern of joint returns.

Instead of pressing that analyst to give an expected return for property that has an equal level of conviction, the analyst could be allowed to specify the level of confidence with which each view is held. *Exhibit 12.27* shows the analyst forecasts together with the assumed long-term returns[7] and confidence level of each forecast.

---

7.   If the optimisation was relative to a benchmark then the long-term returns would be zero, as they have already been embodied in the benchmark.

Exhibit 12.27

Long-term Return, Analyst's Forecasts and Confidence Levels

Asset class	Long-term return	Analyst's forecast	Confidence level
Equities	5.00%	10%	?
Property	2.75%	−2%	5%

In the above table the level of confidence for the equity forecast has not been specified.

Exhibit 12.28 shows how the forecasts for both equity and property vary as the confidence in the equity forecast grows.[8] When there is no confidence, both the equity and property forecasts are at their long-run values. As the level of confidence increases, the equity forecast moves toward the analyst's forecast. Interestingly, the property forecast rises, *away from the analyst's forecast*. Equities are strongly correlated with the property market, as the confidence in the analyst's forecast grows, it implies that property will also rise. This indirect influence has a greater impact because the direct view on property is held so weakly.

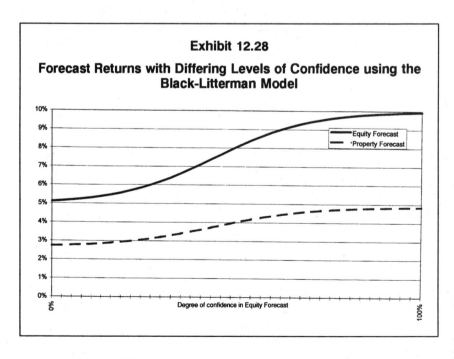

Exhibit 12.28

Forecast Returns with Differing Levels of Confidence using the Black-Litterman Model

8.   Refer to Appendix II for more details of the Black-Litterman model.

Although this two asset example is unrealistic, the approach becomes much more valuable as the number of assets increases. Consider a group of analysts with the task of analysing a few hundred stocks to create an equity portfolio. It is unreasonable for every stock to be analysed and forecast with the same level of detail. The Black-Litterman model allows for a varied level of analysis to be performed, even accommodating stocks on which there has been no analysis.

5. OTHER OPTIMISATION APPROACHES

This section will explore some other approaches to creating an "optimal" portfolio.

5.1 Scenario-based optimisation (goal programming)

As previously noted, one criticism from practitioners of the mean-variance model is that it requires single estimates of the mean return for each asset. Investment analysts often think in terms of scenarios. Scenario-based optimisation allows for forecasts to be input in terms of a number of sets of forecasts (usually at least three), each with an associated probability. *Exhibit 12.29* shows an example of three forecast scenarios along with their associated probability. *Exhibit 12.30* shows an example benchmark and some lower and upper bounds for a portfolio.

Exhibit 12.29
Forecast Real Returns for Three Scenarios

	"Boom" Scenario	"Normal" Scenario	"Bust" Scenario
Probability	15%	70%	15%
Equities	40.0%	5.0%	−20.0%
International Equities	25.0%	4.5%	−25.0%
Property	3.5%	3.5%	3.5%
Index Bonds	7.0%	3.0%	−10.0%
Nominal Bonds	0.0%	2.5%	−10.0%
International bonds—hedged	0.0%	1.0%	−8.0%
Cash	1.5%	1.0%	−0.5%

Exhibit 12.30

Portfolio's Benchmark, Lower and Upper Bounds

	Lower Bound	Benchmark	Upper Bound
Equities	20%	40.0%	60%
International Equities	15%	25.0%	35%
Property	5%	10.0%	15%
Index Bonds	0%	5.0%	10%
Nominal Bonds	5%	15.0%	25%
International Bonds—hedged	0%	0.0%	10%
Cash	0%	5.0%	20%

A typical example of scenario optimisation is to find the portfolio with the highest expected (probability weighted) return subject to the constraint that the portfolio does not under-perform the benchmark in any single scenario. *Exhibit 12.31* shows the resultant optimal portfolio. *Exhibit 12.32* shows the return of the portfolio and benchmark under each scenario.

Exhibit 12.31

Portfolio with the Highest Expected Return (Subject to not Under-performing the Benchmark)

	Optimal Weights
Equities	60.0%
International Equities	15.7%
Property	15.0%
Index Bonds	0.0%
Nominal Bonds	5.0%
International Bonds—hedged	0.0%
Cash	4.3%

Exhibit 12.32
Returns of Portfolio and Benchmark

	Benchmark	Portfolio	Relative
Normal	4.1%	4.4%	0.4%
Boom	23.0%	28.5%	5.5%
Bust	−15.9%	−15.9%	0.0%
Expected	3.9%	5.0%	1.1%

The difference in the expected return of the portfolio and benchmark is 1.1% and there are no scenarios where the portfolio under-performs the benchmark. So it would appear that the scenario optimisation has been successful.

However, there are some drawbacks with this type of approach. First, the portfolio is largely at the extreme end of the asset ranges. This is known in optimisation as a *corner solution* where the result lies at the boundaries of the problem. The reasons for this are subtle. If *Exhibit 12.29* is studied closely, one can note that in all scenarios the local equities market is forecast to outperform the international equity market. Hence, it is possible to over-weight local equities and under-weight international equities ad infinitum, all the time increasing the expected returns without under-performing in any scenario.

The underlying problem is in using a limited number of scenarios to describe all possible futures. This problem is not easily solved merely by taking care not to produce forecasts with embedded free lunches, as there can be groups of assets with the same problem. For example, in the above set of forecasts, a combination of index bond and international bonds can be constructed that will always out-perform nominal bonds.

The problem of scenario optimisers tending to produce extreme solutions can be mitigated by adding addition constraints (turnover, transaction cost) or penalising the portfolio for an increase in risk. However this needs to be thoughtfully done or it can be unclear as to whether the resultant portfolio is a product of the forecasts or of the choice of "taming" constraints.

Scenario-based approaches are most applicable where the scenarios do describe the complete range of outcomes.

5.2 Generalised (non-parametric) portfolio optimisation

The simple and elegant mean-variance criteria is derived by assuming that return are normally distributed. Hence, disagreement with variance as a risk measure is largely an indirect disagreement with the assumption of normality. In the case of some derivative securities (such as options) the assumption of normality is quite clearly wrong.

An approach that avoids assuming any particular form for the distribution of returns is empirical or non-parametric optimisation. Rather than using return observations (be they historical, from a model, or forecast) to estimate a co-variance matrix and expected returns, the returns are instead used to directly describe the probability distribution. This idea is best explained by way of an example.

Exhibit 12.33 shows the monthly historical returns of two Australian stocks (BHP and CRA) over the period 1990 to 1995. The joint distribution is reasonably well described by the stock means and variances and their co-variance.

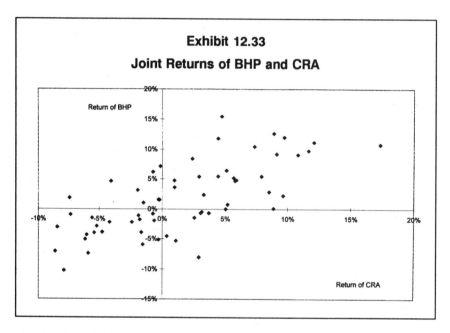

Consider a third stock which has some option characteristics. Assume the stock will either return the highest return of BHP and CRA, or expire worthless if both stocks have a negative return. Further, assume for this example that this option costs 3.5% in each period. *Exhibit 12.34* and *Exhibit 12.35* show the joint distribution of the option with BHP and CRA stocks respectively.

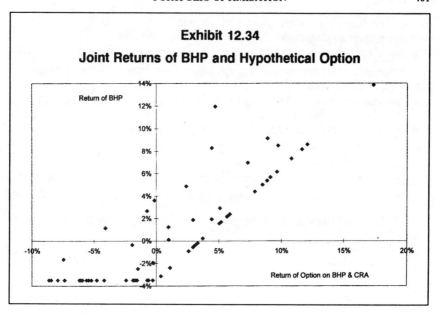

Exhibit 12.34

Joint Returns of BHP and Hypothetical Option

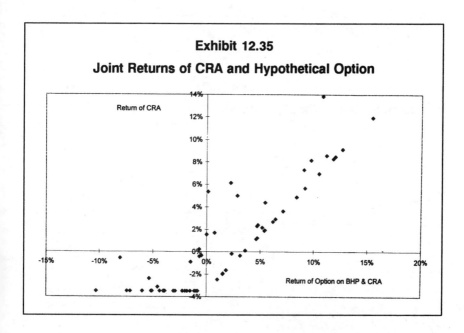

Exhibit 12.35

Joint Returns of CRA and Hypothetical Option

In both cases, using mean, variance and co-variance to describe the joint distribution removes a great deal of information, specifically the asymmetric behaviour of the option. An empirical approach does not try to summarise the entire distribution in a few parameters. Rather, each observation is used directly to represent the future possible outcomes. The most naive approach is to assume that each historical outcome is equally likely to occur in the future. The portfolio optimisation problem then becomes to maximise utility over the empirical distribution.

Exhibit 12.36 shows the summary statistics of the three assets that would be the input into a mean-variance optimiser. The option has a significantly lower expected return and a slightly lower risk. *Exhibit 12.37* shows the resultant optimal mix of BHP and CRA for a reasonably risk-averse investor ($\lambda = 12$) for both the mean-variance approach and the empirical approach. *Exhibit 12.38* shows the optimal portfolio derived from the two approaches when the investor is able to purchase the option stock.

Exhibit 12.36
Return, Risk and Correlation of BHP, CRA and Option

	BHP	CRA	Option
Expected Return	18.3%	20.5%	10.5%
Risk (Standard deviation)	20.4%	20.4%	15.9%
Correlation with CRA	70%	------	------
Correlation with option	85%	88%	------

Exhibit 12.37
Optimal Portfolios for Mean-variance and Empirical Optimisation ($\lambda = 12$)—Option not Included

	Mean-variance	Empirical
BHP	42.4%	40.5%
CRA	57.5%	59.5%

Exhibit 12.38

Optimal Portfolios for Mean-Variance and Empirical Optimisation
($\lambda = 12$)—Option Included

	Mean-variance	Empirical
BHP	42.4%	31.3%
CRA	57.5%	49.5%
Option	0.0%	19.1%

For a risk-averse investor the option is an attractive investment, as it enables the construction of a portfolio with a more limited down-side. As the mean-variance model assumes that returns are symmetrically distributed, it is unable to "see" the asymmetric nature of the option, and only reviews its risk characteristics based on its variance and co-variance with the other assets. The empirical approach uses the actual historical outcomes to characterise its expectation of future behaviour, and hence it is able to "see" the value in the option.

This point is illustrated in *Exhibit 12.39*. On the horizontal axis is the return of the mean-variance optimal portfolio if it had been invested over the sample period from 1990 to 1995. The vertical axis shows the difference in return between the empirical portfolio and the mean-variance portfolio. The empirical portfolio out-performs the mean variance portfolio significantly when its returns are negative and largely matches or marginally under-performs it at other times. Essentially, the empirical portfolio has traded-off a slightly lower expected return for a significantly lower risk of very poor returns. To a risk-averse investor, this is a good deal.

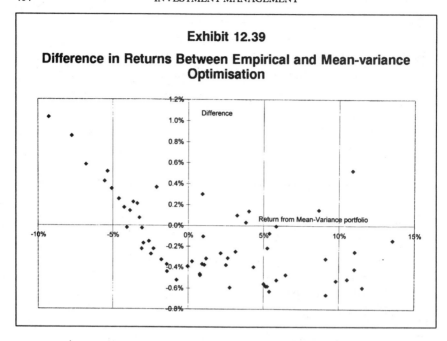

Exhibit 12.39

Difference in Returns Between Empirical and Mean-variance Optimisation

Given the slightly magical ability of a non-parametric optimisation approach to identify and exploit asymmetric distributions, it is tempting to think that it should always be used in preference to a mean-variance model. However, if the underlying distribution of returns are actually (or approximately) normal then the non-parametric approach will magnify the sampling error effect. Also, the non-parametric approach does not lead to a clear definition of risk, which can make interpretation of results more difficult.

6. CHAPTER SUMMARY

The mean-variance model for calculating an optimal portfolio makes two key assumptions:

- investors' preferences can be expressed in terms of well behaved and exponential utility function; and

- returns are modelled with a log-normal distribution.

This leads to the mean-variance criteria for an optimal portfolio (Maximise $\mu_p - \lambda/2\sigma^2_p$). This can be interpreted to mean that an investor will only accept a portfolio with a higher risk provided there is a commensurately higher return. The risk-aversion parameter (λ) can be thought of as the investor's pricing of risk.

Despite its elegant simplicity the mean-variance model has been criticised by practitioners because the output is highly sensitive to small changes in either the expected returns or co-variance matrix. Also the model can produce results that are unrealistic when market factors such as liquidity and transaction costs are considered. There are a variety of methods to overcome these problems, notably:

- using robust methods to calculate the co-variance matrix to reduce unrealistic changes and extreme values in the risk measures;
- using a benchmark as the starting point for an optimisation;
- including transaction costs and turnover limits;
- including legal and practical restrictions in the form of bounds; and
- modifying expected returns to take account of their imperfect nature and to allow for some views to be less firmly held than others.

Successful portfolio optimisation requires more than plugging risk and returns into a mean-variance optimiser and turning the handle. Care needs to be taken to ensure that the inputs are realistic, and that the model is expanded to cover the realities of the financial markets. Used appropriately, the mean-variance model is a powerful tool for efficiently translating estimates of risks and returns into portfolios.

Appendix I

Derivation of the Criteria for an Optimal Portfolio

A rational investor with an exponential utility function will seek to maximise the expected utility. This is defined as:

$$\text{Maximise } E[U(r)] = \int (1 - e^{-\gamma r}) f(r) dr$$

or more simply:

$$\text{Minimise } E[U(r)] = \int e^{-\gamma r} f(r) dr$$

The form of this equation is well known to statisticians as the moment generating function (MGF) evaluated at $-\lambda$. Maximising the exponential utility function over a given distribution is equivalent to minimising the MGF of the distribution. The MGF for the normal distribution is:

$$MGF_{normal}(-\lambda) = e^{\left(-\lambda\mu + \frac{(-\lambda)^2\sigma^2}{2}\right)}$$

The above equation is minimised when the exponent value is minimised, that is

$$\text{Minimise } -\lambda\mu + \frac{\lambda^2\sigma^2}{2}$$

Dividing by $-\lambda$ gives:

$$\text{Maximise } \mu - \frac{\lambda}{2}\sigma^2$$

This is the now familiar mean-variance criteria for an optimal portfolio. An important point is that if the return distribution has a MGF in a closed form *then criteria for an optimal portfolio can be expressed directly.* For example, if the returns were uniformly distributed over the interval $[\theta_1, \theta_2]$ then the criteria for the optimal portfolio would be:

$$\text{Minimise } MGF_{uniform}(-\lambda) = \frac{e^{-\lambda\theta_2} - e^{-\lambda\theta_1}}{-\lambda(\theta_2 - \theta_1)}$$

Similarly, for a gamma distribution (expressed as a function of α and β, the criteria is:

$$\text{Minimise } MGF_{gamma}(-\lambda) = (1 + \beta\lambda)^{-a}.$$

Given the ease by which the criteria for an optimal portfolio can be expressed, why is it that the mean-variance criteria (derived from assuming a log normal distribution of returns) dominates finance, and other criteria are rarely seen?

There are two main reasons for this:

- the log normal distribution is, by and large, the best at describing the observed distribution of returns; and

- only the normal distribution can be generalised into a multi-variate problem without becoming overly complex mathematically.

However, this technique for deriving the criteria for an optimal portfolio is useful to apply to specific problems. The next Appendix gives an example of this.

Appendix II

Implied Risk Aversion from Two Asset Problem

An investor has a choice of two assets to invest in. One will provide a certain return of 3%, the other returning 40%, 10% and −20% with probabilities of 0.25, 0.50 and 0.25 respectively. If it is assumed the investor has an exponential utility function what can be inferred about the investors risk aversion based on the chosen weight in the risky asset?

The exponential utility function takes the following form:

$$U(r) = 1 - e^{-\lambda r}$$

where

λ is a risk-aversion parameter (pronounced lambda);

U is the level of utility for a given level of return; and

r is the return.

A rational investor will seek to maximise the expected utility. This is:

$$\text{Maximise } E[U(r)] = \int (1 - e^{-\lambda r}) f(r) dr$$

where $f(r)$ is the probability density function of r. In the above case the expected value of utility for a given weight (w) in the risky asset is:

$$E[U(r)] = 1 - \left(0.25e^{-\lambda(1+0.4w+(1-w)0.03)} + 0.50e^{-\lambda(1+0.1w+(1-w)0.03)} + 0.25e^{-\lambda(1-0.2w+(1-w)0.03)}\right)$$

The investor will seek to choose such that the expected utility is maximised. That is:

$$\frac{dE[u]}{dw} = 0$$

$$\frac{dE[u]}{dw} = \left(\frac{-\lambda 0.25}{100}\right)\left(37e^{-\lambda(0.97+0.37w)} + 14e^{-\lambda(0.97+0.07w)} - 23e^{-\lambda(0.97-0.23w)}\right) = 0$$

Dividing the above equation through by $\left(\dfrac{-\lambda 0.25}{100}\right)\left(\dfrac{e^{\lambda 0.97}}{e^{\lambda 0.23w}}\right)$ gives:

$$37e^{(-\lambda 0.6w)} + 14e^{(-\lambda 0.3w)} - 23 = 0$$

Let $x = e^{-\lambda 0.3w}$ and substitute in the above equation gives:

$$37x^2 + 14x - 23 = 0$$

Solving this quadratic gives a value for of either −1 or 23/37. As x cannot be negative it can be concluded that:

$$\lambda = \frac{-\ln(23/37)/0.3}{w} \cong \frac{1.58}{w}$$

This gives a simple relationship between the risky asset weight and the investor level of risk aversion.

Appendix III

The Black-Litterman Transformation

The expected return $E[r]$ in the Black-Litterman model is calculated as follows:

$$E[r] = \left[(\tau\Sigma)^{-1} + P'\Omega^{-1}P\right]^{-1}\left[(\tau\Sigma)^{-1}\Pi + P'\Omega^{-1}Q\right]$$

Where

n is the number of assets.

k is the number of views held by the investors. Note the k does not necessarily have to equal n as there may be assets on which the investor does not have a view.

Σ is the n by n co-variance matrix.

Q is the k by 1 vector of investor views.

P is a k by n matrix indicating those assets for which an investor has expressed a view. Z will contain a one where a view has been expressed, and will be zero otherwise. Note that a relative view (excess return of an asset over another) can be expressed by a combination of one and minus one.

Ω is a k by k diagonal matrix showing the uncertainty with which each view is held. The higher the ith *diagonal value the more uncertain is the ith view. It is assumed that* $P'E[r] = Q + \xi$, where ξ is a vector of normal variates with zero means. Ω is the co-variance matrix of ξ. Hence, as the variance of ξ approaches zero, $E[r]$ approaches the investor views.

Π is a n by 1 vector of long-term equilibrium returns.

τ is a scaler ($0 \geq \tau \geq 1$) that reflects the degree of uncertainty in the long term equilibrium returns. Zero would indicate that there is no uncertainty in the long-term equilibrium returns (and the investor views would be redundant).

Chapter 13

Risk Management for Bond Portfolios

by Roger Cohen

1. INTRODUCTION

Bond portfolio management is a major area in the financial markets. Some of the basic principles will be covered here. For further detail, the reader should consult references that specifically deal with this area.

The major areas of portfolio management are asset and liability management. The former applies to managers who purchase, hold and trade assets. Their main aim is to maximise return within specified constraints. Liability managers are trying to minimise their cost of funding by issuing appropriate instruments. They need to be able to service interest payments, to repay principal as scheduled, and to meet cash outflows when required. At times, the liability manager may find it advantageous to arrange refinancing, or to alter the mix of liabilities.

Although asset and liability management are complementary (the liability manager is trying to reduce cost, the asset manager is maximising return), the principles governing both sides are the same. The risks are the same, as are the techniques for managing them.

The following chapter is written mainly from the asset perspective. Implicit in this is the aim to maximise return, and to minimise risk. For liability management, the same techniques are applied to minimise cost.

2. PORTFOLIO MANAGEMENT

2.1 Matching and hedging

Matching and hedging are probably the fundamental concepts required in the management of any portfolio. They allow the portfolio manager to offset both risk and obligation in the portfolio. The former is done by removing sensitivity to possible external changes that may occur. These include changes in market rates, credit and other factors which affect the value of the portfolio.

Matching requires ensuring that a portfolio meets all cashflow obligations set on it. This means that cash inflows and outflows can be met without disrupting the portfolio. A perfectly matched portfolio will deliver exactly the cashflow required when it is needed. Cash inflows will be invested with this criteria in mind. There should also be provisions for emergencies by having a portion of the assets in highly liquid securities, or cash.

A perfectly hedged portfolio should contain no sensitivity to market factors (technically this is impossible, but within normal operating circumstances risk should be minimal). If for example, the portfolio value is going to decline drastically when rates increase, then any hedging strategy will need to hold assets (or liabilities) whose behaviour offsets this decrease.

The function of a portfolio manager is to supply the optimum amount of matching and hedging, and the appropriate choice of assets, so that the portfolio performs to, or exceeds, its goals. This has to be done within set constraints. These can be highly varied. They can govern the types of assets held, the maturity profile, duration limits and allowable trading. At the extremes, consider a long-term retirement portfolio versus an arbitrage trading portfolio. The retirement portfolio would probably hold quality assets with steady yield. The arbitrage portfolio will be traded actively for short-term gain. Style of portfolio management can be as varied as the purpose of the portfolio, and the aims of the manager. There is no perfect management method—rather a number of strategies which can be chosen or adapted. Portfolio management is in many ways a very individual discipline.

Of the many strategies available to the manager of a bond (or indeed other) portfolio, there are two broad categories into which most fall. These are the choice of active versus passive management. The former is used where the portfolio is measured and adjusted over very short time periods. Often this occurs many times a day. The aim is to control risk while taking advantage of intraday market movements. The composition of the portfolio can change rapidly. Passive portfolios tend to be held for longer periods. Because adjustment is not as frequent as for active portfolios, assets need to be chosen to meet the strategic aims of the portfolio rather than short-term goals.

2.2 Passive portfolio management

Passive (bond) portfolios are generally held for the medium to long term.[1] The return on the portfolio depends in general on the yield of the assets in it. Adjustments are made generally when cash inflows or outflows occur, or for strategic reasons (such as a change in economic view). Bonds may be held to maturity. The portfolio manager will aim to get the cashflows in the portfolio to match required outflows, or ensure assets are liquid enough to provide them. Day-to-day market changes will affect the instantaneous value of the portfolio. This may not disrupt the overall investment strategy if obligations are met. They will determine the yield at which assets are purchased, and valued. Cash inflows will be invested to fit the overall time horizon and strategy that is adopted for the portfolio.

The main advantage of passive portfolios are that they do not require a lot of short-term adjustment. This cuts down on both transaction costs, and on the resources required in their management. Provided the assets held in a passive portfolio meet both cashflow and investment return obligations, the risks inherent in these are low. Management is not necessarily (or overly)

---

1. There is no firm delineation between short-, medium- or long-term portfolios. Long-term portfolios can be constructed over years or decades. Medium-term can range from weeks or months to several years, while short-term portfolios can change daily or even intraday.

concerned with day-to-day fluctuations due to market volatility. More important is the overall economic and strategic outlook. The passive portfolio manager may not need to hold liquid assets (however, under disaster situations this could be a problem). This means that access to high-yielding bonds will increase, as assets need not be benchmarks—or have liquidity constraints. Credit exposure becomes important as bonds are held for longer periods.

Passive portfolios require adjustment periodically. This will be due to overall strategic considerations rather than short-term trading opportunities (for example, there may be asset allocation changes, the overall economic view of the manager may be modified, or timing of inflows and outflows needs to be altered). The quality of assets held must reflect the likely holding period.

It is useful for the passive portfolio manager to have, or be aware of, disaster recovery plans. These can be utilised where unforeseen events occur. Such scenarios include market catastrophes—yields plummet or soar—or where a sizeable portion of the portfolio needs to be liquidated. They also include contingencies for issuer defaults or missing interest payments. These can be alleviated by the using of short-term hedges, having the capacity to borrow (money or assets), substituting assets, or by keeping a portion of the portfolio in liquid and tradable assets including cash.

2.3 Active portfolio management

An actively managed portfolio is usually constructed to take advantage of short-term market moves. These are more often relative than absolute. They include changes in the shape of the yield curve or relative movement between different yield curves. As such, actively traded portfolios are often constructed insensitive to overall uniform shifts. They exploit the changes in relativity between assets. Hedging becomes very important. The portfolio needs to be insulated against all changes except those which the manager chooses to exploit. An example of this is where the manager perceives the yield differential between two instruments to be excessively large. To exploit this, the higher-yielding asset will be bought, the lower-yielding sold (or shorted). If this is done so that the portfolio is insensitive to absolute movement of the two bonds, then the only exposure is this relativity.

Active portfolio returns can be measured against a benchmark, or they may just aim to maximise outright return (on capital). Benchmarks are usually market indices, or specific bonds. The aim of the manager is to use short-term trading opportunities to beat the benchmarks or to maximise return. Performance will include transaction costs, which can be significant. Active management of a portfolio must fit within predefined risk limits. These may govern the outright exposure or the exposure to certain assets and parts of the yield curve.

Actively managed portfolios may be used either to generate maximum trading profit, or they may also have some strategic component. In the former case, the manager need not focus on the size and timing of cash inflows and outflows. Profitability is more linked to changes in capital value. Often these portfolios are geared,[2] so funding costs need to be taken into account. Where there is some strategic component, the duration of assets will also need to be managed.

3. BENCHMARKING

The process of benchmarking enables the performance of a portfolio to be measured. It also gives the manager a target for which performance is to be achieved or exceeded. There is no unique benchmark. Generally, a performance benchmark will be the risk/return of an entire market sector, that of a single asset, or an outright return on capital target.

3.1 Single instrument benchmarks

A single instrument benchmark is a bond portfolio where the target return is, for example, that of a ten-year Government bond. The manager must maintain modified duration within (say) one year of the ten-year bond modified duration. Within this constraint, the manager can exactly meet the benchmark if the portfolio consists of just the benchmark ten-year bond, with interest cashflows reinvested in this bond. The major risk then is reinvestment risk. Management of this portfolio would be very passive. The only adjustments would occur when there is a coupon to be reinvested. An active approach would be to hold a series of bonds of maturities around ten years, but not necessarily the ten-year benchmark itself. The manager must choose bonds so that the combination return including costs matches or exceeds the benchmark, whilst maintaining modified duration within the required range around the benchmark. There is greater risk associated with this strategy, however returns can be significantly enhanced if the manager performs well.

Other common benchmarks of this type include cash, or short-dated bills. The actual instruments in the portfolio may or may not be the same as the benchmark itself.

3.2 Market sector or index benchmark

Using indices, the aim of the manager is to construct a portfolio which will replicate or exceed returns of a complete market or market sector. Again, the passive manager can hold (or replicate) the index. The active manager has choice of instruments—usually, but not always—in the sector or index. In the case where the manager is measured against a specific index, but can hold instruments not contained in the index, considerable excess risk may be introduced by the wider choice of instruments available. The return target of the index may become easily attainable if the portfolio can contain other instruments. A common example of this is where a portfolio is benchmarked

---

2.   A geared portfolio is one in which cash is borrowed to buy assets. This means that market exposure can be greater than the capital value of the portfolio.

against a Government bond index. The portfolio is not restricted to holding only Government bonds. Under normal conditions, the portfolio manager can choose to hold higher-yielding corporate bonds. This means that usually returns will exceed the index almost by default. What is not considered however is the additional credit risk associated in holding the more risky corporate bonds.

Sometimes a portfolio is broken down into sub-indices. This is common for very large portfolios, where more than one manager is employed. Consider a very large pension fund whose benchmark is the Government bond index. The portfolio is split into sub-portfolios of various maturities. These may include a cash or bank bill component for durations of 180 days or less, a zero to three year, three- to seven-year and greater than seven-year components. Each is managed against a relevant sub-index. Each contains instruments similar to the sub-index. There may be some overlap. The entire portfolio can be actively managed. The overall strategy is of deciding what proportion of the total portfolio value to allocate to each sub-group. The decision is whether to allocate the portfolio exactly as maturities are apportioned in the index, or to overweight certain maturities. If the overall view is that long-term assets will perform better than short-term ones, the decision might be made to hold less cash and bill type assets in favour of excess weighting in the over seven-year area. Once this strategic allocation is made, each sub-portfolio is managed separately. This gives the managers of these the choice to tilt the portfolio toward areas where overperformance is anticipated. This top down approach provides a number of areas which can be managed. The top level allocation may fit the index, while the sub-portfolios may be tilted, or vice versa.

3.3 Example: top down portfolio management

From the above discussion, consider a large portfolio which is managed against an all maturities index. The table below shows the allocation of the complete portfolio under differing strategic viewpoints.

Maturity band	Average modified duration (y)	Index Weighting	Neutral	Rates increasing	Rates decreasing
Cash–180 days	0.25	16.0%	16.0%	20.0%	14.0%
180 days–3 years	1.6	31.5%	31.5%	34.0%	29.0%
3–7 years	4.4	24.5%	24.5%	22.0%	27.0%
Over 7 years	8.9	28.0%	28.0%	24.0%	30.0%
Total		100.0%	100.0%	100.0%	100.0%
Modified duration		4.11	4.11	3.70	4.36

The table shows the components of the index. A neutral portfolio would exactly mirror this. If the strategic view were that rates were going to increase, then, in general, long-term bonds would perform worse than short-term bonds. The portfolio under this scenario is tilted towards the short end. The modified duration has been shortened from 4.11 years to 3.7 years. The converse is true for the view of rates decreasing. The modified duration is lengthened by 0.25 to 4.36 years.

The above is the overall top level allocation of the portfolio. If the sub-portfolios are separately managed, then there will be tilting within them as well. This can increase or decrease the tilt generated by the top level allocation. If from the above example, the overall allocation is performed with the view that rates will increase, then the sub-portfolios are given a certain proportion of the total portfolio value. The sub-managers may decide to further tilt. If limits are set on the amount each sub-portfolio can be altered from the index, then this effect will be secondary. It may be that the overall asset allocation can move the modified duration plus or minus half a year from the index. The allocation allowed in any sub-portfolio may only be allowed to alter the entire portfolio (including all other sub-portfolios) by plus or minus 0.1 years.

There may be other levels in the asset allocation hierarchy that have not been discussed here. These include global and sector allocation. Global allocation determines what the geographic composition of a portfolio should be. What exposures to what countries or regions are required. Also within a sector, there is the choice of assets. This will include classes such as equities, property, commodities or bonds. It is only the latter that is considered in detail here.

3.4 Return on capital benchmark

As distinct from benchmarks which are an instrument or index, a portfolio may be managed to provide a certain return on capital. Such is the case for many hedge funds and other portfolios with aggressive investment profiles. An outright target return may be set, or the portfolio will aim to achieve a certain margin over cash (or another asset). In this case, the risk profile is usually much higher than for an index benchmarked portfolio. The portfolio will be aggressively managed. There may be little restriction on the instruments the portfolio can hold, and the types of trading activity permitted.

4. CASE STUDY: HEDGING A BOND PORTFOLIO

The following discussion focuses on the hedging of a bond portfolio. It is assumed that the asset allocation and asset choices have been made. Here we show how an asset manager can insulate the portfolio to changes in the market rates (the yield curve). We will use a relatively simple portfolio for this study. These principles can easily be extended to more complex portfolios.

4.1 The portfolio and the yield curve

For simplicity, the portfolio in this study will hold just three bonds. Their characteristics are shown below.

	Bond 1	Bond 2	Bond 3
Spot date	1/6/97	1/6/97	1/6/97
Maturity	15/11/99	15/7/04	1/8/08
Coupon	10.00%	6.50%	8.25%
Coup freq	2	2	2
Yield	7.25%	7.93%	8.12%
Price (per $100)	106.536	94.780	103.659
PVBP (per $m)	114.867	255.392	365.106
DMod	1.083	2.766	3.618
Convexity	0.016	0.087	0.176

The composition and overall characteristic of the portfolio is shown.

	Face val ($m)	Value ($)	PVBP	DMod	Convexity
Bond 1	2	2,130,720	229.734	1.083	0.032
Bond 2	2	1,895,600	510.784	2.766	0.174
Bond 3	6	6,219,540	2,190.636	3.618	1.056
Total	—	10,245,860	2,931.154	2.933	1.262

The portfolio has a total value of just over $10 million. Its modified duration is 2.933 years and the PVBP or sensitivity to a one basis point change in yield is $2931.154.

As hedge instruments, we have available two zero coupon bonds maturing on 15/12/00 and 15/12/06 respectively. The characteristics of these are shown below.[3]

	Hedge 1	Hedge 2
Spot Date	1/6/97	1/6/97
Maturity	1/12/00	1/12/06
Coupon	0.00%	0.00%
Yield	7.50%	8.05%
Price (per $100)	77.283	47.248
PVBP (per $m)	130.369	215.796
DMod	1.687	4.567
Convexity	0.025	0.104

To hedge the portfolio, various combinations of the hedge instruments can be sold (or shorted). This will neutralise some of the sensitivities of the portfolio. There are many choices of combinations for the hedge instruments. It is assumed that the proceeds of the hedge instruments when sold are invested in cash or other readily liquid assets. Funding costs are not considered here. We shall assume that funding costs are negligible—and so do not influence the choice of hedge.

The extremes in the choice of hedge will be all of one or the other zero coupon bonds. Any other combination can be chosen. Generally the

3. The zero coupon bonds are priced as if they had a frequency of two coupons per year. This makes their yield and pricing consistent with that for the bonds in the investment portfolio.

parameter that affects the value of the portfolio most is changes in the yield curve. If the portfolio plus hedge is PVBP neutral, then this will be insulated under small parallel shifts. We consider the hedge performance under a number of scenarios.

4.2 Parallel shifts

Using each hedge instrument separately, the following hedge portfolios can be constructed.

Zero Coupon Hedge Characteristics

	Face val ($m)	Value ($)	PVBP	DMod	Convexity
Portfolio		10,245,860	2,931.154	2.933	1.262
Hedge 1	−22.4835	(17,375,939)	(2,931.154)	1.687	0.562
Hedge 2	−13.583	(6,417,689)	(2,931.154)	4.567	1.413

This means that either $22,483,500 face value of the zero coupon maturing on 1/12/00, or $13,583,000 face value of the zero coupon bond maturing on the 1/12/06, can be used as a hedge. In both cases, the hedge PVBP exactly cancels the PVBP of the portfolio. We now examine what happens to the portfolio and the hedges under various parallel yield curve shifts.

Performance of Hedge 1 Under Parallel Shifts

	Portfolio change ($)	Hedge 1 change ($)	Difference ($)	Diff/bp
−100bp	612,173.41	(597,640.41)	14,533.00	145.33
−10bp	58,863.24	(58,730.69)	132.55	13.25
−1bp	5,863.57	(5,862.88)	0.68	0.68
zero	—	—	—	—
+1bp	(5,858.53)	5,860.62	2.09	2.09
+10bp	(58,359.43)	58,504.69	145.27	14.53
+100bp	(561,744.81)	575,036.94	13,292.14	132.92

Performance of Hedge 2 Under Parallel Shifts

	Portfolio change ($)	Hedge 2 change ($)	Difference ($)	Diff/bp
−100bp	612,173.41	(615,234.15)	(3,060.74)	(30.61)
−10bp	58,863.24	(58,891.66)	(28.43)	(2.84)
−1bp	5,863.57	(5,863.72)	(0.15)	(0.15)
zero	—	—	—	—
+1bp	(5,858.53)	5,858.08	(0.45)	(0.45)
+10bp	(58,359.43)	58,328.25	(31.18)	(3.12)
+100bp	(561,744.81)	558,842.74	(2,902.06)	(29.02)

The tables above show the difference in value of the investment portfolio and the hedge under parallel shifts (where all yields change by the same amount). For small shifts (of plus or minus one basis point), the difference is small. The hedge performs well by countering the change in value of the portfolio. Where the shifts are more extreme (plus/minus 100 basis points), there is significant difference between the change in value of the portfolio and the hedge. Even when expressed as a per basis point change, it is significant.

4.3 Non-parallel shifts

Although the hedge performance is less than perfect when there are large parallel shifts, the hedge still offers a large amount of protection. The worst case above, the unhedged portfolio changes in value by $612,173, while the worst hedge decreases this to less than $15,000.

What happens when the yield curve shifts in a non-parallel manner? To illustrate this, we consider steepening and flattening of the curve.

4.4 Digression: non-parallel yield curve movement

Over short time periods, the yield curve changes. A hedged bond portfolio tries to insulate the effects of these changes from the underlying portfolio. It will never be possible to completely remove sensitivity to change. In practice, hedge strategies are implemented to remove the gross sensitivities. Analysis has shown that most short-period movement of the yield curve is parallel. PVBP matching removes most of this sensitivity. The next most important effect is due slope changes of the yield curve. It is hard to specify exactly how the curve steepens or flattens. Are these changes in the yield curve or the zero curve? Is there a pivot point, or does the curve shift as well? To explore the effect of slope, we will use the modified duration curve as our yield curve. We apply linear slope changes to the curve using the two-year point as a pivot. To gauge effects where the pivot is elsewhere, a parallel shift can be combined with the slope change.

Slope changes (measured in basis points per year) can be superimposed on the modified duration curve. Sample changes are shown on the curve below.

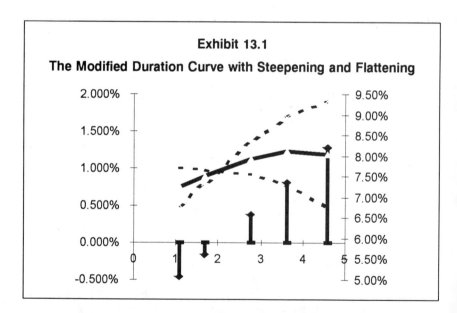

Exhibit 13.1

The Modified Duration Curve with Steepening and Flattening

The original portfolio and the hedge portfolios are revalued under these scenarios.

Performance of Hedge 1 Under Curve Slope Changes

	Portfolio change ($)	Hedge 1 change ($)	Difference ($)	Diff/(bp/y)
+50bp/y	(1,282,135.25)	(371,522.82)	(1,653,658.06)	(33,073.16)
+10bp/y	(358,305.51)	(92,040.48)	(450,345.99)	(45,034.60)
zero	—	—	—	—
−10bp/y	387,200.20	91,486.64	478,686.85	47,868.68
−50bp/y	1,749,027.50	362,660.88	2,111,688.38	42,233.77

Performance of Hedge 2 Under Curve Slope Changes

	Portfolio change ($)	Hedge 2 change ($)	Difference ($)	Diff/(bp/y)
+50bp/y	(1,282,135.25)	2,379,337.48	1,097,202.23	21,944.04
+10bp/y	(358,305.51)	707,856.75	349,551.24	34,955.12
zero	—	—	—	—
−10bp/y	387,200.20	(800,830.20)	(413,630.00)	(41,363.00)
−50bp/y	1,749,027.50	(3,899,959.71)	(2,150,932.22)	(43,018.64)

These changes are now very large. The hedge is not very effective against non-parallel curve changes.

4.5 Duration matching

Under parallel shifts, a single hedge instrument performs well when the move is small. This is due to the significant difference in the structure of the portfolio to that of the hedge. A significant improvement can be attained if a mix of the hedge instruments is used. If a combination is used such that both the PVBP and the modified duration of the hedge and the original portfolio are the same, the hedge is as follows.

Combination Hedge

	Face val ($m)	Value ($)	PVBP	DMod	Convexity
Portfolio		10,245,860	2,931.154	2.933	1.262
Hedge 1	−7.335	(5,668,843)	(956.279)	1.687	(0.183)
Hedge 2	−9.152	(4,323,939)	(1,974.875)	4.567	(0.952)
Hedge Total	—	(9,992,781.936)	(2,931.154)	2.933	(1.135)

Under the parallel shift scenarios, the hedge performance is marginally better than the single instrument hedges. There is still a mismatch when the shifts are large.

Performance of Combination Hedge Under Parallel Shifts

	Portfolio change ($)	DMod Hedge change ($)	Difference ($)	Diff/bp
−100bp	612,173.41	(609,494.25)	2,679.16	26.79
−10bp	58,863.24	(58,839.15)	24.09	2.41
−1bp	5,863.57	(5,863.45)	0.12	0.12
zero	—	—	—	—
+1bp	(5,858.53)	5,858.91	0.38	0.38
+10bp	(58,359.43)	58,385.81	26.39	2.64
+100bp	(561,744.81)	564,126.05	2,381.24	23.81

When the non-parallel shifts of the previous section are applied, the duration-matched hedge performs significantly better than the single instrument hedges.

Performance of Combination Hedge Under Curve Slope Changes

	Portfolio change ($)	DMod Hedge change ($)	Difference ($)	Diff/(bp/y)
+50bp/y	(1,282,135.25)	1,481,878.37	199,743.12	3,994.86
+10bp/y	(358,305.51)	446,892.92	88,587.41	8,858.74
zero	—	—	—	—
−10bp/y	387,200.20	(509,714.77)	(122,514.57)	(12,251.46)
−50bp/y	1,749,027.50	(2,509,293.78)	(760,266.29)	(15,205.33)

Even with this duration-matched hedge, there is still significant deviation between the investment portfolio and the hedge.

4.6 Further improving the hedge portfolio

The portfolio in the above case study was hedged using only two zero coupon instruments. These differ significantly from the underlying portfolio. The timing and size of cashflows is different. They are sensitive to different parts of the yield curve. Despite this, they are effective under parallel shifts, and partially effective with slope changes. There are a number of ways in which hedging can be improved.

4.7 Scenario analysis and optimisation

If more hedge instruments are available, an optimal hedge can be constructed using scenario analysis. This is usually a numerical optimisation procedure. The inputs are the characteristics of the underlying portfolio and the hedge instruments. A number of yield curve scenarios are defined. These include the most likely changes to the curve, plus a few disaster scenarios (large moves or shape changes). The scenarios can be probability weighted. The optimisation procedure finds the portfolio that minimises the mismatch between the hedge and the underlying portfolio. This technique, although numerically complex, can yield very effective results.

4.8 Dynamic hedging

The portfolios in this case study were set up with *static hedges*. Once set up, they were not altered—even where the yield curve changes were large. In reality, the hedge can be adjusted periodically. This is called *dynamic hedging*. A dynamic hedge is rebalanced whenever the value of the portfolio changes. Changes can be due to natural time effects (such as interest payments and maturing bonds), or due to yield movement. Various criteria can be set as to when a rebalance should be performed. These can be a dollar mismatch, or a yield curve change.

With frequent rebalancing, hedging can be very effective—even where the hedge instruments differ markedly from the underlying portfolio. A trade off must be made between hedge cost (both of the hedge portfolio and the resources required to manage it) and effectiveness.

4.9 Use of derivatives

Another method for hedging is by the use of derivatives. Futures contracts are the simplest form of derivative instrument commonly used for hedging. Their use is so widespread that they are often treated as vanilla instruments. More complex derivatives such as options or forward contracts can be very effective in removing risk. They can also allow a portfolio manager to capture upside which would normally be lost with vanilla hedges (for example, an option can protect against interest rate rises whilst allowing the portfolio to profit from rate falls). The main problem with using derivatives is their cost. Options usually have a large premium associated with them. This needs to be considered within the overall portfolio management brief.

Chapter 14

Portfolio Insurance

by Steuart Roe

1. INTRODUCTION

The aim of this chapter is to provide an introduction to the main concepts of portfolio insurance. Portfolio insurance is a generic term used to describe investment strategies that involve the capital protection of an investor's funds. For example, an investor may not be prepared to accept a negative return over a one-year period.

The simplest way to insure an investment is to buy a put option over the investment, struck at the current value of the investment. The put option protects the investor from capital depreciation on the investment by paying the investor the depreciation, if any, at the expiry of the option. *Exhibit 14.1* shows the value of an insured investment at the expiry of the option and the value of the same investment without protection as the value of the underlying investment varies. The difference between the insured investment and the uninsured investment, if the portfolio value rises, is the cost of the option or insurance.

When executing a portfolio insurance program over a portfolio of investments there are many things a fund manager must consider. For instance, how much will it cost? Should the option be purchased or replicated? If an option is purchased, would it be exchange-traded or over-the-counter? How will I pay? How credit worthy is the option seller? What documentation is required? What if I change the composition of my underlying assets? How will I monitor my exposures? How will cash flows be insured? Et cetera. The answers to these questions are rarely black and white.

The chapter examines:

- option-based portfolio insurance;
- cost of protection;
- synthetic option replication;
- constant proportion portfolio insurance; and
- risks associated with portfolio insurance.

Exhibit 14.1

Pay-off from an Uninsured Portfolio vs an Insured Portfolio

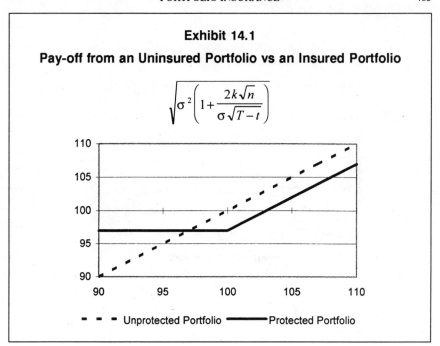

$$\sqrt{\sigma^2\left(1+\frac{2k\sqrt{n}}{\sigma\sqrt{T-t}}\right)}$$

- - - Unprotected Portfolio ———— Protected Portfolio

2. OPTION-BASED PORTFOLIO INSURANCE

When choosing an insurance program the first decision is to decide what and when the payoff is required. A minimum return objective needs to be set, known as the floor. The second question is to decide how the insurance or put option is to be paid. One way to pay for the put option is to sell call options.

Let us suppose an investor wanted to ensure that in one year's time his investments were at least as valuable then as they are today, that is, a floor of 0%. If put and call options struck at the current value of investor's assets cost 4% and 10% respectively then the investor could pay for the put option by selling 40% of the call option. By selling 40% of the call option the investor has limited the capture of any increases in the value of the investments to 60%. *Exhibit 14.2* shows how the investor's portfolio of investments plus a put option less 40% of a call option combine to give the investor a zero floor and a participation rate of 60%. Paying for insurance in this manner is generally referred to as Participation-based Portfolio Insurance (PBPI).

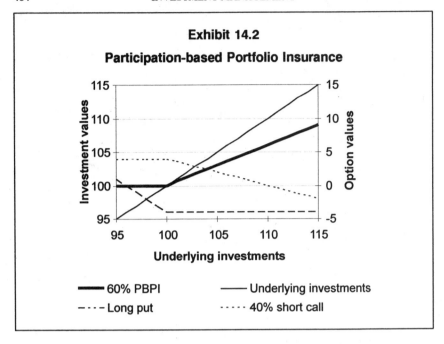

Exhibit 14.2

Participation-based Portfolio Insurance

An alternative to selling call options struck at the same level as the put option is to sell a call option struck such that its value is equivalent to the value of the put option. This method of paying for the protection *caps* the total return the investor can achieve to the strike of the call option. For instance, if, using the previous example, a call option struck at 110% of the investor's assets was worth 4% then the investor could sell this call option to pay for the put option. *Exhibit 14.3* shows how the investor's portfolio of investments plus a put option less a call option struck at 110% combine to give the investor a zero floor and 100% of any upside with the performance capped at 10%.

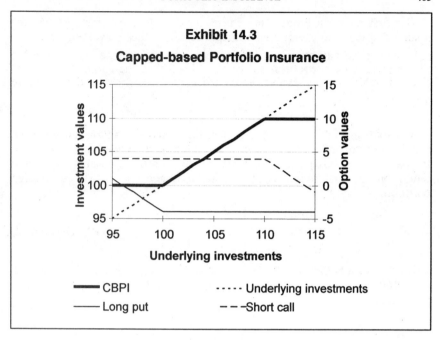

Exhibit 14.3

Capped-based Portfolio Insurance

Legend:
- **CBPI**
- **Long put**
- **····· Underlying investments**
- **– – –Short call**

There are in fact an infinite number of ways the protection can be paid for. Below, I have formally defined three different strategies that provide a fixed percentage of any upside above a floor for some time in the future. For conceptual simplicity, they refer to combinations of cash and call options to construct their desired pay outs. Other combinations using put and/or call options could be created using put-call parity to provide the same pay off.

Each of these strategies involve an investment in a zero coupon bond, maturing on the same day as the protection, with a face value equivalent to the floor. The difference between the face value of the zero coupon bond and the original investment is the amount of money the investor can lose and still meet the capital protection objective. This difference is known as the *cushion*. The cushion is then invested in call options. How many call options (n) and where the call options are struck (K) is dependent upon the desired pay off.

The first of these strategies is known as Option-based Portfolio Insurance (OBPI) and is defined by the following equations:

$$nC_{BS}(P_0, K, T - t, \sigma, i) = P_0 - F_T(1 + i)^{-(T-t)}$$

$$nK = F_T \qquad \text{.... (OBPI)}$$

Where

$$K = \frac{F_T}{n}$$

C_{BS} = standard Black-Scholes value for a call option;

P_0 = portfolio value at time of the start of the insurance program;

F_T = floor value of portfolio at maturity of the insurance program;

σ = volatility of the underlying asset; and

i = annualised risk free rate.

The first equation ensures the entire cushion is invested in options, the second that the total exercise cost equals the floor—thus preventing gearing.

If the desired pay off is to participate in some percentage (n) in the value of the underlying portfolio from the floor level then the strike should equal floor. I refer to this strategy as Participation-based Portfolio Insurance (PBPI).

$$K = F_T \qquad \text{.... (PBPI)}$$

It is sometimes necessary to place a further constraint on this strategy such that if the floor is less than the existing value of the underlying assets then the pay off is a percentage of the return. This constraint ensures that a zero return on the underlying assets results in a zero return on the insured portfolio.

$$K = P_0 - \frac{P_0 \cdot F_T}{n} \qquad F_I + n(P_0 - K) = P_0 \qquad F_T < P_0$$

$$\text{.... (PBPI constrained)}$$

$$K = F_T \text{ otherwise}$$

Exhibit 14.4 plots the pay off structure for each of these strategies. It assumes P_0 is 100, F_T is 95, volatility is 20%, an annualised risk free rate of 7% and a one year term.

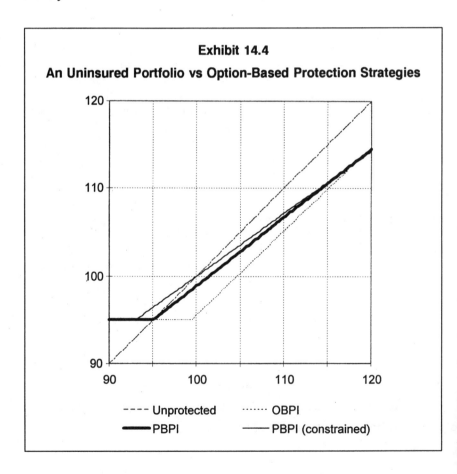

Exhibit 14.4

An Uninsured Portfolio vs Option-Based Protection Strategies

3. COST OF INSURANCE

Once the floor and the method of paying for the insurance premium have been determined, the investor needs to be satisfied as to both the short- and long-term cost of insurance. The cost of insurance is the value of an uninsured portfolio less the same portfolio insured. Likewise, the expected cost of insurance is the expected return on an uninsured portfolio less the same portfolio insured.

Note the distinction between the insurance (or put) premium, the expected cost of insurance and the actual cost of insurance. For example, if the cost of a put option on an investment was 4%, then the expected cost of insurance would be less than 4%, as there is some possibility the insurance will be called. *Exhibit 14.5* shows how the actual cost of insurance varies for a PBPI strategy with 60% participation. If the underlying asset rises then the insurance in that year is an expense to the investor. Conversely, if the underlying assets fall, then the insurance pays off, so the actual cost of protection is negative, that is, there is a claim against the insurance. For instance, a 10% rise and fall result in actual costs of insurance of 4% and minus 10% respectively.

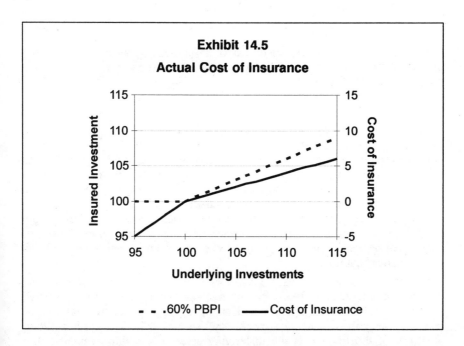

An approximation for determining the expected return on an insured portfolio is to multiply the delta equivalent of uninsured holdings by their risk premium and add the risk free rate.

$$E(\text{cost of insurance}) = E(\text{uninsured return}) - E(\text{insured return})$$
$$= r_f + r_p - (r_f + \Delta r_p)$$
$$= r_p (1 - \Delta)$$

Of course, in any given period the actual cost of protection can be varied. *Exhibit 14.6* shows the distribution of the cost of protection for a CPPI (referred to later in the chapter) program using the same assumptions in *Exhibit 14.4*. A negative cost of protection means the protection paid off.

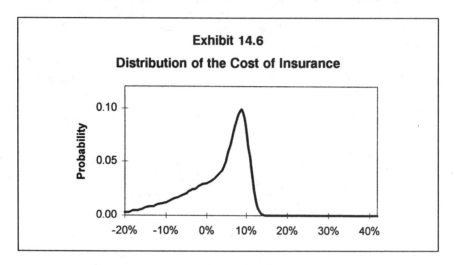

If the variability or the expected cost of insurance are unacceptable to the investor then the floor and/or the method for paying for the insurance premium will need to be modified.

4. SYNTHETIC REPLICATION

After determining the desired pay off the next question to answer is: how to implement the strategy? Probably the easiest approach would be to buy and/or sell the necessary options. Options on a wide range of securities can be traded on the various exchanges around the world. Options are available on individual company shares, stock market indices such as the S&P 500, fixed interest securities, et cetera. Furthermore, there are a large number of investment banks that will buy and sell options on an over-the-counter basis on just about anything.

However, occasionally there may not be any sellers or buyers of the desired options or, more likely, the desired options are either too expensive or too cheap. An initial attempt at deciding an options relative value is to compare the volatility implied by the options price to the expected future volatility of the returns on the underlying asset. When this is significantly different an alternative to trading the options is to replicate the options.

The standard option replication technique is called delta hedging. Delta hedging requires an amount of the asset, which the option is on, to be purchased or sold (known as the hedge) such that a small movement in the price of the asset results in the same value change in the hedge and the option. Theoretical option pricing models, such as the Black-Scholes model, allow the hedge or delta amount to be estimated.

4.1 Example 1: delta hedging

Calculate the value of a one year European at-the-money call option over an asset currently trading at $100 given that the one year annual interest rate is 7% and the expected volatility of the underlying asset is 15%.

$$C_{BS}(100,100,1,15\%,7\%) = 9.6$$

Given these assumptions and the underlying assets value in the table below, calculate the pay out from replicating the option by re-hedging the delta weekly.

The Replication column represents the value of a portfolio that has sold the call option. At time zero $9.6 is received for selling the call option, $60.5 (70.1 − 9.6) is borrowed and delta times the value of the underlying asset $70.1 (0.701 * 100) is bought. At the end of the first week the underlying asset has fallen to $98 so that the value of the portfolio at the end of the week is worth the value at the start of the week plus the appreciation in the asset value less the cost of any borrowings. In this case the value of the portfolio at the end of the first week is:

$$9.6 + 70.1 * (98/100 - 1) - (70.1 - 9.6) * ((1.07) \wedge (1/52) - 1) = 8.2$$

Week	Asset	Delta	Equity	Replication
0	100	0.70	70.1	9.6
1	98	0.65	63.7	8.2
2	96.7	0.61	59.3	7.2
3	96.2	0.60	57.4	6.9
4	98.2	0.65	63.6	8.0
5	99.3	0.67	66.9	8.6
6	102.3	0.74	76.1	10.6
7	106.2	0.82	87.2	13.4
8	107.2	0.84	89.9	14.1
.				
.				
.				
50	115.1	1.00	115.1	15.6
51	116.2	1.00	116.2	16.6
52	118.5			18.7

Because the assets value at the end of the year is $118.5, the call option should be worth $18.5. Replicating the option produced a pay-out of $18.7, very similar to the pay-out from the option. This is essentially because the actual volatility of the underlying asset proved to be very similar to the volatility predicted.

The problem with delta hedging is it is dependent upon the same assumptions as the Black-Scholes formula. Most critically, it is dependent upon a continuous and frictionless market. That is, the market does not gap up or down, there is no impact on market prices due to trading and there are no transaction costs. In the real world these assumptions are rarely valid.

The possibility of discontinuous markets (that is, market gaps) increases the value of an option. This is because an option seller risks the possibility that the market gaps. In return for this risk the seller will require a premium. Exhibit 14.7 shows the value of a portfolio attempting to replicate the pay-off of a call option using delta hedging and the pay-off of a portfolio of cash and the same option if the underlying asset were to jump to the level in the x-axis. Note that if the asset were to fall 20% then the value of the delta hedging portfolio would fall to 86 while the value of the portfolio containing the option would only fall to 91. This risk may not be acceptable to an investor considering replicating an option.

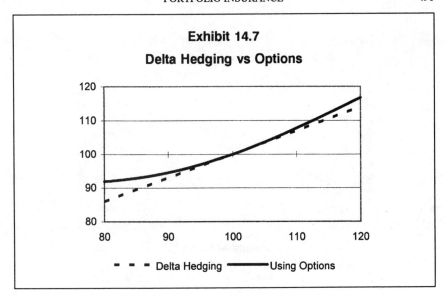

Exhibit 14.7

Delta Hedging vs Options

Where transaction costs exist, they also increase the value of options. The impact on the cost of an option and the option's implied volatility for different transaction costs is approximated in *Exhibit 14.8*. The chart clearly illustrates the sensitivity of an option's value to transaction costs.

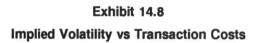

Exhibit 14.8

Implied Volatility vs Transaction Costs

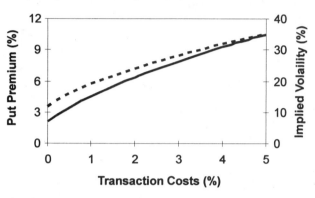

———— Put Premium   - - - Implied Volatility ,

The chart uses the volatility approximation technique developed by HE Leland for incorporating transaction costs

$$\sqrt{\sigma^2\left(1+\frac{2k\sqrt{n}}{\sigma\sqrt{T-t}}\right)}$$

Where k is transaction costs, n is the rebalancing frequency. The chart assumes σ = 12%, n = 83 and T-t = 1.

Another important factor to consider when deciding whether to replicate or not is the management and infrastructure required. Replication requires constant monitoring of positions and exposures, sophisticated computer software and hardware and qualified implementation staff. Each of these cost money. The purchase of an option can be viewed as a mechanism to outsource the management and infrastructure of replicating the option together with guaranteed performance.

Hence, the decision to replicate or not should be based upon a comparison between the value of the option being offered, if available, and the theoretical option value based on future expected volatility plus a margin for transaction costs plus a margin for gap risk plus a margin for management and infrastructure.

4.1.1 Futures

One way to significantly improve the efficiency of a hedging program is to use futures contracts as the hedging instrument. This is because futures normally have far lower transaction costs than their physical equivalents. The amount of futures contracts to be traded to hedge a given amount of underlying is given by:

futures contracts = hedge/futures equivalent

= hedge/(index * contract multiplier * $e^{(i-d)(T-t)}$)

Where

i is the continuous risk free interest rate;

d is the continuous dividend rate; and

T-t is the term of the futures contract.

4.2 Example 2

In Example 1, the delta on the option to be replicated was 0.701 at the start of the period. Using the same assumptions as example 1 calculate the amount of futures contracts required to hedge 1000 of these options if the futures contract expires in three months and the contract multiplier is 25.

$$1000 * 0.701 * 100/(100 * 25 * (1.07) \wedge (1/4)) = 27.6$$

The problem with futures contracts is that they may not be available on the assets to be hedged. One way to compensate for this problem is to use futures contracts on a similar asset or assets and *beta* adjust the amount to be traded. The equation for the amount of futures contracts to be traded to hedge a given amount of underlying becomes:

beta * hedge/futures equivalent

In addition, if futures are used to hedge a portfolio that does not exactly match the futures contract then, even with beta adjusting the hedge, tracking error may arise. In a dynamic hedging approach to portfolio insurance the tracking error can be built into the management. For instance, a portfolio insurance program could be run using index futures as the hedging instrument for an actively managed portfolio of equities. If the equities outperform the index, after beta adjustments, then the strike of the option relative to the index can be lowered. Hence the outperformance serves to reduce the cost of protection. Conversely, and even more importantly, if underperformance occurs then the strike must be raised if the capital protection objective is to be met.

4.2.1 The 1980s experience

During the early to mid-1980s portfolio insurance experienced phenomenal growth in popularity. Funds under management in the US grew from nothing to an estimated $90 billion. When the stock market crashed in October 87 some funds employing portfolio insurance were unable to meet their desired level of protection. In fact, the Brady Commission report into the crash of 1987 found that portfolio insurance was partly responsible for the crash due to the large volume of selling required by the portfolio insurers because of their hedging requirements. As a consequence of this combination of factors, portfolio insurance fell from grace and became a "dirty" word in the investment community. Proponents of portfolio insurance have disputed these findings.

Nonetheless, portfolio insurance is alive and well in some form or other today. This is due to the risk-averse nature of people. In fact, all rationale investors would prefer to have all the upside with none of the downside of investing. It just boils down to the cost of protection versus their risk tolerance.

5. CONSTANT PROPORTION PORTFOLIO INSURANCE

In 1986, Fisher Black published an article proposing Constant Proportion Portfolio Insurance (CPPI). The aim of CPPI is to provide a portfolio insurance technique that protects investors from gaps in markets. CPPI uses a simplistic methodology that does not use option pricing theory and is intuitively appealing. It works as follows:

1. *Establish the floor price.* The floor price is the level that the portfolio's value could fall to and still meet the minimum return objective, if all the assets of the fund were invested in a zero coupon bond that matured on the same day as the insurance program.

2. *Calculate the cushion.* The cushion is the difference between the current value of the portfolio and the floor. The cushion represents how much money the fund can lose at the instant of calculation and still meet the minimum return objective.

3. *Determine exposure to risky assets.* The risky assets are the assets the portfolio is investing whose return the portfolio is aiming to capture. The exposure to the risky assets is the maximum amount that can be invested in the risky assets and still meet the minimum return objective of the portfolio. It is determined by dividing the cushion by the percentage fall (or crash factor) the investors are attempting to protect themselves against from the risky assets. Hence, if the risky assets were to instantaneously fall by the crash factor then the value of the portfolio would equal the floor.

4. *Invest the portfolio.* Invest the portfolio in the risky assets to the level of the exposure determined in step 3 with the balance invested in the riskless asset. The riskless asset is a zero coupon bond that matures on the same day as the portfolio insurance program. For most short-dated, one year or less, insurance programs cash or short-term bills typically act as a reasonable substitute for the riskless asset. Note also that the exposure is bounded to be non-negative and typically by the value of the portfolio. The later boundary condition is to prevent gearing.

5. *Repeat steps 1 to 4.* In practice, step 4 would only be repeated if the theoretically required exposure was significantly different from the actual exposure. What defines "significantly" is typically different from one portfolio insurer to another. Some portfolio insurers have hard trading rules while others have soft rules. Some of the factors that determine whether a portfolio is rebalanced or not include the liquidity of the risky assets, transaction costs and the mandate of the insurer.

The hedging process of CPPI works in a similar way to delta hedging a call option. When the risky assets rise in value, the value of the portfolio rises and hence the value of the cushion rises. If the value of the cushion rises, the fund can afford to risk more and so the maximum exposure the portfolio can have to the risky asset rises. The opposite occurs when the risky asset falls in value. Or, put more simply, you buy when the market rises and sell when the market falls.

One important difference between CPPI and option-based portfolio insurance strategies is that if the value of the portfolio ever falls to the floor level then, under CPPI, the portfolio must be fully invested in the riskless asset. If the risky asset was then to increase in value, then the portfolio would not participate in any of this gain nor could any exposure to the risky asset be taken. Whereas, using options, some of this gain may be captured and, through delta expansion, an exposure to the risky asset may arise.

The formula for CPPI is given by:

$$E = mc$$

Where

E = Exposure to the risky asset

m = risk factor

  = 1/crash factor

c = cushion

  = $P_t - F_T(1 + i)^{T-t}$

i = annualised risk free rate

P_t = Portfolio value at time t

F_T = floor value of portfolio at maturity of the insurance program.

Exhibit 14.9 shows a typical pay-off profile of a CPPI program over a 1 year term. The impact of the insurance program is to smooth the returns relative to the same portfolio uninsured.

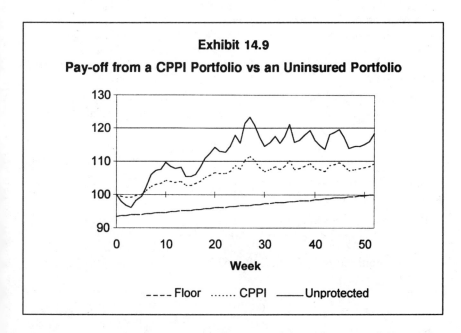

Exhibit 14.9

Pay-off from a CPPI Portfolio vs an Uninsured Portfolio

Exhibit 14.10 is a scatter diagram giving the return from a CPPI program for different returns on the same portfolio uninsured. Unlike the pay-off from options, the pay-off from CPPI is dependent upon the path the market takes over the life of the protection program. This means that for any given return on an uninsured portfolio the return on the same portfolio insured is not fixed. *Exhibit 14.10* also shows the curved pay-off profile from CPPI.

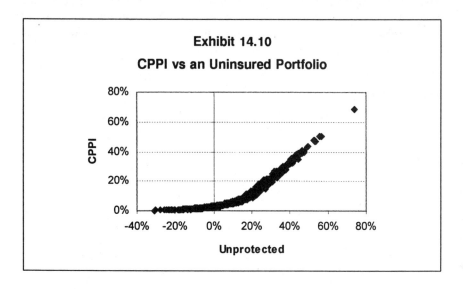

Exhibit 14.10

CPPI vs an Uninsured Portfolio

5.1 Example 3: constant proportion portfolio insurance

Suppose an investor wanted to invest $100 in the asset described in Example 2. Furthermore, the investor wanted to ensure that the capital was insured such that in one year's time it was no less than it is today and that the investor wished to run a CPPI program to achieve this with a crash factor of 20%.

The table below shows the floor, the cushion, the exposure to the underlying and riskless assets and the value of the investment at the end of each week.

For instance, at the beginning of the first week:

Floor   = 100/1.07 = 93.5
Cushion = 100 − 93.5 = 6.5
Exposure = 6.5/0.2 = 32.7
Cash   = 100 − 32.7 = 67.3

At the end of the first week the portfolio's value is:

$$\text{Portfolio} = 32.7 * 98/100 + 67.3 * 1.07 \wedge (1/52) = 99.4$$

Week	Floor	Cushion	Exposure	Cash	Portfolio
0	93.5	6.5	32.7	67.3	100.0
1	93.6	5.9	29.3	70.2	99.4
2	93.7	5.4	27.2	72.0	99.1
3	93.8	5.3	26.3	72.8	99.1
4	93.9	5.8	28.9	70.8	99.7
5	94.1	6.1	30.4	69.7	100.1
6	94.2	7.0	34.8	66.3	101.2
7	94.3	8.3	41.3	61.3	102.6
8	94.4	8.6	43.0	60.0	103.0
.					
.					
.					
50	99.7	8.3	41.7	66.4	108.1
51	99.9	8.7	43.4	65.1	108.6
52	100.0	9.5	47.5	62.0	109.5

At the end of the year the investor's portfolio should be worth $109.5. Using capped, OBPI or PBPI strategies to protect the portfolio would have resulted in portfolio values of $115.3, $112.0 and $112.6 respectively.

CPPI can also be run over multiple assets or asset classes with different crash factors for each different asset or asset class. For instance, a portfolio of domestic equities, international equities and domestic bonds could be run with crash factors of 15%, 12% and a 2% rise in bond yields.

Exhibit 14.11 shows some typical distribution profiles for an uninsured portfolio, the same portfolio insured for a zero floor using CPPI and PBPI. The spike in the PBPI distribution is because all negative returns on the uninsured portfolio result in exactly a zero return insured portfolio.

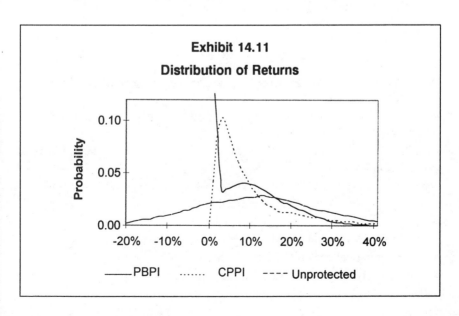

Exhibit 14.11

Distribution of Returns

―――PBPI   ······ CPPI   ---- Unprotected

5.2 Example 4: a basket of options versus an option on a basket

Suppose we have a portfolio comprising $50 of asset A and $25 of asset B. The volatilities of asset A and B are 10% and 20% respectively, the correlation between asset A and B is 0.5, neither asset pays a dividend and one year interest rates are 7%. What are the value of one year at-the-money European put options on asset A and B and the portfolio/basket of asset A and B?

Asset A

$$P_{BS}(50,50,1,10\%,7\%) = 0.689$$

Asset B

$$P_{BS}(25,25,1,20\%,7\%) = 1.195$$

Portfolio A + B

Variance (A + B) = Weight$_A^2$ * Variance(A) + Weight$_B^2$ * Variance(B) + 2 * Weight$_A$ * Weight$_B$ * Volatility(A) * Volatility(B) * Correlation(A,B)

= $0.666^2 * 0.1^2 + 0.333^2 * 0.2^2 + 2 * 0.666 * 0.333 * 0.1 * 0.2 * 0.5$

= 0.01333

Volatility (A + B) = $0.01333^{0.5}$

= 11.55%

$$P_{BS}(75,75,1,11.55\%,7\%) = 1.395$$

Note that the option on the basket cost $1.395 while the basket of options costs $1.884. The basket of options cost more because there is possibility of one of the individual options expiring in-the-money while the basket option expires out-of-the-money. For example, if, at expiry, asset A was worth $40 and B was worth $35 then the put option on asset A would be worth $10 while the put option on the basket would expire worthless.

6. OTHER RISKS

Other factors to consider when considering implementing an insurance program include:

- *Credit* Are the option/futures counter parties of sufficient creditworthiness?
- *Documentation* Does the documentation cover all scenarios? How binding is the transaction?
- *Systems* How stable are the systems? What happens if they go down?
- *Accuracy* Have the systems been audited?
- *Completeness* Do the systems contain every transaction? What reconciliation procedures exist?
- *Error* What happens if there is a dealing error?
- *Liquidity* Is there sufficient liquid capital to support any funding requirements?

- *People*   Are they qualified? Is it overly dependent upon key people?
- *Culture*   Does a control environment exist?

7. CONCLUSION

Portfolio insurance is an investment strategy designed to meet the objectives of investors with specific market risk tolerances. However, before an investor decides to use portfolio insurance it is important that a thorough understanding of the issues involved is gained and accepted. Follow the checklist:

1. define the payoff;
2. understand the cost;
3. determine your tolerance to under performing the desired payoff;
4. appreciate when the program will fail; and
5. accept the non-market risks.

Chapter 15

Indexation of Portfolios

by Frances Cowell

1. WHAT IS INDEXATION?

Tangerines or lemons?

How do you go about choosing securities to hold in your investment portfolio? An approach taken by a Polish investor was to inscribe each of 70 tangerines with a stock code. Then he sat his pet chimpanzee "Karolina" down before the tangerines and recorded which ones she ate. This indicated the stocks to buy and yielded impressive results. Over a three month period Karolina chose five winning stocks, achieving a rate of return of 10%, far superior to the return over the same period achieved by a leading stockbroker.[1]

Most investors will eschew using chimpanzees, pigs' entrails or tea leaves (or at least will not admit to using such techniques). For the serious investor, the answer to this question is "it depends". It depends upon what information can be obtained about various stocks and bonds. The investor who is certain that a particular share is going to beat all others will logically buy as much of the stock as he or she can. The flaw in this approach is that, for the investor to be so sure, he or she must have special information, such as insider information. Access to this cannot always be guaranteed and even if it was, using it to profit from trading risks prosecution in most (but not all) jurisdictions.

Information remains the single most important factor. The job of the professional investment manager is to gain an information edge over her or his rivals. There are two main ways of doing this. The first is to find some legal way of obtaining exclusive access to the best information; the second is to make the best use possible of publicly available information. To this end, stock analysts comb through all the publicly available information they can to identify some new "twist" which will indicate which securities are going to do better or worse than the market. With so much brainpower devoted to working out the true value of this stock or that bond, security prices are usually at about the level they should be to reflect likely returns and risks: their "fair price". This makes it very difficult for the investment manager to consistently choose stocks that will give better returns than the market as a whole. Also, it is expensive.

Another approach is to buy a bit of everything in proportion to its weighting in the market. This is the essence of indexation. If your chimpanzee ate all the tangerines, you have a sort of index portfolio.

---

1. *The Economist*, 6 July, 1996, p 25.

If it is well-constructed, the index portfolio will rise and fall with the market it is designed to match. Because the portfolio does not seek to benefit from the relative returns to individual securities, there is no occasion to "take profits" or "cut losses". Thus the portfolio is effectively a "buy and hold": once set in place the manager can in theory pay it scant attention—although the last statement is true only up to a point.

Because indexation creates a low maintenance buy and hold portfolio, its costs compare favourably to one consisting of selected stocks.[2] Naturally this cost advantage depends on the costs of trading the component securities. For example, a portfolio of Australian equities which has a turnover of 30% will cost the portfolio from 30 to 80 basis points (hundredths of one per cent). For an international portfolio the costs are even higher, because both trading and custodian fees are significantly higher than those for domestic portfolios.

The index portfolio has another cost advantage over the actively managed portfolio: low management fees. The manager passes on to the investor the money saved from not having to conduct expensive research and analysis of the relative value of individual securities. As one would expect, management fees vary widely between markets and between managers. For an Australian equities portfolio, the difference in management fees between active and index portfolios is in the order of half of 1% per year, or 50 basis points. For an international equities portfolio the difference is about 35 basis points.

Indexed portfolios not only cost less to run than the active variety, they are an altogether less risky proposition. While both portfolios will win and lose with the market in which they are invested, the active portfolio runs the additional risk that the securities it has bought will do better or worse than the market. In contrast, the index portfolio reflects only the market performance without the additional excitement of bets placed on individual securities.

Armies of analysts find and apply the all important information which keeps securities prices fair. If all assets within a market were indexed then this information would not be used; it would be wasted, with the result that the market would be inefficient. In such a world it would be easy to achieve better than market returns using publicly available information. Indexation would then become much less popular.

The index portfolio can be sucessful only within a market which is kept efficient by the efforts of active portfolio managers.

Meanwhile, the index portfolio allows the investor something of a free ride, benefiting from all this feverish activity which keeps the market efficient, while incurring only a fraction of the costs and risks involved in achieving and maintaining this market efficiency.

Yet very few portfolios are completely indexed. Most investors recognise the need to combine active and index approaches.

2.   Which must be traded frequently to benefit from the investment manager's judgments.

2. INDEXATION MEETS CAPM

To appreciate how indexation fits into an investment portfolio it is necessary to take a look at the Capital Asset Pricing Model (CAPM). This model was developed in the 1960s and is now used extensively by professional investment managers to analyse and manage the riskiness of their portfolios. CAPM says that investors receive extra returns for taking on additional risk, but only if this extra risk cannot be diversified away: taking on unnecessary (diversifiable) risk does not lead to an improvement in investment returns. CAPM can either be applied to a single asset relative to another, a group of assets within a portfolio or a portfolio of assets—relative to a nominated benchmark.

CAPM is most often applied in the context of domestic equities portfolios, but can also be applied in a more general context. CAPM helps analyse assets against some kind of benchmark. The selected benchmark could, for example, be the local sharemarket or it might be some measure of global markets. Alternatively, the benchmark could be set as a separate portfolio of assets. CAPM divides return and risk into three components which are called alpha, beta and residual risk. The return to asset i (r_i) is expressed as follows:

$$r_i = alpha_i + beta_i \cdot (r_m i - r_f) + residual_i \qquad (1)$$

Where:

r_m is the return to the market

r_f is the risk free rate of return

Thus the return and risk to an asset can be thought of as having three components:

alpha: intentional or active risk

beta: inherent or market risk

residual: incidental risk or error

Past returns are not taken into account. CAPM agrees with efficient market theory that the future returns to an asset do not depend on its returns in the past. CAPM does not take into account transactions costs and other market frictions.

Alpha is the amount by which the market has underpriced asset i. This is what active managers seek to gain their performance advantage. Increasing the expected alpha of a portfolio will increase its expected return. If markets are efficient, alpha is equal to zero.

Beta is the sensitivity, or covariance, of asset i to moves in the market. The market's beta is defined as 1.0, so an asset that moves exactly in line with the market has a beta of 1.0. An asset with a beta of 1.2, for example, will overshoot market rises and falls by 20%. On the other hand, an asset with a beta of 0.9 will match only 90% of moves in both directions. A portfolio consisting entirely of cash will have a beta of zero relative to the equity market. Beta is defined as the covariance of the returns to asset$_i$ and market$_m$ divided by the variance of the return to the market:

$$beta_i = covariance \ (r_i \ r_m)/variance \ (r_m) \qquad (2)$$

Because beta is related to the market return, it cannot be eliminated by diversification without also eliminating the portfolio's market return. Increasing the beta of a portfolio will increase both risk and return.

The residual is that part of an asset's return that is not explained by either alpha or beta and is a random variable. The residual values of a group of assets within a period will average zero; similarly, the residual returns to a single asset will average zero over time. Adding residual risk to a portfolio will do nothing to increase its expected return, so investment managers have every incentive to eliminate this risk. They do this by diversifying the portfolio as much as practicable.

Alpha and residual risk are collectively known as specific risk because they are risks that are unique to that asset or portfolio. In the context of an index portfolio, specific risk is usually called tracking error.

The index portfolio seeks to achieve a portfolio with an alpha of zero; usually, but not always, a beta of one, and a residual as close as possible to zero, which will give zero tracking error. By contrast, the active manager seeks a positive alpha and possibly a beta which is somewhat different from one. Thus the index portfolio is a low risk portfolio with particular emphasis on low specific risk.

Exhibit 15.1 shows the difference in performance between an active and an indexed equity portfolio over a 12 month period. The distance between the the portfolios' performance and that of the market is specific risk.

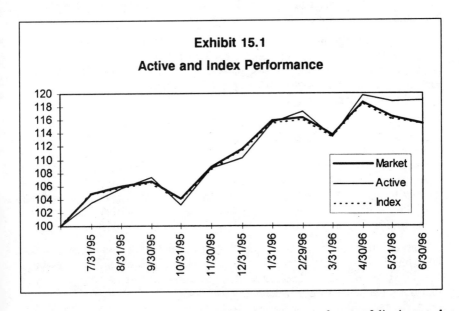

This low specific risk is important in the context of a portfolio invested with many managers over a range of asset classes. This is because investment managers have the resources to analyse easily the *market* risk of each of the markets in which they are invested. In contrast, effective management of the *specific* risk of each individual portfolio in addition to its *market* risk is challenging for even the most sophisticated analytic tools. It follows that portfolios comprising mostly market risk with little or no specific risk are much easier than high specific risk (active) portfolios to integrate to a complex portfolio which is invested in many markets.

This can be a powerful advantage for another reason. Research shows that for such a diversified portfolio, 70% of total performance variation is due to asset allocation, while only 30% is attributable to stock selection. By using index portfolios the investor is able to devote greater analytic resources where these will make the most difference.

Low specific risk portfolios, such as index portfolios, resemble their benchmark. Any futures contract based on that benchmark can therefore be used as a surrogate for the index portfolio. This is particularly so in the case of equities, and can greatly facilitate liquidity management. Futures can be traded quickly and cheaply to match portfolio cash flows without affecting the portfolio balance. Futures contracts and options on futures can also facilitate the implementation of tactical asset allocation decisions, as reweighting can be effected without incurring the substantial costs of transacting physical assets. Low specific risk is also an advantage when entering into stock index arbitrage transactions (more of this later).

The low specific risk of index portfolios is useful when constructing global portfolios because physical assets can be held in the investor's domestic market and the returns swapped for those on international indices. This enables the investor to reap the benefits of dividend imputation tax credits which are lost on physical assets held offshore. It can also reduce custodian and other administrative costs.

An important feature of indexation is its cost effectiveness. Indexation can minimise transaction, management and administrative costs. Because CAPM does not accommodate these costs, index portfolios are a good instrument to use in the context of a diversified portfolio constructed on the basis of a CAPM type analysis.

Transaction costs are minimised within index portfolios because they follow a basic buy and hold strategy which gives extremely low portfolio turnover. A well constructed index portfolio can have zero turnover because the normal cash flows to the portfolio—such as dividends and coupons—are usually sufficient to facilitate periodic rebalancing as it becomes necessary. This reduces the costs of brokerage, commissions, taxes and duties on sale and purchases of securities. It also reduces the cost of market impact, which is the hidden transaction cost.

Market impact arises from adverse changes in the price of a security which are caused by the fact of trading it. It is a particular problem for very large portfolios. When trading less liquid securities, market impact can be so large that the trade becomes a self-defeating exercise.

Because the index fund does not seek to identify outperforming assets, management costs are minimised. It therefore has very low research costs, a saving which is passed on to the investor through very low management fees. Performance analysis is simplified by eliminating the need for elaborate attribution analysis, and administration costs are reduced because transactions are kept to a minimum.

Indexers are sometimes accused of naively believing that CAPM can be strictly applied in real markets. This is often unjust, as indexers are in a good position to recognise the departure of theory from practice. CAPM makes a number of assumptions that clearly do not apply in the real world: zero transactions costs is one; another is that reliable return and covariance data is always available. More importantly, although they can be difficult to identify, non-zero alphas certainly occur in the real world.[3]

Whether or not one subscribes to the efficient market hypothesis, there are several very good reasons why investors choose indexation for most, or even all, of their investment portfolios.

3. WHO USES INDEXATION?

Professional investment managers such as banks and stockbrokers, insurance companies and pension fund trustees and sponsors are the dominant users of indexation for a variety of reasons. Of course the most obvious is cost. Small portfolio investors are another example. Often these investors would prefer to invest in riskier, actively managed portfolios, but cannot because their fund is too small to meet the minimum fee scales which often apply to actively managed portfolios. If they are also unwilling or unable to invest in pooled or comingled funds such as unit trusts or mutual funds, indexation is the logical alternative.

An important and growing group of users of indexation are the large (that is, greater than US$2 billion) pension funds. To these investors, the main allure of indexation is that it is an efficient way of investing large funds, with:

- controlled risk, meaning minimum specific risk;
- minimised transaction costs; and
- minimised market impact.

Some large funds farm out management of their portfolios between several, sometimes dozens, of asset managers all operating in the same market. This leads to a further problem for these investors. This is that the use of multiple managers within a market can have the effect that the sum of all these active managers' investment decisions amounts to a very large index portfolio—but the fund is still paying active fees. This is known as a "closet index" and is clearly suboptimal.

The investor can overcome this problem by adopting what has come to be known as the "core and satellite" approach. Within any given market, the fund invests a core of 50 or 60% of its assets in one index portfolio, with the rest allocated to a small number of active managers with mandates to aggressively manage their portfolios. This approach, if effected properly, has a number of advantages:

1. It minimises the problem of market impact which otherwise would limit the investment manager's ability to assume the risks necessary to achieve acceptable returns.

---

3.   Evidence of this is the superior returns achieved by some investment managers.

2. The active portfolios are more likely to meet their given objectives, because achieving better than market returns is much easier for small to medium portfolios than for large ones.

3. It reduces the likelihood of running a closet index because the investor has appointed a smaller number of active managers in the same market.

4. It facilitates the identification and reward of better than market performance by active managers.

Global asset managers find indexation an attractive means of gaining cost effective exposure to overseas markets. There are two ways in which indexation can improve the efficiency of global portfolio management.

The first is by simply indexing the securities within each target market. This focuses management resources on the choice of which countries to invest in. Empirical research into the performance of globally diversified portfolios supports this decision, because the results usually show that approximately 70% of the variability of returns is attributable to selection of markets, with only 30% due to security selection within markets. Logically, therefore, the global manager will devote management resources to that aspect of the fund which is likely to deliver the best results (that is, country selection and allocation). At the same time he or she eliminates the complexities of trying to manage portfolio specific risk in individual markets—often in an awkwardly different time zone. This leaves time to focus on optimising and managing the risks attributable to the markets themselves and allocating between them. Indexation offers the additional benefits of minimising management, transactions and administration costs.

The second way is to combine indexation with asset swaps. This is very useful to global managers who are subject to domestic tax. This works by arranging for a financial intermediary to swap the return on one asset, or basket of assets, for another. The global investment manager receives, over a fixed period, usually one, two or three years, the return to an agreed international asset or basket of assets. The manager pays the return to domestic assets plus a margin. The benefit to the global manager is that physical assets can be held domestically and so earn tax credits on dividends. Part of this benefit is given up in the form of the margin paid to the intermediary, but part is retained by the fund. Structured correctly, this can be a most efficient means of global investing for a taxable investor.

Exhibit 15.2

Asset Swap Between Investors in Markets A and B

Investor A		Investor B
+ Return on Market A	*Earned on index portfolio of physical assets held*	+ Return on Market B
− Return on Market A	*Swapped asset returns*	− Return on Market B
+ Return on Market B	*Swapped asset returns*	+ Return on Market A
+ Imputation tax credits A	*Earned on index portfolio of physical assets held*	+ Imputation tax credits A
− Margin		− Margin
+ Return to Market B	*Net Outcome*	**+ Return to Market A**
+ Imputation tax credits A		**+ Imputation tax credits B**
− Margin		**− Margin**

Exhibit 15.2 shows an asset swap between investors A and B, each of whom pay tax in their home market but wish exposure to the other. Both parties hold physical assets domestically. Their net outcome is the foreign asset return plus imputation credits in their home market less a margin paid to the intermediary for arranging the swap.

It is usual for the intermediary to seek a taxable investor in another country who can hold physical assets in her or his home market but wishes exposure in another. While this is preferable because the risk incurred in the original deal can be wholly or partially neutralised, it may not always be possible to arrange. Should this be the case, and it often is, the intermediary will be obliged to establish an index portfolio to offset her or his exposure. Thus another group of indexers becomes apparent: the financial intermediary who arranges the asset swap with the global manager.

Another group of indexers seek risk free returns using index portfolios in conjunction with derivative instruments such as share price index futures contracts. Often referred to as arbitrageurs, these indexers usually work for large stockbroking houses and may purchase the index portfolio on behalf of the house or for a client. They differ from most other indexers in that they usually work on a very short time horizon.[4] The opportunities to derive extra-market or arbitrage profits through trading mispriced futures and options contracts tend to be extremely short-lived, rarely more than a few minutes. So, while pension fund trustees and sponsors hold their index portfolios for many years and investment bankers hold theirs for anything from one to three years, the arbitrageur will often buy and sell an index portfolio within a few hours. This time element has important implications for the construction and implementation of the index portfolio.

4.   Arbitrage opportunities depend upon volatility in the price of the derivative relative to that of the underlying physical assets. Volatility in "relative price" or premium is usually associated with volatility in the underlying market.

4. HOW MUCH INDEXATION GOES ON?

The main group of indexers are professional investors responsible for managing large funds over extended periods of time, such as pension plan sponsors and trustees, mutual funds and insurance companies. Taken as a group, these institutions invest approximately 20% of their assets in index portfolios of one sort or another, mostly equities. Indexation has proved most popular with long-term investors in the United States, where nearly 30% of these funds' investments are indexed. In the United Kingdom the figure is closer to 20%. There is as yet little interest in indexation in continental Europe or in Asia. In Australia and New Zealand the proportion indexed is probably just under 15%.

Indexation became popular in the United States in the late 1970s and early 1980s. Interest was first raised by early research into the relative performance of equities managers which indicated that few, if any, active managers consistently did better than the S&P500—the market in which they invested. While each measurement period saw individual managers outperform, it was rare for better than market performance to occur over extended periods under any individual manager. More importantly, from the point of view of the investor, performance was very difficult to predict.[5] Needless to say, the picture was not improved when transactions costs and management fees were taken into account. By early 1987 approximately 9.5% of pension fund assets in the United States were indexed. The following year saw this figure grow to about 11%.[6]

So how much will indexation grow? In the first part of this chapter we found that there is a limit to the amount of indexation that can happen: if all portfolios were indexed, then the market would lose the efficiency upon which indexation relies for its success. So far nobody has succeeded in quantifying this limit. Early guesses put the figure at about 20% but this has already been exceeded in the United States, and is therefore almost certainly an underestimate. The answer will depend in part on the characteristics of the market in question. In particular it will depend on the relative importance in the market of the investors, such as those appearing in section three, who have most to gain from indexation.

For example, a market which is dominated to an unusual degree by very large funds will see more indexation than otherwise, because these funds are likely to favour the passive core and active satellite approach to managing their assets. Similarly, a market with a significant representation by offshore investors will see more indexation, either directly through portfolio share holdings or indirectly through counterparties to asset swaps.

On the other hand, the natural limit to the amount of indexation a market can support will be determined by the effectiveness of the market efficiency counterfoil. A market with even a small number of very efficient and competitive security analysts and traders will support more indexation than

---

5.   A recent study by Lakonishok, Schleifer and Vishny examines this phenomenon in the US equity market over the period 1983 through 1989. Josef, Lakonishok, Andre, Schleifer and Robert W Vishny "Study of the US Equity Money Manager Performance," Brookings Institute Study, 1992.

6.   *The Economist*, 27 August, 1988, p 63.

one where most investors are less aggressive. The former will do more to maintain market efficiency than the latter, who may allow some securities to remain mispriced.

Despite the limits to the amount of indexation within markets, there remains room for indexation to grow as a proportion of total investments. This growth will come from four main sources.

The first of these is pressure on costs. One of the dominant features of the managed funds industry, in most mature markets, is the downward pressure on the general level of management fees and other investment-related costs. This pressure has increased significantly over the decade to the mid-1990s and has a number of sources.

1. The most important of these is increased competition in the managed funds market. While a decade ago this market consisted mostly of life insurers and corporate pension funds, whose clientele were "captive" to some extent, today the range of participants is considerably wider. Evidence of this is that on both the London and New York stock exchanges, the number of listed equity trusts now exceeds that of listed equities. Increased competition is the result of, among other things, a trend in mature markets to the deregulation of financial systems. Deregulation has helped remove many of the barriers which hitherto kept many would-be investment managers from setting up shop.

As the size, in real terms, of managed funds has grown, so management fees have been squeezed. As management fees are usually levied as a percentage of the value of assets under management, the higher the absolute amount under management, the lower the fee in percentage points required to cover the manager's costs.

This real growth has three sources:

(i) deregulation and increased competition: lower fees to managed funds attracts more investment, and so on (this might be called a virtuous circle);

(ii) an increased saving rate in some rich countries, whose populations are entering the period of high savings which precedes the retirement of a large and affluent section of the population; and

(iii) real market returns are mostly reinvested in managed funds, so as markets for financial assets deliver positive real rates of return, the market will continue to grow by the real rate of return.

2. Increased competition in the market for managed funds has necessitated the improvement of capabilities in evaluating the effectiveness of asset managers. This increased efficiency has generally allowed investors to bid down the fees charged by asset managers, although in some spectacular cases the opposite has happened.

3. The early 1990s has seen a trend in most OECD countries toward lower nominal rates of return for most asset classes, mostly driven by lower inflation rates. Investment returns achieved by most asset managers are quoted both before and after fees. The cost factor represented by management fees are more obvious when compared to nominal returns which are low, than to those that are high.

Another source of growth in indexation is the increased use of the core-satellite approach associated with the growth of very large funds. This is partly a function of the growth in the market for managed assets, but it is also determined by how that growth is manifest. Where its main source is increased retirement saving, it is likely that these assets are managed within a small number of very large funds. This effect is, of course, most obvious where the primary vehicle for retirement saving is a public pension plan, but similar effects can be seen where saving is mostly through private pension schemes.

Schemes which are large relative to the market in which they invest may choose the index core-active satellite approach to assume appropriate levels of market risk while avoiding costly market impact. This avoids "closet indexation" and facilitates the identification and reward of active managers who deliver better than market returns.

Market concentration can also contribute to indexation. A recent example of this is given by the merger of CIBA-Geigy AG and Sandoz AG to form Novartis AG. This merger has caused the highly concentrated Swiss equity market to become even more so: together with Roche AG and Nestle SA, the three companies comprise nearly 60% of the Swiss Market Index. This heavy concentration led the Canton of Zurich pension fund to decide to boost passive management from 40% to 85% of its domestic equity allocation.[7]

Increased globalisation is contributing to the growth in indexation because global investors are, on balance, more likely to index some of their offshore assets than are local investors. Global investors are apt to choose indexation because it enables them to focus management resources on country and asset class selection. It is in this area, rather than in intra-market security selection, where they have most competitive advantage. Indexation can also save on global transactions and administration charges.

Investors are choosing to invest increasing proportions of their assets outside their home countries for some very good reasons. Investing outside one's home country can vastly improve the risk-return profile of a portfolio because it increases diversification. Until recently, international portfolio investing was limited in many rich countries by exchange controls and other financial regulations, high transactions costs and the limited ability of many investors to adequately analyse and control the risks of international investing. For investors in most developed markets these restrictions are rapidly falling away, with the result that investors are casting their nets further and further afield in search of returns and diversification not available in their home markets.

The most significant growth in offshore portfolio investing has happened in the United States. As recently as 1989 the proportion of US portfolio investments held internationally was less than 4%; in 1984 it was less than 2%.[8] By the early nineteen nineties the figure was closer to 20%. In contrast, portfolio investors in the United Kingdom are accustomed to investing well over 20% of their assets offshore. International diversification is likely to continue to grow for the following reasons.

7.   *Pensions & Investments*, 8 July, 1996, p 14.
8.   InterSec Research Corp, quoted by Institutional Investor, February 1991, p 97.

- Investors in mature markets in continental Europe will continue to increase international diversification as further deregulation permits, and as returns in their home markets increasingly fail to satisfy their demand for better risk adjusted returns.

- Similarly, investors in newly-emerged markets in Asia and elsewhere will seek increased international diversification as a result not only of deregulation but also because the size of investment funds is already increasing dramatically, relative to investment opportunities at home.

- Emerging markets in south and south-east Asia, Central and South America, Eastern Europe and, in the longer term, Africa, will become increasingly attractive to portfolio investors of all origins seeking to maximise returns and diversification.

As this trend gathers pace, indexation will follow in its wake. Associated with the growth in international diversification of investment portfolios is the growth in the market for asset swaps. The two trends will continue to be closely related as long as there exists a tax advantage to the international investor in using swaps over physical equities or other related instruments.

Both will continue to help fuel the worldwide growth in indexation.

5. APPROACHES TO INDEXATION

The steps to setting up an index portfolio are to:

    (a)   define the benchmark;

    (b)   set target level of tracking error;

    (c)   determine type of portfolio construction;

    (d)   decide rebalancing rules; and

    (e)   plan implementation.

(a) Defining the *benchmark* is not always as simple as it sounds. Most investment managers are acutely aware that, whatever the stated benchmark, the real benchmark is the performance achieved by their competitors.

Nevertheless, a formalised benchmark is a necessary part of any investment management mandate because it provides the investor with a means of objectively assessing the performance of the investment managers who have been appointed (and those who have not). Features which are necessary and or desirable for a benchmark are:

- It must meet the investment objectives of the investor. Usually this means that it must give a broad coverage of the market in which it will invest. In some instances this may necessitate designing a customised benchmark either within a recognised asset class or as a composition of different asset classes or parts of asset classes.

- It should be investable. In other words the securities that make up the benchmark should be freely traded on a recognised exchange.

- Derivatives are a big help. For the purposes of liquidity management and periodic asset class reweighting, there is an enormous advantage in selecting a benchmark on which futures contracts are traded. This is not always possible even for domestic equities portfolios, and is not generally available for international asset classes.

• Public quotation reduces ambiguity. While it is preferable to identify a benchmark which is quoted publicly, customised or less widely recognised benchmarks can work well provided the components are publicly quoted. This allows independent computation of benchmark performance by investor, manager and custodian; so avoiding confusion about the relative performance of the portfolio.

(b) The next step is to decide how much *tracking error* the portfolio can tolerate. This will be determined by the size and purpose of the portfolio and how difficult and/or costly it may be to achieve close to zero specific risk in the portfolio.

Ideally, the indexer will aim for zero tracking error which, combined with a beta of exactly one will give perfect index returns. But this reckons without transactions and other costs, which can have a significant effect on the outcome. In some cases the investor is better off with some tracking error because this flexibility can help reduce the other costs of the portfolio.

(c) Having determined the benchmark and its tolerance for tracking error, the indexer must now decide the best way to go about *portfolio construction*. The inputs to this part of the indexation process are:

• the benchmark;

• the tolerance for tracking error;

• the purpose and expected life of the index portfolio—long-term or short-term;

• the form of the existing portfolio—cash, shares, et cetera.

• estimates of transactions costs for each asset in the sample; and

• estimates of beta values for each asset in the sample.

The first part of this process is to decide whether to fully replicate the benchmark index or to adopt a sampling approach, and, if the latter, how many securities to include in the sample. The names provide apt descriptions: full replication is the process of simply buying every security in precise index proportions, while sampling is where only some securities are bought.

The choice is usually determined by the portfolio's tolerance for tracking error and the structure of the benchmark. If it is made up of a great number of securities then sampling is almost certainly the right approach. If there are only a few dozen securities in it then full replication could be the answer, provided each component is sufficiently liquid and trading costs are not too high.

Full replication will give portfolio performance which is very close to, but not identical with, the benchmark. The difference stems from the fact that all benchmarks change their components from time to time and the replicating indexer must follow suit. This results in trading costs which, together with administrative costs, have a negative impact on performance. Sampling incurs lower rebalancing and administrative costs (because there are fewer securities to trade and changes in the benchmark can be followed less rigidly), but incurs a larger tracking error. Tracking error can be positive or negative. The objective of the sampling indexer is to minimise this error, so delivering portfolio performance with variations from the benchmark which are not only small, but are positive as often as they are negative.

There are a number of approaches to sampling, including random sampling—with or without the assistance of Karolina the chimpanzee. We will concentrate on only two—stratified sampling and optimised sampling—which are often applied in tandem.

Stratified sampling is where the benchmark is broken up into bite-sized chunks and securities selected from each chunk to make up a portfolio. In the case of a domestic equities portfolio, the bite-sized chunks might be determined by industry groupings, with the result that each industry is given proportional representation in the sample portfolio. An international equities index might start with a country by country approach. A property portfolio might seek to separate the index into different property sectors, such as commercial, industrial and residential. For fixed interest one might approach the task by looking at various credit exposures within the index.

Example of a stratified sample

The following example illustrates how a stratified sample might work. The indexer wishes to construct a 100 stock portfolio to track a benchmark which itself has over 300 stocks. The simplest approach would be simply to select the 100 largest stocks by market capitalisation. For the sake of the example this portfolio will be called *TOP100*.

The indexer then notices that the benchmark is divided into 24 industry categories. Since it makes sense to at least try to match industry weightings to the benchmark,[9] the indexer decides to select 100 stocks according to industry categories.

The first step is to decide which stocks to select. Obviously the largest stock in each industry group will be included. (If the number of industry groups exceeded the number of stocks, that is, there were more than 100 industry groups, then one stock would be selected from each of the 100 largest industry groups by market capitalisation.) The next step will select the next largest stock from each industry group.[10]

Next, the indexer must weight the stocks. Industry groups will be weighted according to their weight in the benchmark index. Within industry groups, stocks will be weighted according to their relative weight within the industry. Individual stock weightings will therefore vary from their weight in the benchmark index.

The 100 stock portfolio selected by this process is called *SAMP100*. *Exhibit 15.3* shows the composition of the benchmark and the two portfolios.

9. The usefulness of matching industry weightings depends on the relevance of the industry group definitions to the activities of companies in the benchmark. In many cases companies are arbitrarily assigned to whichever industry group represents the largest of its business lines, despite the fact that, in some cases this may contribute less than half of that company's overall profit.

10. The indexer may omit some stocks because they are unacceptably illiquid. The result will be that some industry groups will have a larger number of stocks in them than others.

Exhibit 15.3

Stratified Samples

Industry Group	Benchmark Weight	No of Stocks	TOP100 Weight	No of Stocks	SAMP100 Weight	No of Stocks	SAMP112 Weight	No of Stocks
Gold	4.83%	43	3.76%	10	4.84%	9	4.09%	10
Other Metals	6.44%	19	6.14%	6	6.44%	6	6.68%	8
Diversified Resources	14.24%	4	16.69%	3	14.24%	3	15.10%	3
Energy	4.19%	14	4.27%	6	4.21%	6	4.19%	6
Infrastructure & Utilities	0.96%	6	0.94%	2	0.96%	1	0.73%	1
Developers	2.97%	12	3.01%	3	2.97%	3	3.03%	3
Building Materials	4.25%	11	4.64%	5	4.24%	6	4.33%	5
Alcohol & Tobacco	2.05%	5	2.20%	3	2.05%	3	2.18%	3
Food	3.37%	8	3.43%	3	3.37%	4	3.49%	4
Chemicals	1.41%	5	1.57%	2	1.42%	1	1.53%	2
Engineering	0.75%	8	0.32%	1	0.74%	1	0.58%	2
Paper & Packaging	2.15%	5	2.39%	3	2.15%	3	2.33%	3
Retail	3.41%	12	3.43%	4	3.42%	5	3.40%	3
Transport	3.07%	11	3.41%	3	3.08%	3	3.24%	3
Media	8.47%	19	9.09%	7	8.47%	5	8.62%	8
Banks	18.61%	14	21.62%	10	18.60%	10	18.91%	9
Insurance	2.31%	9	2.37%	5	2.32%	2	1.88%	4
Telecommunications	0.23%	6	0.00%	0	0.23%	1	0.00%	0
Investment Services	2.07%	22	1.11%	3	2.06%	3	2.52%	7
Property Trusts	4.51%	41	2.67%	5	4.49%	7	4.41%	9
Miscellaneous Services	1.38%	26	0.27%	1	1.38%	3	0.82%	3
Miscellaneous Industrials	1.42%	15	0.59%	2	1.42%	4	1.54%	6
Diversified Industrials	3.96%	12	3.77%	6	3.96%	6	3.96%	4
Tourism	2.95%	21	2.32%	7	2.97%	5	2.44%	6
Total	100%	348	100%	100	100%	100	100%	112

The *TOP100* portfolio is heavily weighted in diversified resources, media and banks, but has no exposure at all to telecommunications. *SAMP100* on the other hand, matches its industry group weightings to the benchmark for each industry group.

Stratified sampling has intuitive appeal and will result in satisfactory risk control so long as the categories are chosen well. If categories are ill-chosen then risk control is liable to fail. Another, often more robust approach is called optimisation, sometimes known as mean-variance optimisation.[11] *Optimisation* seeks the lowest tracking error for the index portfolio by drawing on historical data to maximise diversification relative to the benchmark. To do this it takes into account the historical correlations between securities and groups of securities. From this it constructs a portfolio which will give the lowest expected tracking error. It does this iteratively, in other words it builds the portfolio one "trade" at a time—measuring the expected tracking error of the portfolio after each "trade" until the portfolio

11. For general (active) portfolio construction, optimisation seeks to identify the lowest levels of risk for varying amounts of expected return.

is complete and there is little or no benefit to be derived from further tinkering or iterations.

There are a number of approaches to optimisation, including the linear and quadratic varieties, with a healthy debate raging about the relative merits of each. The two most popular are *factor* models and *industry mean* models. Both are based on the main principle of CAPM, that while future asset returns cannot be derived from past returns, the risk characteristics of an asset (and therefore of a portfolio of assets) tend to be stable over time.

Put simply, the factor model uses either a combination of correlation analysis and intuitive interpretation, or a cross-sectional regression analysis of past security returns. The purpose is to identify factors which are common to groups of securities in the sample, and to quantify the relationship between the factors. It then groups each security in the sample according to its main factor, and tries to achieve a portfolio factor exposure which is similar to the benchmark.

The industry mean model, on the other hand, groups securities according to their main industry and tries to quantify the correlation between these groups. The aim is to give a portfolio which is diversified according to the observed correlation between main industry groups.

To show how optimisation can affect a portfolio's expected risk, the two portfolios above were optimised against the 348 stock benchmark. The optimiser was allowed to change the weightings of each stock but was constrained to the same sample of stocks. Then the optimiser was allowed to add 12 stocks to the *SAMP100* portfolio to give a portfolio called *SAMP112*. The expected tracking error of each portfolio is set out in *Exhibit 15.4*.

Exhibit 15.4

Tracking Error—Stratified Sample vs Optimised

	TOP100	SAMP100	SAMP100	SAMP112
	Stratified	Stratified	Optimised	Optimised
Expected Tracking Error	0.68%	0.56%	0.42%	0.33%

These results show that matching industry weightings to benchmark gives lower expected tracking error, that this result can be improved by optimising the portfolio, and improved even further if extra stocks are added in the optimisation step.

SAMP112 in the first table shows that an optimised portfolio does not necessarily match industry weights to benchmark, although divergences tend to be smaller than those for the *TOP100* portfolio. The optimisation process takes into account correlations between stocks and industry groups to describe a portfolio with the best overall diversification across assets.

As one might expect, the process of portfolio optimisation requires substantial computer resources. For this reason optimisers have been widely used in portfolio construction only for the last decade or so. An endearing feature of optimisers is that they, like all computer models, are subject to the GIGO principle—Garbage In Garbage Out. The optimising indexer must therefore be able to judge if the portfolio defined by the optimiser meets its objectives. A capricious charm of the optimiser is that it can give results which appear much more reasonable than they are. Contrary to the laws of probability, and a sop to the technophobe, the resulting error seems always to be both negative and large.

The combination of stratified sampling and optimisation can be powerful if the benchmark is amenable to stratification, the strata are well chosen, and there exists historical data in sufficient quantity and quality to enable a meaningful optimisation.

There is no single approach to indexation which is always better than others. The successful index portfolio is one that is designed to fit the requirements of the individual mandate even if it requires a customised benchmark. The market, the benchmark, the investment objectives and constraints in the mandate will determine which is the best approach for a given indexed portfolio.

(d) *Rebalancing* rules should be set next. How often this happens will depend on the level of transactions costs and the amount of specific risk that can be tolerated: high risk tolerance allows less frequent rebalancing because the cost of a rebalance will be justified less often by the expected reduction in specific risk. On the other hand, low risk tolerance requires more frequent rebalances. Rebalancing will also be influenced by the frequency and timing of cash flows to the portfolio. If rebalancing can be timed to coincide with cash flows either in or out of the portfolio, then rebalancing costs can be sharply reduced.

(e) *Implementation*: the objective is to minimise transactions costs and execution risk.

The best implementation method depends partly on what shape the existing portfolio has. If for example, it is made up entirely of liquid assets and the relevant share price index futures contract is trading below its fair value, then the indexer can add value by buying futures. These can then be exchanged for physical stock when the futures price is at fair value or higher. However, it is usual for the starting portfolio to comprise an active or indexed portfolio of physical shares and liquid securities. The indexer must then calculate the volume of shares to be sold and bought. If this is relatively small and the trade is made up of a small number of large parcels of stock, then it is most efficiently implemented by simply placing normal buy and sell orders with brokers.

When confronted with the necessity of trading a large volume of stock, however, the indexer must take care to manage the execution cost. In some markets this can be substantial enough to alter the performance of the portfolio or the profitability of the arbitrage. Execution cost consists of a number of elements:

- taxes;
- commissions;
- bid-ask spread;

- market impact; and

- opportunity cost.

The first two of these are usually known or can be accurately estimated in advance. The bid-ask spread is the difference in the prices bid and offered in the market, either by market makers or by other investors. Generally, but not always, the smaller the stock the larger the bid-ask spread.

Market impact can be thought of as the cost of transacting each additional share. For example, consider the buyer of one share; he or she will accept the offer price which will probably remain unchanged after that transaction. If the same investor buys one thousand of the same shares the price may move slightly after the trade is complete, as each marginal seller in turn has completed her or his order. A buyer of one million of the same shares may find that the sale price (and sometimes the bid price) moves even before the trade is complete, as other market participants read the signal that demand for the stock—and therefore its implicit value—has increased sharply.

Opportunity cost applies more to active portfolio managers who have more discretion over the timing of their market activities than do indexers, who are largely bound to follow predefined decision rules. It is the cost incurred when an investor sets out to trade a stock at a certain price and fails to complete the trade because the stock price keeps moving beyond the limit set.

Execution cost and risk can be controlled by executing a "block trade". This is the practice of buying (or selling) the entire portfolio as one parcel of stock. This can reduce the execution risk on the portfolio to zero by transferring this risk to the stockbroker who will effect the transaction. It also reduces the likelihood of dealing errors and can partially streamline the consequent paper trail. The attractiveness of this strategy depends, of course, on how much it costs. This will in turn depend on:

- which stocks are to be traded and in what proportions;

- the amount of liquidity in the market at the time of the trade; and

- the willingness of brokers to execute the trade.

While the portfolio manager has little control over the first two variables, it is possible and desirable to influence the third. The best way of doing this is to seek competing bids from more than one broker. This helps ensure that the price obtained for the transaction is competitive, because the broker with the greatest appetite for the trade will bid the keenest price. It will reflect both the price, including any taxes, at which the broker can buy or sell each stock, either in the market or against existing client business, and some charge to compensate for the risk of taking positions in some of the stocks as principal. The magnitude of this charge will depend on how long the broker expects to have to hold the position, interest rates and other funding costs and hedging costs. A basket of stock which is easy to either trade or hedge in the market will attract a smaller principal charge.

Similar principles will direct the strategy employed to rebalance the portfolio from time to time, although the effect on the portfolio will be smaller.

6. CASE STUDY: DOMESTIC AND INTERNATIONAL INDEXES

The following hypothetical example illustrates how indexation fits into a diversified institutional portfolio.

A medium-sized corporate pension fund, based in Australia, seeks to construct a portfolio that will give optimal long-term gains while controlling risk and cost in the short term. The fund must meet regular redemptions, so it cannot tolerate short term fluctuations in the value of its investments. On the other hand, it also has a regular flow of new funds with a significant quotient of young members with long-term investment needs. The adviser has recommended that about 10% of the overall fund be invested in fairly liquid securities. This will conservatively meet all likely liquidity requirements and allow periodic rebalancing.

The fund's adviser has recommended a mix of growth and defensive assets with a strong emphasis on risk diversification. This is designed to give participation in world growth with controlled volatility. The domestic equity portfolio should be invested mostly in a broad-based share index with a small but significant proportion of the domestic equities portfolio invested in small capitalisation stocks. For the international equities portfolio, both developed and emerging markets should be represented according to their weighting by capitalisation in world equity markets overall.

The fund will also have some allocation to domestic property markets through listed property vehicles. It is recognised that this is not a good substitute for direct property holdings, but the fund size and limited liquidity preclude direct investment in the property market.

Domestic and international fixed interest provide a diversified "defensive" element to the portfolio. Fixed interest markets are usually less volatile than equities and can provide valuable diversification to the overall portfolio.

The pension fund sponsor is aware that transactions costs have in the past contributed significantly to the underperformance of the fund and so is keen to do all that is possible to keep these to a minimum. For this reason the allocation between asset classes is to be held constant. The portfolio will be rebalanced frequently back to the original asset allocation using natural cash flows.

The sponsor therefore determines seven indexing mandates:

(i)   domestic equities—large capitalisation;

(ii) domestic equities—small capitalisation;

(iii) international equities—developed markets;

(iv) international equities—emerging markets;

(v)   domestic listed property securities;

(vi) domestic fixed interest; and

(vii) international fixed interest.

These mandates cover each asset category except cash. Each has a different benchmark and is subject to different market conditions

(i) *Domestic equities large capitalisation* is benchmarked to a broad-based local share price index. In the United States market, for example, the most popular benchmark is the S&P500 index. Our investor has settled on the Australian All Ordinaries Accumulation Index, which satisfies the main requirements of being investable, publicly quoted—in the form of both price and accumulation indices—with a lively futures and options market. The All Ordinaries has some fairly serious shortcomings which are common to many equity benchmarks. That is, it omits some serious sectors of the economy as a whole. The All Ordinaries is designed to capture 90% by capitalisation of all stocks listed on the Australian Stock Exchange, so it misses the smallest 10% of listed securities. More importantly, it misses all unlisted securities[12]—a significant part of the real economy which includes nearly all transport infrastructure, most power generation and most medical services—to name some examples.

(ii) *Domestic equities small capitalisation* is benchmarked to the Australian All Ordinaries Accumulation Index excluding the top 100 stocks. This benchmark is broad-based and publicly quoted but does not have a futures market.

(iii) *International equities developed markets* are benchmarked to the Morgan Stanley Capital International World Index. This benchmark is publicly quoted and has a broad coverage of developed markets. While the MSCI world index lacks a futures market, most of its component countries have actively traded share price index futures contracts.

(iv) *International equities emerging markets* are benchmarked to the Morgan Stanley Capital International Emerging Markets Index. This benchmark, like the domestic equities small cap benchmark, is broad-based and publicly quoted but does not have a futures market.

(v) *Domestic listed property securities* are benchmarked to the Australian Stock Exchange Listed Property Accumulation Index. Again, this benchmark is broadly representative of its sector and is publicly quoted, but does not have any associated derivatives markets.

(vi) *Domestic fixed interest* is benchmarked to the SBC Warburg Semi-Government All Maturities bond index. This benchmark is one of several widely recognised fixed interest indices and its component stocks are publicly available and tradeable. It does not have an associated derivatives market, but futures and options contracts are available on ten and three year Commonwealth Government bonds, which can be used as a surrogate for the purposes of liquidity management and for matching duration.

(vii) *International fixed interest* is benchmarked to the Salomon Brothers World Government Bond Index. This benchmark is widely recognised, with components publicly available and generally tradeable. No single derivatives market covers this index but many component countries have one or more futures contracts on government bonds which can be used as an approximation to the index.

For each international portfolio, currency is to be unhedged. In other words, the portfolio performance will be determined not only by the

---

12. These sectors are held either in unlisted private companies, offshore equity owners or they are publicly owned.

performance of domestic and international stock and bond markets, but also by currency movements.

In recent years index enhancement has gained popularity. Index enhancement seeks to achieve better than market or index rates of return, by adding something to the basic indexing approach. The subject of index enhancement is dealt with in a later section of this chapter. For our example, all of the indexed sectors will avoid risky enhancements.

7. EQUITY INDEX PORTFOLIOS

Following the example set out above, we have four equity index portfolios with four benchmarks:

Exhibit 15.5

Benchmarks

Domestic equity—large cap	Australian All Ordinaries Accumulation Index
Domestic equity—small cap	Australian All Ordinaries Accumulation Index ex the Top 100 stocks
International equity—developed markets	Morgan Stanley Capital International World Index
International equity—emerging markets	Morgan Stanley Capital Index Emerging Markets Index

---

Each portfolio will require its own approach while the general principles of index portfolio construction are applied. This will achieve the twin aims of the indexer, which are the minimisation of cost and risk.

The *domestic equity—large capitalisation* portfolio is best managed using the stratified sampling with optimisation approach already described. Stratified sampling is favoured over full replication because the benchmark index contains well over 300 stocks, many of which trade very rarely. Optimisation can reduce the expected tracking error because there exists sufficient reliable historical stock data to build a useful correlation matrix. From this matrix the diversifying effects of individual stocks can be estimated. This structure will give a portfolio with about 150 stocks in it. It will have an expected tracking error of about 0.25% pa.

The number of stocks selected for the portfolio is important. The index is devised to represent 90%, by market capitalisation, of Australian listed equities: it comprises between 340 and 350 stocks. Too many stocks in the indexed portfolio will increase the transactions and administrative costs of the portfolio, while too few stocks will subject the portfolio to excessive tracking error. The balance between the number of stocks held, tracking performance and estimated rebalancing costs is set out in *Exhibit 15.6*.

Exhibit 15.6
Number of Stocks vs Tracking Error

Number of Stocks	Per cent of Benchmark by Capitalisation	Estimated Rebalancing Costs	Estimated Tracking Error
70	79%	0.40%	0.55%
100	85%	0.45%	0.42%
150	92%	0.69%	0.19%
180	95%	0.86%	0.14%
250	98%	1.05%	0.05%
300	99%	1.22%	0.01%

This shows that reducing the tracking error from 19 basis points to five basis points by increasing the number of stocks from 150 to 250 increases annual rebalancing costs by 36 basis points. In this case the indexer is clearly better off with fewer stocks.

In general, portfolios with more stocks in them will require rebalancing more often because they are more subject to small changes in the benchmark index which can be tolerated by a sample portfolio with higher tracking error tolerance. On the other hand, reducing the number of stocks to 100 can increase the tracking error of the portfolio to approximately 40 basis points, which exceeds the portfolio's specific risk tolerance of 0.25%.

In the case of Australian equities, the choice of the number of stocks held can also have an impact on the beta of the portfolio. This is because, unlike many other equity markets, large Australian stocks tend to have a beta greater than one. Because of this, the beta effect will often show up as a size bias in the portfolio.

An efficient rebalancing strategy is critical to the success of the portfolio.

With about 150 stocks, cash flow to the portfolio needs to be only 3% or 4% per year to allow adequate rebalancing without having to sell any shares. This means that the effective portfolio turnover is close to zero, so transactions costs are very low indeed.

It also means that from time to time the cash balance in the portfolio will be as much as 5%. This liquidity should be "equitised" by buying the appropriate number of futures contracts.

To calculate the number of futures to give equivalent exposure to the equity market, the following algorithm is used:

Number of Contracts = Face Value/(Index Level . Point Value of Futures) (3)

For example, if the investor has $1 million of cash to equitise, the current market level is 2202 and the point value of the futures contract is $25, the number of contracts to be purchased is calculated as:

$$\text{Number of Contracts} = \$1,000,000/(2202 \ . \ \$25)$$
$$= 18$$

Buying futures ensures that the cash component of the portfolio participates in the performance of the equity market. When a rebalance is deemed necessary, futures contracts are sold and physical shares are purchased.

When the portfolio has been optimised and the indexer has determined the portfolio's composition, it remains to be determined how best to purchase the required stocks. The choices will generally include purchasing physical stocks or buying futures contracts which can later be exchanged for physical shares.

Purchasing physical shares often simply means placing an order to buy each of the component assets, but sometimes the indexer may choose to buy the portfolio as a block trade, as described in an earlier section. In some conditions this form of trade can be very cost effective for the indexer, but only if he or she has the capability to accurately evaluate the cost of the trade in comparison to normal on-market transactions.

The other way of implementing an index portfolio is to substitute futures contracts for all or part of the portfolio. This strategy is normally employed for a large trade where the futures market offers better liquidity than the underlying physical assets. It can also happen that using futures contracts can add risk-free returns to the portfolio, which would not be available by a straightforward purchase of physical shares. This type of trade is, strictly speaking, an enhancement, and is dealt with later in the chapter.

The *domestic equity—small capitalisation* portfolio would ideally be constructed following the same principles as the large capitalisation portfolio. The difficulty is that optimisation is precluded by the lack of adequate historical return data—and correlation matrix—for the stocks which make up the benchmark. The indexer must therefore make do with a stratified sample. A portfolio of 100 stocks will cover 73% of the capitalisation of this market. Adding 50 stocks brings this coverage to 88%.

The chosen method of implementation is likely to be limited to ordinary buy and sell orders. Execution may take days or weeks for some stocks.

Both tracking error and rebalancing costs will be higher for this portfolio than for the large capitalisation portfolio. In addition, liquidity management will be complicated by the fact that the only available derivatives contract offers at best an imperfect hedge against the small capitalisation benchmark.

International equities—developed markets: this index portfolio requires a totally different approach to those adopted for domestic portfolios. One reason for this is that the benchmark MSCI index comprises over 1,500 stocks, rendering it unlikley that it would be a full replication portfolio. Another reason is that the indexer is likely to treat each component country as a separate portfolio, mainly because, while the technology exists to optimise a global equities portfolio across borders—representing a more efficient solution in terms of risk diversification—it is still fairly new and requires considerable computing power. Most portfolio construction software therefore makes do with a country by country analysis. Given this approach, the indexer of international assets is much more likely to employ derivatives markets than is the domestic indexer. This is mainly because of economies of scale and transactions costs, but also because the logistics of constructing and maintaining optimised portfolios of physical shares within each country demands a more streamlined approach.

The main approaches to indexing international equities include

- buy physical shares in optimised portfolios within each country, with country weightings matching the benchmark index;
- buy share price index futures in each country, with country weightings matching the benchmark index;
- hold domestic physical assets and enter into an asset swap to achieve exposure to international equities; and
- a combination of the above.

The trade-off between the four approaches is determined by tracking error, transactions and administrative costs and liquidity requirements. *Exhibit 15.7* illustrates how this trade-off might work for a portfolio of approximately AU$300 million.

Exhibit 15.7

Cost-Benefit of Four Approaches to International Equity Indexing

	Physical Shares	SPI Futures	Asset Swaps*	Combination
Transactions Costs	1.03%	negligible	0.50%	0.10%
Administrative Costs	0.17%	0.06%	0.03%	0.05%
Liquidity	good	very good	very poor	good
Tracking Error	0.70%	1.80%	0.25%	0.50%

* Includes costs of maintaining the domestic component of the swap, but not the benefits of domestic dividend imputation credits.

Holding physical shares gives reasonable tracking performance with acceptable liquidity. The main impediment to holding physical assets is transactions and administrative costs. While most developed markets have fairly efficient exchanges and settlement systems, some still impose very high costs on foreign investors. International custodian charges are generally levied at a percentage of the amount under management as well as a fixed fee per transaction. For example, of the total annual administrative costs shown in *Exhibit 15.7*, all but about 0.05% are levied on a fee per transaction basis. This means that holding physical shares is much more expensive for a small portfolio than for a large one. Administrative and transaction costs for physical shares vary enormously from country to country. For example, the costs of holding physical shares in the United States are similar to those for domestic Australian holdings, while some smaller Asian and Scandinavian countries have costs which preclude holding any physical shares.

For a small to medium size portfolio, futures offer a cost efficient means of gaining international equities exposure. This cost efficiency is particularly important if the portfolio has frequent cash flows because the transactions and administrative costs thus incurred are very small. The problem with futures is that of tracking error. Tracking error has two sources. The first is due to the fact that not all countries in the MSCI have liquid share price index futures contracts. The second is because futures contracts do not match the MSCI index within the country.

Countries in the MSCI world benchmark index which have liquid share price index futures contracts cover about 93% of the benchmark by market capitalisation. Some of the countries which do not, such as Singapore and, until recently, Malaysia,[13] have in the past performed very differently to the index overall. Investors who lacked exposure to these markets would have underperformed the benchmark by almost 2% during 1993 and 1994.

Japan provides a good example of the other source of tracking error. This is because the Nikkei 225 contract, the most popular SPI futures contract for the Japanese equity market, is a price weighted index. This differs from the MSCI Japan index which is capitalisation weighted. This means that the smallest stock in the Nikkei 225 can move the index just as much as the largest, resulting in large performance differences between the Nikkei 225 and the MSCI Japan index (nearly 2.5% during 1993 and 1994). Japan does have futures contracts based on capitalisation weighted indices but, partly because of peculiar margining requirements, these have so far proved less popular than those settled to the Nikkei 225, so can introduce liquidity problems.

The use of asset swaps has increased considerably in the last few years. This is unsurprising given the obvious difficulties for the international investor of using physical shares and futures contracts. Asset swaps, if constructed efficiently, can overcome many of the cost and tracking performance problems normally encountered by the international indexer. They have the added charm of being potentially tax efficient too. Tax efficiency derives from the fact that the investor can hold domestic physical assets which may generate dividend imputation tax credits. The return on these assets are then swapped for the return on the desired basket of international assets.

Two important features of asset swaps are that they are not liquid and there exist significant scale economies. Asset swaps can present liquidity problems because they are all dealt as over-the-counter transactions, and so are difficult to terminate or reverse before their prearranged expiry date. The costs of early termination of a swap can be punitive. This means that a portfolio which holds a large proportion of its assets in swaps will be unable to meet a redemption without incurring very high costs. The economies of scale associated with asset swaps derive from the fact that they are always over-the-counter and usually customised to meet the demands of a particular investor. For this reason the set-up documentation and associated costs are normally high. These fees are the same in dollar terms regardless of the face value of the swap, so a large portfolio has a distinct cost advantage in percentage of total assets over a smaller one.

A combination of physical shares, futures and asset swaps can produce the best of all worlds, as can be seen from *Exhibit 15.7* above. *Exhibit 15.8* shows how this would look for a portfolio which requires 10% to be held in liquid assets.

---

13. Futures contracts started trading in Malaysia in late 1995.

Exhibit 15.8
Construction of International Equities Portfolio

	Benchmark	Physical	Asset Swap	Futures	Total
Europe G5*	23.20%	0.00%	0.00%	23.20%	23.20%
Rest of Europe	6.00%	0.00%	6.00%	0.00%	6.00%
North America	46.30%	41.67%	0.00%	4.63%	46.30%
Japan	18.60%	0.00%	16.74%	1.86%	18.60%
Hong Kong	2.00%	0.00%	0.00%	2.00%	2.00%
Rest of Asia	3.90%	0.00%	3.90%	0.00%	3.90%
	100.00%	41.67%	26.64%	31.69%	100.00%

* G5 = UK, Germany, France, Switzerland and Netherlands.

Europe G5 is invested in SPI futures because these give acceptable tracking performance and the costs of physical portfolios are relatively high in some of these countries. The rest of Europe uses an asset swap because the appropriate futures contracts are not generally available and the cost of holding physical assets is high. North America is invested 90% in physical assets because these can be held cheaply, with 10% in futures to meet liquidity requirements. Japan is held 90% in an asset swap to gain cost effective tracking performance, with 10% in SPI futures to meet liquidity requirements. Hong Kong, like Europe G5 is invested all in SPI futures, with the rest of Asia using an asset swap to gain cost effective tracking performance. The portfolio therefore meets the overall liquidity requirement of 10%, with 10% available in liquids for each of the major regions of Europe, North America and Asia. Because the portfolio is 26% invested through asset swaps, it has some capacity to earn domestic dividend imputation credits.

International equities—emerging markets: emerging markets present an entirely different range of challenges. The markets comprising the benchmark index do not have liquid derivatives markets, so the indexer has to decide between physical shares and asset swaps. Moreover, each country needs to be treated as a separate case. For example, many emerging countries discriminate between local and foreign investors, so that foreigners may in fact be precluded from purchasing certain stocks, or they may face discriminatory transaction costs or settlement procedures. Such conditions apply in one form or another in Korea, Philippines, Mexico and Venezuela. On the other hand, some countries offer parcels of their stocks, usually issued by intermediaries such as investment banks, which can be purchased in a unitised structure and may be traded on the stock exchanges of developed countries. While these instruments can simplify the administrative aspects of investing in emerging markets (and some developed markets), they usually incorporate many of the costs which face any foreign portfolio investor. This is because the intermediary, itself a foreign portfolio investor, must pass on the costs incurred in forming the underlying investment.

The composition of the MSCI World Emerging Markets Index is set out in *Exhibit 15.9*.

Exhibit 15.9

Composition of MSCI World Emerging Markets Index

Country	% of index	Mkt Cap USD Bn	GDP USD Bn	No of Stocks
Argentina	2.76%	27.3	268.8	23
Brazil	10.58%	104.7	584.6	61
Czech Republic	1.06%	10.5	40	20
Chile	3.58%	35.4	56.6	32
China	0.39%	3.9	744.9	26
Colombia	0.61%	6	70.3	9
Greece	1.08%	10.7	85.7	36
Hungary	0.31%	3.1	42.3	9
India	5.04%	49.9	327	67
Indonesia	4.42%	43.8	190.1	39
Israel	1.69%	16.7	87.9	51
Jordan	0.11%	1.1	6.4	15
Korea	9.10%	90.1	435.1	116
Malaysia	14.24%	141	80.4	76
Mexico	6.83%	67.6	304.6	42
Pakistan	0.45%	4.5	59.5	32
Peru	0.93%	9.2	55	14
Philippines	3.37%	33.4	72	35
Poland	0.40%	4	107.9	18
Portugal	1.78%	17.6	97	24
South Africa	9.82%	97.2	130.9	53
Sri Lanka	0.06%	0.6	12.6	10
Taiwan	14.93%	147.8	260.8	77
Thailand	4.76%	47.1	159.8	76
Turkey	1.18%	11.7	165.4	45
Venezuela	0.51%	5	65.5	13
Total	100.00%	989.9	4511.1	1019

Source: Morgan Stanley Capital International EMF and Emerging Markets Perspective, November 1996.

To the extent that the indexer invests in physical shares, a stratified sampling approach which tries to match country weights to the benchmark and industry groups within each country will be favoured.

The indexer will seek a combination of asset swaps, listed unitised vehicles and physical shares. The precise composition of the final portfolio will depend on the availability and price of each instrument for each region or country.

The aggregate market coverage of this portfolio is likely to be about 80%. This should allow a tracking error of between 1.5% and 2.0% pa, with a liquidity level of about 10%. Because transactions costs are high, rebalancing will be timed to coincide with cash flows.

8. FIXED INTEREST INDEX PORTFOLIOS

Fixed interest index portfolios require similar considerations as equity indexes. The indexer must first choose between a full replication or a sampling approach, then apply optimisation wherever possible. Mean-variance optimisation is less easily adapted to fixed interest portfolios, because time series data for individual asset returns are less readily available. Most fixed interest assets are traded outside normal exchanges, usually on screen-traded or "telephone" markets. Such trading systems may not include a mechanism for recording trades, so building the type of data base on which a portfolio optimiser works is simply not possible for many fixed interest markets. The Australian fixed interest market is one of these.

The indexer can, however, construct a stratified sample which does almost as good a job, provided care is taken to match duration as well as credit quality, and of course the interaction between the two.

The biggest difference between fixed interest and equity indexes is that fixed interest assets have a defined maturity date, while equity assets generally do not. This means that assets in fixed interest benchmarks can cease to exist from one day to the next.[14] They are usually replaced of course, but the problem remains that the composition of the benchmark index can change suddenly, although usually not without notice. The indexer is thus obliged to purchase the new asset regardless of the price it commands on the day.

Domestic fixed interest is benchmarked to the SBC Warburg Semi-Government All Maturities bond index. For this portfolio, the indexer has decided on a stratified sample. *Exhibit 15.10* shows each asset in the benchmark and the weight each is assigned in the portfolio. *Exhibit 15.11* summarises credit quality and duration of the 17 assets in the portfolio versus its benchmark.

The target tracking error is 0.10%. Liquidity of the portfolio is not a big issue as each security is sufficiently liquid to meet the 10% liquidity requirement.

---

14. This contributes to the problem of the lack of continuous return data.

Exhibit 15.10

Sample Index Portfolio for Domestic Fixed Interest

Description	Maturity	Coupon	Yield	Benchmark Weight	Portfolio Weight
Cash					1.46%
NSWTC	1/04/97	12.50%	7.10%	2.81%	0.00%
NSWTC	1/02/98	7.50%	7.18%	5.39%	7.35%
NSWTC	1/07/99	11.50%	7.31%	4.07%	5.99%
NSWTC	1/02/00	7.00%	7.36%	3.56%	0.00%
NSWTC	1/12/01	12.00%	7.53%	6.57%	9.68%
NSWTC	1/04/04	7.00%	7.75%	5.67%	8.99%
NSWTC	1/05/06	6.50%	7.94%	3.51%	0.00%
NSWTC	1/05/06	12.60%	7.94%	0.39%	0.00%
QTC	14/05/97	8.00%	6.85%	2.53%	0.00%
QTC	15/05/97	12.00%	6.85%	0.22%	0.00%
QTC	14/07/99	8.00%	7.05%	3.97%	6.15%
QTC	14/08/01	8.00%	7.24%	4.89%	6.61%
QTC	15/08/01	12.00%	7.24%	0.40%	0.00%
QTC	14/05/03	8.00%	7.40%	5.22%	7.07%
QTC	15/05/03	10.50%	7.40%	0.54%	0.00%
QTC	14/06/05	6.50%	7.60%	4.52%	5.22%
QTC	14/09/07	8.00%	7.81%	2.86%	0.00%
SAFA	15/10/96	12.50%	6.69%	1.86%	0.00%
SAFA	15/03/98	12.50%	6.82%	2.20%	4.16%
SAFA	15/10/00	12.50%	7.06%	1.88%	0.00%
SAFA	14/01/03	10.00%	7.27%	1.99%	2.53%
TASCORP	15/03/98	12.50%	6.82%	1.37%	0.00%
TASCORP	15/01/01	12.50%	7.09%	1.58%	3.68%
TASCORP	15/11/04	9.00%	7.44%	0.74%	0.00%
TCV	15/09/97	12.50%	6.78%	2.16%	0.00%
TCV	22/10/98	12.00%	6.88%	3.00%	7.72%
TCV	15/09/99	10.25%	6.96%	2.54%	0.00%
TCV	15/07/00	12.50%	7.04%	2.58%	5.36%
TCV	22/09/01	12.00%	7.15%	2.19%	0.00%
TCV	15/10/03	12.50%	7.34%	2.79%	0.00%
TCV	15/11/06	10.25%	7.63%	3.40%	5.39%
WATC	15/01/97	10.00%	6.82%	1.65%	0.00%
WATC	1/04/98	12.00%	6.93%	2.35%	3.51%
WATC	15/04/99	9.00%	7.03%	2.07%	3.76%
WATC	1/08/01	10.00%	7.24%	1.89%	0.00%
WATC	15/07/03	8.00%	7.42%	2.51%	5.37%
WATC	15/07/05	10.00%	7.61%	2.12%	0.00%
				100.00%	100.00%

Exhibit 15.11

Summary of Exposure and Duration

Description	Benchmark Weight	Portfolio Weight	Benchmark Duration	Portfolio Duration
NSWTC	31.97%	32.00%	1.1415	1.1416
QTC	25.16%	25.05%	1.1222	1.1220
SAFA	7.92%	6.69%	0.1917	0.1808
TASCORP	3.68%	3.68%	0.1174	0.1289
TCV	18.67%	18.47%	0.6701	0.6701
WATC	12.59%	12.64%	0.4226	0.4224
CASH	0.00%	1.46%	—	—
Total	100.00%	100.00%	3.6657	3.6657

This portfolio has been matched by credit quality, duration and duration within issuer. The stratified sampling process has taken no account of historical returns or their correlations; it assumes that each bond issue is fairly priced in the market and will remain close to fair price. Deviations from this rule will be the main contributor to tracking error for this portfolio. In practice these are likely to be small because each asset in the portfolio is liquid so mispricings should be quickly traded out.

International fixed interest is benchmarked to the Salomon Brothers World Government Bond Index. The indexer with access to a reliable source of historical data for the component securities in this benchmark will ideally choose an optimised sampling approach, with a target tracking error of about 0.30%. The benchmark index includes the 15 government bond markets of Australia, Austria, Belgium, Canada, Denmark, France, Ireland, Italy, Japan, the Netherlands, Spain, Sweden, Switzerland, the United Kingdom and the United States. In principle, the stratified sample approach will work just as well for this index portfolio as for the domestic fixed interest portfolio. In practice, the number of securities and the volume of data to be analysed favours a more automated version of this approach.

9. DOMESTIC LISTED PROPERTY SECURITIES

This sector is benchmarked to the Australian Stock Exchange Listed Property Accumulation Index.

It is generally accepted among indexers that direct property cannot be indexed because the benchmark consists of a small number of large assets, which are traded so infrequently that regular estimates of asset values are impossible. These obstacles have not deterred the occasional brave attempt to establish indexes of direct property holdings and even derivatives markets based on these. Success has been elusive.

So property indexes and index portfolios are nearly always confined to listed property markets. For the serious property indexer this is highly unsatisfactory because listed property securities do not behave like property markets. This could be because of the liquidity of the listed vehicles which is lacking in the underlying bricks and mortar, or because the prices of listed assets are more likely than direct property assets to incorporate expected future returns to the underlying assets. Or it could be due to other, unidentified factors. The returns to listed property securities are no more similar to those of other listed equities, so the asset class is a useful diversifying element in the portfolio.

From the point of view of the indexer, listed property markets can be treated in very much the same way as other equity index portfolios, except that their liquidity can be a little patchy. The indexer therefore will select a simple optimisation approach for this portfolio, choosing to invest in about three-quarters of the number of issues in the benchmark index, depending on the market's overall liquidity. Tracking error of 0.25% is feasible with negligible turnover.

10. ONGOING MANAGEMENT

It has been said that managing index portfolios is something like patrolling the Bay of Biscay in a Sunderland during World War II. Long periods of tedium are punctuated with bursts of manic activity which end as abruptly as they began. As it is unlikely that any individual has first hand experience of both occupations, the comparison must remain conjecture.

The indexer's aim is to maintain portfolio exposure close to benchmark while keeping costs to a minimum. If the portfolio is well constructed, changes in the composition of the benchmark which come about through normal price fluctuations will not cause problems, as the portfolio's composition will follow automatically.

Changes in the benchmark which are due to external factors may need some action. The guiding principle is that if the capital structure of the benchmark or one of its components changes, then the portfolio needs to follow suit. If there is no change in capital structure, then the indexer can take no action.

Examples of day-to-day changes to benchmarks are:

- Takeovers require no action so long as the portfolio holds both the offeror and the offeree companies. The indexer will usually wait until the takeover proceeds to compulsory aquisition or the bid fails.
- Stock splits require no action because there is no change to the company or the benchmark.
- Cash dividends are used to accumulate cash. This cash must be invested across the portfolio as soon as possible.
- Stock dividends are accepted in the form of physical shares, as the dividend represents an increase in the issued capital of the company.
- Share buy-backs are accepted because the issued capital of the company is contracting.

From time to time the benchmark changes because new stocks are added and others are deleted. For fixed interest benchmarks these changes are known and can be anticipated. For equities the indexer must maintain the appropriate information links.[15] The replicating indexer must buy or sell stock when the index change occurs regardless of prices and costs. The sampling indexer may make a judgement about when and how to buy and sell stock as required by benchmark changes, but will usually implement the required trades within a few weeks of the benchmark change.

Cash flows need to be dealt with on a case-by-case basis. Small cash flows are treated in a similar fashion to cash dividends; that is, they are accumulated as cash and equitised where possible using futures contracts until there is a large enough pool to warrant a purchase of physical stock. This stock purchase can be used to rebalance the portfolio if necessary, so avoiding unwanted transactions costs. If the cash flow is large then the indexer may buy physical assets outright, unless the price of the futures contracts offers an arbitrage opportunity (see the later section on enhancements). Normally the indexer will view any large stock purchase as an opportunity to fine tune the balance of the portfolio thus helping to keep transactions costs to a minimum.

11. MEASURING PERFORMANCE

Investors who place their funds in index portfolios expect unspectacular results. Their investments are expected to rise and fall in value more or less to the same extent as the benchmark or market to which they are indexed.

Performance measurement is therefore relevant only with respect to the benchmark index. For any given period, such as a month, quarter or a year, simple performance comparisons are useful but limited. The apparent performance of the portfolio will depend on the particular period being measured, with little or no indication of what occurred before or after, or in the intervening period. Consider the following series of results for a domestic equity portfolio in *Exhibit 15.12*.

15. Most index services provide periodical information documents about the composition of and changes to the benchmark. These services are usually offered on a subscription basis.

Exhibit 15.12

Monthly Performance of Domestic Equities Index Portfolio

Month	Bench-mark	Portfolio	Differ-ence	Month	Bench-mark	Portfolio	Differ-ence
31/05/94	1.15%	1.00%	−0.15%	30/06/95	0.48%	0.65%	0.17%
30/06/94	−4.03%	−3.95%	0.08%	31/07/95	4.91%	4.91%	0.00%
31/07/94	3.72%	3.80%	0.08%	31/08/95	0.94%	0.80%	−0.14%
31/08/94	3.04%	3.00%	−0.04%	30/09/95	0.74%	0.65%	−0.09%
30/09/94	−3.88%	−4.05%	−0.17%	31/10/95	−2.34%	−2.27%	0.06%
31/10/94	1.29%	1.36%	0.07%	30/11/95	4.43%	4.43%	0.00%
30/11/94	−7.23%	−7.06%	0.16%	31/12/95	2.53%	2.33%	−0.20%
31/12/94	1.65%	1.80%	0.15%	31/01/96	3.93%	3.85%	−0.08%
31/01/95	−4.25%	−4.16%	0.09%	29/02/96	0.39%	0.38%	−0.01%
28/02/95	5.07%	5.00%	−0.07%	31/03/96	−2.28%	−2.18%	0.10%
31/03/95	0.07%	0.02%	−0.05%	30/04/96	4.38%	4.20%	−0.18%
30/04/95	7.78%	7.98%	0.20%	31/05/96	−1.87%	−1.89%	−0.02%
31/05/95	−1.19%	−1.28%	−0.09%	30/06/96	−0.59%	−0.30%	0.29%

Measured to 30 June, 1996, the performance of this portfolio and its benchmark would look like *Exhibit 15.13.*

Exhibit 15.13

Performance Summary, Domestic Equities Index Portfolio to 30 June, 1996

Period	Benchmark	Portfolio	Difference
3 months	1.83%	1.92%	0.09%
6 months	3.82%	3.93%	0.11%
12 months	15.83%	15.53%	−0.31%
2 years	22.44%	22.73%	0.29%

The same performance measurements taken one month earlier would look like *Exhibit 15.14.*

Exhibit 15.14

Performance Summary, Domestic Equities Index Portfolio to 31 May, 1996

Period	Benchmark	Portfolio	Difference
3 months	0.10%	0.00%	−0.09%
6 months	7.08%	6.67%	−0.41%
12 months	17.08%	16.63%	−0.45%
2 years	18.21%	18.24%	0.03%

Neither set of results gives a good indication of the performance of the portfolio relative to the benchmark. In fact, it is not obvious that the two return summaries refer to the same portfolio. Obviously some form of continuous measurement is required to show how well the portfolio is tracking its benchmark. Because the CAPM tells us that asset returns fluctuate all the time but asset risk characteristics are more steady, some measure of the riskiness of the portfolio is required. Fortunately, there are several of these. Together they can indicate how much total risk is in the portfolio. Separately they tell us how much of that risk is due to the portfolio's exposure to its market, in other words its *beta*, and how much is due to other influences, collectively known as *tracking error*.

As we discovered earlier in the chapter, *beta* is a measure of the senstivity of the portfolio to the ups and downs of its market. To arrive at the observed beta measurement for a portfolio, a regression analysis is carried out. This will give an estimate of the historical beta of the portfolio as well as an estimate of how accurate the beta estimate is. This measurement, known as the R square, provides an aggregate measure of the variation between actual results and those predicted by the beta. An R square of 1.0 indicates that the beta calculated explains all of the movement of the portfolio against its benchmark, while an R square of zero says that the beta explains none of the portfolio's movement against its benchmark. In the example above, the beta of the portfolio for two years to 30 June, 1996 is 1.0012 and the R square is 0.9996. For the two years to 31 May, 1996 the beta is 1.0011 also with an R square of 0.9996. This means that, over the previous two year period, the portfolio is moving slightly more than the benchmark, so a benchmark move—up or down—of $100.00 would be associated with portfolio move—up or down—of $100.12. The R square means that this beta explains 99.96% of the portfolio's market driven performance.

In addition to the observed beta, the indexer is usually also interested in what the prospective or ex-ante beta is of the portfolio. This is a useful measure for new portfolios or where an old portfolio has been reweighted. The ex-ante beta of the portfolio is simply the weighted average of the betas of the component securities in the portfolio. (As for portfolio betas, stock betas are calculated by conducting a regression analysis between the stock returns and benchmark returns.) The ex-ante beta of our porfolio is estimated as 1.0009.

As mentioned previously, *tracking error* is a measure of how much of the portfolio's performance is due to risk that is not explained by general market movements

To obtain a measure of observed tracking error the differences in return for each period are calculated. The tracking error is the standard deviation of these differences, usually adjusted to give an annualised figure. The observed tracking error from *Exhibit 15.13* is 0.4404% to 30 June and 0.3958% to 31 May.

A tracking error of 0.4404% pa means that there is a 68% probability that the portfolio's performance will be within that range of the benchmark. In other words, if the benchmark index rises by 15% in a year, then there is a 68% chance that the portfolio will gain between 14.5596% and 15.4404% in that year.

The risk of the portfolio is the variance of its returns. Expected portfolio variance can be estimated from the return variance on the assets comprising the portfolio and the relationship, or covariance, between these assets and the benchmark. The ex-ante tracking error of the example portfolio is 0.45%.

The important thing to note here is that beta and tracking error do not change much over time so, unlike simple performance comparisons, they are not dependent on the period being measured.

Other indications of the performance characteristics of a portfolio include risk analysis and factor analysis. Both are the output of portfolio optimisers: factor models; and industry group models respectively. Although not as widely recognised as beta and tracking error, risk and factor analysis can add insight because they highlight the sources of specific risk, or tracking error, in portfolios. Factor model optimisers deliver factor analyses which allow the investment manager insight into how much portfolio risk is attributable to exposure to various factors. A typical factor analysis would look like *Exhibit 15.15*.

Exhibit 15.15

Factor Analysis, Domestic Equities Index Portfolio

Portfolio Specific Risk (Tracking Error) Factor	0.42% Contribution to Tracking Error
Variability in Markets	−0.02%
Success	−0.02%
Size	0.05%
Value	0.01%
Leverage	−0.01%
Growth	−0.02%
Trading Activity	0.02%
Interest Rate Sensitivity	0.00%
Total Factor Risk	0.01%
Residual Specific Risk	0.41%

The same portfolio analysed using an industry mean model is as follows in *Exhibit 15.16.*

Exhibit 15.16

Risk Analysis using Industry Mean Model, Domestic Equities Index Portfolio

Portfolio Specific Risk (Tracking Error)	0.42%
Sector	0.02%
Residual Specific Risk	0.40%

Both analyses indicate that the portfolio is reasonably well diversified because identifiable factor and sector risk is small. The remaining tracking error can probably be reduced only by increasing the number of stocks in the portfolio.

Performance measurement for indexed portfolios is in many respects more critical than for actively managed portfolios, because the indexed portfolio can generally tolerate less variation from benchmark performance.

12. ATTRIBUTION ANALYSIS

If everything goes according to plan the indexed portfolio's performance will be very close to that of the benchmark, as predicted by the optimiser's risk analysis. Things do not always go so smoothly however, so an attribution analysis may be called for to find out just where things went awry.

As with optimisers, attribution analyses come in a number of varieties, but they do hold some things in common. They try to break the portfolio down into manageable chunks and then see which of these chunks contributed to the unwanted performance variation. In the case of a domestic equities portfolio, industry groups are often used as the basis for attribution analyses; for international portfolios, countries can be used. In extreme cases the attribution analysis may be carried out at the level of individual securities to see which one caused the problem.

To illustrate how an attribution analysis might look, the performance over one month of the *TOP100* portfolio described in Section 5 above is analysed. Remember that this portfolio was compiled simply by selecting the 100 largest of the 300-odd stocks in the benchmark index. It is measurably overweight in diversified resources, media and banks because these sectors claim a disproportionate number of large stocks within the benchmark index.

During the period in question, the portfolio returned +0.21% while the benchmark returned −0.04%. This analysis seeks to identify not only which industry groups contributed to performance variation, but how much of that was due to the portfolio's being over- or underweight in each industry group, and how much can be explained by stock selection within each industry group.

The first of these, the industry mismatch effect can be calculated as follows:

$$IM = (w_{ip}i - w_{ib}) \cdot (r_i - r_b) \qquad (4)$$

The second effect, the stock selection effect can be calculated for each industry group as follows:

$$SS = w_{sp} \cdot (r_{sp} - r_{sb}) \qquad (5)$$

Where:

w_{ip} is the weight of industry i in the portfolio

w_{ib} is the weight of industry i in the benchmark

r_i is the return to industry i

r_b is the return to the benchmark

w_{sp} is the weight of stock i in the portfolio

r_{sp} is the return to stocks in industry i in the portfolio

r_{sb} is the return to industry i in the benchmark

The results of the analysis are set out in *Exhibit 15.17*.

Exhibit 15.17

Attribution Analysis for TOP100 Portfolio

	Industry Group Mismatch	Stock Selection Mismatch
Gold	0.06%	−0.12%
Other Metals	0.00%	−0.02%
Div Resources	0.04%	−0.01%
Energy	0.00%	0.11%
Infra & Utilities	0.00%	0.00%
Developers	0.00%	−0.04%
Building Materials	−0.01%	−0.01%
Alcohol & Tobacco	0.01%	0.03%
Food	0.00%	−0.02%
Chemicals	−0.01%	−0.02%
Engineering	0.00%	0.00%
Paper & Packaging	0.00%	−0.01%
Retail	0.00%	−0.04%
Tspt	−0.02%	−0.01%
Media	0.00%	0.01%
Banks	0.14%	0.17%
Insurance	0.00%	0.01%
Telecommunications	−0.01%	0.00%
Inv Services	−0.01%	0.00%
Property Trust	0.00%	0.01%
Misc Services	0.03%	−0.01%
Misc Industrials	0.01%	0.03%
Div Industrials	0.00%	−0.03%
Tourism	0.01%	−0.01%
Total	0.24%	0.02%

The portfolio benefited from being overweight banks because this sector performed better (+4.47%) than the benchmark (−0.04%) during the period in question. Within this sector the portfolio also benefited from holding large banks in preference to small banks. It also did well to be overweight in diversified resources, although stock selection in this sector contributed little to performance variation because the portfolio held three of the four stocks in the industry group. On the other hand, the portfolio benefited slightly from being underweight gold stocks, but did less well than it would have had it held more small gold stocks rather than only large ones. The portfolio's overweight position in media contributed little to performance variation because the performance of this sector during the period in question was not very different from that of the benchmark index.

It should be noted that this attribution analysis is unusually simple because the portfolio did not trade during the period. When transactions are taken into account an extra column is needed. This column is usually headed "market timing" or "trading activity" and tries to capture value added or subtracted from stock purchases and sales

13. INDEX ENHANCEMENTS

Index enhancements have grown in popularity over the last half-decade. There are a number of possible reasons for this. Probably the most important is the perception by many investors that markets harbour enough inefficiencies to allow risk-free extra market returns, and that indexed portfolios can be well placed to benefit from this "arbitrage" activity. Indexed portfolios bear a closer resemblance in structure to the benchmarks against which derivative instruments, such as share price indices, are settled and because indexing, as a "buy and hold" strategy, can tolerate substitution of individual or groups of stock holdings by futures and options for indeterminate periods of time. Investment managers favour enhancements because they attract higher fees than plain indexing.

Enhancements come in two varieties: risk free and risky. Some might say that a third category is at least as important as these two: risky enhancements masquerading as risk free.[16] If it is so, it is sure to be a short-lived activity[17] and will not be addressed in this chapter.

13.1 Risk free enhancements

An exhaustive treatment is not feasible because so many enhancements are possible, but the main sources of risk free enhancements are mispriced derivatives—such as share price index futures and options; listed stock options; dividend re-investment plans; and tax anomalies.

Mispriced derivatives enhancements characterise immature markets, and markets with particularly high transactions costs. The diversity of strategies

---

16. These can take many forms. Often they combine bought and sold positions in different securities, so that the portfolio's overall level of market risk is unchanged. This is not risk-free because the portfolio is exposed to increased specific risk due to the security mismatches introduced by the enhancement.
17. Because any additional returns will only compensate for the risk added.

which come under this heading is very rich, so a simple specimen will be used to represent the genus. The most straightforward is known as stock index arbitrage. This takes advantage of stock index futures which are trading at a price below "fair price".

Example: stock index arbitrage

Consider the following investment environment:

Date now	July 7
Physical share price index	2202
SPI futures	2215
Expiry date of futures	December 31
Dividend yield	3.2% pa
Interest rate	6.8% pa

The investor has two ways of investing in the stockmarket to the end of December: buy shares or buy futures and place the cash on deposit. The example below looks at what happens in each case.

It is important to note that the level at which the stockmarket closes on December 29 is irrelevant because the futures contract and the physical will be at exactly the same level at that date, however for the sake of illustration we will say that the market closes at 2210.

Strategy	Buy Shares	Buy Futures
Profit (loss) on shares	8	0
Profit (loss) on futures	0	(5)
Dividend income	34	0
Interest income	0	72
Profit (loss)	42	67
Percentage of initial investment	1.9%	3.0%
	42/2202 = 1.9%	67/2202 = 3.0%

In this case the investor holding cash and wishing to invest in the equity market is clearly better off using the futures contract. Another investor who already holds physical shares would sell these in favour of futures, so long as the transactions costs thus incurred are less than 1.1% (3.0 − 1.9) on the round trip. Most mature markets do not allow such easy profits: share price index futures contracts tend to trade in a range—determined by transactions costs—about their fair price. Less sophisticated markets can offer rich pickings in arbitrage activity, but this often comes with exotic sources of risk such as inscrutable trading rules and byzantine settlement systems.

Dividend re-investment plans (DRPs): many listed companies offer their shareholders the opportunity to receive dividends in the form of shares instead of cash. For the company concerned this activity has the advantage of either reducing the effective cash paid out in dividends or encouraging new equity investment in the company—whichever way one likes to look at it. Either way, new shares are issued in lieu of cash dividends. For the investor the attraction is that shares, which probably would have to be purchased anyway, are effectively bought with dividends forgone, saving transactions costs and often adding to return, because the DRP shares are normally issued at a discount to the prevailing market price of the share.

Tax anomalies: other enhancements seek to take advantage of anomalies between tax regimes. Usually this activity centres around the fact that different classes of investor are subject to different tax treatments, especially as they relate to dividends, imputation credits and withholding tax.

The most simple strategy is where the non-payer of local tax, such as a foreign investor, sells stock to a local taxpayer immediately before the ex-dividend date and repurchases the stock immediately after. Such transactions usually have some kind of repurchase agreement attached to protect both parties from unwanted swings in the share price. This may involve some sharing of the imputation benefit to give the non-local taxpayer incentive to carry out the transaction. Alternatively, the stock may be transferred as part of an asset swap or a stock lending arrangement. The principle of transferring the benefits of dividend imputation remains the same in each case but tactics differ in administrative and legal aspects. The only fly in the ointment is that, in some jurisdictions, uncertainties about interpretation of taxation law can seriously modify potential gains from this activity.

13.2 Risky enhancements

Most enhancements add risk as well as return. It is important, therefore, that the nature of the risk being added is understood and quantified. Enhancement strategies aiming to add risk controlled return are many and varied. Most seek to exploit a judgment about which securities or groups of securities will do better than others. Normally this judgment is the result of rigorous and sophisticated analysis. Most enhancement strategies therefore have predefined ''rules'' about when to buy and sell specified groups of assets, and a well articulated strategy for risk control while the strategy is working, and for damage control when it is not. It is these predefined rules and strategies which differentiate most index enhancements from conventional active portfolio management, but in some cases this distinction is one of degree rather than of definition.

Enhancements are generally designed to exploit perceived mispricing of some class of assets. They may also exploit mispriced derivatives such as stock index futures, as in the example above, or options on stocks. Options can present significant opportunities for enhancements because the investor can benefit not only from movements in the asset price but also from mispriced volatility. This is because the price of any option depends not only upon the price of the underlying asset but also, among other things, on the expected volatility of the underlying asset. If the volatility implied by the option price changes over time, the investor can benefit from correctly anticipating the change.

More specifically, if the volatility implied by the price of a particular option series is less than the actual volatility, then the investor can add value. This is done by purchasing the underpriced option—either call or put—and selling or buying the appropriate quantity of physical shares, or another option series which is more fairly priced (or vice versa if the option is overpriced). This position must then be managed closely as changes in the share price as well as the simple passage of time will introduce new, unintended risks to the position. Even when the position is meticulously managed, the investor risks losses if the original volatility estimate was inaccurate. Where the net option position is bought rather than sold, such potential losses can be limited to a quantifiable sum which is set at a level which is tolerable to the investor. Net sold positions, on the other hand, can result in potentially large losses as the maximum loss on a sold option position is usually unlimited.

Index enhancement strategies which employ physical assets must always be carefully managed because, as with sold options positions, the potential risks to the portfolio are very large. Such enhancements are often referred to as portfolio tilts. This implies that the portfolio deviates only slightly—is "tilted" away from true index proportions. The direction of the tilt can be determined by factor considerations, macro-economic variables or active security analysis.

Factor tilts suggest a tilt to a factor which affects the performance of some stocks relative to others. An example of such a tilt would be toward growth stocks rather than value stocks. The portfolio would therefore be expected to outperform in market environments favouring emerging companies, such as those in growth industries like high technology or telecommunications. Conversely, the portfolio will underperform if sectors which represent "value"—which might include countercyclical stocks such as discount retailing and food manufacture—outperform the growth sectors.

Tilts which are driven by macro-economic factors seek to exploit superior economic analysis. This usually results in an opinion about the equilibrium level of some macro-economic variable, such as interest rates. Thus an investor anticipating a change in the level of interest rates might favour stocks which are shown to be sensitive to interest rate changes such as banks and financial services or very capital-intensive industries. An expected fall in oil prices might favour transportation stocks, and so on.

Tilts deriving from active security analysis simply exploit the perceived mispricing by the market of individual securities. This type of tilt is the one which most resembles conventional active management.

Cash enhancements can also add value to an index portfolio if the portfolio happens to hold enough cash. Fortunately, there are enough occasions for this activity (usually where cash is held in the portfolio to provide collateral for derivatives positions) to allow significant value to be added. Cash enhancements add value by adding two types of risk to the portfolio: yield curve risk; and credit risk.

Yield curve risk is added by purchasing interest bearing assets with more than one day to maturity. Under normal circumstances such assets earn higher rates of interest than cash (overnight securities) simply to compensate the investor for the additional risk associated with tying up assets for a longer period. The risk to the investor is that interest rates will rise in the meantime, so increasing the cost of capital and/or the opportunity cost of not having funds to invest at a higher yield.

Credit risk is the risk that the issuer of the interest bearing securities is unable to fulfil its obligations, or will undergo a credit "rerating", which will cause the market value of its issued debt to fall. This is due to the fact that the interest earned on such securities reflects the market estimate of the credit risk for any issuer of debt, so that the higher the interest earned the higher the credit risk.

14. CUSTOMISING INDEX PORTFOLIOS

Index portfolios are particularly suitable to customising because there is no expected outperformance, or alpha to be compromised. The investor may choose to customise either the benchmark, the portfolio or both.

Standard benchmarks are much more popular than customised ones because they are easily measured and widely available. On the other hand, customised benchmarks often provide a more meaningful basis of performance evaluation, particularly if the portfolio specifications are somewhat unusual.

The most popular forms of customisation relate to the level of risk or costs that the portfolio can sustain. In such circumstances the indexer will usually determine the number of securities in the portfolio to give the required results. Or the investor may have specific liquidity requirements and this will determine the portfolio's rebalancing schedule and the use of derivatives.

If the portfolio is held in a jurisdiction where differential tax treatment applies to different classes of investor, the portfolio may be customised to meet specified after-tax objectives.

The investor may have reason to impose embargoes on particular stocks and so demand a customised benchmark. For example, an ethical fund may wish to avoid the arms or tobacco industries. Customised portfolios and customised benchmarks are particularly useful where asset classes overlap, causing a potential double exposure to some asset class. This is often the case where the widely-used benchmark for equities includes both large cap and small cap, but where the investor needs to treat these as separate asset classes. In this instance two customised benchmarks would be constructed. The first would comprise the broad-based benchmark, excluding some collective measure of the small cap stocks. The second would be the broad-based benchmark excluding large cap stocks.

15. TRAPS FOR YOUNG PLAYERS

Constructing and managing index portfolios can look deceptively simple, and some index portfolios are indeed very easy to look after. This perception is reinforced by the continuing downward pressure on management fees.

The biggest pitfall is the expectation that one approach fits all. Often this means that the indexer goes for full replication without considering the implications for the costs of running the portfolio. Probably the next biggest is that of using the optimiser or other stock selection software as a "black box". Experienced indexers will choose their optimiser according to the market to be indexed and will also exercise some care about how data is sourced and applied.

Once the portfolio is up and running the indexer will need to take care to manage liquidity and to avoid unwanted portfolio turnover. Often these are two sides of the same coin because they incorporate the use of derivatives, such as share price index futures.

Corporate actions can cause problems by landing the portfolio with securities which are simply not required for diversification and which merely add to transactions and administration costs. Pre-emptive action is occasionally required to avoid this happening. Similarly, large changes to the benchmark holdings, often resulting from privatised utilities or other publicly owned entities, can present the indexer with quite a challenge. These problems need to be addressed on a case-by-case basis, and require a good understanding of the structure of the underlying market and any relevant derivatives markets.

Where the index portfolio holds derivatives, either by choice or by default, then the indexer must take care that any options holdings do not result, through delta expansion or contraction, in the portfolio being either geared or underexposed. While this problem can also occur in an actively managed portfolio, it is usually more serious in an index portfolio, which usually has less spare liquidity and generally much finer tolerances of performance variation.

16. SUMMARY

Indexation is the answer to the problem of security selection for investors who wish to avoid the costs or the risks of seeking and managing high alpha portfolios. Sometimes investors choose not to chase high alphas because they believe that they represent a wild goose chase.

More often indexation is selected for much more prosaic reasons. This may be that the investor has a very large portfolio and so employs the indexed core-active satellite approach. This effectively avoids both the very high costs of market impact that can result from a large active portfolio, as well as the situation where dividing the fund into many small active mandates results in a very high cost "closet index".

Other candidates for indexation include small or very cost sensitive investors who simply cannot afford active management, and international managers who want to concentrate their efforts on managing beta or market risks without the distracting effects of specific portfolio risks in obscure parts of the world. Still other index portfolios are run as part of a larger strategy deriving from some position in derivatives such as share price index futures or asset swaps, or to meet the requirements of customisation.

Indexation of portfolios will continue to grow as long as pressure on investment management fees continues, and while large funds continue to dominate markets relative to small- and medium-sized investors. Increased international investment will contribute to further growth in indexation, both through indexation of portfolio holdings and indirectly through the increased use of asset swaps as a tax effective means of managing international investments.

The concept of indexing is simple, but eliminating an acceptable amount of a portfolio's specific risk without the costs defeating the very purpose of indexing can be tricky. The best approach is nearly always specific to the situation, depending, among other things, on the market in question and the particular objectives of the investor. The indexer will aim for a balance of minimised cost and specific risk or tracking error, choosing either to fully replicate the target market or to aim for benchmark-like returns using some sample of securities. This sample will be selected either as a cross-section of the market or by using a mean-variance optimiser, or some combination of the two.

The indexer will typically adhere to a rebalancing schedule determined by fixed decision rules, taking into account the likely life span and cash flow requirements of the portfolio.

Performance of index portfolios is best described by evaluating the risk of the portfolio rather than by comparing returns over any given period. This is because the risk characteristics of assets can be thought of as being stable over time while returns are not.

Some index portfolios are subject to return enhancements, which may or may not add alpha risk. Normally enhanced index portfolios seek to exploit mispriced derivative instruments, but some apply wisdom distilled from specialist quantitative or macroeconomic analysis. Still others add value by exploiting anomalies in tax regimes.

Indexation is particularly useful in the context of customised portfolios because it can meet customising requirements without jeopardising the portfolios' other objectives.

The simplicity of indexing is sometimes deceptive and the temptation to apply textbook or black box solutions should be avoided. The skill of the indexer is to achieve the theoretical benefits of indexing while avoiding the practical traps.

Part 5

Risk Management

Chapter 16

Value at Risk Models[1]

by Satyajit Das and John Martin

1. INTRODUCTION

Market risk has emerged as a central issue in financial risk management in recent years. Value at risk (VAR) techniques have also emerged as a central mechanism for quantification and communication of risk on multiple levels ranging from individual traders, trading units to entire businesses, both within financial institutions, and albeit to a lesser degree, in non-financial institutions.

In this chapter, the concept of VAR and its application in market risk management is examined. The structure of this chapter is as follows: the evolution of risk management is considered first. The basic principles of market risk and its measurement is examined later. The VAR technique is then outlined, including consideration of the various types of VAR, the application of VAR to different types of instruments and the interpretation of the VAR statistics in risk measurement as well as consideration of the assumptions underlying the derivation of VAR measures. The application of VAR based risk management techniques to financial institutions and non financial institutions is then considered. The subject of risk adjusted performance measurement is also considered.

2. EVOLUTION OF RISK MANAGEMENT

2.1 Financial risk

All financial intermediation entails the assumption, management and pricing of risk. Risk, in this broader sense, encompasses credit risk, market risk, liquidity risk and operational risks. These risk classes are essential to the process of credit, maturity and market (primarily, interest rate) risk intermediation central to all financial activity.

Credit risk refers to the risk of loss arising from the *default* of the counterparty ie the failure to honour and meet its legal obligation. Market risk refers to the risk of loss sustained as a result of changes in the values of market prices or factors used to value financial instruments. Liquidity risk

---

1. The writing of the chapter was undertaken separately though the authors collaborated on the ideas behind the underlying concepts. Satyajit Das is responsible for the main text of the chapter while John Martin is responsible for Appendices A and B as well as Exhibits 16.8, 16.9, 16.10, 16.11, 16.12, 16.13, and 16.15. The authors would like to thank Suellen Schmidt for her assistance in the preparation of some of the exhibits. The authors would like to thank J P Morgan (Debra Robertson) for consent for the inclusion of the material on measuring the risk of managing option position using analytic VAR and simulation methods in Exhibit 16.17.

refers to the risk of loss arising from either inability to make payments or the inability to re-finance obligations as and when they mature or the inability to re-finance at anticipated rates. Operational risk refers to the risk of loss from a broad range of risks including: operational (processing failure); technology (systems failure); legal (non unenforceability of contracts); and regulatory (breach of regulatory requirements).

Underlying the identified risk factors is the broader issue of management failure or strategic risk wherein the value of the business (in present value terms) is affected by individual risk factors. Examples of this type of failure include the reputation risk where entry into transactions which were not suitable leads to litigation which has the effect of damaging the client perception of the entity.

The important point to make is that trading and market risk management is a part of *the overall risk profile of an entity.*

2.2 Key factors in the evolution of financial institution risk management practice

Most if not all these risks have been present in the process of financial intermediation all along. Several factors have contributed to the increased focus on risk management:

- the deregulation of financial markets;
- the increasing role of securities and derivative products in financial intermediation;
- the increase in the risk profile of organisations, with increased emphasis on activities which require the assumption of risk, deliberately;
- the volatility of markets and its impact on financial institutions;
- the pressure from capital market investors for returns related to the relative riskiness of their investments; and
- the regulatory requirements for a framework for the management of risk.

It is salutary to remember that financial intermediation industries throughout the world have only been de-regulated relatively recently. European markets have only been de-regulated in the last 10-15 years and emerging markets are still subject to varying degrees of regulation.

The presence of regulation impacts on risk in at least two ways: first, it may regulate risk taking itself; and, secondly, the risk taking activity may, to varying degrees be underwritten by the financial system at large *reducing* the requirement for risk management in individual organisations. Elimination of regulation emphasises both risk taking and risk management by individual organisations.

The increased role of securities and derivative products in financial markets affects trading risk management in a number of ways. The increased use of securities in financial markets has resulted in bank financing being gradually supplanted by bonds and other tradeable obligations. This trend has included the securitisation of many hitherto illiquid assets such as mortgages and various types of receivables, extending from credit card, motor vehicle etc loans and lease obligations. The impact of securitisation has included an emphasis on evaluating the risk of these obligations through periodic revaluation of the position, by marking positions to current market values. This trend has replaced, to a large degree traditional methodologies of classical accrual accounting.

The increased role of derivatives in transferring risk and synthesising exposure to asset prices has promoted a focus on risk management for different reasons. The dynamic value characteristics of these instruments, including the potential for leverage, has dictated the need to both frequently and regularly mark to market positions but also to monitor and manage the *potential* value changes to these products as a result of changes in asset prices or other variables.

The increase in trading activities of firms and the resulting volatility of income and the overall increase in risk of the firm's activities has been much commented upon. The reasons underlying this increase in trading include:

• the fall in agency revenues as markets deregulate;

• the increasing pressure from clients for execution based on the financial institution trading as principal rather than agent; and

• the perceived competitive advantage enjoyed by financial institutions in trading, including infrastructure, information, transaction costs etc.

The assumption of risk is often presented as a relatively new phenomenon. In reality, the *nature* of risk taking has changed. Traditional risk taking was confined to balance sheet oriented interest rate risk created by deliberate maturity mismatches. Supplementary risk taking may have been present in areas like currency or securities trading.

Modern risk taking is more diverse in nature. It encompasses traditional forms of risk taking and increased trading in other asset classes. This increased trading focus is driven by both client demands in terms of market-making and proprietary or own account trading, in search of return. This change reflects in no small part the increasing diversity of the activities undertaken by financial institutions which encompass activities in all asset classes (debt, currency, equity, and commodities) and in businesses ranging from balance sheet driven activities (such as lending), off balance sheet activities (such as underwriting and securities distribution and risk management instruments), to pure fee based activities (such as investment management, custody services, cash management services etc).

Underlying the focus on risk is the impact of volatility on values of financial instruments as a result of the change in financial market asset values. While there is little evidence that *overall* levels of volatility have increased it is evident that volatility levels have often become compressed into short time periods when volatility levels rise very substantially. The impact of volatility combined with the increased risk profile of financial institutions dictates a more comprehensive focus on risk management.

The pressure to manage risk is also evident from investor demand for:

1. Understanding of risks taken by financial institutions in a unified and transparent framework; and

2. Measures of return relative to risk for *all activities* of financial institutions.

The external pressure, from increasingly activist shareholders, has its counterpoint in increased internal pressure to measure risk adjusted returns to enable more accurate evaluation of performance and also allocation of capital as between business units.

The final driver of risk management is the regulatory process itself. The transition from a regulated to a deregulated environment requires adjustments in regulatory tools. Traditional tools, such as balance sheet constraints, interest rate controls or specific regulations, regarding participation in specific activities, have gradually been supplanted by capital based controls, requiring minimum capitalisation levels commensurate with risk.

The 1988 Capital Adequacy Accord represents the first concrete step in that process requiring capital resources consistent with the degree of *credit risk*. The credit risk capital framework inevitably creates an adverse incentive in that credit risk taking is discouraged while market risk taking (against which capital does not need to be held) is encouraged. In reality, capital based market risk controls were inevitable from the time the capital based credit risk guidelines were mooted in the mid-1980s.

Underlying the evolution towards risk management is also the process of innovation in capital markets where the product life cycles have shortened and the pace of introduction of new products, reflecting the earnings potential available for the first mover, has increased. Against this background, a more flexible risk management framework was inevitable.

2.3   Risk management versus asset-liability management

It is incorrect to assume that institutions had *no* risk management previously. In fact, most financial institutions had in place frameworks for risk within an overall asset liability management (ALM) framework. The ALM model is now less and less relevant and increasingly replaced by an overall risk management framework. The differences between the two models are considerable:

- ALM is balance sheet oriented while risk management is risk oriented;

- ALM is not easily adapted to off-balance sheet transactions, particularly derivatives;

- ALM risk measures which are interest rate based (gaps and duration) are not necessarily easy to translate across other asset classes;

- ALM provides little mechanism for arriving at an overall risk level for a firm and is not easily adapted to a risk adjusted return framework; and

- ALM, unlike risk management, is difficult to link to either other risks or to return on the firm's equity capital.

Risk management in effect reshapes ALM into the context of modern financial intermediation. Several aspects of this current approach are well worth noting:

- Risk in the modern context of mean variance finance is subject to considerable statistical assumptions which users need to appreciate in utilising the information; and

- While developed largely in the context of trading, particularly derivatives trading operations, it is universally applicable to all aspects of financial intermediation.

2.4 Financial risk management in non-financial institutions

The concepts outlined, while developed primarily for financial institutions active in trading, are equally applicable with some modest adjustments to non-financial institutions. However, the nature of financial risk in non-financial institutions is significantly different.

These differences relate to:

- the financial versus non-financial nature of the underlying assets and liabilities; and
- the source of the underlying risk and the ability to manage this risk.

These differences dictate the nature of risk management processes and approaches for the different types of institutions. An understanding of the identified differences is central to the proper analysis of risk and the concomitant application of derivative instruments to manage that risk.

For financial institutions, the fact that *both* assets and liabilities are financial in nature is central to the task of risk management. This allows risk positions to be matched and the net position to be hedged. The process of hedging is facilitated to a substantial degree by the essential financial nature of these exposures which are correlated to some tradeable financial market variable or index. This allows the risk to be managed synthetically by taking an offsetting position in the physical market or through derivatives.

For non-financial institutions, either the assets in the case of industrial corporations or the liabilities in the case of investment portfolio managers are non-financial in nature. For industrial corporations, the underlying assets include real assets, such as property, plant and equipment, intangible assets, such as goodwill (surplus on acquisition), intellectual property and brand names, as well as financial assets in the form of equity or other investments. For investors, the liabilities may be linked to mortality (life insurance policies), casualty events (fire, earthquake or other physical events) or indexed to inflation or cost-of-living changes.

The most significant aspects of these non-financial assets and liabilities are:

1. they are effectively financed by financial assets or liabilities which have fixed servicing and repayment profiles;

2. the return profile and value dynamics of the non financial assets or liabilities are not driven by the same value drivers that determine the value of the financial assets and liabilities that finance them;

3. the use of mark-to-market methodology to measure risk, at least in a current and static sense, may not be appropriate or even capable of implementation for non financial institution. This will be the case for the non-financial asset and liabilities meaning that marking to market the offsetting financial liabilities and assets may provide an incomplete and potentially misleading profile of risk; and

4.   the capacity to utilise value-at-risk type approaches to model risk on a prospective basis will be constrained for non-financial institutions.

This inherent mismatch reduces the scope to create *net* exposures and, more importantly, the capacity to hedge these exposures with traditional hedging instruments.

The source of risk is also fundamentally different. For a financial institution, risk is to a large degree a matter of choice. The risk assumed is as a result of *creating* the mismatch through a course of dealing—choosing *not* to offset an exposure as a result of a transaction entered into. An example of this would be a foreign exchange transaction entered into with a client which the financial institution chooses not to offset with an equal but opposite transaction. Given the imperfection of certain markets, such as low liquidity and high transaction costs, it may be difficult to *exactly* match the transaction but a surrogate transaction to, at least, lower the exposure, through the principle of a correlation based hedge as noted above, is generally available.

In contrast, for a non-financial corporation, the risk is *inherent* to a substantial degree arising from substantially non-financial sources, such as the business carried out or the business strategy being pursued. For example, for an oil producer, the risk to the commodity price is one which is inherent from the business activities.

The major implications of this source of risk include:

- financial risk for financial institutions is transitory while for non-financial institutions it is permanent;

- the perpetual nature of the risk for non-financial institutions dictates that it is inherently difficult to hedge reflecting the finite maturity characteristic of risk management products;

- the use of capital to manage the risk of loss from financial risk which is mandatory within financial institutions is not applicable in the same manner to non-financial institutions; and

- the measurement of hedge performance is likely to be very different as between the two types of organisations.

The central dominating feature of corporate financial management is the concept of hedging or management of financial exposures to limit the risk to the *cash flow* of the company. This reflects, in part, the central role of cash flow, in modern finance, in determining the value of assets. The acceptance of shareholder value approaches (such as SVA, EVA, MVA, CFROI, et cetera) as the basis of shareholder value, performance measurement metric and, ultimately, strategy formulation is a component of this trend. The need to mange risk in terms of cash flow also highlights its central role in managing the risk of bankruptcy or financial distress of the company.

The acceptance of cash flow as the basis for risk management brings with it a series of distinct problems. For example, it does not necessarily solve the problem of the non-financial assets. However, these approaches do allow capture of a more complete risk profile of non-financial institution's exposures and facilitates their management than traditional risk management methodologies.

3. MARKET RISK AND ITS MANAGEMENT

3.1 Sources of market risk

The concept of risk in finance may be defined as one of uncertainty of values. Specifically, market risk can be defined as the risk to an entity of losses resulting from adverse changes in financial asset prices, including changes in interest rates, currency rates, equity prices, and commodity prices.

Market risk exists in many forms. In the case of a financial institution, this risk arises from financial transactions entered into for the purpose of facilitating a client's requirements (eg to buy or sell assets), financial assets held in inventory or transactions entered into to deliberately expose the institution to the asset price movements in the expectation of being able to profit from anticipated favourable movements. These transactions may be transactions involving securities or off-balance transactions such as derivatives.

In the case of an investor, the exposure arises from the risk of loss in value of investments (direct or indirectly through derivative products) from adverse movements in the value of asset

In the case of non-financial institutions, such as industrial corporations, the risk relates to the financial attributes of business transactions. This may include:

- exposure to interest rates changes on its portfolio of liabilities and liquid investments.

- risk from currency value changes on its revenue or expenses (where these are denominated in a currency other than its functional currency) or on the value of its foreign currency denominated assets and liabilities. The revenue and expenses items as well as assets and liabilities affected are both financial and operating in nature.

- exposure to commodity price changes, either direct or indirect, which impact upon revenue or on its cost of production or operation.

- risk from changes in equity values on equity investments and fund raising.

In each of the above cases, the exposure to market risk necessitates measurement of the quantum of the exposure. This measure is an essential precursor to the management of the risk, either through elimination of the exposure through hedging action, including the use of derivatives, or maintaining capital against the risk to protect the entity from the risk of unacceptable loss.

3.2 Market risk model

The process of measuring market risk entails a series of distinct and separate steps. A market risk measurement model is set out in *Exhibit 16.1*.

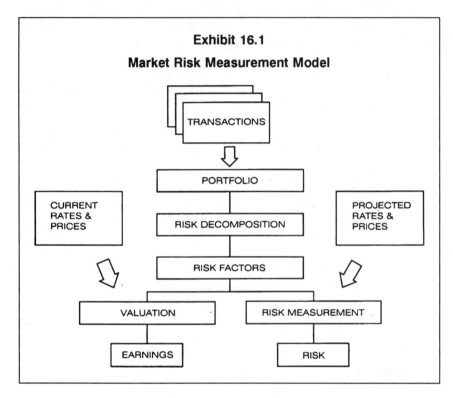

Exhibit 16.1

Market Risk Measurement Model

As set out in the model, the market risk arises from the transactions or positions entered into which are first aggregated to create a portfolio of transactions. The objective of the aggregation process is to combine similar transactions and net positions to the maximum degree possible to arrive at a net or marginal risk position.

The portfolio is then decomposed into the underlying risk factors. The process of risk decomposition entails the breakdown of each instrument, irrespective of its structure or format (on balance sheet or derivative), into its pure risk components (debt/interest rate risk at selected yield curve points, currency risk, commodity price risk and equity risk). The process of risk decomposition as discussed in detail below, is central to the aggregation and consolidation of risk across products and across asset classes. This process of consolidation is essential to capturing the benefit of diversification of risk taking activities within the entity where the risks are non-correlated.

The decomposed portfolio is then processed in two separate ways:

1. *Valuation*—whereby the portfolio is revalued using current prices and rates for the relevant risk factors to estimate the earnings of the portfolio.

2. *Risk Measurement*—whereby projected prices and rates are used to estimate the risk of the portfolio.

The valuation of the portfolio entails marking the portfolio to market using current prices and rates. The mark to market process establishes the value of the portfolio on a liquidation basis. The value established is the value of the portfolio were it to be liquidated at the relevant moment of time. The mark to market value provides valuable information on the success or failure of the transactions entered into, the liquidation value of the portfolio, and the earnings of the portfolio (represented by the change in value of the portfolio from its previous valuation). This information provides the basis for decisions on future action in respect of the portfolio, including transactions to be liquidated or new transactions to be entered into. Where the transactions are designed to hedge certain risks, the mark to market process provides a measure of the performance of the hedge.

The central element of the valuation process within a mark to market framework is its emphasis on *current market prices*. This contrasts with traditional accounting measures of value which emphases accruals. The mark to market valuation approach is consistent with portfolios of liquid and tradeable instruments which allows dynamic management and presents continuous opportunities for value optimisation. The accruals methodology assumes a static framework of management and is consistent with maintenance of these portfolios to maturity.

Risk measurement is concerned with *projecting* futures prices and rates and using these projections to estimate the risk of loss of the portfolio. This can entail, as described more fully below, a wide variety of techniques designed to estimate possible *adverse* changes in market rates and prices and the measurement of the impact of these changes on the value of the portfolio. In essence, the measure of risk entails the following:

*   Estimating the magnitude of any potential adverse changes in individual risk factors (the volatility of market prices) to allow the quantum of any loss to be estimated.

*   The inter-relationship of changes as between market risk factors (the correlations as between changes in risk factors) to allow incorporation of any benefits of diversification of risks within the portfolio.

In addition, the degree of confidence in the estimate of the adverse change (the statistical confidence level) and the time period needed to reasonably efficiently liquidate the portfolio (the holding period) must also be nominated to allow the risk to be estimated.

VAR is a generic term which covers a group of similar techniques designed to specifically measure market risk within this framework.

3.3 Applications of market risk measurement techniques

The market risk management approach described, based on VAR techniques, allows the estimation of market risk inherent in an entity or activity. This facilitates a number of functions, including:

*   management information and oversight;

*   establishment of trading limits and control of trading operations;

- performance evaluation;
- asset and resource allocation, including hedging decisions; and
- regulatory reporting and risk oversight.

Information regarding the risk of activities provides the basis of management of operations exposed to market risk.

Integral to this process of management is the establishment of appropriate trading limits and controls of trading operations. This would entail the setting and monitoring of compliance with limits based on capital or earnings/cash flow at risk in trading activities from adverse market price movements. These limits can be designed for business, individual units as well as traders to allow appropriate risk oversight.

The ability to establish and monitor limits allows the linking of returns from market risk activities to the *capital risked* in the course of such activities. This allows the development of *risk adjusted* performance measurement systems enabling a proper dissection of contribution to overall earnings.

The information available also provides the basis for asset and resource allocation to, at a macro level, activities that provide higher risk adjusted returns allowing diversion of resources away from less attractive opportunities or businesses. At a micro level, the information allows the evaluation of individual transactions allowing trading strategies to be evaluated in terms of the expected return relative to risk allowing maximisation of risk return of trading opportunities. Similarly, it allows the development of hedging strategies based on risk reward trade-offs.

This type of information is integral to the process of regulatory reporting and risk oversight of market risk generating activities being implemented by central banks and other regulators of financial intermediaries. Central to these developments is the impending introduction of capital adequacy requirements in relation to market risk developed by the Bank of International Settlements and being implemented by central banks throughout the world. This follows the European Union's Capital Adequacy Directive (EEC 93/6) which also requires financial institutions to hold capital against market risks assumed in the course of their activities. Parallel developments are evident in relation to investment institutions and corporations where increased disclosure about the impact of market price fluctuations is now increasingly being required.

4. VALUE AT RISK TECHNIQUE

4.1 VAR concept

VAR can be defined as:

"The expected loss on a position from an adverse movement in identified market risk parameter(s) with a specified probability over a nominated period of time."

It is calculated as:

VAR = Current Value of the Position *times* Sensitivity of the Position to a change in the relevant Risk Factor *times* Potential Change in the Risk Factor

The calculation of each component and the overall VAR requires the specification of the numeraire currency. In the case where the positions/instruments are denominated in a foreign currency, the foreign currency equivalents positions, sensitivities and VAR figure will need to be restated in the nominated base currency.

The current value of the position represents the mark-to-market value of the position revalued at current market rates and prices. In effect, the current value of the position specifies the size and direction (long or short) of the risk exposure.

The sensitivity of the position is the equivalent of the present value of 1 basis point (PVBP) or the dollar value of 1 basis point (DVO1) of the position. For example, the sensitivity of fixed interest instruments is the PVBP based on movements of the relevant interest rate. The sensitivity of other assets, currencies, equities, and commodities, will be related to the movements in the underlying price with a US$0.01 movement in the asset price will result in an equivalent change in the value of the position. The sensitivity measure is designed to provide the responsiveness of the position to changes in market prices of the relevant risk factors.

The potential change in the risk factor is central to the calculation of VAR. It is designed to capture potential changes in the relevant risk factors from current levels which will drive changes in the value of the position determining the risk of holding the position. It is, in effect, an estimate of the *volatility* of the relevant risk factor.

The critical elements in selecting the potential change in risk factor are:

- deriving the volatility estimate;
- nominating the level of confidence required; and
- selecting the risk horizon.

Volatility in financial markets is usually calculated as the standard deviation (σ) of the percentage changes in the relevant asset price over a specified period. The volatility for calculation of VAR is usually specified as the standard deviation (σ) of the percentage change in the risk factor over the relevant risk horizon.

As discussed in detail below, the volatility estimate can be derived in a number of ways. These include utilising historical volatilities from a selected time series of data on the risk factor or using implied volatilities from traded instruments.

The concept of the confidence level is designed to allow an estimate to be made regarding the probability that the change in the risk factor will *not exceed*, based on the assumptions made, a nominated level. The use of confidence levels is related to the definition of risk as the variability of the possible changes in the risk factor around an expected change. This assists in allowing the calculation of the level of change in the risk factor and as a consequence the value of the positions that is expected to occur no often than a certain amount of the time.

The selection of the risk horizon relates to the potential liquidation period of the position. Where a trading position is held, the elimination of the risk of holding the position is achieved by liquidating the holding or assuming an equal and opposite position (which in effect is equivalent to the first option). In measuring the risk of any position it is necessary to assume how quickly or slowly the risk can be eliminated as the relative risk of the position will be a function of this time period (the longer the potential holding period, the greater the risk).

The choice of the confidence level and holding period is usually the following:

- *Confidence level*—1.65 σ (equivalent to 95% confidence) or 2.33 σ (equivalent to 99% confidence).[2]

- *Time horizon*—1 day or more.

While the choice, in theory, resides with individual institutions, the following guidelines exist:

- The G-30 Report recommends the use of 95% confidence levels and a 1 day holding period.

- The BIS Market Risk Guidelines recommends the use of 99% confidence levels and a 10 day holding period.

4.2   Application of VAR to estimating market risk—single asset

Exhibit 16.2 sets out the formal mathematical definition of VAR. *Exhibit 16.3* sets out an example of calculating the VAR of a market risk position involving a single asset. The VAR is calculated for 95% and 99% confidence levels and for holding periods of 1, 10 and 30 days.

Exhibit 16.2
VAR Calculation—Single Asset—Definition

$$VAR = V_n . dV/dp . \sigma_{day} . CF$$

Where

V_n	= market value of position n
dV/dp	= sensitivity to price changes per $ market value
σ_{day}	= volatility or standard deviation of daily price changes
CF	= number of standard deviations consist with selected confidence levels (that is, 1.65 for 95% and 2.33 for 99%)

---

2.   The confidence level utilised is statistically the cumulative normal distribution (equivalent to the area under the curve for a normal or Gaussian statistical distribution. In estimating risk, a one tailed distribution is usually used. This reflects that for risk purposes the focus is on potential risk of *losses* only. In these circumstances, 95% (99%) confidence levels are equivalent to 1.65 s (2.33 s).

Exhibit 16.3

VAR Calculation—Single Asset

Position

Assume an organisation has a foreign exchange position whereby it has purchased US$76,550,000 against a sale of A$100,000,000 for spot value. The objective is to quantify the risk of this position over a 1 day (overnight), 10 day and 30 day holding period.

Assumption

The transaction is opened at the current spot of A$1.00 = US$0.7655. The daily volatility (calculated as the standard deviation of the continuously compounded historic price changes) is estimated as 0.4364%.

VAR Calculation

The VAR of the position is calculated as follows:

Asset

Type	US$ Currency
Market Value	$ 76,555,000
Term	Spot

Daily volatility = 0.4364%

Value at Risk Calculation

Holding Period	Volatility	95% Confidence	99% Confidence
1 day	0.4364%	$ 551,196	$ 778,356
10 day	1.3799%	$1,743,035	$2,461,376
30 day	2.3901%	$3,019,025	$4,263,229

The VAR for a 1 day holding period is also often referred to as daily earning at risk (DEAR). The term DEAR has been popularised by J P Morgan.

The calculation of VAR for longer holding period entails the scaling up of the VAR estimate using the following relationship:

$$VAR_n = VAR_1 \times \sqrt{n}$$

Where

VAR_1 = VAR for a 1 day holding period

VAR_n = VAR for a n day holding period

n   = holding period in days

This relationship assumes:

- the daily changes are random and follow a random walk; and
- the daily changes are not cumulative.

4.3   Application of VAR to estimating market risk—multiple assets

Extending the application of VAR to a portfolio consisting of multiple assets entails a similar logic to that utilised for a single asset. The only difference relates to the summation of the risks within the portfolio.

The simple addition of the risks is not appropriate as this assumes that the adverse events are likely to occur simultaneously. This is equivalent to assuming a correlation of 1.00 between the changes in the risk factors. In reality, the changes in the risk factors will rarely be perfectly correlated. In the case of similar risk factors, the direction of change may be the same but the magnitude will be less than one. For example, zero rates for different maturities in the same currency are likely to be positively but imperfectly correlated, implying a correlation of between 0 and 1. The changes in risk factors across asset classes may be *negatively* correlated, that is the change in one risk factor may be accompanied by an opposite change in the second risk factor. For example, an increase in interest rates may accompany a decrease in equity prices.

This requires the incorporation of the correlation between the changes in the risk factors in the calculation of VAR. *Exhibit 16.4* sets out the formal mathematical relationships.

Exhibit 16.4

VAR Calculation—Multiple Assets—Definition

Two asset portfolio

The calculation of the market value of the position and the sensitivity to changes in market price are identical to that for a single asset calculation.

The volatility estimate is given by:

$$\sqrt{[w_1\sigma_1{}^2 + w_2\sigma_2{}^2 + 2\,(w_1 w_2 \sigma_1 \cdot \sigma_2 \rho_{12})]}$$

Where

w_1 = portfolio weighting for asset 1

w_2 = portfolio weighting for asset 2

σ_1 = the volatility of asset 1

σ_2 = the volatility of asset 2

ρ_{12} = the correlation between price changes between asset 1 and asset 2

Multi asset portfolio

For a portfolio of n assets, the volatility estimate is given by:

$$\sigma_p = \sqrt{\sum_{i=1}^{N}\sum_{j=1}^{N} w_i w_j \sigma_i \sigma_j P_{ij}}$$

Where

σ_p = the volatility of the portfolio of asset consisting of n assets

$w_i;w_j$ = the weighting for asset i and j in the portfolio

$\sigma_i;\sigma_j$ = the volatility of the changes in the price of asset i and j in the portfolio

ρ_{ij} = the correlation between the changes in the price of asset i to asset j

---

Exhibit 16.5 sets out an example of calculating the VAR of a market risk position involving two assets. The VAR is calculated for 99% confidence levels and for holding periods of 10 days.

Exhibit 16.5

VAR Calculation—Multiple Assets—Example 1

Position

Assume an organisation (base currency A$) has a US$ asset position (a zero coupon 10 year bond) which it has purchased US$76,550,000. The position gives rise to two risks:

1.   interest rate risk exposure to 10 year zero coupon interest rates; and
2.   movements in the US$/A$ exchange rate.

The objective is to quantify the risk of this position over 10 day holding period.

Assumption

The transaction is opened at a price where security is valued at 100% of original purchase price and the current spot of A$1.00 = US$0.7655. The daily volatility (calculated as the standard deviation of the continuously compounded historic price changes) is estimated as 0.55% for the 10 year interest rate and 0.2630% for the US$/A$ currency rate. The correlation between the two variables is estimated at –0.15.

VAR calculation

The VAR of the position is calculated as follows:

ASSET (FACE VALUE) (USD)	
POSITION AMOUNT (USD)	$76,550,000
CURRENT PRICE (USD)	$76,550,000
PRICE VOLATILITY (PER DAY)	0.5500%
PRICE VOLATILITY (OVER HOLDING PERIOD)	4.0525%
VALUE AT RISK (USD)	$3,102,157
VALUE AT RISK (AUD)	$4,052,459
USD/AUD EXCHANGE RATE	
POSITION AMOUNT (USD)	$76,550,000
CURRENT EXCHANGE RATE	$0.7655
CURRENT PRICE (AUD)	$100,000,000
PRICE VOLATILITY (PER DAY)	0.2630%
PRICE VOLATILITY (OVER HOLDING PERIOD)	$1.9380%
VALUE AT RISK (A$)	$1,938,035
VALUE AT RISK—UNDIVERSIFIED RISK	$5,990,494
VALUE AT RISK—DIVERSIFIED RISK	
PRICE VOLATILITY (OVER HOLDING PERIOD)	$4.2216%
VALUE AT RISK (A$)	$4,221,642
VALUE AT RISK REDUCTION (A$)	$1,768,852

The sensitivity of the VAR of the individual interest rate and currency positions to changes in volatility and holding period are summarised in the following graphs:

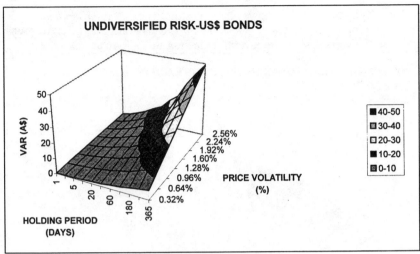

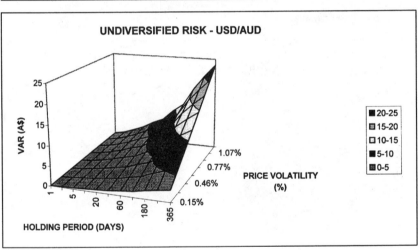

The following graph shows the sensitivity of the *diversified* VAR (incorporating correlations) of the total position to changes in correlations between the variables and the overall reduction in VAR achieved:

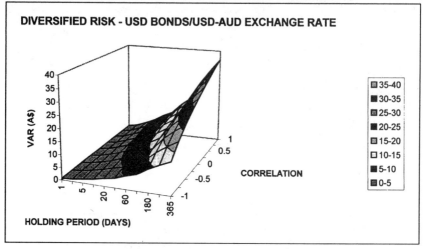

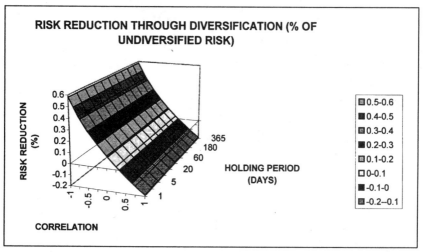

The process of aggregation and consolidation of risk is complex where large portfolios are involved. The process will generally require multiple levels of consolidation. This will be undertaken firstly within each asset class or sub-class with subsequent consolidation across asset classes. *Exhibit 16.6* sets out an example of this process.

Exhibit 16.6

VAR Calculation—Multiple Assets—Example 2

Position

Assume an organisation has a long position in Swiss Franc (CHF) bonds which are offset (partially hedged) by a short position in Deustchemark (DEM) bonds. The positions are predicated on the fact that CHF and DEM interest rates are closely correlated. The VAR of the position is required to incorporate the multiple level consolidations that are necessitated by the positions in two interest rates and two currency pairs.

VAR calculation

The VAR of the position is calculated to incorporate the various correlations at a number of separate levels:

1. correlations between yield curve points at different maturities;

2. correlations between interest rates in the different currencies;

3. correlations between the two currency pairing (against the US$); and

4. correlations between the interest rates and currencies.

The diagram set out below sets out the step by step consolidation process to measuring the risk of the combined positions:

AGGREGATING VAR USING CORRELATION TREE

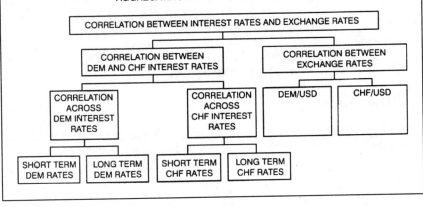

Exhibit 16.6—*continued*

The impact of the correlations in reducing the overall VAR of the combined positions is summarised in the table set out below:

RISK FACTOR	VAR	CORREL-ATION	1ST LEVEL CONSOLID-ATION	CORREL-ATION	2ND LEVEL CONSOLID-ATION	CORREL-ATION	3RD LEVEL CONSOLID-ATION
ST DEM RATES	10000						
		0.69	7483				
LT DEM RATES	−5000						
				0.61	10499		
ST CHF RATES	−15000						
		0.50	−13229				
LT CHF RATES	10000						
						0.19	15232
DEM/ USD	20000						
		0.90	9220		9220		
CHF/ USD	−15000						
TOTAL	75000		29932	19718	15232		

Source: This example is drawn from Chris Matten, "The Capital Allocation Challenge For The Banks" SBC Prospects 4-5/1995 at 4-5.

The calculation of VAR for portfolios of asset requires estimates of the correlations between changes in the prices of assets. The VAR calculation may be sensitive to these correlation estimates.

5.   IMPLEMENTING VAR

5.1   Overview

The basic VAR concept is relatively simple. Implementation of VAR type approaches, in practice, require a number of distinct and separate steps:

- The decomposition of portfolios of transactions into the underlying risk factors.
- The incorporation of adjustments to the framework to accommodate non-linear price risk (primarily, option transactions).
- Estimation of the volatilities and correlation required.

5.2   Risk decomposition in application of VAR

5.21   Concept

The process of risk decomposition entails the process by which individual transactions and products are reduced into cash flows and the relevant factors to enable the measure of market risk.

Exhibit 16.7 sets out the basic model of risk decomposition. The process consists of a number of distinct and separate steps:

1. Similar products and transactions are aggregated to establish net positions in each.

2. The cash flows of each transaction are identified and the products or transactions are then decomposed into the following components:

    (a) the asset class (debt/ interest rates, currency, equity or commodities);[3] and

    (b) the instrument itself—asset, forward, option.

3. The transactions are then restated in terms of the relevant risk factors.

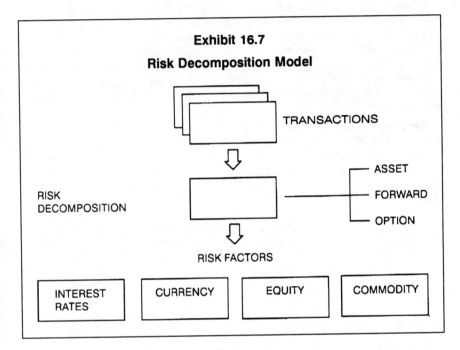

Exhibit 16.7

Risk Decomposition Model

The process of decomposing the position in the asset class into the various instruments (asset or derivative) is designed to facilitate a second order reallocation of the cash flows and risks. For example, a forward on an asset can be decomposed into an asset risk and an interest rate risk reflecting the exposure to changes in the cost of the forward through the carry cost. This process is referred to variously as risk decomposition, risk mapping (J P Morgan in RiskMetrics™), cash flow mapping, and cash flow shredding.

The process of risk decomposition is predicated on a combination of the following factors:

● data requirements;

● flexibility; and

● computational efficiency.

The estimation of market risks using VAR would require either tracking the volatilities and correlations between the price changes on individual

3. It is increasingly feasible to add credit as a separate asset class, particularly with the advent of credit derivatives; see Satyajit Das (ed), *Credit Derivatives* (John Wiley & Sons, London, 1997).

instruments or a series of defined risk factors. The former approach would require information on a very large number of individual instruments. In contrast, the process of decomposing all risk positions into a selected number of risk factors would assist in reducing the amount of information required. For example, thousands of fixed interest instruments would be reduced a series of cash flows allocated to a number of maturity points.

This process also adds to the flexibility of the process. Where estimation of market risk is instrument specific, new products would require individual price volatilities and correlations to enable the market risk to be measured. This may in practice be very difficult particularly where the instruments are not liquid and the establishment of the volatilities and correlations are more difficult. The process of risk decomposition because it allows restatement of any new product in terms of established risk factors greatly increases the flexibility of this framework in accommodating non-standard transactions and innovations.

The computational efficiency of risk decomposition is also superior to that of competing approaches. The number of risk factors dictates the size and number of correlations required. Based on the relationship that the number of correlation is equal to $[n(n-1)]/2$ (where n is equal to the number of risk factors), the rapid growth in the number of correlations can be seen from the following Table:

Number of Risk Factors	Number of Correlations	Increase (times) in Risk Factors	Increase (times) in Correlations
20	190		
50	1,225	2.5	6.4
100	4,950	5.0	26.1
200	19,900	10.0	104.7
500	124,750	25.0	656.6

The use of a limited number of risk factors contains the number of correlations and facilitates efficient calculation of market risk even for very large portfolios.

Despite the fact that the process of risk decomposition may, in certain areas, be artificial and arbitrary, the very real benefits that can be achieved in terms of reducing data requirements, increasing flexibility, and enhancing efficiency makes this approach extremely desirable.

5.2.2 Minimum risk factors

The process of risk decomposition is intrinsically linked to the number of risk factors specified. The selection of risk factors is inevitably a compromise between the accurate and full capture of the market risk of the portfolio and the computational efficiency considerations identified.

In practice, the following minimum risk factors have been nominated by the BIS in its Market Risk Guidelines:

- Fixed Interest—to be represented by cash flows allocated to a number of maturity points (a minimum of six) sufficient to capture exposure to changes in zero and forward rates as well as changes in yield curve shape. The credit risk of fixed income securities is captured through the use of a minimum of two yield curves, namely, a risk free government curve and a credit adjusted yield curve (usually, the swap curve). The credit spread curve is required to be specified such that any specific credit risk is captured in the risk measures.

- *Currency*—represented by the relevant currency cash flows and the individual currency pairings.

- *Equity*—represented by the cash flows in the relevant currency of the position. At a minimum, the risk factor should be related to market wide movements in the relevant equity market, based on the equity market index, with individual stock positions being captured by utilising the beta (relative risk measure) of the stock. Depending on the nature of the trading operation and the risks assumed, more extensive risk factors—ranging from sectoral indexes to risk factors for individual stocks—may be required. The risk factors should encompass the stock specific risks such as the exposure to changes in dividend payments and changes in the stock's beta.

- *Commodities*—represented by cash flows in the currency of trading (usually US$) in the commodity. Risk factors should encompass both the directional price risk and other aspects of the commodity risk including basis risks and risks of changes in convenience yields.

The above risk factors are well adapted to measuring the risk of position in the assets or forward contracts. As described in greater detail below, the risk of option contracts incorporates additional risks which are not completely and effectively captured by the above risk factors.

The specific methodologies of decomposing risk factors by asset class is outlined in the following sections. In each case, the process of decomposing and restating the risk of asset and linear derivatives (forward transactions) is considered. Option transactions are not dealt with in relation to individual asset classes being covered separately in the section on application of VAR to option generally.

5.2.3 Risk decomposition—fixed interest

Fixed income securities are segmented into two fundamental categories: government securities and securities which entail specific credit risk (non government bonds). Within each category, the cash flows of the securities are stated in terms of:

- amount; and

- the timing, that is the date when they are due.

The basic approach requires each individual cash flow to be treated as a separate zero coupon bond which can then be valued using the relevant zero coupon rate (the government or risk free zero rate for government securities and the zero coupon swap rates for all other instruments).

If the bond has any embedded optionality (for example, callable or putable bonds), then the option element is isolated and treated consistently with the treatment of other options.

The major issue with the risk decomposition of fixed interest instruments is the allocation of cash flows to specific maturity points or vertices. This problem arises because of the limited number of maturity points usually used. For example, RiskMetrics™ uses some 18 maturity vertices in each currency ranging from overnight to 30 years.

The allocation process is usually designed to satisfy certain conditions including:

• Ensuring that the present value of the cash flows after allocation is the same as the market value of the instrument.

• The market risk of the cash flows (as measured by, for example, historical volatility) is equivalent to the market risk of the original cash flows.

• The allocated cash flows have the same direction (inflow or outflow) as the original cash flows.

The algorithms for allocating cash flows to individual maturity points are potentially very complex.

Exhibit 16.8 sets out an example of the process of allocating the cash flows of a fixed interest bond to a set of maturity points.

Exhibit 16.8

Risk Decomposition—Fixed Rate Bond

The attached table shows the process of allocating the cash flows of a fixed rate bond into a limited set of maturity vertices. The bond in question is specified in the section entitled Bond Details and is decomposed into a fixed number of vertices (11 in total). The algorithm utilised is that suggested by J P Morgan in its Risk Metrics product[4] which satisfies the three conditions noted. The decomposed cash flows are then utilised to calculate the VAR of the individual cash flows as allocated to individual maturity vertices which are then amalgamated utilising the correlation between the maturity points to calculate the fully diversified VAR of the bond.

Bond Details

Principal	1,000,000
Settlement	1-Jan-97
Maturity	1-Dec-06
Coupon %pa	8
Coupon Frequency	2

Undiversified VAR	6,731
Diversified VAR	6,652
Diversification Benefit	78

	1 Day	1 Week	1 Mo.	3 Mo.	6 Mo.	12 Mo.	2 Yr	3 Yr	4 Yr	5 Yr	7 Yr	9 Yr	10 Yr
Price Volatility	0.000	0.001	0.001722	0.005033	0.01603	0.057673	0.167344	0.268379	0.372298	0.464388	0.645418	0.812764	0.885251
Correlation Matrix													
1 Day	1	0.992	0.178	0.089	0.125	0.03	0.105	0.074	0.051	0.032	0.012	0.007	0.013
1 Week	0.992	1	0.284	0.15	0.178	0.066	0.127	0.095	0.068	0.049	0.03	0.025	0.03
1 Mo.	0.178	0.284	1	0.59	0.509	0.244	0.213	0.185	0.149	0.133	0.139	0.136	0.135
3 Mo.	0.089	0.15	0.59	1	0.744	0.528	0.391	0.384	0.361	0.348	0.322	0.309	0.312
6 Mo.	0.125	0.178	0.509	0.744	1	0.664	0.597	0.59	0.578	0.57	0.556	0.542	0.542
12 Mo.	0.03	0.066	0.244	0.528	0.664	1	0.853	0.863	0.854	0.845	0.806	0.777	0.772
2 Yr	0.105	0.127	0.213	0.391	0.597	0.853	1	0.99	0.969	0.948	0.889	0.847	0.842
3 Yr	0.074	0.095	0.185	0.384	0.59	0.863	0.99	1	0.991	0.976	0.928	0.89	0.885
4 Yr	0.051	0.068	0.149	0.361	0.578	0.854	0.969	0.991	1	0.996	0.961	0.931	0.927
5 Yr	0.032	0.049	0.133	0.348	0.57	0.845	0.948	0.976	0.996	1	0.978	0.955	0.951
7 Yr	0.012	0.03	0.139	0.322	0.556	0.806	0.889	0.928	0.961	0.978	1	0.994	0.989
9 Yr	0.007	0.025	0.136	0.309	0.542	0.777	0.847	0.89	0.931	0.955	0.994	1	0.998
10 Yr	0.013	0.03	0.135	0.312	0.542	0.772	0.842	0.885	0.927	0.951	0.989	0.998	1

4.   See J P Morgan/Reuters, *RiskMetrics™ Technical Document* (4th ed, J P Morgan/Reuters, New York, 1996), pp 117-121.

Exhibit 16.8—continued

Cashflow Map				1 Mo.	3 Mo.	6 Mo.	12 Mo.	2 Yr.	3 Yr.	4 Yr.	5 Yr.	7 Yr.	9 Yr.	10 Yr.
Vertex														
Total Vertex Mapping				—	14,437	31,883	58,428	72,567	67,474	64,375	86,288	105,269	330,972	268,733
Price Volatility					0.0050%	0.0160%	0.0577%	0.1673%	0.2684%	0.3723%	0.4644%	0.6454%	0.8129%	0.8853%
RiskMetrics™ Vertex VAR				—	1	5	34	121	181	240	401	679	2,690	2,379
Date	Flow	Yield	Present Value		Present Value Amount by Vertex									
1 1-Jun-97	40,000	5.62	39,091.85		14,437	24,654								
2 1-Dec-97	40,000	5.90	37,951.37			7,228	30,723							
3 1-Jun-98	40,000	6.04	36,818.36				23,037	13,781						
4 1-Dec-98	40,000	6.14	35,683.00				4,668	31,015						
5 1-Jun-99	40,000	6.25	34,553.72					22,519	12,035					
6 1-Dec-99	40,000	6.36	33,420.53					5,252	28,169					
7 1-Jun-00	40,000	6.43	32,329.49						21,627	10,703				
8 1-Dec-00	40,000	6.49	31,261.68						5,844	25,618				
9 1-Jun-01	40,000	6.54	30,235.54							21,425	8,811			
10 1-Dec-01	40,000	6.59	29,228.43							6,630	22,598			
11 1-Jun-02	40,000	6.62	28,261.53								24,461	3,801		
12 1-Dec-02	40,000	6.66	27,315.13								16,806	10,509		
13 1-Jun-03	40,000	6.69	26,396.90								9,939	16,458		
14 1-Dec-03	40,000	6.73	25,496.56								3,672	21,824		
15 1-Jun-04	40,000	6.75	24,629.03									22,511	2,118	
16 1-Dec-04	40,000	6.78	23,786.71									15,894	7,892	
17 1-Jun-05	40,000	6.81	22,971.72									9,890	13,082	
18 1-Dec-05	40,000	6.84	22,174.75									4,382	17,792	
19 1-Jun-06	40,000	6.86	21,412.44										20,895	517
20 1-Dec-06	1,040,000	6.88	537,408.01										269,192	268,216
			1,100,426.76											

Source: This calculation uses the models provided as part of J P Morgan's *RiskMetrics™ Technical Document*, Fourth Edition, 1996

The approach to linear fixed income derivatives is very similar. The fundamental technique requires restating the derivative in terms of a combination of underlying fixed interest transactions at different maturities. This approach is usually applied as follows:

- *Futures contracts*—are treated as a borrowing (investment) at one maturity and an offsetting investment (borrowing) at a different (more distant) maturity. The first maturity will usually coincide with the settlement date of the futures contract while the second date will relate to final maturity of the security underlying the futures contract.

- *Forward Rate Agreements* (FRAs)—are treated exactly the same as futures contracts.

- *Interest Rate Swaps*—are decomposed into two separate fixed interest transactions. The fixed leg is treated as a position in a fixed rate bond while the floating rate flows are treated as a position in a floating rate note. The risk of each set of cash flows can then be calculated independently. The fixed leg is valued as a bond. The floating leg will generally trade around the par value with only the current coupon (fixed with reference to the last floating rate set) creating an interest rate exposure which will need to be incorporated.

The credit risk of the underlying instrument will determine the market risk of the derivatives. Government or swap risk factors will be used to determine the risk of a futures contract depending upon the underlying asset of the futures contract. Swap risk factors will generally be used to calculate the risk of FRAs and interest rate swaps.

Exhibit 16.9 sets out an example of the risk decomposition of a FRA.

Exhibit 16.9

Risk Decomposition—Forward Rate Agreement

The attached table shows the process of decomposing an FRA. The transaction details are specified in the section entitled FRA Details. The FRA is decomposed into a borrowing and investment for the relevant maturities. The market value of each cash flow is then calculated using the appropriate discount rate for each maturity. The decomposed cash flows are then utilised to calculate the VAR of the individual cash flows as allocated to individual maturity vertices which are then amalgamated utilising the correlation between the maturity points to calculate the fully diversified VAR of the FRA.

FRA — Cashflow Mapping and Value at Risk Calculation

FRA Details

Date		11-Jan-97
Currency	USD	
First Leg (mths)		3
Second Leg (mths)		9
Amount		10,000,000
3m yield		5.25%
9m yield		5.43%
Basis		360

Maturity (days)	Cash Flow	Market Rate	Market Value (2)	Vertex	CF Map	RiskMetrics™ Volatilities			VaR (5)	RiskMetrics™ Correlations	
						Yield (3)	Price (4)				
92	−10,000,000	0.0525	−9,867,610	3M	−9,867,610	6.1875	0.008		789.4	1	0.52
181	10,403,421	0.0543	10,126,947	9M	10,126,947	6.5914	0.068		6,886.3	0.52	1
Total			259,337		259337.116		Diversified		6,510.8		

VaR Simulation

Source: This calculation uses the models provided as part of J P Morgan, *RiskMetrics™ Technical Document*, (4th ed, 1996).

5.2.4 Risk decomposition—currency

Currency positions are decomposed for risk measurement in terms of the cash flows in the relevant currencies. All currency positions are translated and risk measured in terms of a base functional currency presumed to be the home currency of the relevant entity.

The basic approach is to identify the currency positions in terms of the inflow and outflow in the relevant currency pairings as at the relevant maturity point.

Spot positions are stated as the cash flows receivable and payable and the relevant currency pairing VAR factor can be applied.

Currency derivatives are also decomposed in a similar manner:

- *Currency forwards or futures*—are treated as cash inflows and outflows at a forward maturity date. The position is then decomposed into separate spot currency position (calculated by discounting the cash flows back to the spot date using the swap rates for the relevant maturity) and long and short position in the relevant interest rates in each currency. The currency risk VAR is determined by applying the relevant currency VAR to the spot position while the interest rate risk of the position is calculated by applying the interest rate risk factors. The total risk of the position is given by the individual risk which are then consolidated using the correlation between the currency and two interest rate risk factors.

- *Currency swaps*—are treated as two separate fixed interest transactions in the respective currencies with each security being decomposed into the separate interest rate risk factors in the individual currency. The currency exposure is then incorporated, including the impact of correlation as between the interest rate risk factors and the currency, when each fixed interest bond is translated into the base reporting currency. Where one leg of the currency swap is on a floating rate basis, the approach utilised is identical to that used for the floating rate component of an interest rate swap.

Exhibit 16.10 sets out an example of the risk decomposition of a currency forward.

Exhibit 16.10

Risk Decomposition—Currency Forward

The attached table shows the process of decomposing a currency forward. The transaction details are specified in the section entitled Forward Details. The forward is decomposed into cash flows in the respective currencies at the forward date using the contracted forward date. The market value of each cash flow is then calculated by discounting using the appropriate discount rate in each currency. The calculation isolates the risk of the forward into a spot transaction and the borrowing or investment transaction in the respective currency. The VAR of the individual components are then calculated as the VAR of the spot currency and interest rate element, which are then amalgamated utilising the correlation between the separate risk components to calculate the fully diversified VAR of the currency forward.

Currency Forward — Cashflow Mapping and Value at Risk Calculation

This FX Forward to sell USD against the CHF decomposes into:
1. A Spot FX deal to sell USD and buy CHF
2. A 1 year USD borrowing
3. A 1 year CHF investment

Forward Details

FX Rate	USD/CHF	
Spot FX Rate	1.44	
Term (Years)	1	
USD Yield	6.00%	
CHF Yield	2.00%	
CHF Face Value	10,000,000	
1 day time horizon		

Risk Decomposition

Instrument	Cash Flow	Yield	PV	Forward Rate	Price Volatility	VAR Estimate	Correlation Matrix		
							Spot FX Deal	CHF 1 Year	USD 1 Year
Spot FX Deal			-6,808,279		0.6852	-46,651	1.00000	0.23989	0.01768
CHF 1 Year	10,000,000	2.00%	9,803,922	1.38566	0.0322	2,277	0.23989	1.00000	0.16349
USD 1 Year	-7,216,776	6.00%	-6,808,279		0.0577	-3,927	0.01768	0.16349	1.00000

Undiversified VAR	52,854
Diversified VAR	46,363
Diversification Benefit	6,491

Source: This calculation uses the models provided as part of J P Morgan, *RiskMetrics™ Technical Document*, (4th ed, 1996).

5.2.5   Risk decomposition—equity

The risk decomposition of equity transactions will depend on whether it represents a well diversified portfolio of equities which approximates the market index or positions in individual equity securities with a large component of firm specific risk.

This categorisation is related to the risk factors that are applicable. Where the equity positions approximate the risk of the market index, the volatility of the market index is utilised to derive the risk of the transaction. Where the position does not approximate the market index, there are two choices for measuring the risk of the position:

- the market volatility must be adjusted for stock specific risk using the beta of the individual stock; or

- stock specific volatilities must be utilised.

The use of stock beta introduces the problem of basis or correlation risk as between the price changes of the individual stock and the changes in the index.

Irrespective of the risk factors to be used, the decomposition of the position embodies the following approach. Each equity position is restated in terms of the market value of the security as at the specific maturity point. Spot positions are stated as positions in the equity security the risk of which is determined by the application of the market index volatility or the stock specific volatilities. Equity derivatives are also decomposed in a similar manner:

- *Equity forwards or futures*—are treated as a position in the equity as at a forward maturity date. The position is then decomposed into separate spot equity position (calculated by discounting the transaction cash flows back to the spot date using the swap rates for the relevant maturity) and long or short position in the relevant interest rates in each currency. The equity risk VAR is determined by applying the relevant equity VAR to the spot position while the interest rate risk of the position is calculated by applying the interest rate risk factors. The total risk of the position is given by the individual risks which are then consolidated using the correlation between the equity and the interest rate risk factor.

- *Equity swaps*—are treated as two separate transactions; the first being in the equity as at the forward date, and the second being in a floating rate bond. The equity exposure is calculated as a series of forwards and the interest rate exposure on the floating rate leg is calculated using an identical approach to that used for the floating rate component of an interest rate swap. The total risk of the components is consolidated including the impact of correlation as between the interest rate risk factors and the equity.

The process of restating the forward equity position by discounting the future cash flows back to the spot dates requires assumptions to be made regarding the expected dividend income cash flows payable on the security or the portfolio.

Exhibit 16.11 sets out an example of the risk decomposition of an equity position. *Exhibit 16.12* sets out an example of the risk decomposition of an equity forward.

Exhibit 16.11

Risk Decomposition—Equity Position

The attached table shows the process of decomposing an equity position in the spot market. The VAR of equity position is calculated utilising the volatility of *the market index* adjusted by the stock specific risk of the relevant equity security as expressed by the beta (β) of the stock.

Equity Position

Stock Details

Company	GIANT	
Stock Price	$	18.00
Stock Holding		100,000
Present Value		1,800,000
Stock Beta		1.55
Market Volatility		2.21%
95% confidence		3.65%
Holding Period	1 day	

VAR =	Present Value × 95% volatility × Beta
	1,800,000 × .0365 × 1.55
	101,835

Exhibit 16.12

Risk Decomposition—Equity Forward

The attached table shows the process of decomposing an equity forward. The forward is decomposed into a position in the equity by calculating the market value of the forward using the discounted rate for the maturity. The calculation isolates the risk of the forward into a spot transaction and borrowing. The VAR of the individual components are then calculated as the VAR of the spot equity and interest rate element, which are then amalgamated utilising the correlation between the separate risk components to calculate the fully diversified VAR of the equity forward.

Equity Forward Position

Stock Details

Company	GIANT	
Spot Stock Price	$	18.00
Forward Stock Price	$	18.7200
Stock Holding		100,000
Forward Value		1,872,000
Forward Term	1 year	
Stock Lending rate %pa		2.00%
1 year interest rate		6.00%
Stock Beta		1.55
Market Volatility		2.21%
95% confidence volatility		3.65%
Beta Adjusted Volatility		5.66%
Holding Period	1 day	

This FX Purchase of GIANT shares decomposes into:

1. A Spot purchase of GIANT shares
2. A 1 year USD borrowing
3. A 1 year Stock Loan

Exhibit 16.12—continued

Risk Decomposition

Instrument	Cash Flow	Yield	PV	Price Volatility	Undiversified VAR	Correlation Matrix		
						Spot Share Purchase	1 Year Borrowing	1 Year Stock Loan
Spot Share Purchase			-1,800,000	5.6613	-101,903	1.00000	-0.00400	-0.22400
1 Year Borrowing	-1,908,000	6.00%	-1,800,000	0.0322	579	-0.00400	1.00000	0.33240
1 Year Stock Loan	-1,836,000	2.00%	-1,800,000	0.0577	1,038	-0.22400	0.33240	1.00000

Undiversified VAR	103,520
Diversified VAR	102,138
Diversification Benefit	1,382

Source: This calculation uses the models provided as part of J P Morgan, *RiskMetrics™ Technical Document*, (4th ed, 1996).

5.2.6   Risk decomposition—commodities

Commodity positions are decomposed in a manner analogous to that applicable to equities.

Spot positions are stated as positions in the commodity the risk of which is determined by the application of the volatility of the specific commodity or a similar or related commodity.

Commodity derivatives are also decomposed in a similar manner:

- *Commodity forwards or futures*—are treated as a position in the commodity as at a forward maturity date. The position is then decomposed into separate spot commodity position (calculated by discounting the transaction cash flows back to the spot date using the swap rates for the relevant maturity) and long or short position in the relevant interest rates in each currency. The commodity risk VAR is determined by applying the relevant commodity risk factor to the spot position while the interest rate risk of the position is calculated by applying the interest rate risk factors. The total risk of the position is given by the individual risks which are then consolidated using the correlation between the commodity and the interest rate risk factor.

- *Commodity swaps*—are treated as a series of forward contracts on the commodity which are decomposed as above. Alternatively, the swap can be treated as a position in a fixed interest bond (represented by the fixed cash flows to be paid or received calculated as the amount commodity purchased or sold at the agreed forward price) and an opposite position in a floating rate bond (where the cash flows are based on a floating commodity price usually based on the near month futures contract price). The fixed leg can be treated as a fixed interest security while the risk of the floating is analogous to the floating rate note component of the interest rate swap where only the first cash flow is known with a price exposure on the near contract.

The process of restating the forward commodity position by discounting the future cash flows back to the spot dates requires assumptions to be made regarding the convenience yield on the commodity.

5.2.7   Risk decomposition—structured notes

Structured notes can be defined as debt securities with embedded derivative elements. These instruments are decomposed for risk purposes into the individual elements, usually a fixed or floating rate security and the derivative component on the relevant asset, for the purposes of risk decomposition. The individual components are then treated consistent with the framework outlined. *Exhibit 16.13* sets out an example of the risk decomposition of a structured note transaction.

VALUE AT RISK MODELS 583

Exhibit 16.13

Risk Decomposition—Structured Note

The attached table sets out the risk decomposition of an inverse floater.[5] The details of the transaction are set out in the section entitled Inverse Floater Details. The inverse floater is broken up into a fixed rate bond and the embedded interest rate swap. The cash flows on the two transactions are then decomposed into a maturity matrix and are then utilised to generate the VAR both on an undiversified and diversified basis (incorporating the correlation between the relevant rates).

Structured Note — Inverse Floater

Calculate the VAR of an inverse floater transaction which pays 12.2%pa minus 6 month LIBOR for a term of 1 year.

This inverse floater can be decomposed into:

1. A 1 Year Fixed rate bond paying 6% pa
2. A 1 Year Receiving Fixed interest rate swap

Inverse Floater Details

Currency	USD	
Face Value		10,000,000
Fixed Rate Receipt		12.20%
Floating Rate Payment	6mth LIBOR	
Term	1 Year	
Coupon Frequency pa	2	
1 Year Bond rate		6.00%
1 Year swap rate		6.20%
6 Month Yield		5.43%
Time Horizon	One Month	

---

5. For a detailed coverage of all forms of structured note transactions, see Satyajit Das, *Structured Notes and Derivative Embedded Securities* (Euromoney Publications, London, 1996), Ch 4.

Exhibit 16.13—continued

Term Yrs	Bond Cashflows	Swap Fixed Leg	Floating Leg	Net Cashflows	Zero Yield	Price Volatility	Correlations		Present Values	VAR Estimate
0.5	300,000	310,000	−10,000,000	−9,390,000	5.43%	0.1800	1	0.84	−9,141,800	−16,455.2
1	10,300,000	10,310,000		20,610,000	6.21%	0.3900	0.84	1	75,679.3	19,404,952
	Total			11,220,000					10,263,152	

Undiversified VAR	92,135
Diversified VAR	62,498
Diversification Benefit	29,637

Source: This calculation uses the models provided as part of J P Morgan, *RiskMetrics™ Technical Documents* (4th ed, 1996).

The analysis ignores for the sake of convenience the embedded interest rate cap which is incorporated in the structure to prevent the interest rate coupon of the inverse floater becoming negative.

5.3   Application of VAR to options

VAR techniques are well suited to measurement of risk on asset and linear derivatives (forward, futures or swaps). The application of VAR techniques to quantify the risk of options or portfolios containing options presents difficulties. This difficulty arises from a number of sources:

- The price movements of options are non-linear, that is for a given change in the asset price the price change of the option is not constant. This potential acceleration or de-acceleration of the market risk (which is equivalent to the gamma risk of an option) creates difficulties in modelling the exposure of options.

- The impact of changes in volatility on the price of options (the option's vega risk).

- The impact of time decay on the price of the option (the option's theta risk).[6]

In effect, the non linearity of the option price function means that the second parameter required to calculate VAR—the sensitivity of the position to a change in the relevant risk factor—is not constant. This means the VAR estimates may over or underestimate the market risk as it assumes this parameter is constant. The effect of changes in volatility and time decay impact the final term of the VAR calculation as they are additional terms which may impact upon the price of the option and therefore must be incorporated by forecasting potential changes in these factors to derive an accurate measure of risk. Volatility is not a factor in the pricing of assets and forwards and consequently are irrelevant to the quantification of risk of these linear price risk instruments. Theta, in contrast, is not unique to options. The value of both assets (for example, debt instruments) and forwards change as a function of time. However, the degree of change is smaller and the impact on risk less significant.

The difficulties are manifested in two separate contexts: first, where options are included in the portfolio; and secondly, where the portfolio consists of options which are dynamically hedged with positions in the asset (delta hedging). The second position exacerbates the problem of exposure quantification in that changing price exposure of the option requiring re-hedging. This dynamic hedging requirement introduces additional risks such as hedging uncertainties, liquidity constraints, and cashflow constraints. The additional risk impacts on the market risk of the position.

In practice, the difficulties that arise in calculating VAR in the first context are most marked for options with a short time to maturity where the option is trading near to the strike price (near or at-the-money). This holds true where a 1 day VAR estimate is sought to be utilised. Where a longer risk horizon for the calculation of VAR is utilised, the non-linearity of option prices has the potential to distort option prices more significantly, irrespective of the type of option. The problems identified in the second context are present *in all portfolios* where options are dynamically hedged.

6.   See discussion in Chapter 10 on option risks.

There are several possible approaches to the calculation of VAR for options. These approaches are used quite consistently across asset classes. These approaches include:

1. The delta based method;
2. The delta method incorporating adjustments for gamma, vega and theta; and
3. Simulation approaches.

The delta based method entails the risk decomposition of the option position using the following steps:

1. The option delta is calculated using an appropriate option pricing model.
2. The delta is used to determine a position in the asset equivalent to the option.
3. The asset position is then included in the appropriate asset class as the relevant risk position.
4. The VAR of the option is calculated as the VAR of the equivalent asset position using standard VAR techniques.

This approach has the advantage of simplicity and ease of computation. However, the approach has a number of deficiencies:

*   The non-linearity of the option price is not incorporated and a large change in the asset price will result in a change in the option premium which will vary from the VAR estimate.
*   The assumption that the asset volatility remains unchanged. This is because the delta of the option will be volatility specific. Changes in volatility will result in market value changes in the option which are not captured by VAR.
*   The delta estimate may be model dependent in that the choice of option model will dictate the delta and consequently the risk.

The delta method can be expanded to incorporate the gamma, vega and theta risks of an option.

The gamma risk of an option can be illustrated graphically (see *Exhibit 16.14*). The diagram (depicting the option price function for a sold call option) highlights that the delta based method is inaccurate as it measures the slope of the option price function at a specific point in time at the current market price. The delta based method adjusted for gamma requires the incorporation of an adjustment to compensate for the change in slope of the option price function.[7] This adjustment itself will only be accurate for small changes as the change in curvature of the option price function is not constant. This means that for a large change in the asset price will cause gamma to alter rendering any gamma adjusted VAR measure inaccurate.

7.   See J P Morgan/Reuters, op cit n 4, pp 129-133.

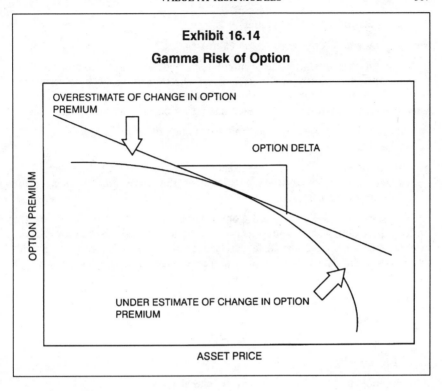

Exhibit 16.14

Gamma Risk of Option

The adjustment for VAR for vega requires incorporating the volatility as a separate risk factor. Volatility risk factors of all assets (effectively, *the volatility of volatility*) for separate maturity vertices as well as correlations would need to be incorporated in the risk data set. The volatilities would then be used to determine the exposure to volatility changes.

Theta is incorporated by estimating the forward price of the option.

The adjusted delta technique is particularly difficult where a longer risk horizon is utilised as each of these risk factors is time sensitive and is characterised by significant non-linearity.

The final approach, discussed in greater detail below, is simulation approaches. These approaches entail the use of various approaches, to simulate the performance of the option over the risk horizon based on expected movements in market risk factors, including asset price and volatility. The simulation approach because it incorporates the full revaluation of option positions captures the problems of gamma and vega risk to a greater extent and more accurately than other approaches.

5.4 Data sources/estimating volatilities and correlations

VAR approaches require volatilities for individual risk factors as well as the correlation between risk factors to measure risks. The major criteria for estimating these volatilities and correlations include:

- consistency of methodology;

- computational efficiency; and
- accuracy and robustness of the estimates.

A major consideration in calculating the relevant volatilities and correlation is the quality of the data. Even small errors in the time series can have a significant impact on the volatilities and correlation which can generate inaccuracies in the risk estimates. Key considerations include:

- inaccurate and missing data and the methodology by which it has been adjusted;
- ensuring that the data is consistent; for example, the data should be synchronous, that is it is calculated at the same time, to ensure the validity of the data set.

Data sets are usually obtained from external providers or collected by the entity. The external data source has the advantage of independence while the maintenance of an inhouse data set has the advantage of allowing greater control over the data collected and the quality. The costs of each approach is also a factor.

There are a number of possible approaches to obtaining these estimates:

1. forecasts;
2. implied volatilities and correlations; and
3. historical data.

In practice, historical volatilities are generally used.

Forecasts would entail development of subjective forecasts of the estimated volatilities of individual risk factors and the correlation between them. This approach suffers from the following deficiencies:

- it is subjective; and
- it may be difficult to implement consistently over a large set of required data.

Implied volatilities and correlation would require extracting the required estimates from existing traded instruments. Volatilities would be derived from traded options while correlation estimates would be backed out of exotic options (quanto options, basket options etc where correlation factors are inherent in the pricing). This approach suffers from the following difficulties:

- Data may not be available for all required risk factors. This is particularly the case with correlation estimates. This unavailability reflects the fact that the universe of options, particularly longer dated options and exotic options, may not be extensive enough to provide the required data.
- The data may be affected by the choice of model used to iterate out the volatility or correlation estimate. The liquidity or other institutional factors may also impact on the estimate.
- There is no evidence that implied volatilities and correlations are a better predictor of future actual volatility or correlations than, say, historical estimates.

These factors favour the use of historical volatility and correlation estimates. For example, the BIS Market Risk Guidelines require the use of a trailing 1 year's historical data for VAR calculations.

The process of deriving the required historical volatility and correlation information usually takes one of the following forms:

- the use of historical estimates calculated and supplied by an external party; and

- the maintenance of extensive data sets to calculate the required estimates.

J P Morgan's RiskMetrics™ is an example of the first approach. RiskMetrics™ consists of daily estimates of the volatility and correlations of a large number of rates and prices covering currency, interest rates (government and swap rates), commodity and equity indexes. The second approach requires the entity to store the data or acquire it from a vendor of financial market data and calculate the necessary information itself.

Irrespective of the source of the estimates, the basic procedure for deriving the estimates entails the following steps:

1. Identify the historical data to be utilised.

2. Adjust the data through smoothing or bootstrapping techniques.

3. Calculate the estimates.

4. Calibrate the results obtained.

In practice, usually high frequency data (daily) prices of the relevant risk factors are used. The length of the time series used is subjective but typically between 1 to 3 years data is utilised. The data set is usually a constantly trailing period which is updated regularly (usually no less frequently than quarterly).

The data may need to be adjusted through smoothing or bootstrapping techniques. Smoothing techniques may be used for the following reasons:

- to allocate greater importance to more recent data than older data;

- to filter out the potential impact of certain events; and

- to overcome inadequacies of the available data sets.

The use of smoothing can be illustrated by reference to RiskMetrics™ which uses an exponential moving averages of historical asset price movements as the basis for deriving volatility and correlation estimates. This is done to increase the sensitivity of the estimates to large price movements and subsequent gradual declines in volatilities. Research by J P Morgan undertaken in conjunction with RiskMetrics™ indicates that the smoothed series generally provides more accurate estimates of volatility and correlations.[8]

Alternative forms of smoothing include the use of adaptive techniques such as the Autoregressive Conditional Heteroskedascity (ARCH) type models for estimating volatilities.[9]

---

8. See discussion in Chapters 8 and 9 of estimation procedures using smoothing techniques.
9. See discussion in Chapter 9 of ARCH type models in estimation of volatility estimates for risk management purposes.

Bootstrapping techniques are generally required for different reasons. They may be useful for allowing estimation from relatively small sample sizes. For example, deriving monthly volatility and correlation estimates from daily volatilities and correlations.

The calculation procedures are relatively straightforward:

- Volatility estimates are calculated as the standard deviation of the (usually) logarithms of the asset price changes.

- Correlations are calculated utilising ordinary least squares or other correlation technique.

Exhibit 16.15 sets out an example of the calculation of volatility and correlation estimates.

Exhibit 16.15—Part One

This exhibit sets out an example of calculating volatility and correlation estimates for the oil price, A$/US$ exchange rate on a monthly basis over ten years. These calculations are used in the case study provided in Appendix A. The table below calculates the parametric 95% confidence loss. The second part of this exhibit calculates the 95% confidence loss using the actual historical distribution.

Time series data

Data Frequency (d,w,m,q)		m		Monthly		
	Price/Yield input			**Asset Return - % change**		Monthly
Name	US$ WTI	AUD/USD	LIBOR	US$ WTI	AUD/USD	LIBOR
Statistics	Absolute Price/Yield Statistics			Asset Return Statistics		
No of obs	121	121	121	120	120	120
Maximum	36.04	0.89	8.82	39.22%	6.17%	11.78%
Minimum	13.77	0.65	2.86	−20.91%	−10.60%	−13.12%
Mean	19.71	0.75	5.46	0.40%	0.15%	−0.08%
Std	3.38	0.05	1.64	7.56%	2.57%	4.03%
95% confidence loss	5.58	0.08	2.71	12.48%	4.24%	6.65%
Kurtosis	7.0797	0.1191	(0.8603)	5.29	2.11	1.03
Skewness	2.0081	0.0629	0.1099	1.00	−0.62	−0.19

		Asset price/Yield			**Calculated % returns**		
Dec-86	1	16.1	0.6648	5.53			
Jan-87	2	18.65	0.6608	5.43	14.70%	−0.60%	−1.82%
Feb-87	3	17.75	0.6748	5.59	−4.95%	2.10%	2.90%
Mar-87	4	18.3	0.7053	5.59	3.05%	4.42%	0.00%
Apr-87	5	18.67	0.7048	5.64	2.00%	−0.07%	0.89%
May-87	6	19.43	0.7137	5.66	3.99%	1.25%	0.35%
Jun-87	7	20.07	0.7203	5.67	3.24%	0.92%	0.18%
Jul-87	8	21.34	0.6978	5.69	6.14%	−3.17%	0.35%
Aug-87	9	20.31	0.7124	6.04	−4.95%	2.07%	5.97%
Sep-87	10	19.53	0.7194	6.4	−3.92%	0.98%	5.79%
Oct-87	11	19.86	0.6757	6.13	1.68%	−6.27%	−4.31%
Nov-87	12	18.85	0.7052	5.69	−5.22%	4.27%	−7.45%
Dec-87	13	17.27	0.7225	5.77	−8.75%	2.42%	1.40%
Jan-88	14	17.13	0.7138	5.81	−0.81%	−1.21%	0.69%
Feb-88	15	16.79	0.7198	5.66	−2.00%	0.84%	−2.62%
Mar-88	16	16.19	0.7388	5.7	−3.64%	2.61%	0.70%
Apr-88	17	17.86	0.7585	5.91	9.82%	2.63%	3.62%
May-88	18	17.42	0.8051	6.26	−2.49%	5.96%	5.75%
Jun-88	19	16.52	0.794	6.46	−5.30%	−1.39%	3.14%
Jul-88	20	15.49	0.8045	6.73	−6.44%	1.31%	4.09%
Aug-88	21	15.52	0.8069	7.06	0.19%	0.30%	4.79%
Sep-88	22	14.53	0.7829	7.24	−6.59%	−3.02%	2.52%
Oct-88	23	13.77	0.8256	7.35	−5.37%	5.31%	1.51%
Nov-88	24	14.14	0.8781	7.76	2.65%	6.17%	5.43%
Dec-88	25	16.38	0.8555	8.07	14.71%	−2.61%	3.92%
Jan-89	26	18.02	0.889	8.27	9.54%	3.84%	2.45%
Feb-89	27	17.93	0.7996	8.53	−0.50%	−10.60%	3.10%
Mar-89	28	19.48	0.8194	8.82	8.29%	2.45%	3.34%
Apr-89	29	21.07	0.7928	8.65	7.85%	−3.30%	−1.95%
May-89	30	20.12	0.7484	8.43	−4.61%	−5.76%	−2.58%
Jun-89	31	20.05	0.7553	8.15	−0.35%	0.92%	−3.38%

Exhibit 16.15—Part One—*continued*

Jul-89	32	19.78	0.7524	7.88	−1.36%	−0.38%	−3.37%
Aug-89	33	18.57	0.7656	7.9	−6.31%	1.74%	0.25%
Sep-89	34	19.59	0.7764	7.75	5.35%	1.40%	−1.92%
Oct-89	35	20.09	0.7831	7.64	2.52%	0.86%	−1.43%
Nov-89	36	19.85	0.7815	7.69	−1.20%	−0.20%	0.65%
Dec-89	37	21.1	0.7927	7.63	6.11%	1.42%	−0.78%
Jan-90	38	22.86	0.7708	7.64	8.01%	−2.80%	0.13%
Feb-90	39	22.11	0.7594	7.74	−3.34%	−1.49%	1.30%
Mar-90	40	20.38	0.7542	7.9	−8.15%	−0.69%	2.05%
Apr-90	41	18.42	0.7509	7.77	−10.11%	−0.44%	−1.66%
May-90	42	18.2	0.7691	7.74	−1.20%	2.39%	−0.39%
Jun-90	43	16.69	0.789	7.73	−8.66%	2.55%	−0.13%
Jul-90	44	18.45	0.7901	7.62	10.03%	0.14%	−1.43%
Aug-90	45	27.31	0.8162	7.45	39.22%	3.25%	−2.26%
Sep-90	46	33.5	0.8265	7.36	20.43%	1.25%	−1.22%
Oct-90	47	36.04	0.7847	7.17	7.31%	−5.19%	−2.62%
Nov-90	48	32.33	0.7745	7.06	−10.86%	−1.31%	−1.55%
Dec-90	49	27.28	0.7733	6.74	−16.98%	−0.16%	−4.64%
Jan-91	50	25.23	0.7849	6.22	−7.81%	−1.49%	−8.03%
Feb-91	51	20.47	0.7851	5.94	−20.91%	−0.03%	−4.61%
Mar-91	52	19.9	0.7752	5.91	−2.82%	−1.27%	−0.51%
Apr-91	53	20.83	0.7817	5.65	4.57%	0.83%	−4.50%
May-91	54	21.23	0.7609	5.46	1.90%	−2.70%	−3.42%
Jun-91	55	20.19	0.7681	5.57	−5.02%	0.94%	1.99%
Jul-91	56	21.4	0.7775	5.58	5.82%	1.22%	0.18%
Aug-91	57	21.69	0.7848	5.33	1.35%	0.93%	−4.58%
Sep-91	58	21.88	0.7995	5.22	0.87%	1.86%	−2.09%
Oct-91	59	23.23	0.7837	4.99	5.99%	−2.00%	−4.51%
Nov-91	60	22.46	0.7848	4.56	−3.37%	0.14%	−9.01%
Dec-91	61	19.49	0.7598	4.07	−14.18%	−3.24%	−11.37%
Jan-92	62	18.78	0.7498	3.8	−3.71%	−1.32%	−6.86%
Feb-92	63	19.01	0.7546	3.84	1.22%	0.64%	1.05%
Mar-92	64	18.92	0.7684	4.04	−0.47%	1.81%	5.08%
Apr-92	65	20.23	0.7593	3.75	6.69%	−1.19%	−7.45%
May-92	66	20.97	0.7589	3.63	3.59%	−0.05%	−3.25%
Jun-92	67	22.38	0.7488	3.66	6.51%	−1.34%	0.82%
Jul-92	68	21.77	0.7442	3.21	−2.76%	−0.62%	−13.12%
Aug-92	69	21.33	0.7134	3.13	−2.04%	−4.23%	−2.52%
Sep-92	70	21.88	0.714	2.91	2.55%	0.08%	−7.29%
Oct-92	71	21.68	0.6954	2.86	−0.92%	−2.64%	−1.73%
Nov-92	72	20.34	0.6823	3.13	−6.38%	−1.90%	9.02%
Dec-92	73	19.41	0.688	3.22	−4.68%	0.83%	2.83%
Jan-93	74	19.03	0.6786	3	−1.98%	−1.38%	−7.08%
Feb-93	75	20.08	0.6957	2.93	5.37%	2.49%	−2.36%
Mar-93	76	20.32	0.7058	2.95	1.19%	1.44%	0.68%
Apr-93	77	20.25	0.7116	2.87	−0.35%	0.82%	−2.75%
May-93	78	19.95	0.6769	2.96	−1.49%	−5.00%	3.09%
Jun-93	79	19.09	0.6722	3.07	−4.41%	−0.70%	3.65%
Jul-93	80	17.77	0.6834	3.04	−7.17%	1.65%	−0.98%
Aug-93	81	17.99	0.6708	3.02	1.23%	−1.86%	−0.66%
Sep-93	82	17.5	0.6453	2.95	−2.76%	−3.88%	−2.35%
Oct-93	83	18.15	0.6661	3.02	3.65%	3.17%	2.35%
Nov-93	84	16.61	0.6586	3.1	−8.87%	−1.13%	2.61%
Dec-93	85	14.51	0.6711	3.06	−13.52%	1.88%	−1.30%

Exhibit 16.15—Part One—*continued*

Jan-94	86	15.03	0.7112	2.98	3.52%	5.80%	−2.65%
Feb-94	87	14.78	0.7178	3.25	−1.68%	0.92%	8.67%
Mar-94	88	14.68	0.7008	3.5	−0.68%	−2.40%	7.41%
Apr-94	89	16.42	0.7124	3.68	11.20%	1.64%	5.01%
May-94	90	17.89	0.7361	4.14	8.57%	3.27%	11.78%
Jun-94	91	19.06	0.7291	4.14	6.34%	−0.96%	0.00%
Jul-94	92	19.65	0.7393	4.33	3.05%	1.39%	4.49%
Aug-94	93	18.38	0.7425	4.48	−6.68%	0.43%	3.41%
Sep-94	94	17.45	0.7393	4.62	−5.19%	−0.43%	3.08%
Oct-94	95	17.72	0.7422	4.95	1.54%	0.39%	6.90%
Nov-94	96	18.17	0.7674	5.29	2.51%	3.34%	6.64%
Dec-94	97	17.16	0.7768	5.6	−5.72%	1.22%	5.69%
Jan-95	98	18.48	0.7583	5.71	7.41%	−2.41%	1.95%
Feb-95	99	18.52	0.7395	5.77	0.22%	−2.51%	1.05%
Mar-95	100	19.18	0.728	5.73	3.50%	−1.57%	−0.70%
Apr-95	101	20.36	0.7299	5.65	5.97%	0.26%	−1.41%
May-95	102	18.88	0.7138	5.67	−7.55%	−2.23%	0.35%
Jun-95	103	17.38	0.7086	5.47	−8.28%	−0.73%	−3.59%
Jul-95	104	17.62	0.7389	5.42	1.37%	4.19%	−0.92%
Aug-95	105	17.89	0.7524	5.4	1.52%	1.81%	−0.37%
Sep-95	106	17.54	0.755	5.28	−1.98%	0.34%	−2.25%
Oct-95	107	17.67	0.7566	5.28	0.74%	0.21%	0.00%
Nov-95	108	18.27	0.7469	5.36	3.34%	−1.29%	1.50%
Dec-95	109	19.54	0.745	5.14	6.72%	−0.25%	−4.19%
Jan-96	110	17.76	0.7447	5	−9.55%	−0.04%	−2.76%
Feb-96	111	19.59	0.7635	4.83	9.81%	2.49%	−3.46%
Mar-96	112	21.43	0.7793	4.96	8.98%	2.05%	2.66%
Apr-96	113	20.95	0.7854	4.99	−2.27%	0.78%	0.60%
May-96	114	19.77	0.7983	5.02	−5.80%	1.63%	0.60%
Jun-96	115	20.92	0.789	5.11	5.65%	−1.17%	1.78%
Jul-96	116	20.45	0.7731	5.17	−2.27%	−2.04%	1.17%
Aug-96	117	22.25	0.7909	5.09	8.84%	2.28%	−1.56%
Sep-96	118	24.2	0.7924	5.15	8.40%	0.19%	1.17%
Oct-96	119	23.25	0.7919	5.01	−4.00%	−0.06%	−2.76%
Nov-96	120	23.7	0.816	5.03	1.92%	3.00%	0.40%
Dec-96	121	25.9	0.7945	5.02	8.88%	−2.67%	−0.20%

Summary Volatility and Correlation Coefficients

Monthly	67% Price Volatility	95% Price Volatility	Correlation Coefficient		
			US$ WTI	AUD/USD	US$ LIBOR
US$ WTI	7.56%	12.48%	1.00	0.09	0.08
AUD/USD	2.57%	4.24%	0.09	1.00	0.16
US$ LIBOR	4.03%	6.65%	0.08	0.16	1.00

Annualised	67% Price Volatility	95% Price Volatility	Correlation Coefficient		
			US$ WTI	AUD/USD	US$ LIBOR
US$ WTI	26.20%	43.24%	1.00	0.09	0.08
AUD/USD	8,91%	14.69%	0.09	1.00	0.16
US$ LIBOR	13.97%	23.05%	0.08	0.16	1.00

Exhibit 16.15—Part Two

Using the historical time series from the first part of this exhibit the actual 95% confidence level price movement is calculated using the actual cumulative frequency distribution for the three data series. As the table shows, in this instance the parametric VAR over-estimates the 95% confidence (or 5% confidence loss).

	US$ WTI	AUD/USD	LIBOR	
Price Exposure	Fall	Rise	Rise	
5% Percentile Loss Price Change	−9.69%	4.21%	6.30%	See Graphs below
Parametric Result	−12.48%	4.24%	6.65%	
Difference	−2.79%	−0.03%	−0.35%	

Cumulative Price Distribution - WTI

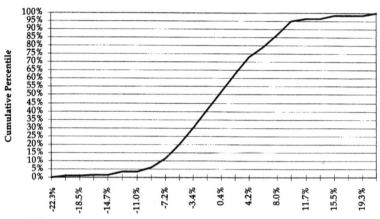

Cumulative Price Distribution - A$/US$

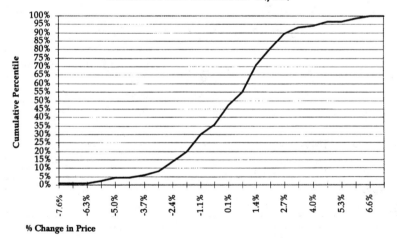

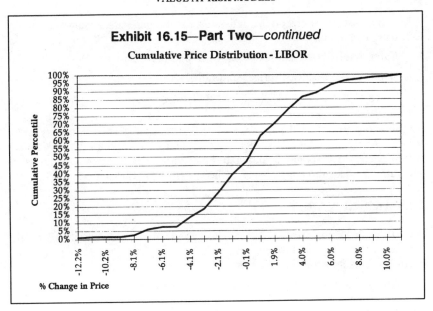

Exhibit 16.15—Part Two—*continued*

Cumulative Price Distribution - LIBOR

The results obtained may be calibrated to test the confidence in the estimates. This is usually done using statistical tests of significance and measuring standard error estimates.[10]

6. TYPES OF VAR

6.1 Technical components of VAR

VAR consists of three elements:

1. The current position in the relevant risk factors.
2. The sensitivity of the position to changes in the risk factor.
3. The forecast adverse change in the risk factors.

The first step is relatively unambiguous being equivalent to the market value of the position calculated at current market prices and rates. The differences in the types of VAR derive from choices in the second and third steps.

The sensitivity of the position can be derived in one of the following ways:

•   *Delta based*—calculated as the first derivative of the instrument or portfolio with respect to a small change in the risk factor; for example, the PVBP or DVO1 of a cash flow.

•   *Full valuation based*—calculated by recalculating the value of the instrument or portfolio using the normal market accepted valuation model relevant for the instrument.

10. See discussion in Chapter 19 regarding tests of statistical significance.

The forecast of future prices and rates can be generated using one of the following techniques:

- Using implied or historical volatilities and correlations.
- Using actual historical prices and rates.
- Using specified price changes or randomly generated price paths.

In practice, the choices in these two steps can be combined in a number of combinations to derive the measure of risk. There are three primary types of VARs: Analytic VAR; Historical VAR; and, Simulation VAR. Choices within each VAR approach and individual variations used by organisations generate various sub-categories of each type of VAR calculation.

6.2   Analytic VAR

Analytic VAR (also referred to as the variance/co-variance method) entails the use of historical volatilities and correlations to derive the market risk of a portfolio. This approach requires the following steps:

1.   Apply a system of risk decomposition to reduce the portfolio to identified risk factors.

2.   Obtain the historical volatilities of individual factors and correlations between risk factors from an external source (such as RiskMetrics™) or calculate them directly from historical data.

3.   Scale the historical volatility by the number of standard deviations consist with the confidence level desired.

4.   Calculate the VAR by applying the volatilities and correlation to the decomposed risk factors.

The techniques described above are an example of Analytic VAR.

In practice, Analytic VAR is generally used with delta based measures of portfolio sensitivity although in theory it is feasible to use full revaluation approaches.

The advantages of Analytic VAR include:

- The elegance and ease of application of the technique.
- Its capacity to be used to analyse complex transaction within a simple framework.
- Computational ease and simplicity, although the size of the correlation matrix can become large and unwieldy.

The disadvantages of Analytic VAR include:

- The need to make a number of statistical assumptions:
  - Assume that the future distribution of changes in the risk factors is normal.
  - Assume stationarity of the volatility and correlation estimates.
- The approach, as already noted, is not capable of accurately capturing the risk of options.
- The need for either historical data sets to generate the volatilities or correlations or availability of external estimates of these parameters.

- It is difficult to incorporate second order risk factors such as gamma (convexity risk), vega (volatility risk) and theta (impact of time decay).

- The process of scaling the risk factor over the risk period by taking the daily VAR estimate and multiplying it by $\sqrt{}$ risk horizon may not accurately capture the risk.

The process utilised to calculate the VAR under this approach suffers from the problem that a certain amount of information is lost in the computational process. The use of deltas, even for assets or forwards on certain instruments, such as long dated bonds, which have a degree of non-linearity or convexity, means that certain aspects of portfolio risk are over simplified leading to potential inaccuracies in the calculation of VAR.

6.3 Historical VAR

Historical VAR is based on revaluation of the current portfolio using historical rates and prices to arrive at the risk of the positions. Application of this approach requires the following steps:

1. The portfolio is defined in terms of risk factors, either as the instruments or risk factors (using the process of risk decomposition).

2. A historical data set is selected.

3. The historical data set is transformed to the current value date for the calculation of VAR.

4. The portfolio is revalued utilising the normal valuation models/ algorithms based on the historical data sets repeatedly to determine the changes in the portfolio values.

5. The VAR estimate is derived from the set of value changes calculated using either a percentile ranking or using statistical methods.

The Historical VAR approach can be based on the value of the instruments or decomposed risk factors. Under the instrument approach, a historical data set of the mark-to-market prices and rates *for each instrument* is required. Under the risk decomposition approach, each transaction is decomposed into the defined risk factors and mark-to-market values *for the risk factors* is required. In practice, for large portfolios the second approach is utilised. This is because of the lower number of price and rates for risk factors that must be stored and, more importantly, the ability to capture the risk of more complex instruments.

The historical data set will usually cover a nominated number of days, ranging between 90 and 500 days (3 to 24 months). This data is usually derived from a data base consisting of the rates and prices used to revalue the portfolio for mark-to-market purposes which has been stored for reutilisation in estimating VAR.

The data set has to be adjusted to the current value date for the VAR calculation. This requires the historical prices and rates to be related to the current rates and prices. There are a number of choices:

- *Absolute rates and prices*—this would utilise the *absolute* historical prices and rates to revalue the portfolios. The current portfolio is revalued using each day's actual price or rate irrespective of the starting rate or price level.

- *Absolute changes in rates and prices*—this would utilise the absolute price *change* in each rate and price to alter the current price and rates to generate a set of future prices based on the changes of the past to revalue the portfolio.

- *Relative changes in rates and prices*—this is similar to the absolute changes in rates and prices except that the relative or percentage changes (usually calculated as price relatives) of historical prices and rates are used to create the set of future prices.

The use of relative changes in rates and prices is the most logical methodology for the following reasons:

- it is consistent with the no-arbitrage approach to financial markets;
- it avoids the possibility of negative asset prices or rates (possible under the second option); and
- it minimises the impact of absolute price cycles in asset prices and rates and the resultant impact on the risk estimate.

The data set used to revalue can merely be the complete set of transformed historical prices and rates utilised continuously. Under this approach, to estimate risk using back data of 90 days would require only 91 days prices to calculate 90 relative price changes which are used to adjust the current prices and rates to generate the revaluation data set. An alternative methodology would be to generate more than the required set of price changes and randomly sample drawing the required 90 price and rate changes for the available data.

The random sampling technique is clearly more computationally demanding. Where the distribution is stable, the choice of method is unlikely to result in significant differences, at least statistically. However, where the distribution is not stable or where the immediate past is not considered a representative sample period, the sampling method may offer advantages in forecasting risk.

The revaluation is usually done using the conventional valuation models employed, such as cash flow models or actual market prices and options pricing models (closed form, numerical or Monte Carlo Simulations).

The risk value is the change in the value of the portfolio is given by:

$$\Delta PV_t = PV_{t+n} - PV_t$$

Where

ΔPV_t is equal to the projected change in the value of the portfolio at time t

PV_{t+n} is equal to the value of the portfolio at time t + n days

PV_t is equal to the value of the portfolio at time t

t is the VAR value date

n is the risk time horizon (usually given in days)

In practice n would be set to either 1, 10 or for longer risk horizons to say 30 days. Notice that the risk is estimated as the actual movement in the portfolio value over the risk period by calculating the *actual* change in value of the portfolio over the risk period. An alternative may be to capture the *single day VAR* and scale it to the required holding period by multiplying by the square root of the holding period (see discussion above).

The actual VAR estimate is derived from the changes in portfolio value calculated in one of two ways:

- *Percentile ranking method*—this requires ranking the price changes by amount from losses to gains. Once ranked, the VAR measure is calculated as the change in the value of the portfolio which is consistent with the percentile ranking that coincides with the confidence level required. For example, if the Historical VAR calculation is done over 250 days, then the appropriate percentile ranking for 99% (95%) confidence is the lowest 1% (5%) percentile ranking which coincides with the 3rd or 13th largest loss. The VAR estimate is equal to that particular loss figure.

- *Statistical (normal distribution) method*—this entails calculating the sample mean and standard deviation of *the changes in portfolio value*. The VAR is then calculated as the mean of the sample minus the standard deviation scaled by the appropriate number of standard deviations for the confidence level required (1.65 for 95% and 2.33 for 99%). The distribution may be reviewed for skewness and kurtosis prior to ensure normality prior to calculation of the VAR estimate.

Where the distribution is normal, either method will produce similar values, albeit not identical ones. The statistical method has the advantage of improving the prediction if the irregularity of the measure is due to sampling error. In the case of a non-normal distribution, the percentile ranking method is to be preferred.

The Historical VAR approach has significant advantages:

- It is simple and easily comprehensible and communicable.

- The capacity to incorporate actual price series incorporating *actual volatilities and correlations,* including any non-normal characteristics (skews, fat tails etc) of the actual distribution. This avoids the statistical assumptions made under Analytical VAR.

- The ability to use actual valuation models matching risk measurement to portfolio valuation and income determination.

- The inherent capacity to capture the effects of gamma (convexity risk), vega (volatility risk) and theta (impact of time decay).

- Ease of implementation as the revaluation models are already present for valuation purposes and limited data requirements as only historical revaluation data is required.

The disadvantages of Historical VAR include:

- The possibility that the historical period selected is not a good predictor of the risk horizon and creates significant inaccuracies in the risk measure. (It is probable that the same problems would affect the risk measures using Analytic VAR under the same circumstances.)

- The time needed to run the Historical VAR calculation which is a function of the time frame needed to revalue the entire portfolio, keeping in mind that the portfolio may need to be revalued 250 times to generate the risk estimate.

- The computational requirements may be large although with a risk decomposition approach the demands are likely to be no greater than for Analytic VAR.

6.4 Simulation VAR

The term Simulation VAR is a generic term which encompasses a number of techniques for modelling the performance of a portfolio and deriving risk estimates. The essential components of a simulation approach include:

1. A large set of random paths for prices and rates is generated.
2. The current portfolio is then revalued based on the generated prices and rates *for each path.*
3. The changes in the value of the portfolio are used to derive VAR and other risk measures by either using the percentile ranking method or statistical techniques as described above.

The Historical VAR calculation described above is a limited form of simulation. In practice, the different simulation models are distinguished by differences in the following components:

- the use of either delta-based or full revaluation models to determine the risks of the portfolio; and
- the process adopted to generate the price paths.

The use of full revaluation is favoured because of its ability to capture the full non-linearity of risk as well as second order impact of changes in volatility and time decay. Delta-based valuation is useful because it utilises existing parameters and provides some computational efficiencies. However, the loss of measurement accuracy and the failure to capture the impact of gamma, vega and theta mean that delta-based measures are generally not accurate.

There are two major forms of Simulation VAR techniques—fixed scenarios and Monte Carlo simulation.

Fixed scenario techniques necessitate the current portfolio being revalued following pre-specified changes in all asset prices and rates. The change in portfolio value provides an estimate of risk under the conditions specified. Given that the fixed scenarios are generally constructed to approximate expected *worst case* movements in the relevant risk factors, the portfolio risk measure is assumed to indicate accurately extreme portfolio risk values.

The major benefit of fixed scenario VAR is that it provides a useful stress test for the portfolio under the forecast conditions.

Fixed scenario simulations also have a number of disadvantages:

- The VAR and other risk estimates suffer from the problem that the risk revealed is dictated by the scenario nominated and has no significance other than in that context. To the extent that the fixed scenario over or under estimates the magnitude of movements in the risk factors the risk measures will inaccurately predict the risk profile of the portfolio.

- The performance of the portfolio will depend uniquely on the structure of the current portfolio. Application of the same fixed scenario stress test to *different portfolios* will predictably yield different views of risk. This lack of consistency and comparability is significant.

- The performance of the portfolio assumes no corrective action or adjustment to portfolio positions. In reality, portfolio managers will take corrective action, to the extent possible, as markets move in the manner forecast. The risk measures derived assuming no action may therefore tend to overestimate risk.

- The number of fixed scenarios run will generally be limited thereby limiting the risk estimates obtained which will not allow generation of a complete distribution of outcomes.

These weaknesses mean that the fixed scenario technique while useful in generating stress tests is not useful in deriving VAR measures.

Monte Carlo simulations entail generation of random multiple paths (between 500 and 10,000) of asset prices and rates which are then used to revalue the portfolio to create a distribution of changes in value of the portfolio which are then used to generate the risk statistics.

The major element in Monte Carlo processes is the choice of path generation mechanisms. There are two choices:

1. parametric; and

2. historical.

Parametric Monte Carlo entails the use of historical volatilities and correlations in conjunction with a selected stochastic price or rate process to generate the price paths. Typical approaches include the use of log normal stochastic processes for returns on assets. Mathematical models may be used to generate the future set of risk factors. For example, interest rate term structure models may be used to generate future interest rate paths. *Exhibit 16.16* sets out some examples of stochastic term structure models that are commonly used.[11]

---

11. Other types of term structure models include Hull-White, Black-Derman-Toy, and Heath-Jarrow-Morton—refer Chapter 6.

Exhibit 16.16

Interest Rate Models

Black Scholes model

The standard Black Scholes relative diffusion model can be used to specific the following stochastic model for interest rates:

$$dr = \mu\, dt + \sigma\, d\omega$$

Where

dr is the change in the short term interest rate

μ is a deterministic drift function per unit of time

dt is a short time interval

σ is the volatility of r

d ω is a standard random number generator

Vasichek model

The Vasichek model specifies the following stochastic model for interest rates:

$$dr = \alpha\,(\gamma - r)\, dt + \sigma\, dz$$

Where

dr is the change in the short term interest rate

α is the parameter (greater than 0) which describes the speed at which r revert to a long run average value

γ is the long run value of r

r is the short term interest rate

dt is a short time interval

σ is the volatility of r

dz is a random variable chosen from a normal distribution with mean 0 and variance dt

The process specified identifies that the change in the short term rate r over the interval dt will have two components:

1. A deterministic component ($\alpha\,(\gamma - r)\, dt$), whereby r will revert to a long run value at a speed parameter (α).

2. A stochastic component ($\sigma\, dz$), which will change randomly.

The structure of the first term implies that if r is close to (away from) its long run value, the deterministic term will be small (large). This term reflects the premise of mean reversion whereby interest rates tend towards some normal rate. The stochastic term will be larger as the time over which change occurs increases. The structure is designed to be consistent with the general pattern of evolution of interest rates in capital markets. The specified process for interest rate changes allows the derivation of valuation formula for a discount bond which in turn facilitates the solution for the value of interest rate derivative products.

Source: O A Vasichek, "An Equilibrium Characterisation of the Term Structure" (1977) 5 *Journal of Financial Economics* 177.

Historical Monte Carlo entails using historical data, rather than mathematical models, to generate the price paths. This approach randomly samples historical price changes (absolute prices, absolute price change, or (the most preferred) relative changes in prices, as described above) to generate the price paths for revaluation.

Common approaches include the use of a nominated stochastic process, which is consistent with valuation approaches, with parameter values being estimated from historical time series.

It is possible to distinguish between two types of Monte Carlo simulations:

1. *Passive*—where the underlying prices and rates follows the selected paths but there is no intervention.

2. *Active*—where the portfolio is rehedged to remain delta neutral as prices and rates alter.

Passive simulation is of limited usefulness in measuring risk, particularly, in portfolios with significant optionality. Active simulation is more valuable for analysis of dynamic trading issues, particularly, in portfolios containing option positions hedged in the asset market (see discussion above). An additional advantage of dynamic trading is the reduction in dependence upon secondary factors (such as drift terms) in the stochastic models used to generate the price paths.[12]

The advantages of Monte Carlo approaches include:

- The large number of price paths and consequently distributions of risk measures generated provide more reliable and comprehensive measures of risk.

- It explicitly captures the convexity of non-linear instruments as well as changes in volatility and time.

- The ability to use full valuation allows greater accuracy in deriving the risk estimates.

- The approach is very flexible allowing development of a wide range of price paths which may enable a fuller view of the risk to be modelled.

The disadvantages of Monte Carlo simulation approaches include:

- The dependence on the accuracy of either the stochastic process specified and/or the historical data used to generate the price path for the validity of the risk estimates.

- The computational requirements which can be formidable and the consequent lack of speed of generating VAR estimates (calculation can take up to several hours). This has cost implications for the user.

6.5   Types of VAR—comparison

The various approaches to VAR are clearly different and not readily reconcilable. The differences as between the approaches predicatably result in different risk estimates.[13] The problem in practice is that a choice has to be made in respect of the approach to be adopted in any particular context or within any organisation.

12. See discussion in Chapter 17 of using Monte Carlo simulations to measure option risks.
13. See Tanya Styblo Beder, "VAR: Seductive But Dangerous" 1995 (September-October) *Financial Analyst's Journal* 12; J V Jordan, and R J Mackay, "Assessing Value At Risk For Equity Portfolios: Implementing Alternative Techniques" in Rod Beckstrom, Alyce Campbell, and Frank Fabozzi (eds), *Handbook Of Firmwide Risk Management* (1996).

The choice between the three general types of VAR is dictated by a consideration of a mixture of the following factors:

1.　Coverage of instruments.
2.　Accuracy and tractability of risk measures, including statistical assumptions underlying approach.
3.　Implementation requirements covering valuation models, risk decomposition and data requirements.
4.　Systems requirements covering information technology issues.
5.　Ease of communicability of concept and results to users.

Coverage issues focus on the capacity of the approach to include all traded instruments and the treatment of options.

Two approaches are evident in respect of the first issue: focus on instruments or the use of risk decomposition to identify and aggregate the risk factors irrespective of the instrument. The first approach requires price, volatility and correlation information to be maintained *on every instrument*. The second approach has the advantage of allowing economies to be achieved in respect of the number of risk factors and thereby improves computational efficiency as well as the capacity to handle newer innovations within the risk factor framework.

Analytic VAR uses risk decomposition and therefore is capable of handling most traded instruments. Historical VAR and Simulation VAR can be undertaken using either instruments price values or risk factors. In practice, the second is favoured for the reasons identified above.

The treatment of options is more problematic. The major issues relate to the additional risks introduced through the inclusion of non-linear risk in the portfolio. Analytic VAR may generate significant inaccuracies in measuring risk because of its weaknesses in capturing the gamma, vega and theta risk of options. Historical and Simulation VARs, particularly, where full valuation models are used and the portfolio is aged to capture time decay (theta) effects, is better at capturing the additional risk of optionality in portfolios. *Exhibit 16.17* sets out a comparison of Analytic and Simulation VAR approaches in deriving risk measures for a portfolio containing options.

Exhibit 16.17

Measuring the Risk of Option Positions—Analytic VAR vs Simulation Approaches

Assumptions

This example compares the differences in risk estimates obtained from measuring risk through analytic VAR as against simulation approaches for a portfolio containing options.

Assume an investor holds the following positions:

- Investment (long) of US$ 1,000,000 (FFR 4,855,000 at US$/FFR spot rate of US$1: FFR4.855) equivalent of French Franc ("FFR") 2 year zero coupon OAT bond at a yield of 7.147%.

- Purchase of 5 week FFR put/US$ call on FFR 4,228,117/US$ 871,044 based on a strike set at the US$/FFR 5 week forward rate of US$1: FFR 4.864.

The investor's base currency is US$ and the investment risk horizon is 5 weeks.

The investor's risk is measured using three approaches:

1. Analytic VAR based on the option's delta.

2. Analytic VAR incorporating gamma changes using estimation procedures.

3. Monte Carlo simulation.

Analytic VAR—Delta Based

Under this approach, the risk is measured using the sensitivity of the individual positions (the option position being approximated by its delta) and using volatility and correlation estimates derived from the RiskMetrics™ data set.

The results are set out below. The undiversified VAR (for a 5 week holding period and for a 95% (1.65 σ) confidence level) is:

Risk Factor	Position (US$)	Volatility (%)	VAR (US$)
2 year FFR OAT zero	871,044	1.22	10,602
US$/FFR	871,044	5.38	20,550

The option VAR reflects the option delta of approximately 0.4386.

Incorporating a correlation between the risk factors of -0.291, the diversified VAR can be estimated as: US$ 20,197.

The relationship between the value of the currency option and the US$/FFR rate is set out in the following graph:

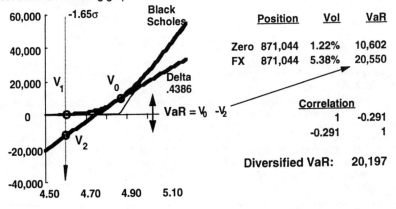

Exhibit 16.17—*continued*

The delta is the approximation of the change in value of the option for changes in the underlying currency measured as the slope of the tangent taken at the current spot rate.

The delta method potentially under or over estimates the change in value of the option. For example, if the spot rate moves from its current level (US$1: FFR 4.85) to, say, US$1: FFR 4.59 (a 1.65 σ change), the value of the option moves from point V0 to V1 in the graph (the option value is calculated using a Black Scholes model). The use of delta would estimate a change in the value of the option from V0 to V2—a much larger fall in value. This would result in an over estimation of the loss. In other words, the undiversified loss VAR estimate of the option of US$20,550 in this case represents an over estimate of the loss.

Analytic VAR—incorporating gamma

The deficiencies of a delta-based methodology for estimation of risk can be overcome by incorporating gamma. This would entail incorporating the option's value by using a non-linear function of the level of the exchange rate. This is set out in the following graph:

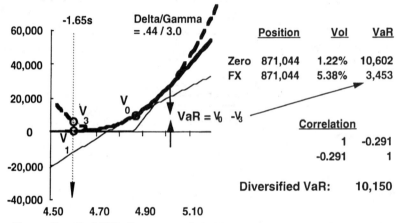

Position	Vol	VaR
Zero 871,044	1.22%	10,602
FX 871,044	5.38%	3,453

Correlation

1	-0.291
-0.291	1

Diversified VaR: 10,150

The undiversified VAR (for a 5 week holding period and for a 95% (1.65 σ) confidence level) is:

Risk Factor	Position (US$)	Volatility (%)	VAR (US$)
2 year FFR OAT zero	871,044	1.22	10,602
US$/FFR	871,044	5.38	3,453

Incorporating a correlation between the risk factors of -0.291, the diversified VAR can be estimated as: US$ 10,150.

As is evident, the VAR estimate *of the currency option* decreases from US$ 20,550 to US$ 3,453.

The use of the delta-gamma non linear function is also not strictly accurate as it under estimates the real change in the value of the option as measured by revaluation of the option using a Black-Scholes model for large changes in the exchange rate. In this case, the estimated risk is too low. The option *real* VAR using full revaluation is US$ 7,405. The underestimation of risk results from the fact that the curvature of the option value function around the current spot price (which is technically what gamma represents) does not accurately represent the curvature of the value function *at other exchange rates*.

Exhibit 16.17—*continued*

Monte Carlo simulation

To estimate the risk using Monte Carlo simulations, it is necessary to generate a substantial number of paths of interest rate and currency value changes. In this case, some 10,000 paths are created. The paths are created consistent with the current volatility and correlation estimates:

FRF 2 year zero volatility: 9.63%

US$/FFR volatility: 5.14%

Correlation: -0.291

The scenario generation requires a number of steps:

1. Decompose co-variance matrix Σ, so that $\Sigma = A*A'$.
2. With 10,000 random numbers X generate 10,000 scenarios of returns $Y = A'*X$.
3. From 10,000 scenarios of returns compute 10,000 scenarios of rate levels around current forwards $Z = F * \exp(Y)$.

The graph below sets out a possible set of scenarios:

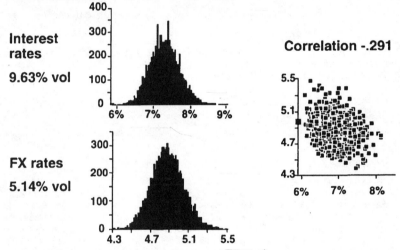

The set of scenarios generated will differ each time the simulation is run although their parameters (volatilities and correlations) are constant.

Once the scenarios are generated, the interest rates and currency values derived are used to revalue the position in each of the 10,000 paths created. The resulting profit and losses are then combined in a histogram. The histogram is then used to calculate the 5% risk estimate.

Exhibit 16.17—*continued*

The graph below sets out the value of the position using the full revaluation method:

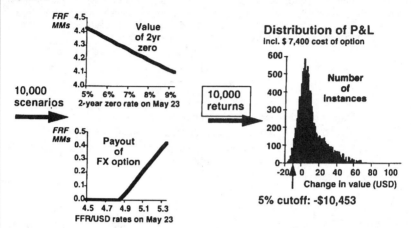

In this case, the simulation indicates that over a 5 week risk holding period and using a confidence level of 95%, the expected loss would not exceed US$ 10,453—the effective VAR of the position.

Summary

The VAR risk estimates generated are as follows:

VAR Technique	VAR Measure (US$)
Analytic VAR—Delta based	20,197
Analytic VAR—Delta Gamma Based	10,150
Monte Carlo Simulation	10,453

As is evident, the delta-based Analytic VAR estimate is flawed because of its inability to capture the non-linearity of the option. The gamma adjusted measure overcomes this problem partially but may incorrectly estimate risk depending on the magnitude of the price moves. The Monte Carlo simulation provides a more robust risk estimate, albeit at greater cost and slower speed, but is subject to the accuracy of the underlying volatility and correlation parameters used to generate the price paths.

Source: J P Morgan, *RiskMetric™—Technical Document* (3rd ed, J P Morgan, New York, (1995), pp 30-37, as presented by Debra Robertson (J P Morgan Australia Limited, "Fixed Income Research"), presentation to AIC Trading Risk Management Workshop, 24 May 1996.

A central criteria in selection is the accuracy and tractability of the risk measures derived from the model. The accuracy of any model is partly derived from the realisation of the assumptions underlying VAR generally, in particular, the representativeness of the historical data or simulation method or stability of estimates (see discussion in full below). However, in general, the following comments are warranted:

- Analytic VAR will provide reasonable VAR measures where the portfolio does not contain significant optionality, although there is dependence on the distribution of actual market outcomes relative to the assumed distribution.

- Historical VAR and Simulation VAR will provide robust estimates, irrespective of whether the portfolio contains significant optionality, provided either the historical period is representative or the stochastic process used to generate simulation paths is reasonably tractable and sufficient numbers of paths are used.

The major issue is the assumptions underlying Analytic VAR of a normal distribution for past asset returns. The assumption which is discussed more fully below is an important aspect of the Analytic VAR approach and non-realisation of the assumption may significantly mis-estimate risk. The emergence of evidence that markets are not consistent with normal or lognormal stochastic processes mean that extreme outliers may occur significantly more often than predicted by a normal distribution. The problem in this regard is that while markets *on the whole* may be consistent with normal distribution it is these outliers that create the most significant levels of risk in the portfolio. Consequently, failure to adequately capture them may reduce the value of the risk measures *in the situation where they are most needed*.

An advantage of historical simulations is that no distribution need be assumed as the *actual* historical price series is used to directly revalue the portfolio. This removes any risk of masking any skew or kurtosis in the distribution. This adds to the robustness of the risk estimates.

Simulation VAR, particularly, that using Monte Carlo techniques, can, depending on its specification avoid the assumption of a normal distribution. However, to aggregate and consolidate individual VAR of the risk factors may require an assumption of normality although this too can be avoided by rerunning the simulations for the total portfolio.

The implementation measures relate to valuation models, risk decomposition and data requirements.

As noted above, there is a choice between delta based valuation methods (Analytic VAR) and full revaluation methodologies using normal pricing models (generally, Historical VAR and Simulation VAR). The simplicity of delta based models is offset by the difficulties in capturing second order (that is, non-asset price) related risks. However, full revaluation is favoured as it overcomes the identified weaknesses and provides considerably greater richness in the risk estimates.

The process of risk decomposition is essentially a concession to data handling efficiencies as noted above. The process has the disadvantage that the process of decomposition, in particular, the decomposition of cash flow to capture interest rate risk into a limited number of maturity vertices, may reduce the accuracy of the risk measure.

The process of risk decomposition is essential to Analytic VAR. It is optional where Historical or Simulation VAR is utilised. However, in practice, the advantages of using a standard set of risk factors rather than the full set of instruments for the reasons already noted favours using risk decomposition methods for both Historical VAR or Simulation VAR without loss of significant precision of the risk estimates.

The data requirements for any type of VAR is significant. Analytic VAR requires volatilities for each risk factor and correlation as between risk factors. This can be either derived from external sources (such as the J P Morgan RiskMetrics™ data set) or internally based on the required data time series.

Historical VAR requires the relevant price and asset parameters for either each instrument or more realistically each risk factor. While this data requirement may appear formidable, in practice, the major proportion of data is available as it is required to mark portfolios to market. As a consequence, ensuring revaluation prices and data is stored in a form facilitating retrieval for VAR calculations reduces the difficulty in obtaining the data required. The internal data may be required to be supplemented by externally acquired data for new instruments or risk factors where the requisite price history is not internally available.

Historical VAR because of its reliance on actual data does not require the extensive computation of volatilities and correlations required under Analytic VAR. This reflects the fact that the volatilities and correlations are implicit in the data set. The data set for Historical VAR requires transforming to the value date for VAR as described above.

The data requirement for Monte Carlo simulations is varied and will relate to the historical market data or correlations or volatilities required by the stochastic processes assumed.

The systems requirements are varied. The requirements relate to the generation of the projected rates and prices, the risk decomposition and finally the generation of the risk measure.

Analytic VAR places considerable demands on systems in the terms of generation the volatility and correlation estimates, the risk decomposition and also the process of VAR calculation, particularly, the aggregation and consolidation of risk within and across asset classes.

Historical VAR is relatively straightforward. It requires merely limited manipulation of the data to rebase it. The risk decomposition (if utilised) will be identical to that required under Analytic VAR. The calculation of VAR requires repeated revaluations of the portfolio, using existing valuation models from which the VAR estimates can be derived.

Simulation VAR entailing Monte Carlo simulations requires the greatest systems resources. The substantial computing demands of generating and running a significant number of price paths makes this technique both slow and expensive. The data requirements and risk decomposition demands (if applicable) are not significantly different to that for Historical or Analytic VAR.

The ease of comprehension and communicability varies significantly as between the methods. The Historical VAR technique is significantly better on this criteria. It is relatively easily understood and its simplicity and relative transparency and flexibility make it a favoured methodology for communicating with less sophisticated users.[14]

Analytic VAR and Simulation VAR are relatively more difficult to communicate because of the inherent statistical techniques involved and the

14. For example, both Merrill Lynch and J P Morgan have used versions of this approach to communicate information about risk to their shareholders.

requirement of an understanding of these to appreciate the use of these models.

The 1996 BIS Market Risk Guidelines do not recommend a standard methodology from estimating market risk. The BIS recommended the use of both qualitative and quantitative standards for internal bank risk management models. The internal VAR based risk models utilised by regulated financial institutions must meet the following general criteria:

1. Daily computation of VAR measures for all trading positions.

2. A confidence level of 99% (2.33 σ) to be utilised.

3. Minimum holding period of 10 business days.

4. Minimum effective historical observation period of 1 year (250 business days) with the data sets to be updated at least quarterly.

5. The models used should capture the non-linear risk of option instruments.

6. Consolidation to be allowed to incorporate both correlations within risk factor categories and between asset classes.

The BIS Guidelines do not recommend any particular form of VAR model. The BIS Guidelines do, however, recommend the use of separate stress testing to measure risk that might not be captured by the models. The BIS also recommends back testing to test and improve risk management systems.

Exhibit 16.8 summarises the differences between the BIS (Basel Committee) proposal with alternative risk management frameworks (such as RiskMetrics™).

Exhibit 16.18

Comparing the Basel Committee Proposal with RiskMetrics

Issue	Basel Committee Proposal	RiskMetrics
Mapping: how positions are described in summary form	• Fixed income: at least 6 time buckets, differentiate government yield curves and spread curves.	• Fixed Income: data for 7-10 buckets of government yield curves in 16 markets, 4 buckets money market rates in 27 markets, 4-6 buckets in swap rates in 18 markets.
	• Equities: country indices, individual stocks on basis of beta equivalent.	• Equities: country indices in 27 markets, individual stocks on beta (correction for non-systematic risk).
	• Commodities: to be included, not specified how.	• Commodities: 80 volatility series on 11 commodities (spot and term).
Volatility: how statistics of future price movement are estimated	• Volatility expressed in standard deviation of normal distribution proxy for daily historical observations year or more back. Equal weights or alternative weighting scheme provided effective observation period is at least one year.	• Volatility expressed in standard deviation of normal distribution proxy for exponentially weighted daily historical observations with decay factors of .94 (for trading, 74 day cutoff 1%) and .97 (for investing, 151 day cutoff at 1%).
		• Special Regulatory Data Set, incorporating Basel Committee 1-year moving average assumption.
	• Estimate updated at least quarterly.	• Estimates updated daily.
Adversity: size of adverse move in terms of normal distribution	• Minimum adverse move expected to happen with probability of 1% (2.32 standard deviations) over 10 business days. Permission to use daily statistics scaled up with square root of 10(3.1). Equivalent to 7.3 daily standard deviations.	• For trading: minimum adverse move expected to happen with probability of 5% (1.65 standard deviation) over 1 business day. • For investment: minimum adverse move expected to happen with probability of 5% (1.65 standard deviation) over 25 business days.

Exhibit 16.18—*continued*

Issue	Basel Committee Proposal	RiskMetrics
Options: treatment of time value and non-linearity	• Risk estimate must consider effect of non-linear price movement (gamma-effect).	• Non-linear price movement can be estimated analytically (delta-gamma) or under simulation approach. Simulation scenarios to be generated from estimated volatilities and correlations.
	• Risk estimate must include effect of changes in implied volatilities (vega-effect).	• Estimates of volatilities of implied volatilities currently not provided, thus limited coverage of options risk.
Correlation: how risks are aggregated	• Portfolio effect can be considered within asset classes (Fixed Income, Equity, Commodity, FX). Use of correlations across asset classes subject to regulatory approval.	• Full portfolio effect considered across all possible parameter combinations.
	• Correlations estimated with equally weighted daily data for more than one year.	• Correlations estimated using exponentially weighted daily historical observations with decay factors of 0.94 (for trading, 74 day cutoff 1%) and 0.97 (for investing, 151 day cutoff at 1%).
Residuals: treatment of instrument specific risks	• Instrument specific risks not covered by standard maps should be estimated. • Capital requirements at least equal to 50% of charge calculated under standard methodology.	• Does not deal with specific risks not covered in standard maps.

Source: J P Morgan/Reuters RiskMetrics™—Technical Document Fourth Edition (1996, J P Morgan/Reuter, New York) at p 39

In practice, the various advantages and disadvantages of the individual techniques are to some extent contextual; that is they depend on the type of portfolio and/or the purpose for which risk is measured. However, based on the analysis set out above, the favoured method of VAR estimation is Historical VAR, supplemented by stress testing using Monte Carlo Simulation. The major advantages include:

• The simplicity of the approach.

• The lack of assumptions regarding the distribution of asset price changes and the capacity to subsume intrinsic shifts in volatilities and correlations embedded in the actual data.

- The limited manipulation of the data utilised and the relative ease of data capture and maintenance.
- The use of full revaluation using normal valuation algorithms which capture second order risks such as gamma, vega and theta.
- The ability to capture non-linear risk of optionality efficiently.
- The flexibility of the approach (where risk decomposition is incorporated) to accommodate all instruments and be adapted readily to new instruments.
- The flexibility of deriving the VAR estimate using a choice of method.
- The lower systems demands of this approach.
- The ease of comprehension and communicability of this technique.

When supplemented with regular Monte Carlo simulations, particularly active Monte Carlo techniques, to stress test the portfolio, the Historical VAR approach provide robust risk estimates. The periodic use of Monte Carlo minimises the cost and speed constraints of this technique but allows it to be used to provide additional insight into portfolio behaviour such as dynamic changes in risk as it is rehedged in a portfolio with significant option contents, the impact of shifting volatility, trading liquidity constraints, cash flow impacts and other dynamic risk aspects.

6.   ISSUES IN USING VALUE AT RISK

6.1   Assumptions underlying VAR

The VAR methodology requires a number of assumptions about the functioning of capital markets. In practice, the most important assumption relates to:

- the estimation interval or time period; and
- the distribution assumptions.

Both have been alluded to earlier in various contexts. The assumption regarding estimation interval affect *all* VAR methodologies. The distribution assumption affects Analytic VAR and may affect Simulation VAR depending upon the type of stochastic process to generate and calibrate the revaluation price paths.

The estimation time period issues arise because all VAR approaches are based on historical information about asset prices and rates albeit in different ways. Analytic VAR uses volatilities and correlations derived from historical information. Historical VAR uses the historical price series directly to generate the revaluation parameters. Simulation VAR, depending on the type of simulation engine, uses historical data indirectly or directly to generate the price paths or determine parameters for the stochastic models utilised.

To the extent that the historical data used is not representative of the actual period in the future, the risk estimates would be inaccurate. The extent of any inaccuracy and its impact would be dependent upon the extent of the variation. The stability of the estimates used to determine risk are very important.

The stability of J P Morgan's RiskMetrics™ volatility and correlation estimates has been tested.[15] The analysis concluded that these estimates based on historical data weighted using an exponential weighting scheme were reasonably stable but were to varying degree time varying.

The use of historical data forces consideration of the estimation interval to be used to minimise estimation error on projecting risk parameters. This question is similar to the issues arising in relation to selection of a time interval to compute historical volatility for derivation of volatilities for option pricing.

There are two choices:

- *Short*—this uses the most recent data and makes estimates responsive to the most recent movements in market prices.

- *Longer*—this uses longer time periods but is subject to the problems that it is not responsive to recent trends, structural changes in markets and any mean reversion tendency make dominate the estimate.

An additional problem is that even with reasonable samples of time series data, it is unlikely that there are sufficient degrees of freedom, from a statistical viewpoint, to accurately discriminate between individual sources of risk. This problem will be greater the smaller the data series used to derive the risk estimates.

The distributional assumption, which affects Analytic VAR most directly, relate to a number of issues including:

1. Normality—that is, are prices changes in financial assets normally distributed.

2. Mean Change—that is, should the volatility be calculated as the difference between zero and the current deviation from the sample mean.

3. Log versus percentage changes—that is, should volatility estimates be based on the distribution of percentage changes or the logarithms of the changes of asset prices.

Each of these issues have been addressed by J P Morgan in the context of its RiskMetrics™ approach which is predicated on the assumption of normality.[16]

The assumption of a normal distribution of asset price changes provides important advantages in allowing predictions about expected price changes. The RiskMetrics™ research focused on establishing the difference between the observed and predicted frequencies and values of observations in the tails of the normal distribution. This methodology, which used a variety of statistical techniques was designed to provide information on both how frequently extreme outcomes *actually* occurred relative to the *predicted* outcomes as well as how *large* these values were relative to the predicted values.

15. See J P Morgan, *Five Question About RiskMetrics™*; (Morgan Guaranty Trust Company; New York, 1995); J P Morgan/Reuters, op cit n 4, Appendix A.
16. Ibid.

The analysis concluded that the observed frequencies and points were not inconsistent with the assumptions of a normal distribution. The most significant exception was money market or short term interest rates which generally did not exhibit the behaviour consistent with normal distributions. The behaviour of money market rates is quite predictable given the impact of intervention by monetary authorities in the setting of these rates which results in non-random changes in value.

Statistically, standard deviation (volatility) measures the dispersion of price changes around a specified mean. This mean is usually assumed to be zero. An alternative may be to utilise the estimate of sample mean or a conditional zero mean return.

The RiskMetrics™ research concludes that for short (1 day) risk horizons the difference between the zero mean and the estimated mean is not significant but for longer risk horizons (1 month) there are larger differences particularly for money market rates. This means that the zero mean estimator is generally unbiased and viable.

The use of logarithm (compounded) price changes are common in finance as they allow continuous time generalisations of discrete time results and returns for in excess of one day are a simple function of the single day return. The alternative is to use simple percentage change returns. The RiskMetrics™ research concludes that the volatilities and correlations calculated under either type of return while different are not significantly so. The original version of RiskMetrics™ utilised percentage returns but subsequently changed to logarithmic returns.

The tractability of the assumptions should be treated with caution. The results of any tests may be contingent upon the test data and different data sets may give rise to different conclusions. The major problem from a practical viewpoint is that even if markets are consistent with normal distribution assumptions *generally* a small departure (which may or may not be statistically significant) from normality has significant implications for risk management as it may lead to an underestimation of risk which in combination with the structure of the portfolio at a given time may lead to unacceptable and unanticipated losses.

The most significant of the above assumptions is that relating to the normality of the distribution of price changes. Given the growing evidence that the behaviour of risk factors do not conform to normally distributed stochastic processes the risk of an outlying event, which may occur more frequently than standard risk models predicated on normality of distributions anticipate, may in fact be the *primary focus* of risk estimation.

The most tractable and useful estimate of risk is one that most comprehensively captures the complexity of the underlying distribution of changes in risk factors, the interrelationship between risk factors, and their impact on individual portfolio structures. In this regard, the absence of significant assumptions makes the Historical VAR approach attractive.

Where distributional assumptions are required, the use of backtesting techniques to review and calibrate risk modelling techniques is essential.

6.2   Backtesting techniques[17]

The concept of backtesting is essential to the process of evaluating and calibrating risk measurement models. The basic concept is to compare the *actual* observed change in the value of the portfolio with the *risk estimate* provided by the VAR calculated. The essential element is to measure the accuracy of the model prediction against actual changes in portfolio value and to ensure that the model estimates the risk consistent with the desired confidence level.

The key steps in backtesting are as follows:

1.   VAR estimates using the relevant VAR model are generated and stored.

2.   Actual portfolio profits and losses are calculated using normal mark to market procedures and stored.

3.   Periodically, the actual daily mark to market gain or loss is compared to the daily VAR measures (the BIS Guidelines recommend quarterly backtesting using a trailing 250 day (1 year) period).

4.   The error fraction (or exceptions) is then calculated as the number of occasions on which the actual trading result exceeded the VAR risk measure.

The VAR estimates should be significantly larger than the trading outcomes for all but a small number of days (for example, at a confidence level of 99%, using a test sample of 250 days (1 year), the error fraction should, intuitively, be around 2-3). To the extent that the error fraction is within or outside acceptable ranges determines the validity of the risk model.

In practice, the process of backtesting is complicated by a number of issues, including:

•   the problem of contamination of the portfolio; and

•   the problem of fee income or other earnings on the portfolio.

The problem of contamination relates to the fact that for the backtest to have validity the actual trading outcomes must not be contaminated by changes in portfolio composition. This means that the portfolio must be held constant during the relevant period.

The problem of portfolio earnings is related to the issue of contamination. Depending on the risk horizon, the portfolio may generate significant earning which may partially offset trading gains and losses. However, the earning may contaminate the backtest and render more complex the interpretation of the results.

The problems of contamination and the inclusion or otherwise of portfolio earnings increases in importance as the risk horizon utilised is longer. This is because the likelihood of changes in portfolio composition and the impact of earning increases.

The guidelines for backtesting suggested by the BIS favour uncontaminated backtesting and non-inclusion of earnings.

17. For an excellent discussion of backtesting, see Basle Committee on Banking Supervision, "Supervisory Framework For The Use of 'Backtesting' In Conjunction With Internal Models Approach To Market Risk Capital Requirements", January 1996.

Evaluation of the backtest can be informal or formal, based on statistics. The Supervisory approach recommended by the BIS is a good example of the latter.

The BIS approach classifies the result into three colour zones (green, yellow, red) based on the error fraction. *Exhibit 16.19* sets out the BIS model.

Exhibit 16.19

BIS Three Zone Approach to Backtesting Interpretation

ZONE	NUMBER OF EXCEPTION
Green	0
	1
	2
	3
	4
Yellow	5
	6
	7
	8
	9
Red	10 or more

Under the model approach, the backtest is interpreted as follows:

- *Green zone*—the backtest does not suggest a problem with the quality and accuracy of the model.
- *Yellow zone*—the backtest results are not conclusive.
- *Red zone*—the backtest results indicate a problem with the quality and accuracy of the model.

The supervisory response to the backtest lies in the adjustment to the scaling factor for capital required to be held against market risk. The base level of this factor is 3 (that is, the capital required to be held equates to three times the VAR estimate). Depending on the results of the backtest, the supervisory authority may increase the factor, at their discretion. *Exhibit 16.20.* sets the increase in scaling factors recommended. For example, where the backtest results are in the red zone, the supervisor would be able to increase the multiplication factor applicable to the model by 1 (increasing it from 3 to 4 times—an effective penalty in capital terms of $33^{1}/_{3}\%$).

Exhibit 16.20

BIS Three Zone Approach to Backtesting
Interpretation—Increase in Scaling Factor

ZONE	NUMBER OF EXCEPTION	INCREASE IN SCALING FACTOR
	0	0.00
Green	1	0.00
	2	0.00
	3	0.00
	4	0.00
	5	0.40
	6	0.50
Yellow	7	0.65
	8	0.75
	9	0.85
Red	10 or more	1.00

The major interpretative problems of a backtest are where the results are inconclusive, that is they are in the yellow zone. The results may be generated by any one of the following factors:

- *Model integrity*—this includes incorrect position or incorrect volatilities or correlations.

- *Model risk factors*—this includes insufficient specification of the risk factors; eg insufficient number of maturity vertices; specific risk (stock specific exposure in equities or credit risk in bonds etc).

- *Market condition*—this covers the occurrence of a low probability event (a stock market crash) or a shift in market volatility levels.

- *Intra-day trading*—this covers income events such as large intra-day changes in the positions.

The analysis of the backtest may be able to isolate the cause of the failure. The second and third factors are potentially the least serious as these events may be expected to occur on some occasions. The first and third are potentially more serious as they point to more fundamental deficiencies in the integrity of the risk measurement process. The supervisory response may incorporate consideration of the likely cause as well as the extent to which the trading outcomes exceeded the VAR measure.

The use of a consistent and regular backtesting protocol is essential to use VAR type model to both measure the accuracy and validity of the risk model as well as allow enhancement and improvements in the basic model.

6.3   Adjustments to VAR methodology

The basic VAR model identified deals adequately with certain elements of risk. It is designed to and fundamentally addresses market risk. However, the basic VAR model provides only limited assistance in measuring liquidity risk and specific risk. It also embodies certain weaknesses in its handling of commodity price risk. In this Section certain enhancements to the basic VAR model designed to address these weakness are considered.

6.3.1   Adjusting VAR for liquidity risk

The concept of liquidity risk encompasses several categories of exposure:

1. *Liquidation risk*—this relates to the fact that a position may be large *relative to the trading liquidity* in that particular security or asset which might impede the elimination of the position by trading.

2. *Trading liquidity risk*—this relates to the volume of trading in a particular asset that might be required, for example to delta hedge a portfolio if the market price moves by a large amount, and the potential risk that the trading volume required may not be able to be executed or can only be executed at larger costs.

3. *Cash flow risk*—this relates to the cash impact of market price movements, for example, in terms of mark-to-market losses on futures positions, and the cash requirements to fund the positions.

Two and 3 are, in reality, extremely important. The best mechanism for quantifying the risk is through simulation methodologies as discussed above.

In contrast, liquidation risk can be encompassed within the VAR model framework. This is because VAR through its risk horizon specifically assumes a liquidation period. A 1 or 10 day risk horizon implicitly assumes that the position held can be eliminated or neutralised *in a period not exceeding the risk horizon.*

In reality, any portfolio will contain a large number of positions with *varying* liquidation periods. Assuming a 10 day risk horizon for risk measurement, a portfolio will generally include a large number of positions which will be able to be adjusted well within that time horizon while there will be other position in less liquid assets which will require a longer liquidation period. This means that the VAR measure may overestimate the risk on liquid positions while underestimating the risk on illiquid positions and the validity of the VAR measure will be contingent on the relative size of the positions.

This problem can be dealt with by amending the basic VAR framework as follows:

*   *The holding period adjustment*—this would entail including a time to liquidation concept whereby the greater of 10 days (the minimum risk horizon) and the actual expected liquidation period could be used to derive VAR. The actual liquidation period could be specified as the size of the position divided by a certain percentage of the daily trading volume to ensure the incorporation of the relative position size in the calculation.

- *The use of bid/offer spread adjustment*—this assumes that the relative liquidity of an asset should be reflected in the bid offer spreads for that asset. Amending VAR by incorporating a bid/offer spread component which is variable depending upon the asset may allow the liquidation risk impact on VAR to be covered.

The above methodologies are relatively crude attempts to address the liquidation risk problem. A more sophisticated technique tries to capture the actual behaviour of traders and institutions in seeking to minimise the loss in closing down risk positions.[18]

The basic model respecifies the liquidation horizon for any position (equating to the VAR risk horizon) as that appropriate to minimise the cost of liquidation. The cost of liquidation is specified as the following:

- *Transaction costs*—covering the bid/offer spread adjusted for the size of the position.

- *Cost of exposure*—covering the cost of capital that must be held against the position until the position is liquidated and any cost of hedging the position until liquidation.

Provided appropriate functions for transaction costs and the cost of exposure can be specified, the optimal liquidation horizon is calculated as the period which minimises the identified costs.[19] The identified liquidation horizon is then used as the relevant risk horizon to derive the VAR risk estimate.

Major advantages of this approach include:

- The explicit linkage created between liquidity risk, transaction cost and risk horizon in deriving risk estimates.

- The capture of the tradeoff between transaction cost and cost of maintaining exposure.

- The attempt to capture explicit trader behaviour and risk management practice.

The difficulties with this approach include:

- Problems in accurately specifying the functions for transaction costs and the cost of exposure.

- Changes in market and trading conditions which may require frequent adjustments in these functions.

- Increased computational requirements and demands.

- Added complexity in the risk measures.

18. The liquidity adjusted VAR approach is set out in Dr Colin Lawrence, Gary Robinson and Matthew Stiles, "Incorporating Liquidity Into The Risk Measurement Framework" (1996) 6 *Financial Derivatives and Risk Management* 24; Dr Colin Lawrence and Gary Robinson, "Value At Risk: Addressing Liquidity And Volatility Risks" (1996) 7 *Capital Market Strategies* 24.
19. For a discussion of the process of specifying the appropriate functions see the references cited in the previous footnote.

6.3.2 VAR and specific risk

The VAR methodology facilitates the capture, measurement and display of market risk in terms of specified risk factors. The risk factors usually are designed to and do in reality capture, reasonably efficiently, *general* market risk. The risk factors are relatively poor at capturing *specific* market risk.

General market risk, in this context, refers to marketwide movements, that is changes affecting *all instruments*. Specific market risk refers to changes which are unique to and affect *individual or specific instruments*. For example, in interest rate risk terms, general market risk refers to changes in general rate levels, embodied in changes in risk free government rates which affects the total universe of fixed interest securities while specific risk refers to changes in the spread relative to the risk free government rate for a specific issuer which affects the value of fixed interest securities issued by the particular issuer.

In practice, the issue of specific risk is evident in two contexts:

1. individual equity securities; and

2. non-government fixed interest securities.

The specific risk relating to individual equity securities only arises where equities are mapped to the relevant domestic market index and the position does not constitute a well diversified equity portfolio. As noted above, in such a case, individual risk factors *for the individual equity securities* are recommended.

The problem of specific risk in non-government fixed interest securities relates to the fact that only two zero rate curves are utilised for risk measurement—a risk free government curve and the swap curve. This assumes that the relationship between the swap curve and the yields on other non-government (and therefore risky) fixed interest securities is constant. In practice, these spreads can be volatile resulting in the residual or specific risk being substantial.

This is particularly the case with non-investment grade securities whose yields are subject to considerable spread volatility. The empirical research[20] indicates that the correlation between the returns on corporate debt and US Treasury yields decreases as the credit quality, as measured by rating

---

20. See Richard Bookstaber and David P Jacob, "The Composite Hedge: Controlling The Credit Risk Of High Yield Bonds" (1986) (March/April) *Financial Analysts Journal* 25; Robin Grieves, "Hedging Corporate Bond Portfolios" (Summer 1986) *The Journal of Portfolio Management* 23; Murali Ramaswani, "Hedging The Equity Risk Of High Yield Bonds" (1991) (Sept/Oct) *Financial Analysts Journal* 41.

parameters, decreases. This decrease in correlation to risk free debt returns is paralleled by an *increase* in the correlation between the bonds and equity of the issuer as the credit quality declines. The relationship can be seen from a comparison of the correlations (see *Exhibit 16.21*).[21] Under these conditions, the lack of incorporation of specific risk can lead to significant weaknesses in the risk measures derived.

Exhibit 16.21

Correlation Between Corporate Bonds, Treasury Bonds and Equity

Rating Level	Corelation With Treasury Bonds	Correlation With Equity
Aaa–A	0.86	0.09
Baa–Ba	0.77	0.25
B–Caa	0.51	0.28

Source: Richard Bookstaber and David P Jacob, "The Composite Hedge: Controlling The Credit Risk Of High Yield Bonds" (1986) (March/April) *Financial Analysts Journal* 25 at 26.

In practice, the problem does not lend itself to easy solution as the incorporation of specific risk factors, say based on credit spreads for different rating categories, while desirable from a model validity viewpoint would substantially increase the number of volatilities and correlations. However, in practice, for entities with large positions in securities or instruments with substantial specific risk factors, the incorporation of specific risk into the VAR model is essential.

6.3.3 VAR and commodity yield risk

The problem of commodity risk relates to practical problems of estimating certain price attributes such as storage costs and the commodity convenience yield[22] (effectively, the asset return earned from ownership of or holding the asset).

In theory, the relevant risk factor for commodity transactions would be to decompose all positions in the spot asset and positions in interest rates at the

---

21. The underlying logic of this relationship is based on the theoretical model which specifies that all corporate securities are claims on the value of the firm. Equity being characterised as a residual claim akin to a call option on the net asset value of the firm (ie assets net of liabilities). Using put call parity, this means that corporate debt equates to the security combined with the sale of a put option structure on the assets of the firm. This analysis is fundamental to the derivation of default risk discussed in detail below. For more detailed discussion of this approach see F Black, and M Scholes, "The Pricing of Options and Corporate Liabilities" (1973) 81 *Journal of Political Economy* 637; R Merton, "On The Option Pricing Of Corporate Debt: The Risk Structure Of Interest Rates" (1974) 29 *Journal of Finance* 449; R Geske, "The Valuation Of Corporate Liabilities as Compound Options" (1977) *Journal of Financial and Quantitative Analysis* 541.
22. See Satyajit Das, "Commodity Swaps: Forward March" (1993) *Risk* 6(2) 41.

relevant maturity vertices in the commodity currency (generally, US$). However, in practice, VAR calculations utilise commodity futures traded on exchanges as the relevant price information and the relevant risk factors.[23]

This reflects a number of factors:

- The fact that commodity transactions, particularly commodity derivatives, such as commodity forwards/swaps etc, are settled against the near or second month futures contract rather than the spot commodity.

- The participation of producers, consumers *and investors* in the commodity futures market which gives this market segment added liquidity and efficiency.

- The higher transparency of the commodity futures markets.

Under this approach, commodity positions are decomposed into equivalent futures positions and the risk factors applied are those related to the futures contracts. The fact that futures contracts have non-constant and decreasing maturities is handled by using a number of adjustment algorithms including:[24]

- Rolling to nearest futures contract (that is the contract which expires closest to a fixed maturity).

- Linear interpolation between the prices of two futures contracts that are adjacent to the relevant fixed maturity.

The methodology identified is generally satisfactory but has a number of deficiencies:

- The liquidity of commodity futures markets, particularly for the very short or longer maturities, can be low.

- The volatility of futures contracts with short terms to maturity may decrease as liquidity declines reflecting the absence of trading interest, illiquidity, and physical delivery concerns.

- The lack of proper capture of the volatility of convenience yields.

These deficiencies may reduce the validity and accuracy of the VAR estimates derived for commodity transactions. In practice, for active commodity traders, it may be necessary to refine the risk factors to encompass these risk aspects to more completely capture the risk of commodity positions.

---

23. RiskMetrics™ follows this convention for all commodities except gold bullion.
24. These algorithms are suggested by RiskMetrics™.

7.   APPLICATIONS OF VAR

7.1   Overview

VAR measures of market risk provide a basis for the management of financial risk in both financial institutions and non-financial institutions. In the first section, applications of VAR to financial institutions are considered while in the following section application for non-financial institutions are examined.

In considering the application of VAR approaches to risk measurement two matters should be noted:

1.   VAR approaches are *a component* of an overall risk management framework.

2.   VAR approaches measure market risk and other risks (such as credit risk, liquidity and operational risk) which may or may not be fully captured by VAR will need to be captured in developing a *complete* risk profile of an entity.

7.2   Market risk management in financial institution

7.2.1   Range of applications

Financial institutions can be taken to encompass two specific types of institutions: dealer and non-dealer financial institutions and investment institutions. Both groups have exposures to asset price exposures as a result of trading positions or investments which can be measured using VAR approaches. While there may be differences in risk horizons or some other aspects in the use of VAR, the principal elements in the application of VAR are similar.

The use of VAR in market risk management in financial institutions will generally encompass the following applications:

1.   Trading risk control and risk management.

2.   Performance evaluation.

3.   Capital allocation.

VAR may also form the basis of the communication of market risk incurred by an organisation in its activities, for example, in the form of disclosure in financial statements or in investor relations more generally.

7.2.2   Trading risk management

The use of VAR to quantify the market risk in a portfolio is one of the most important applications of this technique. The VAR estimate concisely and precisely, within the range of assumptions made summarises the risk of the positions held at a given point of time resulting from an expected large move in market prices. The ability of VAR to capture and consolidate risk across different asset classes and types of activities (proprietary trading, market-making, underwriting, and investment as well as structural exposure embedded in asset-liability balance sheet mismatches) and communicate *the total risk on a firmwide basis* in the form of a *single* $ figure is amongst the most compelling advantages of VAR approaches.

Reports such as the legendary 4:15 PM Report to the Chairman of J P Morgan summarising the total daily earning at risk (DEAR) have enshrined this application of VAR.

This use of VAR also implies the use of VAR based trading limits which are used to control risk taking to acceptable levels within the firm in terms of its capital resources and risk appetite. VAR based limits may still require translation into notional face value amounts for ease of on desk monitoring and trader convenience. VAR based approaches can be used at multiple levels within a trading operation—typical levels would include trader/dealer level, trading desk, asset class or business group, and firmwide. This system of multiple levels would embody the progressive benefits of diversification of risks as the risk is consolidated at increasingly higher levels encompassing greater ranges of activities.

The application of VAR in trading risk control and risk management can also be extended to assisting in enhancing hedging of trading exposures. The use of VAR as the basis for limits and quantification of risk also implies the use of VAR reduction as the basis for optimising hedging behaviour. This approach would seek to reduce risk by entry into transaction which on a portfolio basis reduces the overall VAR or risk of the portfolio. This type of hedging (referred to as correlation based hedges) can overcome deficiencies in the hedge market (for example, because of liquidity, institutional, or regulatory considerations) as well as reducing the transaction costs of the hedge. This contrasts with specific hedges which would be designed to offset *individual* risk positions which may have lower efficiency or higher costs in effecting an equivalent reduction in risk.

7.2.3   Performance evaluation

The ability to quantify the risk of trading positions is essential as both a mechanism for controlling risk as well as aligning risk reward relationships within organisations involved in market risk activities. This entails implementation of risk adjusted performance measurement (RAPM) processes designed to quantify return scaled to the risk incurred in generating that return. RAPM processes are discussed in detail in a following section.

In brief, the linking of return to risk and therefore to the cost of risk capital is essential to the following:

1.   The evaluation of individual trading strategies.

2.   The evaluation of performance at every level ranging from individual dealer to business.

3.   The creation of links between compensation and risk adjusted returns.

These steps are essential to properly aligning the behaviour of traders and business managers with those of shareholders.

7.2.4 Capital allocation

The development of RAPM systems facilitates the evaluation of both products and businesses in terms of their risk adjusted returns. The analysis of risk adjusted returns will take the form of evaluating returns from individual activities and comparing them to the firm's cost of capital. Where the return is lower than the cost of capital, the product or activity should be discontinued or re-positioned to avoid loss of shareholder value. Products or activities returning above the firm's cost of capital will attract risk capital to enhance shareholder value.

The process of capital allocation can be extended using earning volatilities to cover investment in particular lines of business and to determine the amount of capital that must be held against the risk of earning volatility allowing the quantification of the benefit of operating diversified sets of activities within the same financial institutions. *Exhibit 16.22* sets out a simple example of this approach.

Exhibit 16.22

Capital Allocation—Applications of VAR[25]

The use of VAR in capital allocation in financial institutions can be illustrated using the following example. Assume a bank has the historical earning record set out in the following graph:

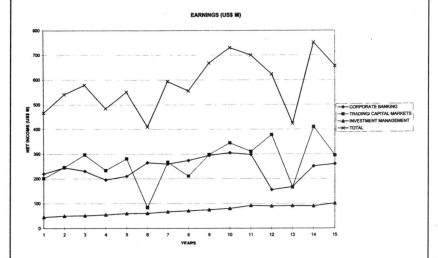

EARNINGS (US$ M)

The earnings are disaggregated into three operating divisions: corporate banking, trading/ capital markets, and investment management.[26]

The overall volatility of earning is summarised in the following table:

BUSINESS UNIT	VOLATILITY (US$ millions)
Corporate Banking	46
Trading/ Capital Markets	83
Investment Management	18
Total	107

25. The approach used here is similar to that outlined in Chris Matten, "Risk Adjusted Performance Measurement" (1996) 6 *Financial Derivatives and Risk Management* 37-43; see also Chris Matten, *Managing Bank Capital: Capital Allocation and Performance Measurement* (John Wiley & Sons, Chichester,1990).
26. The earning analysis could be disaggregated even further into more specific or narrowly focused business units in the same way.

Exhibit 16.22—*continued*

Volatility is measured as the standard deviation of unit earning in US$ million. The volatility of the earnings of the banks is less than the sum of the individual volatilities because of the fact that the earnings of individual units is not perfectly correlated. The correlation of the earnings of the individual units and the impact of the correlations (effectively, the impact of diversification) is summarised in the following table:

BUSINESS UNIT	UNDIVERSIFIED VOLATILITY (US$ millions)	CORRELATIONS	DIVERSIFIED VOLATILITY (US$ millions)[27]
Corporate Banking	46	0.51	23
Trading/Capital Markets	83	0.89	74
Investment Management	18	0.54	10
Diversification adjustment			40
Total	147	1.00	107

As is evident the overall volatility of earning is lower than the component businesses reflecting the less than perfect correlation between the activities.

This analysis can be used for two primary purposes:

1. The calculation of the volatility of earnings and the capital requirements of the bank.

2. The allocation of capital to individual businesses.

Assume the bank is forecasting earnings of US$ 700 million in the next year. The historical volatility of earning can be used to estimate the potential volatility of earnings. Based on 3 standard deviations (99% confidence levels), it is possible to project that earnings will be:

US$ 700 million ± 3 times US$ 107 million or US$ 379 to US$ 1,021 million.

The analysis shows the potential earning volatility and reveals that the bank's earning at risk are US$ 321 million at the nominated 99% confidence level. Based on this type of analysis the bank's management can adjust the risk profile of the bank to bring it into line with levels considered acceptable to shareholders in one of two ways:

1. Reduce the risk profile of the bank by reducing involvement in more risky or more volatile activities (such as trading).

2. Maintain risk capital to offset the earning at risk. For example, to offset the earnings at risk of US$ 321, assuming a risk free rate of 7.00% pa, the amount of risk capital required to be held equals US$ 4,586 million (calculated as the amount of capital invested at the risk free rate which provides earning of US$ 321 million).

This model also lends itself to determining the amount of capital to be allocated to individual activities. This allocation should be based not on the volatility of the earnings of the individual activity but the *marginal contribution* to volatility of the bank's overall earnings. This approach, which is consistent with overall portfolio theory, is based on the fact that a volatile business activity if imperfectly correlated with the earnings of the bank's other businesses may contribute to a reduction in the bank's overall risk as represented by the volatility of the bank's earnings.

27. The diversified volatility is calculated, approximately, by multiplying the correlation (between the earnings of individual unit and the total earnings of the bank) by the original volatility.

Exhibit 16.22—continued

The marginal volatility contribution of each business activity is summarised in the following table:

BUSINESS UNIT	UNDIVERSIFIED VOLATILITY (US$ millions)	DIVERSIFIED VOLATILITY (US$ millions)	MARGINAL VOLATILITY (US$ millions)[28]
Corporate Banking	46	23	15
Trading/ Capital Markets	83	74	56
Investment Management	18	10	9
Diversification adjustment		40	66
Total	147	107	81

The performance of each business unit would then be assessed against its marginal contribution to the overall earnings volatility with capital being allocated to each unit based on its marginal risk contribution.

While theoretically elegant, this approach obviously is difficult to implement in practice:

- The definition of earning is ambiguous. The attribution of earnings for individual business units is difficult and may be arbitrary.
- The method is historical oriented and examines the volatility and correlations that have historically existed. Changes in these volatilities and correlations, as with any VAR analysis, would significantly bias results.
- The distribution of earnings is unlikely to be normal and this creates statistical complications in using this type of approach.

Despite the identified difficulties this approach has considerable benefits in allowing analysis of the risk of individual activities and as a basis for assessing the marginal risk contribution of individual activities as a basis for capital allocation.

7.2.5 Application differences as between dealer financial institutions and investment institutions

The application of VAR as between dealer financial institutions and investment institutions derives largely from the fact that the risk assumed in the former is optional and therefore capable of elimination, while for the latter group is structural and therefore not capable of ready elimination. This flows from the requirement of the investment institution to stay invested at all times.

This difference dictates that the use of VAR as a mechanism for risk management or performance evaluation needs to be amended. The form of amendment would generally take the form of looking at the VAR of a model or benchmark portfolio; this would be the model portfolio prescribed for the asset manager. The VAR measured would be the *incremental risk* of the portfolio assumed as a result of changes in portfolio composition *away from*

28. The marginal volatility contribution is calculated by recalculating the volatility of the total bank earnings excluding each business in turn and taking the difference between the volatility of bank earnings with the business included and excluding the business.

the model portfolio. In essence, the VAR risk estimate would be used to measure the change in risk profile engendered as a result of the investment decisions implemented.

Once this benchmark concept is introduced, the use of VAR as a measure of risk, systems of risk limits, evaluation of optimal hedging strategies and performance evaluation is possible in a manner which is perfectly consistent with the use of VAR in dealer financial institutions.

The concept of capital allocation is also different when applied to investment institutions. The use of risk adjusted returns can aid asset allocation decisions. This may again be allied to model portfolios with the expected returns relative to the VAR risk of a strategy arising from a shift away from the model portfolio composition being utilised to evaluate changes in investment strategy.

A subsidiary problem in application of VAR to investment institutions is the appropriate risk horizon. A short risk horizon (1 day or 10 days) may be appropriate for a dealer financial institution. However, longer time horizons are necessary for investment institutions; for example J P Morgan suggest a risk horizon of 5 weeks.

7.2.6   Market risk management in financial institutions—case study

An example of the application of VAR techniques in the management of risk in a financial institution is set out in *Appendix A* to this Chapter.

7.3   Market risk management in non-financial institutions

7.3.1   Range of applications

Application of VAR techniques to market risk management in non-financial institutions is differentiated by the various factors identified above which distinguishes risk management in non-financial institutions from that in financial institutions. The use of VAR in non-financial institutions is not well developed (see *Exhibit 16.23* which summarises a recent poll of American CFOs).

Exhibit 16.23

Corporate Application of VAR Techniques—US Survey Results

Does your company employ VAR?

Yes	18.0%
No	82.0%

If you do not yet use VAR measurements, have you:

Considered it?	67.6%
Ruled it out?	32.4%

Does your company use the J P Morgan RiskMetrics™ model?

Yes	5.3%
No	94.7%

If your firm uses some form of VAR, what does it measure?

Firmwide risks	40.0%
Investment portfolio	48.0%
Derivatives	36.0%
Interest rate, stock, bond and commodity movements	60.0%
Other	4.0%

Source: Institutional Investor (1996).

In practice, VAR can be applied in non-financial institutions for a number of different applications:

1. Trading risk management where treasuries of industrial corporations operate as profit centres trading for profit in a manner analogous to banks and dealers.

2. Measurement of *financial risk* (such as interest rate exposure on liabilities or investments, currency risk and commodity price risk) and the analysis of efficient hedging alternatives.

3. The measurement of corporate risk from changes in market factors within an integrated risk framework.

The first two applications are fairly restrictive applications which are not dissimilar to the applications in financial institution identified above. The final application is by far potentially the most interesting and valuable use of VAR in corporate context. This application of VAR requires adjustments to the basic VAR framework to expand it into the concept of cash flow VAR.

7.3.2 Concept of cash flow VAR

The concept of cash flow VAR translates the impact of market prices into its impact on an entity's underlying cash flow.[29] The approach is predicated on the fact that for a non-financial corporation cash flow is the major management variable. This reflects the following factors:

- Cash flow discounted to the valuation date at an appropriate discount rate (the cost of capital) is the value of the firm. Consequently, changes in cash flow will have manifest valuation effects.

- Sufficiency of cash flow to meet fixed payments (fixed operating costs as well as fixed debt servicing—interest and principal) is essential as failure may trigger financial distress.

Underlying this approach is the fact that in non-financial institutions, risk is a consequence of operations and the focus of risk management is action to manage the impact of changes in *cash flow*. This is consistent, as noted above, with the cash flow based approaches to shareholder value which are predicated on enhancing shareholder wealth through maximisation of cash flow.

A variation on this approach is to measure the impact of market price changes *on earnings* (a form of earnings VAR).

The overall approach to cash flow VAR is set out in *Exhibit 16.24*.

---

29. The concept of cash flow or earnings VAR has been suggested by a number of writers; for example, see Chris Turner, "VAR as an Industrial Tool" (1996) 9(3) *RISK* 38-40; David Shinks, "VAR for Corporate" (1996) 9(6) *RISK* 28-29; Leslie McNew, "So Near, So VAR" (1996) 9(10) *RISK* 54-56; see also Karen Spinner, "Companies Put Their Own Spin on VAR" (1996) (Aug) *Global Finance* 48-53; Karen Spinner, "Adapting Value at Risk" (April 1990) 14-23.

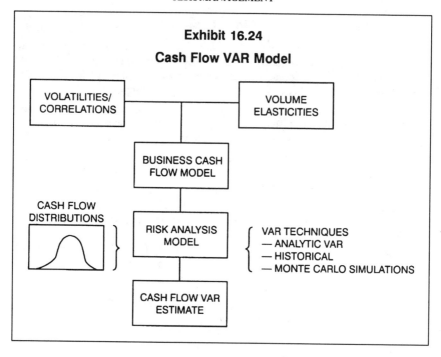

The essential steps in implementing cash flow VAR includes the following:

1. *Risk mapping*—this entails analysis of the entity's exposure to identify the key market prices that affect the cash flow of the firm.

2. *Estimating the historical volatilities and correlations of financial market risk factors relevant to the company*—this is identical to the process developed in the context of more general versions of VAR.

3. *Measuring volume elasticities*—this requires estimation of the *volume sensitivities* of individual cash flow items such as sales and input factors and their correlations to financial market prices. This can be modelled based on historical data series or subjectively based on knowledge of market structures and the industrial economics of the factor. This step is optional in that some approaches to Cash Flow VAR estimation ignore it because of its complexity. However, in reality depending on the importance of volume changes it should be incorporated to capture the changes in portfolio risk composition as a result of volume shifts.

4. *Using the financial variable historical volatilities and correlations and the volume elasticities in the business cash flow model*—this entails incorporating the model variables into the basic cash flow model. This cash flow model will typically incorporate the organisation's own estimates for operating and financial variables which allows analysis of the company's exposures. An example of a business cash flow model is set out in *Exhibit 16.25*. The analysis focuses on the principal traded asset classes and their impact on the projected net cash flow of the entity. Other factors which may be included are alternative sources of

risk such as default (credit) risk on commercial contracts and tax rate changes which may impact on the value of tax losses.

5. *Running the risk model*—the risk model is effectively the VAR risk process. It is identical to that used in the examples used above. In practice, because of the nature of the cash flow model, Monte Carlo Simulation is generally used to create distributions of cash flows based on running a large number of price paths consistent with the historical volatilities, correlations and elasticities.

6. *Derivation of the cash flow VAR estimate*—the cash flow VAR estimate is drawn from the net cash flow distribution generated based on a desired confidence level using a percentile cut-off method. This reflects the typically non normal nature of the cash flow distributions.

Exhibit 16.25

Business Cash Flow Model

IMPACT OF CHANGES IN FINANCIAL MARKET VALUE DRIVERS

CASH FLOW COMPONENTS	PROJECTED CASH FLOW	INTEREST RATES	CURRENCY RATES	COMMODITIES	EQUITIES
Sales Volume					
Sales Price					
Revenue					
Input Volumes					
Input Prices					
Cost Of Sales					
Operating Margin					
Administrative Costs					
Operating Cash Flow Before Tax					
Tax					
Operating Cash Flow After Tax					
Capital Expenditure					
Working Capital Investment					
Net Cash Flow					

The basic approach is consistent for all non-financial institutions, irrespective of industry. The specific industry factors are generally reflected in the risk mapping process and in the design of the business cash flow model.

The risk horizon utilised in estimating cash flow VAR is related to the underlying business cycle. It should be related to the entity's planning horizon over which the cash flows are realised and reaction time scale over which corrective action could be implemented. This means that the VAR risk horizon will be longer than for financial institutions and investment managers. It will generally range from 3 months to 1 year depending on the underlying business dynamics.

7.3.3 Using cash flow VAR in hedging/risk management

The interpretation and the use of the cash flow VAR estimate derived focuses on:

- the risk capital requirements suggested by the estimate; and
- the implicit hedging framework derived.

The cash flow VAR estimate represents the statistical or model based risk of change in the company's cash flow over the risk horizon at the stated level of confidence. The estimate generated may be interpreted as the amount capital that the firm has to commit to absorb the potential risk of a fall in cash flows.

This can be illustrated with a simple example. Assume a company has expected cash flow of $800 million over the forecast period of 1 year. Based on an analysis of its risk profile, it estimates its cash flow VAR is $540 million. This implies that at a confidence level of 99%, the worst case cash flow of the company is forecast at $260 million. This compares to anticipated debt service (interest and principal) of $220 million and forecast dividends of $75 million. The risk analysis therefore indicates that there is a possibility that the cash flow of the company may not be sufficient to cover its fixed costs. Re-examining the distribution of cash flow outcomes, it may be possible to identify that there is a 4% probability that cash flow will not cover the identified fixed payments.

The company might consider this possibility undesirable from the point of view of its risk and credit profile and may wish to reduce the risk to its solvency. This can be achieved by holding sufficient capital against the risk of cash flow shortfall. This can be done by holding risk capital of $540 million to reduce the risk of cash flow shortfall to the company.

The actual cost of minimisation of this risk is the cost of capital incurred. Assume the costs of equity capital to the firm to be 13.60% pa.[30] Based on these cost of capital, the effective capital cost of the exposure is $73.4 million pa (calculated as the equity cost of capital on the amount of capital).

The risk capital requirement can be directly related to shareholder value. The firm value can be regarded as two streams of cash flow:

---

30. This is calculated using the CAPM as follows: Cost of equity = Risk Free Rate (7.00% pa) + Beta (1.1) times Market Risk Premium (6.00% pa).

1. A low risk cash flow stream of $260 which assuming it is sustainable can be capitalised at a low cost of capital.

2. A higher risk cash flow stream of $540 which must be capitalised at a higher cost of capital.

The low risk cash flow stream can be debt financed. The capital held is against the solvency risk presented by the second cash flow stream. In order to minimise the risk of financial distress risk capital must be held against the risk of a cash flow shortfall. This capital can be generated from a number of internal sources (cash reserves, sale of assets, adjustments in capital expenditure etc) or external sources (raising of equity capital). Irrespective of source, the risk capital required to be held will be diverted from other higher returning activity reducing shareholder value; for example, by reducing financial leverage or reducing the capacity to make business investments for a fixed amount of capital.

The analysis of risk can be extended to derive an implicit hedging framework. Hedging action can be considered value creating where the cost of the hedge is lower than the return that can be generated from the released capital. In contrast, hedging activity should not be undertaken where the cost of the hedge exceeds the returns available from the released capital.

In the above example, assume that the underlying price risks can be hedged by a series of transactions. This has the impact of reducing the cash flow VAR to $125 million; a worst case expected cash flow of $675 million. This is considered an acceptable risk level as the fixed payments are effectively adequately covered. The net effect of the hedge is to release approximately $415 million of risk capital which reduces the cost of capital held against cash flow risk by $56.4 million. The hedging action should be undertaken as creating shareholder value where the cost of the hedges is *less than $56.4 million.*

In the above example, the amount at risk was sought to be completely neutralised. In practice, capital allocation or hedging actions designed to adjust risk to within acceptable boundaries consistent with investor preferences.

The use of cash flow VAR in hedging can allow improvement in the efficiency of the hedge. As with financial institutions, the use of cash flow VAR implies the use of VAR reduction as the basis for optimising hedging behaviour through the reduction of risk by entry into transactions which on a portfolio basis reduces the overall cash flow VAR. This type of hedging (referred to as correlation based hedges) can overcome deficiencies in the hedge market (for example, because of liquidity, institutional, or regulatory considerations) as well as reducing the transaction costs of the hedge. This contrasts with specific hedges which would be designed to offset *individual* risk positions which may have lower efficiency or higher costs in effecting an equivalent reduction in risk.

Recent interest in integrated risk management products such as products incorporating correlations or non-linear payoffs can be traced directly to these emerging approaches to the analysis and treatment of risk. An example of this type of product is an interest rate hedge, such as a cap or interest rate swap, which is triggered or activated as a result of an adverse change in a separate defined variable, say a fall in a commodity prices. The structure, a defined exercise option, makes use of the correlation between the interest rates and the commodity price to create a hedge structure which is more cost effective. Central to the structure is the underlying desire to manage the hedger's *cash flow*. An increase in cash flow for the company in this case may be able to be absorbed where it is allied to commodity prices above a specified level. The hedge is designed to operate where a fall in commodity prices *combined* with rising interest rates adversely affects the cash flow of the company outside specified risk tolerances. Similarly, the increased interest in power or exponential options (which pay an exponent of the normal intrinsic value of a standard option) reflect increased understanding of the non-linear nature of certain risks. For example, the impact of demand or supply effects of movements in, say, currency rates on the *volume* of sales or purchases creates specific difficulties in hedging. This is reflective of the assumption underlying hedging generally which is predicated on both known cash flows and linear changes in cash flows.[31]

In essence, the use of Cash Flow VAR to develop an integrated framework for firmwide risk management allows informed and efficient decision-making on:

- Establishing the desired risk profile of businesses.
- Allocating risk capital as between competing business activities based on risk adjusted returns.
- Frameworks for trading and hedging activities to manage financial risk in non-financial corporations.

7.3.4 Market risk management in non-financial institutions—case study

An example of the application of VAR techniques in the management of risk in a non-financial institution is set out in *Appendix B* to this Chapter.

8. RISK ADJUSTED PERFORMANCE MEASUREMENT

8.1 Overview

The accurate quantification of risk is essential to establishing a link between the returns earned from an activity or business and the risks of that activity or business. The evolution of risk management into risk adjusted performance measurement is set out in *Exhibit 16.26*.

---

31. See Satyajit Das, *Exotic Options* (IFR Publishing/LBC Information Services, London/Sydney, 1996).

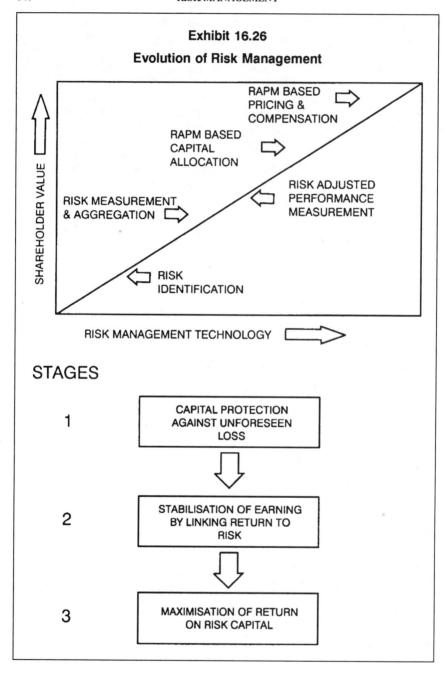

Exhibit 16.26

Evolution of Risk Management

The creation of this link between risk and return entails the implementation of risk adjusted performance measurement (RAPM) systems. Risk adjusted return on capital (RAROC) is one of a number of commonly utilised RAPM systems.

The central element of these systems is the calculation of *risk adjusted returns* of transactions, trading units and businesses. The main advantage of RAPM systems include the ability to facilitate comparability of different businesses enabling capital and resource allocation to be undertaken on a consistent and economically efficient basis consistent with maximisation of shareholder/enterprise value. While primarily developed for financial institutions it can be utilised with some adaptations, as set out above in the discussion of cash flow VAR, for non-financial institutions.

8.2 Concept

Traditional approaches to performance measurement have emphasised revenue or earnings. Typical measures include: gross or net revenue; earning before interest and tax; or net profit.

The major deficiencies of these measures include:

- The earnings are not adjusted for the riskiness of the revenue/earnings stream.

- The earnings are not related to the level of capital required to support the revenue/earning generation activity

RAROC and other RAPM systems overcome these weaknesses in traditional performance measurement techniques by both adjusting earnings for risk and relating it to the level of economic or risk capital committed to the activity. The use of these systems are central to measuring the link between trading activities and shareholder value generation.

8.3 Measurement techniques

The types of measurement techniques utilised can be classified into two separate categories:

- *Generalised measures of risk-return performance*—for example, Sharpe Ratio; Generalised Sharpe Ratio.

- *Risk adjusted return measure*—for example, RORAC models.

The central concept of the Sharpe Ratio is to measure excess return relative to volatility of portfolio value or portfolio returns. Sharpe Ratios are commonly utilised in investment management to measure portfolio performance. The concept of the Generalised Sharpe Ratio is that it relates return from the relevant transaction or activity to the amount of risk measured over a nominated period. This is analogous to the measure of risk adjusted return on the amount of risk capital required. *Exhibit 16.27* sets out details of the calculation of Sharpe Ratios.

Exhibit 16.27

Sharpe Ratios

The Sharpe Ratio is usually defined as:

$$S = (\upsilon - r)/\sigma$$

Where

S = Sharpe Ratio

υ = % return on risky asset portfolio or asset

r = risk free rate

σ = standard deviation of the risky asset or portfolio

As is evident, the Sharpe Ratio determines the return *in excess of the risk free return* relative to the risk of the earnings stream.

The Sharpe Ratio can be generalised to a more broad based measure for any risky activity.

The Generalised Sharpe Ratio is usually defined as:

$$S' = (\upsilon - R)/\sigma \sqrt{T}$$

Where

S' = Generalised Sharpe Ratio

υ = total return on risky asset portfolio or asset over period t (expressed in $)

R = E.r = expected risk free return over time t (expressed in $)

E = equity value invested in asset or activity

r = risk free rate

σ = standard deviation of the risky asset or portfolio

T = number of time periods in time t

Risk adjusted return measures relate to the identification of the economic contribution of an activity through setting income generated by the operation against the shareholder capital required to support its underlying risk. There are a number of risk adjusted capital return measures. The common elements of these measures include:

- adjusting gross earning for the riskiness of the earnings stream;
- determining capital required to be committed to support the activity; and
- calculating the return on the capital base.

The choice of measurement technique focuses on the following:

- RAROC (risk adjusted return on capital);
- RORAC (return on risk adjusted capital); and
- ROVAR (return on value at risk).

The differences between the systems focuses on:

- Whether the adjustment for risk is made by adjusting earnings or the capital held to support the activity.
- The methodology for determining the capital amount which is held.

The generalised RAROC formula is as follows:

Earnings/Economic Risk Capital

Where

Earnings = Revenue − Expenses − Expected Losses ± Adjustments

Economic Capital = Capital required to cover all risks of operation

The individual components of earning are calculated as follows:

- *Revenue* includes all income such as bid-offer spread, fees, commissions, trading income, costs of hedging and funding costs.

- *Expenses* include all direct expenses (salaries, brokerage, premises, technology etc) and allocated costs/overheads.

- *Expected losses* include provisions for expected credit losses, *future* hedging, funding and, operating costs, et cetera.

- *Adjustments* includes any required amendment such as differential tax rates or subsidies.

The individual components of economic risk capital are determined as follows:

- Capital required to cover credit risk (for example, that required under BIS Capital Accord).

- Capital required to cover market risk (for example, the average daily VAR of the activity).

- Capital invested in infrastructure is included as either part of the capital base or treated as an allocated cost (on an amortised basis), which is charged against earnings.

The calculated return allows measurement of the earnings adjusted for risk as a percentage of capital employed.

This return is then compared to a hurdle rate of return required by the entity. This hurdle or benchmark rate can be calculated in several ways:

- The cost of capital of the entity (akin to a divisional cost of capital).

- The expected return on a risk free or risky asset where the quantum is related to the amount of that asset that could be held consistent with risk capital allocated to the relevant business.[32]

The return calculation allows a systematic dissection of performance at several levels:

- The return on economic risk capital earned in absolute terms.

- The capacity on an activity to accrue risk adjusted return on capital at a level adequate to meet the cost of that risk capital.

- The ranking (in relative performance terms) of individual activities.

---

32. For example, in the equity business it would be feasible to use the VAR or indicative risk limit to work back to an equivalent risk position in *the equity market as a passive investment*. The expected return based on this position calculated as the expected return on equities (based on a risk margin over an appropriate risk-free rate) on the amount of investment. This would then form the benchmark return that would have to be met by the business activities.

8.4   Implementation issues

The key implementation issues relate to development of operational systems to dissect earnings and capital allocation consistent with the model proposed. This requires detailed analysis of:

- earnings sources and attribution to individual activities; and
- costs and appropriate allocation systems.

The key organisational issues include:

- ensuring high level commitment to the concept;
- willingness to implement the system across business boundaries; and
- encouraging the adjustment of pricing and capital utilisation behaviour based on the analysis undertaken.

The implementation of the RAPM system will typically have a number of incidental benefits, including:

- improvements in range and quality of financial performance data;
- improvements in systems;
- improvements in understanding of the earnings dynamics of businesses; and
- enhancement of the overall business decision making framework.

8.5   Applications

The principal applications of RAPM techniques include:

- *Return measurement*—the determination of the relative return of any activity. Return can be measured at multiple levels—individual trader/dealer, desk, business unit, economic entity, et cetera.
- *Evaluation of activity*—the process of return measurement facilitates the rational economic analysis of any activity within a shareholder value framework.
- *Capital management*—utilisation of the evaluation process:
  - to determine capital required to support business activities; and
  - to allocate capital based on returns generated on capital to facilitate growth/expansion of existing businesses.
- Performance linked compensation strategies—using risk adjusted return on capital measures as means for establishing accurate mechanisms for aligning employee performance and compensation with shareholder returns.[33]

33. See Mark Rodrigues, "Compensation Methods in Investment Banks: Tackling the Risk Factor" (1996) (June) *Financial Derivatives and Risk Management* 44-48.

9. SUMMARY

The altered business environment is characterised by an increased reliance on trading and acting as a principal to transactions in financial institutions and increased exposure to financial risk in non-financial institutions. This change is reflected in an increase in market risk exposures of organisations. This shift in risk profile requires a corresponding increase in risk management focus and the development of risk quantification techniques. VAR techniques have emerged as the principal mechanism for the unified quantification of market risk. VAR is a generic term which covers a variety of similar approaches to risk measurement. These techniques allow measurement of market risk which, in turn, can be linked to the management and control of risk, performance evaluation and the allocation of risk capital to activities and businesses.

Appendix A

Market Risk Management in a Financial Institution

The example provided in this Appendix is a simplified outline of some of the primary risk management issues of a financial institution. This covers both the interest rate risk created by its underlying business and the implications of hedging these exposures with interest rate derivatives.

1. OVERVIEW

ABC Bank is a financial institution focusing on retail lending products such as home and personal loans. It provides these loans on a standardised basis and views them as a commodity product which represent easily marketable securities (that is, they can be sold into securitisation vehicles or to other financial institutions). Its lending product mix currently includes both variable and fixed interest products with a term of up to three years. All of its assets and liabilities are denominated in local currency. ABC does not undertake any proprietary trading and it uses derivatives primarily to hedge its underlying balance sheet risks.[i]

Historically, ABC has managed its interest rate risk using "gap" modeling and wishes to move to a value at risk (VAR) methodology. After reviewing the available methodologies it decides to adapt the "Standard Model" from the Bank of International Settlements (BIS) Capital Accord Market Risk Guidelines[ii] (hereafter referred to as BIS standard model). While the underlying methodology is based on the BIS standard model the volatilities and correlations will be adjusted to match the interest rate risk management requirements of ABC (for example, a longer holding period and volatilities and correlations which reflect recent history).

The BIS standard model represents a form of Analytic VAR which uses a standard set of historical volatilities and correlations (often referred to as "Parametric VAR"). Using this methodology ABC Bank aims to achieve the following:

- calculate the bank's current VAR;

- determine appropriate VAR limits to assist in the implementation of hedging strategies;

- use the VAR methodology to fix existing "risk holes";

- incorporate the non-linear pay-off structure of options; and

- introduce the concept of risk adjusted performance measurement.

---

i. This case study will not distinguish between "traded" and "non-traded" VAR; the focus is on estimating the overall interest rate risk of the group. This creates some difficulty in assessing performance as not all of the bank's underlying assets can be marked-to-market.

ii. See Bank for International Settlements, "Planned Supplement to the Capital Accord to Incorporate Market Risks", April 1995.

2. CURRENT UNDERLYING BALANCE SHEET EXPOSURE

ABC Bank's underlying business creates a naturally "long" interest rate bias as it funds all of its activities through largely short-term liabilities and then offers a range of variable and floating rate products. The current mismatch in the balance sheet prior to incorporating derivative positions is set out in *Exhibit 16.28*.

Exhibit 16.28

ABC Bank Gap Report—Underlying Balance Sheet (Excludes Derivatives)

Interest rate gap analysis as at end   **Dec 96**

All amounts in $ millions.   Quarterly Asset and Liability Repricing

	Non-interest bearing	Mar 97	Jun 97	Sep 97	Dec 97	Mar 98	Jun 98	Sep 98	Dec 98	Mar 99	Jun 99	Sep 99	Dec 99	Total
Assets														
Non-interest assets	574	0	0	0	0	0	0	0	0	0	0	0	0	574
Retail Loans	0	8,419	329	472	764	285	246	242	211	334	317	283	328	12,233
Overdraft Accounts	0	340	0	0	0	0	0	0	0	0	0	0	0	340
Liquidity Assets	0	1,036	286	0	0	0	0	0	0	0	0	193	0	1,515
Total	574	9,795	615	472	764	285	246	242	211	334	317	476	328	14,662
Liabilities														
Non-interest liabilities	231	0	0	0	0	0	0	0	0	0	0	0	0	231
Savings accounts	0	4,231	0	0	0	0	0	0	0	0	0	0	0	4,231
Investment accounts	0	2,353	2,482	1,515	1,082	25	34	60	42	10	0	0	0	7,603
Wholesale Borrowings	0	1,197	220	0	0	0	0	0	0	0	0	0	0	1,417
Capital Market Issues	0	0	0	0	0	0	0	0	0	0	0	0	0	0
Equity	1,180	0	0	0	0	0	0	0	0	0	0	0	0	1,180
Total	1,411	7,781	2,702	1,515	1,082	25	34	60	42	10	0	0	0	14,662
Net asset/(liability)	(836)	2,014	(2,087)	(1,043)	(318)	260	212	182	169	324	317	476	328	0

Currently ABC only offers fixed rate loans with a fixed interest rate term of one, two or three years.

The gap report highlights the "long" fixed rate interest rate position created by the funding of fixed rate assets out to a three year term with primarily floating rate liabilities (this does not include hedge derivatives). This is illustrated in *Exhibit 16.29*.

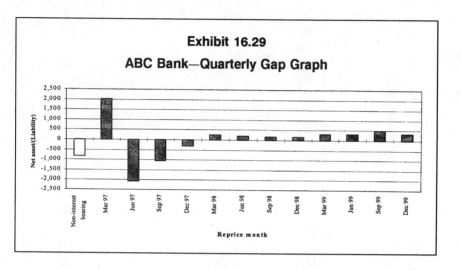

Exhibit 16.29

ABC Bank—Quarterly Gap Graph

3. MODIFIED EXPOSURE—THE IMPACT OF DERIVATIVES

ABC has traditionally hedged fixed rate loans on an ongoing basis. Previous policy has been to hedge between 50% and 90% of fixed rate loans with an interest as they are made. Up until the present all exposures have been hedged with paying fixed receiving floating interest rate swaps. The modified exposure balance sheet after allowing for the current derivatives portfolio is set out in *Exhibit 16.30*.

Exhibit 16.30

ABC Bank Gap Report—Including Derivative Hedge Positions

Interest rate gap analysis as at end   Dec 96

All amounts in $ millions.   Quarterly Asset and Liability Repricing

	Non-interest bearing	Mar 97	Jun 97	Sep 97	Dec 97	Mar 98	Jun 98	Sep 98	Dec 98	Mar 99	Jun 99	Sep 99	Dec 99	Total
Assets														
Non-interest assets	574	0	0	0	0	0	0	0	0	0	0	0	0	574
Retail Loans	0	8,419	329	472	764	285	246	242	211	334	317	283	328	12,233
Overdraft Accounts	0	340	0	0	0	0	0	0	0	0	0	0	0	340
Liquidity Assets	0	1,036	286	0	0	0	0	0	0	0	0	193	0	1,515
Total	574	9,795	615	472	764	285	246	242	211	334	317	476	328	14,662
Liabilities														
Non-interest liabilities	231	0	0	0	0	0	0	0	0	0	0	0	0	231
Savings accounts	0	4,231	0	0	0	0	0	0	0	0	0	0	0	4,231
Investment accounts	0	2,353	2,482	1,515	1,082	25	34	60	42	10	0	0	0	7,603
Wholesale Borrowings	0	1,197	220	0	0	0	0	0	0	0	0	0	0	1,417
Capital Market Issues	0	0	0	0	0	0	0	0	0	0	0	0	0	0
Equity	1,180	0	0	0	0	0	0	0	0	0	0	0	0	1,180
Total	1,411	7,781	2,702	1,515	1,082	25	34	60	42	10	0	0	0	14,662
Derivatives		1,333	0	0	(11)	(164)	(134)	(115)	(107)	(207)	(203)	(181)	(210)	0
Net asset/(liability)	(836)	3,347	(2,087)	(1,043)	(329)	96	79	67	62	117	114	295	118	0

The current hedging policy has reduced the "long" interest rate exposure by converting a large portion of the fixed rate loan portfolio to floating rate. This reduced sensitivity to interest rate movements is reflected in the gap graph provided in *Exhibit 16.31*.

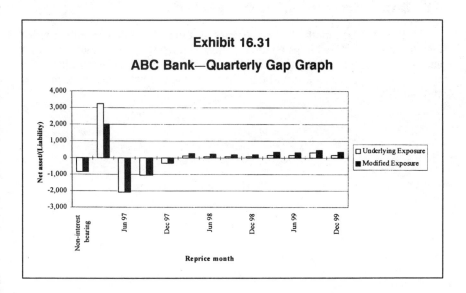

Exhibit 16.31

ABC Bank—Quarterly Gap Graph

4. CALCULATING VALUE AT RISK

Using the modified balance sheet position set out in *Exhibit 16.30* as the starting point we can calculate the VAR by applying the BIS Standard model. The steps in this process are as follows:

1. *Quantify exposure*: Divide the interest rate risks into the ten time bands or "buckets" used by the BIS standard model.

2. *Determine risk equivalents*: Determine the "risk equivalent" position in each time bucket by multiplying the assets and liabilities in each time bucket by the interest rate volatility and assumed duration of each time bucket.

3. *Calculate outright risk*: The outright exposure to interest rates is given by summing across the risk equivalent in each time bucket.

4. *Calculate yield curve risk*: Determine the amount of risk equivalents which offset in the calculation of the outright risk in step 3 (referred to as "horizontal risk") and include an amount for the potential for loss arising from a change in the shape of the yield curve rather than a general rise or fall in rates.

5. *Calculate Basis Risk*: Within each time bucket, determine those assets and liabilities which are offsetting and include an amount for the possibility of loss arising from the fact that the interest rate risk on these assets and liabilities is not perfectly correlated (referred to as "vertical risk").

6. *Calculate VAR*: The VAR is given by summing the outright risk, yield curve risk and basis risk.[iii]

Each of these steps is set out in the following subsections.

4.1   Divide exposures into time bands

The BIS standard methodology assumes that the yield curve can be divided into three "zones" which are then divided into ten "time bands". ABC's current balance sheet structure divides into the following time buckets (the amount repricing in each time bucket reflects the market value of each asset and liability):

---

iii.   All risks are expressed as absolute values.

Exhibit 16.32

Principal Maturity Profile by Time Bucket and Zone
All amounts in millions

Time Bucket	Non-interest bearing	Zone 1			Zone 2			Zone 3				Total
		0-3m	3-6m	6-12m	1-2yr	2-3yr	3-4yr	4-5yr	5-7yr	7-10yr	>10yr	
Assets												
Non-interest assets	574											574
Retail Loans		8,585	329	1,209	939	1,171						12,233
Overdraft Accounts		340	0	0	0	0						340
Liquidity Assets		1,036	286	0	0	193						1,515
Total	574	9,962	615	1,209	939	1,364	0	0	0	0	0	14,662
Liabilities												
Non-interest liabilities	231											231
Savings accounts		4,231	0	0	0	0						4,231
Investment accounts		2,353	2,482	2,597	161	10						7,603
Wholesale Borrowings		1,197	220	0	0	0						1,417
Capital Market Issues		0	0	0	0	0						0
												0
Total	231	7,781	2,702	2,597	161	10	0	0	0	0	0	13,483
Derivatives		1,333	0	(11)	(520)	(771)	0	0	0	0	0	
(-ve net liab)												
Net Asset/Liability	343	3,513	(2,087)	(1,400)	259	582	0	0	0	0	0	
Equity	1,180											
Net A/L by Zone				26			841				0	

Exhibit 16.32—continued

Principal Maturity Profile by Time Bucket and Zone
All amounts in millions

Time Bucket	Non-interest bearing	Zone 1			Zone 2			Zone 3				Total
		0-3m	3-6m	6-12m	1-2yr	2-3yr	3-4yr	4-5yr	5-7yr	7-10yr	>10yr	
Assets												
Non-interest assets	574,178											574,178
Retail Loans		8,585,208	328,724	1,208,856	939,156	1,170,562			0	0	0	12,232,506
Overdraft Accounts		340,186	0	0	0	0			0	0	0	340,186
Liquidity Assets		1,036,200	286,000	0	0	193,160			0	0	0	1,515,360
Total	574,178	9,961,594	614,724	1,208,856	939,156	1,363,722	0	0	0	0	0	14,662,230
Liabilities												
Non-interest liabilities	231,000											231,000
Savings accounts		4,230,732	0	0	0	0			0	0	0	4,230,732
Investment accounts		2,353,120	2,481,732	2,597,122	161,128	10,362			0	0	0	7,603,464
Wholesale Borrowings		1,197,416	220,066	0	0	0			0	0	0	1,417,482
Capital Market Issues		0	0	0	0	0			0	0	0	0
		0	0	0	0	0			0	0	0	0
Total	231,000	7,781,268	2,701,798	2,597,122	161,128	10,362	0	0	0	0	0	13,482,678
Derivatives (-ve net liab)		1,332,879	0	(11,476)	(519,519)	(770,908)			0	0	0	
Net Asset/Liability	343,178	3,513,205	(2,087,074)	(1,399,742)	258,509	582,452	0	0	0	0	0	
Equity	1,179,552											
Net A/L by Zone				26,389			840,961				0	

Given the range of ABC's activities, all of the interest rate exposures fall into the first five time buckets.

The fixed term asset amounts in this table differ from the gap report as an adjustment has been made for the expected level of prepayment on the fixed rate assets.

4.2   Determine risk equivalents

Risk equivalents are calculated by converting the face value amounts from section 4.1 into an amount which represents the "worst case" change in value of the assets and liabilities in each time bucket. Under the BIS methodology this is done as follows:

$$\text{Risk Equivalent} = \text{Market Value} \times \text{Volatility} \times \text{Duration}$$

Where

Market Value =   The Market value of each asset and liability in the time bucket.

Volatility   =   A Historical interest rate 99% confidence volatility for the time horizon used.

Duration   =   The assumed duration of each time bucket

Risk Weight   =   Volatility × Duration

The BIS standard model assumes the combination of volatilities and durations set out in *Exhibit 16.33.*

Exhibit 16.33

BIS Standard Model Risk Weights

Zone Bucket	Zone 1			Zone 2				Zone 3			
	0-3m	3-6m	6-12m	1-2y	2-3y	3-4y	4-5y	5-7y	7-10y	>10y
Volatility(% pa)	1.00%	1.00%	1.00%	0.90%	0.80%	0.75%	0.75%	0.70%	0.65%	0.60%
Duration	0.20	0.40	0.70	1.39	2.19	3.00	3.67	4.64	5.77	7.50
Risk Weight	0.20%	0.40%	0.70%	1.25%	1.75%	2.25%	2.75%	3.25%	3.75%	4.50%

However, the BIS standard model has been developed for a bank trading portfolio which consists of liquid financial instruments held for trading purposes and the assumed VAR time horizon is ten days. Given ABC's underlying assets are less liquid and the time taken to implement risk management strategies may be several weeks then a time horizon of one month is more appropriate to ABC's requirements. Further, ABC would like the volatility factors to reflect recent interest rate history[iv] and also that durations should reflect the current level of interest rates and average term of each time bucket.

Accordingly, ABC has calculated its own 99% confidence risk weights as set out in *Exhibit 16.34.*[v]

---

iv. A feature of interest rate risk volatilities in the 1990s has been greater volatility in the medium term time buckets than the shorter term buckets—this is the inverse of the volatility hue profile assumed in the BIS risk weights.

v. Given ABC Bank operates in an OECD country and if it was applying the BIS methodology to a trading portfolio then the VAR would have to be calculated according to the BIS risk weights.

Exhibit 16.34

ABC Bank Modified Risk Weights

Zone Bucket	Zone 1			Zone 2				Zone 3			
	0-3m	3-6m	6-12m	1-2y	2-3y	3-4y	4-5y	5-7y	7-10y	>10y
Volatility(% pa)	0.62%	0.75%	0.67%	0.45%	1.08%	1.06%	1.03%	1.0%	0.96%	0.96%
Duration	0.20	0.40	0.70	1.39	2.19	3.00	3.67	4.64	5.77	7.50
Risk Weight	0.12%	0.30%	0.61%	1.35%	2.36%	3.17%	3.78%	4.64%	5.54%	7.20%

Applying these risk weights to the market values from section 4.2 gives the risk equivalents set out in *Exhibit 16.35.*

Exhibit 16.35

Risk Equivalent Maturity Profile by Time Bucket and Zone
All amounts in $ millions

Time Bucket	Non-interest bearing	Zone 1			Zone 2			Zone 3				Total
		0-3m	3-6m	6-12m	1-2yr	2-3yr	3-4yr	4-5yr	5-7yr	7-10yr	>10yr	
Risk Weight		0.12%	0.30%	0.61%	1.35%	2.36%	3.17%	3.78%	4.64%	5.54%	7.20%	
Assets												
Retail Loans		10.65	0.98	7.36	12.72	27.65						59.36
Overdraft Accounts		0.42	0.00	0.00	0.00	0.00						0.42
Liquidity Assets		1.28	0.85	0.00	0.00	4.56						6.70
Total	0.00	12.35	1.83	7.36	12.72	32.22	0.00	0.00	0.00	0.00	0.00	66.48
Liabilities												
Non-interest liabilities	0.00											0.00
Savings accounts		5.25	0.00	0.00	0.00	0.00						5.25
Investment accounts		2.92	7.40	15.82	2.18	0.24						28.56
Wholesale Borrowings		1.48	0.66	0.00	0.00	0.00						2.14
Capital Market Issues		0.00	0.00	0.00	0.00	0.00						0.00
												0.00
Total	0.00	9.65	8.05	15.82	2.18	0.24	0.00	0.00	0.00	0.00	0.00	35.94
Derivatives		1.65	0.00	(0.07)	(7.04)	(18.21)	0.00	0.00	0.00	0.00	0.00	(23.66)
(-ve net liab)												
Net Asset/Liability	0.00	4.36	(6.22)	(8.52)	3.50	13.76	0.00	0.00	0.00	0.00	0.00	6.87
Equity	0.00											
Net A/L by Zone				(10.39)			17.26				0.00	

4.3 Outright value at risk

The outright value at risk is ABC's exposure to a parallel shift in the yield curve. It is given by the summation of the risk equivalents across all time buckets. Using the data from *Exhibit 16.34* the outright risk calculation is as follows:

Time Bucket	Risk Equivalents ($m)
0-3m	4.356
3-6m	−6.219
6-12m	−8.524
1-2yr	3.501
2-3yr	13.760
Outright Risk	6.874

ABC has a net "long" interest rate exposure of $6.874 million. If interest rates increase across the yield curve by the amounts assumed in the volatilities determined in section 4.2, the estimated present value of the loss is $6.874 million.

4.4 Calculate yield curve risk

Yield curve risk (or "horizontal risk") represents the exposure to risk from a change in the shape of the yield curve. The outright risk assumes perfect correlation in interest rates across all time buckets, the yield curve risk calculation looks at the net risk equivalent in each zone and time bucket and identifies those time buckets which have been offset (this amount is referred to as the "horizontal disallowance"). Once these offsets have been identified, a risk amount is calculated which reflects the extent to which the offsetting time buckets are not correlated.

The BIS model assumes fixed parameters for the correlation between time buckets and zones. ABC has recalculated this correlation based on actual historical behaviour of its assets and liabilities. Both correlation tables are set out in *Exhibit 16.36*. Once these correlations have been determined then the disallowance or offset rates are given by the difference between 100% and the correlation. Two forms of disallowance are calculated—"intrazone" and "interzone". Intrazone disallowances relate to offsetting risk amounts within a zone while interzone risks relate to offsetting amounts across zones.

Exhibit 16.36

BIS Standard Model Correlations

Assumed Correlation

	Zone 1	Zone 2	Zone 3
Zone 1	60%		
Zone 2	60%	70%	
Zone 3	0%	60%	70%

Resulting Disallowance

	Zone 1	Zone 2	Zone 3
Zone 1	40%		
Zone 2	40%	30%	
Zone 3	100%	40%	30%

ABC Modified Correlations

Assumed Correlation

	Zone 1	Zone 2	Zone 3
Zone 1	70%		
Zone 2	50%	80%	
Zone 3	30%	70%	80%

Resulting Disallowance

	Zone 1	Zone 2	Zone 3
Zone 1	30%		
Zone 2	50%	20%	
Zone 3	70%	30%	20%

The correlation matrices in *Exhibit 16.35* show both the intrazone and interzone disallowances. With the interzone correlations on the diagonal matrix row (for example, the zone 1 intrazone disallowance is given by the zone 1: zone 1 disallowance).

The table in *Exhibit 16.37* sets out the calculation of offsetting risk amounts across zones and time buckets (using the ABC yield curve correlations). The current yield curve risk is $6.501 million—that is, the present value of the loss arising from an unfavourable movement in the yield curve (for example, in ABC's case, a positive steepening in the yield curve).

Exhibit 16.37
Horizontal Disallowance

(Expressed as risk equivalent positions, $ m)

	Zone 1			Zone 2			Zone 3		
	0-3m May-97	3-6m Aug-97	6-12m Dec-97	1-2yr Sep-98	2-3yr Sep-99	3-4yr Sep-00	4-5yr Sep-01	5-7yr Mar-03	7-10yr Sep-05
Net Asset by Bucket	4.356	6.219	8.524	3.501	13.760	—	—	—	—
Net Asset by Zone			10.388			17.261			—

Offset Risk Amounts $'000's

	Zone 1	Zone 2	Zone 3
Zone 1	4.356		
Zone 2	10.388	—	
Zone 3		—	—

Disallowance Rates

	Zone 1	Zone 2	Zone 3
Zone 1	30%		
Zone 2	50%	20%	
Zone 3	50%	30%	20%

Horizontal Disallowance Amounts $'000's

	Zone 1	Zone 2	Zone 3
Zone 1	1.307		
Zone 2	5.194	—	
Zone 3		—	—

Summary VAR

Intrazone	1.307
Interzone	5.194
Total	6.501

4.5   Calculate basis risk

Basis risk arises from the fact that the yields of different assets and liabilities in the same time bucket are not perfectly correlated (referred to as "vertical risk"). As with the other risks areas, ABC has modified the basis risk correlations from the original BIS standard model. The revised basis risk, based on ABC's revised correlations, is set out in *Exhibit 16.38.*

Exhibit 16.38

Vertical Disallowance Calculations

	Total	Zone 1			Zone 2	
		0-3m	3-6m	6-12m	1-2y	2-3y
Offset Risk ($m)	25.644	0.200	0.196	—	7.035	18.213
Vertical Disallowance Rate	—	30%	15%	15%	15%	15%
Vertical Disallowance ($m)	3.877	0.060	0.029	—	1.055	2.732

The estimated present value of losses arising from less than perfectly correlated movements between assets and liabilities is $3.877m.

4.6   Calculate total VAR

The total VAR is given by summing all three elements of risk. This is illustrated in *Exhibit 16.39*. The total VAR of $17.251m represents 1.22% of capital and 5.89% of net interest income (NII). While appearing relatively low at first, the VAR represents the loss over a monthly time horizon, on an annualised basis the loss is estimated to be 4.24% of capital and 20.4% of NII.[vi]

---

vi.   This annual result has been calculated by multiplying the monthly figure by the square root of 12. As such it can only be treated as an approximation as the 99% distribution of annual data is likely to be less than implied by multiplying by the square root of 12 and it assumes nothing would be done to change the exposure over one year.

Exhibit 16.39
ABC Bank Value at Risk Model

As at =　31-Dec-96

Maturity Profile

Time Zone Time Bucket End of Bucket		Zone 1			Zone 2			Zone 3				Totals
		0-3m Mar-97	3-6m Jun-97	6-12m Dec-97	1-2yr Dec-98	2-3yr Dec-99	3-4yr Dec-00	4-5yr Dec-01	5-7yr Dec-03	7-10yr Dec-07	>10yr Dec-09	
Net Asset/(Liability) $m	Bucket	3,513	(2,087)	(1,400)	259	582	0	0	0	0	0	867
	Zone			26,389			840,961					
Risk Equivalents $m	Bucket	4.356	−6.219	−8.524	3.501	13.760	0.000	0.000	0.000	0.000	0.000	6.874
	Zone			−10.388			17.261				0.000	

Value at Risk

Assumed Holding Period:　4 weeks

99% confidence level, actual history	Risk $m	Description of Sensitivity
Outright Exposure to Interest Rates	6.874	Exposure to a rise in interest rates
Yield Curve Risk	6.501	Exposed to a positive move in the yield curve
Basis Risk	3.877	General Asset & Liability mismatch
Total as a present value amount (mthly)	17.251	Worst case loss as a present value amount
Total as a present value amount (annual)	59.759	

Risk comparatives	mthly	annual
VAR as a % of capital	1.22%	4.24%
VAR as a % of Net Interest Income	5.89%	20.40%

After deriving the model it becomes a powerful tool for analysing the risk sensitivity of ABC's balance sheet. For example, it is useful to examine the risk impact of different hedging strategies and *Exhibit 16.40* calculates the VAR of the underlying balance sheet with no derivative hedges, the current position and hedging 95% of the fixed rate assets with an interest term greater than 1 year.

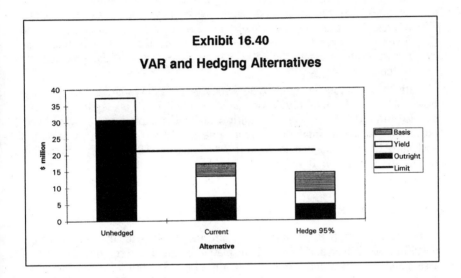

Not surprisingly the VAR of the unhedged position is the greatest. A little more interesting is the fact that the incremental fall from the current position to 95% hedged is fairly small. This is because while the outright and yield curve risk have declined the basis risk has substantially increased. This reflects one of the inadequacies of the methodology used—a basis risk is assumed to exist between the fixed rate assets and the derivatives used to hedge them. While some basis risk obviously does exist, it is substantially less than the VAR estimates suggest and can be reduced by either reducing the basis risk disallowance or by offsetting between derivatives and fixed rate assets. For the purposes of this example, we will continue to leave the basis risk calculations unchanged but will focus more on the outright and yield curve risks.

4.7 Setting VAR-based risk limits

VAR provides a summary statistic of ABC Bank's current interest rate risk and as such provides a convenient method of limiting the bank's interest rate exposures. A common approach is to set VAR risk limits as a percentage of an organisation's capacity to absorb losses—that is, its capital base or operating earnings.

While an overzealous risk manager may wish to remove all risk from a balance sheet this is inappropriate for most financial institutions for the following reasons:

1. By removing all risk from the balance sheet finance theory tells us that it also reduces the likely return.

2. The "positioning" of the balance sheet exposure to take advantage of expected interest rate movements is an important source of income for most financial institutions.

3. A component of the balance sheet position is funded by the banks capital, by hedging all assets and liabilities to a floating rate risk it assumes that the return on capital should be linked to the floating interest rate plus the net interest margin. This cannot be assumed and given the longer term assets being funded by the bank it is likely the return on these assets should bear some relationship to the expected life of the assets.

With these factors in mind, ABC sets a VAR limit relative to its capital base such that the monthly VAR cannot exceed 1.5% of capital (currently $21.15 million). This is viewed to allow sufficient capital and balance sheet positioning while maintaining a reasonable level of risk for an organisation such as ABC. As the line in *Exhibit 16.40* shows, ABC is currently within the limits however if it reduces its level of hedging then this limit will be exceeded.

4.8 Using VAR to fix "risk holes"

As the gap graph in *Exhibit 16.31* indicated, even with the current hedge portfolio, ABC has a substantial mismatch in the interest rate maturity of assets and liabilities under one year. Currently, a $3.3 billion dollar net asset exists in the March 97 time bucket versus net liabilities in the June and September time buckets of $2.1 billion and $1.0 billion respectively.

The Asset and Liability Committee (ALCO) is concerned that short term interest rates will decline over the next nine months leading to a net erosion of interest margin as the yield on assets declines and liabilities remain fixed.

In order to protect this position ABC elects to hedge the exposure by purchasing interest rate floors with at-the-money strikes in June and September 1997 as follows:

Summary of Floors

Expiry	Mar-97	Sep-97
Face Value ($ m)	1,000	500
Delta	48%	36%
Gamma	1.19	0.93
Vega	1.90	2.23

Incorporation of options into the BIS standard methodology can be done in a number of ways, however a reasonably accurate approach is the "delta plus" approach which uses the delta equivalent of positions and then adds an amount for gamma and vega risk. Given the derivative decomposition rules from section 5.2 of this chapter the delta equivalent of the floors is as follows:

Derivatives Portfolio—Floors "Delta Plus" calculation

Time Bucket	Dec 96	Jun 97	Sep 97
Face Value		1,000,000	500,000
Strike		7.00	7.00
Delta		48%	36%
Gamma		Ignore	Ignore
Vega		1.90	2.23
Delta position ($ m)	−666	484	182
Vega Risk ($m)		0.100	0.063

The primary influence of the floors is to increase create net assets in the second and third time bucket of $666 million and a corresponding liability in the first bucket. In this case because the options have positive gamma no VAR "add-on" is required while a vega add-on of $163,000 is required. The total VAR after the implementation of the floors is set out in *Exhibit 16.41*.

Exhibit 16.41
ABC Bank Value at Risk Model—After Executing Caps

As at = 31-Dec-96

Maturity Profile

Time Zone Time Bucket End of Bucket		Zone 1			Zone 2			Zone 3				Totals
		0-3m Mar-97	3-6m Jun-97	6-12m Dec-97	1-2yr Dec-98	2-3yr Dec-99	3-4yr Dec-00	4-5yr Dec-01	5-7yr Dec-03	7-10yr Dec-07	>10yr Dec-09	
Net Asset/(Liability)	Bucket	2,182	−1,603	−1,218	259	582	0	0	0	0	0	202
$'000	Zone		26,389			840,961						
Risk Equivalents	Bucket	2.705	−4.777	−7.417	3.501	13.760	0.000	0.000	0.000	0.000	0.000	7.772
$'000	Zone		−9.489			17.261						

Value at Risk

Assumed Holding Period: 4 weeks

99% confidence level, actual history	Risk $'000's	Description of Sensitivity
Outright Exposure to Interest Rates	7.772	Exposure to a rise in interest rates
Yield Curve Risk	5.556	Exposed to a positive move in the yield curve
Basis Risk	4.249	General Asset & Liability mismatch
Vega Risk	0.163	Long Volatility Risk
Total as a present value amount (mthly)	17.740	Worst case loss as a present value amount
Total as a present value amount (annual)	61.453	

Risk comparatives	mthly	annual
VAR as a % of capital	1.26%	4.36%
VAR as a % of Net Interest Income	6.05%	20.97%

Interestingly, the VAR has increased to $17.7m from $17.21m. This is because by reducing some of the net liability in zone 1 ABC has reduced some of the yield curve offsetting. As a result outright risk has increased more than the yield curve risk has decreased. In addition there is the addition of the vega risk associated with a 25% fall in the implied volatility in the floor of $0.163m.

Appendix B

Market Risk Management in a Resource Company

The example provided in this Appendix is a simplified examination of the calculation of VAR for a corporation—in this case an oil producer. The case study looks to break the oil companies market risk into the three main drivers (the oil price, exchange rate and interest rates) and calculate an estimate of market risk.

1. OVERVIEW

Let us suppose that GIANT Oil Ltd is a limited liability company which produces and explores for crude oil in Asia and Australia. It is an Australian-based company and is listed on a local stock exchange. Expected daily production in 1997 is estimated to be around 10,000 barrels/day rising to around 13,000 barrels/day in 2001.[i]

Traditionally, GIANT has hedged its exposure to the oil price by hedging 30% of the next year's budgeted production. However, it has now decided to manage all of its market risks on a consistent basis and will use VAR to provide a consistent methodology for assessing its expected level of risk.

A summary of GIANT's budgeted balance sheet and income statement for 1997 is set out in *Exhibit 16.42.*

Exhibit 16.42

Budgeted Results for 1997

Assumptions

Oil Price (US$/Barrel)	$	20.00
FX Rate (A$1 = ?US$)		0.7500
Three Month US$ LIBOR		6.00%

Balance Sheet —Dec 97 A$'000's

Total Assets	290,000
Borrowings	80,000
Other Liabilities	53,333
Net Assets	156,667

---

i.   This does not include any estimate for production from new oil fields arising from current exploration.

Exhibit 16.42—continued

Income Statement	A$'000's
Revenues	99,490
Expenses	
Variable Expenses	11,541
Interest Expenses	3,200
Fixed Expenses	33,333
Total Expenses	48,074
Operating Profit (1)	51,415

(1) After interest before tax and depreciation

All oil produced is sold under contract based off a New York Harbour West Texas Intermediate (WTI) price. Because most receipts are denominated in US$ GIANT has denominated its borrowings in US$—the forecast debt level is US$60m (A$80m) for all of 1997. Currently, the borrowings are floating rate and based off US$ LIBOR.

The bulk of the variable and fixed operating expenses are denominated in US$.

2. CURRENT UNDERLYING EXPOSURE

GIANT has three main sources of market risk:

- the US$ oil price;
- the A$/US$ exchange rate; and
- US$ LIBOR.

The list also reflects the order of importance GIANT currently attributes to each of the risk drivers.

Based on a forecast crude oil price of US$20/BBL, exchange rate of 0.7500 and interest rate of 6%, the expected future operating performance is set out in *Exhibit 16.43*.

Exhibit 16.43

Forecast Production Performance—Next 5 Years

(As at 31 Dec 1996)

Year	Av Price	Barrels p.a	Revenues	Expenses	Profit
Dec-97	26.67	3,730,858	99,489,534	48,074,119	51,415,415
Dec-98	26.67	4,033,671	107,564,566	49,677,490	57,887,077
Dec-99	26.67	4,275,707	114,018,849	51,106,187	62,912,663
Dec-00	26.67	4,532,178	120,858,082	52,593,138	68,264,945
Dec-01	26.67	4,803,901	128,104,037	54,141,140	73,962,896

3.   SENSITIVITY TO MARKET RISKS

GIANT carries a substantial exposure to market risk. This is not surprising as a commodity producing company is typically viewed as a risk taking entity and the capital structure and share price usually reflect that structure.

This market risk sensitivity is illustrated in the sensitivity table set out in *Exhibit 16.44*. This shows the sensitivity of GIANT's revenues to movements in both the oil price and exchange rate.

Exhibit 16.44

Revenue Sensitivity — 1997

US$ Oil Price (WTI)

Exchange Rate	$ 17.00	$ 18.00	$ 19.00	$ 20.00	$ 21.00	$ 22.00	$ 23.00
0.72	−11,399,842	− 6,218,096	−1,036,349	4,145,397	9,327,144	14,508,890	19,690,637
0.73	−12,606,551	− 7,495,787	−2,385,023	2,725,741	7,836,504	12,947,268	18,058,032
0.74	−13,780,645	− 8,738,946	−3,697,246	1,344,453	6,386,153	11,427,852	16,469,551
0.75	−14,923,430	− 9,948,953	−4,974,477	—	4,974,477	9,948,953	14,923,430
0.76	−16,036,142	−11,127,119	−6,218,096	−1,309,073	3,599,950	8,508,973	13,417,996
0.77	−17,119,952	−12,274,683	−7,429,413	−2,584,144	2,261,126	7,106,395	11,951,665
0.78	−18,175,973	−13,392,822	−8,609,671	−3,826,521	956,630	5,739,781	10,522,932

A negative sign indicates a decline in revenues

The sensitivity table for the US$ interest expense (converted to A$) is provided in *Exhibit 16.45*.

Exhibit 16.45
Interest Expense Sensitivity (A$)

US$ LIBOR - %pa

	3.00	4.00	5.00	6.00	7.00	8.00	9.00
Exchange Rate							
0.72	2,500,000	1,666,667	833,333	—	-833,333	-1,666,667	-2,500,000
0.73	2,465,753	1,643,836	821,918	—	-821,918	-1,643,836	-2,465,753
0.74	2,432,432	1,621,622	810,811	—	-810,811	-1,621,622	-2,432,432
0.75	2,400,000	1,600,000	800,000	—	-800,000	-1,600,000	-2,400,000
0.76	2,368,421	1,578,947	789,474	—	-789,474	-1,578,947	-2,368,421
0.77	2,337,662	1,558,442	779,221	—	-779,221	-1,558,442	-2,337,662
0.78	2,307,692	1,538,462	769,231	—	-769,231	-1,538,462	-2,307,692

A negative sign indicates a rise in expense

4.   CALCULATING VALUE AT RISK

The methodology for estimating VAR for a corporation is not as clear cut as for a financial institution. In the case study in Appendix A all financial assets and liabilities (except capital) had a defined interest rate term. In the case of a corporation the term of the market risks is unknown and in this case study they are likely to exist as long as GIANT continues to sell oil.

The approach GIANT decides to take in estimating VAR is to determine the likely "worst case" impact of adverse market movements in annual operating profit using a form of the variance/covariance methodology. Accordingly, it will need to estimate the "worst case" movements for each market risk and their correlations, and then apply these to the annual exposures.

4.1   Determine historical volatilities

GIANT takes a long-term view of its market risks and elects to calculate volatilities and correlations based on monthly observations for the past ten years. It will then use this data to calculate the 90% confidence level annual VAR. *Exhibit 16.46* plots the historical oil price, exchange rate and interest rates monthly for the ten years to December 1996.

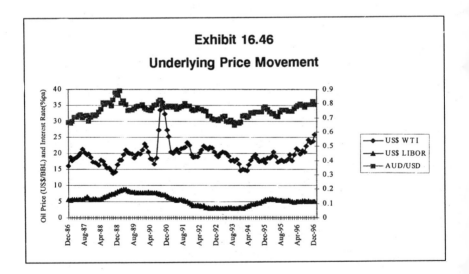

Using this historical data the volatilities and correlations are calculated in *Exhibit 16.47*.

Exhibit 16.47

Summary Volatility and Correlation Coefficients

Monthly	67% Price Volatility	95% Price Volatility	Correlation Coefficient US$ WTI	AUD/USD	US$ LIBOR
US$ WTI	7.56%	12.48%	1.00	0.09	0.08
AUD/USD	2.57%	4.24%	0.09	1.00	0.16
US$ LIBOR	4.03%	6.65%	0.08	0.16	1.00

Annualised	67% Price Volatility	95% Price Volatility	Correlation Coefficient US$ WTI	AUD/USD	US$ LIBOR
US$ WTI	26.20%	43.24%	1.00	0.09	0.08
AUD/USD	8.91%	14.69%	0.09	1.00	0.16
US$ LIBOR	13.97%	23.05%	0.08	0.16	1.00

The analysis assumes that each of these data series is normally distributed. *Exhibit 16.48* compares the actual distribution of each series to a normal distribution. While none of the distributions follow a strictly normal shape as a first estimate they are viewed by GIANT as adequate.

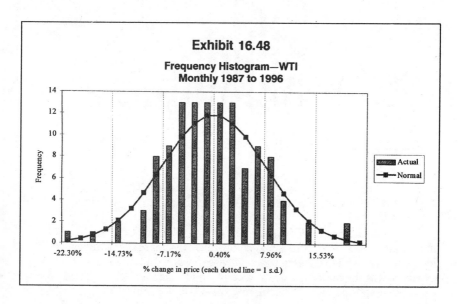

Exhibit 16.48

Frequency Histogram—WTI Monthly 1987 to 1996

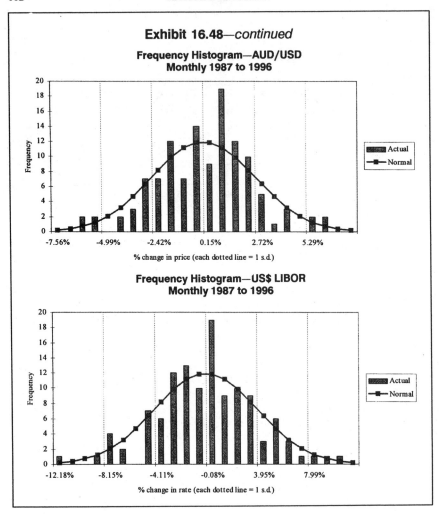

4.2   Outright value at risk

A complicating factor with each of these exposures is that they are interrelated.[ii] For example, a higher oil price inscreases US$ revenues which increases the A$/US$ foreign exchange exposure. Likewise, a lower interest expense will increase net US$ receipts and increase the A$/US$ foreign exchange exposure. When calculating the VAR the impact of these offsetting exposures needs to be incorporated. For our purposes the undiversified VAR will be calculated on an annual basis and it will assume all markets prices move against GIANT's position. The assumed movement in price from current market levels is set out in *Exhibit 16.49.*

---

ii.   Note this is the exposure not the risk factor (that is, the market prices) which determine the market risk of each exposure.

Exhibit 16.49

Volatility Factors

Price	Current	Volatility	Adjusted
WTI	$ 20.00	43.24%	$ 11.35
A$/US$	0.75	14.69%	0.8602
LIBOR	6.00	23.05%	7.38

These price changes represent first estimates only. For example, the oil price has exhibited strong mean reverting behaviour and, based on the last ten years a sustained price movement below US$12/barrel is unlikely. However, as a first estimate it is reasonable.

Using these volatility figures an estimate of the undiversified VAR is set out in *Exhibit 16.50*.

Exhibit 16.50

Undiversified VAR (85% Confidence)

Year	Forecast Profit	Adjusted Profit	VAR	% earnings	% capital
Dec-97	51,415,415	6,671,679	44,743,736	87%	33%
Dec-98	57,887,077	9,269,827	48,617,250	84%	36%
Dec-99	62,912,663	11,218,178	51,694,485	82%	38%
Dec-00	68,264,945	13,306,242	54,958,703	81%	40%
Dec-01	73,962,896	15,542,355	58,420,541	79%	43%

The correlations from *Exhibit 16.46* indicate that the correlations between all three market prices is quite low. That is, a substantial drop in the oil price will not always be accompanied by a sharp rise in the exchange rate and US$ LIBOR.[iii] This lack of any strong negative or positive correlation can lead to a significant diversification benefit when estimating GIANT's VAR.

While a diversification benefit exists across all three market risks, GIANT wishes to manage its interest rate risk independently of the oil price exposure. Accordingly, it looks for diversification benefits arising from the oil price and A$/US$ because it can enter into oil price derivative contracts which hedge just the US$ oil price or the A$ oil price (that is, hedging both the US$ price and the A$/US$ exchange rate).

---

iii. Interestingly the economic argument would generally be a lower oil price should lead to a decline in interest rate and, potentially, a decline in a commodity currency such as the A$.

The diversification benefit can be seen in *Exhibit 16.51* which illustrates the volatility of the US$ oil price and the A$/US$ exchange rate separately and then the A$ WTI price. On an undiversified basis the 95% volatility is 13.54% higher than the diversified A$ oil price.

Accordingly in 1997 the VAR is approximately $6 million less than the undiversified VAR figure.

Exhibit 16.51

Annualised	67% Price Volatility	95% Price Volatility
US$ WTI	26.20%	43.24%
A$/US$	8.91%	14.69%
A$ WTI	26.90%	44.39%

Undiversified US$ WTI and A$/US$	57.93%
Diversified US$ WTI and A$/US$	44.39%
Difference =	13.54%

Chapter 17

Portfolio Simulation: Stress Testing Techniques

by Lance Smith

1. INTRODUCTION

The term "stress testing" refers to an array of risk management techniques that have been developed particularly for portfolios of derivative securities. These go far beyond the traditional methods of simply calculating the current market exposures, and to some extent examine the underlying assumptions of the mathematical models used to calculate these exposures.

In this chapter we will explore a variety of stress testing techniques. These may be classified into two groups: *static* stress testing by input parameters and *dynamic* stress testing by (Monte Carlo) simulation. There are also some interesting connections between these different methodologies, essentially having to do with statistical averages such as volatilities and correlations.

2. WHY STRESS TEST?

Derivative securities exhibit risks that may be inadequately quantified by traditional risk analysis. Greater *leverage* implies a heightened sensitivity to particular market movements, and the potential for such a movement to force liquidation of positions at depressed prices. Such leverage is present not only in options and swaps, but also in long positions that have been financed by repo transactions or purchased on margin.

The introduction of *optionality* or "gamma" means that there is the potential for a sudden *acceleration* in exposure to a variety of market factors; for example, the exposure itself may *increase* as the market levels *drop*, thus compounding the potential losses. As a result, it may now become a requirement to rehedge the portfolio due to market movements. A typical instance of this is commonly referred to as "delta-hedging". For an equity options trader, delta-hedging is an attempt to maintain a net exposure near zero in his options portfolio by reacting to market movements and trading in the underlying security so as to negate the changes in exposure. If he is net short options, this procedure of delta-hedging will require him to "buy high and sell low" as the market moves about. His expectation is that the time decay in his portfolio, which works in his favor, will compensate him for his trading losses incurred in delta-hedging. This implies that the ultimate performance of his portfolio will depend upon the future behaviour of the underlying stock price, and in particular, *patterns of volatility*.

It therefore follows that the risk management of a portfolio containing options (either explicitly or embedded in other securities) should also take into account associated *dynamic trading* issues. The above discussion of delta-hedging, which forms the underpinnings of the Black-Scholes pricing and hedging model, ignores several limitations of the marketplace that do not occur in the theoretical world of stochastic processes.

Liquidity constraints may overwhelm the ability to rehedge this exposure. For example, if an options trader has sold a great many out-of-the-money put options on say, the S&P500, and the market has a gap opening to the downside, he may find himself with a large net long position. Delta-hedging requires him to now sell S&P500 futures against his position. The quantity to be sold may be so large that the actual selling causes the market to drop further, which in turn requires him to sell more, et cetera. This feedback loop can have disastrous consequences. In October of 1987, there were a great many portfolio managers practising "portfolio insurance". In effect each was hedging a short out-of-the-money put option. The market drop of Friday, October 16 caused them to go out net long. On Monday morning, October 19, each was ready to sell. The resulting selling pressure touched off such a feedback loop.

Another example is that of *cashflow constraints*. The theoretical models assume that the trader can borrow as much money as he likes whenever he likes, and at an interest rate that has already been fixed. Most of us aren't that lucky. When hedging a derivatives position, there may arise unforeseen borrowing requirements that exceed our credit lines. As a result we may be forced to liquidate our position at depressed prices (since our trading partners may take advantage of our situation). This has happened to more than one hedge fund recently.

A final example is somewhat philosophical in nature. Option models require a volatility input in order to calculate our exposure. Ideally, this input should correspond to the volatility that will be experienced during the delta-hedging process. Unfortunately, nobody knows in advance what this is going to be. We then have to make a leap of faith just to calculate our risks. Ultimately what this means is that we don't even know with precision what our current exposure really is!

3. TRADITIONAL RISK ANALYSIS

Traditional risk analysis for portfolios focuses on *mathematical* derivatives such as: delta, gamma, duration, convexity, et cetera. These are attempts to quantify exposures and rates of change of exposures at *current levels*. Correlations may then also be used to net exposures to different risk parameters. As discussed above, there is also a dynamic hedging component, usually summarised by a single input number, the *implied volatility*. This single number attempts to encapsulate the cost of delta-hedging the option. The relationship is summarised in the following principle:

The delta-hedging principle

The average P&L (in present value terms) in delta-hedging a portfolio of options is obtained by evaluating the options in the portfolio using the (yet to be experienced) volatility. The P&L dispersion is minimised if the "hedging volatility" is the same as the experienced volatility.

The sensitivity to changes in volatility levels is an additional mathematical derivative, usually referred to as *vega* or *kappa*.

3.2 The role of implied volatility

An option's theoretical value, as well as its risk characteristics (delta, gamma, et cetera) will depend upon the level of implied volatility used in the pricing model. As a result, it is very important to understand the criteria by which an implied volatility is determined. This issue becomes more prominent for a portfolio of options, for trading, risk management and stress testing.

The choice of implied volatilities used by the trader may depend upon the actual strategy being pursued. For example, if the trader is making markets in the options in the portfolio, he will most likely use a volatility surface or "smile". This will ensure that he is hedging the *mark-to-market*. On the other hand, if the portfolio is, say, a portfolio of short dated listed options that is being traded proprietarily (that is, taking a particular view of upcoming patterns of volatility), he may use his expected volatilities to calculate his fair values as well as his exposures.

The risk manager may wish to use an "official" set of implied volatilities to evaluate the risk across a broad collection of portfolios being traded for different purposes. The primary concern here is to ensure that the overall book does not take on risks that may be difficult to hedge under extenuating circumstances, or exposures that may lead to large negative valuations that the firm cannot sustain.

4. STRESS TESTING THE EXPECTED VALUE vs STRESS TESTING THE MARK-TO-MARKET

This latter point leads to two complementary methods of evaluating the risk in a portfolio/book. Should I stress test the potential *mark-to-market* of the portfolio or should I stress test its *expected value*, that is, the value that will be realised if delta-hedged to expiration? The first question may be somewhat difficult to analyse in that it requires an assumption on what the mark-to-market may be after a market event (that is, what will the new volatility surfaces/skews be?). This will also depend upon the liquidity of the securities in the portfolio.

The second question is a little more tractable in that it can be related to potential volatilities, invoking the delta-hedging principle. This approach is certainly a good first step in analysing market risk, but does not capture the "tails", that is the low probability but potentially fatal events. For this reason, the *average* P&L may not be a sufficient measure of potential loss. The firm may also be concerned about a probability of loss greater than some fixed amount.

5. STATIC STRESS TESTING

Static stress tests are performed by pushing the relevant input parameters to unlikely , but possible values and then revaluing the portfolio. For a portfolio of equity options, this might mean imposing gap moves upon each underlying security as well as increasing volatility levels. In essence we are evaluating the expected P&L of the portfolio if the underlying stocks suffer a gap move and we delta-hedge to expiration, experiencing higher volatilities than we expected. Some of the questions that arise are: How do the stocks collectively "gap"? Should we use correlations or betas, or should we assume that under strenuous conditions all stocks move with a beta of one. Alternatively, we could assume that again, under stressful conditions the stocks will move with a correlation of 1.

A more sophisticated version is to evaluate the portfolio under stressful conditions straight out of history. One such way is to introduce a *term structure of volatility*. By this we simply mean that we can use a 30 day volatility for a 30 day option, and a 60 day volatility for a 60 day option. In general, when the market suffers a disturbance, the short term experienced volatility may be very high, but it invariably returns to a lower long-term base level. We can go back into history and record the volatilities actually experienced by the stocks, currencies, interest rates, et cetera, and use these to evaluate a book of derivative securities. In effect, we are calculating the expected P&L of the portfolio, should a similar such historical event occur.

6. MONTE CARLO SIMULATION

In Monte Carlo simulation we generate price "paths" of the underlying risks and examine the portfolio along these paths. For example, in a portfolio of equity options we might generate a path of stock prices; that is, we create a synthetic history of stock prices and see how the portfolio performs, given this particular history. We distinguish between two types of Monte Carlo: *passive* and *active*. In passive Monte Carlo we simply watch the portfolio and bite our nails. In active Monte Carlo we delta-hedge along the way. This latter method is a more reasonable approximation to reality and actually ties in with the underlying mathematical pricing models via the delta-hedging principle. Passive Monte Carlo is frequently used for the *pricing* of some derivative securities, but is less applicable for studying market risk in a portfolio of derivative securities.

According to the delta-hedging principle, the average result from a large number of active Monte Carlo simulations should be obtained by evaluating the portfolio using the simulation volatility. The following example illustrates this point.

7. SAMPLE RESULTS ILLUSTRATING THE DELTA-HEDGING PRINCIPLE

As an example of the delta-hedging principle we consider a portfolio consisting of a short position in 3 month call options on IBM, with a strike price of 125. The initial stock price was 118. The options were sold at an implied volatility of 25%. Unfortunately, the volatility to be experienced in the Monte Carlo simulation is 35%. The expected value (obtained by evaluating the portfolio using a 35% volatility) is then about −$1,000,000, that is, a loss of $1,000,000. The simulation consisted of 1,000 paths, each of length 100 days, stepping daily. The results of the simulation are:

Average Value	−$1,086,826
Worst Path	−$4,011,357
Best Path	+$1,423,509
97.5% Confidence Level	−$2,683,823

Note that the average value is as expected. However the worst path had a loss of an additional $3,000,000. The 97.5% confidence level is $1,600,000 below the average.

It is illuminating to study the behavior of a particular path in *Exhibit 17.1* and *Exhibit 17.2.*

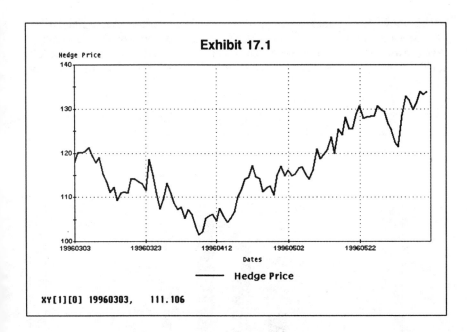

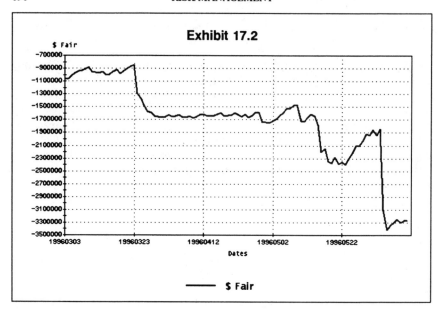

The above two graphs describe Path 14 in our Monte Carlo simulation. The sudden drops in "$ Fair" are explained by the corresponding "whipsaws" in the stock price. The overall distribution of values for all 1,000 paths are described by the following empirical distribution in *Exhibit 17.3*.

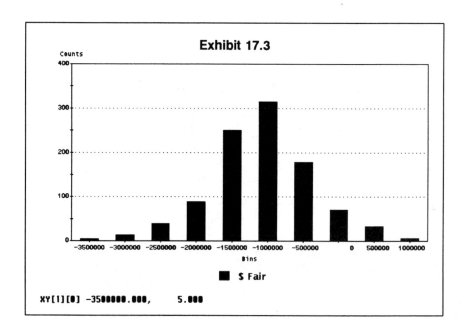

8. STRESS TESTING AN ACTUAL PORTFOLIO

We will next apply these concepts to a portfolio containing some equity options and their underlying stocks. We first examine the static stress test results.

Hedge SPX implied cash 647.4557

Name	Hedge	Delta cntr	Gamma cntr	US$ theta/day	US$vega 0.1%	US$ fair +rlz
SPX	SPX	9.4	−4.8	21,154	−17,728	1,583,602
INTC	INTC	532.3.	2,016.10	−496	649	−23,310
GM	GM	286.9	3,494.70	−1,411	803	−706
IBM	IBM	−2,670.8	312	−5	3,979	49,982
MO	MO	55.7	1,353.60	−1,177	988	−3,930
EK	EK	−1.5	1,075.10	1,259	1,312	6,315

This is a "book" of six portfolios of options. The first one contains options on the S&P500 index, followed by Intel, General Motors, IBM, Philip Morris, and Eastman Kodak. Reading across, we can see the current exposures represented in "Delta Cntr" (literally, delta expressed in contracts). For the stocks these are share quantities and for the S&P500, futures contracts. Adjacent to this column is the "Gamma Cntr"; that is, the change in Delta Cntr for a one point move in the hedge. The vega column indicates that we are net short S&P500 options, but long individual stock options, each approximately hedged. The current expected value of this book is about $1,600,000, using the term structure of volatility in the following table:

Days	EK	GM	IBM	INTC	MO	SPX
30	27.5	30.6	38.0	40.0	21.6	12.9
91	27.4	28.4	36.1	28.0	19.8	11.6
182	25.0	28.0	28.0	27.3	19.5	11.0
365	24.0	27.5	27.5	27.0	19.0	10.5

We also have the betas of each stock with respect to the S&P500, as well as all pairwise correlations. We will first static stress test by stepping the S&P index by (daily) standard deviations, stepping the stocks accordingly, using their betas. We will also re-evaluate the portfolio at current volatilities and after increasing each volatility by 30% (multiplicatively). For example, 30 day INTC volatility will be increased from 40.0% to 52.0%.

Method 1

	−3 std	Current	+3 std	Maximum Loss
Current vols	$1,270,000	$1,600,000	$1,390,000	(330,000)
130% of current vols	$1,380,000	$1,590,000	$1,370,000	(230,000)

This particular test seems to indicate that an increase in volatility is not a major risk in that the stock volatilities will compensate for the S&P500 volatility. However, if we step the volatility differently, the picture looks quite different. Suppose we assume that as volatility increases, the stock volatility only increases *point for point* with the index volatility.

Method 2

	−3 std	Current	+3 std	Maximum Loss
Current vols	$1,270,000	$1,600,000	$1,390,000	(330,000)
Current vols + 5.0	$ 950,000	$1,130,000	$ 910,000	(690,000)
Current vols + 10.0	$ 600,000	$ 690,000	$ 260,000	(1,340,000)
Current vols + 15.0	$ 245,000	$ 265,000	$ 25,000	(1,575,000)

In this example we do progressively worse for each +5.0 shift increase in volatility.

We can also stress test this portfolio by invoking the volatilities incurred by these stocks during the Iraq-Kuwait crisis that began in August of 1990. Here are the actual volatilities these stocks experienced.

Experienced volatilities beginning August 1 1990

Days	EK	GM	IBM	INTC	MO	SPX
30	37.1	42.0	29.5	52.1	39.9	25.6
91	39.6	30.0	25.5	48.1	30.5	22.0
182	33.5	29.0	23.6	32.0	25.5	19.1
365	30.1	28.0	30.0	30.0	24.8	16.4

The table below shows an expected value of −$210,000. In reality, what occurred was that as the 91 day volatility of the S&P500 increased by 10.4, that of IBM actually *dropped* by 10.6. Certainly the volatilities of the underlying stocks did not keep pace with the S&P500 on a percentage basis (with the possible exception of INTC). This is a feature that is not captured in correlations and other such linear measures of risk.

Method 3

Current	Historical	Maximum Loss
1,600,000	(210,000)	(1,810,000)

9. A MONTE CARLO STRESS TEST

The final stress test we will apply will be a full Monte Carlo simulation in which we increase the individual volatilities by 30%, but maintain current correlations. The correlations used are in the following table:

	EK	GM	IBM	INTC	MO	SPX
EK	1.00					
GM	.10	1.00				
IBM	.06	−.06	1.00			
INTC	.17	.14	.47	1.00		
MO	.33	.34	.22	.12	1.00	
SPX	.52	.32	.43	.52	.51	1.00

The results are quite interesting and square up rather nicely with the historical scenario simulation. The 97.5% confidence interval is found to be $150,000, which is fairly close to the previous simulation. The mean of the run is $1,240,000, which roughly corresponds to the numbers obtained in our first static stress test.

Method 4

Current	Mean	2.5% Level	Maximum Loss
1,600,000	1,240,000	150,000	(1,450,000)

If we interpret the "maximum loss" figure, as the value at risk (VAR), we can summarise the calculations for the four methods employed.

Method 1	VAR
Stepping underlyings by beta to ±3 Std	
Increasing volatility by 30%	230,000
Method 2	
Stepping underlyings by beta to ±3 Std	1,575,000
Increasing volatility *linearly* by 15%	
Method 3	
August 1990 Historical Simulation	1,810,000
Method 4	
Active Monte Carlo	1,450,000
Increasing volatility by 30%	
2.5% percentile	

Intuitively, we want a VAR calculation that would incorporate an event such as the August 1990 scenario. Method 1 clearly falls short. Method 2 comes close, but seems somewhat ad hoc. In fact, Method 2 is essentially "vega bucketing", that is, analysing the portfolio assuming a linear change in volatility levels across all underlyings. Method 4, the Monte Carlo simulation, also gives similar numbers and has intuitive appeal. The combination of generally increasing volatility by 30%, but allowing for a dispersion of values by considering the lower 2.50% percentile, seems to incorporate the experience of August 1990: volatility was significantly higher, but not for all stocks as shown in *Exhibit 17.4* and *Exhibit 17.5*.

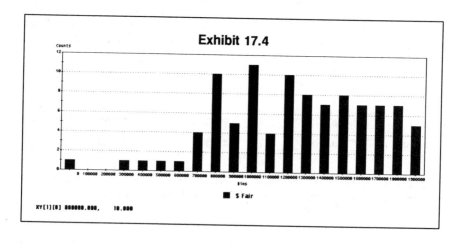

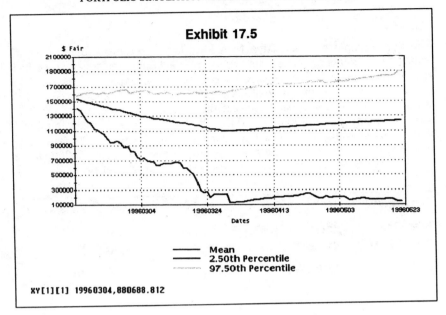

Exhibit 17.5

XY[1][1] 19960304,880688.812

10. OTHER APPLICATIONS OF MONTE CARLO SIMULATION

10.1 Cash flow considerations

Theoretically derived pricing models usually do not take cash flow requirements into account. For example, suppose I have sold an OTC put on, say, the S&P500 index and hedged it with a short position of 200 Index futures. If the market gaps up 10 points, I will need to come up with $1,000,000 of variation margin, since the OTC position cannot be used against the listed futures margin call. This problem is compounded in a portfolio of OTC options with listed hedges. Another example is if I am running, say, a USD interest rate swap book and hedging with listed (Eurodollar) contracts, a change in the yield curve can produce a large variation margin call. Most pricing models assume that you can borrow as much as you like, whenever you like.

10.2 Liquidity constraints

Theoretical pricing models do not usually incorporate liquidity constraints in the dynamic hedging/pricing algorithm. That is to say, the assumptions of the model assume instantaneous rehedging capabilities in as large quantities as desired, with no market impact. As the stock market crash of 1987 demonstrated, (combined with the then current version of "portfolio insurance"), this is not the case in the real world of trading. In reality you may only be able trade a certain amount when rehedging, without distorting the market or accelerating a trend.

Example

In this example we use active Monte Carlo to investigate the impact of liquidity constraints on an options portfolio. The assumption was that we had sold at the money call options, with one month to expiration on 200,000 shares of stock, expecting a volatility of 30.0%. We then experienced 30.0% in our simulation of 100 paths, so that the average P&L was about $14,042, with a standard deviation of $113,608. We then ran two additional simulations in which we imposed a liquidity constraint of 20,000 shares and 10,000 shares. That is, we were not allowed to trade more than 20,000 shares (10,000 shares) at any one time. The results are summarized below.

Simulation	No constraint	10,000 share limit	20,000 share limit
Average	14,042	6,855	4,340
Standard Dev.	113,608	355,867	284,016
2.50% -tile	(216,670)	(1,114,300)	(797,250)

If we use the lowest 2.50% percentile as a "Value-at-risk" (VAR) calculation, we see that the incorporation of a 20,000 share liquidity constraint yields a VAR that is larger than the unconstrained VAR by a factor of almost 4.0! This additional risk is completely ignored by the other stress tests discussed in this chapter.

11. CONCLUSIONS

Proper stress testing of derivatives portfolios should take dynamic trading issues into account. The delta-hedging principle connects these issues with static stress testing, but this is only an average value calculation that may not adequately measure the impact of unlikely but costly events. Testing by historical scenarios can serve as a good "sanity check" on your risk management methodology. Active Monte Carlo simulation provides the greatest flexibility for analysing dynamic trading issues. Confidence intervals of suitably chosen simulations can serve as good value at risk (VAR) calculations.

Chapter 18

Credit Risk Measurement

by Alan Bustany

1. DEFINITION OF CREDIT RISK

"Credit risk" is the risk that a counterparty to a financial transaction will fail to perform according to the terms and conditions of the contract, thus causing the asset holder to suffer financial loss. The risk exposure to a counterparty can be defined as the amount of positive market value of the portfolio of instruments held with that counterparty at any given time. This exposure can be calculated on a gross basis for each instrument in the portfolio or, where netting across transactions is likely to be legally enforceable, on a net basis. In this section we will assume that the "failure to perform" is a default, and we will generally ignore the possibility of recovery of any portion of the loss from the defaulting counterparty.

A key aspect of the definition of risk exposure is the dependency on time. Credit risk is a function of market risk over the remaining life of transactions with a counterparty. It is this dependency on time that adds complications and computational complexity to the measurement, reporting, and control of credit risk.

2. RISK OF COUNTERPARTY DEFAULT

The economic risk associated with a counterparty is the product of three factors:

(i) the exposure to the counterparty (the main focus of this chapter);

(ii) the probability of default of the counterparty; and

(iii) the potential recovery rate following default.

Typical calculations of economic risk simply multiply a single number representing the credit risk by a single number representing a combination of the probability of default and the likely recovery rate. A more sophisticated analysis would recognise that the probability of default is a function of time (as is the credit risk). The product of the two is therefore also a function of time, which can be calculated by multiplication at each point in time (although, for complete accuracy, the correlation between the default probability and the credit risk over time would have to be taken into account).

For debt instruments the exposure is always close to the outstanding principal, so there is little interaction between the size of the exposure and the event of a default. For derivative contracts, however, the exposure is very variable and there may be significant correlation (positive or negative) with the probability of default. Nevertheless it is rare for such correlation to be taken into account in assessing credit risk.

2.1 Counterparty risk weightings

The simplest approach to calculating economic risk is to assign a "weighting", or probability of default, to each counterparty based on a standard rating agency grade such as those from Moody's Investors Service or Standard and Poor's. Aside from the time-based dependency of the economic risk referred to above, the overall economic risk faced by an organisation is (typically) substantially less than the sum of individual counterparty risks. The usual diversification effects apply, especially since there is normally a very low correlation between default risks of counterparties, although concentrations based on industry, country, and so on can lead to some correlation effects. Nevertheless, the conservative approach of summing the economic risk across counterparties is usually applied.

2.2 Exchange traded versus OTC

Exchange traded derivatives offer credit enhancement compared to over-the-counter transactions directly with a counterparty. The credit risk with the counterparty is effectively replaced by the credit risk of the exchange. The exchange would usually have a better credit rating than a counterparty, and it is further protected by the mechanisms of deposits and margin calls. The effect of this protection is to reduce credit exposure to the exchange to the total value of deposits required, and this does not vary significantly over the term of the transactions. Exchange traded transactions, from a credit risk point of view, are therefore normally treated separately from counterparty transactions.

3. RISK INHERENT IN THE PRODUCT

3.1 Credit risk for derivatives = market risk of replacement

The effect of a counterparty default on a derivative transaction, where there is no exchange of principal, can be completely mitigated by replacing the derivative in the market. At default, therefore, the credit risk of a single transaction is precisely equal to the risk of replacing the transaction in the market. This is typically modelled by the current market value of the transaction, although in low liquidity markets this would usually underestimate the credit risk.

This model also assumes that the capital markets are efficient, that the default does not significantly affect the overall market, and that transaction costs can be ignored. Each of these assumptions also tends to underestimate the credit risk, but these effects are marginal where a reasonable volume of trades in the instrument is effected.

3.2 G30 guidelines: credit risk = current exposure + potential exposure

The G30 report on derivatives[1] states that in assessing credit risk, one needs to ask the following two questions:

1. If a counterparty were to default today, what would it cost to replace the transaction?
2. If a counterparty defaults at some point in the future, what is a reasonable estimate of the potential replacement cost?

These questions are formalised in Recommendation 10 of the G30 report, which states that dealers and end-users should measure credit exposure on derivatives in two ways:

(i) current exposure, which is the replacement cost of derivatives transactions (that is, their market value); and

(ii) potential exposure, which is an estimate of the future replacement cost of derivatives transactions.

It further recommends that potential exposure be calculated using probability analysis based upon broad confidence intervals (for example, two standard deviations) over the remaining terms of the transactions. Note, however, that the report aims to reduce credit risk to a single number for each counterparty, rather than representing the risk as a function of time.

The report further refers to tables of credit risk factors (CRFs) for computation of potential exposure based on a transaction's notional principal. These CRFs are pre-computed, conservative estimates of the maximum potential increase in the value of a transaction. They are typically computed using a Monte Carlo simulation at a 97.7% confidence level and choosing a factor which exceeds the maximum value of the transaction at that level of confidence over time. Such CRFs are computed under specific assumptions about, inter alia, instrument, tenor, market levels, and volatilities. These assumptions help reduce the size and complexity of CRF tables, which are then used in a wide range of contexts (not all of which are strictly valid).

3.3 Settlement risk

Settlement risk arises when there is non-simultaneous exchange of value. It is distinct from the pre-settlement risk on which this chapter focuses. For example, paying an A$ amount in Sydney several hours before receiving a US$ amount in New York gives rise to a settlement risk. Were the counterparty to default during this period, the credit loss would equal the entire US$ amount regardless of the market value of the transaction. Measurement of settlement risk poses no special problems and is not further considered here.

1. *Derivatives: Practices and Principles* (Group of Thirty, Washington DC, July 1993).

4. MEASURING EXPOSURE

Most market participants use simple rules to estimate a "loan equivalent amount" for derivative transactions. This is generally the current market value of the transaction (an accurate valuation of the current exposure) plus an add-on based on the notional value and credit risk factors for the transaction (a rough estimate of the potential exposure). This section looks at more accurate ways of calculating the potential exposure, and at the statistical assumptions underlying calculations.

Two measures of potential exposure can be used: "expected" exposure and maximum or "worst case" exposure. Expected exposure is the mean of all possible market values over the life of the contract where the market value (and therefore credit exposure) is positive. Worst case exposure is calculated so that, to within some degree of confidence, the actual exposure will not exceed this value. Expected exposure is a useful measure for assessing capital allocation and pricing decisions. Worst case exposure, however, is more useful for assessing credit allocation since it provides a measure of the maximum that could possibly be at risk to a given counterparty. We will therefore focus on worst case exposure for measuring credit risk. Worst case exposure is also more difficult to calculate than expected exposure, although both are complicated by the non-symmetric nature of the exposure.

The exposure on a derivative contract can be regarded as the payoff from an option on the derivative with a strike price of zero. This is because credit exposure only exists when the derivative has positive value as illustrated in the following graph (familiar as the payoff of a call):

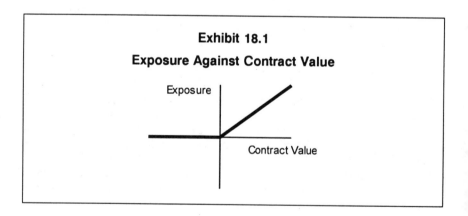

Exhibit 18.1

Exposure Against Contract Value

This fact can be useful in analysing credit risk using option valuation models. The zero exposure part of this graph when the contract has a negative value, however, does have an effect on overall credit exposure when netting agreements are in place. Option valuation models are not therefore of much practical use in measuring credit risk on portfolios.

4.1 Statistics applied to credit risk: normal distribution, "fat tails", worst case

A chief assumption made in almost all evaluations of potential exposure is that the underlying market variable is a random variable with a normal distribution about some expected mean. This assumption is made to make calculations tractable and because it is "near enough" to actual behaviour. The normal distribution is used again in converting a statistical value of potential exposure to a confidence level that this exposure will not be exceeded. Thus two standard deviations corresponds to a 95.45% confidence level, three standard deviations corresponds to a 99.73% confidence level, and so on.

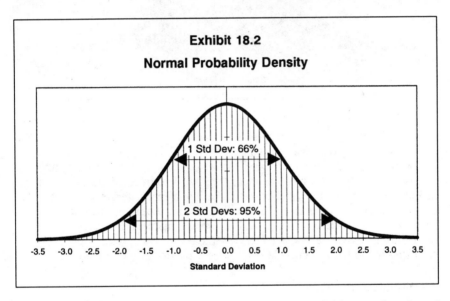

Exhibit 18.2

Normal Probability Density

1 Std Dev: 66%

2 Std Devs: 95%

Standard Deviation

In practice the values taken by almost all market variables can be viewed as near-normal but with "fat tails". That is, for the majority of small deviations from the mean the distribution is almost normal, but the small minority of large deviations occur more frequently than expected. This is of particular concern for credit risk, since worst case exposures occur at the extremes of market variables. Thus we can safely say that 90% of the time the exposure will be less than some value, but it is more difficult to say what value the exposure might have on the other 10% of occasions that, from a credit viewpoint, are more interesting.

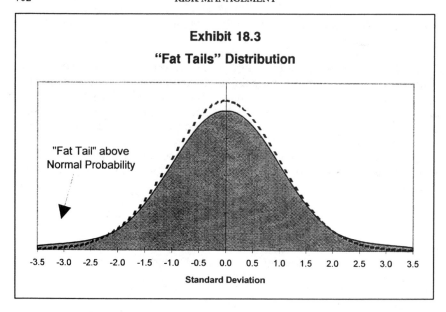

Exhibit 18.3

"Fat Tails" Distribution

To address the problems of "fat tails", worst case stress testing (as described in the preceding chapter by Lance Smith) is used to assess credit risk as well as market risk. That is, the potential exposure to a counterparty at points in the future is calculated for all combinations of specific outlying values of market variables. Note that "market variables" typically needs to include the shape of the yield curve at that point in the future for calculation of the exposure to be completed. Industry experience, more than statistics, is used to choose suitable outlying values, so the mathematical significance of the resulting exposures is not clear. But these stress tested values, applied consistently, do help to provide management control of credit risk.

4.2 Simulation—Monte Carlo

A Monte Carlo simulation builds on the fundamental relationship between credit risk and market risk by calculating market values at discrete intervals of time for discrete values of simulated market variables. A probability is associated with each point in the lattice defined by the combinations of time and market variable values. By calculating the exposure for all transactions at each point in the lattice the probability of a certain level of credit risk exposure to each counterparty can be calculated over time. Since the Monte Carlo method depends only on the ability to price a transaction given a set of market variables, and this ability is a pre-requisite of being able to offer a transaction in the first place, such simulations are an obvious way to calculate credit risk. Further details on Monte Carlo techniques can be found in the chapter by Tom Gillespie (Chapter 19).

Although Monte Carlo simulation is a statistically rigorous approach and is applicable across the full range of transactions, it is a practical impossibility to run the requisite number of simulated portfolio market values in a reasonable time, despite enormous increases in computing power in the last decade. A practical method of measuring credit risk exposure in near-real-time is therefore required, hence the tendency to use tables of credit risk factors which can be based on standard runs of Monte Carlo simulations.

4.3 Regulatory measurement

For obvious reasons, regulators have focused on simple, conservative methods for measuring and reporting levels of credit risk. The Bank of International Settlements method focuses on two components: a credit equivalent and a counterparty factor. The credit equivalent can be calculated by either of two methods:

1. the current exposure method (which uses mark-to-market for current exposure and a credit conversion factor to estimate potential exposure); and
2. the original exposure method (which simply uses a credit conversion factor for the whole calculation).

The original exposure method is intended for use when even a mark-to-market calculation is not available, let alone a full calculation of credit exposure over time.

The credit conversion factors for these two credit equivalent calculation methods are:

| | % of Nominal Principal Amount | |
	Interest Rate Contract	Exchange Rate Contract
Current Exposure Method		
Less than one year	nil	1%
One year and over	0.5%	5%
Original Exposure Method		
Less than one year	0.5%	2%
One to two years	1%	5%
Each additional year	1%	3%

The counterparty factor is then applied to the credit equivalent calculated above. Selected counterparty risk weightings are listed below:

	% of Credit Equivalent Amount
Domestic Banks, and Foreign Banks with an original maturity less than 1 year.	20%
Foreign Banks with an original maturity greater than 1 year, and all corporates.	100%

These simple measures can be calculated easily by all market participants. They provide a rough and ready measure for regulators that is consistent across organisations, even if the measure is only an inaccurate approximation of the true credit risks. Such measures are inappropriate for accurate allocation of credit by an organisation.

5. TYPICAL EXPOSURE PROFILES OF DERIVATIVE PRODUCTS

For accurate measurement of credit risk, the potential exposure of a transaction or portfolio of transactions with a counterparty should be represented as a profile, measured at some confidence level, at a set of forward times (such as monthly intervals) over the remaining life of the portfolio. This provides a portfolio credit curve which more accurately reflects the credit exposure over time. It also provides the capability to compare the credit curve against a corresponding risk limit curve enabling time-based control over exposure to counterparties.

5.1 Forwards and futures

A forward foreign exchange transaction has a simple monotonic increasing credit curve based on the potential movement of the relevant exchange rate away from the current forward rate for the transaction. As time passes there is an increasing likelihood (at any given confidence level) that the rates will have diverged, but the *rate* of divergence will decrease over time. Assuming a confidence level of say 90% for example, we can model exchange rate movements on a day by day basis to determine at what value we can be 90% sure the exchange rate will not exceed that value on any given date in the future. This exchange rate value translates directly into an equivalent value of our forward contract, which is, in turn, the potential credit exposure on the contract at a 90% confidence level for that date in the future. Performing a Monte Carlo simulation on the underlying exchange rate provides a curve of potential credit exposure.

Ignoring effects from forward rates based on yield curves and other time-based dependencies, the statistical shape of the credit curve is given by exposure increasing as a function of the square root of time. This is simply the effect of assuming that today's exchange rate is a reasonable estimate of future rates, and the "random" movement of the rate will be statistically normal. The typical credit curve for a forward transaction therefore looks similar to the illustration below.

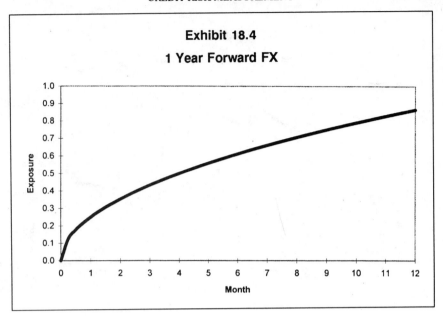

Exhibit 18.4

1 Year Forward FX

Any forward transaction, including forward rate agreements and over-the-counter futures transactions, will have a similar credit curve analysis based on the movements and volatility of the underlying market variable.

5.2 Swaps

When an interest rate swap is first entered into (at market prices) there is no market value and no credit exposure. If interest rates move in your favour the swap has a positive value, thereby creating an exposure whose expected profile over time is a function of expected interest rate moves and the remaining cash flows on the swap. As for forwards and futures, the expected divergence (at any given confidence level) of the interest rate move will increase over time. The reducing number of cash flows on the swap, however, tend to decrease the exposure in discrete steps as each payment is made. To establish the potential credit exposure curve, we therefore need a simulation of the interest rate to provide the relevant rate at the chosen confidence level, which is then multiplied by the remaining cash flows on the swap (suitably discounted) at that time.

The result is a stepped curve starting at zero, peaking during the life of the swap, and decreasing back to zero as the swap matures. The basic shape of this curve is consistent from swap to swap, but specific values depend on the notional principal, term of the swap, and payment frequencies as well as the usual market conditions. A two year quarterly swap might have a profile as follows:

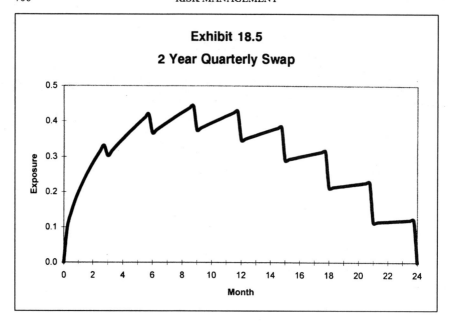

A five year semi-annual swap might have a profile as follows:

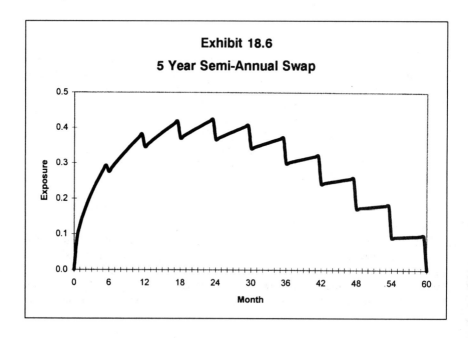

The basic shape of a swap credit profile has a peak at approximately one third of the time to maturity. The precise location and size of the peak is of course dependent on market factors including volatilities and the shape of the yield curve.

Cross-currency swaps which do not include an exchange of principal have essentially the same credit profile as interest rate swaps, but with the added computational complexity of two currencies and two yield curves. Where an exchange of principal is involved, there is effectively a forward FX agreement for the reverse exchange of principal at maturity in addition to the swap's interim cash flows. The credit profile is a combination of the swap and forward, as illustrated below, which is typically dominated by the forward exposure especially as maturity approaches.

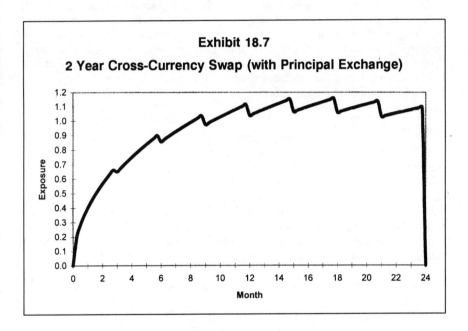

Exhibit 18.7

2 Year Cross-Currency Swap (with Principal Exchange)

5.3 Options

The credit risk on an option is one-sided, unlike the situation with forwards and swaps. The buyer of an option typically pays in full when the option is bought. The seller, however, is not required to perform until the option is exercised. This exposes the buyer, but not the seller, to credit risk (which is the inverse of the market risk exposure of the two parties).

Although the value of a simple option is not a linear function of the underlying market variable, it does have extremes at extreme values of the underlying. This is a critical fact when considering simulation models for credit risk which typically follow the highest and lowest possible values (at some confidence level) for, say, the interest rate. Since a simple option will have a corresponding extreme value at these points, this is a valid way of evaluating the credit risk associated with the option. As a result the credit profile of a simple option is again similar to a forward contract.

Combinations of options, and exotic options, however, present a more serious problem for valuation of potential exposure. The pay-off, and therefore the credit exposure for the buyer, can have a peak at *any* value of the underlying market variable including, of course, the current market rate. This is quite unlike other derivatives which, like simple options, typically have extremes of value at extremes of the underlying rate. As a result accurate calculation of the potential exposure of a portfolio of options and exotics with a counterparty requires simulation of all future rates, as well as all time points, to maturity.

The value of an exotic can also be made as sensitive as desired to a particular rate which further complicates the analysis required to establish within the desired degree of confidence what the potential exposure will be. Adding further complications is the fact that the liquidity for exotic options may be limited, resulting in large bid-offer spreads. This affects the underlying assumption throughout this chapter that the credit risk on a transaction can be accurately modelled by a well-defined current market value. Detailed analysis of the valuation and credit handling for exotics is beyond the scope of this chapter.

6. PORTFOLIO EFFECTS

Adding the future potential exposure to the current exposure of a portfolio will almost always overstate the credit risk on the portfolio. Typically, a significant part of the current exposure will settle before the future exposure has time to develop. Secondly, various offsets imply that the exposure on individual transactions cannot logically increase together. Finally, the statistical procedures used for reducing potential exposure on individual transactions to a single number do not permit the simple addition of the resulting numbers—for example adding a peak that occurs at three months to a peak that occurs at two years does not result in the peak of the combined transactions.

The errors involved in the simplifications above are always conservative: that is they are guaranteed to over-estimate the risk. Such conservatism, however, restricts an organisation's ability to do business with a counterparty. It will also lead to poor allocation of risk-adjusted capital. It is therefore a serious problem where credit is in short supply, and it is becoming increasingly important as credit becomes a significant factor in the pricing of transactions.

6.1 Netting

Netting allows the counterparty to a default to add together the positive and negative market values of derivative agreements and either remit the net negative amount or make a claim for the net positive amount. This is a significantly different credit position to the situation in which the gross negative amount is remitted and a claim is made for the gross positive amount, but it depends on the existence and the enforceability of netting agreements. At present netting agreements typically don't apply across the full range of instruments, or across the full range of legal jurisdictions, or to all contracts with counterparties or their subsidiaries. In practice it is therefore necessary to calculate and track nettable exposures as well as non-nettable exposures.

Netting current exposures is a straightforward exercise of summing current market values which can be positive or negative. Netting potential exposures is more difficult since the potential exposure is a statistic summarising the likely worst case at some point in the future. In practice such netting must be embedded in the procedure for calculating potential exposure rather than being applied after the potential exposure is calculated.

6.2 Timing offsets

The fact that potential exposure is a function of time implies that the combination of two exposures with peaks at different times will result in a combined exposure with the following properties:

- the peak of the combined exposure is less than the sum of the peaks of the individual exposures; and
- the combined peak may not occur at the same point in the future as either individual peak.

The fact that a short-term exposure combined with a long-term exposure will produce a combined exposure that is less than the sum of the two individual exposures is referred to as a timing offset. Viewing credit risk as a profile over time, of course, means that the combined exposure is indeed equal to the sum of the individual exposures on a point-by-point basis over the profile.

6.3 Economic offsets

Economic offsets share the properties of netting and timing offsets. The fact that a market variable, say an interest rate, cannot be at both an extreme high and an extreme low at the same time means that a fixed-for-floating swap and a floating-for-fixed swap cannot both have credit exposure at the same time. At one extreme, one swap would have a credit exposure and the other would have no exposure (or could contribute in a netting arrangement). At the other extreme the latter swap would have the exposure and the former none. By combining potential exposures at a point in the calculation where the assumed market variables are known, the benefits of these economic offsets can flow through to the overall exposure.

By viewing potential exposure as a function of a market variable the parallel with timing offsets can be seen. This is particularly so when exotic options are included in the portfolio, since their potential exposure as a function of the underlying market variable can have peaks in the middle of the range similar to the credit profile (over time) of a swap.

6.4 Curve addition

Curve addition is intended to be short-hand for the combination of two credit risk profiles to get the combined profile. Unfortunately, the addition of curves involves more sophisticated mathematics than simple addition if the benefits of the netting, timing, and economic offsets mentioned are to be obtained. Nevertheless, significant improvements over summation of simple numeric credit exposures can be obtained by one or more of:

- netting current exposures (where applicable);
- combining potential exposures point-wise over time; and
- noting which extreme of which market variable drives the potential exposure.

These techniques require representing the credit exposure as a profile in time with various annotations. Note, however, that this approach does not allow for correlations in the instruments or underlying market variables giving rise to the credit exposure. Full evaluation of correlations across multiple variables requires all of these to be incorporated into the initial simulation used to derive relevant values over time.

To be effective as a management tool, the increased sophistication of representing credit exposures needs to be reflected in the representations for reporting and limit setting.

7. MANAGING CREDIT RISK

Credit risk on derivatives cannot be considered in isolation from the credit risks arising elsewhere in an organisation. The credit risk associated with derivatives may be more complex than those associated with, for example, debt instruments, but they need to be aggregated to give a complete picture. This requires the credit risk to be expressed in a comparable manner across all products. Ideally the risk should be translated into the most flexible form (such as that used for representing derivative credit profiles). In practice, a "lowest common denominator" tends to be used, giving inaccurate but conservative "credit equivalents" for derivatives.

Recommendation 11 of the G30 report states that:

> "Credit exposures on derivatives, and all other credit exposures to a counterparty, should be aggregated taking into consideration enforceable netting arrangements. Credit exposures should be calculated regularly and compared to credit limits."

This recommendation emphasises the need to aggregate exposures, but also suggests the two key management criteria of frequent measurement and the imposition of limits for each counterparty.

7.1 Frequency of measurement

The G30 report states that credit exposures should be calculated regularly. In particular, dealers should monitor current exposures daily; they can generally measure potential exposures less frequently. End-users with derivative portfolios should also periodically assess credit exposures. For them, the appropriate frequency will depend upon how material their credit exposures are.

Full measurement of potential exposure on a portfolio basis is a computationally intensive task which cannot, at present, realistically be performed more frequently than daily. A combination of accurate over-night measurement followed by intra-day conservative updates can, however, provide real-time measurements. These real-time credit risk profiles can take into account netting, timing, and economic offsets and allow management against credit limit profiles (as described below). Techniques allowing some form of real-time credit measurement are becoming increasingly important as credit is incorporated into the pricing of transactions.

7.2 Limits

Credit limits should be established for all parties with whom an organisation is willing to have a credit exposure. In addition to counterparties this should include brokers, banks, and clearing houses. Typically, organisations impose two or three credit limits for each counterparty: a short-term limit for transactions of less than, say, one or two years; a medium-term limit out to say three or five years; and a long-term limit for greater maturities. They may also impose a limit on the maximum tenor for each counterparty.

Whilst multiple limits can capture some of the time-dependent features of credit risk, a more sophisticated approach is to have a credit limit profile. Such a profile provides a credit limit for the potential credit exposure at each point of time in the future. The chief advantage of this approach is that it avoids the discontinuity that occurs at the boundary between any two specific limits. For example, an organisation's credit profile with a particular counterparty may be perfectly acceptable at all points except for a month or two at the short end of the medium-term period. Given the amount of "room" available above the credit risk profile except at particular points, it seems unreasonable to restrict all transactions.

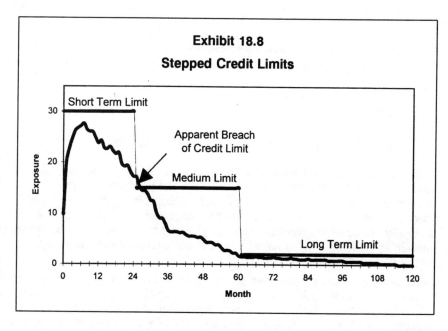

Exhibit 18.8

Stepped Credit Limits

The nature of the risk with any given counterparty can be more accurately reflected with a credit limit profile. This can acknowledge certain acceptable peaks with a counterparty and provide limits that gradually decay over time. With such a limit profile, it is less likely that there will be an unrealistic restriction on transactions when there "ought to be" credit available. Equally, a breach of the credit limit will be a "real" breach rather than an artefact of how the risk is measured.

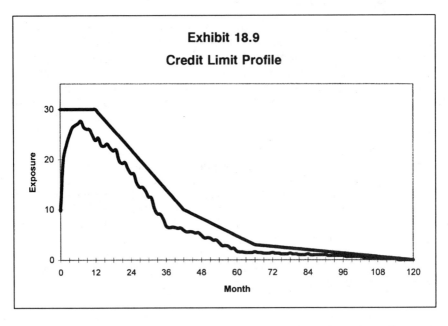

Exhibit 18.9

Credit Limit Profile

The fact that credit risk on derivatives moves with market prices (far more than does the credit risk on non-derivative products) means that a credit limit can be breached without any new transactions occurring. Management procedures to cover monitoring, authorising, and correcting credit limit excesses need to cover the effects of both new transactions and price movements.

7.3 Minimising risk: netting, margin calls, collateral, guarantees

Having analysed and measured credit risk, organisations should take all practical steps to minimise those risks through the use of netting agreements, margin, collateral, or other forms of credit enhancement. We have already referred to the beneficial effects of netting on credit risk exposure (provided a legally enforceable agreement is in place). The use of margins and so on, outside an exchange traded environment, is quite rare but can be particularly useful in dealing with higher risk counterparties.

At present most over-the-counter derivative transactions proceed without either party placing cash margin or any form of collateral as security with the other party. Where such security is provided, it should be noted that the posting of margins or collateral can itself involve a credit risk which should not be left out of the measurement. Margins and collateral can, of course, dramatically change the exposure profile of a transaction. In the case of particularly large, difficult, or unusual transactions, they can be the best means of managing the credit risk.

7.4 Hedging effects

Sophisticated measurement of credit exposure, especially with netting agreements in place, can result in an additional transaction *reducing* the overall credit risk. It can also result in altering the credit risk profile such that it is reduced at one part of the profile whilst being increased at another. These effects can result in a transaction being viewed as a "credit hedge" with one of its purposes being a reduction in credit risk which is of benefit to the organisation.

Given the cost of credit, the effect of a transaction on an organisation's credit risk profile with a counterparty should be taken into account in pricing a transaction. This could enable the organisation to pay slightly more for a credit effective transaction, or to improve the price offered for a product.

Clearly, credit hedges are a secondary consideration to market risk hedges. They are, however, an important consideration especially when credit with a particular counterparty is in short supply. Effective use of such hedges requires relatively sophisticated real-time measurement of credit risk profiles.

Part 6

Mathematical Techniques

Chapter 19

Mathematical Techniques

by Thomas R Gillespie

1. INTRODUCTION

In 1900, one of the most eminent mathematicians of the time, David Hilbert, addressed the second congress in Paris with a talk titled "Mathematical Problems". Hilbert went on to describe 23 of the most important and unsolved problems to mathematics at the time. Most of these problems are still unsolved and hundreds have replaced the few for which a definitive answer has been found. In the meantime hundreds of new avenues of research have sprung up and the sum total of mathematical knowledge has exploded. Mathematical finance is one of these new areas of work.

To summarise all of mathematical knowledge to date in a few dozen pages would be impossible to say the least. To most professional mathematicians today, the bulk of mathematical knowledge is as incomprehensible as it is to the lay person. Mathematicians typically have an intimate knowledge of a few related areas as well as the fundamentals, if they can remember enough of their undergraduate lectures.

The aim of this part of the book is to give a brief introduction to mathematics, so that readers of this book will have a starting point to further enquiry. The bibliography is extremely important, as it gives the direction of the next point of reference. Hopefully, this chapter also makes the book more complete and introduces some of the more common mathematical notation and terms. This chapter has been designed to be referred to, while reading the main part of this volume, by people with little or no training in formal university level mathematics but a desire to better understand the notation and formalism of financial mathematics.

For a general reference to mathematics, *Advanced Engineering Mathematics* by Kreyszig[1] is a good start and covers a lot of territory. For an introduction to statistics in particular, Mendenhall, Scheaffer and Wackerly, *Mathematical Statistics with Applications*[2] or Hogg and Craig, *Introduction to Mathematical Statistics*[3] are useful. These books are not alone, a quick browse through an academic bookshop will yield many alternatives, which are probably just as serviceable. Every mathematician will have their favourites.

The only prerequisite for this chapter is a fair grasp of ordinary calculus as taught in most high schools. The reader is expected to know the difference

---

1. E Kreyszig, *Advanced Engineering Mathematics* (John Wiley and Sons, 1993).
2. W Mendenhall, R Scheaffer and D Wackerly, *Mathematical Statistics with Applications* (4th ed, Duxbury Press, 1990).
3. R Hogg and A Craig, *Introduction to Mathematical Statistics* (5th ed, Prentice Hall, 1995).

between $\dfrac{\partial}{\partial x}$ and what the symbol $\dfrac{d}{dx}$ means and how to manipulate it, and so forth. It is also assumed that the reader is familiar with standard mathematical notation such as $\sum\limits_{i=1}^{n}$ and $\prod\limits_{i=1}^{n}$, standard mathematical functions such as $\exp(x)$ or e^x, $\log(x)$, $\sin(x)$, $\cos(x)$ and so on. In all following material, the notation $\log(x)$ will denote the natural logarithm function, that is, $\log(e^x) = e^{\log(x)} = x$. For readers not familiar with these concepts see any good high school text or for more detail, see Kreyszig.[4] The notation used in this chapter is the standard form used by most writing in financial mathematics, and summarised in Appendix II.

It is one thing to understand the mathematics, the next job is to code it into a computer to give precise numerical solutions to actual problems. Some people wish to apply a recipe approach to this process. Press, Flannery, Teukolsky and Vetterling, *Numerical Recipes in c*[5] is popular with versions in other languages and now in its second edition. Extreme caution must be exercised with this approach as one volume cannot hope to expound all of numerical mathematics, nor cover recent developments. Another problem is that it gives people a false sense of security; nothing is ever as simple as transcribing a programme out of a book. A little understanding of the basic mathematics and numerical techniques is invaluable.

In section 2 a brief introduction to matrix algebra is covered. Matrix algebra is used to simplify the notation and concepts in areas such as portfolio optimisation and linear regression.

Section 3 gives an introduction to probability theory which is the firm basis for all of statistics. Section 4 discusses random variables and distributions and covers the important distributions in mathematical finance such as the normal distribution. Distribution theory provides a formalism in which to describe random variables such as stock price movements or interest rate movements.

Section 5 covers estimation, that is, it explains how best to derive values for parameters from a model given historical data. The classical example of estimation is deriving estimates for volatility from historical price data.

Section 6 covers the estimation of linear models and describes general optimisation issues. Portfolio optimisation is an ideal example of the use of least squares theory and constrained optimisation, where, usually, tracking error must be minimised given constraints on asset weights and total expected returns.

Section 7 describes random processes. Random processes describe the path a random variable such as a stock price will take from the current level going forward in time. Also covered in section 7 is an introduction to stochastic calculus and the derivation of the Black-Scholes equation.

Section 8 covers simulations and the Monte-Carlo method. Monte-Carlo methods are sometimes the only method for valuation of exotic options and

---

4. Kreyszig, op cit n 1.
5. W Press, B Flannery, S Teukolsky and W Vetterling, *Numerical Recipes in c* (2nd ed, Cambridge University Press, 1992).

always provide a backup method to check valuations from more analytical methods. Section 8 covers the generation of random numbers and some recent advances.

Appendix I is a brief glossary of names and standard terms used throughout the chapter. Appendix II lists all of the notation used in this chapter and the rest of the book. Finally, please refer to the bibliography at the rear of this book as the first point of reference if the content of this chapter is not detailed or specific enough.

Where possible, examples have been given using Microsoft Excel[6] so that readers may replicate results and understand better the mechanics of the problem. While there are better mathematical programming languages, Excel is serviceable and accessible. These sections are enclosed in shaded boxes and separated from the rest of the discussion.

2. MATRIX ALGEBRA

A *matrix* is simply a rectangular array of numbers. A *vector* is a matrix with either one row or one column only. Matrix algebra is also known as *linear algebra*.

In financial mathematics and risk management the main interest in matrices is that they simplify a lot of the tedious and repetitive calculations in a more elegant formalism. Portfolio optimisation theory lends heavily on this formalism as often portfolios are constructed with hundreds of different but correlated securities. See section 6.5 for a simple finance example. In statistics, linear regression and multivariate statistics are ideal examples of this.

Most undergraduate maths texts[7] contain a more complete discussion of matrix algebra, but the information contained below should suffice for the purpose of this book.

2.1 Notation

A matrix is characterised by its size or the number of rows and number of columns in the array. For example consider the following matrix

$$A = \begin{pmatrix} 1 & 2 & 2 \\ 4 & 1 & 7 \end{pmatrix}$$

This is a matrix with two rows and three columns called A. The entries of A are usually denoted a_{ij} or $[A]_{ij}$, the element in the ith row and jth column. For this example $a_{2,3} = 7$. The size of A is denoted 2 by 3 or 2×3, 2 rows and 3 columns. Notice that the name is usually written in bold type face but sometimes it is inferred by the context of the matrix equation.

---

6. Microsoft Excel is a registered trademark of Microsoft Corporation.
7. For example see Kreyszig, op cit n 1, Ch 7.

In Excel, matrices (also called arrays) can be entered into joining cells of a worksheet. Look up the Excel User's Guide for a description of how to enter and manipulate arrays. It is especially important to remember to use the [Ctrl][Shift][Enter] keys when inputting array formula instead of just [Enter].

2.2 Addition

Matrices can be added only if they have the same number of rows and columns. The addition of two matrices is simply the addition of each corresponding element. For example if **A** and **B** are defined as

$$\mathbf{A} = \begin{pmatrix} 1 & 2 & 2 \\ 4 & 1 & 7 \end{pmatrix} \quad and \quad \mathbf{B} = \begin{pmatrix} 2 & 3 & 4 \\ 1 & 3 & 7 \end{pmatrix}$$

then

$$\mathbf{A} + \mathbf{B} = \begin{pmatrix} 1+2 & 2+3 & 2+4 \\ 4+1 & 1+3 & 7+7 \end{pmatrix} = \begin{pmatrix} 3 & 5 & 6 \\ 5 & 4 & 14 \end{pmatrix}$$

Also notice that **A** + **B** = **B** + **A**.

In Excel, matrices can be added simply using the + operator. Using the above example enter the **A** matrix into cells A1:C2, the **B** matrix into A4:C:5. Select a range consisting of 3 rows and 2 columns and enter the formula A1:C2 + A4:C:5, press [Ctrl][Shift][Enter] and Excel will calculate the matrix addition. Notice the curly braces "{" and "}" around the formula once it has been entered to indicate an array formula.

2.3 Scalar multiplication

Multiplication by a scalar is element wise, that is $[3\mathbf{A}]_{ij} = 3[\mathbf{A}]_{ij}$. For example

$$\frac{d \log(L)}{d\mu}$$

then

$$\frac{d \log(L)}{d\sigma^2}$$

and so we have the desirable property $3\mathbf{A} = \mathbf{A} + \mathbf{A} + \mathbf{A}$.

In Excel, matrices can be multiplied by a scalar easily using the * operator. Using the above example enter the A matrix into cells A1:C2. Select a range consisting of 3 rows and 2 columns and enter the formula 3*A1:C2, press [Ctrl][Shift][Enter] and Excel will calculate the scalar multiplication. Excel uses the * operator to denote element wise multiplication and so in the above example will automatically expand the scalar 3 to a 2 by 3 matrix of 3s.

2.4 Matrix multiplication

The matrix product $C = AB$ is defined if and only if the number of columns of A equals the number of rows of B, if A is an m × n matrix and B is r × p matrix then n = r and the product C is of size m × p. The entries of the product are defined to be $[AB]_{ij} = \sum_{k=1}^{n} [A]_{ik} [B]_{kj}$ that is, the ijth element of the product is the sum of the element wise multiplication of ith row of A and the jth column of B. If

$$A = \begin{pmatrix} 1 & 2 & 2 \\ 4 & 1 & 7 \end{pmatrix} \quad and \quad B = \begin{pmatrix} 1 & 2 \\ 9 & 4 \\ 3 & 8 \end{pmatrix}$$

then

$$AB = \begin{pmatrix} 1*1+2*9+2*3 & 1*2+2*4+2*8 \\ 4*1+1*9+7*3 & 4*2+1*4+7*8 \end{pmatrix} = \begin{pmatrix} 25 & 26 \\ 34 & 68 \end{pmatrix}$$

Notice that for this example

$$BA = \begin{pmatrix} 9 & 14 & 16 \\ 25 & 22 & 46 \\ 35 & 14 & 62 \end{pmatrix} \neq AB$$

Hence there is usually a distinction made between multiplying A by B on the right as in the first example and on the left in the second example.

In Excel, the * operator is reserved for scalar multiplication as discussed above. Excel provides a built in function MMULT() for matrix multiplication. See the online documentation. Remember when inputting matrix formulae to press [Ctrl][Shift][Enter] instead of just [Enter].

2.5 Identity matrix

Just as with real numbers there is a special number 1 such that 1a = a there exists an *identity* matrix **I**. The identity matrix **I** is a square matrix that is composed of mostly 0s but with 1s on the diagonal. For example the 3 × 3 identity matrix is

$$\mathbf{I} = \begin{pmatrix} 1 & 0 & 0 \\ 0 & 1 & 0 \\ 0 & 0 & 1 \end{pmatrix}$$

and if

$$\mathbf{A} = \begin{pmatrix} 1 & 2 & 2 \\ 4 & 1 & 7 \end{pmatrix}$$

then **AI** = **A**. Notice that for **IA** to be defined **I** must be the 2 × 2 identity matrix and again **IA** = **A**.

The identity matrix is an example of a *diagonal* matrix because its only non zero entries are on the diagonal. Often a diagonal matrix is written in shorthand notation as

$$\mathrm{diag}(a_1, a_2 \ldots a_n) = \begin{pmatrix} a_1 & 0 & \cdots & 0 \\ 0 & a_2 & \cdots & 0 \\ \vdots & \vdots & & \vdots \\ 0 & 0 & \cdots & a_n \end{pmatrix}$$

Excel provides no built in function to return an identity matrix. For those familiar with Visual Basic, the following code can be used to return an n × n identity matrix.

```
Function MIDENTITY(n As Integer) As Variant
  Dim i As Integer, j As Integer, result() As Double
  ReDim result(1 To n, 1 To n)
  For i = 1 To n
    For j = 1 To n
      If i = j Then
        result(i, j) = 1
      Else
        result(i, j) = 0
      End If
    Next
  Next
  MIDENTITY = result
End Function
```

2.6 Inverse

In real algebra the inverse of a number is well understood and lets us easily solve equations such as $2x = 4$. In matrix algebra, the *inverse* of a square matrix A is denoted A^{-1} and satisfies the following equations, $A^{-1}A = I$ and $AA^{-1} = I$. For example if

$$A = \begin{pmatrix} 1 & 2 \\ 2 & 3 \end{pmatrix}$$

then

$$A^{-1} = \begin{pmatrix} -3 & 2 \\ 2 & -1 \end{pmatrix}$$

Just as in real algebra the inverse of 0 is not well defined, not all square matrices are invertable for example the matrix $\begin{pmatrix} 1 & 2 \\ 2 & 4 \end{pmatrix}$ has no inverse. Such a matrix is called singular as opposed to one which has an inverse which is called non-singular. Actually calculating the inverse of a matrix is problematic and tedious, the mechanics of which are not enlightening and beyond the scope of this chapter. Most spreadsheets can invert matrices and well-established computer codes exist [8]

> Excel provides a built in function MINVERSE() to calculate the inverse of the specified matrix. If no inverse exits then the error #NUM! is returned. The function MDETERM() calculates the determinant and can be used to indicate if the matrix is singular. Singular matrices have a zero determinant.

2.7 Solving simultaneous linear equations

Now that all of this formalism has been establish it will let us solve a simple problem. Consider two simultaneous equations

$$3x + 4y = 6$$
$$2x + y = 9$$

A quick substitution in the second equation of $y = \dfrac{6 - 3x}{4}$ gives the solution

to be $x = 6$ and $y = -3$. These equations can be more concisely written as

$$AX = B$$

Where

---

8.   See Press, Flannery, Teukolsky and Vetterling, op cit n 5.

$$A = \begin{pmatrix} 3 & 4 \\ 2 & 1 \end{pmatrix}$$

$$X = \begin{pmatrix} x \\ y \end{pmatrix}$$

$$B = \begin{pmatrix} 6 \\ 9 \end{pmatrix}$$

Left multiplying both sides of this equation by A^{-1} gives

$$A^{-1}AX = A^{-1}B$$
$$IX = A^{-1}B$$
$$X = A^{-1}B$$

Calculating the inverse of A gives the solution to be

$$X = \begin{pmatrix} 3 & 4 \\ 2 & 1 \end{pmatrix}^{-1} \begin{pmatrix} 6 \\ 9 \end{pmatrix}$$

$$= \begin{pmatrix} -0.2 & 0.8 \\ 0.4 & -0.6 \end{pmatrix} \begin{pmatrix} 6 \\ 9 \end{pmatrix}$$

$$= \begin{pmatrix} 6 \\ -3 \end{pmatrix}$$

As was calculated before. Of course, this example is almost trivial but it can be seen that the dimension of the problem may be simply expanded to any size and basic matrix calculations are the same. To solve a set of 10 simultaneous equations in 10 unknowns would be tedious and error prone, but with matrix algebra almost trivial.

Excel can of course be used to solve this set of equations. One such calculation would be to enter the A matrix in the range A1:B2, the B vector in D1:D2 and enter the equation =MMULT(MINVERSE(A1:B2),D1:D2) in the range F1:F2.

2.8 Transpose

The *transpose* of a matrix is sometimes a useful concept. The transpose of a matrix A is denoted A^T or A', and is simply the swapping of the rows and columns, that is $[A^T]_{ij} = [A]_{ji}$. For example if

$$A = \begin{pmatrix} 1 & 2 & 2 \\ 4 & 1 & 7 \end{pmatrix}$$

then

$$\mathbf{A}^T = \begin{pmatrix} 1 & 4 \\ 2 & 1 \\ 2 & 7 \end{pmatrix}$$

A bit of algebra can show the important relationship $(\mathbf{AB})^T = \mathbf{B}^T\mathbf{A}^T$.

> Excel provides a built in function TRANSPOSE() to calculate the transpose of the specified matrix.

3. PROBABILITY THEORY

Probability theory forms the basis of most of mathematical statistics. A fundamental understanding of the basics and laws of probability is essential to a deeper understanding of statistics.

In financial mathematics, the pricing of most financial derivatives is made by assuming the probability of future events and so inferring a "fair" price to pay today for the derivative. Probability is an important concept to the valuation of most exotic derivatives as the payoffs are usually expressed as a complex series of events or conditions.

3.1 Definitions and axioms

Most people have a good understanding of the concept of *probability*. A fair coin has a probability of $\frac{1}{2}$ of landing heads up, a fair dice roll has a probability of $\frac{2}{6}$ of showing a 1 or 2 on its upper face, a particular horse has a probability of winning a race, and so forth. A fully rigorous definition of probability is not very illustrative, and so a more heuristic one will be employed to highlight the fundamentals.

The probability of an event A, a subset of a sample space S consisting of finitely many, equally likely points is defined to be

$$\text{Pr}\{A\} = \frac{\text{Number of points in } A}{\text{Number of points in } S}$$

To take the coin tossing example, the sample space of equally likely points is $S = \{1,2,3,4,5,6\}$ and the event of interest is $A = \{1,2\}$ and so trivially $\text{Pr}\{A\} = \frac{2}{6}$.

The probability of any event satisfies the axioms of probability

1. $0 \le \text{Pr}\{A\} \le 1$
2. $\text{Pr}\{S\} = 1$
3. For two mutually exclusive events A and B (no point of S lies in both A and B)

$$\text{Pr}\{A \text{ or } B\} = \text{Pr}\{A\} + \text{Pr}\{B\}$$

3.2 Conditional probability and independence

The *conditional probability* is the probability that an event B will happen given another event A has already happened. This probability is written $\Pr\{B|A\}$ and pronounced "probability of B given A". This conditional probability is defined to be

$$\Pr\{B|A\} = \frac{\Pr\{B \text{ and } A\}}{\Pr\{A\}}$$

and so we get the identity

$$\Pr\{B \text{ and } A\} = \Pr\{B|A\}\Pr\{A\} = \Pr\{A|B\}\Pr\{B\}$$

Two events A and B are defined to be independent if

$$\Pr\{B \text{ and } A\} = \Pr\{A\}\Pr\{B\}$$

or equivalently

$$\Pr\{B|A\} = \Pr\{B\} \text{ and } \Pr\{A|B\} = \Pr\{A\}$$

Conditional probability is an important concept in financial mathematics. The price for a particular share today is always implied in any statement or assumption of that share price tomorrow, next week or next year.

3.3 Counting events

Some notation and concepts are useful for counting events, so that one may calculate probabilities.

The number of ways of arranging n distinct objects in order (without replacement) is

$$n(n - 1)(n - 2)...(2)(1) = n!$$

This is easily shown by observing that there are n choices for the first place, $n-1$ for the second as one has already been placed, $n-2$ for the third and so forth.

For example, if we are to consider a 5 horse race there are $5! = 120$ ways the 5 horses can be placed.

This simple construction can be used to show that the number of ways of arranging only k of n distinct objects in order (without replacement) is

$$n(n-1)(n-2)...(n-k+1) = \frac{n!}{(n-k)!}$$

To take our example of a 5 horse race, the number of different combinations for the top 3 places is $\frac{5!}{(5-3)!} = 60$.

If we allow replacement then it is easy to see that the number of ways of ordering only k of the n objects is

$$n \cdot n ... n = n^k$$

For example, if 10 tosses of a coin are to be considered there are 2^{10} different combinations of the sequence of heads and tails.

If the order of the k outcomes is unimportant, the number of ways of arranging only k of n distinct objects (without replacement) is

$$\frac{n(n-1)(n-2)\ldots(n-k+1)}{k(k-1)\ldots1} = \frac{n!}{(n-k)!\,k!} = \binom{n}{k}$$

Sometimes $\binom{n}{k}$ is pronounced "n choose k". In the five horse race example the number of combinations for the top 3 places (where order is unimportant) is $\binom{5}{3} = 10$. Calling the horses A, B, C, D and E, it would be a simple matter to write out all 10 combinations ABC, ABD, ABE, ACD, ACE, ADE, BCD, BCE, BDE, CDE. Note that the order is unimportant and so just ABC has been listed instead of ABC, ACB, BAC, BCA, CAB and CBA.

Microsoft Excel provides some counting functions built in

$$\text{COMBIN(n,k)} = \binom{n}{k}$$

$$\text{PERMUT(n,k)} = \frac{n!}{(n-k)!}$$

$$\text{FACT(n)} = n!$$

---

4. RANDOM VARIABLES AND DISTRIBUTIONS

Real variables make a convenient form of abstraction to solve equations such as $ax^2 + bx + c = 0$. Random variables are also convenient to express values that may change.

Financial mathematicians use random variables and distribution theory to describe uncertain stock prices, foreign exchange rates or interest rates. From the assumed distribution the financial mathematician may make various statements about the likelihood of events, the "expected value" of various quantities and finally derive valuation formulae. Distribution theory is used to derive the Black-Scholes equation in section 4.13.

4.1 Definitions

A *random variable* is a real valued function that can take any value from a specified sample space. The value a random variable will take will change with every sampling, test or observation. The frequency that a random variable will take a particular value will depend upon the *probability distribution* that defines the random variable. An alternative definition of the distribution of a random variable X is to define the *distribution function* F() or *cumulative distribution function* such that

$$\Pr\{X \le x\} = F(x)$$

The cumulative distribution function, because it is a probability, must obey the axioms of probability; that is $F(-\infty) = 0$, $F(\infty) = 1$ and $F(x) \geq F(y)$ if $x \geq y$.

The actual distribution is not always known but can be approximated by assuming the form of distribution and estimating the unknown parameters. Most practitioners agree that stock prices are random variables, the actual form of the distribution is not known but section 4.6 below will discuss a popular choice.

4.2 Discrete random variables

A *discrete random variable* is a random variable that can only take a countable number of values. For expediency we will assume that a discreet random variable will only take positive integer values, that is 0, 1, 2, and so forth. A discrete random variable X is defined by its probability function $p(i)$ or p_i,

$$p(i) = \Pr\{X = i\}$$

And so the probability distribution is

$$F(i) = \Pr\{X \leq i\} = \sum_{j=0}^{i} p(j)$$

Each of these probabilities $p(i)$ must satisfy the axioms of probability as discussed in section 2.1; that is, $0 \leq p(i) \leq 1$ for all i, and $\sum_{All\ i} p(i) = 1$.

For example, consider tossing a coin. A random variable X takes the value 1 if a head is observed otherwise it takes the value 0. If the coin is assumed to be fair then the probability function of X will be $p(0) = 0.5$ and $p(1) = 0.5$. Consider tossing this coin 10 times and let $X_1..X_{10}$ be the outcomes. These variables are identically distributed and independent with probability function $p_X(i) = 1/2$, $i = 0,1$. If a new random variable Y be the total number of heads, that is $Y = X_1 + .. + X_{10}$, what probability function does Y have? The answer is $p_Y(i) = \binom{10}{i} \frac{1}{2^{10}}$, $i = 0..10$, there are $\binom{10}{i}$ ways of getting i heads and 10-i tails in a sequence and each independent toss has a probability of $1/2$ coming up head or tail.

The random variable Y is said to be a *binomial* random variable and each of the X's is said to be of type *Bernoulli*. Another important type of random variable often found to be a good approximation is the Poisson random variable.

4.3 The Poisson distribution

If Y is a Poisson random variable it is defined by a characteristic parameter λ and its probability function is

$$p(y) = \Pr\{Y = y\} = \frac{e^{-\lambda}\lambda^{y}}{y!}, \quad y = 0,1,2,\ldots$$

The probability function can be represented graphically. For $\lambda = 10$ the probability function takes the following shape in *Exhibit 19.1*.

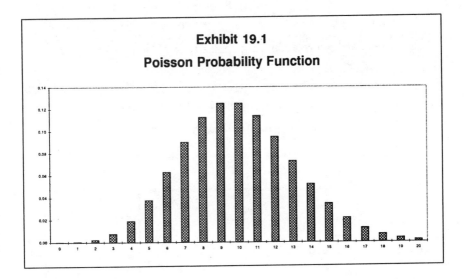

Exhibit 19.1
Poisson Probability Function

The Poisson distribution is often used as a good approximation to the number of rare events that occur in a fixed unit of time or space. It can be shown that λ is the mean number of events per unit time. One model used to explain stock price moves is the so-called "jump diffusion process", where there are a Poisson number of stock price jumps in a small interval of time.

4.4 Continuous random variables

A *continuous random variable* is a random variable that can take any real value. A continuous random variable X is defined by its probability density function $f(x)$:

$$f(x) = \lim_{dx \to 0} \frac{\Pr\{x \le X \le x + dx\}}{dx} = \frac{dF(x)}{dx}$$

And so the probability distribution function is:

$$F(x) = \Pr\{X \le x\} = \int_{z=-\infty}^{x} f(z)\,dz$$

The axioms of probability dictate that $f(x) \ge 0$, but as $f(x)$ is not a probability, the function can take values greater than 1.

Continuous distributions are of great use in mathematical finance, as they represent a good framework in which to deal with random stock prices, interest rates and foreign exchange rates.

4.5 The uniform distribution

The uniform distribution is probably the simplest of continuous distributions. A uniform random variable U is defined by its probability density function:

$$f_U(u) = \begin{cases} 1 & for\ 0 \le u \le 1 \\ 0 & otherwise \end{cases}$$

The density has been reproduced graphically in *Exhibit 19.2*.

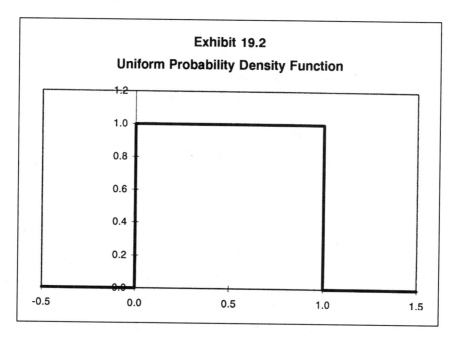

Exhibit 19.2

Uniform Probability Density Function

Uniform random numbers are of great use in the generation of random numbers. Section 8 discusses the generation of random numbers and simulations in some detail.

4.6 The normal distribution

The normal, or Gaussian, distribution is one of the most important in all of statistics. The central limit theorem discussed in section 4.9 shows why this distribution appears again and again in real world applications, approximations and theoretical statistics. The normal distribution is parameterised by a location parameter μ and a spread parameter $\sigma > 0$, the probability density function is

$$f(x) = \frac{1}{\sqrt{2\pi\sigma^2}} e^{-\frac{1}{2}\left(\frac{x-\mu}{\sigma}\right)^2}$$

If a random variable X has this probability density function then it is written as $X \sim N(\mu,\sigma^2)$. The sign "$\sim$" is read as "distributed as" and "$N(\mu,\sigma^2)$" indicates the exact form for the distribution. The probability density function for a normal distribution with $\mu = 10$ and $\sigma = 3$ has been reproduced graphically in *Exhibit 19.3*.

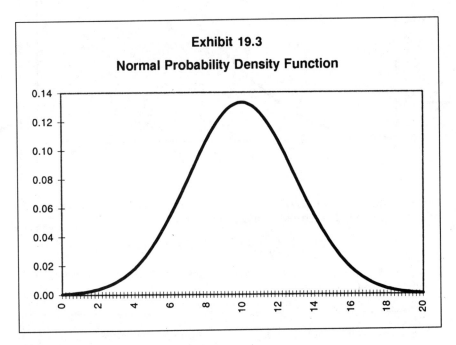

Exhibit 19.3

Normal Probability Density Function

A standard normal variable has $\mu = 0$ and $\sigma = 1$ and is the foundation of all normal variables because if $Z \sim N(0,1)$ then $\mu + \sigma Z \sim N(\mu,\sigma^2)$. Another important property of the normal distribution is that it is closed under addition, that is if $X_1 \sim N(\mu_1, \sigma_1^2)$ and $X_2 \sim N(\mu_2,\sigma_2^2)$ are independent then $X_1 + X_2 \sim N(\mu_1 + \mu_2, \sigma_1^2 + \sigma_2^2)$.

The cumulative distribution function has no closed form. The cumulative distribution function for a standard normal variable is denoted

$$\Phi(x) = N(x) = \int_{z=-\infty}^{x} \frac{1}{\sqrt{2\pi}} e^{-\frac{1}{2}z^2}\, dz$$

This function is well tabulated in statistics texts and most spreadsheets can calculate these values. See Abramowitz and Stegun[9] for various polynomial approximations.[10] *Exhibit 19.4* below shows a graphical representation.

---

9. M Abramowitz and I Stegun, *Handbook of Mathematical Functions* (9th ed, Dover, 1972).
10. Equation 26.2.17 of Abramowitz and Stegun, ibid, is the most popular choice having an error less than 7.5×10^{-8}. J Hull, *Options Futures and Other Derivative Securities* (2nd ed, Prentice-Hall International, 1993) advocates an inferior approximation.

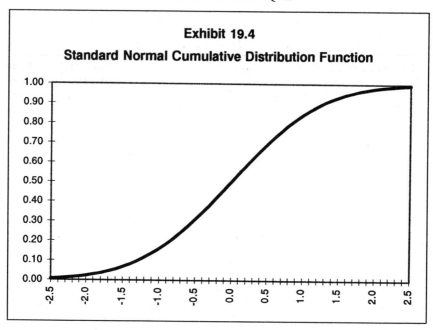

Exhibit 19.4

Standard Normal Cumulative Distribution Function

The central assumption of the Black-Scholes[11] equation is that the stock price is log normally distributed, more precisely

$$\log\left(\frac{S_t}{S_0}\right) \sim N\left(\left(r - \tfrac{1}{2}\sigma^2\right)t, \sigma^2 t\right)$$

Section 4.9 will discuss this assumption further and indicate theoretical and practical reasons for its use.

Excel has built in functions to calculate normal cumulative distribution functions and probability density functions

NORMDIST = The normal cumulative distribution or density function.

NORMINV = The inverse of the normal cumulative distribution.

NORMSDIST = The standard normal cumulative distribution, $\Phi(\ )$.

NORMSINV = The inverse of the standard normal cumulative distribution.

11. F Black and M Scholes, "The Pricing of Options and Corporate Liabilities" (1973) 81 (May-June) *Journal of Political Economy* 637.

4.7 Expected value and variance

The distribution function uniquely determines the distribution of a random variable. To compare two random variables of different types of random variables we can talk about their location and dispersion. These statistics provide descriptive measures of a particular distributions properties. The location or *expected value* of a random variable X is defined to be:

$$E[X] = \overline{X} = \begin{cases} \displaystyle\sum_{i=0}^{\infty} i p(i) & \text{for a discrete random variable} \\[2ex] \displaystyle\int_{z=-\infty}^{\infty} z f(z) dz & \text{for a continuous random variable} \end{cases}$$

This statistic corresponds to our heuristic concept of mean or average.

The spread parameter or *variance* is defined to be:

$$\text{Var}[X] = E\left[(X - \overline{X})^2\right] = \begin{cases} \displaystyle\sum_{i=0}^{\infty} (i - \overline{X})^2 p(i) & \text{for a discrete random variable} \\[2ex] \displaystyle\int_{z=-\infty}^{\infty} (z - \overline{X})^2 f(z) dz & \text{for a continuous random variable} \end{cases}$$

Sometimes a more convenient measure of spread is the *standard deviation*, which is defined to be:

$$\text{StDev}[X] = \sqrt{\text{Var}[X]}$$

For continuous distributions, neither the expected value nor variance need exist. This is a technical point and such cases are rare in practice.

Also, the expected value of a function $g(\cdot)$ of X can be defined as:

$$E[g(X)] = \begin{cases} \displaystyle\sum_{i=0}^{\infty} g(i) p(i) & \text{for a discrete random variable} \\[2ex] \displaystyle\int_{z=-\infty}^{\infty} g(z) f(z) dz & \text{for a continuous random variable} \end{cases}$$

For the normal distribution a little bit of integration can show that if $X \sim N(\mu, \sigma^2)$ then $E[X] = \mu$ and $\text{Var}[X] = \sigma^2$.

For the Poisson distribution, it can be shown that if $X \sim Poisson(\lambda)$ then $E[X] = \text{Var}[X] = \lambda$. Hence λ represents the mean number of jumps or events per unit time.

4.8 Higher moments

It is useful to define some more general moments, the nth moment about the origin is defined to be

$$\mu'_n = E[X^n]$$

and the nth central moment to be

$$\mu_n = E[(X - X)^n]$$

A few special functions of these central moments are *skewness* and *kurtosis*, defined as

$$\text{Skew}[X] = \frac{E\left[(X - \bar{X})^3\right]}{\left(E\left[(X - \bar{X})^2\right]\right)^{3/2}}$$

$$\text{Kurtosis}[X] = \frac{E\left[(X - \bar{X})^4\right]}{\left(E\left[(X - \bar{X})^2\right]\right)^2} - 3$$

One particularly useful expectation is the *moment generating function* defined as

$$m(t) = E[e^{tX}]$$

A bit of calculus will show that

$$\mu'_n = E[X^n] = \frac{d^n m(t)}{dt^n}\bigg|_{t=0}$$

and hence the name. Section 4.10 tabulates most standard probability distributions, their expected value, variance and moment generating function.

For the normal distribution both skewness and kurtosis are 0. Stock prices are commonly described as heavy tailed or *leptokurtic*, which indicates that the observed kurtosis is greater than that of a normal distribution, 0. *Exhibit 19.5* below shows the daily and return distribution for the Australian All Ordinaries Index and the normal approximation.

Exhibit 19.5
All Ordinaries Index Standardised Return Distribution

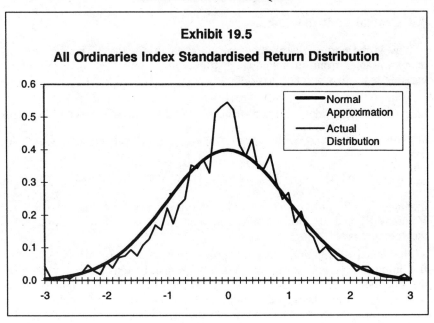

Notice that the actual daily returns have a narrower distribution with heavier tails. For this sample the estimate for skewness is -0.608 (the distribution is mildly tilted to the left by the outliers) and the estimate for kurtosis is $+6.124$ (the empirical distribution has significantly narrower body and fatter tails). This observed skewness and kurtosis impacts on option pricing and is thought by most practitioners to explain the *volatility smile*.[12] The observed skew and kurtosis have been used by Jarrow and Rudd[13] to derive correction terms to the Black-Scholes formulae and so take into account observed departures from normality.

Microsoft Excel has built in functions to calculate sample moments. These functions are discussed at the end of section 5.2 on sample estimates.

12. The volatility smile is a description of the implied volatilities observed in most options markets. Out-of-the-money and in-the-money options trade at higher volatilities than at-the-money options and so giving the smile shape when plotted against strike.
13. R Jarrow and A Rudd, "Approximate Option Valuation for Arbitrary Stochastic Processes" (1982) 10 *Journal of Financial Economics* 347.

4.9 Central limit theorem

Why is the normal distribution so important in statistics? The reason is if many variables from an unknown distribution are mixed, then the resulting variable tends to a normal distribution.

A formal statement of this theorem[14] would be useful. Let $Y_1, Y_2 .. Y_n$ be independent and identically distributed random variables, with mean μ and finite variance σ_2. The mean $\overline{Y} = \frac{1}{n} \sum_{i=1}^{n} Y_i$ will converge to a normal distribution $N\left(\mu, \frac{\sigma^2}{n}\right)$. The reader is referred to Feller's excellent monographs *An Introduction to Probability Theory and Its Applications*, Volumes I[15] and II[16] for a more complete discussion of the central limit theorem and proof.

The actual distribution for stock prices over very short intervals such as five minutes may not be known. When these distributions are mixed to give the distribution for one day or one week they become very much like a normal distribution. Using daily and monthly data, *Exhibit 19.6* below shows the standardised return distribution for the Australian All Ordinaries Index over 8 years.

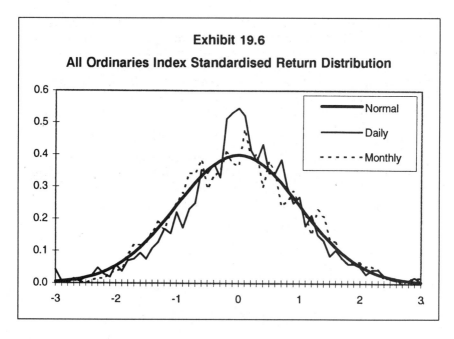

Exhibit 19.6

All Ordinaries Index Standardised Return Distribution

14. For a statement and proof of the full central limit theorem see W Feller, *An Introduction to Probability Theory and its Applications* (Vol II, 2nd ed, Wiley, 1971). What follows is a special case of the more general theorem but should suffice for our purposes.
15. W Feller, *An Introduction to Probability Theory and its Applications* (Vol I, 3rd ed, Wiley, 1968).
16. Feller, op cit n 14.

It is the central limit theorem which guarantees[17] the fact that longer and longer averages tend to a normal distribution. The normal distribution is a good approximation to the more complex but unknown stock return distribution. For this reason the Black-Scholes[18] formula is still widely used.

4.10 Common probability distributions

Some common discrete probability distributions are shown in *Exhibit 19.7*.

Exhibit 19.7
Common Discrete Probability Distributions

Name	Probability Function $p(y)$	Mean	Variance	Moment Generating Function
Bernouli	$\begin{cases} p & \text{if } y = 1 \\ 1-p & \text{if } y = 0 \end{cases}$	p	$p(1-p)$	$pe^t + (1-p)$
Binomial	$\binom{n}{y} p^y (1-p)^{n-y}$ $y = 0, 1, \ldots, n$	np	$np(1-p)$	$\left[pe^t + (1-p) \right]^n$
Geometric	$p(1-p)^{y-1}$ $y = 1, 2, \ldots, n$	$\dfrac{1}{p}$	$\dfrac{1-p}{p^2}$	$\dfrac{pe^t}{1-(1-p)e^t}$
Poisson	$\dfrac{\lambda^y e^{-\lambda}}{y!}$ $y = 0, 1, \ldots$	λ	λ	$e^{\lambda(e^t - 1)}$
Negative Binomial	$\binom{y-1}{r-1} p^r (1-p)^{y-r}$ $y = r, r+1, \ldots$	$\dfrac{r}{p}$	$\dfrac{r(1-p)}{p^2}$	$\left[\dfrac{pe^t}{1-(1-p)e^t} \right]^r$

Source: Mendenhall, Scheaffer and Wackerly[19] and Abramowitz and Stegun.[20]

Some common continuous probability distributions are found in *Exhibit 19.8*.

---

17. Given a few regulatory conditions.
18. Black and Scholes, op cit n 11.
19. Op cit n 2.
20. Op cit n 9.

Exhibit 19.8

Common Continuous Probability Distributions

Name	Probability Density $f(y)$	Mean	Variance	Moment Generating Function
Uniform	$$\dfrac{1}{\theta_2 - \theta_1}$$ $$\theta_1 \le y \le \theta_2$$	$\dfrac{\theta_2 + \theta_1}{2}$	$\dfrac{\left(\theta_2 - \theta_1\right)^2}{12}$	$\dfrac{e^{t\theta_2} - e^{t\theta_1}}{t\left(\theta_2 - \theta_1\right)}$
Normal	$$\dfrac{e^{-\frac{1}{2}\left(\frac{y-\mu}{\sigma}\right)^2}}{\sigma\sqrt{2\pi}}$$ $$-\infty < y < \infty$$	μ	σ^2	$e^{\mu t + \frac{t^2\sigma^2}{2}}$
Gamma	$$\dfrac{y^{\alpha-1}e^{-y/\beta}}{\Gamma(\alpha)\beta^\alpha}$$ $$0 < y < \infty$$	$\alpha\beta$	$\alpha\beta^2$	$\left(1 - \beta t\right)^{-\alpha}$ $t < 1/\beta$
Chi-Square	$$\dfrac{y^{\frac{v}{2}-1}e^{-y/2}}{\Gamma\left(\frac{v}{2}\right)2^{\frac{v}{2}}}$$ $$0 < y < \infty$$	v	$2v$	$\left(1 - 2t\right)^{-v/2}$
Beta	$$\dfrac{\Gamma(\alpha + \beta)}{\Gamma(\alpha)\Gamma(\beta)}y^{\alpha-1}\left(1 - y\right)^{\beta-1}$$ $$0 < y < 1$$	$\dfrac{\alpha}{\alpha + \beta}$	$\dfrac{\alpha\beta}{\left(\alpha + \beta\right)^2\left(\alpha + \beta + 1\right)}$	No Closed Form

Source: Mendenhall, Scheaffer and Wackerly[21] and Abramowitz and Stegun.[22]

21. Op cit n 2.
22. Op cit n 9.

Microsoft Excel has many built in functions to calculate the probability density/function, cumulative distribution function and the inverse of the cumulative distribution function:

BETA = cumulative beta distribution function.

BETAINV = inverse cumulative beta distribution function.

BINOMIAL = binomial probability function and cumulative distribution function.

CRITBINOM = inverse cumulative binomial distribution function.

CHIDIST = cumulative chi-squared distribution function.

CHIINV = inverse cumulative chi-squared distribution function.

EXPONDIST = exponential probability density and cumulative distribution function.

FDIST = cumulative F distribution function.

FINV = inverse cumulative F distribution function.

GAMMADIST = gamma probability density and cumulative distribution function.

GAMMAINV = inverse cumulative gamma distribution function.

HYPGEOMDIST = hypergeometric probability function.

LOGNORMDIST = lognormal cumulative distribution function.

LOGINV = inverse cumulative lognormal distribution function.

NEGBINOMDIST = negative binomial probability function.

NORMDIST = The normal cumulative distribution or density function.

NORMINV = The inverse of the normal cumulative distribution.

NORMSDIST = The standard normal cumulative distribution, $\Phi()$.

NORMSINV = The inverse of the standard normal cumulative distribution.

POISSON = Poisson probability function and cumulative distribution function.

TDIST = cumulative Student's t distribution function.

TINV = inverse cumulative Student's t distribution function.

WEIBULL = Weibull probability density and cumulative distribution function.

4.11 Bivariate and multivariate distributions

So far the discussion has centred around univariate distributions, probability distributions in one variable. Often in mathematical finance, distributions of more than one random variable are of interest, or *multivariate* probability distributions. A typical example of this is if the joint distribution of the all ordinaries index and the S&P 500 index is of interest because of a suspected causal relationship between the two equity indices.

The discussion below will focus on continuous random variables; a corresponding derivation for discrete random variables would be an easy extension.

Two random variables X and Y are said to have a *bivariate distribution* if a function $F()$ can be found such that

$$F(x,y) = \Pr\{X \le x, Y \le y\}$$

which satisfies the following criteria

1. $F(-\infty,-\infty) = F(x,-\infty) = F(-\infty,y) = 0$ *for all* x, y
2. $F(\infty,\infty) = 1$

3. $f(x,y) = \dfrac{\partial^2 F(x,y)}{\partial x \partial y} \ge 0$ *for all* x, y

The function $F()$ is usually called the *joint distribution function* and the function $f()$ is usually called the *joint density function*.

The *marginal density* of X is defined to be:

$$f_X(x) = \int_{y=-\infty}^{\infty} f(x,y)\,dy$$

A similar definition can be made for the marginal distribution of Y. The *conditional density* of X given Y is defined as:

$$f_{X|Y}(x,y) = \begin{cases} \dfrac{f(x,y)}{f_Y(y)} & \text{if } f_Y(y) > 0 \\ 0 & \text{otherwise} \end{cases}$$

which of course corresponds directly to the definition of conditional probability given in section 2.2.

Two random variables X and Y are said to be *independent* if

$$F(x,y) = F_X(x)F_Y(y) \ \text{ or } \ f(x,y) = f_X(x)f_Y(y)$$

The introduction of more than one random variable introduces the concept of an expected value of more than one random variable. The expected value of a function $g()$ of random variables is defined as

$$E[g(X,Y)] = \int_{x=-\infty}^{\infty} \int_{y=-\infty}^{\infty} g(x,y)f(x,y)\,dx\,dy$$

A special expectation is the *covariance* of two random variables defined as

$$\text{Cov}[X,Y] = E[(X-\bar{X})(Y-\bar{Y})] = E[XY] - E[X]E[Y]$$

Notice $\text{Cov}[X,X] = \text{Var}[X]$. The *correlation* between two random variables is defined as

$$\text{Corr}[X,Y] = \frac{\text{Cov}[X,Y]}{\sqrt{\text{Var}[X]\text{Var}[Y]}}$$

If two random variables are independent then it can easily be shown using the definition of independence that $E[XY] = E[X]E[Y]$ and so

$$\text{Corr}[X,Y] = \text{Cov}[X,Y] = 0$$

The reverse is not true in general, two random variables may be uncorrelated but may not be independent.

The *conditional expectation* of X given Y is defined as

$$E\left[X\middle|Y=y\right]= \int_{x=-\infty}^{\infty} xf_{X|Y}\left(x,y\right)dx$$

A *multivariate distribution* is defined as the distribution of a number of random variables $X_1,X_2,...,X_n$ more conveniently expressed as a column vector

$$\mathbf{X} = \begin{pmatrix} X_1 \\ X_2 \\ \vdots \\ X_n \end{pmatrix}$$

The definitions above for joint distribution function, joint density function, marginal densities and conditional densities have analogous versions for the multivariate case.

The *covariance matrix* is defined as

$$\text{Cov}[\mathbf{X}] = E\left[(\mathbf{X}-\overline{\mathbf{X}})^T (\mathbf{X}-\overline{\mathbf{X}})\right]$$

$$= \begin{pmatrix} \text{Var}\left[X_1\right] & \text{Cov}\left[X_1,X_2\right] & \cdots & \text{Cov}\left[X_1,X_n\right] \\ \text{Cov}\left[X_2,X_1\right] & \text{Var}\left[X_2\right] & \cdots & \text{Cov}\left[X_2,X_n\right] \\ \vdots & \vdots & & \vdots \\ \text{Cov}\left[X_n,X_1\right] & \text{Cov}\left[X_n,X_2\right] & \cdots & \text{Var}\left[X_n\right] \end{pmatrix}$$

4.12 Bivariate normal distributions

The *bivariate normal distribution* of two random variables X and Y is defined by the probability density function

$$f(x,y)= \frac{\exp\left(\frac{-1}{2(1-\rho^2)}\left(\left(\frac{x-\mu_x}{\sigma_x}\right)^2 -2\rho\left(\frac{x-\mu_x}{\sigma_x}\right)\left(\frac{y-\mu_y}{\sigma_y}\right)+\left(\frac{y-\mu_y}{\sigma_y}\right)^2\right)\right)}{2\pi\sigma_x\sigma_y\sqrt{1-\rho^2}}$$

It can be shown that the five parameters that characterise the bivariate normal distribution are

μ_x = E[X]
μ_y = E[Y]
σ_x^2 = Var[X]
σ_y^2 = Var[Y]
ρ = Corr[X,Y]

It can be shown that by substituting $\rho = 0$ in this equation that two uncorrelated bivariate normally distributed variables are also independent.

A simple extension of this definition is appropriate to define the *multivariate normal distribution*.

4.13 The Black-Scholes equation and expected value

The Black-Scholes equation is easily derived with the use of expected value introduced in sections 4.7 and 4.8. In section 4.6 it was stated that the central assumption of the Black-Scholes equation was that the stock price S_t, of a non dividend paying stock, at a time t in the future is distributed as

$$\log\left(S_t\big/S_0\right) \sim N\left(\left(r - \tfrac{1}{2}\sigma^2\right)t, \sigma^2 t\right)$$

or a convenient change of variables gives

$$S_t = S_0 e^{\left(r - \sigma^2/2\right)t + \sigma\sqrt{t}z}, \quad Z \sim N(0,1)$$

Where S_0 is the current stock price, r is the risk free interest rate and σ is the spread parameter commonly known as *volatility*. This statement was made without proof, but *Exhibit 19.6* of section 4.9 and the central limit theorem itself show that the distributional form is reasonable. The seemingly strange choice of mean parameter is easily explained by computing $E[S_t]$,

$$E[S_t] = \int_{z=-\infty}^{\infty} S_0 e^{\left(r-\sigma^2/2\right)t+\sigma\sqrt{t}z} \frac{1}{\sqrt{2\pi}} e^{-z^2/2} dz$$

$$= S_0 e^{\left(r-\sigma^2/2\right)t} \int_{z=-\infty}^{\infty} \frac{1}{\sqrt{2\pi}} e^{-\frac{1}{2}\left(z^2 - 2\sigma\sqrt{t}z + \sigma^2 t\right) + \frac{1}{2}\sigma^2 t} dz$$

$$= S_0 e^{rt} \int_{z=-\infty}^{\infty} \frac{1}{\sqrt{2\pi}} e^{-\frac{1}{2}\left(z - \sigma\sqrt{t}\right)^2} dz$$

$$= S_0 e^{rt}$$

Notice that $S_0 e^{rt}$ is simply the arbitrage free price for the forward.

Consider a European call option,[23] whose strike is K and time to expiry is t, the value of the call option at expiry, as a function of the random stock price, is simply

$$\max(S_t - K, 0)$$

If we define the fair price as the discounted expected value, that is

$$C_{K,t} = e^{-rt} E[\max(S_t - K, 0)]$$

This last expression may be easily integrated by making the convenient substitution given above

---

23. A European call option is the right but not the obligation to purchase the underlying asset at a fixed price (strike price), on a certain date (expiry date).

$$C_{K,t} = e^{-rt} \int\limits_{z=-\infty}^{\infty} \max\left(S_0 e^{\left(r-\sigma^2/2\right)t+\sigma\sqrt{t}z} - K, 0 \right) \frac{1}{\sqrt{2\pi}} e^{-z^2/2} dz$$

$$= e^{-rt} \int\limits_{z=-\frac{\log\left(S_0/K\right)+\left(r-\sigma^2/2\right)t}{\sigma\sqrt{t}}}^{\infty} \left(S_0 e^{\left(r-\sigma^2/2\right)t+\sigma\sqrt{t}z} - K \right) \frac{1}{\sqrt{2\pi}} e^{-z^2/2} dz$$

Separating the two integrals and completing the square on the first gives

$$C_{K,t} = e^{-rt} S_0 e^{\left(r-\sigma^2/2\right)t} \int\limits_{z=-\frac{\log\left(S_0/K\right)+\left(r-\sigma^2/2\right)t}{\sigma\sqrt{t}}}^{\infty} \frac{1}{\sqrt{2\pi}} e^{-z^2/2+\sigma\sqrt{t}z} dz$$

$$-e^{-rt} K \int\limits_{z=-\frac{\log\left(S_0/K\right)+\left(r-\sigma^2/2\right)t}{\sigma\sqrt{t}}}^{\infty} \frac{1}{\sqrt{2\pi}} e^{-z^2/2} dz$$

$$= S_0 \int\limits_{z=-\frac{\log\left(S_0/K\right)+\left(r-\sigma^2/2\right)t}{\sigma\sqrt{t}}}^{\infty} \frac{1}{\sqrt{2\pi}} e^{-\frac{1}{2}\left(z-\sigma\sqrt{t}\right)^2} dz$$

$$-e^{-rt} K \int\limits_{z=-\frac{\log\left(S_0/K\right)+\left(r-\sigma^2/2\right)t}{\sigma\sqrt{t}}}^{\infty} \frac{1}{\sqrt{2\pi}} e^{-z^2/2} dz$$

$$= S_0 \int\limits_{z=-\frac{\log\left(S_0/K\right)+\left(r+\sigma^2/2\right)t}{\sigma\sqrt{t}}}^{\infty} \frac{1}{\sqrt{2\pi}} e^{-\frac{1}{2}z^2} dz$$

$$-e^{-rt} K \int\limits_{z=-\frac{\log\left(S_0/K\right)+\left(r-\sigma^2/2\right)t}{\sigma\sqrt{t}}}^{\infty} \frac{1}{\sqrt{2\pi}} e^{-z^2/2} dz$$

Using the properties of the cumulative standard normal distribution function $\Phi(\cdot)$ introduced in section 4.6 simplifies the integrals to

$$C_{K,t} = S_0 \left(1 - \Phi\left(-\frac{\log\left(S_0/K\right) + \left(r + \sigma^2/2\right)t}{\sigma\sqrt{t}} \right) \right)$$

$$- e^{-rt} K \left(1 - \Phi\left(-\frac{\log\left(S_0/K\right) + \left(r - \sigma^2/2\right)t}{\sigma\sqrt{t}} \right) \right)$$

$$= S_0 \Phi\left(\frac{\log\left(S_0/K\right) + \left(r + \sigma^2/2\right)t}{\sigma\sqrt{t}} \right)$$

$$- e^{-rt} K \Phi\left(\frac{\log\left(S_0/K\right) + \left(r - \sigma^2/2\right)t}{\sigma\sqrt{t}} \right)$$

which is the celebrated Black-Scholes equation.

The value of a European put[24] option may similarly be calculated to be

$$P_{K,t} = S_0 \left(\Phi\left(\frac{\log\left(S_0/K\right) + \left(r + \sigma^2/2\right)t}{\sigma\sqrt{t}} \right) - 1 \right)$$

$$- e^{-rt} K \left(\Phi\left(\frac{\log\left(S_0/K\right) + \left(r - \sigma^2/2\right)t}{\sigma\sqrt{t}} \right) - 1 \right)$$

This derivation of the Black-Scholes equation is called the *risk neutral derivation* because it relies on the risk neutral property for assets $E[S_t] = S_0 e^{rt}$ and for options $C_{K,t} = e^{-rt} E[\max(S_t - K,0)]$. The Black-Scholes equation is also derived in section 7.7 using stochastic differential equations which are discussed in section 7.

5. ESTIMATION

Given a theoretical model of a process, and a sample of results, the method of *estimation* will dictate how to guess at the values of unknown parameters of the model. In this way we can establish quantitative measures of the theoretical model that fit the observed sample.

24. A European put option is the right but not the obligation to sell the underlying asset at a fixed price (strike price), on a certain date (expiry date).

For example, given that a Poisson model is thought to explain the move in stock prices and some stock price information, estimation will dictate how to guess at the unknown value of the Poisson model λ. Given the normal model for stock price returns, estimation will indicate how to establish the value of the dispersion parameter σ.

In finance, estimation is used to derive actual values for the parameters of models from historical data. One typical example of this is the derivation of volatility estimators which will briefly be discussed in section 5.4.

Hypothesis testing is the process whereby a rigorous framework is set up to determine within a certain bound of error, if a parameter takes a certain fixed value. Such a test would be to test if the mean of a distribution was zero for instance. Estimation theory can also be used to derive *confidence intervals*. Instead of point measures, confidence intervals are ranges that a parameter can take, based upon the sample data. For example, the mean of a distribution may be estimated to lie in the range $[-0.1, 0.2]$ with a 95% confidence. This section will not touch on hypothesis testing nor confidence intervals. Most standard statistics texts such as Mendenhall, Scheaffer and Wackerly[25] or Hogg and Craig[26] will cover these areas in detail.

5.1 Statistics and estimation

A *statistic* or *estimator* is defined as a rule or algorithm used to calculate a quantitative measure of a sample. For example, the sample average is a statistic calculated using the rule

$$\bar{x} = \frac{1}{n}\sum_{i=1}^{n} x_i$$

and the sample of observations $x_1, x_2, ..., x_n$.

Consider an estimator $\hat{\theta}_n$ of a population parameter θ using n abbreviations, two desirable characteristics of the estimator are

1. It is *unbiased*, $E[\hat{\theta}_n] = \theta$
2. It is *consistent*, $\lim_{n\to\infty} Var[\hat{\theta}_n] = 0$

There are two principal means for finding estimators, method of moments and maximum likelihood.

Method of moments estimators are based on the sample moments

$$m_k' = \frac{1}{n}\sum_{i=1}^{n} x_i^{\ k}$$

These sample moments correspond to the moments of the distribution μ_k' which can be expressed as functions of the unknown parameters. Using the assumption that the sample moments are good estimates of the actual moments of the distribution, the equations $m_k' = \mu_k'$ are solved for the unknown parameters.

25. Op cit n 2.
26. Op cit n 3.

A *maximum likelihood estimator* is based on the *likelihood* of a sample $x_1, x_2, ..., x_n$ which is the joint density of the variables $X_1, X_2, ..., X_n$ evaluated at the realised sample $x_1, x_2, ..., x_n$. The likelihood is usually denoted $L(x_1, x_2, ..., x_n)$. Maximum likelihood estimates are derived by calculating (usually using calculus) the values for the unknown parameters that maximise the likelihood. More often than not, it is convenient to maximise the log likelihood and using the fact that the log() function is strictly increasing.

A few common examples will clarify these points.

5.2 Sample average and standard deviation

Consider n independent and identically distributed variables $X_1, X_2, ..., X_n \sim N(\mu, \sigma^2)$. Let $x_1, x_2, ..., x_n$ be a sample of these variables. What estimators are useful to estimate the two parameters μ and σ^2.

Consider $\hat{\theta} = x_1$. This is unbiased, as section 4.7 above showed that $E[X_1] = \mu$, but it is not consistent because $Var[X_1] = \sigma^2$ and so $\lim_{n \to \infty} Var[\hat{\theta}_n] \neq 0$.

Consider the method of moments from above and note that

$$\mu'_1 = \mu$$
$$\mu'_2 = \sigma^2 + \mu^2$$

Equating these equations with the sample moments

$$m'_1 = \frac{1}{n} \sum_{i=1}^{n} x_i$$

$$m'_2 = \frac{1}{n} \sum_{i=1}^{n} x_i^2$$

gives the method of moments estimators

$$\bar{x} = \frac{1}{n} \sum_{i=1}^{n} x_i$$

$$s'^2 = \frac{1}{n} \sum_{i=1}^{n} (x_i - \bar{x})^2$$

It can be shown that $\bar{x}$ is unbiased and consistent for μ but s'^2 is biased for σ^2. Defining a new estimator s^2 as

$$s^2 = \frac{1}{n-1} \sum_{i=1}^{n} (x_i - \bar{x})^2$$

It can be shown that the estimator s^2 is unbiased and consistent for σ^2. For most purposes s^2 is used in preference to s'^2.

The same estimators $\bar{x}$ *and* s'^2 can be derived using the method of maximum likelihood discussed above. Noting that it is assumed that $X_1, X_2, ..., X_n$ are independent, the likelihood can be written as a product of normal probability density function. The log likelihood can be written

$$\log(L) = -\frac{\displaystyle\sum_{i=1}^{n}(x_i - \mu)^2}{2\sigma^2} - \frac{n}{2}\log(\sigma^2) - \frac{n}{2}\log(2\pi)$$

Using standard calculus, it can be shown that setting the derivatives $\frac{d\log(L)}{d\mu}$ and $\frac{d\log(L)}{d\sigma^2}$ to zero, the log likelihood, and so the likelihood is maximised by setting $\mu = \bar{x}$ and $\sigma^2 = s'^2$.

Microsoft Excel provides many estimation statistics as built in functions

AVERAGE = Sample average $\bar{x}$

STDEV = Sample standard deviation s

STDEVP = Population standard deviation s'

VAR = Sample variance s^2

VARP = Population variance s'^2

DEVSQ = Sum of squares of deviations

SKEW = Sample skewness estimator

KURT = Sample kurtosis estimator

CORREL = Sample correlation estimator

COVAR = Sample covariance estimator

FREQUENCY = Sample density function sampled at discrete points.

5.3 Robust estimation

In the previous section on maximum likelihood estimation, it was shown that the estimator $\hat{\mu}$, for the mean of the normal distribution $N(\mu, \sigma^2)$ based upon the sample $x_1, x_2, ..., x_n$ was the solution to the equation

$$\sum_{i=1}^{n}(x_i - \hat{\mu}) = 0$$

That is, $\hat{\mu}$ was the sample mean. It is easy to see that if one of the sample was abnormally large or small, an *outlier*, it would have a great impact on the value of the estimator. The estimator is not *robust*.

The mean is one of a more general class of estimator. This more general class of estimators are the solutions to

$$\sum_{i=1}^{n}\Psi(x_i - \hat{\mu}) = 0$$

for some predefined function $\Psi(\cdot)$. For example if

$$\Psi(x) = \begin{cases} 1 & \text{if } x \geq 0 \\ -1 & \text{if } x < 0 \end{cases}$$

then the resulting estimator $\hat{\mu}$ will be the median. This is a robust estimator, as an outlier will not change the value of the estimator a great deal.

For example consider the samples from a $N(0,1)$ *Exhibit 19.9* below and note that the second column is the same as the first except the last point is an outlier.

Exhibit 19.9

	Sample 1	Sample 2
DATA	−1.191730	−1.191730
	0.696167	0.696167
	0.099973	0.099973
	0.337278	0.337278
	−0.053640	−0.053640
	0.690118	0.690118
	−0.802490	−0.802490
	0.630671	0.630671
	0.421836	0.421836
	1.379594	5.000000
Mean	0.220777	0.582817
Median	0.379557	0.379557

Huber[27] suggests the use of the following $\Psi(\cdot)$ function

$$\Psi(x)=\begin{cases} -a & \text{if } x < -a \\ x & \text{if } |x| \le a \\ a & \text{if } x > a \end{cases}$$

for $a = 1.5$, and solving (usually numerically) the equation

$$\sum_{i=1}^{n}\Psi\left(\frac{x_i - \hat{\mu}}{\hat{\sigma}}\right) = 0$$

where the estimator $\hat{\sigma}$ is a robust one such as

$$\hat{\sigma} = \frac{\text{median } [|x_i - \text{median } [x_i]|]}{0.6745}$$

This is just a brief introduction to a new and developing branch of statistics. For further reference consult Huber[28] or Launer and Wilkinson.[29]

27. P Huber, *Robust Statistics* (Wiley, 1981).
28. Ibid.
29. R Launer and G Wilkinson, *Robustness in Statistics* (Academic Press, 1979).

Microsoft Excel provides many built in functions useful for generating robust statistics

MEDIAN = Sample median

TRIMMEAN = Mean of an interior subset of a sample

MIN = minimum of a sample

MAX = maximum of a sample

PERCENTILE = the kth percentile of a sample

QUARTILE = the quartile points of a sample

AVEDEV = average of the absolute deviations from the mean

5.4 Volatility estimators based on historical data

A common estimation problem in financial mathematics is the estimation of volatility from a historical time series, also known as *historical volatility*. This section will discuss a few commonly used estimators for historical volatility as an example of an estimation problem.

Consider 20 days of data in late 1995 for BHP,[30] the prices and returns (as defined by $\log\left(S_i/S_{i-1}\right)$) were

---

30. Broken Hill Pty Co Ltd, Australia's largest traded stock.

Exhibit 19.10

Price	Return
18.42	
18.18	−0.01311
18.30	0.00658
18.14	−0.00878
18.16	0.00110
18.08	−0.00442
18.22	0.00771
18.20	−0.00110
18.36	0.00875
18.44	0.00435
18.60	0.00864
18.48	−0.00647
18.62	0.00755
18.36	−0.01406
18.24	−0.00656
18.10	−0.00771
18.30	0.01099
18.10	−0.01099
17.96	−0.00776
17.90	−0.00335

Using the model from section 4.6 for the stock price distribution

$$X_i = \log\left(\frac{S_i}{S_{i-1}}\right) \sim N\left(\left(r - \tfrac{1}{2}\sigma^2\right)\tau, \sigma^2\tau\right)$$

where τ is the average time between stock price samples.

The standard method for calculating historical volatility is to use the estimator s^2 for σ^2 and assume there are 260^{31} trading days per year and so $\tau = {}^1\!/_{260}$. Hence the classical estimator for $\hat{\sigma}_c$ volatility is

$$\hat{\sigma}_C = \sqrt{\frac{1}{2}\frac{\displaystyle\sum_{i=1}^{n}x_i^2 - \frac{\displaystyle\sum_{i=1}^{n}x_i}{n}}{n-1}}$$

For this data set $\hat{\sigma}_c = 0.1324$.

This estimator is not quite the maximum likelihood estimator as the mean of the distribution is a small function of the volatility and the constant interest rate r.

Using the techniques of section 5.2 the log likelihood can be written as

---

31. This figure will vary slightly from country to country, and for different times of the year.

$$\log(L) = -\frac{\sum\limits_{i=1}^{n}\left(x_i - r\tau + \frac{\sigma^2\tau}{2}\right)^2}{2\sigma^2\tau} - \frac{n}{2}\log(\sigma^2\tau) - \frac{n}{2}\log(2\pi)$$

The maximum likelihood estimator for σ is the solution of the equation $\dfrac{\delta\log(L)}{\delta\mu} = 0$. There are in fact four separate roots of this equation, two are complex and one is negative, and so the only solution of interest is

$$\hat{\sigma}_{MLE} = \sqrt{\frac{2}{\tau}\left(\sqrt{1 + r^2\tau^2 - 2r\tau\frac{\sum\limits_{i=1}^{n}x_i}{n} + \frac{\sum\limits_{i=1}^{n}x_i^2}{n}} - 1\right)}$$

For this data the estimator is $\hat{\sigma}_{MLE} = 0.1322$, not overly different from the classical estimator because the mean term of the distribution $(r - 1/2\sigma^2)\tau$ is always much smaller than the standard deviation $\sigma\sqrt{\tau}$. Hence, for the purposes of estimating volatility from a frequent data set, an equally good assumption is that

$$X_i = \log\left(\frac{S_i}{S_{i-1}}\right) \underset{approx}{\sim} N(0, \sigma^2\tau)$$

and so based on this approximate assumption, the maximum likelihood estimator is

$$\hat{\sigma}_{Approx} = \sqrt{\frac{1}{\tau}\frac{\sum\limits_{i=1}^{n}x_i^2}{n}}$$

For this data the estimator is $\hat{\sigma}_{Approx} = 0.1311$.

An alternative is to use a robust estimator as introduced in section 5.3 with this new approximate assumption.

The robust estimator is

$$\hat{\sigma}_{Robust} = \frac{median\left(|x_i|\right)}{0.6745} \times \sqrt{\frac{1}{\tau}}$$

For this data the estimator is $\hat{\sigma}_{Robust} = 0.1842$, this deviation is partly a result of the unrealistically small sample size and partly a result of the non normality of returns.

Often it is assumed that the return distribution is non stationary, the volatility fluctuates as well as the stock price. Management of companies, core business activities and other fundamental reasons indicate that only a short period of historical data should be used to predict future volatility. To accommodate this reality either a short estimation period is used compared to the entire data set. Often it is possible to observe price data for 10 years or more on a daily basis but an estimator based on approximately 2,600 will be very efficient but will be little or no use to predict future volatility.

Another method is to use a weighted average of the returns squared. A popular scheme is the exponentially smoothed volatility

$$\log\left(P_i\middle/P_{i-1}\right)$$

Notice that $w_i = \alpha w_{i+1}$, the most recent data is given the most weight and each preceding piece of data is given slightly less weight. For this data, and choosing $\alpha = 0.97$, the estimator is $\hat{\sigma}_{ES} = 0.1318$. The selection of α will influence the decay of the weights, the closer α is to 1 the more the estimator is influenced by past data and the more stable it is.

More sophisticated estimators are based on open-high-low-close data instead of the close-close data, see Garman and Klass[32] and Parkinson.[33]

6. LEAST SQUARES AND OPTIMISATION

A common problem in mathematical finance is finding the best estimators for a linear model. An example of this sort of problem is fitting a model such as $y = \alpha + \beta x$ where y represents a stock return such as BHP, x is the market return and α and β are constants to be estimated. This is the single index model which is a generalisation of the commonly used CAPM. Section 6.5 discusses another application in mathematical finance.

The broad method used for estimating constants from such models is called *least squares*, the reason will become apparent in the later discussion. Special cases of this technique are called *linear regression and multiple linear regression*. The least squares method will be introduced by discussing these two models in detail.

A discussion of least squares leads naturally to more generic problems of *optimisation* and *constrained optimisation*.

6.1 Linear models

Consider a stochastic model of the form

$$Y_i = \alpha + \beta x_i + \varepsilon_i$$
$$\varepsilon_i \sim N(0,\sigma^2)$$

There are many cases where such a linear model may be appropriate. For example, take the relationship between the returns from a stock such as BHP and the Australian all ordinaries index. For a period of 20 days in late-1995 the stock and index prices were

32. M Garman and M Klass, "On the Estimation of Security Price Volatilities from Historical Data" (1980) 53(1) *Journal of Business*.
33. M Parkinson, "The Extreme Value Method for Estimating the Variance of the Rate of Return" (1980) 53(1) *Journal of Business*.

Exhibit 19.11

BHP Price	All Ordinaries Price
18.42	1902.4
18.18	1891.6
18.30	1891.2
18.14	1883.2
18.16	1877.5
18.08	1868.9
18.22	1884.5
18.20	1885.5
18.36	1904.3
18.44	1908.9
18.60	1921.2
18.48	1904.5
18.62	1914.7
18.36	1892.4
18.24	1890.9
18.10	1897.2
18.30	1908.8
18.10	1899.7
17.96	1893.0
17.90	1884.6

The returns (as defined by $\log\left(P_i/P_{i-1}\right)$) plotted against each other with BHP returns on the vertical axis and the all ordinaries index returns on the horizontal axis appear as in *Exhibit 19.12*.

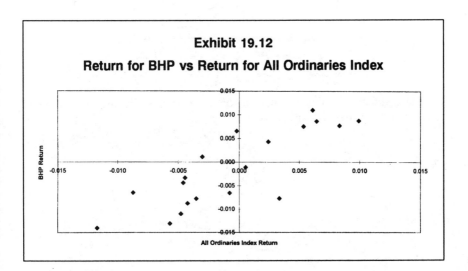

Exhibit 19.12
Return for BHP vs Return for All Ordinaries Index

A linear relationship such as $BHP = \alpha + \beta.AOI$ seems a plausible explanation for this data. There seems to be a number of possible choices because of the random terms ε_i. One commonly used choice for α and β are the least squares estimators.

Consider an estimate for Y_i denoted $\hat{y}_i = \alpha + \beta x_i$, the least squares estimates $\hat{\alpha}$ and $\hat{\beta}$ for α and β are those which minimise the sum of the squares between the actual observed data y_i and the estimate $\hat{y}_i$, that is

$$SS = \sum_{i=1}^{n} \left(y_i - \hat{y}_i\right)^2 = \sum_{i=1}^{n} \left(y_i - \left(\alpha + \beta x_i\right)\right)^2$$

The actual minimum point is found by taking partial derivatives with respect to α and β and setting equal to zero

$$\frac{\partial SS}{\partial \beta} = \sum_{i=1}^{n} 2\left(y_i - \alpha - \beta x_i\right) \cdot -x_i = -2\left(\sum_{i=1}^{n} y_i x_i - \alpha \sum_{i=1}^{n} x_i - \beta \sum_{i=1}^{n} x_i^2\right)$$

$$\frac{\partial SS}{\partial \alpha} = \sum_{i=1}^{n} 2\left(y_i - \alpha - \beta x_i\right) \cdot -1 = -2\left(\sum_{i=1}^{n} y_i - \alpha \sum_{i=1}^{n} 1 - \beta \sum_{i=1}^{n} x_i\right)$$

Setting both of these partial derivatives to 0 and solving for $\hat{\alpha}$ and $\hat{\beta}$ gives

$$\hat{\beta} = \frac{n \sum_{i=1}^{n} y_i x_i - \sum_{i=1}^{n} y_i \sum_{i=1}^{n} x_i}{n \sum_{i=1}^{n} x_i^2 - \left(\sum_{i=1}^{n} x_i\right)^2}$$

$$\hat{\alpha} = \bar{y} - \hat{\beta}\bar{x}$$

These equations are also the maximum likelihood estimators for α and β if the error terms ε_i are assumed to be normal and independent.

Given the estimator for the correlation between the BHP returns and the all ordinaries returns is

$$r = \frac{n \sum_{i=1}^{n} y_i x_i - \sum_{i=1}^{n} y_i \sum_{i=1}^{n} x_i}{\sqrt{n \sum_{i=1}^{n} x_i^2 - \left(\sum_{i=1}^{n} x_i\right)^2} \cdot \sqrt{n \sum_{i=1}^{n} y_i^2 - \left(\sum_{i=1}^{n} y_i\right)^2}}$$

and the estimates for the variance of the BHP returns and the all ordinaries returns are the usual estimates, that is

$$s_x^2 = \sum_{i=1}^{n} x_i^2 - \frac{\left(\sum_{i=1}^{n} x_i\right)^2}{n}$$

$$s_y^2 = \sum_{i=1}^{n} y_i^2 - \frac{\left(\sum_{i=1}^{n} y_i\right)^2}{n}$$

then the important relationship

$$\hat{\beta} = r \frac{s_y}{s_x}$$

can be derived. This relationship is often used to calculate the estimator of β from the estimate for the correlation coefficient and vice versa.

Using these equations and the data above, the estimates for α and β are $\hat{\beta} = 1.1503$, $\hat{\alpha} = -0.0009$. Charted with the data as in *Exhibit 19.13* below, it can be seen that this selection of parameters explains the variation in the data reasonably well.

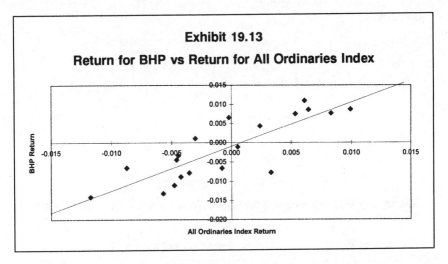

Alternatively, the errors, when plotted against the all ordinaries returns, as in *Exhibit 19.14* below, show no systematic deviation.

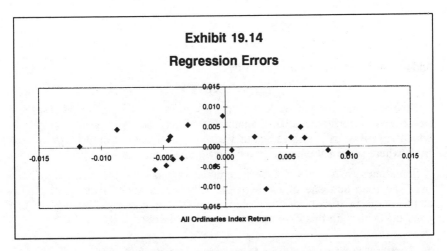

This is only a brief summary of the major results of linear regression; the full theory derives estimates for the variance of the Y estimates, confidence intervals for the parameters and Y estimates, and test statistics for a variety of different hypothesis. The interested reader is referred to Neter and Wasserman,[34] Neter, Kutner, Nachtsheim and Wasserman[35] or any similar book dealing with linear regression.

6.2 Multiple linear models

The theory of multiple linear regression extends the simple theory derived above to more than one X variable. Matrix algebra considerably simplifies the derivation and calculation of the estimators. The methods of section 6.1 above can easily be rewritten using matrix algebra. If we redefine the problem as

$$\mathbf{Y} = \begin{pmatrix} Y_1 \\ Y_2 \\ \vdots \\ Y_n \end{pmatrix} \quad \mathbf{X} = \begin{pmatrix} 1 & x_1 \\ 1 & x_2 \\ \vdots & \vdots \\ 1 & x_n \end{pmatrix} \quad \beta = \begin{pmatrix} \alpha \\ \beta \end{pmatrix} \quad \varepsilon = \begin{pmatrix} \varepsilon_1 \\ \varepsilon_2 \\ \vdots \\ \varepsilon_n \end{pmatrix}$$

$$\mathbf{Y} = \mathbf{X}\beta + \varepsilon$$

and the sum of squares expression can be rewritten as

$$SS = (\mathbf{Y} - \mathbf{X}\beta)'(\mathbf{Y} - \mathbf{X}\beta)$$
$$= \mathbf{Y'Y} - 2\beta'\mathbf{X'Y} + \beta'\mathbf{X'XB}$$

Minimising this expression with respect to the vector β yields the estimator

$$\hat{\beta} = (\mathbf{X'X})^{-1}\mathbf{X'Y}$$

This equation may be easily extended to p dimensions, that is

$$\mathbf{Y} = \begin{pmatrix} Y_1 \\ Y_2 \\ \vdots \\ Y_n \end{pmatrix} \quad \mathbf{X} = \begin{pmatrix} x_{11} & x_{21} & \cdots & x_{p1} \\ x_{21} & x_{22} & \cdots & x_{p2} \\ \vdots & \vdots & & \vdots \\ x_{n1} & x_{2n} & \cdots & x_{pn} \end{pmatrix} \quad \beta = \begin{pmatrix} \beta_1 \\ \beta_2 \\ \vdots \\ \beta_p \end{pmatrix} \quad \varepsilon = \begin{pmatrix} \varepsilon_1 \\ \varepsilon_2 \\ \vdots \\ \varepsilon_n \end{pmatrix}$$

$$\mathbf{Y} = \mathbf{X}\beta + \varepsilon$$

and again the estimators are given by

$$\hat{\beta} = (\mathbf{X'X})^{-1}\mathbf{X'Y}$$

Note that one column of $\mathbf{X}$ may be 1's as in the simple linear case, and hence give a constant value. Columns of $\mathbf{X}$ may be entirely 0's and 1's in which case it is called an indicator variable. Such a use would be in clinical trials where some patients are given a drug and some are not.

Sometimes $(\mathbf{X'X})$ may not be invertable; in this case the model has been over specified and one or more of the x variables must be dropped out. A simple case is if two of the columns of $\mathbf{X}$ are entirely 1's, that is two constant factors. In this case one can easily be dropped.

34. J Neter and W Wasserman, *Applied Linear Statistical Models* (Irwin, 1974).
35. J Neter, M Kutner, C Nachtstein and W Wasserman, *Applied Linear Statistical Models* (4th ed, Irwin, 1995).

Microsoft Excel has a comprehensive multiple linear regression function built in. LINEST will return an array of information such as the estimates themselves, standard deviation estimates for the estimates, the correlation coefficient, and an F statistic. See the comprehensive online documentation for a description of the input and outputs of this function. Excel also provides other associated functions, FORECAST and TREND to calculate values along a linear trend, FDIST and FINV for interpreting the calculated F statistic from LINEST, TDIST and TINV for interpreting the standard deviation estimates for the estimates from LINEST.

Excel also provides regression functions LOGEST for a regression using log transformed y's and x's, but it is usually more convenient to use LINEST and transform as required.

6.3 Nonlinear models

In more complex situations a linear model may not be appropriate. Consider the error estimates plotted against the original x values as in *Exhibit 19.15 below.*

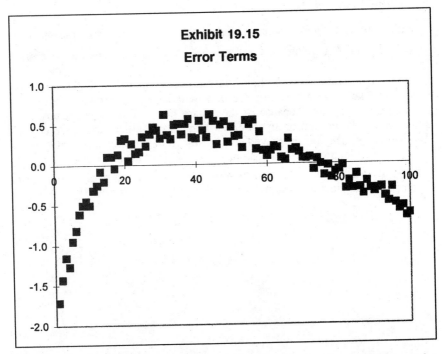

Exhibit 19.15
Error Terms

Obviously the linear model is not appropriate description of the data and a more complex model may fit better. Sometimes the required model can be rewritten as a linear model. Consider a model like

$$Y_i = \alpha x_{1i}(1 + \beta x_{2i}) + \varepsilon_i$$
$$\varepsilon \sim N(0,\sigma^2)$$

This can be rewritten as

$$Y_i = \alpha x_{1i} + \alpha\beta x_{1i}x_{2i} + \varepsilon_i$$
$$= \alpha x_{1i} + \beta'x_{3i}$$

where $x_{3i} = x_{1i}x_{2i}$ and $\beta' = \alpha\beta$. This is obviously linear in the transformed variables now and standard multiple linear regression may be used to estimate the variables.

More often than not, the equation can not be transformed to a linear one, such as

$$Y_i = \alpha\left(1 - e^{-\beta x_i}\right) + \varepsilon_i$$
$$\varepsilon_i \sim N\left(0, \sigma^2\right)$$

For this kind of problem it is more convenient to return to first principals. The sum of squares to be minimised is

$$SS = \sum_{i=1}^{n}\left(y_i - \alpha\left(1 - e^{-\beta x_i}\right)\right)^2$$

This expression may be minimised either analytically (rarely) or numerically. For a discussion of some numerical methods see section 6.6 below.

6.4 Robust regression

With ordinary least squares estimators the sum of the squares $SS = \sum_{i=1}^{n}\left(y_i - \hat{y}_i\right)^2$ is minimised and the error terms are assumed to be normal.

It is a simple calculation to show that the least squares estimators are also maximum likelihood estimators. Outliers will have a pronounced effect on the sum of the squares because of the square function. If the error terms are known not to be normal or an abnormal number of outliers are observed then the estimates can be improved either by transforming the data, using maximum likelihood estimates or using robust estimators.

Consider the case where a linear model has been fit to data and the error when plotted against the original x values appear as in *Exhibit 19.16* below.

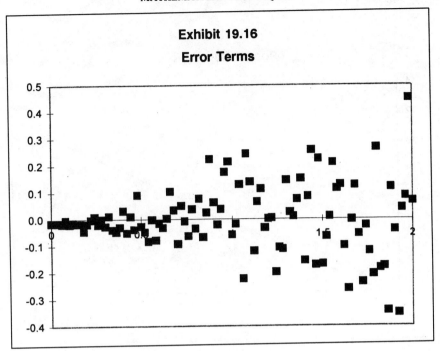

Exhibit 19.16

Error Terms

The increasing error magnitude as shown in *Exhibit 19.16* above indicates that the linear model is not a good description of the data and maybe a log transform may be appropriate.

If the error terms are known to be of a certain distribution then the ordinary least squares estimators can be replaced by the appropriate maximum likelihood estimators. The likelihood is simply a function of the known density function and the observed data. The estimates may have to be estimated numerically (see section 6.6 for a brief discussion of numerical methods).

The effect of outliers on a least squares fit are pronounced, for example consider the bulk of the data in *Exhibit 19.17* below and the outlier.

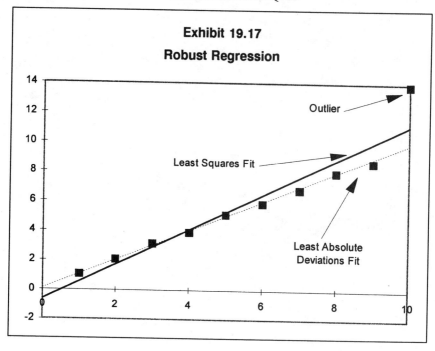

Exhibit 19.17

Robust Regression

Some authors advocate the use of least absolute deviations as a robust methodology to fit this kind of data. Here the sum of the absolute deviations

$$SAD = \sum_{i=1}^{n} |y_i - \hat{y}_i|$$

is minimised with respect to the parameters of the model. In this way outliers have considerably less impact on the result. *Exhibit 19.17* illustrates this point.

An alternative sometimes used is weighted least squares. Each point is given a weight w_i and the weighted sum of squares is minimised

$$WSS = \sum_{i=1}^{n} w_i \left(y_i - \hat{y}_i \right)^2$$

The determination of the weights is non-unique and may be adaptive. For a more thorough discussion of robust parameter estimation readers are referred to Huber[36] or Launer and Wilkinson.[37]

6.5 Constrained optimisation and the method of Lagrange multipliers

Sections 6.1 to 6.4 above are examples of optimisation. In section 5.1 the concept of the ''sum of the squares'' was introduced and it was shown how this was minimised using calculus.

36. Op cit n 27.
37. Op cit n 29.

In most practical cases it is desirable to constrain the parameters or a linear function $f(\cdot)$ of the parameters. Constraints can be either *equality constraints* such as $f(\mathbf{X}) = c$ or *inequality constraints* such as $f(\mathbf{X}) \le c$. Such a constraint in the simple linear regression example given above would be to constrain the β parameter to be greater than or equal to zero.

For equality constraints the method of *Lagrange multipliers* is useful. If the original problem involves minimising the *objective function* $h(\mathbf{X})$, the constrained problem can be solved by defining the *Lagrangian* as

$$L = h(\mathbf{X}) - \lambda(f(\mathbf{X}) - c)$$

and solving the equations

$$\frac{\partial L}{\partial \mathbf{X}} = 0 \ \text{ and } \ \frac{\partial L}{\partial \lambda} = 0$$

The new parameter λ is called a *Lagrange multiplier*. If more than one equality constraint is required, these equations may be extended in the logical manner.

Consider the example where we wish to replicate an equity index such as the Australian all ordinaries index with two stocks from the index such as BHP and CRA. Letting Y be the index return, x_1 be the BHP return and x_2 be the CRA return. The model will be of the form

$$Y_i = \beta_1 x_{1i} + \beta_2 x_{2i} + \varepsilon_i$$

The parameters β_1 and β_2 can be estimated using the method of least squares and some data. Using the methodology discussed in sections 6.1 and 6.2 above, these estimators will satisfy the equations

$$\begin{pmatrix} \sum\limits_{i=1}^{n} x_{1i}^{\ 2} & \sum\limits_{i=1}^{n} x_{1i} x_{2i} \\ \sum\limits_{i=1}^{n} x_{1i} x_{2i} & \sum\limits_{i=1}^{n} x_{2i}^{\ 2} \end{pmatrix} \begin{pmatrix} \hat{\beta}_1 \\ \hat{\beta}_2 \end{pmatrix} = \begin{pmatrix} \sum\limits_{i=1}^{n} y_i x_{1i} \\ \sum\limits_{i=1}^{n} y_i x_{2i} \end{pmatrix}$$

These equations may easily be solved for the estimators $\hat{\beta}_1$ and $\hat{\beta}_2$.

If it is desired to constrain the solution so that the portfolio is fully invested in the market, that is $\beta_1 + \beta_2 = 1$. The Lagrangian is now

$$L = \sum_{i=1}^{n} \left(y_i - \left(\beta_1 x_{1i} + \beta_2 x_{2i} \right) \right)^2 - \lambda \left(\beta_1 + \beta_2 - 1 \right)$$

The three equations that now must be solved are

$$\frac{\partial L}{\partial \beta_1} = 0 \Rightarrow \hat{\beta}_1 \sum_{i=1}^{n} x_{1i}^{\ 2} + \hat{\beta}_2 \sum_{i=1}^{n} x_{1i} x_{2i} - \frac{\lambda}{2} = \sum_{i=1}^{n} y_i x_{1i}$$

$$\frac{\partial L}{\partial \beta_1} = 0 \Rightarrow \hat{\beta}_1 \sum_{i=1}^{n} x_{1i} x_{2i} + \hat{\beta}_2 \sum_{i=1}^{n} x_{2i}^{\ 2} - \frac{\lambda}{2} = \sum_{i=1}^{n} y_i x_{2i}$$

$$\frac{\partial L}{\partial \lambda} = 0 \Rightarrow \hat{\beta}_1 + \hat{\beta}_2 = 1$$

Notice that the last equation guarantees the constraint will be satisfied by the solution. In matrix notation these equations are

$$\begin{pmatrix} \sum_{i=1}^{n} x_{1i}^{2} & \sum_{i=1}^{n} x_{1i}x_{2i} & -\frac{1}{2} \\ \sum_{i=1}^{n} x_{1i}x_{2i} & \sum_{i=1}^{n} x_{2i}^{2} & -\frac{1}{2} \\ 1 & 1 & 0 \end{pmatrix} \begin{pmatrix} \hat{\beta}_{1} \\ \hat{\beta}_{2} \\ \lambda \end{pmatrix} = \begin{pmatrix} \sum_{i=1}^{n} y_{i}x_{1i} \\ \sum_{i=1}^{n} y_{i}x_{2i} \\ 1 \end{pmatrix}$$

which may be easily solved using matrix inversion.

For inequality constraints, the method of Lagrange multipliers may be extended with an iterative scheme to alternatively satisfy the constraints.[38]

6.6 Linear, quadratic and integer programming

Consider the more general problem

minimise $h(\mathbf{X})$

subject to $f_i(\mathbf{X}) \leq c_i$ for $i = 1...p$

$f_i(\mathbf{X}) = c_i$ for $i = p + 1...p + q$

If the *objective function* $h(\mathbf{X})$ and the *constraint functions* $f_i(\mathbf{X})$ are linear the problem is called a *linear programming* problem. The *simplex method* is used to solve such problems. Such problems are often a good approximation to a more complex problem.

If the objective function $h(\mathbf{X})$ is quadratic in $\mathbf{X}$ (that is, it can be expressed as $h(\mathbf{X}) = \sum_{i,j} a_{ij}x_i x_j + \sum_i b_i x_i$, the problem is one of *quadratic programming*. The example in section 6.5 above was an example of this type.

If a linear problem is further constrained so that the parameters X are to be integers, the problem is one *integer programming*.

These sorts of problems are part of the field of *operations research*. The solutions to these types of problems are reasonably involved and beyond the scope of this discussion, the interested reader is referred to Taha[39] or similar treatments in this field.

More often than not, a numerical approach must be used to solve any realistic problem. Optimisation theory is an active area of research in numerical mathematics, generating new more efficient methods. For a rudimentary and somewhat dated approach, the reader is referred to Press, Flannery, Teukolsky and Vetterling.[40] For an up-to-date but advanced discussion of the implementation of one efficient algorithm see Lawrence, Zhou and Tits.[41]

38. See H Taha, *Operations Research: An Introduction* (5th ed, Macmillan Publishing, 1992), section 18.2.2.
39. Ibid.
40. Op cit n 5.
41. C Lawrence, J Zhou and A Tits, *Users Guide for CFSQP Version 2.4: AC Code for Solving (Large Scale) Constrained Nonlinear (Minimax) Optimisation Problems, Generating Iterates Satisfying All Inequality Constraints* (Electrical Engineering Dept and Institute for Systems Research, University of Maryland, College Park, MD 20742 USA, 1996).

Microsoft Excel incorporates an optimiser, called Solver, as an add in. Solver is easy to use and can handle quite general and complex problems. Solver can analyse linear, nonlinear and integer problems. Solver is more than adequate to prototype most problems but slow to tackle any problem with a large number of dimensions or complex constraints. Refer to the online documentation or the Microsoft Excel User's Guide.

7. RANDOM PROCESSES AND STOCHASTIC CALCULUS

Up until now the discussion of asset price probability distributions has been concerned with one point in the future, typically the expiry date of the option as in section 4.13. More often than not mathematical finance is concerned with how the stock price moves in the intervening time or the path it takes over the time interval. The theory of random processes provides a convenient framework to study these paths

With a European option the value at expiry depends only on the value of the asset at expiry. With a path dependent option, the value depends upon the actual path the asset price takes from its initiation to expiry. The class of path-dependent options includes American, average or Asian, lookback and barrier options. The results of delta hedging an option will also depend upon the path the asset price takes. Section 7.7 covers the classical derivation of the Black-Scholes first presented in Black and Scholes.[42]

More than any other, this section is a summary of the most important points and results from a difficult area of mathematics. Interested readers should consult Ross[43] for an introduction to this topic. For a more thorough and complete coverage of this material the reader is referred to an excellent and topical coverage in Malliaris and Brock.[44] Also of use could be Schuss[45] or Bhattacharya and Waymire.[46] Many other books exist on this subject, but most are of an extremely technical nature.

7.1 Definitions

A *random process* or *stochastic process* is a collection of random variables $\{X(t), t \in T\}$. The index set T may be either discrete or continuous and the random variables $X(t)$ may be either discrete or continuous. If the index set T is discrete then the process is said to be a *discrete time* process and if the index set is continuous then the process is said to be *continuous time* process.

42. Op cit n 11.
43. S Ross, *An Introduction to Probability Models* (4th ed, Academic Press, 1989).
44. A Malliaris and W Brock, *Stochastic Methods in Economics and Finance* (North-Holland, 1982).
45. Z Schuss, *Theory and Application of Stochastic Differential Equations* (Wiley, 1980).
46. R Bhattacharya and E Waymire, *Stochastic Processes with Applications* (Wiley, 1990).

Consider the number of trades in a day for a particular stock, this can be represented as the process $\{N_1, N_2 ...\}$ where N_1 is a discrete random variable representing the number of trades on the first day, N_2 represents the number of trades on the second day and so forth. This is an example of a discrete time random process of discrete random variables.

Consider the price of a particular stock over time, this can be represented as the random process $\{S(t), t \geq 0\}$ where $S(t)$ represents the stock price distribution a time t in the future. This is an example of a continuous time random process of continuous random variables. Most of the discussion will focus on these types of random processes as they are a good framework in which to model asset price processes.

One sample $\{x(t), 0 \leq t \leq t_{max}\}$ of the random process $\{X(t), t \geq 0\}$ is called a *path* or a *realisation* of the random process.

7.2 Markov processes

A *Markov process* is one where only the present state of the process is important and the actual path taken to reach the present state is unimportant. More formally for $0 \leq s \leq t$

$$\Pr\{X(t) \leq y | X(u) = x(u), 0 \leq u \leq s\} = \Pr\{X(t) \leq y | X(s) = x(s)\}$$

That is, a Markov process is one that depends upon the present only, all of the information contained in the past is also contained in the present state of the process.

It is usually assumed that asset prices follow a Markov process. Hull[47] argues strongly that the Markov property of observed processes is a result of market efficiency. Although impossible to empirically prove, the Markov property has been shown to be at least a good first approximation.

7.3 Wiener process

The standard *Wiener process* or *Brownian motion* $\{X(t), t \geq 0\}$ is defined by the properties

1) $X(0) = 0$.

2) $\{X(t), t \geq 0\}$ has stationary and independent increments, that is $X(t + y) - X(t)$ and $X(t + 2y) - X(t + y)$ are independent and have the same distribution.

3) $X(t) \sim N(0, t)$ for all $t > 0$.

Property 2) can be used to show that the Wiener process has the Markov property.

These properties can be used to show that

$$X(t) - X(s) \sim N(0, t - s) \text{ for } 0 \leq s < t$$

The Wiener process was used by Einstein to describe the motions of particles in liquids that are due to a large number of small movements. Mathematical finance also uses the Wiener process to describe the movement of stock prices over time. The statement in section 4.6 claiming that the stock

---

47. Op cit n 10.

price distribution is normally distributed is equivalent to claiming the stock price process is a Wiener process.

7.4 First passage times and maximum variables

Some useful characteristics of any Wiener process are the time it takes for the process to first reach a level and the maximum of the process over a finite period. Let T_a denote the first time the Wiener process $\{X(t), t \geq 0\}$ exceeds the level $a \geq 0$. Using conditional probability it is easy to show that

$$\Pr\{X(t) \geq a\} = \Pr\{X(t) \geq a | T_a > t\} \Pr\{T_a > t\} + \Pr\{X(t) \geq a | T_a \leq t\} \Pr\{t_a \leq t\}$$

If $T_a \leq t$, then as the process is symmetric, there is just as much chance the process is above a at time t as below a, hence

$$\Pr\{X(t) \geq a | T_a \leq t\} = {}^1/_2$$

Also if $T_a > t$, then it is impossible for $X(t) > a$ and so

$$\Pr\{X(t) \geq a\} = 0.\Pr\{T_a > t\} + {}^1/_2\Pr\{T_a \leq t\}$$

or

$$\Pr\{T_a \leq t\} = 2\Pr\{X(t) \geq a\}$$

$$= 2\left(1 - \Phi\left(\frac{a}{\sqrt{t}}\right)\right)$$

This distribution is also known as the hitting time distribution. One interesting feature is that $E[T_a] = \infty$, that is, although the process will reach a in finite time, the expected value is infinite.

Let $M(t) = \max_{0 \leq s \leq t} X(s)$ be the maximum level the process reaches over a finite time t, it can easily be shown that

$$\Pr\{M(t) > a\} = \Pr\{T_a \leq t\}$$

$$= 2\left(1 - \Phi\left(\frac{a}{\sqrt{t}}\right)\right)$$

and the expected value is

$$E[M(t)] = \sqrt{\frac{2t}{\pi}}$$

These equations are the foundations for the valuation of lookback[48] and barrier[49] options.

It can also be shown that given $A>0$ and $B>0$ that

$$\Pr\{T_A > T_{-B}\} = \frac{B}{A+B}$$

This is just the probability that the random process will hit A before it passes through $-B$. This equation can also be used to solve the Gambler's

---

48. An option with a payoff that depends upon the maximum or minimum of the asset price over a fixed period of time.
49. An option that terminates or is initialised if the asset price passes through a certain fixed barrier.

Ruin Problem and evaluating the probability of being "stopped out" of trading positions before a trade is closed out at a profit.

7.5 Stochastic calculus

Consider a Wiener process $\{Z(t), t \geq 0\}$ as introduced by section 6.3. For a small time Δt it can be shown that

$$Z(t + \Delta t) - Z(t) \sim N(0, \Delta t)$$

Alternatively, if $U \sim N(0,1)$ then

$$Z(t + \Delta t) - Z(t) = \sqrt{\Delta t}\, U$$

Taking the limit $\Delta t \to 0$ this equation may be written

$$dZ(t) = \sqrt{\Delta t}\, U$$

Notice that the usual expression $\dfrac{dZ(t)}{dt}$ does not exist, a Wiener process is nowhere differentiable. A more general stochastic process, also known as an *Itô process* may be written as

$$dX(t) = a(t,X)dt + b(t,X)dZ$$

which represents a Wiener process with drift $a(t,X)$ and intensity $b(t,X)$. The assumption of the stock price distribution introduced in section 4.6 as

$$\log\!\left(S(t)\big/ S(0) \right) \sim N\!\left(\left(r - \tfrac{1}{2}\sigma^2\right)t, \sigma^2 t \right)$$

can be rewritten as a stochastic differential equation as

$$\frac{dS}{S} = \left(r - \tfrac{1}{2}\sigma^2\right)dt + \sigma dZ$$

This differential equation may be integrated to yield

$$\int_{u=0}^{t} \frac{dS}{S} = \int_{u=0}^{t}\left(r - \tfrac{1}{2}\sigma^2\right)du + \int_{u=0}^{t}\sigma dZ$$

The first integral may be formally integrated to yield

$$\int_{u=0}^{t} \frac{dS}{S} = \log(S(t)) - \log(S(0)) = \log\!\left(S(t)\big/ S(0) \right)$$

The second integral may also be formally integrated to give

$$\int_{u=0}^{t}\left(r - \tfrac{1}{2}\sigma^2\right)du = \left(r - \tfrac{1}{2}\sigma^2\right)t$$

While the last integral is not of the usual calculus type, but observing that σ is a constant it may be simplified to

$$\int_{u=0}^{t}\sigma dZ = \sigma\int_{u=0}^{t} dZ = \sigma(Z(t) - Z(0)) = \sigma Z(t)$$

where $\{Z(t), t > 0\}$ is the usual Wiener process. Hence, the stochastic differential equation $\dfrac{dS}{S} = \left(r - \tfrac{1}{2}\sigma^2\right)dt + \sigma dZ$ is identical to the statement about the probability distribution of $S(t)$.

7.6 Itô's lemma

One of the most important result of stochastic calculus is Itô's Lemma. In section 7.7 it will be shown how this lemma is applied to deriving the Black-Scholes equation.

Consider a function $f = f(X(t),t)$ of an Itô process $dX(t) = a(t,X)dt + b(t,X)dZ$ and time. Then Itô's Lemma states that

$$df = \left(\frac{\partial f}{\partial t} + \frac{\partial f}{\partial X}a(t,X) + \frac{1}{2}\frac{\partial^2 f}{\partial X^2}b(t,X)^2\right)dt + \frac{\partial f}{\partial X}b(t,X)dZ$$

The interesting thing about this equation is the term $\dfrac{1}{2}\dfrac{\partial^2 f}{\partial X^2}b(t,X)^2\,dt$.

Consider a two dimensional Taylor expansion of $f(X(t,t)$

$$f(X+\Delta X,t+\Delta t) - f(X,t) = \frac{\partial f}{\partial X}\Delta X + \frac{\partial f}{\partial t}\Delta t$$

$$+\frac{1}{2}\frac{\partial^2 f}{\partial X^2}\Delta X^2 + \frac{\partial^2 f}{\partial X\partial t}\Delta X\Delta t + \frac{1}{2}\frac{\partial^2 f}{\partial t^2}\Delta t^2$$

$$+ \text{ higher order terms}$$

By replacing Δt with dt and ΔX with dX this equation simplifies to

$$df = \frac{\partial f}{\partial X}(adt + bdZ) + \frac{\partial f}{\partial t}dt$$

$$+\frac{1}{2}\frac{\partial^2 f}{\partial X^2}(a^2dt^2 + 2abdtdZ + b^2dZ^2) + \frac{\partial^2 f}{\partial X\partial t}(adt^2 + bdtdZ) + \frac{1}{2}\frac{\partial^2 f}{\partial t^2}dt^2$$

$$+ \text{ higher order terms}$$

Notice the term in dZ^2, we know from the properties of the standard Wiener process and the normal distribution that $E[dZ^2] = dt$ and $Var[dZ^2] = 2dt^2$, hence in the limit dZ^2 becomes a constant value of dt. Taking the limit $dt \to 0$, only terms in dt and dZ are significant. This yields the lemma.

7.7 Black-Scholes equation revisited

Using Itô's Lemma it is a simple matter to derive the Black-Scholes equation. Using the assumption above that the instantaneous change in value of the stock S over time t is governed by Itô process

$$\frac{dS}{S} = \left(r - \tfrac{1}{2}\sigma^2\right)dt + \sigma dZ$$

Consider the value of a European call option[50] $C_{K,t}(S,t)$ with strike K and time to expiry t, as only a function of the stock price S and time. Itô's lemma shows that $C_{K,t}(S,t)$ is governed by the stochastic differential equation

$$dC = \left(\frac{\partial C}{\partial S}\left(r - \tfrac{1}{2}\sigma^2\right)S + \frac{\partial C}{\partial t} + \frac{1}{2}\frac{\partial^2 C}{\partial S^2}\sigma^2 S^2\right)dt + \frac{\partial C}{\partial S}\sigma dW$$

---

50. A European call option is the right but not the obligation to purchase the underlying asset at a fixed price (strike price), on a certain date (expiry date).

We construct a portfolio P, of long (purchase) of 1 call option and short (sale) of δ shares

$$P = C - \delta S$$

Then the instantaneous change in value of the portfolio is given by

$$dP = dC - \delta dS$$

$$= \left(\frac{\partial C}{\partial S} \left(r - \tfrac{1}{2}\sigma^2 \right) S + \frac{\partial C}{\partial t} + \frac{1}{2} \frac{\partial^2 C}{\partial S^2} \sigma^2 S^2 - \delta S \left(r - \tfrac{1}{2}\sigma^2 \right) \right) dt$$

$$+ \left(\frac{\partial C}{\partial S} - \delta \right) S\sigma dW$$

If δ is chosen such that

$$\delta = \frac{\partial C}{\partial S}$$

this choice implies

$$P = C - \frac{\partial C}{\partial S} S \qquad and$$

$$dP = \left(\frac{\partial C}{\partial t} + \frac{1}{2} \frac{\partial^2 C}{\partial S^2} \sigma^2 S^2 \right) dt$$

Then the portfolio is riskless and so its return must be the risk free interest rate r and so

$$dP = rPdt$$

Thus we have derived the celebrated *Black-Scholes differential equation* for the value of a call option

$$\frac{\partial C}{\partial t} + r \frac{\partial C}{\partial S} S + \frac{1}{2} \frac{\partial^2 C}{\partial S^2} \sigma^2 S^2 = rC$$

This second order linear parabolic partial differential equation must be solved with regard to the boundary condition

$$C_{K,t} = \max(S - K, 0) \text{ at } t = T$$

It can be shown that solution

$$C_{K,t} = S_0 \Phi \left(\frac{\log\left(S_0 / K \right) + \left(r + \sigma^2 / 2 \right) t}{\sigma \sqrt{t}} \right)$$

$$- e^{-rt} K \Phi \left(\frac{\log\left(S_0 / K \right) + \left(r - \sigma^2 / 2 \right) t}{\sigma \sqrt{t}} \right)$$

satisfies the boundary condition and the Black-Scholes partial differential equation. Note that $\Phi()$ is the standard cumulative normal distribution.

Note that the Black-Scholes partial differential equation holds for all types of securities; the only difference is the boundary conditions change. For example, exactly the same partial differential equation holds for European put option,[51]

$$\frac{\partial P}{\partial t} + r\frac{\partial P}{\partial S}S + \frac{1}{2}\frac{\partial^2 P}{\partial S^2}\sigma^2 S^2 = rP$$

but the boundary condition has changed to

$$P_{K,t} = \max(K - S, 0) \text{ at } t = T$$

This solution is important because it shows how a riskless portfolio of options and underlying asset may be constructed. For more advanced options it is not always so easy to solve the partial differential equation; numerical methods are often resorted to.[52] Note also that this method does not rely on the drift of the stochastic process being $r - \frac{1}{2}\sigma^2$ as the risk neutral derivation of section 4.13 did.

8. SIMULATIONS

Simulation, or Monte Carlo, techniques are an important tool in the valuation of financial securities. For many types of exotic derivatives, no closed form solution for the value exist. In these cases either the partial differential equation needs to be solved or a Monte Carlo technique may be adopted. Simulation can also be used to measure the effect of changing the underlying stochastic process.[53]

One of the Black-Scholes[54] assumptions is that the option may be continuously hedged. This is plainly unrealistic as markets tend to move very quickly (gap) and the transaction costs associated with this scheme would be prohibitive. Monte Carlo methods are useful to estimate the effect of different hedge methodologies.

The term "Monte Carlo" refers to a broad class of techniques that use random numbers to simulate the possible outcomes of a system. In mathematical finance, typically the random stock or asset price is assumed to be normally distributed and so normal random numbers are used to simulate the possible asset price at some point in time. From these asset prices the value of the derivative security may be easily evaluated and so the long run average may be established if enough sampling is performed. Mathematically, the basic principal of Monte Carlo simulation is to approximate the expected value $E[f(X)]$ with $\frac{1}{n}\sum_{i=1}^{n}f(x_i)$ where x_i are samples from the same distribution as X. Moreover, the Central Limit Theorem tells us, under a few regulatory conditions, that

51. A European put option is the right but not the obligation to sell the underlying asset at a fixed price (strike price), on a certain date (expiry date).
52. See P Wilmott, J Dewynne and S Howison, *Option Pricing: Mathematical Models and Computation* (Oxford Financial Press, 1994).
53. For example see J Hull and A White, "The Pricing of Options on Assets with Stochastic Volatilities" (1987) 42 (June) *Journal of Finance* 281.
54. Black and Scholes, op cit n 11.

$$\frac{1}{n}\sum_{i=1}^{n} f(x_i) \xrightarrow[n\to\infty]{d} N\left(E[f(X)], \frac{\text{Var}[f(X)]}{n}\right)$$

Note that the standard deviation of the estimate is of order $\frac{1}{\sqrt{n}}$. This criteria will determine how many samples is enough to estimate the average within a specified tolerance.

8.1 Generation of uniform deviates

Generation of random deviates from the uniform distribution (section 4.5 above) is the starting point for generating other types of deviates. The reason is simple to justify, because if X is a random variable with cumulative distribution function $F(\cdot)$, then $F(X)$ is distributed as a uniform random variable. Hence if U is a uniform random variable then $F^{-1}(U)$ is a random variable with cumulative distribution function $F(\cdot)$. This is called the *transform method* of generating random deviates from a known distribution.

Most programming languages have routines built in to generate uniform deviates but care must be taken with these routines. Most built in generators use the linear congruential method calculated by the integer recurrence formula

$$I_{j+1} = (aI_j + b) \bmod m$$

where a, b and m are pre-set integers. This calculation will be extremely fast but only generate m distinct values. This method can be quite unacceptable if the implementation uses small integers or the three constants a, b and m are poorly chosen.[55] In short, do not use these routines for important calculations.

Many portable random number generators that produce high quality and fast uniform deviates exist, see Press, Flannery, Teukolsky and Vetterling,[56] or for a more up to date discussion see Tezuka.[57]

Microsoft Excel provides a built in uniform random number generator RAND. Exercise care.

55. For a discussion of these problems see D Knuth, *The Art of Computer Propgramming: Seminumerical Algorithms* (Vol II, 2nd ed, Addison-Wesley, 1981) or Press, Flannery, Teukolsky and Vetterling, op cit n 5.
56. Op cit n 5.
57. S Tezuka, *Uniform Random Numbers: Theory and Practice* (Kluner Academic Publishers, 1995).

8.2 Sobol quasi random numbers

As discussed above, the convergence of Monte Carlo techniques is of order $\frac{1}{\sqrt{n}}$. As an alternative consider using n equally spaced points on a grid. Such an example would be to choose 100 points on the two dimensional plane as in *Exhibit 19.18* below.

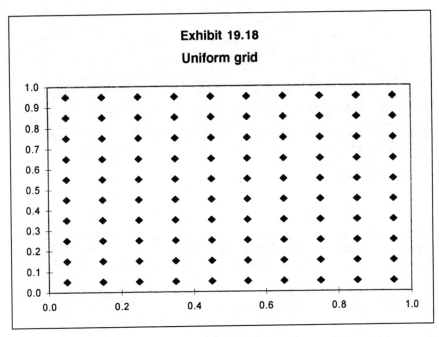

Exhibit 19.18

Uniform grid

Using this scheme, the sum $\frac{1}{n}\sum_{i=1}^{n} f(x_i)$ will approximate the integral $E[f(X)]$ with an error of $\frac{1}{n}$, a worthwhile improvement for large n. The problem with this type of scheme is that, once started, the whole scheme must be completed, otherwise a biased sample will be taken.

The aim of quasi random or low discrepancy sequences is to choose points in the p dimensional space as uniformly as possible. With these methods, each successive point is chosen to be "as far away" from the previous points as possible. In this way the clustering of points observed with random number generators is avoided. *Exhibit 19.19* shows 127 points generated with a uniform random number generator and also with a low discrepancy sequence.

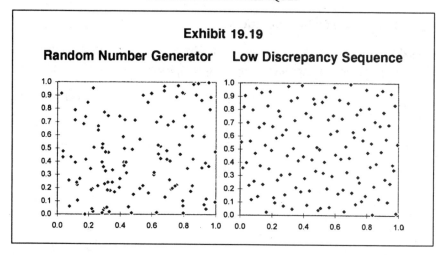

Exhibit 19.19

Random Number Generator   Low Discrepancy Sequence

There is more than one way of generating these low discrepancy sequences. Common types are Sobol, Halton and Faure sequences. Each differ markedly in their operation and their asymptotic properties. For example, the Sobol sequence used to generate *Exhibit 19.19* above has a

$$\text{convergence rate of } \frac{(\log n)^p}{n} \underset{n\to\infty}{\cong} \frac{1}{n}.$$

The derivation of these sequences is based on advanced number theory and is beyond the scope of this chapter. For a detailed discussion and an example of an implementation of a Sobol sequence see Press, Flannery, Teukolsky and Vetterling,[58] or for a more up-to-date discussion see Tezuka.[59] For an example of how these sequences have been applied to mathematical finance see Papageorgiou and Traub.[60]

8.3 Generation of standard normal deviates

For financial applications, the generation of normally distributed random variables is important. Once standard normal deviates are generated and rescaled, stock prices may be simulated using the usual normal assumption (see section 4.6).

Some authors[61] advocate the use of the formula

$$X = \sum_{i=1}^{12} U_i - 6, \quad U_i \sim Uniform$$

to generate normally distributed random deviates. It does not take long to see that this method is fairly crude and slow. In addition, this type of estimate would be incompatible with Sobol or quasi random numbers, using the routine 12 times to generate one normal deviate would destroy the low discrepancy behaviour of the routine.

58. Op cit n 5.
59. Op cit n 56.
60. A Papageorgiou and J Traub, "Beating Monte Carlo" (1996) 9(6) *Risk Magazine.*
61. See Hull, op cit n 10, for example.

A common alternative is to use the Box-Muller method of generating standard normal random numbers. If U_1 and U_2 are uniform deviates then

$$Z_1 = \sqrt{-2\log(U_1)}\cos(2\pi U_2)$$

$$Z_1 = \sqrt{-2\log(U_1)}\sin(2\pi U_2)$$

are normally distributed. There is an elegant explanation of these transformations. Consider two independent standard normal variables specifying the horizontal and vertical distance from the origin of a point on the two-dimensional plane. It is easy to see that the angle the line joining the point with the origin makes with the horizontal axis will be distributed Uniform$[0,2\pi]$. Furthermore, the distance squared of the point from the origin will have cumulative distribution function $F(x) = 1 - \frac{1}{2}e^{-x/2}$. This last function may be easily inverted using the transform method discussed above. While elegant in derivation, this method is reasonably slow[62] to calculate and cannot be used with Sobol sequences.

A further alternative is to use the transform method by inverting the normal cumulative distribution function directly. Just as there is no closed for solution for the normal cumulative distribution function there is no closed form solution for its inverse. Fortunately, this function can be approximated by a function of two polynomials. See Abramowitz and Stegun,[63] or Moro[64] for a particularly good example. This type of approach can be used with Sobol and low discrepancy sequences.

62. A slight modification exists to avoid the computation of the two trigonometric functions, see Press, Flannery, Teukolsky and Vetterling, op cit n 5, or Ross, op cit n 43.
63. Op cit n 9.
64. B Moro, "The Full Monte" (1995) 8(2) *Risk Magazine*.

Appendix I

Glossary

Bivariate distribution

A probability distribution that describes the distribution of two, not necessarily independent, random variables.

Brownian motion

See **Wiener process**.

Consistent estimator

An **estimator** whose variance tends to zero if enough samples are taken.

Estimator

A function or algorithm based on an observed sample that gives a numerical value to a parameter of the underlying system.

Historical volatility

An estimate of the annualised standard deviation of asset returns based upon an observes time series of asset prices.

Lagrange multiplier

A dummy variable introduced in constrained optimisation to reflect an equality constraint.

Linear programming

A constrained optimisation problem where the objective function is linear in the unknown parameters.

Markov process

A **stochastic process** where the increments are independent.

Matrix

Rectangular array of numbers.

Monte Carlo

A method where the random variable is numerically simulated and so the long run average of a function of the random variable may be evaluated.

Normal distribution

The classical "bell shaped" distribution that underlies most of statistics because of the central limit theorem.

Outlier

A lone observation that deviates markedly form the behaviour of the rest of the data.

Quadratic programming

A constrained optimisation problem where the objective function is quadratic in the unknown parameters.

Random process

See **Stochastic process**.

Random variable

A mathematical concept for a variable that has no fixed value, but can be described by a probability distribution. Random variables may take on either discrete values or continuous values.

Robust estimator

An **estimator** that is not overly influenced by outliers.

Simplex method

A procedure used to solve a **linear programming** problem.

Stochastic process

A set of random variables, indexed by time, that describes the evolution of a probabilistic system. Also known as a random process.

Sobol pseudo random sequence

A sequence of numbers chosen to be as far away form the previous numbers in the sequence. Used in **Monte Carlo** techniques to speed convergence. Also known as *low discrepancy sequences*.

Unbiased estimator

An **estimator** whose mean is the parameter to be estimated.

Vector

A **matrix** with either one row or one column.

Wiener process

A **stochastic process** whose increments are independent and normally distributed. Also known as *Brownian motion*.

Appendix II

Summary of Notation and Symbols

$\begin{pmatrix} a_{11} & a_{12} \\ a_{21} & a_{22} \end{pmatrix}$ The 2 × 2 matrix with entries $a_{11}, a_{12}, \ldots$

$[\mathbf{A}]_{ij}$ The element of the matrix $\mathbf{A}$ in the ith row and jth column.

$\mathbf{A}^{-1}$ Inverse of the matrix $\mathbf{A}$.

$\mathbf{A}^T$ or $\mathbf{A}'$ The transpose of the matrix $\mathbf{A}$.

^nC_r or $\begin{pmatrix} n \\ r \end{pmatrix}$ $\begin{pmatrix} n \\ r \end{pmatrix} = \dfrac{n!}{r!(n-r)!}$

$\mathrm{Corr}[X,Y]$ The correlation of two random variables X and Y.

$\mathrm{Cov}[X,Y]$ The covariance of two random variables X and Y.

$\dfrac{\partial f(x,y)}{\partial x}$ The partial derivative of $f(x,y)$ with respect to x.

$\dfrac{df(x,y)}{dx}$ The total derivative of $f(x,y)$ with respect to x.

$\exp(x)$ or e^x The exponential function where $e = 2.71828\ldots$

$E[g(X)]$ Expected value of a function $g(X)$ of a random variable X.

$!$ Factorial that is $n! = n \cdot (n-1) \cdot (n-2) \cdots 2 \cdot 1$. Note $o! = 1$.

$\Gamma(x)$ The gamma function, that is $\Gamma(x) = \displaystyle\int_{u=0}^{\infty} u^{x-1} e^{-u}\, du$.

$\mathbf{I}$ The identity matrix.

$\displaystyle\int f(x)\, dx$ The indefinite integral of $f(x)$ with respect to x.

$\displaystyle\int_{x=y}^{z} f(x)\, dx$ The definite integral of $f(x)$ with respect to x from $x = y$ to $x = z$.

$\displaystyle\lim_{x \to 0} f(x)$ The limit of $f(x)$ as x tends to zero.

$\log(x)$ The natural logarithm function, the inverse of e^x, that is $\log(e^x) = e^{\log(x)} = x$.

$N(\mu, \sigma^2)$ A normal distribution with mean μ and variance σ^2.

$\Phi(x)$ or $N(x)$ The cumulative normal distribution

$$\Phi(x) = N(x) = \int_{z=-\infty}^{x} \frac{1}{\sqrt{2\pi}} e^{-\frac{1}{2}z^2}\, dz.$$

$\Pr\{A\}$ Probability of an event A.

$\Pr\{B|A\}$ Conditional probability of event B given A.

$$\prod_{i=1}^{n} a_i$$ The product $a_1 \cdot a_2 \cdots a_n$.

$$\sum_{i=1}^{n} a_i$$ The summation $a_1 + a_2 + \ldots + a_n$.

Var[X]   The variance of a random variable X.

~   Distributed as.

Index

Entries in italics refer to illustrations